THE SOCIOLOGICAL OUTLOOK

EIGHTH EDITION

THE SOCIOLOGICAL OUTLOOK

EIGHTH EDITION

Reid Luhman

ROWMAN & LITTLEFIELD PUBLISHERS, INC.
Lanham • Boulder • New York • Toronto • Plymouth, UK

ROWMAN & LITTLEFIELD PUBLISHERS, INC.

Published in the United States of America
by Rowman & Littlefield Publishers, Inc.
A wholly owned subsidary of The Rowman & Littlefield Publishing Group, Inc.
4501 Forbes Boulevard, Suite 200, Lanham, Maryland 20706
www.rowmanlittlefield.com

Estover Road
Plymouth PL6 7PY
United Kingdom

British Library Cataloguing in Publication Information Available

Library of Congress Cataloging-in-Publication Data

Luhman, Reid.
The sociological outlook / Reid Luhman.— 8th ed.
    p.   cm.
  Includes index.
  ISBN-13: 978-0-7425-4331-7 (pbk. : alk. paper)
  ISBN-10: 0-7425-4331-5 (pbk. : alk. paper)
  1. Sociology.   2. Social problems.   I. Title.
  HM586.L85 2006
  301—dc22   2006001555

Printed in the United States of America

The paper used in this publication meets the minimum requirements of American National
Standard for Information Sciences—Permanence of Paper for Printed Library Materials,
ANSI/NISO Z39.48-1992.

PHOTO CREDITS

CONTENTS

PART 1

INTRODUCTION TO SOCIOLOGY

THE SOCIOLOGICAL OUTLOOK: THE INDIVIDUAL AND SOCIETY

SOCIETY AS A HUMAN CREATION
Coordination as a Mode of Adaptation
The Development of Culture: Reason and Rules for Coordination
HUMANS AS A SOCIAL CREATION
Socialization: The Internalization of Culture
Freedom versus Conformity in Society
READING: "INVITATION TO SOCIOLOGY," BY PETER BERGER

We humans seem endlessly fascinated by the other members of the animal kingdom with which we share our planet. We keep them as pets, visit them in zoos, and even name them as beneficiaries in our wills. In particular, our fascination focuses on the ways various species of animals "earn their living." Spiders spin webs and wrap up their catches for midnight snacks; cheetahs hunt their food by running faster than any other animal; termites attack our houses in organized groups; and honeybees create small factories to manufacture their food and provide their housing. All of these creatures go about their business on a planet that we dominate, at least temporarily.

What talents do we humans possess that have allowed us to dominate the earth? We are not very strong in proportion to our body mass, nor very swift afoot. Our senses of smell and hearing are well below par for mammals, although we do have fairly good stereoscopic vision. Our body hair is minimal, which would leave us quite cold in winter without our clothes. Our claws are neither strong nor sharp, and our fangs are nonexistent. There are, of course, some points to be made on the other side. We have thumbs, for example. Specifically, we have opposable thumbs, which gives us the ability to grasp and operate tools of all kinds. A great variety of human products and skills would be impossible without the thumb. But thumbs are not usually the first thing we think of when the secret of human dominance is in question. The first thought is usually of the human brain.

Humans don't have the largest brains in the animal kingdom; whales, for example, have much larger ones. But whales also have large bodies for their brains to operate, so their brains are busy directing muscles and supervising bodily processes, with little leisure time for solving equations. In terms of having a relatively large brain for their body size, humans are right up at the top of the animal world, along with dolphins—and dolphins don't have thumbs. A large brain coupled with a relatively small body mass has given humans a facility in thinking that sets us apart from other animals. But how have we used that facility to dominate the planet? At first glance it would seem that our tools—from the stone axe to the nuclear reactor—are the secret of our dominance. Yet there is a much more basic and more important product of our intelligence: before we became great toolmakers, we used our intelligence to organize ourselves into coordinated groups.

Humans are not the only animal to hit upon this secret of survival. Many other species of mammals live in coordinated groups, and, of course, the most striking examples come from the insect world. Whatever the species, the benefits are more or less the same. Baboons, wolves, bees, ants, and humans all have less difficulty surviving because they live in groups. The one distinctive feature about human groups, however, is that whereas other animals make their societies by instinct, we consciously create the kind of coordination our groups will have and then consciously teach that way of life to our children in each successive generation. Although we get attached to a way of life over time and may not want to change, the fact that we organize ourselves and teach each other consciously means that we have the potential to change the way we live. Bees have never been known to retool their industry when pollen becomes scarce.

The manner in which humans organize themselves into coordinated groups inspires the outlook of sociology. Sociology, like some other perspectives, tries to explain why people think and act in the ways that they do. The unique feature of the sociological outlook is that it looks for answers by examining the social groups within which people do their thinking and acting. Humans are born into social groups and are dependent on them for everything from the outset of their lives. Older individuals in those social groups teach the younger members about the particular way they live. As those younger members become older, they come to look and act remarkably like the members who initially taught them. The sociological outlook examines social groups and the pattern of coordination within them to gain a fuller understanding of why people behave as they do.

In this chapter we focus on the ways humans coordinate a variety of activities in their attempts to live their lives and how that overall coordination develops over time into larger human societies. As we look at the social groups that humans have created, we also look at how those groups, in effect, create humans. It is as impossible to imagine a human being without a human society as it is to imagine a honeybee without the hive. This chapter provides an overview of the rest of the book. We introduce some of the basic terms used by sociologists in order to emphasize the connections among these terms; all the terms will be developed in greater detail in later chapters. We also look at some examples of sociologists at work, showing how research applies the sociological outlook to help understand everyday life.

SOCIETY AS A HUMAN CREATION

When sociologists talk about societies, they are thinking not so much about people as about the ways particular groups of people live. The difference is that the ways of living change much more slowly than the people who learn to live by them. Specifically, a **society** is a relatively large, self-sufficient collection of people that (1) shares and transmits a common heritage from one generation to another, (2) contains patterns of behavior that govern interaction, and (3) occupies a given territory.

When you notice that large numbers of people in any society tend to be doing similar things on any given day, and that those same people tend to keep doing those same things from one day to the next, you are observing patterns of behavior. If you are reading this paragraph for a sociology class, for example, you can be assured that many other people are reading similar paragraphs today in similar books for more or less the same reasons that you are. Furthermore, students behaved that way in the previous generation and more than likely will continue to behave that way in the next. As we grow up in a society, we learn about the standard patterns of interaction that others already follow, and ultimately we follow them ourselves.

The sociologist is interested primarily in the ongoing patterns of behavior that people follow. These patterns of behavior in a society are far more than just random forms of interaction; they are highly coordinated, so that while one kind of need is being taken care of through one set of patterns, other kinds of needs are being tended to through other patterns. It is the *coordination of behavior patterns* that makes a society a useful means of survival.

COORDINATION AS A MODE OF ADAPTATION

Coordinated patterns of behavior in a society permit a variety of needs to be taken care of simultaneously. When different activities form in a society and different people come to specialize in those activities, sociologists refer to this phenomenon as a **division of labor.** We could imagine a simple society in which certain people might specialize in caring for children, others might specialize in gathering food from the environment, and still others might specialize in hunting and group protection. Thus, a variety of needs are taken care of simultaneously, and each need is probably taken care of quite well, since the individuals entrusted with it would have ample opportunity to perfect their skills through repetition.

Once a division of labor occurs, the number of divisions that can arise becomes unlimited. Looking just at hunters, for example, we could imagine a group of twenty or so individuals out to capture a large animal—a task none could accomplish alone. One subgroup might be in charge of fashioning a trap, another might specialize in driving the animal toward the trap, and still another might have perfected the art of slaughtering the animal after it has been trapped. The image of humans as tool-makers is striking in this example, but even more striking is the complex coordination of activities without which the tools would be useless. Primitive tools cannot fell an elephant, for example, unless they are used by coordinated groups in some kind of systematic fashion. Modern tools (such as an elephant gun) can accomplish the same end with only one hunter, but the complicated nature of modern tools requires coordination in the manufacturing process. Tools may be the secret of our success, but coordinated groups are the secret behind the secret.

Coordination and Communication How would it be possible for groups of people to work together if they were unable to communicate? Indeed, how would it be possible for any coordinated group to function without communication? A beehive requires communication. If the hive is attacked, the "guards" will sound an alert. If a worker bee finds a pollen source, it is able to communicate both the direction of and the distance to the source upon returning to the hive so that the other workers can retrieve the pollen (Dadant and Sons, 1975). Human groups take this process one step further: humans are conscious of their communication as they communicate.

The importance of being conscious of communication becomes apparent when you look more closely at communication itself. In its most fundamental sense, communication means that an idea or thought or experience of mine can become known to you through your experience of my behavior. My experience of pain, for example, can be communicated to you through your experience of watching me writhe in agony and hearing me scream. But this communication is not conscious on my part; in such pain, I would probably not care about communicating effectively. Nevertheless, my experience is communicated. As far as we know, this is the kind of communication that goes on in beehives.

At another level, I can communicate consciously with you through the use of symbols. A **symbol** can be anything that you and I both agree will stand for (or communicate) something else. A colored piece of cloth can stand for a nation-state; a hand gesture can communicate respect or disrespect; a sound produced by the vocal cords can stand for an object or an idea. These black marks on white paper that you are looking at right now stand for the ideas I was thinking as I entered them by means of my keyboard. Symbols are both limitless and flexible. They are limitless in that any new thing or idea can be communicated through a symbol designed for that purpose. They are flexible in that you and I can alter the meaning that we want a particular symbol to communicate. Symbols are tied to the things they communicate only in the specific ways and for the length of time that people in groups choose to have them serve that purpose.

The ultimate human symbol use is in the symbol system of language. A **language** is essentially a code (like Morse code or a spy's secret code) in which meaning is encoded into (or changed into) particular symbols according to the rules of the code, which are referred to as *grammar*. It is then possible for anyone who knows the rule system to decode (or change back into meaning) the symbols used in communication. To communicate through language, two people have to agree on which words will stand for which ideas and, in addition, on the rules by which the words will be strung together. In English, for example, "John hit Mary" communicates a very different meaning from "Mary hit John," even though the three words are identical in both cases. If all this makes language sound complicated, it is. Symbolic communication is truly one of the great and complex human creations.

Coordination allows social animals to function as groups. The worker bees surrounding the queen illustrate the kinds of coordination found in all societies, whether human or nonhuman. The main difference between the two (as far as we know) is that humans are conscious of the forms of coordination by which they live.

Coordination and Human Values As human behavior becomes coordinated in social groups, it is organized into ongoing patterns that are accepted as proper within the group. Language use, for example, depends on people following a particular symbol system from one day to the next so that they can understand each other. Such patterns endlessly fascinate the sociologist; the people in the social group who follow the patterns are aware of them also, though they don't have the same kind of awareness that the sociologist has as an outside observer. A fish probably has less understanding of swimming than we do since the fish is not aware of alternatives. But the fish has a greater attachment to swimming. A similar situation is found within human social groups: people get attached to their patterns.

Habitual patterns of behavior are hard to break. When habits are not just individual but are followed by everyone in a group, the force of others' expectations is added to the force of habit in general. Such patterns of behavior may begin because they are useful in dealing with some problem the social group has; over time they become important in their own right simply because they are there. They may continue when they are no longer useful or perhaps even destructive to the social group. In short, habits, or patterns of behavior, can become values in a social group.

A **value** is an ideal agreed on by a social group as to what is good or desirable. Americans, for example, value freedom, technology, motherhood, apple pie, and money—not necessarily in that order. Within the general range of values, the everyday patterns of behavior come to be valued by the people who follow them. Thus, wearing clothes in public is not only a pattern of American behavior, it is also valued as a desirable behavior. We come to believe strongly in our habits. And all of this results from the conscious manner in which humans coordinate themselves in social groups. Whatever patterns develop, those who follow them will notice them and think all manner of thoughts about them. Sociologists sum up this phenomenon by saying that humans develop cultures.

THE DEVELOPMENT OF CULTURE:
REASON AND RULES FOR COORDINATION

Culture is the most general concept used by a sociologist. It refers to all the objects, skills, ideas, beliefs, and patterns of behavior that are developed and shared by members of a social group. In short, anything that is created and shared by given groups of humans is part of culture. The patterns of everyday behavior in social groups that have held our attention up until now in this chapter form the core of culture and develop only as culture develops. All the elements of culture, from tools to religious beliefs, develop simultaneously and in an interconnected manner; changes in one element of culture result in changes in the other elements of culture. The development of the automobile for the mass market in the United States, for example, affected patterns of living, traveling, eating, praying, romancing, and consuming, to name just a few. Conversely, the automobile could not have been developed had not other elements of American culture provided large-scale industry, cities filled with wage workers, assorted technological advances necessary to the production of the automobile, and so on.

As patterns of behavior become habitual over time for a group of people, their consciousness of those patterns is reflected in their culture. The members of the group come to agree that certain things should be done by certain people in certain ways at certain times and in certain places. Such agreements come to be expressed as the norms of a culture. **Norms** are the shared rules that govern the wide variety of patterned behavior within the culture. Norms cannot be seen or touched, but their existence can be unmistakably felt through the negative responses of others when we violate the agreed-upon rules of behavior. We are probably most keenly aware of norms, however, when we are confused as to what they are. Such confusion typically occurs when cultures change quickly or when people move. Box 1.1 illustrates this problem through showing the confusion faced by immigrants in their new surroundings.

Norms provide only the what, where, how, and when of patterned behavior; it is left to values to provide the *why*. Values back up norms by providing the reasons for following them. Values may hold individuals to the norms when the force of habit fails and the utility of following the norm is called into question. Values may also keep individuals following norms when no one is watching to see that the norm is adhered to. People give their lives in the defense of values they believe in strongly, so it is small wonder that values play a major role in maintaining conformity to cultural norms. Unlike bees, which follow their patterns without question, humans develop elaborate systems of justification in their cultures so that individuals following current norms will not consciously search for alternatives. They would undoubtedly find some if they looked.

As culture develops, it organizes patterned behavior into **roles,** the expected behavior patterns that develop for specific activities or positions in a society. Because roles respond to the expectations of others, they may also be described as norm-governed behavior. To play a role is to follow a set of norms; conversely, to not play a role is to break a set of norms. Roles are often conveniently labeled in a culture. In American society, for example, one individual might simultaneously be a daughter, sister, cousin, aunt, mother, wife, student, church member, best friend, shopper, political activist, newsgroup member, soccer coach, and professional sociologist, just to scratch the surface of possibilities. Each of these roles demands different kinds of behavior, and each role carries with it a pattern such that each individual behaves more or less like other individuals playing the same role. Most individuals take to this variety as a duck takes to water, finding little difficulty in keeping track of the variety of expectations within each role and the different expectations from one role to the next.

BOX 1.1

Bride Theft among the Lao Hmong in Southern California

The Hmong (pronounced "Mung") people traditionally lived in what is now Laos and Thailand. The Vietnam War disrupted their lives tremendously, forcing many of them to immigrate to the United States. As with many immigrants to the United States, they have found adaptation always curious and often difficult. Anthropologist George M. Scott Jr. (1988) offers a case study involving several Hmong families in southern California, showing that it's hard for a man to find a wife when the rules of courtship change.

In Southeast Asia, the "normal" (or most typical) form of courtship for Hmong people involves extensive discussion, celebrations, and negotiations over bride price between members of two families from different clans. The marriage takes place after all parties in both families are satisfied with the arrangement. When negotiations break down, however, there is an alternative to this process. Bride theft occurs when a prospective groom (with the help of a few friends) kidnaps his prospective bride and holds her for three nights of sexual intercourse (with or without her consent). During these three days, his kinsmen approach the abducted girl's family and attempt to continue the negotiations from a position of somewhat greater strength (given that their daughter would now be less desirable to some other man as a result of having lost her virginity). Even in Southeast Asia, bride theft is not the norm, but at least it is tolerated. (Indeed, it once was the norm in the Western world and was legal in England as recently as the thirteenth century [Ackerman, 1994].)

Scott picks up his southern California case study with the frustrations of an Orange County Hmong man who wanted a wife. The man met an attractive sixteen-year-old Hmong girl at a wedding in San Diego and arranged a visit to her family some weeks later. During the visit, he suggested the girl accompany him on a trip to the supermarket but instead kidnapped her and took her back to Orange County. The girl (who knew of the practice) was apparently not overly upset about the turn of events, but the girl's mother was distressed enough to contact the local (American) authorities. Subsequently, an Orange County resettlement worker located the young man and woman and explained to the man that what he had done (kidnapping and rape) was a very serious offense in the United States. The man was instructed to return the girl or face criminal charges. Disgusted, the young man returned the girl. He was furious with the girl's mother and her clan for bringing in American authorities. Interestingly, the girl's clan was furious with the mother for exactly the same reason and attempted to convince her to arrange a wedding. By the time they convinced her, the Orange County man had become even angrier; he refused to marry the girl, arguing that if they could follow American laws when they felt like it, so could he. This made the girl's clan furious and led to permanent bad feeling between members of the two clans within the immigrant community.

As you can see from this brief account, most of the problems occurred because the players weren't sure which set of rules they were following—Hmong or American. As the events played out, members of both clans switched from one set to the other when it was to their immediate benefit. Social norms, when agreed upon, prevent this kind of problem.

In a manner of speaking, being born into a human society and its culture is like entering into an ongoing game. Whether field games like baseball or board games like Monopoly, games provide positions or roles for the players, rules that govern the play, artifacts with which to play, and ready-made values in the player's desire to win. Also, as with our cultures, we tend to get caught up in the playing of a game, perhaps feeling hate for our best friends when we go bankrupt in Monopoly. Just as the game provides a context for the patterned behavior that makes up the game, so culture provides a context for the patterned behavior that allows humans to survive in their societies. Culture provides them with technology, skills, knowledge, norms, values, and roles.

Because culture develops far more slowly than the individuals who learn about it and keep it thriving in each generation, it is easy to forget that culture is a human creation. Even though culture was begun by humans and is added to or changed by each generation of humans, it in turn creates the humans of each generation who will live within it. Parents who are caught up in the playing of their cultural "games" pass on that culture to their children, who generally accept it simply because it is there. This observation brings us to one of the central problems for the sociologist. Societies and cultures are simultaneously the creations and the creators of human beings. We make up the games ourselves, but we often forget that fact in the excitement of play.

HUMANS AS A SOCIAL CREATION

Few other creatures in the animal kingdom are dependent for so many years after birth as humans. Long after puppies and kittens are out on their own, human infants are just learning to crawl. Part of the reason for this difference is physiological—human bodies have slow maturation built into their design. But another reason brings us back to human societies: humans do not inherit their forms of coordination, as bees do; they must learn them from other humans. This process takes time and requires that young individuals remain around older individuals. A growing physical maturity then comes to be accompanied by a growing social maturity. Both are necessary to function as a human being in society.

How much of what people do is learned, and how much are they born with? Do murderers, for example, learn their behavior from others, are they born with murderous instincts, or both? This basic question—usually called the heredity versus environment question—is far from being answered. Humans begin learning from the moment of birth, if not before, so it becomes almost impossible to sort out the learning from the genetic input in a particular individual's life. One thing we do know, however, is that there are few limits to the things humans can learn from their cultures.

Remarkable cultural variation occurs around the world. There are some things that every human group must do, such as take care of dependent children, but the ways they carry out these activities vary considerably. Families can be large or small, male dominated or female dominated, run democratically or with an iron hand. They can be geared toward religious concerns, economic concerns, warfare concerns, or all three. However families are organized, the children born into them find little difficulty learning how they work and learning to believe in them. Unlike bees, humans have a wide variety of means for organizing the hive. A child born to parents in one culture can be adopted at birth by parents from another culture and have no problems with adjustment (unless members of the new culture reject the child). The hearts and minds of humans are both highly moldable and highly flexible. In the terminology of sociology this process is called *socialization*.

SOCIALIZATION: THE INTERNALIZATION OF CULTURE

Socialization is the ongoing process by which humans come to learn about and believe in their cultures. It is a process that begins at birth and continues until death. The process is different, of course, at different stages of life. Infants start from scratch and require the broad brushstrokes of the basics from the culture they are born into, whereas older people generally face a continuing series of "finishing touches" of socialization from their associates. Whatever the case, socialization never stops.

The persistence of socialization in social groups can be attributed to the group members themselves. Group members never tire of watching the behavior of others and of noting when that behavior is out of line with the shared norms of the group. That "noting" can take the form of comments, snickers, ridicule, withholding of affection, exile, or violence, depending on how strongly the group members feel about the norm that has been broken. Any of these responses serves to communicate to the offending members (1) the fact that a norm has been broken, (2) a definition of the norm so that it can be followed in the future, and (3) the importance of the norm. Along with this information comes enforcement; ridicule, for example, not only communicates the group's displeasure but is, in itself, an unpleasant experience that most of us seek to avoid. We can use the information so communicated to help us avoid such penalties in the future. Any enforcement of group norms (by any means) is called **social control** by sociologists. (The reading by Peter Berger following this chapter provides an in-depth look at this process.)

Just as group members never tire of socializing us, we seldom tire of helping them do so. Human beings are irretrievably social creatures. The social isolation of an adult is one of the most extreme punishments that can be inflicted; the social isolation of an infant leads to either death or mental disorder. Our need for each other makes each of us a willing participant in the process of socialization. In many cases we will seek out the norms of our social groups at the same time that other group members are virtually shining spotlights to help us find them. This situation of avid learners coupled with determined teachers gives tremendous strength and vitality to the process of socialization.

The study of socialization is not as simple as its theoretical description. In actuality American society is filled with disagreements and violence as "learners" rebel at the best efforts of the "teachers." Socialization is often less than smooth, and social control is not always effective. The reason stems in large part from the cultural diversity in American society. Within our overall society are many smaller groups, and these groups often hold values that differ both from those of the mainstream culture and from each other's norms. The average American adult comes into daily contact with a variety of groups and social situations that are incompatible with one another in terms of norms and values. A professional criminal can be a dedicated church member or a ruthless businessman can be a loving father and husband. The problem in the study of socialization is not that social groups don't have great power over their members but that there are so many different groups doing the socializing. The more influence one group has, the less open individuals of that group will be to the socialization and social control of other groups. Consider the enthusiasm with which many members of the People's Temple apparently followed their cult leader Jim Jones into mass suicide in Jonestown in 1978. After persuading his followers to move to South America, he then convinced many of them that their suicides could have significant religious meaning. They lined up to drink poisoned drinks. Or consider the experience of the Branch Davidians under David Koresh, who went down in flames in Waco, Texas, in 1993 during a shootout with federal government agents. These situations illustrate both the failure of socialization by the mainstream American culture and the power of socialization within a closed group.

While the results of socialization vary considerably within one culture, as with the examples above, the greatest differences occur between cultures. Consider the case of al-Qaida and the Islamic fundamentalist movement. The 9/11 attacks on the United States could only have occurred through incredibly strong group ties and effective socialization practices among the perpetrators. From the standpoint of American culture, both the goals and the socialization outcomes of such groups are alien and repugnant. From the standpoint of the Islamic fundamentalist movement, American culture is alien and repugnant. Yet the socialization processes

This poster on a wall in a Jenin refugee camp in the West Bank glorifies a Palestinian suicide bomber. The boy in the background is the aim of the socialization.

themselves—the manner in which individuals become loyal group members—are not all that dissimilar.

Socialization leads to a curious development in the thinking of the individuals it affects. As infants, we see ourselves as pretty much the center of the universe. As socialization continues, we become more aware of how others view us; our emotional needs are changing, and we will want to ensure the continued affection of those most important to us. As we focus on the views others have of us and our behavior, we come to look at ourselves more and more as others do. If others treat us as an unpleasant nuisance, we will come to see ourselves as an unpleasant nuisance. Once we get used to seeing ourselves this way, we will not even need others physically around to respond to us; we will be able to imagine their responses, based on our knowledge of their past responses.

As we come to see ourselves in terms of our social group, we are internalizing the culture of the social group. **Internalization** is the process by which we come to know the norms of a culture and, more important, come to hold the values of a culture as our own. When you accept someone else's view of who you are, you also accept many other aspects of that person's values. If, for example, your social group believes that women should be homemakers and mothers and it communicates to you that you are a good little girl for playing with dolls, you will tend to internalize this general value for women while also internalizing the view of yourself as a "good little girl." All members of society seek positive views of themselves from others whose views are important to them; more general values tend to sneak in the back door at the same time. This process happens more or less unconsciously, so that one day you wake up and the values are your own. Once they are established, they may be almost immovable, even if you become aware of them, don't like them, and desire to change them. The example of women's roles illustrates this phenomenon, but consider a simpler and more graphic example. We are taught in American society to value cow flesh as a food but not grasshopper flesh, even though both are good sources of protein. Try to eat grasshopper for dinner tonight, and you will experience an internalized value.

Internalization involves more than accepting the values of our society. We also internalize the knowledge of our culture. Some parts of that knowledge are obvious— for example, the skills and general information that we learn. Learning how to read, how to fry chicken, how to drive a car, how to vote, and how to play baseball are all parts of knowledge that we are conscious of, both when we teach them and when we learn them. We internalize them in the sense that they become added to the repertoire of things we can do. But our cultural knowledge also provides us with a **worldview,** or general perception of the world. A cultural worldview is seldom either taught or learned consciously but develops along with the skills and information that are. For example, most Americans believe that individuals are all different and should have some personal liberty; that private property is fundamental to social life; that dreams aren't real events and aren't overly important; and that the earth is here for humans to live on rather than live with. We don't have to look too hard to find cultures that differ from our own on each of these elements. Sociologists are interested in the internalization of a cultural worldview because it colors (or, from another point of view, limits) what people see. As the United States deals with the growth of Islamic fundamentalism in the Middle East and the values and perspectives that drive its adherents, the limitations in outlook caused by culture appear to be an increasingly important obstacle to peace in that area.

The overall picture of socialization painted by sociologists is that every part of the individual's personality is in some way affected by membership in a social group. The fact that we are conscious of much of this socialization gives us a false belief that we are aware of all of it. Our very desire to be members of and accepted by at least one social group overrides our ability to stand back and understand what the social group does to us in return. Such an understanding is a fundamental part of the sociological outlook. But in calling attention to the ways in which we are unconsciously manipulated by our social groups, the sociological outlook brings up questions of freedom and conformity in society that are not necessarily comforting.

FREEDOM VERSUS CONFORMITY IN SOCIETY

Sociology paints a picture of social groups as coercive. Members of social groups demand conformity from each other and employ ruthless tactics of social control when they don't get it. At the same time, group members facing social control seem desperate to learn the group's norms so that they might conform voluntarily. In spite of this overall orientation, however, few sociologists would relegate humans to the status of behavioral robots. The variety of social groups that most people associate with lessens the influence of each—ridicule from one group will not be quite as devastating if we get respect from some other group. Moreover, socialization may not be the sledgehammer that sociologists describe; people are very likely more than just blank sheets of paper waiting for the writing of society. But, for all of this, we still come back to the basic observation that many people are more than happy to turn over their freedom of choice to the social group.

Looking at the ways social groups provide basic patterns of behavior for their members offers a new perspective on the question of freedom. If we fit ourselves into the ongoing patterns that our social groups provide, we give up our freedom to decide what to do, but we are also saved from the responsibility of having to decide. A soldier who fires at the enemy in wartime has been given an order, and if he is a good soldier (if he has internalized the role), he will not feel guilty. It was the decision of the officer who gave the order that made the enemy soldier die, not the action of the private who pulled the trigger. When our roles carry with them directives of this sort, we can always blame the role for what we do and hold it, rather than ourselves, responsible.

On the other side of the coin, people are far from being role robots; indeed, social experiences often place us in too many conflicting situations for roles to be followed with unquestioned obedience. Soldiers who take orders share uniforms with other soldiers who ignore orders. New roles can develop within such situations, as, for example, the "fragging" of officers in Vietnam by enlisted personnel, who quietly killed their commanding officers when they disapproved of the orders given. Less dramatically, some soldiers in the 2004 Iraq War refused orders to drive poorly armored supply trucks into dangerous territory. The same situations can look very different to different people.

The basic question of freedom versus conformity is one for which sociology has no answer; sociology simply provides better ways to ask it. Too much personal freedom is highly disruptive and can be dangerous to personal welfare; we don't want to give others the right to murder on the pretext of not limiting their liberty. On the other hand, some of the horrors of history—the Spanish Inquisition, Hitler's Third Reich, and the mass suicide of People's Temple followers at Jonestown— all happened in the name of conformity. People didn't have the power or weren't psychologically able to say no; they fit into the patterns provided for them and passed the responsibility for their own actions on to others. All these cases of individual submersion in the group raise interesting questions about human behavior.

The social groups we create turn around and seduce us into being loyal members. By focusing on the processes of socialization, sociology brings that seduction more into the light. Individuals can thus use the sociological outlook to watch the process of manipulation in action. That does not mean that we will be immune from those processes, as everyone needs some kind of social group to survive, but at least we will have some protection provided by the understanding.

On a more general level, the sociological outlook focuses on the sources of social groups themselves. It is easy to forget that society and culture are the creations of humans and, as such, are open to change by humans. Living in a social group, playing its roles according to its norms, and accepting its values take on the characteristics of a game played for so long that the participants forget they're playing it. Just as people become caught up in the playing of a game, so people become caught up in their social groups. Being rich and powerful in American society can make you feel good and important, just as owning the major properties in a Monopoly game can make you feel good for an afternoon. By bringing society itself into question, sociology places all the rules and values we live with into a sharper perspective. We become aware of where they come from, how we came to accept them, and how they make us feel. This understanding gives them a little less control over our freedom.

SUMMARY

This chapter is both an introduction to and an overview of sociology. It defines society as the coordination of human activities, with this coordination being a source of strength for and an aid to human survival. Unlike other animals, humans consciously build societies. Thus they have the flexibility of being able to change their societies should circumstances require it and of having a changeable system of communication. In spite of the conscious nature of their societies, however, humans become attached to their particular forms of coordination and include within their cultures a system of values supporting their lifestyle.

The conscious and flexible nature of human societies requires that each generation become socialized into the culture. Socialization results in internalization as the individual comes to hold cultural values as his or her own. As social creatures, humans desire the company and acceptance of others; they are capable of freedom, yet they often desire conformity to the ways of their cultures.

These general observations about human societies can be applied more specifically toward understanding everyday life. Even the most trivial social situations are norm-governed, and other participants will expect us to follow those norms. If we are not familiar with the norms, the other participants will generally attempt to socialize us into behavior that follows the norms and perhaps into an acceptance of the values behind those norms. If a newcomer to the social group internalizes these values, the newcomer comes to see himself or herself in a new light.

Glossary

Culture The configuration of humanly created objects, skills, ideas, beliefs, and patterns of behavior that are learned and transmitted by members of a society in a shared fashion.

Division of labor The separation of activities within a society, coupled with specialization in these activities by different members of the society.

Internalization The process by which individuals come to see themselves in terms of the roles they play and come to share in the values of the social group, making those values their own.

Language A symbol system that functions as a code into which meaning is encoded and from which meaning is decoded according to particular rules.

Norms The shared rules that govern the wide variety of patterned behavior within a given culture, forming the expectations for specific behaviors in particular social situations.

Roles The expected behavior patterns that develop for specific activities or are typical for specific positions within a society.

Social control The enforcement of group norms by any means through the imposition of sanctions in response to behavior.

Socialization The ongoing process by which humans come to learn about and believe in their cultures, from learning the roles to sharing the values. Through socialization the individual becomes a member of the social group and develops a sense of self.

Society A relatively large, self-sufficient collection of people that (1) shares and transmits a common heritage from one generation to another, (2) contains patterns of behavior that govern interaction, and (3) occupies a given territory.

Symbol A word, gesture, object, or image of any sort that, by the agreement of two or more people, stands for another idea or object.

Value An ideal agreed upon by a social group as to what is good or desirable.

Study Questions

1. How does the coordination built into both human societies and nonhuman societies produce increased survival potential for societal members?
2. Why is communication necessary for societies to exist?
3. Unlike other species, humans communicate by using symbols. What are symbols and how do they improve communication?
4. Unlike other species, humans are self-conscious. How does this ability make human societies more flexible and therefore more adaptable?

5. What is culture? How does it relate to the forms of coordination in societies? In particular, how do values affect that coordination?
6. What are social norms and social roles? How do norms define roles in everyday life?
7. What is socialization and why is it so crucial in societies? How and why do we learn from others? What things do we learn?
8. What is internalization, and how does it naturally result from the way we live in societies? What kinds of things can we internalize?
9. Once we have learned to live in a society, becoming adult societal members, just how free are we in our thoughts and behaviors? What choices are left to us?

Peter Berger   **READING**

INVITATION TO SOCIOLOGY

Peter Berger has explored a variety of areas within the discipline of sociology throughout the course of his career, but his *An Invitation to Sociology* is particularly well suited not only for the beginning sociologist (for whom it is intended) but for this chapter, as it explores the sociological perspective on human freedom. Since most of us are brought up to believe ourselves to be individuals who make our own decisions and chart our own courses in life, the sociological perspective presents us with a challenge by emphasizing how our thoughts and behaviors are affected by outside influences. In the following section from his book, Berger explores the influences (termed *social control* by sociologists) that tend to keep us in line, with or without our consent.

Social control is one of the most generally used concepts in sociology. It refers to the various means used by a society to bring its recalcitrant members back into line. No society can exist without social control. Even a small group of people meeting but occasionally will have to develop their mechanisms of control if the group is not to dissolve in a very short time. It goes without saying that the instrumentalities of social control vary greatly from one social situation to another. Opposition to the line in a business organization may mean what personnel directors call a terminal interview, and in a criminal syndicate a terminal automobile ride. Methods of control vary with the purpose and character of the group in question. In either case, control mechanisms function to eliminate undesirable personnel and (as it

was put classically by King Christophe of Haiti when he had every tenth man in his forced-labor battalion executed) "to encourage the others."

The ultimate and, no doubt, the oldest means of social control is physical violence. In the savage society of children it is still the major one. But even in the politely operated societies of modern democracies the ultimate argument is violence. No state can exist without a police force or its equivalent in armed might. This ultimate violence may not be used frequently. There may be innumerable steps before its application, in the way of warnings and reprimands. But if all the warnings are disregarded, even in so slight a matter as paying a traffic ticket, the last thing that will happen is that a couple of cops show up at the door with handcuffs and a Black Maria. Even the moderately courteous cop who hands out the initial traffic ticket is likely to wear a gun—just in case. And even in England, where he does not in the normal course of events, he will be issued one if the need arises.

In Western democracies, with their ideological emphasis on voluntary compliance with popularly legislated rules, this constant presence of official violence is underemphasized. It is all the more important to be aware of it. Violence is the ultimate foundation of any political order. The commonsense view of society senses this, and this may have something to do with the widespread popular reluctance to eliminate capital punishment from the criminal law (though this reluctance is probably based in equal measure on stupidity, superstition and the congenital bestiality that jurists share with the bulk of their fellow citizens). However, the statement that political order rests ultimately on violence is just as true in states that have abolished capital punishment. Under certain circumstances the use of their weapons is permitted to state troopers in Connecticut, where (much to their freely expressed gratification) an electric chair graces the central penal establishment, but the same possibility exists for their colleagues in Rhode Island, where police and prison authorities have to get along without this facility. It goes without saying that in countries with less of a democratic and humanitarian ideology the instruments of violence are much less gingerly displayed—and employed.

Since the constant use of violence would be impractical and also ineffective, the official organs of social control rely mostly on the restraining influence of the generally known availability of the means of violence. For various reasons this reliance is usually justified in any society that is not on the brink of catastrophic dissolution (as, say, in situations of revolution, military defeat or natural disaster). The most important reason for this is the fact that, even in dictatorial and terroristic states, a regime tends to gain acceptance and even acceptability by the simple passage of time. This is not the place to go into the sociopsycho-

logical dynamics of this fact. In democratic societies there is at least the tendency for most people to share the values on behalf of which the means of violence are employed (this does not mean that these values have to be fine—the majority of the white people in some Southern communities may be, for instance, in favor of using violence, as administered by the police agencies, in order to uphold segregation—but it does mean that the employment of the means of violence is approved by the bulk of the populace). In any functioning society violence is used economically and as a last resort, with the mere threat of this ultimate violence sufficing for the day-to-day exercise of social control. For our purposes in this argument, the most important matter to underline is that nearly all men live in social situations in which, if all other means of coercion fail, violence may be officially and legally used against them.

If the role of violence in social control is thus understood, it becomes clear that the, so to speak, penultimate means of coercion are more important for more people most of the time. While there is a certain uninspired sameness about the methods of intimidation thought up by jurists and policemen, the less-than-violent instrumentalities of social control show great variety and sometimes imagination. Next in line after the political and legal controls one should probably place economic pressure. Few means of coercion are as effective as those that threaten one's livelihood or profit. Both management and labor effectively use this threat as an instrumentality of control in our society. But economic means of control are just as effective outside the institutions properly called the economy. Universities or churches use economic sanctions just as effectively in restraining their personnel from engaging in deviant behavior deemed by the respective authorities to go beyond the limits of the acceptable. It may not be actually illegal for a minister to seduce his organist, but the threat of being barred forever from the exercise of his profession will be a much more effective control over this temptation than the possible threat of going to jail. It is undoubtedly not illegal for a minister to speak his mind on issues that the ecclesiastical bureaucracy would rather have buried in silence, but the chance of spending the rest of his life in minimally paid rural parishes is a very powerful argument indeed. Naturally such arguments are employed more openly in economic institutions proper; but the administration of economic sanctions in churches or universities is not very different in its end results from that used in the business world.

Where human beings live or work in compact groups, in which they are personally known and to which they are tied by feelings of personal loyalty (the kind that sociologists call primary groups), very potent and simultaneously very subtle mechanisms of control are constantly brought to bear upon the actual or potential deviant. These are the mechanisms of persuasion, ridicule, gossip and opprobrium. It has been discovered that in group discussions going on over a period of time individuals modify their originally held opinions to conform to the group norm, which corresponds to a kind of arithmetic mean of all the opinions represented in the group. Where this norm lies obviously depends on the constituency of the group. For example, if you have a group of twenty cannibals arguing over cannibalism with one noncannibal, the chances are that in the end he will come to see their point and, with just a few face-saving reservations (concerning, say, the consumption of close relatives), will go over completely to the majority's point of view. But if you have a group discussion between ten cannibals who regard human flesh aged over sixty years as too tough for a cultivated palate and ten other cannibals who fastidiously draw the line at fifty, the chances are that the group will eventually agree on fifty-five as the age that divides the dejeuner from the debris when it comes to sorting out prisoners. Such are the wonders of group dynamics. What lies at the bottom of this apparently inevitable pressure towards consensus is probably a profound human desire to be accepted, presumably by whatever group is around to do the accepting. This desire can be manipulated most

effectively, as is well known by group therapists, demagogues and other specialists in the field of consensus engineering.

Ridicule and gossip are potent instruments of social control in primary groups of all sorts. Many societies use ridicule as one of the main controls over children—the child conforms not for fear of punishment but in order not to be laughed at. Within our own larger culture, "kidding" in this way has been an important disciplinary measure among Southern Negroes. But most men have experienced the freezing fear of making oneself ridiculous in some social situation. Gossip, as hardly needs elaboration, is especially effective in small communities, where most people live their lives in a high degree of social visibility and inspectability by their neighbors. In such communities gossip is one of the principal channels of communication, essential for the maintenance of the social fabric. Both ridicule and gossip can be manipulated deliberately by any intelligent person with access to their lines of transmission.

Finally, one of the most devastating means of punishment at the disposal of a human community is to subject one of its members to systematic opprobrium and ostracism. It is somewhat ironic to reflect that this is a favorite control mechanism with groups opposed on principle to the use of violence. An example of this would be "shunning" among the Amish Mennonites. An individual who breaks one of the principal tabus of the group (for example, by getting sexually involved with an outsider) is "shunned." This means that, while permitted to continue to work and live in the community, not a single person will speak to him ever. It is hard to imagine a more cruel punishment. But such are the wonders of pacifism.

It is possible, then, to perceive oneself as standing at the center (that is, at the point of maximum pressure) of a set of concentric circles, each representing a system of social control. The outer ring might well represent the legal and political system under which one is obligated to live. This is the system that, quite against one's will, will tax one, draft one into the military, make one obey its innumerable rules and regulations, if need be put one in prison, and in the last resort will kill one. One does not have to be a right-wing Republican to be perturbed by the ever-increasing expansion of this system's power into every conceivable aspect of one's life. A salutary exercise would be to note down for the span of a single week all the occasions, including fiscal ones, in which one came up against the demands of the politico-legal system. The exercise can be concluded by adding up the sum total of fines and/or terms of imprisonment that disobedience to the system might lead to. The consolation, incidentally, with which one might recover from this exercise would consist of the recollection that law-enforcement agencies are normally corrupt and of only limited efficiency.

Another system of social control that exerts its pressures towards the solitary figure in the center is that of morality, custom and manners. Only the most urgent-seeming (to the authorities, that is) aspects of this system are endowed with legal sanctions. This does not mean, however, that one can safely be immoral, eccentric or unmannered. At this point all the other instrumentalities of social control go into action. Immorality is punished by loss of one's job, eccentricity by the loss of one's chances of finding a new one, bad manners by remaining uninvited and uninvitable in the groups that respect what they consider good manners. Unemployment and loneliness may be minor penalties compared to being dragged away by the cops, but they may not actually appear so to the individuals thus punished. Extreme defiance against the mores of our particular society, which is quite sophisticated in its control apparatus, may lead to yet another consequence—that of being defined, by common consent, as "sick."

DISCUSSION QUESTIONS

1. Berger says that violence is the basis of social control but that it is also generally impractical. What does he mean by this? Why isn't violence practical?

2. Ostracism, or "shunning" (among the Amish), is singled out by Berger as being one of the most devastating and effective means of social control. Why should a lack of response from others be more effective than either a violent or nonviolent direct response from other group members? If Berger is right, what does that say about the importance of social group membership to most individuals?

SOCIOLOGY AS A SOCIAL SCIENCE

S ociology is an outlook, a way of looking at people in hopes of understanding why they do the things they do. Of course, in order to explain why people act as they do, sociology must also pay some attention to the what, where, how, and when of human actions, but the ultimate aim of sociology is always to explain why. In the search for explanations of human action, the sociological outlook is only one perspective among many. It differs, for example, from religious explanations of human action and, to a lesser extent, from psychological explanations of human action. Different perspectives provide different kinds of explanations since they begin with different assumptions about how the world works. Specifically, **sociology** is a social science that seeks the causes of human behavior in the workings of the social groups and institutions within which people live. This book invites you to add the sociological perspective to your arsenal of outlooks; it will give you access to an additional kind of explanation for the people and situations you encounter.

This chapter looks more closely at sociology in practice. After comparing sociological explanations with psychological explanations of human action, sociology is shown in a more formal manner, as a social *science*.

SOCIOLOGY VERSUS PSYCHOLOGY: DIFFERENT KINDS OF EXPLANATIONS

In order to compare two kinds of explanations, we first need something to explain. For that purpose, consider the following fictional account:

> Johnny Smith had spent the last half of his twelve years in and out of trouble. He had been a polished shoplifter at the age of six. Older boys on the block would create some kind of distraction in the corner grocery to cover the theft they had assigned to Johnny. Needless to say, Johnny finally got caught—which enhanced his reputation in the neighborhood as well as providing an additional frustration for his mother.
>
> Johnny's mother worked as a shipping clerk in a nearby factory and tried to apply her small paycheck and limited free time to the raising of her three children. Johnny was her oldest and had been only four when his father deserted the family.

With his father absent and mother working, Johnny had a lot of free time on his hands without the restrictions of parental supervision.

Johnny's experience in the first grade was less than adequate, and it went downhill from there. He never learned to read and fell farther and farther behind the expectations of the grades into which he was constantly promoted. As the years went by, Johnny began to associate almost exclusively with other boys having the same frustrating school experience as he was. Johnny became the leader of a group of seven boys, who began to specialize in petty theft and minor extortion. By the time he was eleven, Johnny was well known to the police and apparently beyond the control of his mother.

By the time he turned twelve, Johnny was well established as the leader of his gang (which now had a name, a secret handshake, and an official meeting place in an abandoned building). After an unpleasant run-in with school authorities and a subsequent suspension, Johnny organized his gang into an evening's activity of vandalizing their school. When Johnny was arrested for this action, he told the authorities that he was very sorry for what he had done and hadn't meant to. From time to time, Johnny said, he simply lost control of his actions.

This brief description of Johnny gives us some factual information on the hows, wheres, and whens of Johnny's childhood but leaves open the question of why. Why did Johnny spend much of his time in trouble with the police and why did he finally vandalize his school? Of the many answers that could be given, consider the following explanations:

1. Johnny is the victim of a basic personality disorder (or is "mentally ill"). He has consistently had trouble with personal relationships in his family and at school, reacting violently to the best efforts of his mother and teachers to help him. His constant aggressive behavior toward others and his final senseless aggression toward the school building itself indicate his inability to cope. His own admission that he often feels not in control of his actions supports this explanation.
2. Most of the experiences Johnny has faced in his life have attacked his self-esteem. First, his father deserted the family, leaving Johnny without a significant male role model and giving him the feeling that perhaps something he did made his father leave. Later, his failure at school made him feel unworthy and led him to look for social experiences in which he could be successful. He found these experiences as the leader of a young gang in which other boys looked up to him and respected his decisions. As his gang increased in importance in his life, his family and school experiences decreased in importance and lost influence over his behavior. By ignoring his family and attacking his school, he was attacking the situations that he felt had attacked him.
3. Public education in the United States today does little to help the poor to advance; poor children tend to fail in the classroom while the children of high-

income families tend to succeed. The institution of education also serves to cluster children of the same age and to draw their attention to their peer group. When schools introduce children to each other and then give poor children the experience of failure in the classroom, those children have much in common. One of the things they have in common is opposition to the school that does not serve them well. In this manner the institution of education as it operates in the United States today helps to create youth gangs among the poor and stimulates those gangs to commit acts of violence against the school.

Explanation 1 could be characterized as a psychological explanation. As a perspective, psychology focuses on individuals, emphasizing their attitudes, emotions, and abilities to cope with other individuals. In a manner of speaking, psychology finds the "causes" of human behavior to be inherent in (or inside) human beings themselves. Thus, Johnny's actions are seen as reflections of other occurrences (frustration, anger, and so on) that are going on inside Johnny.

Explanation 3, at the other extreme, could be characterized as a sociological explanation. Sociology finds the causes of human behavior somewhere in the workings of the social groups and institutions within which humans live. It is even possible (as suggested by explanation 3) to provide a sociological explanation of an individual's behavior without ever looking inside the head of the individual whose behavior is being explained.

Explanation 2 includes a little of both psychology and sociology; it finds the "causes" of Johnny's behavior in the groups and institutions within which Johnny lives, but it also suggests that Johnny's personal response to those social situations plays a major role in explaining his behavior.

The three explanations are perhaps as fictional as the story of Johnny they were designed to explain. Explanations 1 and 3, in particular, are extreme (or ideal types of) psychological and sociological explanations; it would be rare today to find a psychologist who completely ignored the social environment of an individual or a sociologist who completely ignored an individual's response to his or her social experiences. Psychology and sociology differ from each other primarily in the emphasis they place on different factors in their explanations. Social psychology, which sees the importance of both factors, is a recognized subdiscipline of both sociology and psychology.

Before we leave this comparison of different outlooks, it might be interesting to note a few more possible explanations outside the realms of both sociology and psychology. It could be argued that Johnny behaved as he did because:

4. He was possessed by the devil.
5. He was under the influence of an alien being from another planet.
6. His astrological sign periodically led him into conflict with the astrological signs of his mother and teachers.

Whereas a psychologist would be interested in the scores that individuals attained on a test like the one these people are taking, a sociologist might be interested in trends shown by certain subgroups or even in the overall phenomenon of mass testing.

7. He inherited a group of genes from his parents that gave him a body chemistry prone to violence and aggression.
8. He normally consumed an unbalanced diet with large quantities of sugar (or some other behavior-altering substance) that increased his aggressive tendencies.

This short list of explanations by no means exhausts the possibilities. The important point to remember is the connection between different outlooks and the explanations they provide. A religious outlook might lead to explanation 4, while biochemistry might suggest explanation 7. We might think explanation 5 is limited to the realm of science fiction, but remember that traveling in rockets to the moon used to be limited to it, too. It is important to consider also how different explanations for problems lead to different "remedies." A psychological explanation leads us to change Johnny, whereas a sociological explanation leads us to change social factors, such as the school environment. A biochemical explanation would lead us to treat Johnny with medication. Accepting a sociological outlook and its explanation does not replace other outlooks and explanations; it can be added to them and applied when it seems most useful. One of the clearest statements on the sociological perspective has been offered by American sociologist C. Wright Mills (see the reading at the end of this chapter). As he puts it, the sociological imagination turns your private troubles into public issues by the way you come to think about them.

SOCIOLOGY AS A SCIENCE

Unlike a religious outlook, a sociological outlook is *scientific*. Unlike biochemistry (which is also a scientific outlook), sociology is a *social scientific* outlook. Understanding the sociological outlook requires an understanding of **social science**. Sociology does not always live up to its scientific ideals, but an understanding of those ideals should bring the nature of sociological research into clearer focus. Knowing what sociologists are trying to achieve in their research should help you understand why they go about it in the ways they do.

Science, whether social, natural, or physical, is a way or a method for understanding. To the scientist, *understanding* means explaining why something under study acts or behaves the way it does. The explanation is the product of the scientist's thought and involves constructing concepts and specifying how those concepts relate to one another. Thus, for example, a scientific explanation of how you catch a cold would involve concepts such as *bacteria* and *antibodies*. It would then proceed to explain how bacteria enter the human body and how the body attacks them. A logically organized scientific explanation is called a **theory**. A scientific orientation does not stop at that point, however. The theory must be tested according to scientific methods. If the theory predicts that certain kinds of behavior (of bacteria, people, or whatever) will occur under certain kinds of circumstances for certain kinds of reasons, it is up to the scientist to check that prediction. If the behavior does in fact occur under the specified circumstances, there is a good chance the reasons offered for that prediction are correct (in other words, the theory is correct). We discuss theories further in the following section.

Ideally, science proceeds in the same manner regardless of the object under study. Social scientists should differ from other scientists only in their concern with human behavior as opposed to the behavior of bacteria or electrons; a social science is a scientific discipline that studies human behavior through a perspective on the social context of that behavior. The actual situation, however, is much more complicated. Bacteria and electrons rarely object to being studied, nor do they offer suggestions directly to the scientist while under investigation. Perhaps even more important, the physical or natural scientist has no direct vested interest in the behavior of the objects under study; the scientist will not have a brother or sister married to a bacterium. The social scientist, on the other hand, faces all of the above complications plus many more. The biologist can create and destroy bacteria during experiments, but the social scientist *cannot* (or certainly *should not*) experiment on people that way. In other words, the human subject matter affects the research methods of the social scientist as well as presenting a unique object of study.

In the rest of this chapter, we look at the methods of science as practiced by the social science of sociology. For purposes of clarity, this examination is separated into two sections: we look first at ways sociologists create and use concepts and theories, and second at the methodologies they use to test those theories. Remember, however, that this logical separation is not generally a practical separation; the collection and testing of scientific data are part of the process of building concepts and theories (and vice versa).

Concepts and Theories in Sociology

The concept is the building block of science, but the use of concepts is not limited to scientists. Concepts are the building blocks of all human thinking; scientists are just more systematic and self-conscious about the way they use them. A brief look at the way we use concepts in everyday life might therefore aid us in understanding scientific concepts.

CONCEPTS

A **concept** directs our perceptions of the world around us by specifying what we should notice and what we should ignore; it calls our attention to certain similarities among objects or ideas and at the same time directs us to ignore all differences. A chair, for example, is a concept that directs our attention to objects that provide a place to sit and include some kind of backrest. Chairs can be large or small and can be constructed of a variety of materials, but the concept directs us to ignore all those differences and to focus on two basic similarities. The concept *chair* is useful because people like to sit and they want to be able to recognize places to sit, even in an otherwise strange environment. Concepts therefore reflect the interests of the people who created them.

All concepts are human creations. Chairs are not inherently similar to each other; they are similar only because we want to think of them that way. Likewise, hamburgers and apples are both food because we think of them as things to eat. Grasshoppers, on the other hand, are not normally included within the concept *food* in our culture—not because we cannot eat them, but because we don't want to eat them. People create and use concepts to deal with an otherwise impossibly complex situation. We live in a world in which no two things or events are ever exactly the same; to cope with that complexity, we must simplify the variation. Concepts are the tools we use to do that.

While concepts direct our attention, they simultaneously limit us. By calling attention to some basic similarities among objects or ideas, they discourage us from looking for other similarities unspecified by the concept. We get used to our concepts just as we get used to our other habits. If we look at the world in one way long enough, we might not want a new concept that will give us a different perspective. Because we see most of the world through our concepts, those parts of the world not highlighted by our concepts must necessarily pass us by until we develop concepts to corner them.

This discussion of concepts is of crucial importance to scientists because they attempt to use concepts in a systematic and self-conscious manner. Scientists must always be aware of how their thoughts and observations are subject to conceptual limitations. If the wrong concepts are used, a scientific problem can be stared at forever and never be understood. In medicine, for example, the concepts *bacterium, virus,* and *protozoan* made it possible to understand disease and respond to it effectively. Until that conceptual breakthrough, disease was a vast puzzle; it was known only to be contagious. Malaria, for example, was narrowed down to swampy areas in the summertime, especially where large numbers of people slept outside at night. If you're not looking at a problem with useful concepts, staring at it won't solve it, even if the malaria-carrying mosquito lights on your nose.

We can illustrate the effects of concepts on observations with some of the sociological concepts introduced in Chapter 1. Consider the concept *role,* for example. A nonsociologist would probably attempt to understand a particular individual's behavior by thinking about the similarity of the behavior in question to other behaviors of that individual. The concept *individual* directs your attention to those similarities, and it is certainly a useful concept. But role sheds a different kind of light on the problem. The concept *role* redirects your attention to the behavior of other individuals in the same situation. The norms that govern roles in that particular situation may explain the behavior in question. If you currently occupy the role of student, is your behavior totally predictable from knowledge about you in other situations, or would it help to know something about the expectations of teachers and other students with whom you interact as a student? The noisy extravert at a party is sometimes a quiet, passive student in the classroom.

THEORIES

Concepts are important to science, but the real goal of scientific inquiry is theory construction. A theory specifies relations among concepts, predicting the degree to which they affect each other, and why. The concept *bacteria,* for example, is not very useful in preventing disease without a theory that explains how bacteria enter bodies, their impact on life processes within bodies, and the means by which bodies counteract that impact. In fact, this germ theory of disease made possible the development of vaccinations, which make the individual immune to specific bacteria in the future.

How scientists create theories is one of the great mysteries; although scientists are generally imagined to be very down-to-earth and methodical, there is something truly creative and artistic in theory creation. Many aspects of Albert Einstein's famous theory of relativity could not be tested until the development of space flight many decades later. How could he have formed such a theory without the ability to test his preliminary ideas against the world?

A theory states that one concept causes changes in another concept and specifies the degree of those changes. The germ theory of disease specifies the changes in the body caused by disease-causing microorganisms. It also specifies the degree of those changes, which has enabled researchers to develop the correct dosage of vaccine.

Sociology has a vast array of concepts to offer, but exact predictions of how they cause each other to change are few and far between. We know, for example, that group pressure can cause an individual to change his or her attitudes. But how much can those attitudes be changed, and why are some individuals more vulnerable to group pressure than others? Sociology can demonstrate relationships among concepts, but exacting predictions seem to be blocked by the complexity of human beings and their societies.

At least part of the problem in the development of sociological theory stems from problems inherent in sociological research. A scientist can manipulate bacteria in the laboratory, but there are limits to the kinds of experiments humans can be used in. The question of human experimentation is, in fact, a major concern of sociologists today, as some past experiments have stepped close to or over the line of ethical research. But even if sociologists were not limited in their laboratory research, how do we know that an individual's reaction in a laboratory situation would be anything like his or her reactions in real social situations? We already know that people play different roles in different situations; laboratory experiments may tell us a lot about laboratory roles and not much else. The problems of theory building are closely tied to the methods of scientific inquiry, but before turning to those methods, we examine some of the major theoretical traditions that have developed in sociology.

MAJOR THEORETICAL PERSPECTIVES IN SOCIOLOGY

Although sociological theorists have devised a wide variety of theoretical approaches, three main perspectives have emerged that warrant our attention: structural-functionalism, conflict theory, and interactionism.

STRUCTURAL-FUNCTIONALISM: THE ORDER THEORISTS

Structural-functionalism is a perspective that views the various parts (or structures) of society in terms of the functions they fulfill for the overall society. Just as your heart fulfills the function of pumping blood so that the rest of your organs receive the oxygen they need to operate, so the different "organs" in the social body do their bit to keep the society healthy. Religion, for example, could be viewed as having the positive function of maintaining social values by effectively teaching those values to members of the society—socializing them. One such religious value might be that people should work hard, so those who believe in that value will go out to work hard at jobs that fulfill other functions for the society. To the structural-functionalists, society is a finely tuned machine (or a complex organism like the human body) in which all the parts are interdependent and operate for the good of the whole.

This concern about the interdependence of parts of society and the roles played by each to further the harmony of the whole developed during the nineteenth century, when European societies were going through massive changes as a result of industrialization. Economies and governments were changing rapidly, and individual lives were caught up in those changes as people found their current jobs and locations (usually farming in rural areas) to be no longer viable. Cities grew rapidly as workers flocked to new industrial employment. This general upheaval in people's lives affected their feelings about family, religion, and many other aspects of life that had previously been taken for granted. Thus, the cohesion of society was called into question for the first time. It was during this period, and largely because of it, that the discipline of sociology entered its infancy.

Nineteenth-century French sociologists such as Auguste Comte (1798–1857), who gave sociology its name, and Emile Durkheim (1858–1917) helped to develop the functionalist perspective by raising an interesting first question. Instead of asking, "Why is society changing so much?" they asked, "What normally holds society together?" The cohesion of society, formerly taken for granted, was now a topic of investigation. The search for this "social glue" helped produce many basic tenets of functionalism as sociologists searched for the forces that bound people together. In short, these early sociologists wondered what caused social consensus.

Given the other scientific advances of the time, it is not unusual that comparisons between social structures and the parts of organisms were made. In addition, the idea of biological evolution, which viewed biological change as responsive to environmental changes over time, seemed an appealing model for early sociological theorizing. Perhaps the ultimate example of this point of view came from English sociologist Herbert Spencer (1820–1903), who viewed societies as becoming increasingly complex in structure over time (just as humans had become more complex

French sociologist Emile Durkheim (1858–1917). Durkheim played an important role in the early growth of sociology through his refinement of the theories and methods of sociological inquiry.

BOX 2.1

The Sociological Study of Suicide: Emile Durkheim

How would you view suicide through the sociological outlook? Very few actions seem as personal and individualistic as suicide, yet, as with most of our behavior, the sociological outlook points out the social and group aspects of even this apparently solitary action. One of the first pieces of sociological research into suicide is also considered by many sociologists to be a research classic—*Suicide*, an 1897 study by French sociologist Emile Durkheim.

Durkheim theorized that suicide results from certain specific ways people might be connected to their social groups. For example, individuals very tightly connected to their social groups might see themselves as insignificant and think nothing of terminating their lives for the benefit of the group. Durkheim termed this *altruistic suicide* and pointed to the behavior of soldiers during warfare as an example. Overly loose connections between the individual and the group can also lead to suicide. Individuals not closely connected to others in their social groups and to group goals might be likely to take their own lives in what Durkheim called *egoistic suicide*. Finally, Durkheim proposed a third type of suicide based on the amount of control the social group has on the individual. Our social groups give us our goals, convincing us to strive for certain ends while ignoring others. In this sense, our social groups also make us happy or unhappy; if we are taught to want things we are capable of getting, we will be happier than if we are taught to want the unobtainable or if our desires are not limited in some way. Durkheim identified the situation of unlimited desire, which he termed *anomie*, as a cause of suicide.

How would you test Durkheim's theory of suicide? Durkheim set out in search of social situations that would foster altruism, egoism, and anomie. According to his theory, each of these situations should produce higher rates of suicide than situations lacking those theoretical elements. But where would you find the social situations in question?

Durkheim looked to the military for his example of altruism. He found that soldiers were more likely than civilians to commit suicide. Carrying his measure of group cohesion one step further, he also found that officers had a higher rate of suicide than enlisted men; officers are presumably more highly committed to the military group than enlisted men, and this finding concerning suicide among officers supported Durkheim's theory.

How would you find social situations of varying degrees of egoism for which you could compare suicide rates? One piece of information Durkheim had was the religion of individuals who committed suicide. Of Protestants, Catholics, and Jews, Protestants seemed the most egoistic, with their emphasis on individualism, while Catholicism placed more emphasis on the group. Judaism emphasized the individual, yet the persecution Jews faced created a strong group cohesion. As Durkheim predicted, Protestants had higher suicide rates than Catholics, and Catholics had slightly higher rates than Jews.

Finally, Durkheim looked for anomie in various social situations. The lack of societal regulation of our desires that characterizes anomie occurs during economic depressions as individuals are forced to reevaluate their goals. But it would seem that economic depressions could also cause suicide by increasing poverty and thereby adding to human unhappiness. Durkheim solved this dilemma by pointing out that rapid economic growth, as well as economic depression, creates anomie. If anomie is a cause of suicide, rates of suicide should increase with rapid changes in the economy, *regardless of the direction of those changes*. By comparing suicide rates with economic statistics, Durkheim discovered just such a double connection, finding support for his theory.

Durkheim's theory is not perfect, nor were his research methods beyond criticism (although both were amazingly sophisticated for 1897). His study of suicide does, however, illustrate one of the ways that sociologists go about the business of building a theory and testing the predictions that come from that theory. *Suicide* remains one of the true classics in sociology.

than single-celled animals), with each part of that structure responsible for helping maintain the overall functioning of the system. Just as animals evolve so as to better adapt to their environment, a society must change through a natural and gradual process. An implication of this perspective is that no part of a society should be altered unless all of the society's functions are clearly known; otherwise, the meddling social surgeon might remove an essential kidney rather than an expendable appendix. Spencer became progressively more conservative over the years, arguing that any attempt to meddle in the natural state of society would, by definition, counter the laws of nature and produce social problems.

Later thinkers, such as American sociologists Talcott Parsons (1902–1979) and Robert Merton (1910–2003), developed and refined functionalism without altering its basic nature. These two promoted the functionalist perspective to a point of dominance in American sociology during the 1950s. Merton observed that functions could be divided into manifest and latent functions. **Manifest functions** are the obvious functions provided by social structures. For example, educational systems serve to pass on cultural knowledge to each generation. **Latent functions** are the unintentional or hidden functions provided by social structures, which may not be known or understood until the structure is altered. For example, educational systems tend to keep wealth in the hands of the wealthy across generations because the children of the wealthy have access to better schools and do better in school, and people with more education get better jobs and earn more money. (We examine both of these points in much more detail in Chapters 10 and 11.)

Are all social structures functional by definition? Is every aspect of society necessary by the fact of its existence? Herbert Spencer seemed to think so (although even he had a moment or two of doubt), but other sociologists in this tradition have considered the possibility of nonfunctional social structures. Early American sociologist William Graham Sumner (1906) believed that some of the most basic elements of culture occasionally outlive their usefulness and end up either serving no function or creating problems by their continued existence. Robert Merton coined the term *dysfunction* to refer to social structures that seem to produce negative consequences for society.

The structural-functionalists are sometimes called *order theorists* by critics who suggest that the theory focuses attention on maintaining social order and the status quo at the expense of understanding social change. These critics say that structural-functionalists look at social change as if it were a sickness in society rather than a common process. Defenders of the perspective point out that the functional perspective offers a unique and clear picture of social cohesion in society by unearthing the forces that build consensus among its members.

CONFLICT THEORY

The sociological perspective known as **conflict theory** is generally traced to the pioneering work of Karl Marx (1818–1883), in particular his study of the social inequality characteristic of capitalist economies in industrial societies. Marx and later sociologists with this perspective observed that human inequality is not just a result of some individuals being stronger or smarter than others; rather, a structural inequality is built into the very fabric of society. Over time, for example, certain kinds of positions in society (such as a lord in feudalism) come to exercise power and hold wealth. Individuals come and go from the positions, but it is expected that someone will occupy such positions at all times. In this sense, we can say that inequality is structured into society because the inequality is part of the social structure itself. Even the strongest and most intelligent individuals will not hold power and wealth if their social position prohibits them access.

Conflict theorists assume that built-in differences in power and wealth will produce conflict in society between those who have them and those who don't. The favored few will fear those less favored while the have-nots will feel envy. The favored will work to maintain the status quo (as it clearly benefits them), while the remainder of society will be encouraged to compete for greater power and wealth. In short, conflict theory focuses on the structured inequality of society, which produces conflict as individuals and groups with different interests compete with one another.

If all these assumptions are correct, why are most social relations apparently so peaceful? The conflict theorists answer by pointing to efforts by the powerful to maintain the status quo. Power and wealth give the haves greater access to weapons, for example, with which they might dominate others. But weapons are not a very efficient means of control if they have to be used on more than a small minority of a society's members (see the reading by Berger following Chapter 1). Power also provides access to less obvious means of control. Power and wealth mean that you can publish the books (and determine their content), structure the school curriculum, purchase the politicians (or buy an office yourself), make the movies, influence the major religions, and, in general, have a major impact on the kinds of ideas and beliefs that most members of your society are likely to have.

Many of these ideas are part of a set of coordinated ideas, termed an **ideology;** conflict theorists say that the set of ideas promulgated by the ruling members of society always support their own interests. Most Americans, for example, believe firmly that private property is a fundamental right of all Americans. We are taught this in school and read it in our newspapers. Does such a belief benefit the average American as much as it does the Rockefellers or the DuPonts? Conflict theorists would point to this idea as an example of attempts by the more privileged to control the less privileged. Of course, the result is a fairly high level of agreement among members of a society. Note, however, how structural-functionalists and conflict theorists look at exactly the same thing—this high level of agreement—but provide very different explanations for its existence. Instead of looking for value consensus, conflict theorists roam the corridors of power relations, asking questions about how power develops, how it is used, and what its results are. Unlike structural-functionalism, conflict theory provides a definite insight into social change, showing how internal contradictions in societies can lead to change over time.

We return to the debate between structural-functionalism and conflict theory in Chapter 7, when we examine the social stratification system—the system through which inequality is structured. The differences and strengths of the two approaches stand out most clearly when applied to that topic. In the meantime, the sociological research you will encounter in this book is more easily understood if you look for the underlying theoretical perspective each researcher takes.

THE INTERACTIONIST PERSPECTIVE

Both structural-functionalism and conflict theory can be described as macro theoretical perspectives in that they take the wide view, starting their explanations of human behavior by examining some of the most basic aspects of society. Individual behavior sometimes gets lost in such approaches, appearing only as the actions of robots responding automatically to social forces. While it is in the nature of the science of sociology to focus on group processes, sociology is not blind to the thoughts and feelings of individuals. As we saw at the opening of this chapter, the realm between sociology and psychology often provides fruitful insights into individuals' thoughts and feelings. If we enter that realm from the sociological point of view, we come prepared with the interactionist perspective.

The **interactionist perspective** (sometimes called the *symbolic interactionist perspective*) maintains that human behavior is a meaningful response to an agreed-upon social reality shared by members of society; in order to understand a response, we need to understand that social reality. But what exactly is "social reality" to the interactionists? Why does it need to be "agreed upon"? And how does it come to be agreed upon? The answers to these questions make up the central focus of this perspective.

To the interactionists, the reality of society exists only in the imaginations of society's members. Why do you wear clothes when you leave your home in the morning? Because in American society, covering the body in public in certain specified ways is considered appropriate. I feel that way, you feel that way, and your neighbor feels that way. More to the point, your neighbor would act out his or her sense of inappropriateness if he or she were to see you walking to the bus stop unclothed; even unclothed, you would understand that feeling because you are able to interpret your neighbor's negative reactions, guessing the meaning that lies behind them. As your neighbor and other observers react similarly and you interpret their behavior, you come to understand their shared sense of social reality: they agree that public nudity is inappropriate and act upon that belief. Each person's action reinforces the belief in others who had already shared the belief but have come to hold it more strongly upon confronting so many allies. In short, public nudity is inappropriate in American society because Americans believe that to be the case and maintain the shared nature of that belief by reminding one another as they interact. The belief lives in their shared imaginations and nowhere else. In this sense, the social world is a collective imagination and survives only so long as we agree to continue imagining it. If new imaginations arise and come to be shared, society changes.

The interactionist idea of social reality as a shared imagination places the individual social actor on center stage. But a person does not have total freedom to act, because he or she is constrained by the actions of others, who act out their own imaginations. Individuals also tend to be constrained by their own imaginations because humans can only imagine actions they have experienced or have learned. Nevertheless, this perspective presents a view of social reality on the level of individual interaction and the possibility of changing that reality as an outcome of that interaction. It also sends a clear message to the sociologist researcher: if your subject matter (the individual) is free, then so are you; there is no reason why sociological knowledge cannot be consciously used to bring about social change (with, sometimes, the sociologist leading the charge) (Farberman, 1991).

The interactionist perspective arose from many sources within sociology. German sociologist Max Weber (1864–1920), who took sociology in many different directions, is often credited with nudging the interactionist perspective into existence through his emphasis on the importance of meaning in social action. To Weber, we can only understand, explain, and predict an individual's action if we first know what that action means to the individual. Individuals, argued Weber, act only after interpreting the actions of others in some way that is meaningful to them. Sociologists must gain an understanding of this meaning (Weber termed this attempt at sociological understanding *Verstehen*).

American sociologists George Herbert Mead (1863–1931) and Charles Cooley (1864–1929) continued this tradition in sociology and are generally credited with laying the foundation of the interactionist perspective. Mead, in particular, outlined an approach to human behavior in his lectures at the University of Chicago. The human mind, said Mead, is the product of social interaction. As we think about ourselves, we do so in terms of how others react to us. Over time, the mind comes to reflect the general attitudes and perspectives of an individual's social community. Cooley used the term *looking-glass self* to refer to this process. Our interactions with others result in our carrying society around inside our heads, as the attitudes of the social groups to which we belong become our own personal attitudes.

We return to the interactionist perspective in Chapter 4 (when we look more closely at the process of socialization); its focus on individuals' responses to their social environment gives it particular value in helping us understand the force of socialization in shaping individuals. Beyond that, however, look for aspects of the interactionist perspective in other sociological theories and studies that you come across in this book; as one example, the interactionist perspective helps structural-functionalists picture the growth and maintenance of consensus in society.

In general, understanding the theoretical perspective of a scientist will help you understand not only what that scientist sees but what that scientist does not see. When you shine a light in one direction, it makes the darkness in other directions seem all the denser.

THE METHODS OF SOCIOLOGICAL RESEARCH

A fundamental part of the scientific approach is testing theories through research. The relationship between theory and research runs both ways: the theory must be transformable into hypotheses, the elements of which can be measured and tested repeatedly. A **hypothesis** states a prediction, which follows from the theory ("If this happens, then that will happen"). Research proceeds by finding a way to measure the elements of the hypothesis and then to test the relationship between the measurements. It should be possible for anyone to repeat the research under the conditions specified in the theory and to achieve the same results.

Continuing our example of bacteria and disease, the germ theory of disease would lead to a hypothesis such as, "If I inject this bacterium into these laboratory animals, then I should be able to detect specific disease symptoms in the animals as the bacteria multiply." This hypothesis (which would actually be stated in more specific terms) can be tested in the laboratory. If some or many of the injected animals do not respond as predicted, the scientist must either reexamine the experiment or reexamine the theory that led to the experiment. As is common in all scientific inquiry, the theory is likely to need either change or development. The new theory that results from this process will then lead to further hypotheses, which, when tested, will lead to further changes in theory. Although greatly oversimplified, this is one way science changes.

When testing hypotheses, scientists must measure the predicted changes. We usually think of **measurement** as the assignment of numbers to some characteristic according to some specified rule. We turn length, for example, into feet or meters so that we can speak of it in an exact sense. For sociologists, measurement often has this traditional meaning. We might measure an attitude, for example, by asking individuals a series of questions relating to the attitude and then ranking their responses along some kind of numbered scale as to how strongly they responded to the questions. We might measure an individual's personal ties to a social group by asking other group members whether they think of the individual as a friend and then counting the number who responded affirmatively. Measurement takes on an additional problem for the sociologist, however. The concept of length is clearly the distance from here to there. But what, exactly, is an attitude?

Sociological concepts such as attitude, group cohesion, social role, and so on are not easily turned into any kind of systematic measurement (numbers being the most systematic). If it were possible for observers to watch groups and determine their degree of cohesion with a method of observation that others could copy, we could say that the concept was measured. But what looks like cohesion to one observer may seem to be disunity to the next. One solution is the **operational definition,** or definition of a concept in terms of the way it is measured. Thus, intelligence could be defined as a score on an intelligence (IQ) test. The nature of sociological concepts makes measurement an ever-present problem. Sociologists often have the feeling that the concept they have imagined in their theory is not quite being tapped through whatever measurement techniques they have developed. And if measurement is not precise, the outcome of research will carry the same imprecision.

THE FORMAL EXPERIMENT

Hypothesis testing is best carried out through the formal experiment, whether the hypothesis relates to physics or sociology. An **experiment** consists of randomly assigning people (or laboratory rats, chemical compounds, and so forth) to two groups: the control group and the experimental group. It is important that the assigning be random so that any differences among the research subjects will be found equally in each group. The *control group* is left alone, while the *experimental group* is subjected to whatever experimental treatment is prescribed by the hypothesis. The experimental treatment consists of some variable the sociologist thinks important in causing other things (attitudes, behavior, and so on) to happen. Scientists refer to this treatment as the *independent variable.* (A **variable** is a trait or characteristic subject to changes from case to case.) The changes caused by manipulation of the independent variable are seen as changes in a *dependent variable.* In other words, the dependent variable is the thing you want to explain, while the independent vari-

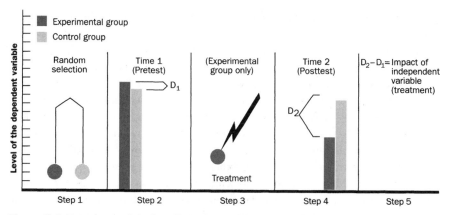

Figure 2.1 Experimental design. (Based on a drawing by Vance Wisenbaker)

able is what you believe to be its cause. At the end of your experiment any differences between the groups (D_2 D_1 in Figure 2.1) are assumed to be the result of whatever you did to the experimental group, as the two groups were the same (or contained the same variety of difference) when the experiment began. This process is depicted in Figure 2.1, but perhaps an example would make the process clearer.

Consider the following hypothesis. If individuals experience frustration, their attitudes of prejudice toward others will be increased. To test this hypothesis, you must first develop some kind of method for measuring attitudes of prejudice, presumably some kind of written questionnaire or structured interview. Second, you will need to think of some kind of frustrating experience to which you can subject people without getting arrested. Finally, you will need some people. Now you need to randomly assign these people to control and experimental groups, at which point their respective levels of prejudice can be measured. This is called the *pretest* (see Figure 2.1). If, by chance, the experimental group members are more prejudiced than the control group members, the pretest will discover this difference. The next step is to have the individuals assigned to the experimental group face the frustration you have devised for them (the independent variable); then have the individuals in both groups undergo your prejudice-measuring technique again (the *posttest*). If the experimental group members exhibit significant changes in attitudes of prejudice (the dependent variable) when compared with control group individuals, you will have support for your hypothesis.

The formal experiment is certainly a powerful research method, but the reactions of individuals in a laboratory situation may be very different from their reactions in everyday life. Though it is not often feasible, it is possible to conduct an experiment in a natural setting. The main problem is finding naturally occurring control and experimental groups—two groups that are alike in every way in terms of the range of individuals that make them up. You could then subject one of these groups to your experimental situation and compare the two groups later. Generally speaking, however, two groups of people found in a natural setting would already have differences in membership. Two university classrooms would have different kinds of people in them since, for example, different kinds of people take art classes than take business classes. How about using two business classes? Perhaps different kinds of people prefer each of the two instructors. How about two sections from the same teacher's classes? Perhaps different kinds of people sign up for morning classes than for afternoon classes. The possibilities for built-in differences are endless. If you find differences in the two groups after your experiment, you will never know whether those differences are the result of your experiment or were present when you began.

A more typical but less powerful sociological method is to begin with groups that you *pretend* are the control and experimental groups. For example, how would you test a hypothesis concerning the effects of religious beliefs on political attitudes? You could find a group of people who adhere to one kind of belief, evaluate their political attitudes, and then compare that evaluation with the attitudes of another group of people who adhere to some other religious belief. But is that an experiment? The problem is that two religious groups (Catholics and Protestants, for example) already differ from each other in so many ways that you will never know whether the difference in political attitudes is caused by differences in religious beliefs or by some other difference. For example, as a group, Protestants in the United States are wealthier than Catholics. Protestants also vote Republican more often. Do they vote Republican because they are Protestants, because they are wealthier, or for some other reason? In this kind of research, cause and effect are difficult to pin down. Figure 2.2 graphically illustrates the shortcomings of such research when compared to the formal experiment (Figure 2.1).

PARTICIPANT OBSERVATION

In **participant observation** the sociologist becomes personally involved in the everyday lives of the people under study—lives with them, talks to them, jokes with them, dines with them, works with them, and worships with them. The sociologist is half an observer of their lives and half a participant in their lives. This style of research gives the sociologist an idea of how the people under study think and feel about themselves and others. The general sociological observer might know where and how people work, but the participant observer knows what they think about their jobs. Following our earlier example about religious beliefs and political attitudes, the participant observer might learn about the political concerns of the people under study and whether those people link their political concerns to their religious beliefs.

Participant observation has some disadvantages along with its advantages. The personal nature of this research makes it impractical for any kind of large-scale study. It is also limited directly by the perspective of the sociologist, who may have difficulty separating personal values and beliefs from observations. Furthermore,

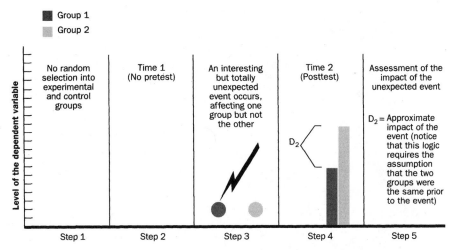

Figure 2.2 Design of nonexperimental research. (Based on a drawing by Vance Wisenbaker)

there is no guarantee that the people under study will tell the truth to the sociologist. They may lie intentionally or, more likely, present a side of themselves that reflects the way they prefer to be perceived rather than how they actually are. Finally, and to some most important, participant observation does not lend itself to the scientific rule of replication. Because a second sociologist is likely to get different information or have a different perspective from the first, a study is almost impossible to repeat.

OTHER SOURCES OF INFORMATION

In addition to creating their own data (or information) through some of the methods I have described, sociologists frequently gather a wide variety of information on social characteristics and behavior. Probably the best known method is the personal interview or questionnaire (the national census proceeds in this manner). Through such means the sociologist can collect both factual information about individuals and less concrete information such as attitudes and beliefs. A questionnaire might ask for your religious affiliation and then ask you to agree or disagree with a series of political statements in order to arrive at a relationship between political and religious beliefs. Sociologists also make use of voting results, economic trends, consumer behavior, and figures on population change or geographical movement; anything people do that can be counted finds its way sooner or later into sociological research. Keep in mind as well that social behavior in the past is also fair game for sociological inquiry. Historical data make up an important part of the sociological undertaking in that history allows sociologists to deal with issues of social change.

Sociologists frequently gather information about people's behavior and attitudes by simply asking them—either by means of questionnaires or, as here, in face-to-face interviews.

RESEARCH ETHICS

Before leaving this brief discussion of sociological methods, a word about research ethics is in order. Sociologists are bound by the same rules of ethics that are followed outside the boundaries of scientific inquiry. For example, it might be useful in a scientific sense for the sociologist to observe behavior after starting a revolution, setting fire to a crowded theater, or generating hatred between two racial groups— but it certainly wouldn't be ethical. The question of ethics in research is complicated; experts often disagree as to exactly where the line should be drawn. It is impossible to develop a single code of ethics for sociological research without raising objections from some sociologists. In particular, one branch of sociology known as *applied sociology* seeks to use sociological knowledge to bring about social change. Social change, by definition, invariably ruffles someone's feathers, and that person would no doubt declare the applied sociologist unethical. By the same token, a sociologist working to prevent social change might be viewed as unethical by the applied sociologist. Beyond following basic rules of human decency, the line of ethics in sociological research is difficult to nail down.

Applied sociologists make their values and goals clear from the outset; at least everyone knows where they stand. In contrast, Max Weber introduced the goal of *value-free* sociology in which the scientist would take on the role of the objective observer, not allowing his or her values to cloud theories, observations, or conclusions. Applied sociologists (along with many others) argue that the value-free stance is inherently impossible, for, as we have seen throughout this chapter, the sociologist is a social person as well as a sociologist; it is difficult to be objective when you are part of your own investigation. Nevertheless, some modern sociologists feel that a value-free position is still possible and might lead sociology to a stronger scientific position in which its theories would provide greater predictability.

MAKING SENSE OF RESEARCH FINDINGS: STATISTICS

A stereotypical view of the sociologist is someone who goes out into the world armed with a questionnaire and returns with a mountain of statistics. As with most stereotypes, there is some truth to the image. For the beginning sociologist, statistics seem to make research results more complicated even though the reason for using them is to simplify results. The purpose of statistics is to turn observations into numbers so that (1) they become subject to the rules of mathematics, which makes analysis of the observations more flexible, and (2) it becomes possible to compare large numbers of observations. It is important to remember that statistics are just a means of communication. For some kinds of observation they are not feasible; for others they are useful.

Descriptive Statistics The numbers provided by statistics allow the sociologist to describe observations in a simplified manner, commonly called **descriptive statistics.** The most simplified form is the basic tally. For example, we tally votes after an election; we can then say that candidate X received 972 votes rather than describing each voter's trip to the polls followed by a rundown of Mr. Jones's vote and Ms. Smith's vote.

Now that you can think of numbers as simplifications rather than complications, consider the following observations. The same test is given to students in several different classes with different teachers who are supposed to be covering the same material. The purpose of the test is to locate outstanding students. Two students achieve a score of 98 on the test (known as a raw score), one student from a morning class and one from an afternoon class. Are the students equal? They certainly are in terms of knowing the material on the test, but are their achievements in learning that material equal? The rest of the tests in each of those two classes reveal that all of the scores in the morning class are quite high; the average (or mean) score is 81. In the afternoon class, however, the students as a group have done much more poorly on the test; their average (or mean) score is only 63. Why the difference?

Because we didn't run a formal experiment with random assignment to classes, the difference could be the result of any number of factors. One possibility we might want to explore is the quality of teaching in the two classes. Assume we discover that the afternoon-class teacher has missed over half the classes during the semester and has delivered poorly organized lectures in the other half. Our afternoon student with the 98 has probably had to work much harder for that score than the individual from the morning class. But how much harder?

Descriptive statistics allow us to change the number scores so that we will know exactly how far ahead of the rest of her or his own class each student who scored 98 was. The two students now have newly assigned scores (called standard scores) that reflect how far ahead of the pack they are. The two students may be equal in knowledge but unequal in perseverance. The raw score on the test will give us information on the first observation, whereas the standard score will tell us about the second. Descriptive statistics allow us to manipulate numbers so as to provide different kinds of observations or to view the same observations in different lights.

Because scientists are often interested in how measurements of variables relate to one another (which is what theories are all about, after all), they often subject those measurements to correlational analysis. **Correlations** indicate the degree to which measurements of variables go up and down together. A high positive correlation means that as one observation goes up, so does the other. If we measured the heights and weights of one hundred people, we would find a high positive correlation, since taller people generally weigh more than shorter people. This is not true in every case, of course, but it is true in general. With this example, however, we know the cause. "Tallness" causes greater weight since it creates a bigger frame upon which to hang extra pounds. Scientists must be careful, however, as correlational statistics don't provide causal information along with the correlational information. Furthermore, they may lead the scientist in a totally wrong direction. For example, there is a correlation between rape and ice cream consumption: when more ice cream is consumed in a community, the incidence of rape goes up, and vice versa. Yet ice cream does not cause rapists to attack; a third factor is involved. Both rape and ice cream consumption go up in warm weather (see Figure 2.3), and the two have no connection other than that (Field, 1992). On the other hand, early correlational research connecting cigarette smoking with health problems has since been shown to reflect a causal relation. Correlations can be useful, but they can also be hazardous to scientific inquiry.

Inferential Statistics A second important use of statistics in sociological research is somewhat more complicated. **Inferential statistics** basically convey information on probabilities. The scientist is always on the lookout for the relations among the objects of study; when relationships pop up, one important question concerns the probability that they might have occurred by chance. Inferential statistics are used to analyze descriptive statistics in order to find out how likely the findings were to occur by happenstance.

With regard to our two classes and the different test scores in each, how likely is it that, purely by chance, the average student in the morning class scored 81 while the average student in the afternoon class scored 63? Perhaps the teachers were of

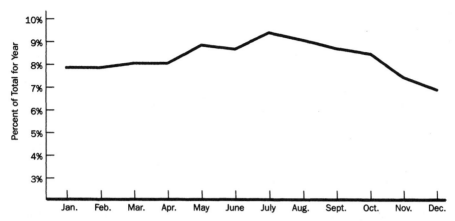

Figure 2.3 Reported forcible rape by month, 1996 (percent distribution). Imagine how closely a graph of ice cream consumption would match this one. (Data from U.S. Department of Justice, 1997b)

the same quality after all. It's also possible to flip a coin ten times and come up with ten heads, but it's unlikely; inferential statistics tell us just how unlikely.

Use of inferential statistics in sociology ranges from relatively simple applications to elaborate manipulations of numbers possible only with computers. A computer can look at a set of observations in a thousand different ways simultaneously, providing relationships among the observations that the lone scientist could never achieve. However elaborate some of these modern techniques are, we still return to the original assertion with which we began this section: numbers simplify. Some of the most elaborate techniques take a great many observations and reduce them to just a few numbers.

You have probably noticed that in this short section on statistics you have not learned to do anything. At this stage of your encounter with sociology, it is more useful just to acquire a general picture. Beginning students of methods and statistics sometimes miss the forest while they spend time inspecting the trees. There is much to be learned in the area of sociological research, but it is important not to lose sight of what you are doing while you are doing it. Research is a means for testing theory, and statistics are a means for doing research. If you find the sociological outlook worth pursuing, you will have the opportunity to return to the methods of research when you have an important question that needs an answer.

SUMMARY
The sociological outlook is distinctive in the kinds of explanations it provides for human behavior. The sociologist looks for the "causes" of behavior in the coordinations of social groups, viewing individuals as group members and their actions in terms of group norms and values. Sociology differs from the discipline of psychology

largely in the emphasis it places on the importance of social groups in individual behavior: Sociology seeks explanations in social groups, whereas psychology seeks explanations within the individual.

Though the sociological outlook is a distinctive perspective on human behavior, sociology as a social science has many similarities with other social sciences in the formation and testing of theories. Theories are the organized and logical explanations produced in any scientific endeavor. Theories are composed of concepts, which provide distinctive ways to view objects under study. Theories also predict the relations among those concepts, suggesting how changes in one concept would produce changes in another and why.

The sociological tradition has produced a wide variety of theories, many of which fall under three major headings. The structural-functionalist tradition focuses on the causes of consensus in society by investigating social structures to see how they help maintain agreement among members of a society. The conflict tradition focuses on the manner in which social inequality arises from the basic nature and structure of society; theoretical research in this tradition attempts to explain how the strains caused by social inequality lead to social change or, alternatively, how members of society in positions of power attempt to prevent that change from occurring. The interactionist tradition focuses more on the individual in society, emphasizing the manner in which individuals create social reality as their ongoing interactions lead to agreements (as well as changes in those agreements) concerning the basic norms and values of society.

Because sociology is a science, sociologists are under an obligation to test their theories according to the rules of the scientific method. Generally, the most accurate test is the formal experiment, in which the predicted "cause" of change is isolated. An experimental group of individuals is subjected to this isolated cause, while a similar control group is not; if changes are found to occur in the first group after the experiment, this result is an indication that the theory is accurate.

Although the formal experiment is a powerful research technique, sociologists are often unable to use it because of the kinds of questions they are interested in. Moreover, some theories in sociology emphasize the voluntary nature of human action in the natural setting, which leads to less formal means of data collection.

Sociologists commonly transform the data they collect into numbers. This process, known as statistics, consists of two basic parts—description and inference. Descriptive statistics simplify observations by placing many observations into the same frame of reference; this process more fully describes the matter under observation. Inferential statistics, on the other hand, test theories by predicting the probability that a certain relationship found among the phenomena under study might have occurred by chance.

GLOSSARY

Concept An idea or notion created by focusing on specific similarities among perceptions while ignoring differences.

Conflict theory A school of sociological theory that focuses on the inherent strains and conflicts in social relations and the use of power by members of society to further their interests in light of that conflict.

Correlation A descriptive statistic (usually varying from −1.0 to +1.0) that measures the degree to which two or more observations (or variables) rise and fall together, suggesting a relationship between the two.

Descriptive statistics The transformation of observations into numbers in such a way that the observations are described (how many, to what extent, etc.).

Experiment (formal) A method of hypothesis testing in which the objects to which the hypothesis applies (people, white rats, or whatever) are assigned randomly to two groups, the experimental and the control groups. The experimental group is then subjected to a particular experimental condition (the presumed "cause"), while the control group is not. Resulting differences between the two groups should be due to the experimental condition.

Hypothesis An experimental prediction based on a causal theory ("If this happens, then that should happen").

Ideology An idea or set of ideas that represents a particular interest of a particular social group. As defined by Karl Marx, it refers specifically to the set of beliefs that supports the interests of a ruling class in society.

Inferential statistics The analysis of scientific observations that assesses the probability of certain relationships occurring by chance.

Interactionist perspective A school of sociological theory that perceives human behavior as a meaningful response to an agreed-upon social reality shared by and created by members of society.

Latent functions The unintentional or hidden functions provided by social structures that may not be known or understood until the structure is altered.

Manifest functions The obvious (or intended) functions provided by social structures.

Measurement The assignment of numbers to some specific characteristic according to a specified rule.

Operational definition The definition of a concept in terms of the way it is measured.

Participant observation A form of sociological analysis in which the sociologist becomes personally involved in the everyday lives of the people under study, hoping to learn how they see their world and how they feel about it.

Science A form of knowledge that attempts to provide causal explanations of phenomena and tests of those explanations through empirical research.

Social science A scientific discipline that studies human behavior through a perspective on the social context of that behavior. Included are such disciplines as sociology, psychology, anthropology, political science, and geography.

Sociology A social science that seeks the causes of human behavior in the workings of the social groups and institutions within which humans live.

Structural-functionalism A school of sociological theory that focuses on the inter-relations among the elements of a society, emphasizing how elements of the social structure function to maintain the society.

Theory A specification of relationships among concepts that predicts the degree to which they affect each other and explains why.

Variable A trait or characteristic subject to changes (or variations) from case to case (such as height, weight, level of education, or income). Independent and dependent variables make up a pair of such traits or characteristics in which one (the independent variable) is believed and demonstrated to cause changes in the other (the dependent variable).

Verstehen A method of sociological interpretation in which the sociologist attempts to gain an understanding of what an individual thinks about or means by his or her social behavior.

STUDY QUESTIONS
1. Science is a method for understanding and explaining observations. How does it differ from other forms of knowledge in the way it provides that understanding and explanations? It what ways is science limited?
2. How are scientific concepts similar to the generalizations we use in everyday life? How are they different? What are scientific theories, and how are they created from concepts?
3. Three broad theoretical traditions in sociology are structural-functionalism, conflict theory, and the interactionist perspective. How does each tradition provide a distinctive picture of society through its theories? What assumptions does each make?
4. Science requires that theories be tested. How does the scientific method approach that testing? What are hypotheses and how do they provide tools for the scientist? What is scientific measurement? How does it help the testing process? What are the pitfalls in attempting to measure concepts?
5. What is a formal experiment? Why is it a particularly useful method for testing hypotheses? Why is it often not available to sociologists?
6. What is participant observation? What unique kinds of information does it provide about the social world? What are its scientific limitations?
7. What is the role of ethics in scientific inquiry? What are some of the particular ethical problems inherent in sociology?
8. How do statistics help in scientific inquiry? What is the difference between descriptive statistics and inferential statistics?

C. Wright Mills

THE SOCIOLOGICAL IMAGINATION

C. Wright Mills became a prominent American sociologist in the 1950s, bringing both enthusiasm and a critical attitude to the discipline. The following excerpt is from his book *The Sociological Imagination*, published in 1959. In it he points out the basic difference between private troubles and public issues. Private troubles are those that occur at the individual level, whereas public issues are those problems that have their root in the workings of society. A fundamental aspect of the sociological imagination, says Mills, is to understand the impact of society on its members.

Perhaps the most fruitful distinction with which the sociological imagination works is between "the personal troubles of milieu" and "the public issues of social structure." This distinction is an essential tool of the sociological imagination and a feature of all classic work in social science.

Troubles occur within the character of the individual and within the range of his immediate relations with others; they have to do with his self and with those limited areas of social life of which he is directly and personally aware. Accordingly, the statement and the resolution of troubles properly lie within the individual as a biographical entity and within the scope of his immediate milieu—the social setting that is directly open to his personal experience and to some extent his willful activity. A trouble is a private matter: values cherished by an individual are felt by him to be threatened.

Issues have to do with matters that transcend these local environments of the individual and the range of his inner life. They have to do with the organization of many such milieux into the institutions of an historical society as a whole, with the ways in which various milieux overlap and interpenetrate to form the larger structure of social and historical life. An issue is a public matter: some value cherished by publics is felt to be threatened. Often there is a debate about what that value really is and about what it is that really threatens it. This debate is often without focus if only because it is the very nature of an issue, unlike even widespread trouble, that it cannot very well be defined in terms of the immediate and everyday environments of ordinary men. An issue, in fact, often involves a crisis in institutional arrangements, and often, too, it involves what Marxists call "contradictions" or "antagonisms."

In these terms, consider unemployment. When, in a city of 100,000, only one man is unemployed, that is his personal trouble, and for its relief we properly look to the character of the man, his skills, and his immediate opportunities. But when in a nation of 50 million employees, 15 million men are unemployed, that is an issue, and we may not hope to find its solution within the range of opportunities open to any one individual. The very structure of opportunities has collapsed. Both the correct statement of the problem and the range of possible solutions require us to consider the economic and political institutions of the society, and not merely the personal situation and character of a scatter of individuals.

Consider war. The personal problem of war, when it occurs, may be how to survive it or how to die in it with honor; how to make money out of it; how to climb into the higher safety of the military apparatus; or how to contribute to the war's termination. In short, according to one's values, to find a set of milieux and within it to survive the war or to make one's death in it meaningful. But the structural issues of war have to do with its causes; with what types of men it throws up into command; with its effects upon economic and political, family and religious institutions, with the unorganized irresponsibility of a world of nation-states.

Consider marriage. Inside a marriage a man and a woman may experience personal troubles, but when the divorce rate during the first four years of marriage is 250 out of every 1,000 attempts, this is an indication of a structural issue having to do with the institutions of marriage and the family and other institutions that bear upon them.

Or consider the metropolis—the horrible, beautiful, ugly, magnificent sprawl of the great city. For many upper-class people, the personal solution to "the problem of the city" is to have an apartment with private garage under it in the heart of the city, and forty miles out, a house by Henry Hill, garden by Garrett Eckbo, on a hundred acres of private land. In these two controlled environments—with a small staff at each end and a private helicopter connection—most people could solve many of the problems of personal milieux caused by the facts of the city. But all this, however splendid, does not solve the public issues that the structural fact of the city poses. What should be done with this wonderful monstrosity? Break it all up into scattered units, combining residence and work? Refurbish it as it stands? Or, after evaluation, dynamite it and build new cities according to new plans in new places? What should those plans be? And who is to decide and to accomplish whatever choice is made? These are structural issues: to confront them and to solve them requires us to consider political and economic issues that affect innumerable milieux.

Insofar as an economy is so arranged that slumps occur, the problem of unemployment becomes incapable of personal solution. Insofar as war is inherent in the nation-state system and in the uneven industrialization of the world, the ordinary individual in his restricted milieu will be powerless—with or without psychiatric aid—to solve the troubles this system or lack of system imposes upon him. Insofar as the family as an institution turns women into darling little slaves and men into their chief providers and unweaned dependents, the problem of a satisfactory marriage remains incapable of purely private solution. Insofar as the overdeveloped megalopolis and the overdeveloped automobile are built-in features of the overdeveloped society, the issues of urban living will not be solved by personal ingenuity and private wealth.

What we experience in various and specific milieux, I have noted, is often caused by structural changes. Accordingly, to understand the changes of many personal milieux we are required to look beyond them. And the number and variety of such structural changes increase as the institutions within which we live become more embracing and more intricately connected with one another. To be aware of the idea of social structure and to use it with sensibility is to be capable of tracing such linkages among a great variety of milieux. To be able to do that is to possess the sociological imagination.

DISCUSSION QUESTIONS

1. What is Mills's distinction between private troubles and public issues? In your own life situation, how might you tell whether a particular difficulty is one or the other?

2. Why is Mills's perspective on public issues specifically a sociological perspective?

3. Pick a problem that you currently face in your life. Describe it first as a private trouble (you probably already have) and then list possible kinds of solutions to it. Second, describe that same problem as a public issue, placing it more into a sociological perspective as described by Mills. What different kinds of solutions arise now?

P A R T 2

SOCIAL PROCESSES AND INTERACTION

THE GROWTH OF CULTURE: THE BASIS OF SOCIETY

As we have seen, humans are the only animals that live in coordinated groups self-consciously, which gives them the possibility of consciously changing the coordinated patterns by which they live. In Chapter 1 we introduced the concept of culture. A **culture** contains all the objects, skills, ideas, beliefs, and patterns of behavior that are developed and shared by members of social groups; anything that is created and shared by groups of humans is part of culture. This chapter returns to the discussion of culture, providing a more detailed look at the elements of culture and how they develop.

CULTURE AND SOCIETY

Culture is commonly divided into two aspects. The physical creations of humans are referred to as **material culture.** This book you are holding and the technology that produced it, for example, are elements of your material culture; the book exists not only as a result of my actions as author but as a result of the actions and inventions of a great many other people, both alive and dead. Also included within material culture are those physical objects that are naturally created but given meaning by humans. Gold, for example, is a very important part of every culture in the industrial world. The way naturally occurring objects can become part of culture suggests an important facet to material culture that will be developed later on: objects become part of culture not just because people create them but because of the way people think about them.

Nonmaterial culture refers to all human creations that are not physical—ideas, beliefs, skills, language, and so on. Nonmaterial culture is the foundation of culture, for it is ideas that make objects a part of culture. Those ideas also stand behind and give meaning to every human activity. To the sociologist, nonmaterial culture represents a vast array of ideas, beliefs, and traditions that are developed over time and passed on to each new generation. A major portion of this chapter will be devoted to an examination of the many elements that make up nonmaterial culture.

In a large and complex society such as the United States it is difficult to speak of a single culture, either material or nonmaterial. Although many things, ideas, and beliefs are common to much of the population, poor people, for example, use different things, think different thoughts, and hold different beliefs than rich people. Catholics are different from Muslims, rural people are different from city people, sociologists are different from used-car salesmen, and hip hoppers are unlikely to spend their afternoons mingling with retired couples. The people in each of these pairs live in some degree of physical or social isolation from each other. They all share some elements of American culture, but their isolation makes them different over time. We can use the concept of *subculture* to describe these differences. A **subculture** refers to specific objects, skills, ideas, beliefs, and patterns of behavior that are unique to individual segments of an overall population and that differ from those of the larger culture. Subcultures develop through isolation, whether that isolation is caused by physical separation or social separation. Subcultures develop from differences in geography, occupation, age, race, ethnicity, income, education, hobbies, politics, or religion, to name a few of the possibilities.

The concept of subculture is particularly useful to the sociologist because it focuses attention on degrees of cultural difference and similarity. For example, you and I both speak English, but I can use terms specific to the discipline of sociology that you may not understand. In return you could use terms specific to your background that I would not understand. If we met, these differences might seem large and important, making us feel very separate from each other. If we were joined by someone from Outer Mongolia, however, our cultural differences from each other would seem less important in contrast to our mutual differences from our foreign guest. In the terms of sociology we share the same culture but occupy different subcultures. In trying to understand us, the sociologist might emphasize either the similarity of culture or the difference in subculture, depending on the question under investigation.

CULTURAL VARIATIONS

Outside the forms of coordination necessary to human survival that it provides, culture can vary tremendously from one social group to another or even within the same social group from one time to another. For example, in the United States, major changes have occurred in the family just within the last three generations. People do different things for entertainment, have different standards for behavior, and hold different values. Box 3.1 documents a few of the many changes in sexual behavior that have occurred in Western culture over time, fluctuating between times of sexual openness and sexual repressiveness.

More striking examples of cultural variation can be found in different cultures around the world. The Semai of Malaya live with the utmost cooperation in their daily lives, and they have no system of social stratification. They avoid violence at all costs and have an extremely nonviolent view of themselves. At the other extreme the Yanornamo tribe in South America has turned fighting and aggression into the reason for its existence. Hostile behavior occurs in almost all social situations, and warfare with neighboring tribes is an ongoing state with a beginning no one can remember and with no end in sight.

BOX 3.1

Sex through the Ages

No two cultures are alike, but even the same culture can look as different as day and night at two different time periods. Consider Judd Marmor's (1971, 165–166) description of the changes in sexual practices in Western culture over the years:

> Even a cursory look at the recorded history of human sexuality makes it abundantly clear that patterns of sexual behavior and morality have taken many diverse forms over the centuries. Far from being "natural" and inevitable, our contemporary sexual codes and mores, seen in historical perspective, would appear no less grotesque to people of other eras than theirs appear to us. Our attitudes concerning nudity, virginity, fidelity, love, marriage, and "proper" sexual behavior are meaningful only within the context of our own cultural and religious mores. Thus, in the first millennium of the Christian era, in many parts of what is now Europe, public nudity was no cause for shame (as is still true in some aboriginal settings), virginity was not prized, marriage was usually a temporary arrangement, and extramarital relations were taken for granted. Frank and open sexuality was the rule, and incest was frequent. Women were open aggressors in inviting sexual intercourse. Bastardy was a mark of distinction because it often implied that some important person had slept with one's mother. In early feudal times new brides were usually deflowered by the feudal lord (*jus primae noctis*). In other early societies all the wedding guests would copulate with the bride. Far from being considered a source of concern to the husband, these practices were considered a way of strengthening the marriage in that the pain of the initial coitus would not be associated with the husband.
>
> It was not until the Medieval Church was able to strengthen and extend its control over the people of Europe that guilt about sexuality began to be a cardinal feature of Western life. Even the early Hebraic laws against adultery had nothing to do with fidelity but were primarily concerned with protecting the property rights of another man (the wife being considered property). Married men were free to maintain concubines or, if they preferred, multiple wives; also, there was no ban in the Old Testament on premarital sex. The Medieval Church, however, exalted celibacy and virginity. In its efforts to make license in sexual intercourse as difficult as possible, it sanctioned it only for procreative purposes and ordained laws against abortion—laws that had not existed among the Greeks, Romans, or Jews. At one time it went so far as to make sexual intercourse between married couples illegal on

(continues)

BOX 3.1

Sex through the Ages (continued)

Sundays, Wednesdays, and Fridays, as well as for forty days before Easter and forty days before Christmas, and also from the time of conception to forty days after parturition. (By contrast, Mohammedan law considered it grounds for divorce if intercourse did not take place at least once a week.)

The ideals of romantic love and marriage for love which are taken for granted today are a relatively late development in Western history and did not make their appearance until the twelfth century AD. Clearly, there is nothing about our current sexual attitudes and practices that can be assumed to be either sacrosanct or immutable. They have been subject to much change and evolution in the past, and they will undoubtedly be different in the future.

Variations in culture over time show us that although any one way of living may seem right to us, it is not the only way to live. The description of changes in sexual practices also reminds us that current lifestyles often convince us to alter our memories of the past. The way we live now seems more valid if we can convince ourselves that "it's always been that way."

Everyday practices in cultures around the world often seem strange from our perspective. In Eskimo tradition, male visitors to a home might have sexual intercourse with the host's wife as part of the general hospitality shown them. This practice carries much of the symbolic meaning that sharing food and drink has in American culture. Lest you think Eskimos are simply promiscuous, having intercourse with a man's wife without his permission is considered adultery and is a serious offense. The Etero and Marind-anim tribes in New Guinea follow norms that prohibit sexual relations between men and women during most of the months of the year; as a result, both of these tribes are primarily homosexual in their behavior. The Caribs in South America practice the *couvade,* in which women return to their daily routine immediately after having babies while their husbands take to bed for a lengthy recovery from the ordeal of childbirth. Some Indian tribes in Canada used to practice the *potlatch,* a ritual gift-giving social occasion during which gifts of great value would sometimes be destroyed by the giver as a symbolic gesture aimed at tribal rivals.

Although cultures around the world seem to show infinite variation, they are nonetheless somewhat limited by the necessities of survival. Culture must provide for basic human needs and, in so doing, must take the local environment into account. A culture that effectively satisfies human needs in the jungle will not work well in the desert. Sociologists and anthropologists deal with these limitations through the concepts of cultural universals and cultural adaptation.

CULTURAL UNIVERSALS

Cultural universals are those beliefs, behavior patterns, and institutions that are found in all known cultures. This concept is difficult to work with. Since no two cultures could ever be exactly alike, it becomes necessary to decide when similarity can be called "the same." For example, all cultures regulate sexual behavior and specify people between whom sexual relations must never occur; anthropologists call these specifications the *rules of incest,* or *incest taboos.* In American society the rules of incest prohibit sexual relations between parents and children, between siblings, and usually between first cousins. With only a few and highly unusual exceptions, every human culture prohibits sexual relations between parents and children and between siblings; many cultures in fact go much further in their incest restrictions. Presumably, therefore, some form of incest prohibition can be called a cultural universal.

Could the family be called a cultural universal? This question brings us face to face with the ambiguity of the concept. To the extent that a family is a social organization that creates and cares for babies, yes. A culture that does not get that job done will not be around long enough for an anthropologist to discover it. On the other hand, you will not find the same family organization in any two cultures. All families create and care for babies but they do so in endlessly creative ways.

The concept of cultural universality calls our attention to many of the basic problems all humans must solve if they are to survive. The more alike different cultures are with regard to a particular element—such as incest rules—the more necessary that element probably is to survival. Presumably, cultures that ignored the regulation of sex ran into difficulties somewhere along the line.

CULTURAL ADAPTATION

Cultural adaptation refers to the manner in which people adapt their cultures to the necessities of survival. These necessities may stem from our animal needs or from the physical or social environment (see Durham, 1992; Graves, 1991). Some sort of family organization, for example, is necessary because of the manner in which humans are born and their long period of helplessness; a culture must adapt to that requirement. In a society that has become industrialized and densely populated, small families would be valued; we can see this in changes over the last fifty years in American culture. A culture adapted to a desert would, of necessity, develop means for coping with sand and conserving water. Whatever the source of the necessity, culture can adapt.

If we look at cultural adaptation together with cultural universals, some interesting questions about human cultures arise. The universality of incest rules, for

Cultural universals are those elements that are found more or less in all cultures. All cultures have some sort of rite to recognize marriage, the start of a new family, though the ceremonies can vary greatly. Shown are a traditional Israeli Jewish wedding and an American formal civil wedding.

example, suggests that all cultures must have faced the same necessity to have adapted in the same way. One suggestion is that rules of incest are necessary to keep peace in the family—imagine the jealousies that could develop if mothers left their husbands for their sons. Other observers have suggested that rules of incest are necessary to eliminate confusions in inheritance, since property follows kinship lines in most cultures. Still others suggest that mating within families leads to genetic complications and that cultures have coped with this problem by creating rules of incest either instinctively or through trial and error (see Leavitt, 1990, for a discussion). Whichever (if any) explanation is true, the universality of incest rules as a cultural adaptation sheds some light on the problems of survival that human cultures attempt to solve. All cultural adaptations direct our attention to the relation between culture and human survival and the many variations that human beings have developed for dealing with the problems of survival.

MATERIAL CULTURE

As we have seen, the concept of material culture includes all the physical things that humans create for their use and also naturally occurring objects to which humans add meaning. Not only is this general definition practical, it also calls attention to the unbreakable connection between material and nonmaterial culture: an object cannot be part of the material culture unless people think about it in the realm of the nonmaterial culture. Nevertheless, there are important differences between the two realms. In this section we look first at how material and nonmaterial culture affect each other and then at the ways in which meanings are attached to elements in the material culture.

HOW MATERIAL AND NONMATERIAL CULTURE AFFECT EACH OTHER

One theory about the connections between material and nonmaterial culture is William Ogburn's (1964) theory of **cultural lag**. Ogburn observed that elements of culture seem to change at different rates. In particular, he noted, the things that people think and believe are often more appropriate to the lives they used to live than to what they are currently doing. For example, in the United States today one in two marriages ends in divorce, yet ideals of married bliss and "till death do us part" are still very much part of our nonmaterial culture.

Part of the reason for this "lag" is that humans don't always know what will result from their technology; building something new may significantly affect the way people live before they really have a chance to think about it. The automobile, for example, was initially seen as a cute new toy that would never replace the horse. It wasn't until Henry Ford began mass-producing cars that their impact on every aspect of American life could be seen.

Other reasons for cultural lag stem from the attachments that people come to feel for their cultures. The force of habit and tradition keep elements of nonmaterial culture thriving even when they appear to be fighting a losing battle against the changing times.

As we will see later in this book, many of our strong values about the importance of the family were formed at a time when family unity was necessary for human survival. Today, a single person can hold a job and provide for his or her survival needs quite well; the divorce rate is a testimony to the existence of such alternatives. But most Americans still value the family above most other aspects of their lives.

Ogburn's theory of cultural lag doesn't deny the connection between material and nonmaterial culture. Even if nonmaterial culture lags behind developments in technology (and the like), it is nevertheless affected by those developments and changes accordingly. The automobile did come to be an integral part of American nonmaterial culture. We even value cars in their own right, desiring certain models and styles. Some observers suggest that the cars we buy are extensions of our sexual feelings about ourselves, providing us a sense of power and mastery over our environment. A technological development in this case turned into a love affair. Another inescapable part of American life now is the Internet. This technological advance is changing the ways in which we communicate, learn, play, shop, commit crimes, and even meet our mates. That is quite a list for a development originally designed to maintain governmental communication during times of crisis. Our cultures sometimes seem to be at the mercy of technological development as we struggle to respond to the genies we set loose upon the world. In the world today we see only minimal political control over science and technology—a situation that should become increasingly problematic as technology becomes globalized while politics remain localized within national boundaries (Kirat, 1992).

While the technology of material culture affects the nonmaterial culture, changes in the nonmaterial culture affect technology in return. The introduction of the automobile led to many changes in American life as values related to cars and their use developed, but those new values in turn affected cars. The speed of cars led us to value speed, which led us to create cars that could go faster. As cars went faster, it became necessary to improve the technology of road construction so the new cars would have a place to run. As roads were built, it became possible to develop a trucking industry for the transportation of goods. Trucks made waterways and railroad tracks less important, so cities grew in different places. Such interrelations between material and nonmaterial culture could be continued indefinitely. As Ogburn pointed out, the elements of culture don't always change at the same rate, but they are all part of the whole, and none changes alone.

THE ATTACHMENT OF MEANING TO MATERIAL CULTURE

"Things" become part of material culture only when humans think about them and attach meaning to them. A church building for example, could be just another building, but any member of American culture knows the difference. Americans think about their church buildings differently than they think about banks or supermarkets. Consider, for example, how different your reaction would be to hearing that a local church was vandalized as opposed to hearing the same about the local minimart. You would probably assume that the vandal also thought and felt differently in each case. Such differences in meaning are not inherent in the objects themselves but are added to them by social groups. As the members of social groups come to think about objects differently over time, so the objects become different objects for all intents and purposes.

The meanings attached to material culture can be seen in all walks of life and at all levels of society. How do you act, for example, when you have guests in your home? You might offer them something to eat, but in offering that part of your material culture you are also offering a symbolic welcome to your home in the nonmaterial culture. Inviting someone to eat with you does far more than satisfy the hunger of the guest; it communicates a facet of your social relationship. Is your guest thirsty? Consider the difference between offering a glass of water, a cup of coffee, or a glass of fine (and expensive) wine. A glass of water contains only a small welcome, while the glass of wine contains a large one. It could be argued that the money invested in each item determines the size of the welcome, but coffee (or tea) has traditionally carried a symbolic welcome, whether expensive or inexpensive. Or perhaps it is the labor of the host in making the coffee that carries the meaning. All of these explanations are possible. But a piece of material culture can also contain meaning for no other reason than that the members of a social group agree it should. You may think gold is valuable because it's hard to find, but albino squirrels are also hard to find.

Perhaps an even better example of this process can be seen in the world of art. What makes a painting expensive? Obviously, the demand for the work of a particular artist makes certain paintings expensive, but where does the demand come from? The demand comes from decisions made and agreed to by certain people who are influential in shaping the tastes of the art-buying public. If those influential people decide that Rembrandt does good work, Rembrandt's work becomes important and then valuable. It is common for the paintings of an artist unknown during his or her lifetime (van Gogh, for example) to become highly valuable after the artist's death. Do the paintings change, or is it just that new meanings become attached to them? The material culture doesn't change, but in a sense it becomes transformed as the meanings change. Objects such as paintings come to be looked at more closely or perhaps just in a different light as the nonmaterial culture assigns them new meanings.

Even our bodies are assigned meaning by nonmaterial culture. Consider the values we attach to body weight. At the moment, thin is in. It is difficult to find someone who doesn't want to lose at least a little weight. Those of us who would like to lose a little (and find it difficult) envy those who can eat almost anything and never gain an ounce. But consider how the values would be different if food were scarce. Being obese in a society with a food scarcity would be symbolic of wealth and

In some cultures dogs are cherished pets. This gravestone commemorating Dolly is in France, where dogs are welcome to accompany their owners into many restaurants. In other cultures, dogs may serve a more utilitarian need, as in this market in China.

no doubt would be assigned a symbolic value of beauty. The obese person may have a more efficient metabolism, able to survive on less food, which would clearly have survival value. But this advantage is lost when there is a food surplus such as industrial societies produce; as a result, the values change (see Brown, 1991; Smuts, 1992).

The examples of art, gold, and socializing over food and drink all illustrate a fundamental aspect of the relationship between material and nonmaterial culture: the meanings attached by the nonmaterial culture must be shared by the members of the social group if they are to be considered part of the culture. You may personally decide that albino squirrels are important and begin collecting them, but unless you can convince others to value them similarly, your personal meanings regarding them will remain personal and will not be cultural. By the same token, welcoming a guest with coffee or wine carries no significance unless your guest recognizes those objects as symbols of welcome (that is, shares the meaning that you attach to those objects in that situation). As we saw earlier, an Eskimo host may offer his wife's sexual favors to a guest as a symbol of welcome, but such an action would conjure up very different ideas within most segments of American culture.

You may wonder why this discussion of material culture has focused largely on nonmaterial culture. The emphasis has been intentional. It points to the central nature of nonmaterial culture in all human affairs. The only complexity in material culture is that introduced by the nonmaterial culture. Of particular interest to sociologists is the fact that nonmaterial culture is the product of collective human imaginations and is ultimately shared by the humans that create it. The remainder of this chapter examines the primary elements that make up the nonmaterial culture in human societies.

NONMATERIAL CULTURE

In turning our attention to the nonphysical realm of human creations in nonmaterial culture, we encounter a wide range of ideas, beliefs, expectations, and meanings. All these facets of the human imagination are learned through socialization; are added to, deleted, or changed over time; and are subsequently passed on to the next generation. As human societies persist, their nonmaterial cultures can grow extremely complex. This complexity can be made a little more manageable by separating nonmaterial culture into two basic categories: modes of social interaction and meanings of social interaction. The *modes of social interaction* include concepts such as norm and role, which call our attention to the patterned behavior that members of society follow and the society's expectations that others should follow these patterns. The *meanings of social interaction* include cultural elements such as values and knowledge that direct our attention to the thoughts that members of a society have about their behaviors and the reasons they develop for performing them.

In practice, both modes and meanings of social interaction exist together. For example, a student in modern American society plays the role of student in response to the normative expectations to be found in the institution of education. Playing that role and following those norms involve conforming to a wide variety of patterned behaviors. At the college level these patterns include registering, securing living arrangements, developing a major program of study, getting up in the morning to go to classes, finding classrooms, taking a seat, buying books, taking notes and tests, avoiding direct insults to teachers and administrators, and so on. All of these behaviors typical of the student role fall under the heading of modes of social interaction. But why play the role in the first place? American culture values education and the people who get it from acceptable (accredited) sources. You may hope to attain occupational and other rewards in the future for playing that role today. If you have accepted the American value of education, you may enjoy playing the student role in its own right as you move toward a goal of graduation and thinking of yourself as an "educated person." These meanings attached to education give people reasons for playing the roles.

MODES OF SOCIAL INTERACTION: NORMS AND ROLES

Social scientists observe that human behavior is both patterned and coordinated. But the repetition of social life is not lost on the social actors themselves. People come to plan on following the patterns of behavior within their cultures and, perhaps more important, come to expect that others will do the same. Such shared expectations are referred to as **norms.**

Norms In referring to norms as shared expectations, sociologists mean that two individuals who share a culture also share expectations as to each other's behavior. If you and I share a culture, this means that the plans I make for what I will do next are more or less in tune with what you expect me to do next. And one of the things I will take into consideration as I plan is my expectation that you will have an expectation that corresponds with my plan. Putting this into words makes it sound confusing, but in everyday life the process itself is not difficult. In making our plans of action, we spend much of our time guessing others' expectations. Generally, we become aware of this guessing process only when we guess wrong and others respond to us in ways we had not prepared for. This can happen when behavior is misinterpreted ("No, Maria, that's not what I meant by that") or when others hold norms we are unaware of ("No, Michael, going out to dinner with you does not mean that you're welcome to spend the night").

Norms make up the rules we follow in our social behavior, and they can become as complex as we want to make them. Imagine meeting a good friend on a street corner, starting a conversation, and then being joined in turn by a priest, your employer, the town mayor, a homeless person, and one of your parents. Consider how the social situation would change with each new addition to the group. Each newcomer might make it necessary to change the topic of conversation, alter your word selection, and even change your physical posture. Any such changes would be responses to social norms as you alter your behavior in response to new expectations.

To understand norms, you must have an extensive knowledge of your culture and of all the slight differences among social relationships within it. Children, who haven't had time yet to learn all this, often embarrass their parents in public by saying the wrong thing at the wrong time to the wrong person ("No, William, Daddy's boss doesn't want to hear what Daddy calls him at home"). The irony is that once we learn all the complexity for our particular culture, it seems simple, and we alter our behavior automatically in response to slight changes in norms.

Cultures differ in the importance they place on various norms. In American society, for example, slurping your soup is not looked upon with as much concern as murdering the cook. While norms vary across a gradual range from trivial to serious, they are often divided into two general categories, identified by early American sociologist William Graham Sumner (1840–1910) as folkways and mores. **Folkways** are the less serious norms, which, when broken, bring only mild disapproval from others. Slurping your soup would clearly fall into this category. **Mores,** on the other hand, are the norms that are adhered to more forcefully in a culture. They comprise the basic beliefs and patterns of behavior common to a social group that form a foundation for the everyday patterns of life. In American society, the unauthorized taking of a human life falls into this category. The only real way to

The Japanese culture's custom of bowing in greeting is an important folkway. Failing to bow or bowing incorrectly for one's status can be an insult to others or bring shame to oneself.

distinguish folkways from mores is to watch what happens when the norm is broken. An emotional or violent response from others means that you have assaulted one of their mores; snickers, frowns, and mild ridicule indicate a violated folkway.

Mores commonly find their way into the rule of law. A **law** is perhaps the ultimate model of the norm, for it is an expectation for behavior that is written down and backed with the force of the society. But as complicated as law is, it can only scratch the surface of societal norms; as a result, only the more important norms (the mores) usually receive this treatment. Of soup slurping and murder, only a prohibition against the latter has found its way into our law. In the United States, where the norm is to have only one spouse at a time, we have laws against bigamy (having more than one spouse). In cultures where bigamy coincides with the mores, having more than one spouse at a time is not only tolerated but respected. Even though bigamy does not do the damage that murder does, sanctions against it are equally a part of American mores and are represented by law.

Differences often exist between what we claim to expect from others and what we actually expect from them. In American society, for example, we claim to expect that marriages will last a lifetime and that adultery will not occur; in reality, however, we know that half of all marriages will end in divorce and that adultery is both a common and popular activity. Sociologists refer to these two kinds of expectations as ideal and real norms. **Ideal norms** are the expectations that people value and want to think will be followed. **Real norms** represent the patterns of behavior that people actually follow.

Differences exist between ideal and real norms because norms are always backed up by values. As patterns of behavior (or norms) develop in a society, reasons for following them (**values**) develop simultaneously. As observed earlier, humans come to value the forms of their sociability consciously. As society changes, however, it may become necessary to develop new patterns of behavior. Because norms change more rapidly than values, we may find ourselves having to do things in opposition to our values. One way we cope with this conflict is to create ideal norms, which represent our values, and real norms, which guide our everyday lives.

The distinction between ideal and real norms helps explain some of the inconsistencies in our society, but it also calls attention to a basic problem confronting the sociologist. If a sociologist wants to learn the norms in a social group, asking group members how they act will only bring forth the ideal norms. The real norms may well be hidden from observation and thus hard to locate. One possible but sometimes impractical and dangerous approach is for the sociologist to break norms intentionally and observe how people react. The sociologist may be told that a norm is important to a social group but, upon breaking it, discover that it is an ideal norm that many group members do not follow anyway.

Roles Norms and roles are closely connected in any society. Norms represent expectations for behavior, while **roles** represent the patterned behavior that follows these expectations. The term *role* comes to us from the theater. Actors step into roles in a play. The actors must be creative about how they portray their roles, but much of the work has already been done for them. The playwright provides all the lines, some background on the character, and stage directions. The actor follows these directions and knows when to move, where to stand, and what to say and to whom. Actors come and go, but roles remain for each new generation of actors.

Social roles are not as well planned or as restrictive as theatrical roles, but there are many similarities. An employee, for example, must arrive for work on time and accomplish the work that he or she was hired to do. The employee will also soon discover how the supervisor expects to be treated, how co-workers expect to be treated, and so on. Some of these expectations may be written down as job descriptions; some will simply be "understood" and will be learned on the job. The employee does not, however, have exact lines written down to be said word-for-word in each situation, as the actor does. A role consists only of general directives and limitations, within which the role player may be creative. An employee might be a little on the talkative side or more quiet and reserved without stepping beyond the boundaries of the role. A college student can quietly take notes or join in class discussions without stepping outside the role. In any case, roles are very real, with very real boundaries set by social norms. And like theatrical roles, social roles must be learned and practiced to be played properly.

From the individual's point of view, living in a society is the process of learning many roles and playing them according to the norms that govern different social situations. In a fairly complex society such as the United States, the average adult will play a great many roles just in the course of one day. You might wake up in the morning and step into a variety of family roles (husband or wife, son or daughter, father or mother, sister or brother). You may switch from one of these roles to another in a matter of seconds, planning the day's activities with your husband in one room and then talking to your child in the next room, for example. As you switch roles, you will be responding to different norms, and your behavior will be quite different. You might stop at a store on your way to work and play the role of consumer in response to some stranger who is playing the role of retail clerk. (That clerk probably kissed his or her family good-bye shortly before, but you encounter the clerk only within the clerk role.) When you arrive at work, you will encounter another variety of roles, perhaps simultaneously playing the roles of employee, co-worker, and boss (if you have people working under you). You might then go to lunch with a co-worker who is also a close friend and, while in the restaurant, play the role of customer to someone else playing the role of waiter. We have only arrived at lunchtime, and already the complexity is evident. The amazing thing is that most of us have no difficulty whatever keeping track of all these roles. We step into and out of them automatically, change our behavior drastically as we do, and rarely become aware of ourselves as actors.

Playing roles takes much of the guesswork out of living. Of the many millions of things we say and do every day, only a small number require any conscious planning.

The plans come to us ready-made with the role. I can walk into a strange drugstore and buy a strange pack of chewing gum from a strange clerk without giving a thought to the process. I can automatically play the consumer role that I've played in other stores in the confidence that the clerk will behave much the same as many other store clerks I've encountered. Daily life under any circumstances would be difficult without roles, but consider how impossible city life would be without them. Cities are full of people who are strangers to us, but luckily those strange people play familiar roles. Without such patterns of behavior in daily life we would never be able to get through the day.

As we encounter others in their roles, so they encounter us in ours. As a result, no single person will ever know the "whole you." Even your best friend may not know the side of you that comes out in the role of son or daughter or perhaps in the role of employee. You may discuss those roles with your best friend, but that friend will never experience you in those roles firsthand; it would be inappropriate to treat your best friend as you treat your mother or your boss. In fact, you probably would not be able to keep a straight face if you tried it. This "compartmentalization" of ourselves into our roles becomes even more evident when we deal with strangers in roles or with less personal roles. The drugstore clerk no doubt has a full life, but your encounters with the clerk will give you the illusion that he or she lives in the store and has no other activities or interests. You will encounter only a very small part of that person, and he or she of you. Similarly, though you may have an everyday, ongoing relationship with your employer, it may be limited to formal kinds of conversations relating to your work. Roles allow us to interact with people constantly without ever getting to know them, if that is our choice.

The picture of role playing presented thus far gives the impression that roles make society a well-oiled and smooth-running machine. Few societies, however, exist without conflict. People may make mistakes in their roles through not having learned them properly, or they may choose not to play their roles according to the expectations of others. Either of these situations would lead to a disruption in the patterns of interaction. But additional problems exist in the realm of the role playing that sociologists term *role conflict*.

Role conflict occurs when people become confused as to how they should play their roles or even which role is appropriate in a given situation. In the first circumstance (sometimes called *role confusion* or *role strain*) people must play their roles to an "audience" whose members hold varying expectations as to how the role should be played (Goode, 1960). All teachers, for example, face this kind of role conflict. In any classroom, differences of opinion will inevitably occur among the students regarding whether the teacher should emphasize lectures or discussion. Some students will find certain modes of explanation and examples useful and interesting, while other students will find those same explanations and examples meaningless and boring. The teacher can't please everyone and must make a decision as to which expectations should be followed. In a highly diverse society, such as the United

States, this kind of role conflict occurs to some degree in almost any situation where two or more people are responding to a role.

The second circumstance of role conflict is less common but a little more colorful. Usually, we keep our many roles separate from each other since they are specific to social situations that occur in different places at different times. But what do you do when two of those situations overlap? I was teaching an evening sociology class once when my four-year-old son came running into the classroom shouting "Daddy!" Should I continue to play the role of teacher or play the role of daddy? (I suppose my only realistic choice was the latter, which was what I did.) This kind of role conflict generally requires a choice on the part of the role player. The two roles may well be mutually exclusive to the point where no single role could please both audiences.

MEANINGS OF SOCIAL INTERACTION: VALUES AND KNOWLEDGE

As we have seen, all the meanings that culture provides have come about through the thinking that people do about the lives they lead. Much of this thinking, which falls under the general heading of what we call *knowledge,* ultimately finds its way into cultural *values.*

Our culture gives meaning to our lives. It tells us how to live, but, more important, it tells us why to live. For example, unless you are an orphan, you are or were a son or a daughter. Son or daughter is a role in American culture, and, while everyone plays this role a little differently, definite similarities nevertheless occur, especially in comparison to the behaviors for this role in a very different culture. Sons and daughters respond to specific norms regarding how they should behave toward their parents. In American culture that relationship has a highly valued meaning, providing us with notions of family importance and leading us to see the family relationship as a central part of our lives. When was the last time you heard a politician attack motherhood? When you are interacting with your parents, a culturally provided voice in your head tells you that you are doing something important and meaningful. If you dislike your parents, that same voice will probably try to make you feel guilty, even if your parents are thoroughly unlikable people. Without that cultural meaning, interacting with your parents would be on a par with your interaction with the drugstore clerk.

In a similar manner, culture provides meaning for every role we play. I am a teacher, and my culture explains to me the importance of communicating knowledge to others and the importance to our society of educating people. You are likely a student; American culture values students, for they acquire socially useful skills, learn how to think clearly, and expand their horizons of knowledge. You may or may not think all these beliefs are accurate, but the meanings are nevertheless present and can't help influencing at least a part of how you think of yourself. Just as important, they influence how others see you. If you lose interest in going to school, perhaps a stern talking to by your cultural values will convince you to give it another try.

Cultures don't do their own talking, of course, but the shared nature of cultural values leads individuals to act as stand-ins for those values in convincing you of their worth. If you drop out of school to become a dishwasher, the values will find you.

Symbols The ability to create and use *symbols* is the basis for the way culture assigns meaning to human behavior. **Symbols,** as we discussed in Chapter 1, are anything that people agree will stand for (or communicate) something else. The symbol can be a gesture, an object, a mark, a sound—anything that is recognizable will do. Cultural meaning is shared meaning, and before it can be shared it must be communicated. I must be able to communicate to you what I think of your actions before you can know what those actions mean to me. The flexible nature of symbols allows us to be endlessly creative in the way we assign meaning to our actions. Symbols are cultural building blocks.

Social Status One of the clearest illustrations of the way culture assigns meaning and uses symbols is the concept of social status. **Social status** is an individual's social

Cultural meaning is communicated through symbols. Symbols are anything that people agree will stand for (or communicate) something else. Through our responses to symbols, we communicate how we feel about the "something else" being symbolized. People at this convention are proudly waving the flag—symbol of America—to show their loyalty and support. Others have burned the flag to demonstrate displeasure with the country.

position within the social group, particularly in terms of prestige. Typically, social status is closely tied to roles and the ranking of those roles within a system of social stratification; if your primary occupation is medical doctor, for example, you will have a high social status in the United States. The concept of status ignores what you actually do and focuses on what people think of what you do. For obvious reasons it is pleasant to be well thought of.

Social status is also useful for the acquiring of specific ends. For instance, when you apply for a job, you will wear your best clothes and try to present yourself to your prospective employer in the best light possible. When you do this, you are trying to create the image of high social status so that you will be seen as a valuable person and a good candidate for the job. When you apply for a loan, you will want to present an image of respectability and responsibility so that you will be seen as a good credit risk. If you are going out on a date with a person for the first time and hope to see him or her again, you will want to be viewed as a valuable person. You may try to drop hints regarding your skills, abilities, accomplishments, and possessions to create this image. Your image of high social status may even lead the drugstore clerk to treat you a little more courteously during your brief encounter. The impression others have of you affects all the details of your everyday life, from the most important to the most trivial.

Social status is conveyed through **status symbols,** anything that communicates your social position to others. An expensive possession communicates that you have the wealth (or the credit) to purchase it; having particular knowledge or skills communicates the kinds of people you associate with and activities you engage in; your style of speech communicates the kinds of people you talk with; and the color of your skin or your last name communicates the ethnic group you come from. Just as others are aware of these symbols, you, too, are aware of them. Putting on your best clothes and manner for a job interview indicates a basic way that status symbols are manipulated to create specific and hoped-for impressions. The most obvious status symbol is the expensive possession. Because American culture values wealth, you can be valued if you have it or appear to have it. The car you drive, the neighborhood you live in, and the clothes you wear all communicate this aspect of your status. But note that possessions serve this function only when their value is clear to others. In his classic *Theory of the Leisure Class* (see Box 3.2), Thorstein Veblen discusses two of the most common symbols of wealth: conspicuous consumption and conspicuous waste.

In any society social status can be acquired through two basic means: ascription and achievement. **Ascribed status** is any status you acquire through birth. In American society both your sex and racial or ethnic status are acquired in this manner and will affect the rest of your life no matter what else you do. Other aspects of status are at least partially acquired through ascription. You are born into the social class of your parents, and, at least initially, your society will respond to you in terms of that status. Although it is possible in American society to change your social class, it is far from easy to do so; much of that difficulty stems from the skills and abilities

BOX 3.2

Conspicuous Consumption and Waste as Status Symbols:
Thorstein Veblen's Theory of the Leisure Class

Thorstein Veblen was an American sociologist of the late 1800s and early 1900s. He was quite a colorful figure in the quiet academic world of his day. His critical perspective on society, along with his unorthodox lifestyle, led him into a number of controversies. *Theory of the Leisure Class* (1899) is one of the best remembered of Veblen's writings. In that book Veblen trained his critical eye on the people of wealth in the United States—the leisure class. Within this class he found that the primary symbol of high status was the visible waste of time (conspicuous leisure) and goods (conspicuous consumption).

The truly wealthy should not have to work for a living; their work should be done for them by others, such as servants. If they want other people to be aware of their high status, however, they must make their nonwork visible. The presence of servants symbolizes this lack of activity, as do a number of leisure pursuits. Veblen pointed out that wealthy individuals who privately pursue some obscure form of scholarship or who engage in the breeding of race horses or exotic dogs are making visible the fact that they need not concern themselves with their own survival. This "conspicuous leisure" communicates to others that the individual in question has made it into the leisure (and upper) class.

Veblen was also interested in a new phenomenon of early twentieth-century America—the front lawn. At a time when agriculture was the predominant use of land, a purely decorative lawn in front of a house seemed to Veblen to be a statement from the owner. In a sense, the owner was advertising the ability to waste land on decoration rather than putting it to some more functional purpose. And putting that lawn in the front of the house made it conspicuous.

The wealthy not only waste time, they also waste consumable items. By *waste* Veblen referred to consumption that is not directly related to survival. All humans must seek food and drink, for example, but when food becomes a fancy and expensive gourmet dish and drink a rare and expensive wine, conspicuous consumption is going on. As with conspicuous leisure, the point of conspicuous consumption is to symbolize status. An individual who can visibly and extravagantly consume nonessentials conveys to observers that he or she need not worry about money. Conspicuous consumption thus makes a statement to the community about social position.

One of the more interesting and less obvious modern examples of both conspicuous leisure and conspicuous consumption is the suntan. In times past, a suntan symbolized low status since it meant that the tanned individual engaged in hard and lower-class work, such as agriculture, which occurred mostly outside. In fact, to have absolutely white skin used to be a mark of high status, for it meant you never worked. In the United States today, however, most lower- and middle-class jobs occur indoors during the hours of sunshine. Under such circumstances an individual with a tan communicates that he or she has the leisure to lie in the sun for hours, doing nothing but accumulating progressively darker skin. In the colder climate areas of the United States an early spring tan also communicates that the bearer has the income to travel to sunnier areas and the leisure to lie in the sun while there. Consequently, most of us see a suntan as attractive since it symbolizes attractive social position. Not surprisingly, there is a thriving industry in sun lamps, artificial tanning lotions (that don't require the sun), and tanning salons that give you a quick tan during a January snowstorm in Michigan. As with all status symbols, there is always an interest in acquiring the symbol even if you can't achieve the status.

It is interesting to predict yet further changes in the relation between tanned skin and social status. Throughout the 1980s and early 1990s, Americans were warned continually about the dangers of skin cancer and its relation to exposure to the ultraviolet rays of the sun. What price are we willing to pay for beauty? Cigarette smoking used to be an integral part of every movie romantic scene as well as symbolic of macho tough guys. Now, with symbols like Humphrey Bogart and John Wayne dead of cancer, cigarettes have come to carry a different cultural meaning. Perhaps the suntan will follow a similar route, and, in this case, the situation will return full circle to the positive value placed on a pale complexion.

you get or don't get from your family. This topic will be examined in greater detail in Chapter 7.

Achieved status is any status you acquire through your own actions (or achievements). In American society a job gives you an achieved status, since few jobs are assigned at birth (although many are influenced by birth—you might inherit millions and spend your life in the occupation of stock investor). The fact that most status in American society is based on achievement provides an interesting comparison with other cultures. Industrial societies tend to be based more on achievement, while nonindustrial societies are based more on ascription. In the latter, it is not unheard of for an individual's entire life to be set at birth—including future spouse, occupation, and place in the community. Societies such as the United States must necessarily place more emphasis on achievement to match the demands of their diverse and competitive economic system.

Cultural Values Our discussion of social status should underscore the importance of values in understanding cultural meaning. High or low social status is assigned to roles or individuals according to how that role or individual fits into dominant

BOX 3.3

Where Do You Put the ⊗*?*

Thorsten Veblen's theory of conspicuous consumption seems applicable in modern American society in ways he probably never dreamed. Status has always been important to Americans, but our current consumer-oriented society has opened many new means of expression. Sylvia Sansoni from *Forbes* magazine describes one of the newer entrants into this game:

> A fair number of car companies got their starts as bicycle makers, and now the circle is closing: The leading German car companies have begun designing and selling two-wheelers. You won't find a Mercedes bike in Wal-Mart, though. You'll have to visit a Mercedes-Benz dealer and pay $3,300 for a high-performance mountain bike or a retro-look $1,795 city bike. A Porsche mountain bike will set you back anywhere from $2,250 to $6,000 at a Porsche dealer.
>
> Neither company expects to make a lot of money from bikes. They're a marketing tool. "We are using this to attract younger consumers who would not think of Mercedes as dynamic and fun," says accessories product manager Steven Beaty.
>
> Mercedes is promoting the bikes as a kind of accessory for its sportier models. Some dealers display Mercedes' sport utility vehicles with matching Mercedes mountain bikes mounted on roof racks.
>
> Volkswagen offered a mountain bike as an accessory to its 1996 and 1997 Golf and Jetta models. Since 1994 BMW has been marketing a now $795 bike that folds into a car trunk; it is looking into higher-end bikes, in the $2,000 range.
>
> The bikes are image-builders, not traffic-builders. In the past two years Mercedes has sold only 1,000 bikes in the U.S.; Porsche expects to sell 1,000 this year and BMW sells between 1,200 and 2,000 units per year. It appears that most bikes are purchased by people who already own one of their models.
>
> No surprise that bike fanatics scorn the fancy new German models. "It's the ultimate bourgeois accessory for bourgeois car owners," scoffs Zapata Espinoza, the executive editor of Burbank, Calif.-based *Mountain Bike* magazine. We suspect that the car folks take that as a compliment.

Source: Sylvia Sansoni, "The Two-Wheeled Status Symbol," *Forbes*, August 24, 1998, p. 52. Copyright Forbes, Inc. 1998.

cultural values. In American society, we value doctors above garbage collectors, for example. Ironically, most doctors would probably agree that more lives are saved through good sanitation than through medical treatment, yet doctors have our respect. Why? That is always a difficult question. Perhaps we want to value people who are trying to save our lives, or perhaps doctors have had good public relations. Whatever the reason, we can see a clear connection between cultural values and the way social status is assigned.

Although their existence indicates nothing more than the fact that we have convinced ourselves which things, people, or activities are good and which are bad, values provide the ultimate basis for the assignment of meaning to life. If you convince yourself (with the help of others) that your activities are good, they become inherently meaningful. You now have a reason to continue. Professional ballplayers are paid large sums of money to perform, but what is meaningful about being able to hit a small ball with a stick? In some societies it is in fact a meaningless activity, but in American society (where we value competitive sports in general and baseball in particular) it is a highly valued skill. Not being sociologists, however, ballplayers probably do not spend a great deal of time questioning the meaning of their existence, for most people accept their cultural values without question.

Humans tend to accept their cultures along with the air they breathe and the ground they walk on. Cultures are far more powerful than the individual—they are there waiting for us when we are born, and they go on existing after we die. Whatever habits and values we acquire through socialization will come to seem both reasonable and natural to us as adults; other cultures will often seem silly, stupid, or immoral. Sociologists refer to this perspective on other cultures as **ethnocentrism** (Sumner, 1906). The ethnocentric individual (which each one of us is, to some extent) values only his or her own cultural ways and is unable to look on other cultures objectively. Ethnocentrism is inherent in cultural values: as you internalize the values of your culture, you become ethnocentric.

Values are part of culture, and through socialization, they become part of us. They are the basis of everything we do since they are the way we "make sense" of what we're doing. Interpreting someone else's actions must begin with an understanding of that individual's values. We must, in short, be able to look at the world from others' perspectives before we will be able to understand how their actions are meaningful to them. Ethnocentrism makes this difficult for both the layperson and the sociologist. And just as ethnocentrism makes it difficult to look at other cultures objectively, it also makes it hard to look at our own culture objectively; it's hard to be objective about something you love. (See the reading by Winther following this chapter for a good example of this problem.)

Cultural Worldviews At perhaps their most basic level cultures direct how we think and how we express the things we think about. The most basic assumptions in the knowledge structure of each culture are referred to as a **cultural worldview.** These assumptions relate to some of the most basic questions of life, such as, "What is real and what is unreal?" or "How do we prove to ourselves that something is real?" Different cultures provide their members with very different ways of making sense of themselves and the world they live in (Berry and Bennett, 1992). The very "basicness" of these differences makes them difficult for an outsider to understand.

Just as scientists' concepts direct their observations to certain phenomena (leaving other phenomena to be ignored), every individual acquires a conceptual orientation from his or her culture that has the same effect. Sometimes these different orientations are lower-level products of the more general cultural worldview; sometimes they reflect differences among groups that share a general cultural worldview but share in it differently. The latter circumstance can easily be seen by looking at the differences in subcultures within American culture. Artists and architects are much more likely to notice shape, color, and design than the rest of us, as they have been trained to observe them. Botanists will have a different experience walking through the woods than the rest of us who simply see a lot of trees. When carpenters walk into a bank building, they will notice methods of construction, whereas bank robbers will note alarm systems and the presence or absence of rear exits, and sociologists will note the group dynamics before, during, and after a bank robbery. But perhaps the best example comes from children. Being too young to have fully accepted and understood the way their culture looks at the world, children are endlessly creative in their perceptions. Most of us write this off by observing that children have vivid imaginations, but a child's perceptions tell us as much about what we have lost as what we have gained by accepting the knowledge of our culture.

Cultural worldviews come to the forefront when cultures meet (and sometimes collide). Differences in worldview between the Western world and the Islamic world came to a head with the 9/11 attacks on the United States by al-Qaeda. Things taken for granted in the West—women's rights, separation of church and state, considerable skin showing in Western fashion, and the like—violate many of the basic assumptions inherent in the Islamic fundamentalist movement. And those Islamists so offended are allowed or encouraged by their worldview to engage in terrorist acts against Western civilians and to commit suicide in so doing. As they act, the Western world has its worldview challenged and is just as offended. Neither side can imagine having the perspective of the other. When differences get so basic, communication and understanding become virtually impossible.

Knowledge, Language, and Culture The relationship between knowledge and language is unclear. One argument (called the Sapir-Whorf hypothesis, after its originators) states that the form and structure of language limits the way we think (Whorf, 1956). Languages also differ in their use of pronouns, verbs, sentence structure, and so on, all of which direct and limit an individual's perceptions. For instance, if you forget to bring something with you, you say, "I forgot it," taking personal responsibility for the forgetting. In Spanish, however, you would say (in rough translation), "It forgot itself on me," seemingly placing all the blame on the object you forgot. Does this mean that Spanish speakers refuse to take responsibility for their actions?

An alternative perspective on the relation between knowledge and language suggests that many language forms are simply conventions and don't actually limit our perception. The difference between Spanish and English in expressing forgetting would not necessarily indicate two different ways of thinking but rather two different ways of putting the same thought into language. This quickly becomes a chicken and egg question: does the experience lead to the language changes, or do the language changes lead to new experiences? Both are possible. A student, for example, might learn the language of botany along with knowledge of the subject in a classroom and discover that his or her observations are now more precise because of the new labels for acquiring and storing those observations in memory. (It's easier to distinguish oak trees from maples when you can label them accordingly.)

One linguistic example that lends support to the second perspective comes from the use of pronouns in English as compared with other European languages (Brown and Gilman, 1960). For the second-person pronoun, English has only one choice—*you*. In French, Spanish, and German, however, there are two choices (*tu* and *vous* in French, *tu* and *usted* in Spanish, and *du* and *sie* in German). In each of these languages you must first decide on your relationship to the person you are addressing before you can decide which pronoun to use. In French you would use *tu* for close friends and *vous* with strangers. Even more important for our discussion, social class differences are also noted by this means. A French employer might use *tu* to address an office boy, but the office boy would have to use *vous* in speaking to his employer. Ironically, English used to have this same distinction (*thou* served the *tu* function), but the term dropped out of use long ago because it was seen as antidemocratic. The question, therefore, is whether English speakers are less aware of status differences because those differences don't receive attention in their pronoun choice.

Obviously, we English-speaking Americans are very aware of status differences. Linguistically, we can make the same distinction in other ways—for instance, in the use of titles ("Dr. Jones" as opposed to "Bob" or, under slavery, "Massa Jones") or in speech styles ("Would you mind closing the door while you're up?" as opposed to "Go close the door") (Brown and Gilman, 1960). This example suggests that parts of important knowledge in a society (in this case, status distinctions) will continue regardless of language forms. As with the expulsion of *thou* many years ago, political movements often seek to change thinking by changing speech. The women's movement has worked to substitute *Ms.* for *Mrs.* and *Miss,* and *chairperson* or *chair* for *chairman.* A change in language can be an important starting point for getting people to change the way they think, but language changes only become truly meaningful when accompanied by changes in the social world to which the language refers.

While language may not be a determinant of culture, it is most certainly a reflection of culture. Beyond providing an abstract symbol system designed to communicate meaning, language use is also a social act that, like all other social acts, is governed by the norms of culture. Before we speak, we interpret the social situation confronting us to determine what (if anything) should be said, how it should be said, and to whom it should be said (Fishman, 1971; Hayashi, 1991; Hymes, 1974). A social situation can be changed by the addition or subtraction of only one individual. How would your speech change if you were discussing your date last night with a few friends and were suddenly joined by your priest, minister, or rabbi? You would probably alter your choice of words, your sentence structure, your pronunciation, and, most probably, your topic. Knowing such rules regarding language use is just as important as knowing the basic grammar rules of the language.

Not all language is verbal. Basso (1970) shows how silence communicates effectively among the Apache Indians of the United States. In many of their social situations, particularly those marked by ambiguity, Apache will generally remain silent, which, depending on the situation, communicates deference, uneasiness, or other social meanings. Newly courting couples will always remain silent on their first "dates" because of the strangeness of their being together. Edward Hall (1959) has focused attention on **body language**—communication through gestures, expressions, body position, and the like. We can communicate a great deal by making (or breaking) eye contact, looking at our watches while someone speaks, or slumping back in classroom chairs while a professor drones on. Within this general area, the topic of personal space has received considerable research attention. *Personal space* refers to the distance we maintain between ourselves and others. This preferred distance will vary depending on the social situation in which we find ourselves. Burgoon and Jones (1976) have found that preferences in personal space vary by degrees of friendship and differences in age, race, and social status. Pederson (1973) notes in general that men stand farther apart than women. Hall and Hall (1971) emphasize the cultural aspect of all this by noting variations in such preferences from one culture to another. Germans, for example, prefer a lot of space between them when conversing, whereas Latin Americans and Arabs like to stand quite close. The implications are clear: people from different cultures may never be able to find an appropriate distance at which both individuals are comfortable.

Language and Social Groups Groups vary in the kinds of things or experiences they find important and in the ways they add meaning to those things and experiences. As thinking varies, so, too, does talking. Technically, different groups may all speak the same language, but they use different words, different sentence structure, and different pronunciation. Is your carbonated beverage pop, soda, or a soft drink? When your frying pan is covered with grease, is it greasy with an *ssss* sound or with a *zzzz* sound? And is the pan itself a frying pan or a skillet? All these language forms vary according to geographical regions of the United States; language also varies according to occupation, interest group, and, perhaps most important, social class.

William Labov, a researcher in sociolinguistics (a discipline combining sociology and linguistics), has done considerable work in relating speech differences to other social differences. For example, he discovered that the *th* sound is pronounced slightly differently by the members of each social class in New York City (Labov, 1970). The upper class uses one pronunciation and the lower class another; the social classes in between vary between the two extremes. It could be possible, therefore, to know a lot about a person's background from his or her pronunciation of one word.

Linguists are trained to notice these differences, but do other people? In spite of many claims to the contrary, the average person is as good a listener as a talker. Most people are not aware of the exact variations in speech from one social class to the next, but they can tell the difference. We are, of course, consciously aware of differences in word choice and grammar among the people we listen to, but we also hear the differences in pronunciation. In my own research on language, I've found that most people can accurately place the geographical location of a speaker from listening to an audiotape (although they can't always tell you what exact differences in pronunciation they are hearing) (Luhman, 1990). Dean Ellis (1967) found that a significant number of people could identify the social class of speakers on a tape recording when the speakers were counting from one to twenty; the only possible differences from speaker to speaker could be in pronunciation of the various sounds in those twenty words.

When it enables us to tell a person's social group, speech can be described as a **boundary marker** of that social group—it communicates to all who know about it just who is in the group and who is not. And by giving us that information, it allows us to place the boundaries between social groups, separating the people of different classes simply by listening to them. There are a great many such boundary markers in addition to speech. The upper and lower classes generally dress differently, for example, but clothing can be altered much more easily than styles of speaking or the styles of thinking expressed by speech, so dress is not a reliable boundary marker. Any boundary marker can become a basis for discrimination, as we will see in Chapter 5.

Language can also mark the boundaries between social groups by preventing communication between them (Gumperz, 1968). This may seem a strange function for language, but the members of social groups often go out of their way to alter their speech so outsiders will not understand them. Criminal groups, for example, may use a lot of slang so as to more easily recognize a police undercover agent through speech errors. A revolutionary group would have a similar motive. A religious cult might create language differences so that its members would feel set apart from the rest of society and therefore be less likely to return to it. Professionals such as doctors, lawyers, government bureaucrats, and sociologists express themselves

Both dress and hair styles can function as boundary markers. It is hard to imagine the young men above doing Mormon missionary work.

in speech that only their colleagues can understand. This specialized language, or jargon, makes it more difficult for outsiders to evaluate the services they provide. Clouding their activities in mystery keeps these activities under their own control. To put that same thought in sociological jargon, "One latent function of highly differentiated linguistic patterns within the subcultures of occupational categories is to legitimate an ideological orientation which maintains the authority position of the category" ("If it's my job to understand society, and if you can't understand how I do it, you'll either have to come to me when you want advice or continue reading").

Power and Authority **Power** is the probability that you can control the behavior of others. Holding a club over a man's head, for example, may lead to a high probability that he will do what you want him to. **Authority** is a special kind of power in which the people under your control feel that you have the right to give orders. Under these circumstances you don't need a club most of the time. Power that relies basically on raw force or intimidation exists in both the human and the nonhuman world. Authority is a relationship specific to human society that gains its force in the meaning system of culture.

In all but the most simple societies, relationships of authority make possible the coordination on which the society runs. Authority means that people in certain roles or positions within the society typically give certain kinds of orders to certain kinds of people. It is the work of culture to convince all concerned that this is a practical, reasonable, and just arrangement: the leaders must be willing to lead, and the followers must be willing to follow.

When authority becomes established in a culture, most members of the society come to take that authority for granted, just as they accept the rest of their culture. While some argue that this kind of acceptance is changing in American society, Americans generally believe what their doctors tell them about health, what their judges tell them about law, what their presidents tell them about government, and what their teachers tell them about knowledge. Even if we do question authority, it usually requires an effort for us to get out of the habit of acceptance. We believe our president unless forced to believe otherwise, for example. The Milgram experiment described in Box 3.4 illustrates how many Americans follow even a presumed authority just because they are so used to taking orders. The existence of authority in any society creates a strange chain of responsibility for actions—individuals used to taking orders are also used to passing on the responsibility for their actions to the authority that gave the orders.

Following World War II the government of the United States called the principle of authority into direct question with the Nuremberg Trials of Nazi war criminals. The now-famous plea of "I was only following orders" became the dominant line of defense for many of the men whose actions were on record. The decision that many of them were guilty of war crimes implied that people who follow orders are responsible for their actions along with the people who give orders. This decision returned

BOX 3.4

Obedience to Authority:
The Milgram Study

In what has become one of the most famous studies on human behavior, Stanley Milgram (1974) conducted an experiment to determine the degree to which people would take orders. Subjects solicited through advertising were told that they would be taking part in a memory experiment designed to test the effectiveness of punishment on learning. The punishment was to consist of electric shocks administered whenever mistakes on the memory test occurred. The experiment was to consist of two individuals—a "teacher," who would administer the shocks upon receiving wrong answers, and a "learner" whose job was to remember meaningless word pairs and receive shocks for memory lapses. In reality, however, experimental subjects who answered the advertisement were always placed in the role of teacher, while the learner was an actor and not actually hooked up to the impressive-looking shock machine. The teacher's instructions were to increase the voltage on the shock machine for each subsequent wrong answer. The shock machine was marked with switches ranging from 15 to 450 volts. The real point of the experiment was to determine how long subjects would continue to administer what they thought were painful electric shocks while the "learner" screamed for the experiment to end and the experimenter calmly insisted that the experiment continue.

Would you have obeyed those orders? Milgram asked a variety of people, including professional psychiatrists, how far they thought most people would go before refusing to continue the experiment. The psychiatrists agreed that most subjects would discontinue the experiment at the first request of the "learner" to terminate it and that only one in a thousand would continue long enough to administer 450 volts. When he conducted the experiment, Milgram discovered that approximately 50 percent of the subjects could be convinced without excessive pressure to continue until the 450-volt level—over the screams of agony and complaints of heart trouble from the actor in the next room.

Are people naturally sadistic? No, says Milgram. They are just accustomed to taking orders in their everyday lives and easily slide into that role in the laboratory. The subjects who continued the experiment to the end were visibly upset and unhappy about what they were doing but became convinced that the researcher, not they, was responsible for their actions.

The sense of responsibility is perhaps the key to understanding both these experimental results and the functioning of authority in society. When we become used to taking orders from an established authority (such as a government), we also become used to holding that authority responsible for the things we ourselves do. A soldier is not supposed to feel responsible for the people he kills in war because he is just "following orders." Industrial societies such as the United States are based on elaborate systems of authority to which their members become accustomed. Many Americans have looked on the ruins of Nazi Germany and proclaimed, "It can't happen here." According to the Milgram study, it can happen anywhere.

to haunt the U.S. government during the Vietnam War, when draft resisters stated that they were responsible for their own actions and would not kill Vietnamese people. The U.S. government, not surprisingly, looked on the situation differently. The curious fact of authority in a culture is that no society functions without authority, yet the authority relations in some other cultures seem arbitrary and pointless while our own seem reasonable and essential. Nevertheless, in spite of both the Nazi trials and the Vietnam experience, the sense of responsibility that people feel following the orders of an authority has changed little.

An important early study of authority in society was done by Max Weber (1864–1920), a versatile and creative German sociologist. Weber separated authority into three basic types: traditional, charismatic, and legal/rational. *Traditional authority* refers to those forms of authority that people follow through the sheer weight of time and tradition. Monarchs are clear examples of traditional authority, the king or queen generally being a member of a royal family that has governed for some time. When a society's members get used to taking certain orders from certain people for generations, the tradition itself gives force to the authority and increases the probability that orders will be followed. As we will see, the force of time affects other forms of authority as well. The presidency of the United States is not an example of traditional authority, yet the two hundred-year tradition of that office gives modern presidents an authority that George Washington did not have.

The second and, in some ways, the most interesting authority type that Weber presented is charismatic authority. *Charismatic authority* exists when an individual possesses particularly persuasive personality traits that convince others to obey his or her orders. Some charismatic individuals base their authority on a claim of spiritual closeness to a deity, but others are just as effective through the force of their personality and their ability to persuade. Charisma cannot be easily defined or measured, as it is an intangible quality. It can perhaps best be described by naming some leaders in recent history who possessed it: Adolf Hitler, Martin Luther King Jr., John F. Kennedy, Franklin D. Roosevelt, Charles De Gaulle, and Charles Manson all had charismatic control over people. As is obvious from the list, they were very different people who used their charisma to very different ends—yet they all had the quality in common.

Finally, and to Weber most important, we come to legal/rational authority. *Legal/ rational authority* is authority specifically and consciously attached to a given office or position in a society for the purpose of producing a certain kind of societal coordination. A classic example of legal/rational authority is the U.S. Constitution, which created a variety of offices from thin air for the purpose of governing the new United States. In the Constitution we find the presidency, the justices of the Supreme Court, senators, representatives, and so on. The Constitution specifies exactly how these offices are to be filled and exactly what kind of authority each is to have. Once the offices were created, all members of society were subject to their authority, including the individuals who created the offices in the first place.

An important aspect of legal/rational authority is that it is attached to roles or offices and not to individuals. Individuals have authority only while they occupy an office of authority, and they have only the authority that has been specifically given to that office. If they go beyond those bounds, as Richard Nixon did in his presidency, there are usually means by which they may be removed from office. It is very easy for both leaders and followers to forget this source of authority in everyday life; the individual in the office begins to "own" the part and others begin to associate that individual with the authority he or she wields. Nevertheless, legal/rational authority is not a personal possession.

Weber felt that legal/rational authority was clearly the dominant form of authority in any modern or industrialized society and would become increasingly dominant over time. The clearest example is the modern bureaucracy (to be described in Chapter 6), which delineates a chain of command among offices and provides clear specifications for who gives orders to whom and exactly what those orders may be. A modern military organization is one of the best examples of such a system. With each office backed up by still another office with still more legal/rational authority, the control over behavior becomes awesome. The old expression "You can't fight city hall" indicates something of this force. Nevertheless, as with all forms of authority, legal/rational authority gets its strength from the meaning system of the culture. Societies can and do have revolutions in which an entire structure of authority may be terminated, usually to be replaced by another one. Russia turned into the Soviet Union in 1917 and the Soviet Union turned into the Commonwealth of Independent States in 1991; now we are yet again back to Russia. Similarly, the British colonies in the New World turned into the United States a couple of centuries back. Authority is always bestowed by the people who are willing to take orders; if the people remove that acceptance, authority figures are left only with power (such as the military). And power without authority is a cumbersome and generally ineffective way to run a society.

SUMMARY

Culture is the ultimate human creation. It refers to all of the objects, skills, ideas, beliefs, and patterns of behavior that are developed and shared by members of societies. It provides the basis for human societies, creating ongoing coordinated patterns of behavior for survival and giving meaning to human existence. As the problems of survival change or vary from place to place, culture is capable of adapting. Beyond the necessity of providing for the survival of societal members, cultures vary considerably around the world.

Culture can be separated into material and nonmaterial realms. Material culture consists of all the physical creations of humans as well as naturally occurring physical objects to which humans attach meaning (such as gold). Nonmaterial culture is the source of that meaning, specifying both patterns of behavior (modes of social interaction) and reasons for following those patterns (meanings of social interaction). From the meanings of social interaction humans acquire knowledge, along with a system of values that directs their desires and encourages them to follow the patterns of their culture.

The concept of culture is the foundation for the basic theme of social coordination that runs throughout this book and sociology in general. In this chapter we've examined the many facets of culture. Our cultures provide us with ready-made patterns of behavior, and they give us appropriate thoughts and feelings to have about those patterns. Humans are not robots, and they can change those patterns, thoughts, and feelings, but that process of change is also part of culture. More than any other single concept from sociology, culture describes the way we live our everyday lives and provides a realm of meaning within which we experience our lives.

GLOSSARY

Achieved status Social status acquired through an individual's actions or achievements.

Ascribed status Social status acquired by and set at birth.

Authority The probability for control over the behavior of others based on their belief in the right of the authority figure to issue orders.

Body language Nonverbal communication in which body movements such as gestures, expressions, and body placement carry social meaning.

Boundary marker Any symbol that communicates group membership.

Cultural adaptation The manner in which people adapt their cultures to the necessities of survival.

Cultural lag A theory by William Ogburn that suggests elements of culture change at different rates as changes in one area would cause later changes in another area. In particular, changes in material culture often have later impact on nonmaterial culture.

Cultural universals Particular cultural elements (beliefs, behavior patterns, etc.) that are found in all known cultures.

Cultural worldview The most basic assumptions in the knowledge structure of each culture.

Culture The configuration of humanly created objects, skills, ideas, beliefs, and patterns of behavior that are learned and transmitted by members of a society in a shared fashion.

Ethnocentrism A positive value placed on the cultural elements of one culture by its members, typically coupled with negative evaluations of cultural alternatives.

Folkways Less serious social norms, which, when broken, bring only mild disapproval from others. As originally defined by William Graham Sumner, folkways are the habitual patterns of behavior common to a social group.

Ideal norms Expectations for behavior within a social group that are based more on group values than on the realities of everyday life.

Law An expectation for behavior that is written down and backed with the force of the society.

Material culture Physical creations or objects to which people assign cultural meaning.

Mores Basic beliefs and patterns of behavior common to a social group that form a foundation for the everyday patterns of life. Mores are norms that are adhered to forcefully by members of the social group.

Nonmaterial culture All culturally shared human creations that are not physical, including ideas, beliefs, skills, and language.

Norms The shared rules that govern the wide variety of patterned behavior in a culture, forming the expectations for behaviors in particular social situations.

Power The probability for control over the behavior of others.

Real norms Expectations for behavior within a social group based on past experiences of what individuals are likely to do.

Role The expected behavior patterns that develop for specific activities or as typical for specific positions in a society.

Role conflict Confusion on the part of an individual as to how a given role should be played or which role is appropriate in a given social situation.

Social status An individual's social position within the social group, particularly with respect to his or her prestige.

Status symbol Anything that communicates the social status of an individual to others.

Subculture Specific objects, skills, ideas, beliefs, and patterns of behavior unique to specific groups within a larger culture.

Symbol A word, gesture, object, or image of any sort that stands for another idea or object through the agreement of two or more people.

Value An ideal agreed upon by a social group as to what is good or desirable.

STUDY QUESTIONS

1. What are the differences between material culture and nonmaterial culture? How can each affect the other? How can cultural lag be produced through that interaction? (Consider the role of technology and values here, in particular.)

2. How does human biology and the nature of human societies limit the variation found in culture? What are cultural universals? How many of them are rooted in those limitations?

3. How is cultural adaptation a fundamental part of social change?

4. Explain how norms govern social interaction. What are the differences among folkways, mores, and laws? Why are norms sometimes ideal and other times real?

5. How can one individual play many different roles? Why are some roles rigid while others leave more room for the role player's imagination? When do roles come into situations of role conflict and how do we respond when that happens?

6. What is the relationship between personal preferences and social values?

7. What is a social status? How does ascribed status differ from achieved status? Which type increases when societies become industrial and why?

8. How (and why) do conspicuous consumption and conspicuous waste become status symbols?

9. The Sapir-Whorf hypothesis deals with the connection between how we think and how we talk. What relation is suggested by that hypothesis?

10. How does speech come to symbolize social group membership? When can speech differences come to be boundary markers?

11. What is the difference between power and authority? What different kinds of obedience do they produce? What are the differences among traditional authority, charismatic authority, and legal/rational authority?

Paul Winther

"The 'Killing' of Neni Bai"

Our culture is composed not only of the things we do every day but also of the meanings we give to that everyday life. We cannot, for example, separate the act of going to church from the religious beliefs of individuals who attend; going to church is different from going to a ballgame because of the meanings we attach to these two activities. Understanding culture is difficult for all social scientists, but it is a particular problem for cultural anthropologists, who study cultures around the world and must learn to cope with kinds of meanings vastly different from those they are used to.

In the following reading, cultural anthropologist Paul Winther describes his research in a small traditional village in India. In particular, he describes an event that was very upsetting to him—the murder of a teenage girl by her own father. He was upset not so much by the "crime" as by the fact that few of the people in the village viewed it as a crime; within their cultural outlook, the act was justified. His task as an anthropologist was to learn to look at the world in such a way that this act could take on the same insignificance for him that it had for the villagers.

Winther's account is separated into two parts. Part One describes his role in the village as an anthropologist and the circumstances surrounding the death of the girl Neni Bai. Part Two explains the cultural outlook of the villagers. Part Two may be more difficult for us to deal with, but as Winther explains, the central ideas and assumptions of one culture cannot be easily transformed into the modes of expression of another culture. If you do have some difficulty in understanding the villagers' point of view, you will learn something about the fundamental differences between the cultures humans create.

PART ONE

It is not an exaggeration to say that seldom does a visitor to India soon forget the experience. The number, variety, and intensity of feelings can multiply as a tour evolves into months and years. The contrasts between beauty and ugliness, real and disturbing, alternately assault and soothe your sensitivities. That these emotions may persist suggests that you don't so much travel in India as the place begins to occupy you. You don't "see" the country; you "feel" it. It is a phenomenon that can alter your consciousness

Essay © 1982 by Paul Winther. Used by permission of the author.

in ways much more subtle and ultimately more profound than merely recognizing differences in wealth and reacting to deprivation.

For me India was, and continues to be, a surreptitious encounter that changed my attitude to existence. I want to relate to you how this happened to me. I want to tell you about a young girl who died. Or was she killed? Perhaps murdered is a better word for it. Maybe nothing really ever happened to her.

More than twelve years have passed, but the events are still vivid. I was a graduate student in anthropology, doing a participant observation study in north central India. Participant observation simply means learning the rudiments of a society's language prior to arrival, supplemented by intensive study of its history and culture, and then residing in a specific locale for one to two years—in my case, a village of approximately 2,000 people. You attempt to become "part of the furniture," so to speak, being very cautious not to violate any local rules of etiquette or taboos. As you ask questions, you observe, and in the quiet moments of the day you write about what you have seen, heard, and felt in the form of field notes. This is the material from which you abstract ideas for future publications.

During the innumerable walks I took through the village and adjoining land as part of my work, I often met people tending fields. These were landowners, sharecroppers, and hired labor; usually from the community. They would acknowledge my presence with a look or a wave and a smile. And, occasionally, I would stop to have a cup of tea with those I knew particularly well. Boiled in prodigious amounts of buffalo milk and sugar, the beverage was compensated only by the relaxed flow of talk. I learned much about the village and its people from these encounters. It was as if the shade and the privacy in which we sat encouraged people to speak about things they would normally keep to themselves.

One series of meetings was particularly memorable. It involved two brothers, both Brahmans, a caste of high ritual status. The men were very friendly and always asked the same questions con-

cerning me and the United States, to which I replied with the same answers. They responded with the same expressions of amazement or partial comprehension. I believe the inquiries were intentionally repetitious because they thought me to be a bit weird. Their questions, which I came to know by heart, were demonstrations of friendship, discreetly phrased in such a way as not to strain my apparently limited mental capacities. How else to explain and treat a foreigner 12,000 miles away from home, who sits and asks questions about such things as lineages, clans, and the like? Pancham Ram, one of the brothers, was an oddity for me as well. He wore a beard, and a bearded Brahman in the village was a rarity. We joked about this and compared respective lengths.

Pancham Ram was married and had six children, the oldest of whom, a girl, was deceased. Then there was another girl, Neni Bai, followed by four brothers down to the age of one and a half years. Pancham Ram, his wife, and children lived in a small dwelling with his unmarried brother. The family had a high ritual status but modest economic resources. The small amount of land they owned yielded sufficient produce to feed them, although it left little to sell at the market beyond the village.

Pancham Ram's daughter, Neni Bai, was in her early teens. I never talked to her or made inquiries about her until after her disappearance. An unmarried male, and a foreigner at that, does not ask questions about single females of high caste and marriageable age in the community and expect to remain in the village. But I noticed her each time I left my room above my landlord's cow pen and walked down the path to the village platform where the "important" men gathered when I took the shortcut to the highway where I waited for a bus to the nearest city. Often she would be there when I returned. She, like so many residents, became part of the animated scenery, stopping whatever was being done, the old women staring, the younger casting furtive glances beneath veils, the little girls giggling, and the boys shouting "White monkey!" and scampering away in good-natured mock fright. I grew accustomed to these acknowledgments of my presence, and, cut off from everything resembling my previous American existence, they helped make occasional bouts of loneliness less difficult and prolonged.

Neni Bai was in that field the first winter when temperatures were unexpectedly low and I nearly froze; she was there in the incredibly dry heat of May and June; and she was there during the monsoon season, seemingly oblivious to the danger of the water-inundated gully threatening to engulf the village. And she was there the autumn day I left to visit distant New Delhi. It was a cool, clear morning. With the same dull, expressionless look she observed my departure. The only thing that ever seemed to move was her eyes, insufficiently striking to detract from her exceedingly plain face. A beauty Neni Bai was not, even less so because she had a club foot. Others said that she was retarded, and I believed them. It would cost her father much money to find her a husband. She was a human being, however, and I felt sorry for her.

Neni Bai was gone when I came back. But I was so absorbed in data collection that initially I only dimly sensed her absence. The people I met that first day seemed pleased to see me again. I felt good. I remember meeting one man who looked vaguely familiar and hearing him greet me. But I was in a hurry, said hello, and went to an appointment. I met the same man later with his brother in Pancham Ram's field. Then I realized it was Pancham Ram, but without a beard. I kidded him about the hairless jaw, and when I asked him why no beard, he and his brother laughed, Pancham waving his hand in that typical Indian way signifying so many things. I assumed he had become tired of the growth and didn't give my debearded friend's new appearance any more thought.

Only several days later did one of my informants mention the village meeting that had taken place during my absence. It had been called by the village headman (sarpanch). Other people's descriptions suggested that it had been a perfunctory occasion, serving to satisfy inquiries initi-

ated by the police. I was sorry that I had not witnessed the events and issues prompting the meeting. I was politely insistent that they tell me more. The sarpanch, I was told, had ordered Pancham Ram's beard shaved. Furthermore, no one was to talk to him for three days, and if they did, their crops would fail. (Nobody refrained from talking with Pancham Ram during this period, and no crops failed due to the infringement of the sarpanch's admonition.) I sensed that Neni Bai's absence, the village meeting, and Pancham Ram's beardless condition were related. In retrospect, maybe I should have left the puzzle unsolved, for what I was to discover was disquieting.

Neni Bai was indeed gone. She had become pregnant by a lower caste male. Her throat had been cut and her body thrown into a dry well on Pancham Ram's land. Pancham did not deny having perpetrated the act. My shock was intensified when I was told that he had strangled another daughter—the one he had mentioned months before—two years before my arrival. The same well had been used as a disposal site. The agitation I experienced during these sessions may have been evident, but my feelings did not appear to be shared by others. It is difficult to describe the villagers' reactions in exact terms, but they gave the impression of a perplexing indifference, a casually nonchalant attitude, and one I thought was merely a disguise affected so as to calm me. However, unobtrusive inquiries during the remainder of my stay generated similar reactions.

In those early days I was convinced that these people had been just as upset as myself. It was, after all, merely human to be ashamed of a fellow villager who had committed such a horrible act. I assumed without question that they felt as I did, and I strove to discover reasons why their reactions were not following these assumptions. I realize now how engrained in my consciousness were my assumptions about the act of killing called into question because of Neni Bai. The villagers' awareness of the girl, of her father, and of the significance of their relationship attained in my eyes seemed to be predicated upon different principles. So much for justice, I thought. But I was unsatisfied. Being able to comprehend the underlying logic intellectually is different from accepting it emotionally without feeling estranged. I had prided myself on beginning to understand how the villagers viewed the world around them. I was reacting to the contradiction between what I felt to be an exceptional event and my friends' treatment of it as less than exceptional. As I walked back to the village that day, I felt lonely, depressed, and apprehensive. The community appeared unappealingly foreign to me. They had become strangers all over again. The hard part of the research lay ahead, I thought—a realization that my concept of "human being" might not be shared by the people amongst whom I was living.

PART TWO

What I ultimately gained from trying to understand Neni Bai's departure and the milieu in which it took place was a heightened awareness of the power of culture to condition an individual's perception of reality. My informants, friends, and acquaintances and I shared perceptions of Neni Bai. For example, she was a female, young, unattractive. This overlapping made the disagreement regarding the significance of her death so disconcerting to me. Given my need and desire to remain in the community and accomplish my goals, I was impelled to examine engrained assumptions and modify basic attitudes typical of our society's world view. I was divesting myself of the cocoonlike security, the complacency such unquestioned assumptions provide, and was assimilating in subtle, albeit commanding, ways aspects of a fundamentally different consciousness. It is a trip I perhaps never fully returned from.

It is impossible to convey the complexity of thought my co-villagers were employing in their interpretations of Neni Bai; only an inadequate attempt can be made. What they were articulating were themes found in the classical texts of Hinduism and their idiosyncratic interpretation at the local level. These ideas pertain to their notion of time and the phenomenal world it embraces.

One dominant idea in classical Hinduism is that of transcendental reality underlying and sustaining all of the phenomenal world. While this does not discourage recognition of different objects, "in the end" all entities having status as "facts" and articulated by all languages are not the absolute. In the Hindu worldview the things perceived may not possess emotive potential identical to that of the Judeo-Christian world. Both Western and Indian cultures have the concept of time, but even a cursory reading of the texts of Hinduism suggests a different kind of sensitivity toward its nature and, by implication, those entities "occupying" time.

For those dominated by such ideas, things populating their world are seen as always in movement. Neni Bai's birth, for example, was not denied. Her actions during the course of her short life were acknowledged, but it was an acknowledgment of different significance from that I accorded her. For me her actions, all those qualities I had perceived as well as those I had not had a chance to observe but accorded her, were *her*. They defined her.

Her uniqueness in time was my reality. But the villagers envisaged Neni Bai—as they probably do all human entities—as a surface phenomenon. Reality to them is something other than the outward appearance that I deemed as significant. Neni Bai, myself, them—and you, the reader—are part of a ceaseless flux, the underlying reality of which is left unchanged. Lives are created, lives are stopped, but the substance of things remains unchanged. And what I label dynamics, in motion, is perceived by my Hindu friends as but a manifestation of ultimate "unchange."

Although I could accept, rather than merely say I understood, that time was not a distinct entity and absolute in its independence, I still had difficulty seeing how Neni Bai related to this esoteric intellectual orientation. In other words, I was uncomfortable with their conceptualization of form. Gradually I realized that it is the "ultimate nonreality of any instant" that provides the foundation for their conception of human beings. I held a distinction between living and dead, between existence and nonexistence. These sets of contrasts are, for Westerners, facets of the human condition. We believe there exists a physical life, and the majority of us posit a spiritual existence also. The Western religions vary in how they perceive the latter after cessation of physical life, but the notion that one "lives on" after the other is familiar.

The people attempting to educate me in this south Asian community reflect an absence of this duality. For them existence and nonexistence are not different aspects of a thing residing in time and do not entail physical bodies evolving and culminating in cessation. Rather, existence and nonexistence are the thing itself, different manifestations of the same underlying unfathomable sameness. Life and death, then, need not have the identical moral implications they do for us. Their indigenous cultural code conditions them to perceive, experience, and react in a manner I did not anticipate. The physical demise of a person can occur, the villagers perceive it, but the range of reactions does not automatically generate synonymous responses. Death taking place in time was not accorded the same status in regard to "reality" as I accorded it. The result was the curious, and for us probably unnerving, realization that Neni Bai's extinction was the dissolution of a "form," but her consequent "nonexistence" was coequal with her "existence." For them what was important was neither the death of Neni Bai as an event-in-itself nor a concern with the injustice I thought had been inflicted upon her.

The notions of the village people, while different from ours, are neither more barbaric nor more civilized. They do have definite perceptions of time and of the "human beings" populating it, but it is a concern with time on a cosmic order. While we attach importance to the passing events of a person's life and to grand historical episodes, they tend to see these events not as indications of change, progress, and evolution, but as revelations of the eternalness of the social order, of the world, and of the universe. On a far less grandiose level each person—Neni Bai, you, myself—is but a transient instance, an inconsequential "form" repeatedly appearing in a limitless "time."

Neni Bai and the milieu in which she lived forced me to become aware of how I had unquestioningly accepted one culture's definition of common sense. It now also enables me to recognize the usually unrecognized contradictions in the Judeo-Christian legacy regarding the creation, appearance, continuance, and cessation of human life. My problem is that I see and feel these contradictions in an environment not conducive to acting upon such realization; your problem may be that you see no contradictions at all. If you are among the latter, it will be difficult for you to accurately comprehend the phenomenon of violence and crime in a comparative perspective. You will engage in assigning labels to people and events that will be dramatically different from the interpretations of the participants themselves.

There is little in our genetic makeup that makes us prone, or not prone, to engage in ending human life. Rather, our responses are situationally defined. And it is our culture, through its numerous institutions, that conditions our consciousness. The irrationality of killing humans is transformed into the rational, the legitimate, and the acceptable, by society. Our institutions define when killing is to be condoned and when the annihilation of others warrants censure because of inappropriate circumstances. Stand aside for only a moment and reflect upon how our society—or any society—constructs the proper setting for extermination of individuals or groups of humans.

There are probably many of you who, with some encouragement, would readily kill "for your country," or for your God. But we seem to be disturbed by merely killing, or by the label used to designate it.

We feel better, we are ethical, if the institutional fabric of our society can satisfy our need for the legitimation of its performance. So killing for Christ and the U.S.A. is effectively conveyed to us in the form of protecting ourselves from some amorphous devil. One subtle function of the groups to which we belong is to lift us out of the emotional quagmire of morality. Not only do such institutions provide us with a sense of identity, security, and the satisfaction of human needs, they also alleviate us of the burden of serious reflection. We are free, but free to conform. Our institutions define the situations when we can kill with gusto, without debilitating feelings of guilt, or at least categorize the act(s) as unfortunate but necessary.

I could understand the phenomenon called Neni Bai only with an eventual willingness to recognize, and to shed, the ethnocentric tendencies inculcated since my childhood. And only by engaging in a similar process can you begin to comprehend "crime" in your society and "crime" as it is defined and conceptualized by inhabitants of the many societies around the world. While all peoples may possess an intellectual category called crime, the contents of the compartment are shaped in numerous ways by their respective cultures. A heinous act in one culture may be a nonevent in another, or a performance of remarkably different emotional significance for those involved. This status is not due to any barbarism of the practitioners; it is a reflection of culture's ability to condition us and to invest acts with a multitude of equally logical, sensible interpretations. No one explanation is correct or constitutes a more perfect approximation of some ultimate "truth" existing independently of us, residing "out there." There are, according to the wise men in that Indian village, merely many diverse ways by which human beings express their self-deception.

DISCUSSION QUESTIONS

1. What is the source of ethnocentrism in any culture? How are social scientists limited in their ability to understand other cultures by their own ethnocentrism?
2. Consider the difficulties that anthropologist Winther had in explaining in the English language the worldview of the people he studied. To what degree do you think a person's language limits the thoughts that he or she is capable of having?
3. How is culture differently understood by the people who live it and outsiders who observe it? Is one picture more accurate than the other?

SOCIALIZATION: LEARNING THE GAME AND BECOMING A PLAYER

S

ocialization—the ongoing process by which humans come to learn about and believe in their cultures, from learning the roles to sharing the values—is one of the most basic concepts social science has to offer; it calls attention to the fact that humans learn about ways to live their lives rather than inherit them. Both the personalities people develop and the actions they perform in their social groups are highly related to other personalities and actions that have existed before them. There is no one else exactly like you in any way, but there are many other people who are much like you in most ways. That similarity is the result of common patterns of socialization within your social group. Of all the activities coordinated within a society, the preparation of new members is one of the most important and most closely looked after. Both slow learners and uncooperative learners are apt to face some form of social control from other members of their social groups as group norms are enforced. The pressures you face every day (as others attempt to change your behavior) are far from accidental. As we will discuss in Chapter 6, adults can be very similar even though they grew up in different places. Such similarity is possible because of coordinated socialization.

Because of its central position in the social sciences, the concept of socialization was introduced in Chapter 1. This chapter explores socialization in much greater detail. The first section covers the agents of socialization, analyzing the many sources in society that provide us with both cultural information and coercive forms of social control. The following two sections detail the processes of socialization, with a focus on the changes at different stages in the life cycle and in different situations. The fourth section examines the **self,** that ongoing product of socialization, with an eye to better understanding where individual personalities come from and why people view themselves the way they do. The final section is concerned with *resocialization,* an extreme form of socialization that produces dramatic changes in adult personalities and behavior.

AGENTS OF SOCIALIZATION

An **agent of socialization** is any social source that communicates elements of the culture or requires conformity to them. Your parents, for example, are important agents of socialization because of the amount of time you spend with them and the crucial stage of your life when you spend that time. They communicate information to you about the culture you live in and spend a good deal of energy enforcing their teaching. The television shows you watch, however, are also important agents of socialization. They communicate a great deal of cultural information and, in methods varying in subtlety, "encourage" you to behave in certain ways (people won't like you if you have bad breath, lack fashion sense, or act "nerdy"). And, in fact, if other people have been watching the same programming and are influenced by it, they may not like you if you exhibit those characteristics. Living in any society means that you will encounter agents of socialization at every turn. You are even being socialized when you play with Barbie (see Box 4.1).

INDIVIDUALS AS AGENTS OF SOCIALIZATION

Most of us enter families as defenseless infants and spend quite some time at their mercy before we have the skills or the independence to receive socialization elsewhere. The first socialization we receive in life is by far the most important; a five-year-old is more like an adult than like a newborn infant. Additionally, this first, or primary socialization consists of time spent with a few individuals; the infant is little affected by or interested in strangers, abstractions, television, acts of Congress, or fluctuations in the economy. Parents may encounter interference from society if they abuse the child physically, but short of that, they pretty much have a free hand. People may need a license to drive a car and formal education to get a job, but anyone can have and raise a child. This overall situation makes parents extremely important agents of socialization; their impact can be seen throughout their child's life.

Other family members can also be important agents of socialization for the child. Although they are less important than parents because they don't satisfy as many needs, brothers and sisters certainly play a major role in early training. Other adult family members, such as aunts, uncles, and grandparents, are socialization agents of steadily declining importance in American society as family living units become smaller and families become geographically more dispersed. If you grew up in a nuclear family (with only parents and children), consider how different you might be today had you shared your home with a set of grandparents and perhaps an uncle or two. It is not uncommon in other cultures to find the major childrearing role bestowed on someone other than the biological parents. The American mode, in which parents do the raising while grandparents do the spoiling, suggests something of how we delegate our childrearing duties.

While the American family has declined in size, it has also been declining in influence over its offspring. Many American children today attend day-care centers or nursery schools, and most attend some kind of formal schooling by the age of six. Beyond increasing the importance of the school (which we look at in the following section), this shift places greater importance on peers as agents of socialization. It is

BOX 4.1

Barbie's Missing Accessory: Food

Ever since her "coming out" in 1959, Mattel's Barbie has been "on the scene" worldwide, with 700 million dolls sold in more than 140 countries. The typical American girl owns eight Barbie dolls, not to mention the clothes and other accoutrements specially designed for her, her boyfriend Ken, and her bevy of companions. At one time membership in the Barbie Fan Club was second only to membership in the Girl Scouts.

But little girls who view Barbie as a model of feminine good looks may be getting the wrong message about what a healthy woman's body looks like. If the long-limbed blonde were a real woman, she'd be so lean she probably wouldn't even be able to menstruate, according to a group of researchers reporting from University Central Hospital in Helsinki, Finland.

Judging by their calculations, Barbie's svelte thighs, hips, and stomach—areas where nature intended women to carry fat for the purpose of childbearing—would have far too little padding to give her the 17 to 22 percent body fat a woman needs to have regular periods. And lack of menstruation is one of the signs of anorexia nervosa.

Barbie's not the only plastic beauty that could stand to gain some weight. When the researchers looked at the measurements of fashion mannequins manufactured throughout the U.S. they found that since the 1950s and '60s, about the time Twiggy and other lanky-looking models came into vogue, clothing-store dummies have had on the order of only 10 percent body fat. Mannequins dating back to the 20s, however, are proportioned more like healthy women of normal weight.

Source: *Tufts University Diet and Nutrition Letter,* Vol. 11, No. 11, January 1994.

---

at this stage that the growing child often encounters the first major contradictions in socialization, for the demands of the peer group may be either different from or in opposition to the expectations of the parents. From the child's perspective, increased interactions within the peer group often make peer expectations more important than the parents' expectations. The domination of certain fads within adolescent peer groups and the rapidity with which they change suggest the importance of conformity to peer demands.

As life goes on, the importance of individuals as agents of socialization may decrease somewhat. This change is due partly to the process of maturation, but much of it results from the increasing numbers of individuals that most of us face as adults; the more individual agents we face, the less significance any one is likely to have. Nevertheless, as adults, most of us live with or around a small group of "significant" individuals who have a major influence over us. And most of our relationships with those significant individuals are characterized as personal, often intimate, yet simultaneously loose and playful (Baxter, 1992).

INSTITUTIONS AS AGENTS OF SOCIALIZATION

Most of the activities we engage in every day are parts of interrelated clusters of activities known as **institutions** (this concept is presented in detail in Chapters 9–13). Institutions include education, work/the economy, politics, the mass media, and religion. If you are currently a student, for example, you are involved in one of the many activities that make up the American institution of education. The sum total of a great many individuals involved in a great many activities within an institution affects you on a different scale than the day-to-day socialization you experience by family and friends. Television as an agent of socialization falls into this category.

Television joins radio, magazines, newspapers, and other forms of communication under the general heading of mass media. What you see on television, hear on the radio, or read in the paper is not the work of one individual but the result of a great many individuals working in concert. If your experience with the media socializes you by teaching or influencing you, that influence can be explained only through an understanding of the institution it comes from. For example, a child watching cartoons on Saturday morning will learn that candy and sugar-coated cereals are desirable things to eat. This message is conveyed not because the cartoon makers want young Americans' teeth to rot but because they must have sponsors if they wish to appear on commercial television. In this case financing within the institution of the media leads to a certain form of socialization. There have also been some interesting changes in television program content since its early days. Heintz (1992) calculated that conflictual situations in story lines occur almost twice as often as in the past; it is indeed hard to picture *Will and Grace* running alongside *Leave It to Beaver.*

Singer and Miller (1999) found a clear relation between the amount of violence watched by children and their self-reported violent acts. (This relation was particularly strong when coupled with low parental monitoring of their behavior.) Potter and Smith (2000) found that the lower level of graphic violence on television (as compared with films) was often linked with positive and attractive social values. Brown and Newcomer (1991) found a relationship between the number of adolescent viewing hours of sexual content on television and the amount of sexual behavior exhibited by those viewers (presumably between programs); this relationship held regardless of peer encouragement, race, or gender.

Lawmakers have considered placing some form of control on advertising for children, but the questions concerning program content raise more complicated issues involving censorship. This dispute figured prominently in the 2000 presi-

Children growing up in a society torn by violence will be socialized to deal with things never encountered in peaceful societies. These two Chechen boys learned all about weapons and their handling during their state's rebellion against Russia.

dential campaign as candidates George W. Bush and Al Gore argued about the role of Hollywood in increasing levels of violence among America's youth. The U.S. Congress sought testimony from Hollywood business leaders regarding their effectiveness in keeping programs with high levels of violence and sex away from younger viewers (Finnigan, 2000). Particular concerns were voiced about the focused marketing of such programs directly to those younger viewers.

Like television, the institution of education is an important agent of socialization in American society. Children enter this institution around the age of six and generally remain under its influence for a minimum of ten years. (It should be noted, however, that socialization cannot be measured in contact hours; the life satisfaction of children and young adults is generally related more closely to the quality of their family relationships than to the quality of their school experience and the grades they receive [Huebner, 1991].) Like the media, education is the result of many individuals occupying roles that act in concert. If you are interested in understanding why teachers teach the way they do or why they teach what they teach, you will have to understand the overall workings of the institution. Who trains the teachers? Who trains the trainers? Who writes the textbooks? Who buys the textbooks? How are schools funded? How are schools affected by legislators or by the electorate? All of these questions (plus many more) must be answered before you will understand why Johnny and Jeannie have specific experiences in their third-grade classroom. Ask yourself how many decisions, influences, and activities resulted in your holding this book in your hands right now. If you are a college student reading this book for a sociology class, a conscious attempt is being made by the institution of education to socialize you into looking at the world sociologically.

The growth of the Internet has added yet another outside force that affects your daily life. The Internet combines elements of the mass media with your home mailbox as it provides information others want you to have and sometimes actually delivers it to your cyber doorstep. At the same time, the Internet opens more democratic doors than are available in the traditional media. If you have an opinion (or many opinions), perhaps you should create your own weblog (or "blog") where others can read your insights. And if you want to research those opinions before their public display, you can "Google" your way to a variety of information sources.

All of the institutional arenas in American society shape your experience. As an adult, you will respond to the world of politics and alter your life in response to changes in the economy. Your experiences on the job, both intended and unintended by your employer, will change you in many ways. If you are drafted and sent to fight a war, you will return a different person. Coming full circle, you may discover that your parents raised you according to a book written by someone within the institution of education and published by a firm with clear economic interests in the book's success.

Institutions are impossible to escape. As agents of socialization, they permeate modern American life and ultimately are responsible for much of the individual socialization we confront. But while individual socialization seems obvious (as when our friends try to change us), socialization from institutions often affects us without our knowledge, unless we're looking for it. The sociological outlook directs you to look for it—to become aware of the many norms that are enforced and values supported through the ongoing activities within societal institutions and the ways you and your friends mirror the institutions that have already socialized you. If you think that wearing Levi's, Nikes, and a T-shirt with the emblem of your favorite band is an expression of your individuality, think again—you might have been watching too much television.

PRIMARY SOCIALIZATION: THE EARLY YEARS

Primary socialization is the socialization that occurs during the first several years of life, from whatever source. It is distinctive because (1) it is the first socialization encountered in the life cycle, and (2) the infant or young child is biologically immature and responds very differently than older children or adults. Since the biological development of the child will be an important point in our discussion, it might be useful at the outset to address the heredity versus environment dispute with a basic question: how much is a child born with and how much does he or she learn?

BOX 4.2

Why Do Men and Women Talk Differently? Carli's Study on Gender Socialization of Speech

Men and women obviously speak differently. They use different kinds of words and expressions; it's hard to imagine an American man saying, "My, how marvelous for you!" They also raise and lower their voices in different ways (called intonation) when they speak so that rises and falls in pitch come in different places and to different degrees; women are more likely to use a greater range of pitch variation (we often call this *expressiveness*) and are more likely to raise pitch at the end of a declarative sentence (making it sound almost like a question in English). Women are also more likely to use disclaimers ("I may be wrong, but . . . ."), add hedges ("Well, *perhaps* the best way would be . . . ."), add tag questions (". . . and I think that would be best, *don't you think so?*"), and interrupt less than men. Since language is obviously learned after birth rather than linked to instinct, it would be safe to say that one of the many ways the two sexes are socialized differently is in their speech.

Differences in speech according to sex could provide little more than a sociological footnote, joining all the other differences we note (and often enjoy) in the opposite sex. But some sex-linked speech variation carries more important meaning beyond just its association with the sex of the speaker. Consider the examples given above. All of them (including the questioning intonation at the end of a statement) could be taken as examples of low self-confidence and lack of assertiveness. Women often invite men to contradict them through their speech. And what kinds of impressions do we have of people who speak tentatively? Are you as likely to trust them with an important position involving responsibility? Are you going to vote for a president who begins a debate with, "I'm not sure, but . . . ."? Sex-specific speech may have more general importance.

Psychologist Linda Carli (1990) studied gender differences in speech, focusing on the way that men and women think about each other based on the way they speak. Specifically, she wanted to know how women who conformed to the speech characteristics described above (those who spoke tentatively) were perceived *as people* by *both* other men and women; she also wanted to know how women who *violated* those norms (those who spoke assertively, more in the male style) were perceived. She also wanted to know if women changed their speech to the more tentative style when they were interacting with men but used more assertive speech when only other women were present.

(continues)

BOX 4.2

Why Do Men and Women Talk Differently?
Carli's Study on Gender Socialization of Speech (continued)

Carli first noticed that women did indeed change their speech depending upon whether the listener was a man or woman. With other women as an audience, women speakers used more expressive speech; with men for an audience, women speakers used more tentative language such as increased use of hedges and tag questions. Women, it seemed, were clearly responding to some of the social expectations learned through previous socialization. Carli encountered the source of that socialization in the next part of her study.

Carli had both male and female subjects listen to a speech given by a male and a female speaker, each delivering the speech twice, once in tentative speech and once assertively. She then asked her listening subjects about their reactions to the speakers they had just heard. The response? Men found the tentatively speaking woman to be more trustworthy and likable than the assertively speaking woman; they also were more likely to agree with the position she was arguing. Women listeners, on the other hand, responded in just the opposite way. They found the *assertively* speaking woman to be more trustworthy, likable, and believable.

One conclusion leaps out at you from the above research: if women wish to influence men or be well thought of by them, women must speak the way men want. And since men are generally likely to be the ones in power, holding the gates to employment, it is clearly in the interest of women to respond to men's expectations. If a woman does this consciously, we could call it manipulation, but whether it's done consciously or unconsciously, it is clearly a response to the power of socialization.

HEREDITY VERSUS ENVIRONMENT

All organisms inherit their biological makeup and then must survive in some sort of environment. As we watch them (or ourselves) behave in that environment, we might wonder where the behavior came from. At one extreme we might assume that they inherited their behavior genetically, which would lead us to label that behavior instinct. The natural world is full of many examples of obviously inherited behavior. How do spiders know how to spin webs or bees to make honey? Even birds seem to find their way south without a roadmap or a guide. These sorts of observations give weight to the heredity side of the argument.

At the other extreme we might observe the lessons provided for the organism by the environment—either the physical environment or other organisms like itself.

The socialization that goes on when a toddler "learns" a task from a parent involves vastly more than the learning of a skill. The child cannot help but take in attitudes about responsibility or irresponsibility, dedication or carelessness, and pride or heedlessness.

On the environment side of the argument we note all instances in which organisms "learn" behavior, either through their own trial and error or by watching others. As spiders tend to lend support for the heredity side of the argument, human beings—with the tremendous amount of learning they do after birth—provide a good example for the environment side.

The dispute over heredity and environment has been going on for centuries and is far from concluded, even though the battlefields have changed many times. One hundred or so years ago, the heredity side of the dispute was in command, and even many human behaviors were explained genetically. It was assumed that criminals were genetically predisposed to crime, musicians were all born with great musical talent, the insane inherited mental instability, and different races and ethnic groups inherited specific mental and physical talents or deficiencies. "Everybody knew" that murderers had "bad blood," Latins had "hot blood," and aristocrats had "blue blood."

More recently, the environment side of the dispute has practically displaced the heredity side, largely as a result of the growing influence of the social sciences. While the social sciences have allowed many other animals to have their instincts, they constantly attack assertions that humans have them. Murderers now come from a "bad environment," Latins live in a culture that encourages displays of emotion, and aristocrats rule not because they are superior but because their culture and weapons give them the power.

Still more recently, we have seen some stirrings for a return to genetic explanations of human behavior. Some psychologists have argued that there may be racial differences in intelligence. There is also a growing field of scientific inquiry known as **sociobiology,** defined by Edward O. Wilson, one of its founders, as "the systematic study of the biological basis of all social behavior" (Wilson, 1975, 595). Sociobiology seeks to determine what genetic basis may exist for animal social behavior, particularly that of monkeys, apes, and humans. For example, Wilson notes that there are ongoing social systems in which males dominate females among almost all the primates (in other words, there is a similarity between ape societies and most human cultures) and asks whether it is possible that male members of the species inherit more aggressive behavior, particularly through the male hormones. The willingness of human beings to sacrifice ourselves for others (especially our children) is argued to be biologically based in that parents who engage in such behavior are more likely to have their children survive and, therefore, their genes survive (see Fisher, 1992, for a good overview). Sociobiology has been criticized, however, for the inability of its adherents to verify their theories according to the scientific method (Kitcher, 1985) and for their unwillingness to integrate biological theories with sociological theories (Allison, 1992).

There is no definitive answer to the questions posed by sociobiology or even to Wilson's theory. Our inability to answer these questions stems directly from the nature of human socialization and the inseparable bond between humans and their societies. No other animal depends as much on learning as humans do. Once we begin to socialize our infants, it becomes impossible to separate learned behavior from inherited behavior. The difference between the two could not be tested for practical reasons as well as the obvious ethical ones; as noted in Chapter 1, human infants require sociability in addition to food and shelter if they are to survive, and such a test would require removing that sociability. Locating cross-cultural similarities is also not a complete answer, as similarities in human adaptation (such as male dominance) might have more to do with our planet's environment than with our genes.

The best possible position regarding the heredity versus environment dispute at this point is to keep an open mind. You should also be aware of the biases of the individual or discipline that responds to the dispute. Sociology, as a social science, is biased toward the environment side of the dispute, and this book is no exception (a point you should remember while reading the rest of it). Nevertheless, the topic of socialization brings us the closest that sociology comes to the biological position. As we look at the processes of socialization, you will see something of this interplay as the social forces of society encounter a growing and biologically changing child.

FREUD'S THEORY OF PSYCHOSEXUAL STAGES

Sigmund Freud (1856–1939) is known as the father of psychoanalysis (although many of his ideas have been dropped or modified by modern psychoanalysts). More generally, his insights provided some of the major turning points that shaped the modern social sciences, sociology included. Perhaps his greatest contribution was his idea of the human unconscious.

Freud theorized that people are not consciously aware of many of their desires, angers, lusts, fears, and other feelings. In particular, they are unconscious of whatever feelings their society defines as wrong or inappropriate. Through socialization individuals *repress* these inappropriate feelings; **repression** involves moving such feelings from the conscious mind into the unconscious. After repressing these feelings, an individual can see himself or herself as a "good" person (as defined by society). The inappropriate feelings don't disappear, however; they just go beneath the surface into the unconscious. They may respond to this inhospitable treatment by giving one ulcers, headaches, bad dreams, fits of depression, or a variety of other ailments. Opening up the unconscious, Freud felt, could bring some of these feelings back into the conscious mind of the individual and stop the damage they were doing. Such tapping of the unconscious was the purpose of Freud's approach to therapy, which he dubbed *psychoanalysis*.

The knot that ties Freud's theory to sociology is repression. Without society and the values that are socialized into us, repression would not be possible. Hating your mother or father, for example, would cause you fewer problems if your society did not place a strong value on loving one's parents. Freud became interested in the processes of socialization in hopes of learning just how the values of society come to be part of an individual; as a result, he developed his theory of the stages of *psychosexual development*.

The newborn infant is in the *oral stage*. At this stage the infant receives sexual satisfaction through biting and sucking; everything encountered goes into the mouth. (This can be a trying stage for a parent.) In approximately the second and third years of life the child is in the *anal stage*, during which the child's attention shifts from the mouth to the anus. Commonly the period in which toilet training occurs, this stage was of great interest to Freud. The young child has no inborn interest in becoming toilet trained, but the parents are greatly interested. The child must acquire the parents' value of using the toilet (being "clean" as opposed to "dirty") and come to view himself or herself as they do. When the child becomes happy at being toilet trained, the value has been *internalized* and socialization is progressing.

Freud's third, or *phallic, stage* begins around age three or four and continues until five or six. During this stage the child once again shifts the focus of sexual interest, from the anus to the penis or clitoris. Freud posited that at this time the *Oedipus complex* develops. The young male comes to desire his mother and hate his father (who presumably is first in line for his mother's attentions). The young female, on the other hand, desires her father and fears her mother. By repressing these inappropriate feelings, boys and girls come to identify with their same-sex parent.

The fourth, or *latency, stage* begins at around age six and continues through the school years until puberty, when the fifth and final stage, the *genital stage,* begins. During these stages the developing child becomes increasingly bound up in his or her social environment and learns to develop a wide variety of "appropriate" feelings. The true power of society can be seen in these stages, as the values of society become increasingly internalized. We return to this topic at the end of the following section on secondary socialization when the socialization of older children is discussed. The importance of Freud's stages for our discussion here is their emphasis on the maturation of the child. The concerns of the parents change as the child grows older, but so do the concerns of the child. Freud's stages are focused somewhat narrowly on the sexual and emotional concerns of the child. We can broaden our perspective by considering the work of Jean Piaget and his theory of cognitive development.

PIAGET'S THEORY OF COGNITIVE DEVELOPMENT

Cognition is the process of perception or knowing; *cognitive development* refers specifically to the mental development of the child and focuses our attention on changes in the mental capabilities of children as they mature. Just as a five-year-old is biologically incapable of understanding adult sexual desire or throwing a football very well, so the same child is biologically incapable of understanding calculus. Jean Piaget (1896–1980), a Swiss psychologist, concluded that the best method for understanding the thinking processes of adults is to begin with infants and trace their development. His work in this area has been truly monumental, and as with Freud, it offers many lessons for the sociologist.

Piaget constructed a general theory of knowledge, part of which must be understood in order to follow his theory of cognitive development. Piaget posited that humans, like all organisms, adapt to their environment. Desert dwellers, for example, would have to develop special means of adaptation to find and conserve water. The same principle holds true for the infant, who must learn to cope with the strange environment outside of the womb. The newborn enters the world knowing how to suck, grasp, and make noise, and for a while does quite a bit of all three. Previously unencountered objects, such as a mother's breast, can be grasped and sucked. This early adaptation to the new environment is the first step on the road of cognitive development.

Adaptation continues as the child builds from these rudimentary skills. New elements in the environment are dealt with in old ways (a thumb can also be sucked, for instance), and over time old elements can be dealt with in new ways. Piaget calls these growing abilities *psychological structures*. Structures involving physical manipulation are referred to as *schemes*. The infant develops a sucking scheme, for example, and can learn by applying that scheme to other objects in the environment.

A second type of psychological structure is the *operation*. Whereas the scheme is a behavioral adaptation, the operation is an intellectual adaptation. Like schemes, operations develop through maturation as the child becomes increasingly able to think in more complicated ways. As just one of the many examples from Piaget's research, younger children find it difficult to answer the question, "Are there more girls or more children in the room?" This apparently easy (to an adult) question is tough for young children because they find it hard to think of the girls twice—first as girls and second as children. The question involves two levels of generality.

Piaget concluded through his studies of children at different ages that cognitive development occurs in definite stages as children reach new levels of understanding. His first stage of cognitive development is the *sensorimotor period,* which lasts roughly from birth until age two. This period is dominated by the acquisition of motor skills, eye-hand coordination, and so on. While the young infant may go through great effort to grasp a rattle, the older infant in this period may be experimenting with elaborate patterns of imitation, developing new schemes.

The second stage, which Piaget calls the *preoperational period,* lasts from ages two to seven. The preoperational child is going through considerable mental development, especially in the area of language. Of particular interest to sociologists is the *egocentrism* typical of this period: the preoperational child has difficulty in separating herself of himself from others, or looking at anything from the perspective of someone else. As we will see, this is a fundamental skill to be derived from socialization. Piaget tells us that until a certain age a child is simply not mature enough to learn it.

The third stage, the *concrete operational period* (ages seven to eleven), is followed by the fourth and final stage of *formal operations* (age twelve and over). In both of these stages the child is developing increasingly sophisticated mental skills, becoming capable of systematic logic and finally abstract thought. The fundamental difference between the two stages is suggested by the word *concrete;* the child at the concrete operations stage can achieve fairly sophisticated thought provided the objects of that thought are physically present.

The ages given for each stage are far from absolute; individual children might move from one stage to the next before or after the years specified. The important points are that (1) all children go through these stages in order (each stage builds upon the one before it as the child adapts), and (2) these stages are part of the child's biological maturation; adult socializers should exercise patience and wait for the child to be ready to acquire certain kinds of information.

The impressiveness of both Piaget's theoretical framework and his research should be considered in light of other research that highlights variables other than just biological maturation (see Wellman and Gelman, 1992). For example, Gruber (1992) found in a study of school-aged children that an interest and competence in games with rules was related to social class, with middle- and upper-class children turning toward those activities at younger ages; interest was also greater among boys than girls. Such findings point to the need for further research on the environmental impact on cognitive abilities.

TAKING THE ROLE OF THE SIGNIFICANT OTHER: GEORGE HERBERT MEAD

George Herbert Mead (1863–1931), an American sociologist particularly concerned about socialization, reached many conclusions similar to those of both Freud and Piaget. He was convinced that the "self" is a product of society (through socialization), and he set out to discover how it develops (Mead, 1934). His groundbreaking work has influenced most subsequent theoretical efforts in this area, setting the direction for its development (Winter and Goldfield, 1991).

To Mead the infant's first experience with social interaction comes through her or his understanding of communication. The child may discover, for example, that crying brings Mother to the crib or that laughing makes Mother laugh. This interaction, which Mead referred to as a *conversation of gestures,* represents the child's first efforts at communication. Specifically, gestures are forms of communication that begin randomly but come to be associated with elements in the environment. Communication is, of course, the first step on the road to socialization.

Around age two the child begins to develop the ability to use language. Language is the ultimate symbol system of human societies, and, for Mead, this development increases communication greatly and opens many more doors to socialization. As the child's communication skills increase, he or she will simultaneously be learning to **take the role of the other.** To communicate, the child must learn to imagine how

American sociologist George Herbert Mead (1863–1931). Mead was influential in turning the attention of American sociologists toward the importance of socialization and the development of the self.

he or she looks to others. When someone makes a negative response, the child realizes that his or her behavior is being seen in a negative light and comes to look at himself or herself in the same light.

When two people communicate through language, the words presumably create the same meanings in the minds of both people simultaneously. And since each person can look at the communication from the perspective of the other, each can be assured that the other is receiving the intended meaning. The ability of the child to see himself or herself from the perspective of others thus allows the child to understand fully language and all forms of symbolic communication. This process is in many ways the foundation of Mead's theory of socialization; the *social self,* to Mead, develops only as we come to see ourselves through the responses of other people.

As the child begins to take the role of the other, he or she enters the *play stage* of development. During this stage, the child's imagination leads to an actual playing out of the many "others" the child has encountered. Probably the clearest example of this stage is the childhood game of dress-up, in which the child puts on Mommy's or Daddy's clothes and, in play, actually becomes Mommy or Daddy. This kind of physical acting out is necessary because taking the perspective of another person is a difficult mental operation for the developing child; using some props and talking out loud like Mommy or Daddy helps make the understanding more meaningful. I recall an argument I had with my son when he was three. He was sent to his room, and for the next half-hour I heard our argument continuing, with my son playing

Playing dress-up is an important part of primary socialization as children learn to see the world through their parents' eyes.

both parts. Not only did he get rid of some of his anger this way, but he also produced in his own mind a clearer image of my expectations (however unreasonable they might have been). He was learning to see himself as I saw him.

Taking the role of the other is fundamental to socialization and to the communication that makes up that socialization. The basic form of the process is present even in young children, though it is difficult for them because of their level of maturation. Recall Piaget's description of children at the preoperational stage: they are focused strongly on their own desires and have difficulty realizing that others have similar strong desires. Mead's explanation is that the child can take the perspective of others but only one "other" at a time—and even then with some difficulty. Young children clearly can distinguish between different expectations from one person to another. The child may discover that some behavior tolerated by Mommy will result in punishment from Daddy, and vice versa. The expectations of grandparents will likely be something else entirely. It is very interesting watching a child of three or four in the company of both parents and some grandparents—which "other" is in charge? The answer comes through an experience of trial and error, often painful to all concerned.

The overall picture of primary socialization that emerges from the various theories is a composite. Freud, Piaget, and Mead all emphasize the maturation of the child as an important factor in determining the process of socialization. Just as your thinking processes can never return to where they once began, no adult can ever experience primary socialization. Furthermore, as all three theorists emphasize, the child's coming to view himself or herself through the perspectives of others is the true source of the developing end product—the social self. As we turn now to a discussion of secondary socialization, we will get a still clearer picture of this process, as the child becomes biologically more receptive and the agents of socialization become more insistent.

SECONDARY SOCIALIZATION: A LIFELONG PROCESS

Consider all that goes into adult conversation, even at its most basic level. For example:

> **John:** Hello, Mary. Where are you going?
> **Mary:** Hello, John. I'm walking to the library to get a book.
> **John:** I just came from there. The library is closed.

How is it that John and Mary understand each other? This very brief communication is more than enough to make the point. Here is the same conversation as it occurs inside the heads of John and Mary:

> **John:** (There's my friend Mary. I think I'll give her a friendly greeting along with a polite question about her activities. I speak English, and I know from past

experience that Mary does, too, so I'll string some English words into a sentence that will communicate my thoughts to Mary.)

Mary: (John has just said, "Hello, Mary. Where are you going?" Now what would I have been thinking to myself if I had just met someone like myself and selected those particular words to say? I would probably have simply wanted to convey a friendly greeting coupled with a polite question as to current activities. Assuming that John meant what I would have meant if l had spoken those words, I'll return the friendly greeting along with some information about my current activities. I'll try to create an English sentence that conveys my thinking as nearly as possible.)

John: (Mary has just responded to my original remarks by saying, "Hello, John. I'm walking to the library to get a book." Before she decided on that reply, she placed herself in my original position and asked herself what she would have meant had she made my original remark. She then made assumptions that I actually meant what she would have meant under similar conditions, responded to that meaning in her own thoughts, and tried to place that response back into English for my benefit. Now if I had been making those assumptions about what I originally meant and had then produced the utterance that she just produced, what would I have meant? I will assume that she actually meant what I would have meant under those conditions and respond as if that is actually what she did mean. If all my assumptions are correct, I think that she might find it useful to hear about my recent experience at the library. I'll try to create an English sentence that will convey that recent experience.)

It is a wonder of human communication that we can do all that thinking and assuming in a split second with very little conscious effort. We must constantly place ourselves in someone else's position throughout a conversation if we are to understand each other. We usually become aware of this process only when communication breaks down. People sometimes make faulty assumptions about another's meaning and take offense at a comment that was not meant that way; it can be difficult to backtrack along a conversation to find exactly where the mistaken assumption occurred.

The process by which we "take the role of the other" tells us as much about socialization in general as it does about human communication. **Secondary socialization** is the socialization that occurs after the first few years of life, when the individual is capable of symbolic communication and developing a social sense of self. It has truly begun when a child can imagine himself or herself in someone's position as automatically as John and Mary do in the above conversation. Such imagining requires considerable mental agility, which a very young child does not possess. The secret of this automatic "role taking" according to Mead, is not just the speed but the complexity with which it occurs. On numerous occasions we must take into account the perspectives of many roles simultaneously; for this we need what Mead calls a generalized other.

THE DEVELOPMENT OF THE GENERALIZED OTHER

A **generalized other** is your mental idea of what you believe a large number of people (or people in general) expect of you. For all practical purposes your generalized other will relate not to a group of actual people but to roles. When you walk into a supermarket, you can imagine how other customers and clerks expect you to behave; your imagination need not get more specific than that because the coordination of society creates enough regularity in roles. The expectations held of one role by other roles have already been defined as *norms;* thus we can simplify the definition of generalized other to your understanding of social norms and how they affect you. Everyday social interaction could not occur without generalized others; patterns of social behavior depend on people constantly checking their own behavior against norms.

When the child is mature enough to construct a generalized other, he or she has moved from Mead's play stage to the *game stage.* A child can play by himself or herself (even if other children are in the play group), but a game requires the child to view a common activity from many perspectives at once. Mead uses the game of baseball as an example.

How do you play first base in the game of baseball? Physically you play only one position, but mentally you play every position. You imagine yourself as the batter and take on that perspective. The batter probably wants to get a hit and make it to first base. Let's assume the batter does hit the ball on the ground to the second-base player. You now have to imagine yourself as the batter and the second-base player simultaneously: The batter will be trying to run to first base, and the second-base player will try to catch the ball and throw it to first base ahead of the runner. Since you are the first-base player, you had better run to first base in anticipation of the throw that you expect from the second-base player. You anticipate all this because you can imagine what you would do in both of the other positions simultaneously. In short, says Mead, you understand how to play a game. But before you can play a game, you must be able to construct a generalized other.

Piaget (1965) noticed the same phenomenon in his study of how children learn to play the game of marbles. The Swiss children he studied seemed to play marbles at very young ages, but upon watching them closely and talking to them, Piaget discovered they didn't understand what they were doing as a "game." They were just shooting marbles at other marbles. They were not competing against the other children, since to compete one must understand how a game is played with winners and losers. The key to any game is its rules. Young children do not understand a rule and are unable to look at the game from the perspective of others simultaneously and then win or lose accordingly. Piaget further discovered that, at a certain point in life, a "light went on" in the minds of the children, and they comprehended the rules of the game. From then on they didn't just play; they played a game.

Note the similarity between Piaget's idea of the child's relation to the rule and Mead's idea of the generalized other as an understanding of norms. A norm, after all, is nothing but a rule in a social game; it specifies who should do what and when. A very young child may understand what Mommy expects (the "rule" of an individual) but cannot understand what people in general expect (the norms). To a child every new situation is new because the people are different; to an adult situations that are technically new may in fact be nothing more than an old game played with new players at a new location. A supermarket, after all, is a supermarket, wherever you find it.

If we want to understand how children react to socialization, we must know something about how they come to understand norms. The very young child can deal only with individual others because he or she is biologically limited to that kind of mental perspective. This limitation is one of the reasons the actions of our parents are so important to the way we turn out. We perceive Mommy's expectations as extremely important; they fill the whole world of our imagination. As adults, however, we see the expectations of other individuals often as just representations of more general group norms. We are also more capable as adults of associating with a variety of groups that may have different norms (and we will develop a different generalized other for each group). Having this variety in our experience gives us a different perspective altogether on the importance of norms: we may come to see them as arbitrary rules agreed upon by a social group. The young child, on the other hand, experiences the expectations of an individual other as virtually carved in granite.

But socialization conveys more than just norms; socialization also conveys *values*. The ultimate goal of socialization is not only to teach you the norms but to make you want to follow them. Values provide reasons for following the norms or, more basically, convince you that following your group's norms is important. If values were not part of socialization, we would be spending most of our time policing other members of social groups, seeing to it that they followed the norms. The process in which individuals respond to socialization by coming to believe in the values of their social group is called **internalization**.

INTERNALIZATION: THE BASIS OF MORALITY AND SOCIAL CONSTRAINT

Try the following experiment. Cover your hands with honey, chocolate, or anything you can find that is sticky. Then leave them that way for an hour or two. If you have internalized the American value of cleanliness, it will drive you crazy ("Cleanliness is next to Godliness"). Babies are not born wanting to be clean; if anything, they seem to be inclined the other way. How is it possible to take a nice sticky baby and turn it into an adult who can't stand a little goo? This may not seem an important question, since similar changes happen to all of us, but to a sociologist it's a miraculous transformation.

Piaget understood this function of socialization very well in his study of children and their marble games, titled *The Moral Judgment of the Child* (1965). What's moral about marbles? Not much. But the basis of any kind of group morality is an understanding of how your group looks at its rules. As with the Ten Commandments, there is always an inseparable bond between a group's rules and its values. Morality, therefore, can begin with marbles. The child's first understanding of adhering to a moral code will occur simultaneously with his or her understanding of the rules in a game.

Perhaps the most famous part of Freud's theory is an elaboration on this idea. The human personality, says Freud, contains a facet called the *id,* which consists of our basic drives and desires. Humans are born with a well-developed id; a baby is concerned with its own wants and, as we have seen, is incapable of appreciating the wants of anyone else. The part of the human personality controlled by the id is referred to by Freud as the *primary process.* As socialization occurs, the id is joined by a growing *superego,* that portion of the personality that has internalized the values of the social group. Freud refers to the part of the personality controlled by the superego as the *secondary process.* Repression occurs when the superego comes into conflict with the id and wins, driving the desires of the id into the unconscious. The third, and final, facet of the human personality is the *ego,* which acts as something of a mediator between the id and the superego, striving to satisfy basic desires as much as possible while dealing with the realities of the world.

Freud's concept of the superego is similar to the common idea of the conscience— that part of you that keeps track of "right" and "wrong" and makes you feel guilty when you do "wrong." Freud's observation was that the conscience is very real, but it must be understood as a social creation. The conscience contains the values of the social group; if it makes you feel guilty, that means that you have internalized those values to the point where they are now part of you.

Mead conceived of value internalization in a manner similar to Freud. According to Mead, there is a part of every human personality, which he termed the **"I,"** that is spontaneous and creative; it initiates or encourages action by the individual. Mead also conceived of another part of the personality that he termed the **"Me."** Much like Freud's superego, the **"Me"** is the part that is socialized by the group and contains the group's values; it sometimes battles the **"I"** for control over your behavior. The **"Me"** directs or channels action by the individual into socially approved forms.

Mead's somewhat unusual choice of pronouns as names for his concepts relates to his conception of the reflective manner in which socialization occurs. The pronoun *I* is always used as a subject in a sentence, as in "I saw Mary"; it always refers to something active. The pronoun *me,* on the other hand, is grammatically an object, as in "Mary saw me." While *I* does the doing, something is being done to *me.* Since

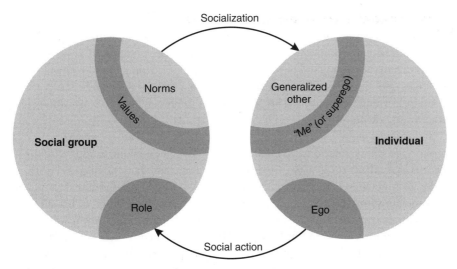

Figure 4.1 The process of socialization.

socialization occurs as we come to look at ourselves as objects viewed by others, it is fitting that the socialized part of the self should be a grammatical "object" rather than a "subject." We are fully socialized when we carry our social group around inside us, constantly evaluating our own behavior according to the group's standards. Though our generalized other tells us what those standards are, we must also have internalized values if we are to care about adhering to those standards. We have a police force to enforce many of these standards, but that force could never be large enough if most of us didn't police our own behavior.

Figure 4.1 graphically sums up the connections among all the concepts in the sociological view of socialization. On one side we find the social group with its norms, values, and roles. The goal of socialization (to the socializer) is to place those norms and values firmly into a potential new group member, in hopes of producing a new role player. The process of socialization itself turns group norms into a generalized other (the individual's knowledge of the group norms), and group values into a "Me" (or a superego). The individual may then choose to play an appropriate role. Along with each role comes appropriate feelings and emotions; we acquire these emotions through socialization and also learn how, when, and where to express them (Kagan, 1984).

An individual will never be a carbon copy of the group; one individual will seldom be aware of all the group's norms, nor will he or she be likely to have internalized all the group's values. Unlike the painter who declares the painting finished, members of social groups never tire of putting a few finishing touches of socialization into their interactions.

LEARNING NORMS AND INTERNALIZING VALUES

Whenever you enter a new social situation or begin interacting with members of an unfamiliar social group, you will likely have a limited or confused knowledge of the norms that operate, and as part of the process of learning them, you will make mistakes. No matter how old you are, you relive a little of the experience of childhood in learning new norms. The "new kid on the block" has to learn slowly just where and how to fit in.

In a highly mobile society such as the United States, wherever you find social groups and social situations, you will also find newcomers trying to cope with them. Because socialization is a two-way street, the newcomer is often as anxious as older group members for the socialization to be successful. In the case of **anticipatory socialization,** the newcomer may even begin socializing himself or herself in an imaginatory sense before real socialization begins; a high school student who wants to be a doctor may start to "feel the part" long before medical school.

An individual who enters an official training program (or college major) will "learn" many things at various levels. Beyond the program content, the individual will face a variety of efforts from teachers and others in the program to change his or her values and perceptions of self. A professional college program (nursing, education, law enforcement, and the like) not only passes on knowledge related to the prospective job but also seeks to make students think of themselves as future practitioners of the job. The school may offer official courses on the ethics and values of the occupation, but more important are the informal settings (clubs, associations, casual conversations) that slowly but surely make the student identify with others in the occupation and, ultimately, with the occupation itself.

Another newcomer situation is that of immigrants. America is often labeled the nation of immigrants, and we can look to the history of the many who came (and are still coming) to learn the problems of newcomers. The problems were much the same for a German immigrant in 1800, an Italian immigrant in 1900, or a Vietnamese immigrant in the 1980s. Immigrants encounter differences in language, religion, political processes, occupations, clothing styles, food, childrearing practices, education, gender roles, entertainment forms—the list could go on forever. The newcomer problem for the immigrant is made even more difficult because, unlike some other newcomer situations with avid socializers, the "old-timers" may keep the immigrant away from experiences needed for socialization. Old-timers with particular job skills, for example, may not want an immigrant to learn those skills and become a competitor.

Such complexity makes the socialization of the immigrant take a long time. In general, the individual who immigrates as an adult will always be a newcomer, even after forty or fifty years. A "foreign accent" is only a concrete sign of a great many other elements of the original culture that the immigrant retains. The immigrant's children, however, face a different situation. Even though they may not have access to many sectors of the society because of discrimination against their group, they

Secondary socialization is the socialization we experience as adults. This young woman, in the course of becoming a helicopter pilot—an occupation totally dominated by males in the past—had to learn many new norms.

nevertheless will be native-born members of their parents' adopted society. They have fundamentally different experiences from those of their parents and, as a result, will think and act differently from them.

THE DEVELOPMENT OF THE SELF: SOCIETY AND PERSONALITY

If we look at people as learners who are "taught" how to be human by other members of their social groups, we can see that your self and your personality have more to do with your social group than with your own hopes and desires. By the time you are old enough to form definite goals and preferences, your social group has already had sufficient time to affect the kinds of goals and preferences you'll create. When you look to your adult self for a little decision making about your future, many of those decisions will in fact have been made for you by others and hidden in your personality for you to discover later on. You may decide, for example, that you want to have a job with power over others, that you like art and want to paint, or that you want to get married and have babies. In each case it will be your decision—but, as with much in society, it will come with a little help from your friends [see Burkitt (1991) for an overview on theories relating to the development of the social self].

CHARLES COOLEY: THE LOOKING-GLASS SELF

Charles Cooley (1864–1929) was an American sociologist who helped direct sociological attention to the study of the primary group and its importance to the socialization of the individual. He is best known today for one of the concepts he used in describing his process: the **looking-glass self,** the process by which we acquire a sense of self from the way others view us. We constantly (1) imagine how others see us, (2) imagine how others judge us, and (3) add those imaginations to our overall view of self, consequently feeling, for example, proud or ashamed (Cooley, 1909). Other people, of course, are interested in socializing us and may go out of their way in helping us be clear about exactly what their views and judgments of us are. If other people think you are physically unattractive, for example, they may tell you that (1) you are ugly, and (2) being ugly is a characteristic that disgusts them. As a result, according to Cooley, you will come to see yourself as (1) an ugly person and (more important in the long run) (2) a disgusting person.

Cooley's concept of the looking-glass self is consistent with the theories of Freud, Piaget, and Mead. In each case there is an emphasis on the reflective nature of socialization as we come to view ourselves through the eyes of others, who represent the norms and values of our social groups. Our self develops as a mirror image; we can only see ourselves as a reflection from the responses of other people. To some extent your adult self will be the sum of other people's responses to you throughout your life. Keep in mind, however, that not all other views will affect your self-image equally. Your parents' views will have a much greater impact on you than a neighbor's impression; your best friends will have much more effect on your self-image than casual acquaintances will.

Your view of self is also flexible because of its dynamic nature. For example, you could spend several years in a social situation where everyone responded to you as if you were unintelligent; others might ignore your opinions, ridicule your thoughts, or (if they wished to leave no doubt in the matter) simply call you stupid. Almost certainly you would come out of this situation with the impression that you were not too bright. If you changed social situations, however, you could conceivably encounter others who were greatly impressed with your mental skills and abilities. In this new situation you would slowly but surely acquire a new self-image as an intelligent person. To explain your past, you might also become convinced that your former associates were not too bright themselves and therefore unable to appreciate your true gift of intelligence. While the looking-glass self seems somewhat passive, Cooley recognized the ability of the individual to respond creatively to life's decisions (Franks and Gecas, 1992).

HOW TO AVOID A SELF: AN ACTIVE APPROACH TO ROLE PLAYING

Your self-image is a reflection of other people's responses to you in a specific role. As an adult, you will discover that you have acquired a variety of self-images specific to certain roles. Your employer may think you're incompetent, while your spouse may think you're very capable (or vice versa). This situation would give you a negative self-image in the role of employee and a positive self-image in the role of spouse (or, again, vice versa). Most of us are in fact very aware of the roles that give us positive feedback and try to spend as much time in them as possible. A bad situation at work will find us rushing home at the end of the day to a positive family life; a bad situation at home might make us workaholics, dedicated to our jobs. We slip fondly into the roles we find the most comfortable.

Responses to you depend on how well others feel you play a particular role, but they can also vary according to the role itself. The role of prisoner, for example, produces a negative self-image no matter how well other prisoners and guards feel that you play it. The same could be said for the roles of slave, welfare recipient, garbage collector, janitor, or mental patient. In each case the role itself tends to have a negative connotation in American society; identifying yourself as a player of that particular role thus tends to produce a negative self-image. You may know in your heart that being a really good janitor is difficult and that you do your job very well indeed, but the responses of others to "what you do" will always make you feel as if you are in a second-class occupation. You may conclude that you are "not as good" or "not as smart" as other people—a conclusion to avoid.

Because your view of yourself comes from roles, an alternative view of yourself depends on an alternative role that will provide you with a more positive self-image. Such an alternative role can be achieved through the imagination. John Updike's (1960) novel *Rabbit, Run* tells the story of an ex-high school basketball star (nicknamed Rabbit) for whom nothing has gone well since school. He responds to his current problems by reliving his past fame on the court in his mind. Although still a young man in his twenties, Rabbit turns his back on his dead-end job and nagging wife to "run" his imagination back into his days of glory and a self-image he found satisfying. People can also imagine themselves in the future and avoid identifying with a current unpleasant job, for example, by imagining some position of importance they plan to occupy in the future. College students often put up with unpleasant summer jobs in this way. Ely Chinoy (1952) noted some similar imaginings among full-time automobile workers in the United States. Most of the men he interviewed recognized, when pressed, that they would probably never be doing anything but what they were doing, yet many had alternative activities alive in their imaginations. For example, many of them talked of leaving the factory one day to operate some kind of small business. A light at the end changes a hole into a tunnel.

The human imagination is amazing, but it can't compete with the reality and involvement of everyday life. The habit of role taking that is so necessary for even the most basic forms of communication opens the door to socialization. An employer who thinks poorly of you, for example, will communicate that thought with every interaction between the two of you. And you can't refuse to interact with your employer. Your imagination will remind you that better times are ahead and that your boss is a feeble excuse for a human being (whose opinions should therefore be disregarded), but the everyday experience of negative responses will have a wearing effect. You may come to doubt the reality of both past and present alternative roles as your current situation imperceptibly alters your self-image.

The social self that individuals develop over the years is in fact a shaky construction that is constantly in need of strengthening and repair. Most adults will think this assertion contrary to their own experience, for most of us perceive no major changes in our personalities over the years and think of ourselves as "set." Selves are seldom set, however. Most people never find themselves in social situations that drastically attack the social self they have developed; in fact, most of us go out of our way to avoid such situations. We like to remain around familiar places, people, and social situations, where we're comfortable. This kind of constancy hides the effect our social lives have on our selves; we are unaware of how our everyday experiences have become a "fix" to which we become addicted in order to maintain our personalities. If you receive respect in your everyday life, for example, you will feel happy, content, and strong and you may have the impression that you will be basically that way in any situation. An unpleasant new role could change all that, however.

As stated earlier, the most effective way to minimize the impact of a particular role on your self-image is to cultivate another self-image in another, more positive role. A good job can make a bad family situation more bearable, and vice versa. The positive self-image we acquire in one role helps counteract the negative self-image offered to us in another. We can also add groups of friends, club memberships, and so on to further extend the roles available to us. With such a variety of messages concerning our selves available, we can use the more positive messages as psychological ammunition against the negative messages. A bad day at work makes you even happier than usual to get home; you've probably used up your ammunition that day and need to reload.

We sometimes need to convince others along with ourselves that a particular role does not represent who we think we are. We respond to this need with **role distance**—playing our roles in some creative fashion that communicates to others that "our heart is not in it." Erving Goffman (1961a), who has researched role distance in various settings, observed it among adolescent boys on merry-go-rounds. Feeling that riding the merry-go-round might undermine their growing sense of maleness, those boys would make fun of the merry-go-round and its horses as they rode, hopping from horse to horse, not holding on, or perhaps holding onto a horse's tail. They wanted to make it quite clear both to themselves and to others that they had not taken the childlike role of merry-go-round rider to heart.

Role distance can also be maintained through the artful creation of alternative roles to play alongside a distasteful role. When I was a sophomore in college, a good friend dropped out of school and took a job as a janitor in the cafeteria of the student union building. We sometimes coordinated our evening coffee breaks, his from dishwashing and mine from the library. One evening, as we were sitting in the empty cafeteria with two cups of coffee, a middle-aged male janitor came in and asked, "Might I avail myself of a sponge?" *Avail?* Even people who use that word normally would be unlikely to use it in regard to a sponge. The question, as it turned out, had much more to do with us than it had to do with sponges. The janitor told us his life story, which included many advanced university degrees, a prison sentence for refusing the draft during World War II, and a dedication to doing common work with his hands so as not to prostitute his intellect. Nevertheless, it was obviously important to him that we not mistake him for a "common" janitor; if we didn't, neither would he. As he joined our coffee break, moved the topic of discussion to a theological debate (which was over our heads), and invited us to join the evening discussion group he had organized, it became clear that his alternative role was working well for him.

Wherever distasteful roles are found, role distance will be found. It is perhaps a natural response from any individual in a modern, complex society. The vast number of roles that all of us play make us aware of the differences among them as well as the different kinds of effects they have on us. If a role doesn't fit, try on a new one; if you can't get out of the old one, add one to it. Even though most of us prefer to see ourselves as having one basic personality, the large number of roles we play provide many facets to our personalities. Our multiple roles give us multiple selves.

MULTIPLE SELVES: THE MODERN INDIVIDUAL

As we've seen, the image you view when you look at yourself was put there by others as they have responded to you throughout your life. The infant, in spite of being clearly self-centered, really has no view of self, since the infant is unable to imagine how he or she appears to others. When individuals develop this ability, they begin building a self-image that becomes quite complex over time. As an adult, you probably make a great many fine points and subdistinctions in your self-image; you may see yourself as skilled to a certain specified degree in certain specified tasks while finding yourself just as specifically lacking elsewhere. You are not just attractive or unattractive—your hair looks good, your mouth is acceptable, your nose is too big. We make similar fine distinctions in all aspects of our self-images because the responses we get from others come complete with those distinctions. Do all of these elaborate fine points describe just one person or many?

Our cultural knowledge contains the idea that all individuals are different from each other, but nowhere do we hear that each individual has parts that are different from each other. This might even sound to you like a description of some form of mental illness such as the "split personality." But are you the same person all the time? Do you always act the same way, or even with the same style? Are you the same person in a peaceful mood that you are when you lose your temper? When you pause to reflect, you no doubt justify all this diversity as parts of your one "self." But do you even see the same self when you are in different situations or in different moods?

A modern industrial society is characterized by an extremely high division of labor. This means that each individual will generally have more roles than in a non-industrial society. Roles are highly specialized in a modern industrial society, with each one requiring different skills and providing different activities. And each one provides a different "self."

Besides being specialized, roles in a modern society tend to be highly compartmentalized (or segregated). Particularly in the world of work, people engaged in one activity frequently don't know (or care) much about the activities of others. The ideal of the well-rounded individual is fast being replaced by the competent but limited specialist who knows more and more about less and less. As individuals keep their roles separate, played in special arenas for special audiences, the possibilities for multiple selves become endless. People come to direct a specific part of their personality toward each role they play, and as a result, a different version of self emerges. A hired contract killer can become president of the PTA and feel little if any contradiction.

RESOCIALIZATION

Resocialization is an extreme form of secondary socialization in which drastic changes are deliberately brought about in the thinking and behavior of an adult. It can occur only when the agent of socialization has almost total influence or control over the individual to be socialized. The process of resocialization requires a systematic breaking down of the already socialized adult individual so that his or her previous patterns of behavior and thought become disorganized. Once the individual's previous "selves" have been displaced, it then becomes possible for the agent of socialization to replace those selves with a previously selected "self," coupled with appropriate patterns of behavior. Resocialization typically occurs in total institutions (such as prisons, mental institutions, and political "reeducation" programs) and in extreme social movements (such as revolutionary political groups or religious cults). As these examples suggest, individuals can be subjected to resocialization against their will, or they may submit to it willingly. In either case the result is an almost complete transformation of the individual.

This section discusses resocialization techniques in two types of settings. First, the basic techniques of resocialization are highlighted through an examination of their most common setting: the total institution. Second, we turn to the world of everyday life and look at how some individuals are lured out of that world into religious cults by techniques of resocialization that do not require either compulsory participation or physical control over the individual.

THE IMPACT OF THE TOTAL INSTITUTION

A **total institution** provides a regimented living and working existence for its members, who are isolated from the rest of society. The most common examples are prisons, mental institutions, and, to some extent, the military (see the reading on Marine recruit training at the end of this chapter). Some total institutions are organized solely to provide a highly controlled custody for those whom social authorities want isolated.

Even when resocialization is not a conscious goal in such situations, it occurs through the institution's control over the behavior of inmates. A custodial total institution requires submission to the rules. With no alternative, many individuals come to take on a self-image appropriate to their role of submissive inmate. It is quite common, in fact, for individuals who have spent many years in total institutions to be incapable of living elsewhere. People who have spent many years in prison, for example, have been known to commit very obvious crimes upon their release for the sole purpose of regaining entry to the prison. This process whereby individuals become completely adjusted to and dependent on the total institution is known as **institutionalization.**

If the total institution is an effective resocializer even in the absence of conscious effort, its influence is awesome when directed consciously. The first goal of resocialization is to create a break between the individual and his or her previous life. Incoming mental patients, for example, may be stripped of their clothes and have all their personal possessions removed (Goffman, 1961b). Similarly, Westerners who went through "brainwashing" at the hands of the Chinese during the Korean War were cut off from the outside world and confined to cells (Lifton, 1969; Schein, Schneier, and Barker, 1961). Whatever the particulars, the intent is to disorient by separating the individual from all past social realities. It is at this stage of resocialization that the social nature of the self is very evident. Even a piece of clothing can provide a tie to a past life; when removed, it makes that past life (and self) more remote.

Initial separation is followed by introduction of the individual to the new reality of the total institution. In more extreme cases of resocialization various forms of physical abuse may introduce the individual to the rules of the institution. In our modern world of elaborate technological advances in torture, some of the most effective techniques are the most simple. Solitary confinement, sleep deprivation, and hunger will make anyone disoriented and susceptible to suggestion. The agent (or agents) of socialization offers suggestions in the form of attacks on the individual's previous self and behavior, together with instructions for improving both. Americans "brainwashed" during the Korean War were constantly reminded of their past "sins" as capitalists, were encouraged to feel guilt for that behavior, and were constantly instructed on the advantages of a communist state (Schein et al., 1961).

Similar procedures occur in most total institutions, although they are not always coupled with physical disorientation. Part of "curing" the "mentally ill," for example, consists of convincing patients of their illness in the past; patients who do not see themselves as "sick" will find that attitude taken as a further symptom of illness. People imprisoned for criminal activity must feel guilty about their past behavior if they are to achieve the label *rehabilitated*. The Marine recruit will learn to see his past self as a soft civilian compared to the tough Marine he now is.

Perhaps most important, the total institution places the individual among a select group of associates. The more total the institution, the more clearly this situation occurs. Those individuals being "reeducated" during the Korean War were placed in carefully selected cells with other successful converts (Schein et al., 1961). As we will see in the next section, this social aspect of resocialization is extremely important among converts to religious cults. If the institution is not total enough, inmates may find a variety of ways around the hoped-for results. Goffman (1961b) describes the variety of relationships mental patients form with staff members or outsiders in attempts to achieve distance from the mental patient role. Prisons are famous for their underground drug rings, gang relationships, and homosexual activities, all of which subvert the presumed goals of rehabilitation.

The basis of resocialization is to be found in the social nature of the self and the day-to-day interactions that maintain it. Control over the individual and those interactions (which the total institution provides) gives the agent of socialization enormous influence over the individual's self-image. Once the individual has been pried from former personalities and well situated into the ongoing roles of the total institution, resocialization is already well on its way. The amazing ease with which this process occurs is illustrated with frightening clarity in the experiment described in Box 4.3. As is apparent, you control your personality only to the extent that you control the social groups with which you interact and the roles you play. As the total institution takes that control from you, it is also essentially free to remove your personality.

THE POPULARITY OF RELIGIOUS CULTS

Most of the resocialization situations I've described involved unwilling participants. The realization that you are totally at the mercy of someone else (whose motives and goals you may only partially understand) would place you in a naturally weak position for holding up against resocialization. How is it possible, therefore, for resocialization to occur when individuals are physically free to walk out the door? The popularity of religious cults in the United States has shown that it is not unusual for this to happen.

The 1970s brought us Scientology, the Unification Church, Krishna Consciousness, and the People's Temple. The 1980s witnessed the rise of fundamentalist religious sects as new religious leaders such as Jimmy Swaggert and Jim Bakker came to have large followings. In the 1990s, the Branch Davidian and Heaven's Gate tragedies showed the power of a cult and its leader. With the exception of the most revolutionary political movements of the 1960s, none of the political organizations

BOX 4.3

The Pathology of Imprisonment: The Zimbardo Study of Prison Roles

Your sense of self is the continuing product of the socialization you receive from your social groups. It develops in response to the way others treat you in the roles you play, and it is continuous in that it is never finished forming and always open to change, even drastic change, if the social situations you encounter demand it.

In 1972, Philip Zimbardo, a professor of psychology at Stanford University, created such a social situation by forming a mock prison on campus. He advertised for college students to take part in an experiment (paying $15 a day) in which half would be placed in the role of prisoners while the other half would play the role of guards. Those placed in the prisoner roles (through the flip of a coin) were unexpectedly picked up at their homes, run through normal booking procedure at the local police department, and taken blindfolded to the university, where they were stripped, deloused, put in a prison uniform, and placed in a cell. The "guards" were instructed to make up rules for maintaining law, order, and respect. Beyond that, the subjects were on their own. Zimbardo was forced to cancel the experiment after six days. As he describes the situation,

> In less than a week the experience of imprisonment undid (temporarily) a lifetime of learning; human values were suspended, self-concepts were challenged and the ugliest, most base, pathological side of human nature surfaced. We were horrified because we saw some boys (guards) treat others as if they were despicable animals, taking pleasure in cruelty, while other boys (prisoners) became servile, dehumanized robots who thought only of escape, of their own individual survival and of their mounting hatred for the guards. (Zimbardo, 1972, 4)

Some of the prisoners had to be released from the experiment after the first four days because of such behavior as hysterical crying. Others asked for parole (part of the experiment), were turned down, and seemed to forget that they were really college students who could leave at any time by simply giving up their pay. The guards seemed similarly caught up in the experiment, several of them engaging in brutal behavior (such as locking up one of the prisoners in a small closet for refusing to eat).

These research results have particular importance for similar roles in American society such as prison guard, police officer, or soldier. For example, Johnson (1991) found that police officers often responded to the conflict inherent in their jobs by

(continues)

BOX 4.3

The Pathology of Imprisonment:
The Zimbardo Study of Prison Roles (continued)

"depersonalizing" citizens. This is similar to a soldier thinking of his enemy as, for example, a "gook" (as in the Vietnam War) rather than a human being; it's much more difficult psychologically to injure a fellow human being than a depersonalized "gook." Zimbardo's only conclusion to these phenomena is that the self is more the result of social situations than it is the possession of the individual.

All roles affect us, and most of us play or will play roles with built-in stress and conflict. Knowledge of what roles can do may not prevent their effect, but at least you might understand as you watch your personality change.

Prisoner abuse in Iran's Abu Ghraib prison by American soldiers may well have its roots in Zimbardo's pathology of imprisonment.

resocialized their members; they attracted members only as long as they satisfied members' political interests. The religious cults, by contrast, developed a much stronger hold on their members, often resulting in blind obedience to the cult's leaders; the mass suicide of People's Temple followers at the command of leader Jim Jones may be the most sensational illustration, but all of the cults mentioned were able to achieve amazing loyalty. While none of them applied the initial physical coercion of the total institution, their methods were otherwise very similar.

Bridge-Burning Activities: Examples from the Unification Church A prime example of religious cults is the Unification Church founded by Korean Sun Myung Moon. The problems faced by the Unification Church in finding and resocializing converts are common to most of the religious cults. These problems can be summarized under the heading of bridge-burning activities. When you burn your bridges behind you, leaving the cult and returning home becomes difficult, if not impossible. With the total institution social bridges are burned automatically when the individual is placed under the physical control of the institution and is prevented from leaving. With religious cults the individual must be convinced to burn slowly one bridge after another before resocialization can occur. John Lofland's (1977) study of the Unification Church (published as *Doomsday Cult*) makes the nature of bridge burning clear.

The power of the Unification Church in resocializing the cult's members is obvious in this photo of a mass wedding ceremony. The brides and grooms did not choose each other but were matched up by the Church.

The most important element in the success or failure of conversion is the human relationships of the potential convert. Lofland found that the most successful converts were "loners" before their meeting with cult members, and they came to develop intense and satisfying social relationships with cult members. This is similar to the enforced techniques used during the Korean War, when individuals were placed among those who had already converted to communism. A former loner takes on the new cult role and new cult self in return for sociability. Individuals who had preexisting social ties outside the cult were unlikely converts if those preexisting relationships were strong enough to withstand the individual's first brief attraction to the cult.

The maintenance of social ties outside the cult is always a direct threat to the conversion process. Thus, part of the bridge-burning activities is convincing the potential convert to break ties with other people, who may be defined either as "agents of Satan" or just "negative influences," depending on the cult in question. The following quotation from a Unification Church member (a response to her mother's rejection of her conversion) illustrates the style with which cults deal with this issue:

> At first it was the deepest hurt I had ever experienced. But I remember what others in our [Unification Church] family have given up and how they too experienced a similar rejection. But so truly, I can now know a little of the rejection that our beloved Master experienced. I can now begin to understand his deep grief for the Father as he sat peering out of a window singing love songs to Him because he knew that the Father would feel such grief. I can now begin to feel the pain that our Father in heaven felt for 6,000 years. I can now begin to see that to come into the Kingdom of heaven is not as easy as formerly thought. I can now see why many are called but few are chosen. I begin to understand why men will be separated, yes, even from their families. I begin to see the shallowness of human concern for God as a Father and their true blindness. Oh, my heart cries out to Our Father in grateful praise and love for what He has given. (Lofland, 1977, 56)

The majority of religious cults provide for communal living for their members, ranging from the almost total isolation of the People's Temple members in Jonestown (in the South American country of Guyana) to having members share apartments within a city. Whatever the arrangements, communal living decreases the time spent by converts with noncult people while simultaneously increasing the time spent with (usually) veteran cult members, already at a further stage of conversion. As Lofland noted, one of the most effective alterations in changing potential converts to converts was moving them into one of the cult's communal living situations.

Last, but not least, we come to money and other material possessions. Many religious cults, like the Unification Church, encourage or insist that the convert turn all worldly possessions over to the cult; others, like the Church of Scientology, achieve almost the same end by charging extremely high prices for the essential services they provide for their members. In either case the result is the same: the convert (no longer potential) winds up very poor. Meanwhile, not only does the cult become wealthy (and ultimately powerful), but the individual burns both practical and psychological bridges away from the cult; leaving the cult will require new means of support. On the psychological level, an individual would later find it difficult to justify having turned over wealth should he or she return to a lifestyle that valued it. Ironically, most of us would find it easier to justify time wasted with a cult than money wasted. By the time the Unification Church acquired the wealth of its converts, it could rest assured that it had in fact converted them.

Resocialization: A Final Look If young children are amazingly adaptable to their cultures in primary socialization, it appears that adults can be made equally adaptable under the pressures of resocialization. In primary socialization the child acquires his or her first self; in resocialization the adult replaces an old self with a new one. Remarkably similar principles appear to be at work in each case. Our sense of who we are (our self) comes initially from the social group, and it must continue to come from that group on a day-to-day basis if it is to survive. If your personality appears to you to have remained fairly stable during your life, it is likely that there has been considerable continuity among your roles and social groups. If there is one major point to this discussion, it is this: continuity is not guaranteed, and if change comes, you are likely to change with it.

SUMMARY

Socialization is the process by which, through agents of socialization, individuals learn about and come to believe in their culture. These agents may be other individuals (parents, for example), or they may be societal institutions, the experience of which can be an effective socialization force.

Primary socialization is the first socialization faced by the young child. During this period the interests of the socializers collide with the biological development of the child. Freud described this development in terms of stages of psychosexual development, as the child slowly internalizes the perspective of society (known as the superego), which often restricts inborn desires (known as the id). Piaget described the child's intellectual development during this same period as an increasing ability to master abstract thought. One element of this abstract thought is the child's ability to understand rules, which reflects the child's ability to look at himself or herself in terms of general expectations. Mead focused his attention on the emotional identification of the child as the child comes to view himself or herself in terms of significant others and later in terms of the generalized other. When this stage has been reached, secondary socialization has begun.

Secondary socialization begins when the child is biologically mature and capable of understanding the rules of society through the general expectations of others.

Internalization occurs when the values of the social group become the values of the group member (or become the superego of the group member).

From the very beginning the child develops a self-image that is a reflection of other people's views. The child develops this image through the responses of others so that ultimately he or she can predict those responses and view himself or herself accordingly. This process is called the looking-glass self. To the extent that everyone has a variety of roles, an individual may acquire a variety of selves, each appropriate to the responses received in specific roles. This variety permits role distance—the ability of an individual to avoid acquiring a self-image from the responses of a specific role.

Although they can never return to primary socialization, adults can be resocialized. Resocialization results in a major personality transformation brought about by rigid socialization techniques. These techniques usually require placing the individual in an isolated and highly controlled environment where, shut off from the past, a new self begins to develop. Resocialization is common to total institutions (such as prisons or mental institutions) and also occurs in organizations such as religious cults.

GLOSSARY

Agent of socialization Any social source (a person, an institution, etc.) that communicates elements of culture or requires conformity to them.

Anticipatory socialization Socialization in anticipation of acquiring a specific role at some time in the future.

Cognition The process of perception or knowing.

Generalized other An individual's mental idea of what a large number of people (or people in general) expect in social behavior.

"I" As defined by George Herbert Mead, the element of the self that is creative, is spontaneous, and tends to initiate action.

Institution A cluster (or sphere) of interrelated activities within a society coupled with the knowledge, beliefs, and objects that relate to those activities. Institutions are typically stable configurations of social forms that meet social needs in specific areas.

Institutionalization The psychological adaptation of an individual to life in a total institution to the point of dependence on the institution.

Internalization The process by which individuals come to see themselves in terms of the roles they play and come to share in the values of the social group, making those values their personal beliefs.

Looking-glass self As defined by Charles Cooley, the process by which an individual acquires a sense of self through imagining how he or she looks to others.

"Me" As defined by George Herbert Mead, the element of self that has internalized the expectations and values of others in the social group.

Primary socialization Socialization that occurs during the first several years of life, distinctive due to the individual's biological immaturity.

Repression The "placement" of inappropriate feelings and desires in the unconscious mind as opposed to the conscious mind. Part of Freud's psychoanalytic theory, repression occurs as the individual responds to the demands of society.

Resocialization An extreme form of secondary socialization in which major changes are deliberately brought about in the thinking and behavior of an adult.

Role distance An individual's introduction of unusual or creative elements in role playing that communicate to others a distance between the individual and the role being played.

Secondary socialization Socialization that occurs after the first few years of life, when the individual is capable of symbolic communication and developing a social sense of self.

Self The process by which the individual develops a sense of who he or she is based on the responses of others. The emergence of a social self indicates that the individual shares with others in the social group a set of common meanings, including a definition of the individual's place in interactions with others.

Socialization The ongoing process by which humans come to learn about and believe in their cultures, from learning the roles to sharing the values. Through socialization the individual becomes a member of the social group and develops a sense of self.

Sociobiology The systematic study of the biological basis of all social behavior.

Taking the role of the other The ability of an individual to view the self from the perspective of others in the social environment, making the self an object and allowing for the development of common symbols.

Total institution A social group that provides a regimented living and working existence for its members, isolated from the rest of society.

STUDY QUESTIONS
1. How do agents of socialization influence an individual's thoughts and behavior? How does that influence vary depending upon whether the agents are individuals or institutions?
2. What is the difference between primary and secondary socialization?
3. Human behavior can have its roots in either an individual's heredity or an individual's social environment (or socialization). How can we determine the causes of any given behavior?
4. What are Freud's stages of psychosexual development? How are they related to the process of socialization?

5. Piaget's theory of cognitive development traces the development of human thinking as children mature. How is cognitive development fundamental in understanding Mead's theory of how individuals learn to take the role of the other?

6. What is the difference between taking the role of the other and taking the role of the generalized other? How is the latter similar to an adult's understanding of a social norm?

7. How does socialization lead to the internalization of social values (or the internalization of a superego or *me*)? How does that internalization come to control a person's thoughts and behavior?

8. What is anticipatory socialization? What does it suggest about how willing most of us are to be socialized?

9. What kind of a picture of everyday life does Charles Cooley's looking-glass self paint? How does the process he describes relate to Mead's notion of taking the role of the other?

10. Compare the opposite concepts of role internalization and role distance. Why do people tend to internalize the roles they play? What are the techniques of role distance? How do both of these concepts help us understand resocialization?

Steven A. Gilham

THE MARINES BUILD MEN: RESOCIALIZATION IN RECRUIT TRAINING

Before being socialized into his present occupation of sociologist, Steven Gilham was a dedicated U.S. Marine, the successful product of the intensive resocialization program known as recruit training. This reading takes you through that experience with him, from the fright of the first day to the pride of recruit graduation. The recruit program is typical of many resocialization programs in the techniques it uses to transform the adult individual. Gilham shows how that transformation occurs, both from his experience of the program then and from the sociological perspective he employs now.

Perhaps a warning should be issued to the fainthearted before beginning: the United States Marines have many differences from other social groups in American society, and one of the most notable is their use of language not normally found in polite company. Recruit training in particular is unimaginable without four-letter words. This reading is recommended for mature audiences.

Night, about 9:30, San Diego. Chillier than I had expected for southern California in mid-November. Several of us—I do not remember now how many; seven or eight, maybe—standing around outside the airport, waiting. Anticipatory, anxious, excited maybe. When I had asked the recruiter about training and job opportunities, he had glared flatly at me and said in a deep voice, "Look, I can't promise you anything but a hard time. We generally find that the people who make the best Marines just wanna be Marines." That is how he got me. No song and dance, just plain old macho. Well, we would soon see.

Here it came. A long, olive green, double-cab pickup, with an emblem on the front doors and covered in the rear. The driver's door opened, slammed shut; crisp, clicking steps behind the truck. Then he appeared at the rear: stocky, erect, a recruiting poster Marine. Closest to the truck, I reached for the handle of the passenger-side door to the rear seat. I was cut short by a booming, guttural voice. "Get your goddam hand off the truck! Spit out that gum and get your fuckin' hand out of your pocket, you fat piece of shit." Brief, stunned silence all around. "Get in the rear of the truck. Everybody. Hurry up, hurry up, hurry up!"

Scrambling. "Sit with your eyes front and your mouths shut. I don't wanna hear a fuckin' word." "Jeesus" (a low whisper). "Shut up, maggot!" Silence. Was he still outside the truck? No matter. More footsteps approaching; several people, muted voices. "Shut up and get in the truck. Keep your eyes straight ahead. Hurry up, hurry up." Then we were off.

After several turns I had lost my sense of direction. We made a few halting attempts at conversation, but soon we passed through a gate with an MP at a guardhouse. We heard one low wail from somewhere outside, "You'll be sorree!" We had arrived at the Marine Corps Recruit Depot (MCRD). Then we stopped, and seconds later the tailgate was unlatched and dropped. "Get out and form lines on the yellow footprints. On the double! Keep your eyes straight ahead and don't move. Lines, asshole, not ranks. You know what a fuckin' line is? When you're called, go one at a time through that hatch on the right, right line first. First three, move!" We waited. "Next . . . Next . . . Next." My turn. Inside, the barbers' chairs on the left. "Here. Sit down, look straight ahead." It took twenty, maybe thirty, seconds; hardly any hair left, only a couple of nicks. "Out to the left. Next!"

Moving past a counter like a coat-check stand, each of us was given our basic issue: a galvanized pail; a wooden scrub brush; a pair of high-top tennis shoes; a pair of olive green socks; heavy, olive green cotton trousers (never again to be called pants under any circumstances); a matching cap (ever after, a cover); a long web belt and brass buckle; underwear (skivvies); a book of coupons (chits) redeemable at a recruit base exchange (BX); red shorts with yellow stripe and Marine Corps emblem; and a bright yellow sweatshirt emblazoned with an equally bright red eagle, globe, and anchor, and the words *U.S. Marine Corps*. Thus supplied, we filed into yet another room and lined up along opposite sides of two very long tables divided into stalls. The guy across from me could not keep his eyes still. They darted, clicked, rolled in a frenzy as he scanned everything, trying, it seemed, even to

see behind himself. Mine, too, maybe; but I was watching him. Suddenly a big square face was next to his, booming, "What the fuck you lookin' at maggot-eyes?" "Nothing." "Yer ass! You callin' me nothing, puke?" "No, sir." "Bullshit! Sir! The first fucking word out of your mouth is always sir. Do you understand that!" (Not, of course, a question at all.) "Yes, sir!" "Bullshit!" "Sir! Yessir!" "What the fuck you laughin' at you big stringy hunk of shit . . ."

And so on until we were all in and were once again addressed as a group. "When I give you people the word, you will strip and place everything you brought with you in the bin in front of you. You will then stand with your eyes front and your hands at your sides until further word. You have thirty seconds. Do it! Hurry up, hurry up, goddam it! Stop! If that fat piece of shit at the other end doesn't freeze right now, I'm gonna come down there and take his goddam head off!"

We next boxed up our belongings—everything except watches and wallets, which we could keep but not wear for the next twelve or so weeks—to be sent home. After showers and bedding issue we joined earlier arrivals in a dorm (squadbay) where we slept—interrupted by another group of later arrivals—until 5:30. We were then awakened and led off, shuffling and stumbling, to breakfast. (Chow. All meals are chow, distinguished only by time of day.) Upon return we were settled into a classroom and introduced formally to the United States Marine Corps by the same thick-necked staff sergeant who had met us at the airport. Of course, we would not call him Sergeant or Staff Sergeant anything. He and all uniformed personnel, we learned, would be addressed as *sir*, irrespective of their ranks. Our trainers were drill instructors (DIs), who would always be called *sir*, except when spoken to or about in the third person, when they would be called by their positions—drill instructor or platoon commander—rather than by rank. These were the people to whose care we would be entrusted when enough of us to form a training company (or series) had collected at Receiving Barracks. We were then instructed in forms of address: "Sir, Pvt. (last name) requests permission to speak to the drill instructor." "Sir, Pvt. _____ reporting as ordered." Knock three times. "Sir, Pvt. _____ requests permission to enter the duty office." Each of us was then given a pocket-size, red vinyl, ringbound book with nearly everything we would need to know in it. Finally, we were put to work policing the barracks and its surroundings, picking up cigarette butts, polishing brass fixtures (brightwork), cleaning windows (portholes), sweeping and mopping floors (swabbing decks), and emptying trashcans (shitcans). If we looked about us at all, we could see strategically placed red and yellow signs: "To be a Marine you have to believe in: Yourself . . . Your fellow Marine . . . Your Corps . . . Your Country . . . Your God. Semper

Fidelis." Or, quoting Field Marshall Erwin Rommel (Hadn't he been "the enemy" once? I thought): "The more we sweat in peace, the less we bleed in war."

Recruits sometimes wait for days in receiving; we did not. Within forty-eight hours we had been taken by two of our DIs to four corrugated steel quonset huts—two on either side of and opening onto an asphalt strip we would call the platoon street—that would be home for nearly three months. Immediately began the task of preparing us for the actual training routine. For over a week they instructed us in the fundamentals of our new lives—how to make a bed (rack), stand at attention, mark and wear our clothing—and marched us all over to MCRD for additional clothing issue, tests, dental checks and physical

The U.S. Marine Corps has had considerable success over the years with its unique methods of resocialization.

examinations, and purchases at the BX. There we all bought the same items—identical brands of razor, shave cream, soap, shoe polishes and brushes, toothbrush, and toothpaste—which we were later taught to arrange, along with issued gear, identically in our footlockers.

After this we settled into the routine that would prevail over the remainder of boot camp, to be interrupted only by two weeks at the rifle range (actually a wholly separate facility at Camp Pendleton, near Oceanside) and a week of mess or maintenance duty. Reveille, exercise, head call (toilet and shave), chow, classes, chow, classes, exercise, chow, review sessions, head call (with shower), free time, taps. "Academic" classes—in military history, weapons, military justice, hygiene and first aid, and so on—were held indoors; "practical" ones—close order drill (COD), bayonet training, calisthenics and distance running—outdoors. We would spend over two hours a day on the drill field (parade deck, grinder) alone. There were breaks between, usually for exercise, and occasional business tasks such as swimming tests (twice), weapons and web gear issue, BX run, measurement and fitting for dress uniforms. Everywhere we went, we went in formation at either a march or a run. And always we carried in the hip pockets of our utility trousers the little red book we were to study anytime we might find ourselves waiting for some scheduled activity.

Throughout the routine we acquired numerous physical skills and some "book" knowledge that few of us had previously possessed. But just as important, perhaps more important from our trainers' point of view, were the lessons we would learn about ourselves. It was not that we would acquire deeper insight into our extant, already formed selves; rather, we would acquire new selves. By the end we would look, walk, and talk remarkably alike. Some of our attitudes and general beliefs, no doubt, would be relatively unmoved—for example, our tastes in music, literature, art, civilian dress, and recreation—but those were inessential to the transformation at hand and were of little interest to the Corps. What was essential was that we learn and adhere

to a new code of conduct. That code comprises several stipulations: Obey immediately and unquestioningly. ("When I tell you people to jump, you jump and ask how high on the way up.") Do not quit. Be sharp, mentally and in appearance and demeanor. It will not be particularly helpful to attempt an exhaustive listing of the rules here—some of them will be clear later on anyway—but they conjoin to form the exhortations "Be a man! Be a Marine!"

The transformation from civilian to Marine involves little or none of the exploration, experimentation, and curiosity typical of infants' and children's learning. It is also effected with a rapidity, efficiency, and self-consciousness on the part of the trainers that far exceed the gradual socialization of the young. It is that process to which I now turn. The first stage of the process is a deliberate stripping of all our ties to our old selves—what Erving Goffman has called a *degradation ritual*. The basic recipe goes something like this: Plunge recruits into a situation in which numerous, repetitive failures of all sorts are virtually inevitable, strip them of as many distinguishing characteristics as possible, sever their ties to preexisting networks of association, prevent or restrict as far as possible the formation of new linkages except those to their trainers, and ritualize their relations to the trainers. In short, leave them with as few resources—as little that is useful, valued, or a source of positive evaluation—as possible. All of that can be achieved with great predictability through any or all of the following devices: introducing and requiring the use of a new and unfamiliar "language," holding recruits accountable for violations of rules or standards of performance of which they have not been informed, continually escalating standards of performance some measure beyond actual achievement, and/or applying rules or commands arbitrarily or contradictorily. At each breach the recruits' failures are announced loudly and publicly in a literal bombardment of negative sanctions. One of the favored techniques is the use of games that cannot be won (by recruits).

"Private Gilham to the duty office! On the double!"

Knock, knock, knock. "Sir! Pvt. Gilham reporting as ordered, sir."

"Well, well, well. Is that a little goddam mouse at my hatch? You better put some balls in that little pussy voice, maggot! I can't hear you!"

"Aye, aye, sir!" THUMP! THUMP! THUMP! "SIR! Pvt. Gilham reporting as ordered, SIR!"

"Get your ass in here, Private."

Next time:

THUMP! THUMP! THUMP! "SIR! Pvt. Gilham requests permission to speak to the drill instructor, SIR!"

"Jeesus H. Christ, Private! Don't break my fuckin' hatch! What the fuck you screamin' at me for? I'm only ten feet away. Try again, asshole."

"Aye, aye, Sir!" THUMP! THUMP . . .

"Bullshit! Didn't your mother ever teach you how to knock?" He rises and demonstrates a polite knock at the door.

Such experiences help demolish any unified, positive sense of self, create confusion and apprehension, and deliver a message that neither old habits nor present efforts will do. It matters little how well recruits have previously known themselves, for the persons they were are repudiated as "scuzzy civilians," and, in any event, all the props that would support their former identities are gone. And their present selves are hardly desirable—confused, clumsy, and (some at least) frightened (frightened enough, for example, that most of us were awake and moving before reveille as soon as the electronic pop of the PA system signaled that it was on in an attempt to avoid the unavoidable harangues about our slothfulness). Add to this disorientation the recruit's appearance, and the degradation is complete (but by no means over). Their haircuts and uniforms are constant reminders of the recruits' new status,

but they also make recruits, by both civilian and military standards, ugly, or at least funny-looking. The tremendous contrast between them—shorn, rumpled, sweaty, dusty, and stinking—and the clean, fresh, well-tailored appearance of their overseers (who sometimes change uniforms two or three times a day to maintain that appearance) further reinforces recruits' conceptions of their own worthlessness.

Thus, each of us who had come to the situation with a variety of ideas of ourselves as somehow good or distinctive—smart, tough, good-looking, nice, and so forth—discovered almost instantly that we had been wrong: that we were instead ugly, stupid, soft, and inept and that no initiative on our part was safe. You need only assume that each individual wants or needs to think of him- or herself as basically "okay" to understand how susceptible recruits are made to taking on a new self that will confer on them some measure of respect or dignity. Nearly any praise, and the conduct required to "earn" it, seems acceptable.

That this stripping away of self-esteem takes place as it does illustrates dramatically its reliance on some preestablished conditions that confine recruits to the situation and subordinate them to their trainers' control. First among these are the rules and contingencies that bind recruits to the training regimen. For we have no reason to expect any individuals to voluntarily shed a positive sense of self, to endure a process that strips them of it, or to accept a bombardment of verbal and physical abuse if other, more attractive, options are freely available. In this case they are not; any attempt to leave, or even successful flight, would cost dearly.

Any separation from others to whom we are bound by some agreement—informal or formal, traditional or contractual—has costs that will exceed some of the unpleasantness we might experience within those relationships. Most institutions rely on a concerted effort to escalate these costs as high as possible so that they exceed markedly (for most folks) any nastiness we may experience while "in" the institution. (Some, of course, like many employers, simply benefit from conditions over which they may have little or no direct control, such as a wretched labor market.) But leaving Uncle Sugar (Uncle Sam) is not like leaving a friend, lover, club, college, family, or spouse whose charms have worn thin or become aggravating, with prospects of bluer skies or greener grass ahead. For Uncle Sugar's agreement with his recruits is a contract that only he is legally free to terminate.

Recruits, or any service personnel, who leave or even try to leave will not only forfeit some benefits such as pay or, where possible, rank, they will also face some actual punishments ranging from extra duty through restriction to quarters, brig time, and hard labor to expulsion via a bad conduct (BCD), undesirable, or dishonorable discharge (DD). These are not penalties among which the violator has choices, nor are they mutually exclusive. The lesser penalties may be linked to, and very many on one's record will lead to, the most severe ones. And discharge at any level below an honorable, or at worst a general, discharge means additional post-service costs by way of reduced job opportunities after release. Even a successful escape from recruit training would necessitate years of separation from family or friends if the other penalties are to be avoided, as the ex-recruit would become a fugitive. Add the promise of better days after boot camp to this scheme of punishments, and the recruit's interest in staying and enduring even considerable misery is clear, so long as life "inside" is not on balance worse than the potential consequences of flight.

It is not the DI's principal responsibility to enforce these rules even though his job depends on them. Neither are the punishments outlined above ones a DI is authorized to employ or to decide. Those available to the DI are both less enduring in their consequences and more immediate, requiring no juridical procedures prior to their use. Their potential effectiveness is not ensured merely by recruits' enforced presence; it is necessary that the sanctioning resources be securely under the control of the drill instructors

only. That monopoly is ensured by two general types of rules: those that isolate recruits from any other effective source of positive sanctions and those that deprive them of any negative sanctions of their own. Let us take the first.

Not only are symbolic ties severed by returning civilian articles home, but communication with the world outside MCRD is strictly limited: no phone calls in or out, no radios or TV, no liberty (time off-duty, off-base); newspapers and visitors (if a boot is lucky enough to have relatives near enough to visit) only on Sundays, and then only after the seventh week. Outgoing mail is limited practically, if not officially, by the amount of free time allotted recruits. Usually thirty to forty-five minutes per evening and one to two hours on Sundays (after the first two or three weeks) are set aside for rifle cleaning; polishing of boots, shoes, and belt buckles (all mandatory); and, finally, letter writing. Incoming mail is regulated in other ways: no scented letters ("Well, Private, you just tell that little skirt of yours that if she keeps this up, you aren't gonna be getting any mail. I might read 'em, though."), no money ("Tell those folks back home you got plenty."), and no food.

> "You don't need that fruitcake do you, fat boy?"
> "Sir, No." "Shitcan it."
> "Aye, aye, Sir." PLUNK.
> "Now you write those people and tell 'em that was the best fuckin' fruitcake you ever ate, y' hear?"
> "Sir! Yes, Sir."
> "There aren't enough of those cookies for everybody to have some are there, Private?"
> "No, SIR."
> "Then I guess you'll just have to eat 'em, won't you?"
> Faint, hopeful smile. Pleased. "Yes, Sir!"
> "Now." "Sir?"
> "Every goddam one of 'em. Do it."

Indeed mail call itself, and certainly the time to read the letters, might be treated as a privilege that could be suspended, even if for no more than a day or two. And, of course, talk, simple small talk among recruits—"Where you from? What'd ya do before this?"—is never authorized. Speak only when spoken to or, if on a detail, when giving orders. Important as all of those rewards are, they are not the source of livelihood. The latter kind of resources—pay, promotion, and the service records on which all decisions about Marines depend throughout their service—belong only to the Corps from the beginning.

Just as recruits are deprived of effective alternative sources of reward, so are they deprived of means, other than compliance, of influencing their keepers. No hitting back, no name calling, no sneering, no votes, no strikes. Resorting to any of these could constitute punishable offenses under the Uniform Code of Military Justice (UCMJ). The only possible sources of clout, since the DI's pay and career are also controlled from above, are a request for mast (a meeting with the commanding officer) or connection to a political official who might instigate an investigation. Mast might get the DI a mild reprimand, and no investigation of a DI will be undertaken without accusations of extreme malfeasance. In either case any attempt to initiate an investigation, or cooperation in one, would brand a recruit as a trouble maker throughout MCRD.

The most any recruit can do is simply refuse to yield to the Marine role. If he does so, he may retain something like dignity or integrity, though he gains no power; he simply deprives the Corps of its power over him. Neither side can get what it wants from the other—a stalemate in which the costs for the recruit are momentous, for the Corps, trivial.

The last real threat to the Corps's power over its recruits (and its other personnel) is collective action. Both the sanctions at the drill instructors' disposal and their use of those sanctions are calculated to prevent that.

The DI thus becomes the sole effective, legitimate source of rewards and punishments. Your compatriots may care when you get nailed, but there is precious little they can *do* to support you. ("From now on, girls, I am your mother, your father, your sister, your brother, and your girlfriend; and you aren't even gonna screw me.") Among the negative sanctions DIs use, most are relatively mild. ("Well, no shit, dippy. What the fuck you think you're doin' there?" or "Jeesus Keerist! You are the stupidest piece of shit I ever saw." or "Whoa, mob! Look around. You really fucked that move up good, didn't you? You look like a bunch of dumbfucks.") Some are more serious. A recruit drops his rifle or calls it a gun, offenses almost equal in severity: "You dickhead! You'll sleep with that sonofabitch tonight. Field strip it and sleep on it. I'll be there to be sure you do."

A recruit scratches his nose while in formation. "You like to scratch, maggot? Scratch! Scratch that sonofabitch until I give you the word. And tell all the rest of these turds how much you like to scratch. Say, 'I like to scratch.'" He says repeatedly, "I like to scratch," and scratches until his nose bleeds.

A recruit is caught sleeping, seated on his footlocker with a newspaper on his lap, during Sunday free time. His rack and the footlocker's contents are dumped and strewn over part of the squadbay. "You've got three minutes to square that shit away." His neighbor joins to help, and the DI returns. "So you wanna clean up, too?" He dumps both racks and both footlockers. "Now you two have exactly two minutes to get squared away." He returns. Replay. "Clean up this mess. When I come back you will be at attention beside your racks." Moral: A Marine on duty (twenty-four hours a day for recruits) has no friends.

It is possible to go on ad nauseum with similar examples. Rust on a rifle at a weekly inspection. The rifle is buried in sand, two or three buckets of water poured over it, and it lies there for several hours before the recruit is allowed to retrieve and clean it. Or we do poorly at COD and are banished to the platoon street for exercise. We begin push-ups or squat thrusts, say fifty repetitions. We do not count (sound off) loudly enough. We start over after ten or so. We do not count in unison. We start over. Somebody quits.

We start over. Or someone leaves the padlock on his footlocker or his rifle (to be locked to the rack) unlocked. We return from classes to find the squadbay a shambles. And so on.

Finally there are the most severe penalties—expulsion to the Special Training Unit (Special Training Platoon, STU, STP, fat farm) or Correctional Custody (CC).

> "Keep draggin' your ass, shitbird, and you'll
> find yourself breakin' rock with the other
> discipline problems over in CC."
> "Drop out of this run, lardass, and you'll go
> straight to the fat farm."

It is important to note, however, that, as often as these sanctions are employed, their threat is actually more important than their actual use. It is not that, if they were used constantly, recruits would get used to them; rather, there must be some real difference in consequences between good performance and ready compliance, on the one hand, and poor performance and recalcitrance, on the other hand. Only then does anyone have an interest in compliance unless the things to be learned are intrinsically rewarding to the learner. The boot camp regimen is obviously calculated to create incentives for recruits to do things (at times, to an extent, and in ways) that few if any of them find intrinsically rewarding. The more recruits learn and the more quickly, the more free of penalties their lives become. The threat and the actual administration of punishment are calculated to keep them from backsliding.

There are additional considerations that discourage frequent actual punishment. The DI is not utterly free in his use of sanctions, for he too is evaluated by his peers and superiors. Any DI who constantly resorts to punitive measures is regarded by superiors as one who cannot effectively maintain order and train troops. Such evaluations diminish his chances for promotion and may ultimately lead to relief from duty and a transfer, a blemish on his record with potentially serious long-term consequences. And, finally, time

spent in punishment is time not spent in the teaching and practice of skills recruits are to learn, and the DI does have a schedule to meet.

This last point does not imply that punishment teaches nothing; for in fact many sanctions are loaded with information that constitutes (and in turn depends on) a whole worldview. In particular, certain evaluative standards have to be established so that invidious comparisons to which recruits are subjected are clearly undesirable in their eyes as well as their trainers'. Some examples are explicit in their ordering of the universe ("You people are boots. That's lower than whaleshit and that's on the bottom of the ocean.") Some are less clearly so. ("Whatsamatter, girls? Are we tired?" or "My four-year-old daughter could do this shit.")

It soon became clear to me that there was a distinct hierarchical order to the world, at the top of which sat Marines—a goal we had not attained. ("You turds wouldn't make a pimple on a professional Marine's ass.") Beneath that were three general categories in approximately the following order of inferiority: the other services and their members, civilians, and all things not American. Marines' only peers, in this view, are British Marines and, with some reservations, elite units such as Army Green Berets, Navy Seal Teams, and Korean Marines (utterly ruthless, so the mythology went)—all bested, of course, by the Marines' elite Force Reconnaissance units.

Racial and ethnic categories were out for purposes of denigrating recruits because of the recruit population's heterogeneity. They were, however, used—usually jokingly. And they were used often enough to remind us that we were not, after all, entirely alike and to discourage any fellow feeling strong enough to serve as a basis for banding together in opposition to our trainers' interests.

This was all, by the way, a distinctly male world. Another wholly separate hierarchy, paralleling the first but lower at each of its levels, was women. Apart from references to body parts and body functions, the most frequent negative evaluations we heard involved civilians and women;

but the two were used in significantly different ways. The former usually referred to appearance or demeanor—hands in pockets, slouching—the latter almost always were used when our performance was to be impugned. Furthermore, the references were not to *women* or *females* but to *girls* and *weak sisters*, or any of the multitude of genitally based terms by which women could be called. It soon became clear to us that there could be no worse judgments of our performance than those likening it to women's. The message was clear: Women were regarded as weak, not very bright, generally incompetent, sexual objects. The status of women Marines illustrates that neatly. As Marines, they would presumably be regarded as superior to civilians or other servicewomen. They were, indeed, regarded as tougher, but they were also presumed to be largely failures as women—not as attractive as civilian women, unable to get men, and simultaneously more sexually accessible and less desirable (because tougher).

This image of women was linked to the only real taboo, homosexuality. Since it was impossible that any of us were women (sex change operations notwithstanding), being called a girl or worse always retained a metaphorical character that allowed occasionally (and increasingly frequent as training progressed) joking usages. *Queer,* however, was always a vicious epithet, even though jokes about "them" were permissible and even desirable (keeping in mind that all jokes come from the DIs). We were warned repeatedly that actual homosexuality would bring dishonorable discharge from the Corps, the consequences of which—immensely restricted job opportunities in the outside world (no government agency or government subcontractor could hire a BCD or DD)—were so severe that we should never regard calculated engagement in homosexual activity as a reasonable way of trying to get kicked out. It would be better to go crazy.

The way in which these evaluative standards were used implies a lesson in language. When name calling was used, it was always the disvalue of the referent and/or the traits it implied rather than the crudity of the language itself that carried the greatest weight. Thus, terms like *asshole, shitbird,* or *fucking maggot* were indignities not so much because they were ugly but because they implied that we had no human value. And in *fat/scrawny/weak/stupid piece of shit* it was the *fat/scrawny/weak/stupid* that carried the greatest weight. Similarly, all of the uglier synonyms for women were indistinguishably degrading as against the fact that our performance had been judged feminine or inferior to that. The other terms, in fact, became commonplace. You should have noticed by now that the simple word *fuck* could be adapted to any part of speech—noun, verb, adverb, adjective, interjection, conjunction. Indeed, all of us not only heard jokes about, but lived through, experiences after boot camp in which we would embarrass ourselves by the use of any number of such terms in "polite" civilian company. That language and the special military vocabulary we were taught would further serve to distinguish us from others and to bind us as a brotherhood.

But it is a brotherhood bound together only against the "outside" world; within there is fragmentation sufficient to prevent the group from developing and enforcing norms opposed to the interests of their trainers. Sanctions are administered so as to keep each recruit mindful of his own interests and to encourage him to act on those interests. Action on the basis of collective interests or in the name of some greater good is generally given mere lip service ("Get down on your knees and pray, girls. Pray for war. 'Cause that's the only way you're gonna get promoted.") This fragmentation is a consequence of the fact that most rewards and punishments are directed at individuals. Should there ever arise, for example, conflict between the DI's order and perceived expectations of a boot's peers, the DI's virtual monopoly of punitive sanctions creates a clear interest in compliance with the order. In addition, the competition for the scarce individual rewards available—personal orderly (mouse) to a DI, platoon secretary, and the positions of platoon guide and squad leaders (which almost automatically carry with them promotion to PFC at graduation from recruit training)—further encourages recruits to look out for themselves.

For purposes of controlling an entire group, however, it would be inefficient and impractical to rely always on individual rewards and punishments. Sending an entire platoon to STU or CC would be horrendously costly, and discharges of large numbers of recruits would deprive the Corps of the troops it demands. One of the DI's problems, therefore, is how to get maximum effectiveness and efficiency out of the sanctions at his disposal. The solution is occasionally to punish or to withhold rewards from an entire platoon for the misdeeds of one or a few of its members.

This device has an interesting result from the point of view of socialization theory. Assume that any recruit has an interest in avoiding punishment and/or obtaining rewards. So long as he can do so by his own compliance, his primary interest is in his own behavior. When he is punished or deprived of some reward for others' errors, however, he acquires a direct interest in their behavior, as does everybody else in his. That is true even in matters where he would otherwise be tolerant of or indifferent to their conduct or would himself want to act as he now wants to prevent others from acting. Each recruit, of course, will grant some latitude to others for outright error, just as he expects some tolerance of his own mistakes; but when one recruit (or a few) consistently provides occasions for collective punishment or loss of promised rewards, his peers may move to control him. If a platoon does not spontaneously initiate such controls, the DI will remind it that, while he cannot hit anyone, he cannot prevent someone from slipping in the shower, falling over a footlocker, or otherwise "injuring himself."

The message is not lost on recruits. However, they do not resort first (or even often) to physical force as a means of control. Warning glances, whispers, and mutters usually suffice, but less subtle measures are also available. A miscreant

recruit may get his heels kicked during COD or a run, or he may find that Sunday afternoon athletics become contact sports. If he protests aloud, it is he who is out of order and who will suffer the DI's wrath. Finally, he may be the guest at a nighttime blanket party at which his hosts cover his head with a blanket (to protect their anonymity) and pummel him. The entire platoon need not join in; they merely assent by "looking the other way," as will the DI. ("What happened to you Pvt. Dodo? You slip on a bar of soap?" "Sir! No, Sir! They hit me." "Someone hit you? Is that true platoon?" In unison: "Sir! No, Sir!" "You calling all the rest of these recruits liars, Private?")

Alternatively, the DI may use the platoon more directly. I remember one such incident in particular. I do not remember the person's infraction or series of infractions, but I do recall our part in his humiliation. It sickened me then; it chills me in retrospect.

> "You're crazy aren't you, Pvt. Dodo?" "Sir! No, Sir!"
> "Oh, yes, you are. Isn't he platoon?" A chorus: "Sir! Yes, Sir!"
> "See? The platoon thinks you're crazy. You must be crazy. Aren't you, Private?"
> "Sir! No, Sir!"
> "Bullshit. Tell 'im, platoon. Tell 'im. 'You're crazy, Pvt. Dodo!'"

And we did. Until he cried. It is unlikely that we convinced him he was crazy, but his isolation from any peer support could not have been made more clear. He was dropped—to STU—within a week.

The points to be made by all this are, first, that making a whole group liable for the wrongs of one or a few engenders a collective control mechanism that looks much like normative control; and, second, that it would be a mistake to regard the rules thus enforced as norms arising from group interaction. Some general societal norms such as cleanliness, it is true, merely get additional "official" support in boot camp; but most of the rules are ones imposed on one group by another. They differ, in content and in the interests underlying them, from norms that arise out of collective preferences or collective concern for the harms done by some acts. None of that implies that recruits do not develop some norms among themselves. Given their common interests in avoiding negative sanctions or getting positive ones and in minimizing the burdens of an already onerous training schedule, the strongest are "Don't squeal on your peers (let the DI's catch them)," and "Don't give them any ideas for additional things for us to do." Even these, clearly, are formed in response to the organizational structure of the recruit training situation.

Finally, something remains to be said about the nature of the transformation into Marines. There are, as I have implied, some rewards along the way. There are cigarettes. ("The smoking lamp is lighted for one cigarette!" "Sir! The smoking lamp is lighted for one cigarette! Aye, aye, Sir!" "Light 'em. Burn 'em." "Sir! Aye, aye, Sir!") And there are movies. (We went to two during the twelve weeks; Marines figured heavily in both. *The Sands of Iwo Jima* must play six times a year at every Marine Corps base in the world.) Cigarettes are optional (nonsmokers may write letters for five minutes); movies are not. ("You *will* enjoy this flick, and you will keep your goddam mouths shut or the shit'll hit the fan when we get back.")

We needed no telling to understand that these were rewards. But some—the symbolic rewards associated with being Marines—required construction of a proper evaluative base, just as some punishments do. To that end we heard lectures, classroom reviews, and countless sea stories ennobling the Corps's history (first to fight), extolling the toughness and courage of its heroes, and recounting the pugilistic and sexual exploits of Marines on liberty. Much of this included no small bit of bragging on the part of the DIs. Marines, it was to be understood, are men like no others and an exclusive fraternity the uninitiated would never truly understand.

On that foundation we were then given periodic indications of our gradual progress toward the exalted goal. First we were allowed to starch and block our covers (so that they held a recognizable shape) and to send one pair of utilities to the base laundry service to be starched. The crisp feel of truly clean clothing and the change in our own appearance wrought by pressed, sharply creased uniforms helped dissolve some of the feeling of slovenliness and ugliness with which we had been burdened; it also clearly distinguished us from newer recruits.

We were then "allowed" to blouse our trousers (turn the trouser leg up inside an elastic blousing garter so that the trouser "blouses" over the boot-top.) We were thus known on sight as at least fifth-week recruits. Then we began to be accorded the honor of learning songs to sing as we ran. ("One, two, three four; we love the Marine Corps.") Later came fittings for dress uniforms and, still later, inspections during which we wore them. All of these events, of course, also tempered our suffering by providing milestones on the twelve-week road to graduation. Even better were those moments of simple, overt verbal praise. (We march in rhythm with the sing-song cadence. "Hehp, toop, threep . . . keep parallel, toop, keep parallel. . . . Good. Keep it up, keep it up. One heel. I want to hear the sound of one heel. . . . Outstanding! Co-o-olumn, right! Har! . . . Out-fucking-standing! You people are starting to look like Marines!")

Any of this can be taken away. ("Oh, that's right. Don't march; just mill around. Stop. Un-blouse your trousers. You turds think you can come out here and embarrass me in front of my peers? Get off my fucking grinder! Now! Run! Assholes and elbows!") But such occasions become even more rare until, finally, graduation. Even then there is one last show. After the ceremony, complete with the base band, we were granted a four-hour base liberty during which we got our first phone calls, junk food, beer (if we were old enough; most of us were not), and unlimited smokes since twelve weeks before. We returned to the platoon area for our last afternoon and night at MCRD. "Well, girls, I hope you had a good time, 'cause now we're gonna sweat all that shit out. You got five fuckin' minutes to give me a for-fuckin'-mation out here in utilities. Do it!" Then we ran—five or six miles; most of us believed six—singing and clapping our hands to the rhythm of seventy or so pairs of boots stomping double-time in unison.

This time they all ran with us—platoon commander and both DIs.

Finally we stopped, and the platoon commander, the "head honcho," asked, "You girls tired?" "Sir! No, Sir!" "Well I sure as shit am." It had never before happened. From this man who had never allowed an imperfection, never wavered in his cold sternness, never shown humility or admitted human frailty, never permitted himself to breathe hard after exercise or shiver in the cold, always made us hate him and then never let us beat him at any games, we heard it. "I'm tired." It is unlikely he was any more tired than we, probably less; but he said it. And the next morning he and both junior DIs spoke to each of us, in formation of course, and found something praiseworthy to say about every recruit in the platoon. The rite of passage was over and the illusion complete. We were now Marines.

The bubble would be burst soon enough as we discovered the secrets from which our isolation had protected us—for example, that there were also tough soldiers, sailors, and aviators—and as we rediscovered that we were really not all that different from others in the world. But in the heady atmosphere of graduation we were hardly encouraged to think about that.

These final days are important for fixing the transformation; for there is an irony in the whole process that graduation resolves. Anyone subjected permanently or indefinitely to the conditions recruits live through would have little reason for pride. More likely they would feel like slaves. But the final ritual dissolves that prospect, even though the remainder of service differs mostly in degree from training and in one's eventual promotion to higher positions. (Many of us expressed plans to try for DI school later.) Having been scum and become cream, we were able to

look at our past indignities as tests, as proof of our worth, rather than as humiliations. And we were able to claim that, having survived, we had triumphed (even though that had been planned for us by others) and were in some permanent way different from everyone who had never done what we had done.

This is similar to what people experience emerging from college, police training, mental hospitals, or prisons. What really separates "graduates" from "inmates," however, is what happens to them afterward—the laurels (or stigma) attached to the end of the process, their associations and their work—rather than the process itself. Ultimately, it is life afterward that will account most for the permanence or impermanence of the changes wrought in behavior and self-concept.

In the absence of the recruit training regimen, many of the changes we had undergone showed little permanence. They did not evaporate; they simply no longer "worked" or proved necessary. Maintaining the level of disciplined dress, walk, posture, efficiency, and obedient responsiveness we had learned at MCRD has fairly high costs (in effort, for example, or time taken from other pursuits), which rather soon clearly exceed any benefits to be derived from them. There are those persons, of course, who come to love the discipline itself—perhaps those few for whom their identities as Marines are their best sense of self to date and their best hope for the future. Most, however, eventually slouch again, put their hands back in their pockets, stop spit-shining all their shoes, cease daily exercise except when required, stop walking in step with others when not in formation, and let their hair grow longer (even pushing military regulations). Most also openly complain about the Corps generally ("this fucking Green Machine"), even though they bristle at anyone else's attack on the institution and the implicit attack on themselves. (You are what you belong to?) Whatever happens, the Marine does not remain a boot. He becomes an old salt, who takes liberties with the rules; a former Marine, who revels in past glories; or an ex-Marine, who wonders how he ever allowed himself to be taken in in the first place.

DISCUSSION QUESTIONS

1. What techniques are used to separate Marine recruits from their previous "selves"?

2. Resocialization typically relies on breaking down the support for the past "reality" of an individual and replacing that vacuum with supports for a new "reality." How do the Marines do this?

3. Social control operates in diverse ways in most social groups, ranging from formalized sanctions to the informal ways group members pressure each other to conform. What kinds of social control techniques are found in Marine recruit training? Which are the most important and why?

4. Are the Marines a subculture in American society? What kinds of beliefs and behaviors set them apart?

SOCIAL CONTROLS AND DEVIANCE

T he coordination of society provides people with ready-made roles coupled with norms; "normal" human behavior is behavior that follows those norms. This is the behavior you see every day and take for granted. But what of the other kind? You no doubt frequently encounter people new at a particular role (still learning the norms) who make "mistakes." You also meet people who choose not to follow a particular set of norms for a role you would prefer them to play. Many of the people in this second category are in fact following other norms that apply to other roles. For example, individuals who dress differently from you (and who may look strange to you) are likely conforming to the fashion dictates of their social group at the same time they violate the fashion dictates of your social group. The more complex a society, the more such disagreements are likely to occur concerning which behavior is appropriate when and where. The United States contains a large array of social groups that differ greatly from each other; the disagreements that arise from all these differences make up the sociological study of deviance.

Sociological definitions of deviance vary. One common point, however, is that **deviance** is always behavior that violates the norms of a social group. No behavior is inherently deviant; a behavior is deviant only from the point of view of members of a particular social group in relation to their particular social norms. Behavior that is deviant here may not be deviant there; behavior that is deviant today may not be deviant tomorrow.

This basic definition of deviance provides a start but does little in the way of pointing a direction for understanding the phenomenon. Knowing that deviance is behavior that meets with disapproval doesn't tell us why it meets that disapproval, the form that disapproval will take (a smirk or a firing squad), or how the disapproval will affect the deviant behavior. Our definition also leaves out one of the most important questions: why do people engage in deviance? We consider all of these questions in this chapter as we look at the place of deviance in society, at some theories of why deviance exists, and at group responses to the deviance of others. To understand these topics, however, we first need to examine some of the types of behavior that are generally labeled as deviant in American society today (keeping in mind that there is not total, or sometimes even general, agreement that these behaviors are deviant). Let's look, then, at the crooks, weirdoes, freaks, sluts, maniacs, and perverts that keep the study of deviance from getting boring. As we turn to all these broken norms and the people who break them, don't become immediately convinced that you've encountered a major break in the wall of social coordination. Prostitution, for example, has been considered deviant and has been engaged in enthusiastically for centuries. Such consistency both in behavior and in attitudes toward it suggests that much deviant behavior is just one more facet of the social organization within which we live.

TYPES OF DEVIANCE

Deviant behavior produces a wide variety of responses from observers, depending on their attitudes toward the norms that are in the process of being violated. Breaking a casual norm may bring only a stern look one's way, while violating a norm felt to be central (or sometimes sacred) in a culture can result in violent responses. Societies typically systematize such reactions into law, reserving special punishments for behavior that breaks norms encoded in a legal system. Because laws change over time as the importance placed on individual norms changes, the distinction between illegal (or criminal) deviance and legal (or noncriminal) deviance provides a clear starting point for the study of deviance.

CRIMINAL BEHAVIOR

Criminal behavior is behavior that violates the laws of a society. Strictly speaking, that behavior must also occur during the time those laws are in effect. For example, heroin was legal in the United States until 1914, and therefore its use was not criminal behavior until after that time. Behavior becomes criminal when a social norm becomes a law. A *law* is nothing but a formalized social norm in which the prohibited behavior and sanctions against it are specified. Law is extremely important for understanding deviance because it represents a major societal response to a particular behavior. It is also important because those who break laws are generally fully aware of the deviance in their behavior and continue with it anyway.

Criminal behavior is as varied as the number of laws on the books. For purposes of this discussion we will break down crime into four basic categories: (1) juvenile delinquency and the role of young people in crime; (2) the "standard" crimes, including murder, robbery, burglary, larceny, and so on; (3) white-collar crimes; and (4) victimless crimes, which include gambling, prostitution, and drug use.

Juvenile Delinquency **Juvenile delinquency** includes all illegal behavior committed by individuals who are legally minors (usually under age eighteen). Much of this behavior is identical to crimes committed by adults, although some of it is criminal behavior only if committed by a juvenile. Adults, for example, cannot get into legal trouble for running away from their parents' home. Such crimes, which are illegal only for people in a certain social status, are called **status crimes**.

Young people in general make up far more than their share of arrests in the United States. Individuals between the ages of 15 and 19 make up only 7.1 percent of the U.S. population yet they account for 21.3 percent of all arrests; by contrast, individuals over the age of 25 constitute 64.9 percent of that same population yet are involved in only 53.5 percent of all arrests (U.S. Department of Justice, 2003a; U.S. Bureau of the Census, 2004a). This proportion of young people in the arrest records has been growing steadily in the United States. Moreover, the age at which young people have their first encounter with the police has been dropping steadily. Later in this chapter, we look at some of the research that sociologists have conducted to explain why people engage in criminal behavior. Much of that more general research applies to adolescents as well as adults, but the uniqueness of adolescence calls for a corresponding uniqueness in the focus of research. Juvenile crime, especially when violent, often has sources in the turbulence associated with coming of age. Considering that the majority of adult offenders began their careers as juveniles, this area of research takes on added importance.

Social psychological studies have a prominent place in juvenile delinquency research. The assumption behind most of them is that the emotions associated with adolescence play a major role in adolescent crime. Pakiz, Reinherz, and Frost (1992) explored the background of over four hundred European American juvenile offenders in a northeastern American community. They found that prior aggressive conduct was strongly associated with delinquency for both males and females. Both genders also reported difficulties with family and other relationships. (Other research, however, indicates that parents' reports of family interactions are more reliable than those coming from adolescents; see Krohn et al., 1992.) An important difference between the sexes involved the manner in which each responded to their difficulties; males were found to have low self-esteem, while females were more likely to suffer from depression. In a study of African American youth offenders, Boone (1991) found that a history of aggression at home in family settings was the strongest predictor of committing crimes of violence; other factors, such as parents' social and economic status, were far less important.

Peer associations have been much studied, particularly with relation to juvenile gangs. In short, and not surprisingly, a strong association exists between adolescent delinquency and having close ties to other adolescent delinquents (Agnew, 1991; Pabon et al., 1992). On the other hand, research has found that adolescent delinquents also adhere to many mainstream American values; for example, many attempt to maintain friendships with nondelinquent adolescents (Gilmore et al., 1992). A significant relationship has also been found between dropping out of high school and subsequent delinquent behavior (Rosen et al., 1991). The picture that emerges from this research suggests that a combination of social psychological and sociological factors come into play, as adolescents who are already aggressive or live in aggression-filled environments find outlets for those emotions through relationships with other adolescents of a similar bent.

Juvenile offenders often encounter a distinctive aspect of the criminal justice system known as the *juvenile court*. The juvenile court limits publicity and places the offender within a distinctive system in which specialized juvenile judges work closely with attorneys and social service workers. The existence of this system parallels the research described earlier in which youthful offenders are viewed as distinctive within the overall criminal justice system. When Brown et al. (1991) traced the records of youth offenders in a Pennsylvania county, they found that the intervention of the juvenile court system in an adolescent's first offense greatly decreased the likelihood of that individual being sentenced to prison as an adult.

Index Crime **Index crimes** are those crimes considered by the FBI to be major crimes; the list includes murder, forcible rape, robbery, aggravated assault, burglary, larceny/theft, and motor vehicle theft. Figure 5.1 gives a breakdown by offense. We cannot be exactly sure just how many such crimes were committed, however, as a great many of such crimes are not reported. The level of inaccuracy varies somewhat from crime to crime. The number of murders reported probably comes very close to the actual number; murders are hard to hide, as people are missed and bodies are found. At the other extreme, no doubt a great many more forcible rapes are committed than reported; it was estimated that between 1992 and 2000 only about 36 percent of rapes were reported to the police (U.S. Bureau of the Census, 2004a). The underreporting occurs because people dislike the publicity that follows rape, and perhaps more important, because the rape victim often finds herself on trial along with the rapist. This situation is particularly ironic in that a majority of rape victims know their assailant beforehand; the phenomenon of "date rape" has come to be recognized as a "crime" by women yet is still typically defined as "normal behavior" by men (Adams-Curtis and Forbes, 2004; Bogal-Allbritten and Allbritten, 1992; Holcomb et al., 1991).

Who is responsible for index crime? We have already seen that young people are heavily represented in all arrest records. Arrested individuals are also much more likely to be African American than European American, based on their percentages in the population; in 2002 African Americans made up over 26.9 percent of the arrests for index crimes while making up slightly more than 12 percent of the overall population (U.S. Bureau of the Census, 2004a; U.S. Department of Justice, 2003a). Perhaps most important, individuals arrested for index crimes are poorer than the rest of the population. It has been estimated that 80 percent of prisoners in the United States are ranked in the lowest 15 percent of the population in terms of income (Reiman, 1998).

Who is victimized by index crime? For the most part, the victims of index crime are much like the people arrested for it, particularly when it comes to violent crime. Tables 5.1 and 5.2 show the 2002 victimization rates as they vary according to the victim's gender, age, race/ethnicity, income, marital status, region, and residence. Looking first at age, we can see that young Americans have much higher victimiza-

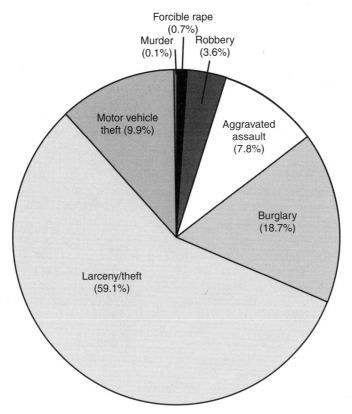

Figure 5.1 Crime index offenses for 2002. (Note: Due to rounding, the percentages do not add to 100.0.) (Data from U.S. Department of Justice 2003a)

tion rates than older Americans. While it is not depicted by these tables, rates drop with increased age for all racial and ethnic groups and for both men and women. Looking at the population as a whole for 2002, we can see that over 58 of every 1,000 Americans in the 16–19 age group were victimized by violent crime, compared with fewer than 11 of every 1,000 Americans in the 50–64 age group (U.S. Department of Justice, 2003b). Table 5.1 also suggests a strong relationship between both race and gender and victimization; in almost every age category, men have higher victimization rates than women, particularly with regard to crimes of violence. In addition, African Americans tend to have higher victimization rates than European Americans, although more so for men than for women (particularly true for young African American and European American men). We could add two more statistics to this summary: an African American man is over seven times more likely than a European American man to be murdered, and an African American woman

TABLE 5.1

RATES OF VIOLENT CRIME AND PERSONAL THEFT, BY GENDER, AGE, RACE, AND
HISPANIC ORIGIN, 2002

Characteristic of victim	Population	Victimizations per 1,000 persons age 12 or older						Personal theft
		Violent crimes						
			Rape/ sexual assault	Robbery	Assault			
		All			Total	Aggravated	Simple	
Gender								
Male	112,241,930	25.5	0.3	2.9	22.3	5.2	17.1	0.6
Female	119,347,330	20.8	1.8	1.6	17.4	3.4	14.0	0.7
Race								
White	192,956,980	22.8	0.8	1.9	20.0	4.1	15.9	0.7
Black	28,871,440	27.9	2.5	4.1	21.3	6.7	14.6	0.7*
Other	9,760,850	14.7	1.2*	2.4*	11.0	0.9*	10.1	0.4*
Hispanic Origin								
Hispanic	26,991,490	23.6	0.7*	3.2	19.7	6.1	13.7	0.4*
Non-Hispanic	203,062,880	23.0	1.1	2.1	19.8	4.1	15.8	0.7
Age								
12–15	16,676,560	44.4	2.1	3.0	39.3	5.0	34.3	0.9*
16–19	16,171,800	58.2	5.5	4.0	48.6	11.9	36.7	0.6*
20–24	19,317,740	47.4	2.9	4.7	39.8	10.1	29.7	1.6*
25–34	37,329,720	26.3	0.6*	2.8	22.8	52	17.6	0.5*
35–49	65,263,580	18.1	0.5*	1.5	16.1	3.5	12.7	0.7
50–64	43,746,850	10.7	0.2*	1.6	8.9	1.7	7.2	0.3*
65 or older	33,083,000	3.4	0.1*	1.0	2.2	0.7*	1.5	0.6*

Note: The National Crime Victimization Survey includes as violent crime rape, sexual assault, robbery, and assault. Because the NCVS interviews persons about their victimizations, murder and manslaughter cannot be included.

*Based on 10 or fewer sample cases.

Source: U.S. Department of Justice (2003b).

is over three times more likely than a European American woman to be murdered (U.S. Bureau of the Census, 2004a). But this breakdown of the statistics doesn't present the full picture.

Perhaps the most striking information in Table 5.2 is the importance of family income in victimization. While high income does not make one immune from index crime, it does apparently protect those fortunate enough to have it from *violent* crime. Looking at the violent crime total column, we can see that those with family

TABLE 5.2

RATES OF VIOLENT CRIME AND PERSONAL THEFT, BY HOUSEHOLD INCOME, MARITAL STATUS, REGION, AND LOCATION OF RESIDENCE OF VICTIMS, 2002

		Victimizations per 1,000 persons age 12 or older						
		Violent crimes						
					Assault			
Characteristic of victim	Population	All	Rape/ sexual assault	Robbery	Total	Aggravated	Simple	Personal theft
Household income								
Less than $7,500	8,347,650	45.5	2.5*	6.3	36.7	11.2	25.5	1.7*
$7,500–$14,999	15,608,210	31.5	3.2	4.1	24.2	5.8	18.4	0.5*
$15,000–$24,999	23,872,200	30.0	2.1	2.9	25.0	6.1	18.9	0.8*
$25,000–$34,999	24,104,810	27.0	1.2*	2.9	22.9	4.1	18.9	0.3*
$35,000–$49,999	31,655,160	25.6	0.9*	2.2	22.4	5.2	17.2	0.4*
$50,000–$74,999	33,713,640	18.7	0.2*	2.1	16.5	2.5	14.0	0.6*
$75,000 or more	43,139,380	19.0	0.4*	1.0	17.6	2.8	14.8	0.7
Marital status								
Never married	74,029,810	43.3	2.6	3.7	37.0	7.3	29.7	1.1
Married	117,296,790	10.6	0.2*	0.9	9.5	2.2	7.2	0.3
Divorced/ separated	24,768,200	30.7	1.1*	4.0	25.6	5.9	19.7	1.1*
Widowed	13,699,370	7.1	0.3*	2.0*	4.8	2.2*	2.7	0.6*
Region								
Northeast	43,705,120	18.8	0.7	1.5	16.7	2.7	13.9	1.2
Midwest	54,065,070	25.7	1.0	2.2	22.6	4.3	18.3	0.5*
South	83,470,930	19.7	1.0	2.6	16.2	4.7	11.5	0.6
West	50,348,150	29.4	1.6	2.3	25.5	5.0	20.6	0.5*
Residence								
Urban	64,533,840	33.1	2.2	4.3	26.7	6.5	20.2	1.2
Suburban	111,164,070	20.0	0.7	1.8	17.6	3.5	14.1	0.6
Rural	55,891,360	17.5	0.6	0.7	16.2	3.3	12.9	0.2*

Note: The National Crime Victimization Survey mcludes as violent crime rape, sexual assault, robbery, and assault. Because the NCVS interviews persons about their victimizations, murder and manslaughter cannot be included.

*Based on 10 or fewer sample cases.

Source: U.S. Department of Justice (2003b).

incomes less than $7,500 were victimized at a rate of over 45 individuals for every 1,000 Americans. By comparison, for Americans making more than $75,000, victimization rates drop by more than half. The income levels between are almost perfect stairsteps between the two extremes; as income goes up, violent crime victimization drops. Much of the explanation for these statistics is hinted at by the differences in crime rates between central cities and other areas; when you have money, you can move away from the poor people who, as we've seen, are more likely to be the index criminals. But an important factor not included among the data in Table 5.2 is that the relation between family income and violent crime victimization exists, regardless of race. The higher rates of violent crime victimization for African Americans appear to be caused primarily by higher levels of poverty among African Americans coupled with a greater likelihood of living in a central city. Safety seems to come to people, one way or another, in their pay envelopes.

Turning our attention to the nonviolent crimes (personal theft) in Table 5.2, we see an altogether different relationship between family income and victimization. In fact, there is very little relationship between the two. There is also little relationship between race and theft victimization. Theft generally is a premeditated crime, and it would certainly make sense to steal from those who have more of value. On the other hand, considerable premeditated theft is perpetrated on those closest at hand to the thief. This combination perhaps results in the widespread distribution of theft across the population.

Additional important information about victimization comes from interpreting the relationship between victim and perpetrator. The European American population of the United States has been taught to fear African Americans as potential criminals, yet the victimization rates suggest something else. Looking just at murder rates in 2002, 84 percent of white murder victims are murdered by white perpetrators; 91 percent of black murder victims are murdered by black perpetrators (U.S. Department of Justice, 2003a). The segregation of American life by race seems to include even the world of murder (see also Palley and Robinson, 1990).

Another important aspect of victimization is gender. When men are victimized, they typically are victimized by men who are strangers to them; when women are victimized, they are typically victimized by men who are known to them (U.S. Department of Justice, 2003c). The common gender of the perpetrator in each case probably comes as no surprise, but the difference in relationship might. One might imagine a man and a woman walking home after a night on the town and having to pass a dark alley. While the woman might fear that a stranger is lurking with criminal intent, statistics suggest that the real threat to her is much more likely to be the man who is escorting her.

White-Collar Crime American sociologist Edwin Sutherland popularized the idea of white-collar crime in his book by that name published in 1949. **White-collar crime** refers to specific types of criminal behavior typical of middle-class and upper-class people. Crimes such as tax evasion and antitrust violations fall into this category; some sociologists also include crimes with harsher penalties such as embezzlement, fraud, and forgery. These crimes are essentially closed to lower-class people, who don't have the skills or the access to commit them; you can't embezzle until you get access to the company funds, and you can't evade taxes until you earn some money. Upper-class people, on the other hand, are unlikely to hold up a liquor store when they can engage in a little insider trading and earn millions. They clearly cannot be argued to have motives of escaping poverty (as with many index criminals) yet the volume of white-collar crime is surpassed only by its creativity (Benson and Moore, 1992).

There is no question that white-collar crime results in far greater losses of property each year than index crimes. Estimates are that white-collar crime amounts to from three to ten times the dollar loss of all the index crimes put together (Reiman, 1998). Estimates are necessary here since a large proportion of white-collar crimes go undetected, unreported, or unprosecuted. Tax evasion and price fixing are difficult to detect; employee theft is often not reported; and the influence of wealthy criminals often prevents prosecution. When white-collar criminals are prosecuted, penalties are either nonexistent or minimal compared to the sentences imposed on those accused of index crimes.

One famous example is the 1961 conspiracy trials of forty-five executives from twenty-nine major American electrical equipment companies (including General Electric and Westinghouse). These men were convicted of price fixing—they had met regularly for a period of time and agreed to set prices artificially high on the items their companies produced. As a result, consumers paid around $1.75 billion extra over a period of eight years. After pleading *nolo contendere* (no contest) to the charges, the men were sentenced to thirty days in jail (Reiman, 1998).

Have times changed? Consider the case of the Archer Daniels Midland company, the world's largest grain processor. In 1996, the company was trapped in a federal sting operation attempting to fix prices for two of its products. It was fined $100 million and faced more than that much again through civil lawsuits. Extra profits gained through the price fixing of just one of the affected products netted the company $170 million. How did Wall Street react to the case? ADM stock rose (Sherrill, 1997).

If anything, the twenty-first century has witnessed an increase in illegal corporate activities. The Securities and Exchange Commission opened 570 new investigations in 2002 alone, bringing such corporations as Enron, WorldCom, and ImClone into the consciousness of the average American (Drutman and Cray, 2002). Corporate executives lined their own pockets (and sometimes their corporation's pockets) through a variety of accounting tricks, insider information, and insider loans. In the case of Enron, smaller investors were left holding the bag when the corporation went down. Many of these cases are still in the courts. It will be interesting to see how many executives wind up joining Martha Stewart in serving prison time.

White-collar criminals receive lighter sentences than index criminals do but, as Martha Stewart discovered, there may be some consequences.

There are indications that American public opinion has been turning against such wrist slaps. In a 1999 survey, one in three Americans reported having been the victim of white-collar crime. Many people surveyed rated some such crimes—knowingly selling tainted meat that caused illness, for example—as the equivalent of armed robbery (Mokhiber, 2000). Nationwide, from 1993 to 1997 about one white-collar defendant was sentenced to prison for every two convicted (Higgins, 1999). But most corporate criminals still avoid jail time or prison sentences, even when their crimes cause death (Sherrill, 1997). The American public is still not ready to fill its prisons with white-collar criminals (Multinational Monitor, 1998).

Victimless Crimes Now we come to the interesting and somewhat peculiar topic of crimes without victims. **Victimless crimes** are those crimes in which the criminal is the only victim (if there is a victim) (Schur, 1965). Whereas most laws, such as those relating to murder and robbery, seem designed to protect innocent victims, laws relating to homosexuality, prostitution, drug use, and gambling have a different intent. The implication seems to be that society in general is the victim of these behaviors and so they should be prohibited. With drug use, for example, we seem to feel that certain drugs are so bad for people that those who use them should be put in jail to prevent them from becoming victims of their own behavior.

The behaviors that fall under this heading are a curious group. Prostitution is often called "the oldest profession," yet it is illegal in most of the United States. Gambling is illegal in most states unless the state itself chooses to run it, with lotteries or horse racing. Sexual relations between consenting adults of the same sex are still illegal in many states, although gay rights organizations are attempting to change such regulations through political action. Like prostitution and gambling, homosexuality is as old as human memory. In addition, as with the other two activities, it has been fully legal in many times and places. Finally, drug use is perhaps the most curious of the group. Which drugs? As noted, heroin was legal in the United States until 1914. It was once one of the most popular ingredients (along with chloroform and chloral hydrate) in a variety of nineteenth-century infant remedies for coughs and teething troubles (Douglas and Waksler, 1982). It is now illegal on the grounds that it is dangerous to health, yet cigarettes and liquor, which are clearly severe health hazards, are both legal (although somewhat restricted).

American attitudes toward illegal drugs are expressed clearly in the U.S. prison population. Prisoners incarcerated for drug offences made up 54.7 percent of the federal prison population and over 20 percent of the state prison population in 2002 (U.S. Department of Justice, 2003d, 2003e). See Box 5.1 for a more complete view of changes in the way drug offenses have been treated by the American criminal justice system.

The existence of victimless crimes tells us more about a society than it does about the people who commit the crimes. Although all laws make a statement about which behaviors a society approves or disapproves, crimes without victims are the clearest examples of this process. When we return, later in this chapter, to look at the role of deviance in society, a closer examination of these "crimes" will provide some insight. We need to remember, however, that the scope of "victimhood" is a matter of dispute. Prostitutes, for example, sell a service to people who want it, but some could argue that the legal presence of prostitutes in a society also affects those who choose not to patronize them. And a prostitute who carries the AIDS virus raises a series of complex questions not only for the sociological study of deviance but also for legislators.

NONCRIMINAL DEVIANCE: ALCOHOLISM, MENTAL ILLNESS, AND MENTAL RETARDATION

Alcoholism refers to the behavior of an individual who is not able to control either the frequency or the amount of alcohol he or she consumes. *Mental illness* is not so easily defined, for it refers to a wide variety of human behaviors; the common threads that run through these behaviors are that (1) other people are unable to

BOX 5.1

Drug Convictions and Crowded Prisons

One of the most confusing statistics in criminology is the combination of a steadily dropping crime rate coupled with overflowing prisons. If fewer crimes are being committed, why do we have more prisoners? The answer lies not in raw numbers of crimes but in changes in how crimes are defined by law and sentenced by the courts.

Without a doubt, America's newest prisoners find their way into cells via drug convictions. This change, which began in the 1980s, is surprisingly not really connected to drug use in the United States. The use of all drugs, including tobacco and alcohol, has been dropping steadily over the last two decades (Tonry, 1995). What has changed is the effort placed by police on drug arrests and the sentencing of drug-related crimes by America's judges. The Anti-Drug Abuse Act of 1986 mandated stiffer federal sentencing for drug possession and trafficking. Those convicted were more likely to be placed in prison and more likely to have long sentences. As prisoners with shorter sentences for other crimes came and went, the overall prison population became increasingly drug related and increasingly larger. In 1985, drug offenders made up 8.6 percent of the state prison population in the United States; by 2001, they had risen to 20.4 percent (U.S. Department of Justice, 2003e). In federal prisons, drug offenders increased their share of the prison population from 16.3 percent in 1970 to 55 percent in 1998 (U.S. Department of Justice, 2003e). And not only the percent of drug offenders has climbed. The American prison population has grown radically in the last few decades. From 1930 to 1975, the American incarceration rate remained constant at about 100 prisoners for every 100,000 Americans. Since then, the rate has risen to a peak in 2002 of 476 prisoners for every 100,000 Americans (U.S. Department of Justice, 2003e). Very few countries in the world imprison a higher percentage of their citizens.

During this same period of time, America's prisoners were also becoming increasingly nonwhite. Much of this change can also be traced to changes in the way drug offenses are handled. Consider cocaine. It is normally produced as a powder but that powder can be transformed into another form popularly termed "crack" cocaine. The powdered form is much more expensive, ounce for ounce, and is generally trafficked and used by wealthier people. Crack cocaine is cheaper and is more likely to be used by poorer people. And poorer people are more likely to be nonwhite. According to federal sentencing guidelines, an individual arrested with one gram of crack cocaine should receive the same penalty as an individual arrested with 100 grams of powdered cocaine. The stated logic behind this is that crack cocaine is believed to be more quickly addictive. In 2002, 81.4 percent of individuals sentenced in U.S. District Courts for crack cocaine were African American. By contrast, only 30.9 percent of powdered cocaine sentences involved African Americans (U.S. Department of Justice, 2003d). The result is that nonwhite (and poor) drug offenders fill the prisons (U.S. Sentencing Commission, 1997).

imagine themselves engaging in the behavior with any rational purpose, and (2) the behavior is thought to be a danger either to the individual or to others. *Mental retardation* refers to the apparent inability of an individual to exhibit intellectual characteristics thought typical of his or her age. Generally, these characteristics are measured through the use of some standardized intelligence test.

These apparently strange bedfellows can share the same heading because of their similarities in the sociological study of deviance. First, the individuals engaging in each of these types of behaviors are assumed to be either temporarily or permanently incapable of behaving any other way; the fact that both alcoholism and mental illness are commonly thought to be "diseases" suggests this perspective (see Erickson, 1992). None of these behaviors can therefore be considered criminal, because the individual is presumed not responsible for his or her behavior. Second, each of these behaviors breaks social norms and often results in a social control response from some sector of society. Alcoholics receive tremendous informal social pressure and often find their way into alcoholic treatment groups or facilities. The mentally ill may be incarcerated (voluntarily or involuntarily through a court order) in a mental health facility, where attempts are made to alter their behavior. The mentally retarded are often removed from a standard school curriculum in favor of a program designed specifically for their category. In each case the individual is set apart from others. These examples of noncriminal deviance will help us later to understand more about deviance in general.

TYPES OF DEVIANCE: HOW MANY?

One danger of categorizing anything is that it leads you to forget things not included in the typology. Keep in mind that deviance is a general concept; behavior that breaks norms can vary from some of the extreme forms we've looked at here to a vast number of milder forms. People who are too tall or too short, too fat or too thin can be deviants in the eyes of others. Some people are considered deviant because they are mentally retarded, but how about people who appear to be more intelligent than the rest of us? The physically handicapped are often forced into forms of behavior that others consider deviant (see Sagarin, 1971). How about people with extreme political views? The list is endless—just as endless as the social norms that apparently exist only to be broken. Too close a focus on the more extreme forms of deviance can make us lose track of the way deviance is integrated into everyone's behavior and into every social situation.

THEORIES OF DEVIANCE

Theories that attempt to explain deviance can be separated into two basic types. *Deviant-centered theories* attempt to understand deviant behavior by learning more about the deviant himself or herself and trying to explain why individuals engage in acts of deviance. *Society-centered theories* attempt to explain deviance by understanding the social groups within which deviance occurs. Not surprisingly, most sociologists fall into the second category. When we look at this second collection of theories, you'll note a variety of questions being asked. Some focus on those factors within the social group that encourage individuals to engage in acts of deviance, while others are concerned less with the deviants themselves and more with the social group whose members find the behavior deviant. By the end of this section you should understand deviance as a complex interplay between the individual and the social group on a battlefield of social norms.

DEVIANT-CENTERED THEORIES

Traditionally, notions about deviance have focused on the individual deviant. In the Middle Ages unusual individuals were often thought to be possessed by the devil, and aggressive individuals were thought to have inherited their tendencies. Today, most deviant-centered theories are found in the fields of biology and psychology.

Biological Explanations It is both an appealing and a sobering thought that our biological makeup directs much of our behavior. It is appealing in the sense that it gives hope to the idea that severe mental disorders, for example, might be "cured" by a particular drug. It is sobering because too much knowledge in this area could be used to turn us all into robots. In any case, biological theories and experimentation related to behavior continue.

One of the earlier and more colorful efforts in this area was the work of criminologist Cesare Lombroso (1836–1909). He assumed that criminal deviance was inherited and that this inheritance was visible in the shape of the human skull. He isolated particular jaw structures and the like that he claimed illustrated inherited deviance. Although none of Lombroso's work is applied today, it does explain why most butlers in murder mysteries have close-set eyes and weak chins.

Interest in sociobiology (see Chapter 4) has also influenced research in criminology. Van den Berge (1974) argues that aggressive behavior should be studied from a biosocial standpoint. Gabrielli and Mednick (1983) studied over 14,000 adopted children to see whether their criminal (or noncriminal) behavior more closely followed the behavior of their natural parents or that of their adoptive parents. While they found a significant relation between adopted children and their natural parents with regard to property offenses, they found no relationship between the two with regard to crimes of violence. If aggressive behavior were inherited, it would not be likely to appear in property crime.

Biological explanations of deviance have generally been more popular in the study of mental illness than in criminology. Mental illness is hardly a simple research question, but the wide variety of behaviors that fall under the criminology umbrella exceed what little we know about genetics. Clearly, individuals arrested for illegal substance possession, repeated burglary, or the murder of a family member during an argument are all engaging in very different behaviors in terms of motivation. Thus, it seems highly unlikely that genetics will ever be able to predict criminal behavior.

Psychological Explanations The most famous of the psychological explanations of deviance come from the psychoanalytic tradition of Sigmund Freud (see Chapter 4). Freud's theory of the inborn id, the superego with its internalized values, and the rational ego provides one possible explanation of deviance: the deviant might be someone who has never properly internalized social group values; with little self-restraint, the id would run wild into deviance. Or the deviant might have internalized group values too strongly, leading to almost total repression of the id's desires and subsequent mental disorder. In either case the deviance would be the result of forces within the individual. Freud's *Civilization and Its Discontents,* published in 1930, started the ball rolling in this direction.

Other psychological approaches, particularly in the study of criminal behavior, have sought to isolate "psychopathic" personalities. The idea behind this approach is that many criminals have basic personality defects, which become reflected in criminal (and other antisocial) activities. Hirschi and Hindelang (1977) sought to forge a link between the lack of intelligence and criminal activity. With regard to juveniles, for instance, they argued that low IQ leads to frustrating school experiences, which in turn lead to delinquent behavior.

From the sociological point of view, psychological and biological explanations overlook much of the meaning that deviance has for the people who engage in it. Most deviant behavior is, in fact, just like any other ongoing patterned social behavior, governed by its own set of norms and values. In short, for sociologists deviance is a phenomenon of social groups.

SOCIETY-CENTERED THEORIES

Sociological, or society-centered, theories of deviance are distinctive in that they call attention to the deviant's social groups, to the social groups whose norms the deviant breaks, or to both. Although the theories in this section vary considerably, they all have one point of similarity: they all place the deviant firmly in a social context.

Differential Association The **differential association theory** was introduced by the American criminologist Edwin Sutherland (1962). The core of this theory is both simple and important: deviants generally learn to be deviant from ongoing deviant social groups. The juvenile learns to steal from other juveniles who have stolen before and who support the behavior; the prostitute learns her (or his) trade from those with experience in the field. People become deviants, says Sutherland, because they associate with deviants.

The theory of differential association focuses on changes in the thinking of the prospective deviant as he or she associates with established deviants, the most important change being the definitions of legal and illegal, right and wrong. As the prospective deviant associates with established deviants, he or she acquires a new set of attitudes that condone or even promote criminal activity, thus motivating the newcomer to future deviant acts.

Subcultural Theory As we saw in Chapter 3, a **subculture** is a social group or collection of social groups that exists within a larger culture yet has distinctive norms and values that set it off from the larger culture. Any subculture might be somewhat deviant, since its members might have to violate the larger culture's norms in order to follow their own. The question is: how different are the subculture's norms? A **deviant subculture** is a subculture viewed by both its members and outsiders as having fundamentally, and often threateningly, different norms and values. To become part of such a subculture is to enter the world of deviance. Aside from that, the processes of socialization and internalization are much the same as those that occur when any individual encounters a new social group.

Subcultural theorists tend to view criminal deviants as coming from a fundamentally different culture and, as a result, adhering to a fundamentally different set of values. Walter Miller (1958) explained the large number of lower-class criminals by such logic, suggesting the existence of a "lower-class culture" with values supporting toughness, excitement, trouble, and the immediate gratification of desires. Such values tend to lead individuals into criminal activity.

Labeling Theory **Labeling theory** looks beyond the social groups to which the deviant belongs and focuses attention on the groups whose norms the deviant breaks. As Howard Becker (1963) describes it,

> social groups create deviance by making the rules whose infraction constitutes deviance, and by applying those rules to particular people and labeling them as outsiders. From this point of view, deviance is not a quality of the act the person commits, but rather a consequence of the application by others of rules and sanctions to an "outsider." The deviant is one to whom that label has successfully been applied; deviant behavior is behavior that people so label. (9)

From this definition we can extract the basic ideas of labeling theory:

1. No action or behavior is ever inherently deviant, and no individual is ever inherently a deviant.
2. Deviance exists only when members of social groups label the violation of their norms as deviance.
3. Deviants exist only when individuals are labeled as such by members of social groups.

Let us look at these ideas one at a time.

First, the reason no act or behavior can ever be inherently deviant is that norms change from group to group and from time to time. Actions considered to be deviant today or in the eyes of a certain group may well be considered "normal" behavior tomorrow or somewhere else. We have already seen some of this variation across cultures in Chapter 3, but the same variation occurs within one culture. During Hitler's leadership in Germany, murdering Jews and burning books were considered normal, while going to certain churches or supporting programs to aid the mentally retarded was considered deviant. Probably an even better example would be the early Christian movement. In the eyes of the state (as it then was) Jesus was considered a supreme deviant and suffered the ultimate sanction—execution. Today, of course, belief in Christianity is highly respectable in the Western world. Times and people change. It is a sobering thought to realize that some of the people we think of as deviants today may be looked upon in the future as the greatest figures of our time.

Second, certain violations of certain social norms must be labeled as deviance before deviance is considered to exist. Becker's argument here is that the members of social groups must reach some kind of consensus as to which kinds of behavior are deviant and which are not. They must also decide how deviant that behavior is in relation to others. In the United States during the 1920s, for example, alcoholic drinks were illegal but marijuana was legal; today it is just the reverse. Such changes are indicative of the group decision-making process and the manner in which consensus can change. In a court of law you cannot be prosecuted for an act you committed before a law was passed declaring it illegal. By the same token, you cannot count on being released from prison should your offense be subsequently removed from the inventory of illegal acts.

Being poor in the United States unavoidably leads to deviant behavior and to a variety of deviant labels.

Finally, individuals become deviants (in the sociological sense) only when they are labeled as such by members of social groups. According to this aspect of labeling theory, you are not a deviant until people think of you as a deviant and, more important, treat you as a deviant. If you are a mass murderer who has never been caught, you are not strictly speaking a deviant. At the other extreme, if you have been unjustly accused of a deviant act and are believed by others to have committed it, you will be treated as a deviant even though you've done nothing. As far as Becker is concerned, a deviant is an individual who is treated as a deviant and forced by others into a deviant role. Deviance belongs to the group, not to the individual.

This last idea offered by Becker is in keeping with Edwin Lemert's (1967) distinction between primary and secondary deviance. **Primary deviance** refers to the commission of an act that has been labeled as deviant. Primary deviance is a behavior that only you know about; the fact that others treat you as if it hadn't occurred minimizes its importance in your everyday life. (You can probably think of a few deviant acts out of your past that you would just as soon not have spread around.) **Secondary deviance** begins when you get caught, when others become aware of your behavior. Secondary deviance gains its importance from the nature of the social self (as described in Chapter 4). If others treat us as deviants, that treatment will become a very real factor in our everyday life and will ultimately change the way we look at ourselves.

Because of its focus, labeling theory directs our attention away from the deviants themselves and toward the people who do the labeling. We must now ask several new questions. Whose norms are being broken? Why are those people in a position to label others effectively—why are they "respectable" and deviants "deviant" instead of the other way around? What is the process by which they apply labels to actions and to the people who engage in those actions? These questions can draw our attention to the people who hold power and authority in society (the people who make their labels "stick"). The questions direct us further to examine police, courts, judges, prisons, psychiatrists, mental hospitals, educators, and everyone else who takes an active part in the labeling process. We become aware, through labeling theory, of which people are caught, processed, and labeled, as opposed to those who aren't. We become aware of why certain behaviors may be labeled as deviant today but not tomorrow. In short, labeling theory calls our attention to deviance as a label that is created and applied in social groups.

A role with authority in a social group is a role with, among other things, the right to label. Typically, such rights are specific to certain kinds of labels; that is, a judge can label you a criminal; a psychiatrist can label you as mentally ill; and a teacher can label you as a poor student. The label can act as a *self-fulfilling prophecy:* if everyone (including the person labeled) treats the label as accurate, ultimately it may become accurate. Mental institutions often turn people into excellent mental patients, and prisons are famous for producing more and better criminals. As labeling theory tells us, the label carries its own reality.

The norms of American society demand that people clothe their nakedness, even if it's with the briefest of bikinis. We label those who want to wander about without clothes as deviant. These "deviants" often band together and create camps and other places where they can participate in the lifestyle they prefer.

Anomie Theory French sociologist Emile Durkheim (1858–1917) used the term **anomie** to describe a state of normlessness in society, when many people are unclear as to the expectations others have of them (Durkheim, 1951). Durkheim applied this concept to his famous study of suicide (see Chapter 2), explaining that suicide rates went up with increased anomie. The importance of his study for an understanding of deviance is his focus on the way a society can actually create strains in the lives of its individual members. Labeling theory examines the manner in which deviants are labeled but ignores the question of what causes deviance. **Anomie theory,** as it has been applied in the study of deviance, offers one solution to the question of what causes deviance: deviant behavior is encouraged by strains built into the very fabric of society.

Durkheim's concept was borrowed by American sociologist Robert Merton in his study of deviance. Merton was particularly interested in the problems people had in adapting to certain cultural goals (or values) and their ability or inability to acquire certain goals through established means (or norms). For example, all Americans are socialized to value success and material goods, but not all Americans can achieve those goals through the legitimate means that are available in our society. If you want a new car and a fine house but can't find a job that will allow you to acquire them, you might find some creative (deviant) way of achieving the same ends.

Merton (1956) analyzed societal strains by pointing out the variety of ways that people might respond to such strain. As the strains occur in all walks of life, so too do the (often deviant) adaptations. Consider how each of Merton's types of adaptation occurs in the world of everyday work.

1. *Conformity.* By far the most common response, conformity occurs when individuals adhere to cultural norms and values in spite of strain. A janitor might prefer to have his or her occupation better thought of and better paid but, failing that possibility, learns to live with it and do the job. The strains are still there, but they don't appear in behavior.

2. *Innovation.* A clear deviant response, innovation occurs when individuals accept cultural values (such as success) but find alternative means for achieving them. The quiet bank teller who has been cleverly removing bank funds for years has found an alternative to the promotion that didn't happen. We can also see innovation in the actions of a bureaucrat who, frustrated with organizational graft and ineptitude, steps outside the organizational role by blowing the whistle to authorities. Innovation is a clear case in which the structure of society encourages actions of individual deviance.

3. *Ritualism.* The ritualist response to strain involves giving up goals that seem impossible to achieve in favor of adhering to the standard means (or norms). The once-dedicated high school teacher who now settles for just law and order in the classroom is a classic ritualist. Rules concerning student behavior were instituted in public schools with the idea that they would lead to more effective education. If that more effective education does not appear forthcoming, the ritualist can nevertheless cling to the ritual of following the established means. Under this heading we also find the bureaucrat more interested in following rules than helping people or the librarian who is only really happy when all the books are safely on the shelves and the doors locked. A great many occupations appear to have unreachable goals built into them. One response to this strain is to forget them and concentrate on "doing your job" even if the point of the job seems forgotten.

4. *Retreatism.* The retreatist responds to strain by giving up on both cultural values and norms. Not even criminal occupations would fit in here since most criminals are interested in making money illegally (an innovative response). Merton's example is the "occupation" of hobo—the individual who thumbs a deviant nose at the whole society. The hobo wants none of society and has no desire to change it.

5. *Rebellion.* The last response, rebellion, rejects both cultural norms and values but seeks to change both. A radical political activist who makes bombs and plans of revolution in his or her spare time is a classic example. Islamic jihad in the Middle East embodies these strategies and goals.

All of Merton's adaptive types (except for conformity) can be thought of as deviant responses to societal strain. In each case the "cause" of the deviance lies outside the individual and in the state of anomie that exists in society. If these deviant individuals also have "personality disorders" or choose to associate with deviant subcultures, those attributes are only symptoms of more general social forces.

Anomie theory has found particular application with regard to juvenile delinquency. Cloward and Ohlin (1960) pointed out that lower-class juveniles are subject to acquiring the same values as middle-class juveniles but with far fewer legitimate means of acquiring them. The delinquent subculture is not so much an ongoing part of lower-class culture (as subcultural theories suggest) as an adaptive form of social organization designed to meet the needs of otherwise frustrated juveniles. Criminal behavior thus becomes a reaction to their feeling of injustice at being deprived of what middle-class youths are given.

Cohen (1955) offered a similar view of the juvenile gang. Lower-class juveniles feel a sense of material deprivation relative to middle-class juveniles, but they also feel a status loss. Middle-class juveniles, for example, are likely to acquire favorable evaluations of their worth from established social institutions, such as schools, whereas lower-class juveniles are likely to acquire negative attitudes about themselves from those same institutions. The gang becomes a source of self-esteem for the lower-class juvenile, providing a sense of "fitting in" somewhere. If you don't get respect at home or at school, you can always get it from fellow members of the gang.

The positive responses and "legitimacy" provided by gang members have more recently been combined with the more immediate experiences connected with criminal behavior. Is stealing a "rational" way to get ahead? No, if the chances of getting caught are at all high. But theft can also be inherently exciting. If this excitement becomes at all connected with city street life (such as the need to impress others with both acts of courage and their fruits), anomie becomes only one of many causes of such behavior.

Social Control Theory Like anomie theory, **social control theory** attempts to explain why individuals engage in deviant behavior. Unlike anomie theory, however, social control theory explains why only certain deprived individuals turn to criminal behavior while others in remarkably similar situations resist the temptation. The answer focuses on the standard sociological concept of social control—the means by which individuals are convinced (or coerced) to follow the norms of respectable behavior.

Reckless (1967) separates these mechanisms of social control into outer containment and inner containment. *Outer containment* comes from the strength of the social group and its commitment to noncriminal behavior. If members of the social group are bound together tightly enough, they will police each other's behavior, thus prohibiting individual members from attempting any criminal behavior. *Inner containment* stems from the process of the internalization of values—individuals come to police their own behavior through a desire to live up to their (socially constructed) conscience. According to Reckless, when either of the social control processes breaks down as individuals interact within their social groups, deviant behavior will result.

Radical Theories The **radical theories** of deviance follow in the tradition of Karl Marx (1818–1883), whose ideas will be examined more fully in Chapter 6, on social stratification. Marx's concern with social stratification has a definite bearing on deviance for, as we've already seen, the rich and the poor in the United States have very different experiences with the criminal justice system.

Marx's primary interest was to gain an understanding of capitalist industrial society—a society based on private property in which the means of production and distribution (all economic power) are in the hands of a few—the capitalists, or, more simply, the ruling class. Marx was particularly curious about how the ruling class, a very small percentage of the population, could control most of the wealth. He was also interested in the reasons that the rest of the population (who work for members of the ruling class) would either decide to put up with their situation or seek to change it. These decisions, Marx felt, have a lot to do with actions taken by members of the ruling class. They are in a position to control the living situations of those who work for them and even control the ideas that these people have by controlling the flow of information in society. According to the modern radical theories of deviance, one of the ways they exercise this control is through the way they define and respond to "crime."

Jeffrey Reiman (1998), one of the modern radical theorists, raises an interesting question. What kind of criminal justice system would you form, he asks, if you wanted to "maintain and encourage the existence of a stable and visible class of criminals" instead of eliminating crime and rehabilitating criminals? First, he says, you would need "irrational" laws on the books (such as laws against possessing or using heroin) that would encourage people to engage in other forms of criminal activity (such as burglary, in order to support an expensive habit). Second, give police, prosecutors, and judges broad discretion as to which people go free and which people go to prison. Third, make the prison experience painful and demeaning. Fourth, make sure the prisoners acquire no skills while in prison and have no jobs when they get out. Finally, make sure that a prisoner's record colors the rest of his or her life, separating the individual socially, economically, and politically from those who have never been in prison. In short, says Reiman, you would set up a criminal justice system exactly like the one we have.

Reiman's radical criticism is that our criminal justice system is designed to maintain a certain percentage of the population, mostly of the lower class, involved in activities labeled criminal so that they may be presented to the rest of the population (the middle class) as an ever-present danger. If the middle class is concerned about lawbreaking among the lower classes, they will favor a strong government and, more important, they won't come to recognize the upper classes as a danger to them. For example, middle-class Americans are afraid of being murdered. As a matter of fact, two Americans die every hour as the victims of homicide, whereas eleven Americans die in the same time period from diseases brought about by unhealthy conditions in the workplace (Reiman, 1998). In addition, women workers may suffer more from corporate crime than men (Gerber and Weeks, 1992). Where, Reiman asks, is the real danger?

Why is armed robbery or assault a serious crime, while ignoring an industrial safety regulation that results in a death is only breaking a regulation? The difference, says Reiman, is in the criminal. In the first case the criminal will usually be poor; in the second case the criminal will never be poor. This is similar to the difference between index crime and white-collar crime discussed earlier. Any behavior by the middle and upper classes somehow doesn't seem quite as criminal as the things lower-class people do. Yet, as Reiman points out in an analysis of occupational hazards and unnecessary surgery, the upper classes are often far more dangerous than the lower classes.

A serious example of corporate disregard for the health of workers is presented by Paul Brodeur (1985) in his history of the lawsuits spawned by the actions of the major U.S. manufacturers of asbestos. Asbestos is a mineral that causes serious health problems when it enters the lungs; even a brief exposure can produce cancer thirty years later. For years, workers knew nothing of the danger they were in as they worked with this product. As they began to die and as lawyers began to gather evidence, it turned out that the major manufacturers had known (in some cases) for fifty years about the dangers of their product. Rather than notify their employees (which might have resulted in lawsuits) or institute safer work situations (which would have been expensive, producing a drop in profits), they chose to prepare themselves by taking out more insurance. The insurance companies investigated also discovered the risks of asbestos exposure, and then sold more insurance at higher premiums rather than tell anyone. All these actions were motivated not by the evil intent of the individuals involved but rather by the way the business world is structured around the profit motive. From the perspective of radical theory, it is the structure of the corporate world that produces such abuses.

How do we view different types of crime? To most of us, the armed robber looks more dangerous than Enron executive Jeffrey Skilling, even though corporate theft involves far greater sums of money.

Another radical theorist, Richard Quinney (1980), points out a service that criminal justice provides for the economy. Capitalists, says Quinney, often have a problem coping with workers as the economy fluctuates downward and people are put out of work. What do you do with all the people? Many go on one or another government program (food stamps, unemployment compensation, etc.) until things start looking up. One of these unemployment programs, says Quinney, is prison. Prison certainly keeps people off the streets, and if you are a member of the ruling class, the last thing you will want is a large number of unhappy unemployed people out on the streets. Quinney's findings are also far from unique in connecting prison commitments with unemployment. Along with age (more younger people in the population means more crime), unemployment is consistently shown to be one of the strongest predictors of growth in the prison population (Cappell and Sykes, 1991; Smith et al., 1992).

In sum, the radical theorists argue that criminal justice is a far more pervasive means of social control than we normally think. Crime is defined in such a way that potentially dangerous members of the lower class are the only people truly affected. In addition, these lower-class criminals are held up to the rest of us as a threat to our well-being; if we accept this picture, we are more likely to prefer a strong protective government and less likely to notice other threats to our well-being perpetrated by members of the ruling class.

POWER AND AUTHORITY IN THE CONTROL OF DEVIANCE

As noted in earlier chapters, **power** is the extent to which you can control the behavior of others, while **authority** is the right that others give you to exert that control. Both of these concepts are important in the study of deviance. Social control techniques that are common responses to deviance are generally backed by raw power. The police and prison systems in the United States, for example, operate through armed might. Authority may be even more important than power, however.

The theories of deviance we've examined thus far bring us naturally to the role of authority. When social groups that violate each other's norms come into conflict—police and burglars, for example—only one group ends up with the label *deviant*. Clearly, some groups have the authority to label, and others do not. The burglars find the behavior of the police highly unattractive, but that opinion does not become a societal label. Similarly, when legislators and courts tell us that car theft is a "crime" but that industrial deaths are "safety violations," we abide by the labels; legislators and courts have the authority to make those decisions for us. The kinds of behavior that are labeled as deviant obviously have a lot to do with the positions of authority in a society.

In this section we look at the role of deviance in relation to power and authority with two basic questions in mind. First, to what extent is deviant behavior labeled as such because it in some way threatens positions of authority? Second, how does the label of deviance become a social definition that most of us accept without question?

DEVIANCE AS A THREAT TO AUTHORITY

People come and go from positions of authority, and the positions themselves have been known to come and go as societies change. When Richard Nixon resigned the U.S. presidency, he lost the authority he had been receiving from that position. If a revolution had occurred as well, the position itself might have been replaced by a new position of authority. In short, authority can be a somewhat slippery social possession. And the more slippery it becomes, the more avidly it will be sought and clutched. Not surprisingly, therefore, the quickest way for behavior to earn a deviant label is for it to threaten authority or to be perceived as a threat to authority.

Probably the clearest example of this aspect of deviance is the distinction between index crime and white-collar crime. Burglary (which is a nonviolent index crime) results in prison sentences twice as long as those for embezzlement and almost four times as long as those for income-tax fraud (Reiman, 1998). The irony is that the two white-collar crimes each result in a far greater dollar loss each year than burglary. Why the difference? As an index crime, burglary is typically a crime of the lower classes and represents an attempt to move wealth from haves to have-nots. On

Authority was threatened mightily by the civil rights movement of the 1960s and its leaders. Militant blacks—even though avowedly and actually acting in nonviolent ways—appeared deviant to many authorities in both North and South. Here, Dr. Martin Luther King, Jr., is shown during one of his several jail stays. Dr. King, of course, was eventually acknowledged as an American hero; there is a national holiday honoring him.

the other hand, white-collar crime shifts wealth from one set of haves to another. Perhaps more important, the people who commit white-collar crime are typically in positions of authority themselves and are the same "kind of people" as others in positions of authority (such as judges) who may be called upon to label the act (see Box 5.2).

Perhaps an even better example comes from the history of labor relations in the United States. The success and respectability of labor unions today makes it easy to forget the long period of extreme violence in the early history of unionization. Whereas a strike today attracts a federal negotiator, a strike at the end of the nineteenth century usually attracted the police, the National Guard, or the U.S. Army. Such repressive responses lasted well into the 1930s and are still not unheard of with some unions today. Why the violent response? Workers were not just asking for money and better working conditions; they were demanding some authority over their lives. Once an industry was unionized, management would thereafter always have to consider the union in all decisions. This pill has been well swallowed and digested by American industry, but it was an extremely bitter one at the outset.

Of all the labor history that could serve to illustrate this violent response from a threatened authority, one of the most interesting incidents is the Sacco-Vanzetti execution on August 23, 1927. Nicola Sacco and Bartolomeo Vanzetti were Italian American members of a radical labor organization. They had both had brushes with the law because of their labor activities; they were finally arrested, charged with, and convicted of the robbery and murder of a paymaster and guard at a shoe factory in South Braintree, Massachusetts. Even though another prison inmate subsequently confessed to the murders, Sacco and Vanzetti were executed anyway (Rolle, 1972). They were on trial for their labor activities, which had little to do with the crime of which they were accused.

Other examples of threatened authorities could be cited from any situation in which social authority exists. Jesus was crucified not so much for his religious beliefs as for his rebellion against Roman authority. In turn, the Catholic Church, which formed in response to the teachings of Jesus, came to a position of authority itself and responded with hostility to scientific advances, such as Galileo's idea that the sun (and not the earth) was at the center of the universe. Examples are abundant in our own time, too. Doctors often want you just to take the pills without wasting their time with questions. Students who want decent grades must use care not to impugn their professor's knowledge and expertise. Employees of all descriptions must show proper deference to their employers if they wish to remain employed. In each case those in positions of authority jealously guard their right to decide and will label as deviant any behavior that gets in the way.

DEVIANCE AS A SOCIAL DEFINITION

American sociologist W. I. Thomas (1863–1947) is best remembered today for his concept of the **definition of the situation.** Thomas meant by this that **social reality**

BOX 5.2

The Saints and the Roughnecks

William Chambliss (1973) offers us a view of deviant labeling through his study of two teenage boys' gangs: the Saints and the Roughnecks. These gangs had two striking differences between them: (1) The Saints were all middle class or upper class, while the Roughnecks were all lower class. (2) The Saints engaged in a variety of deviant acts equal to or surpassing the delinquency of the Roughnecks, yet they were seldom in trouble with the police and were well thought of in the community. The question is: how does social class play a role in the way behavior is interpreted?

The primary difference between the Saints and the Roughnecks was in style. The Saints presented an image of middle-class respectability by following middle-class norms, of which they were well aware, while the Roughnecks violated these norms. For example, the Saints were good students and were involved in school activities. They managed this even though they were truant much of the time. They always managed to leave school "legitimately" (forging excuses, etc.) so that their behavior was not widely known among teachers. When their grades did fall as a result of truancy, teachers always gave them the benefit of the doubt because they were "good students."

When truant or on weekends, the Saints got drunk, drove their cars recklessly, shouted obscenities at passing women, and engaged in acts of vandalism. If, for example, they found a street being repaired, they enjoyed removing the barriers and watching cars drive into the open holes. Abandoned houses were also considered fair game for vandalism. They were careful, however, to limit all this activity to a nearby city so as not to lose their "good name" in their hometown. They generally were able to avoid the police. When caught, they were extremely polite and contrite and were generally let off with a warning.

The Roughnecks had little money for liquor and seldom had cars. They generally hung around a town street corner, regularly getting into fights among themselves or sometimes with rivals. They engaged in acts of theft, although the community was not aware of the extent of the stealing, thinking the boys were primarily drinkers and fighters. The Roughnecks' drinking, though limited by their lack of funds, was highly visible when it did occur since the boys had no place to go and no cars in which they could achieve some privacy. Ironically, most of the Roughnecks attended school regularly, but they were not particularly successful students and had a bad reputation among the teachers.

The Saints were viewed by the community as good boys who sowed a few wild oats from time to time. The Roughnecks were viewed as a bad bunch. Not only were the Saints given the benefit of the doubt because of the prestige of their social class,

> they were able to use that class position to manage the impression they made on others. They used their knowledge of middle-class norms to appear respectable and their money to obtain privacy for their delinquent behavior. The Roughnecks had neither advantage. The different perspectives on these two gangs is almost identical to the more general distinction in the United States between index crime and white-collar crime—both the crimes and the criminals are viewed differently.

(norms, values, knowledge, etc.) is largely a matter of definition; if we all agree that something is real, then it will become part of social reality, as it will be real in its consequences for all concerned. Consider the situation of the American college classroom. What makes that situation real? A collection of people making noise in a room becomes a college classroom as soon as everyone decides it should be. When employers tell you that you must spend time in college classrooms before they will hire you, they help give that situation reality. If you then go through the experience and subsequently get a job, you will taste the real consequences of an agreed-upon social definition. Note that it's not important that you actually learn anything; it's only important that you and others agree that you have. You could become very well educated through your experiences outside the classroom but never get credit for that education if no one will treat it as "real." Similarly, the grouping of people by race is an agreed-upon definition in American society; we could just as well separate people by eye color. If we all agree that the definition is real, then it will have very real consequences for all of us. Those consequences create social reality.

The function of labeling in deviance is similar to Thomas's definition of the situation; as with other aspects of social reality, deviance is an agreed-upon definition of reality. We have seen that positions of authority have the right to label, but we have yet to see why most people accept the decisions of authorities without question. Why are we more apt to accept someone else's definition of the situation as opposed to creating our own? For sociologists this is the question of how authorities maintain legitimacy.

"Legitimate" Definitions of Authority Authority is not authority without legitimacy. The sense of legitimacy we feel when confronting an authority comes from the right we feel the authority has to make certain decisions that affect us. As authorities decide, they also define social reality. To decide that burglary is more serious than embezzlement is to define burglary as a more socially dangerous act than embezzlement. If you engage in either of these acts, you will experience the reality of that definition in the responses of others to your behavior; those who accept the definitions of authority will reflect that acceptance in the way they treat you. Knowing what keeps the decisions of authorities legitimate will therefore also tell us what keeps their definitions legitimate.

In a modern industrial society such as the United States, the predominant type of authority is *legal/rational authority* (see Chapter 3). A distinctive feature of legal/rational authority is that it is attached to positions and not to individuals; individuals can exercise it only while they occupy positions of authority. If we search out these positions of authority in the United States, we find they are firmly embedded in the dominant institutions of the society. Judges are part of the criminal justice system, which is tied into the political institution (judges are elected by the people or appointed by politicians) and into the economic institution. Teachers, psychologists, and others who make decisions about students are part of the educational institution. Your spiritual conduct will be evaluated by religious officials, who are part of the institution of religion. Your ability to sell your labor will be decided upon by employers, who are part of the economic institution. In short, disputing the decisions (and definitions) of authorities will get you into a fight with a societal institution.

Institutions represent huge hunks of society; it is difficult to imagine their scope or their influence. We can see part of that scope and influence, however, in the unquestioning way that most of us accept their reality. People in prison look dangerous because they are in prison; the very environment gives you that feeling (Reiman, 1998). People in mental institutions look crazy because they are in mental institutions (Goffman, 1961b). The Rosenhan study described in Box 5.3 shows that anyone and any behavior becomes suspect just by existing within a mental hospital. Presumably, professors look knowledgeable because they are standing in the front of a classroom.

Social Definitions in Action: The Case of the Mentally Retarded What do we mean by the term *mentally retarded,* and who decides when it should be used? Both questions have almost the same answer. We generally accept the meaning provided by educational psychologists (the position with authority over that particular label), and educational psychologists decide when the term should be used. Typically, a mentally retarded individual is thought to be intellectually challenged, unable to grasp certain concepts or master certain mental operations. We also usually think of this trait as inherent in people; no matter how much they learn or what kinds of experiences they have, they will always be "slow."

Sociologist Jane Mercer became suspicious of this label in her research with the Riverside, California, school system (Mercer, 1973). Her suspicions came from the ethnic membership of classes for the mentally retarded; Mexican American children had been placed in those classes in far greater proportions than their numbers in the school system should warrant. Why? Either Mexican Americans were racially (and therefore genetically) inferior to the rest of the (Anglo) school population, or being mentally retarded actually meant that an individual was just culturally different from the people who labeled him or her as retarded.

When she looked a little more closely at the situation, Mercer discovered that one of the main reasons children were placed in classes for the mentally retarded was

BOX 5.3

Being Sane in Insane Places:
The Rosenhan Study

How do people get into and out of mental hospitals? How do they acquire the label *mentally ill?* Psychologist David Rosenhan (1973) set out to study this question by sending eight "sane" people to twelve different mental hospitals with the complaint that they were hearing voices saying things like "empty," "hollow," and "thud." Rosenhan knew these symptoms to be standard symptoms of schizophrenia that would gain these pseudopatients entry into the hospitals. From that point on, the pseudopatients were under instructions to tell no more lies and to declare the symptoms vanished. They were also instructed to take notes of their experiences for the experiment.

None of the pseudopatients was correctly identified as sane by the hospital staffs, despite their public display of their sanity on the hospital wards after their admission. The length of hospitalization ranged from seven to fifty-two days, with the average being nineteen days. Ironically, during all this time only the other mental patients recognized pronounced symptoms of sanity among the pseudopatients, with 35 of 118 real patients questioning their "craziness"; the hospital staff members tended to view the pseudopatients as cooperative but sick. The pseudopatients told their true life stories when asked, detailing the good and bad spans of their experiences and relationships such as we all have. These stories were generally viewed in a negative light by the mental health staff so as to better "explain" the mental illness they were sure existed. One nurse even took notes on the pseudopatient's note taking, putting on the nursing record, "Patient engages in writing behavior." On a mental health ward all behavior looks pathological.

Upon release the patients were labeled *schizophrenia in remission.* The implication of "remission" is that they were not cured; rather, the illness was quieted but might reappear at any time. Such a label, in these cases applied incorrectly, colors the remainder of one's life, affecting both personal relationships and public activities. Would you vote for a vice president with this label or even want such a person to teach your child?

Some mental hospital administrators told Rosenhan they doubted whether such mistakes could occur in their hospitals. Rosenhan told them he would send some pseudopatients to see how accurately they were able to pick them out. He sent none. After 193 real patients had been admitted to the hospitals, Rosenhan questioned the staff as to which were real and which were pseudopatients. Of the 193 patients,

(continues)

BOX 5.3

Being Sane in Insane Places:
The Rosenhan Study (continued)

43 were selected by at least one staff member (with a high degree of confidence) to be pseudopatients.

Rosenhan's study tells us about labeling the mentally ill and also provides some more general insights about our society. The fact that the pseudopatients looked crazy to the hospital staffs suggests the ease with which we accept the "rightness" of our institutions. An individual's existence under a label tends to be accepted as truth when an entire institution operates on that basis.

their score on an intelligence (IQ) test. How can a test measure intelligence? A test can measure what you know about something, your ability to handle certain kinds of problems, and (perhaps most significantly) your ability to take tests. But if you don't know about something or can't handle a problem, does that mean you're retarded or simply that you're lacking a certain experience? In looking more closely at the IQ tests themselves, Mercer found that they were based almost entirely on the experiences typical of a middle-class European American child. If you had any other ethnic background, your experience with the content of the test items would be limited, and, ultimately, so would your score. Children were being labeled as mentally retarded because they lacked some of the cultural experiences common to other children in their school system.

Like other deviants, the mentally retarded have been judged and labeled by an established societal authority—in this case, the educational psychologist. And as with all such labeling situations, a social definition is created that most of us come to accept.

Boundary Maintenance: Victimless Crimes and Respectability One of the most important social realities created by the deviant label is separation of groups. Sociologists refer to this phenomenon as **boundary maintenance** (as we maintain the boundary between us "good" people over here and you "bad" people over there). Labels of deviance are very effective in maintaining boundaries in that the label givers are able to contrast the wonderfulness of themselves with the horribleness of the deviant. Just as you seldom become aware of your culture until you meet someone from another culture, you seldom become aware of your norms until you meet someone who breaks them. Then you (and all who share those norms) can communally label the deviant, reaffirm your common membership in one social group, and remind yourselves where your group ends and the other begins. It is, in fact, essential for members of social groups to maintain their boundaries in this way. The label of deviance will be created from thin air if necessary just to have something to point to as a violation. In short, group members create deviance; deviant individuals are but pawns in the game (Erikson, 1966).

Boundary maintenance theory suggests that the desire of the respectable people in society is often more to punish others than to protect themselves from becoming victims. We can see boundary maintenance operating in the area of crimes with victims by looking at capital punishment in the United States. Repeated research has shown consistently that the presence of capital punishment is not a significant deterrent to criminal activity (see Peterson and Bailey, 1991). Yet most Americans favor capital punishment. Because it doesn't keep them safer, it presumably makes them feel better in some other way.

Of all the laws on the books in the United States, those that most clearly serve this function are laws against victimless crimes. These, you'll recall, are those forms of criminal behavior in which no one "gets hurt," unless you want to count the criminal. Consider a case that could be made for heroin. Contrary to popular opinion, there is little evidence that heroin is as physically damaging as laws against it suggest, especially compared with the effects of cigarettes and alcohol. Heroin is more addictive than cigarettes (although some have argued the opposite), and addiction isn't a pleasant idea to most of us, but why is that the government's business? The physical problems most generally associated with heroin are, in fact, withdrawal symptoms, and those symptoms wouldn't occur if heroin weren't illegal and were, on the contrary, inexpensive and readily available. Most deaths due to overdoses (except those that are intentional suicide) are caused by variations in the strength of heroin bought on the street. By making the possession or sale of heroin a serious crime, the government has managed to push the price of heroin sky high, which leads those who use it to commit crimes to earn money to support their habit. (There is indeed a strong association between drug use and being booked for a criminal offense; Harrison and Gfroerer, 1992.) The cost of this drug-related crime plus the cost of drug-related law enforcement easily runs into billions of dollars a year. American taxpayers (most of whom would rather not consume heroin personally) are apparently willing to pay this price to keep current drug laws on the books. Are they getting their money's worth? To the extent that such expenses provide the satisfaction of boundary maintenance, it would seem reasonable to assume that boundary maintenance is a very valuable commodity indeed. (See Courtwright, 1991, for a further discussion of this side of the argument.)

Similar arguments could be made concerning laws against homosexuality, gambling, prostitution, and other activities entered into by consenting adults. Note the difference in the way the law deals with alcohol (which is currently respectable in the United States). Alcohol use becomes a crime only when it threatens someone besides the user (such as in drunk driving) or when the "criminal" is too poor to

Prostitution is sometimes called "the oldest profession," yet it continues to be thought of as a deviant activity in the United States. Those who hire and pay prostitutes, however, are rarely considered deviant. There appears to be a boundary maintained here between sellers (female) and buyers (male).

have a classy place to drink and gets arrested for public intoxication at the corner of Tenth and Main. Crimes without victims are illegal anywhere under any circumstances, even if kept totally private and off everyone's toes. Such laws represent a public statement about our group's norms and values and, ultimately, allow us to define "respectability." An example of these sorts of values in action is reflected in American attitudes toward various aspects of homosexuality. According to a 2004 Gallup Poll, 89 percent of Americans believe that homosexuals should have equal rights in job opportunities (compared with 71 percent in 1989 and 56 percent in 1977). Lest you think that all attitudes regarding homosexuals reflect such a "liberalization," however, only 52 percent of that same sample believes that sexual relations between homosexuals should be legalized; that figure went up a scant 9 percentage points between 1977 and 2004 (Gallup Poll, 2004a). Since these laws involve consenting adults in the privacy of their own homes, public attitudes that support restricting relations suggest the lack of respectability that continues to be associated with homosexuality.

Respectability means being well thought of by others, but we'll need a more precise definition to capture the real meaning. An expert safecracker may be well thought of by other safecrackers, but is that really respectability? We return once again to the question of authority. To be respectable, you must be well thought of by the "right" people because you exemplify the "right" norms and values. As we've seen, being "right" means being in power and having authority. Because victimless crimes are defined by those in authority (as is all criminal behavior), such laws serve to define respectability at the same time they define deviance. And that is why they are so important. The exercise of authority that creates victimless crimes becomes necessary to justify the lifestyles of the very people who currently hold that authority. It reiterates their moral right to hold that authority. Boundary maintenance is just one aspect of the overall process through which social reality is created.

RESPONSES TO DEVIANCE: COURTS AND PRISONS

Some form of social control is the standard response to deviance. Group members typically take a dim view of having their norms broken, and their response will generally be in keeping with the importance they place on the norm(s). Acts of deviance considered mild (becoming too loud at a party, for instance) will receive milder forms of social control (such as not being invited back). Most of us commit such acts of deviance every day and are used to these forms of social control. As acts of deviance violate increasingly important norms, however, social control escalates accordingly. If your social blunders become too severe, you may face general ostracism from your community. At some point in this progression informal means of social control will give way to formal means. If your behavior becomes seen as criminal, the police, courts, and prisons will intervene. If it becomes seen as dangerous and irrational, the police, courts, and mental health practitioners will intervene. This section examines some of these formal means of social control.

In dealing with criminal behavior, courts are entrusted with determining guilt and assessing a penalty on guilty parties. Prisons are entrusted with carrying out the penalties involving incarceration or execution, the most severe penalties currently used in the United States. All citizens are supposed to be equal before the law and should therefore receive treatment consistent with others charged with the same law violations. In addition, most people have hopes that the system of criminal justice might play some role in the rehabilitation of the lawbreaking individuals it processes. As we look more closely at the system of criminal justice in the United States, however, we find considerable variation from these goals.

Whatever else they may or may not do, courts and prisons serve to keep large numbers of people off the streets. In 2002, about 2.8 percent of Americans were incarcerated or under correctional supervision; this percentage had risen from 1.3 percent in 1985. For African Americans in 2002, 9.0 percent lived within the criminal justice system (U.S. Department of Justice, 2003d, 2003e; U.S. Bureau of the Census, 2004a). Many of these people had not even been convicted of a crime but were merely awaiting trial. The dominant orientation of jails and prisons is custodial. Prisoners generally learn how to play the role of prisoner and, perhaps more important (and it almost goes without saying), they get very angry regardless of their guilt or innocence.

Beyond the inability to turn convicted criminals into law-abiding citizens, there is also some question as to the fairness of both courts and prisons as far as who goes through the system and who doesn't. This question focuses in part on racism in the criminal justice system. African Americans make up a little more than 12 percent of the U.S. population, yet they account for 27 percent of all arrests and 45 percent of the state and federal prison populations. Perhaps more significant is that fact that these percentages have been rising in recent years (U.S. Department of Justice, 2003e). Moving these statistics to more individual terms, an African American individual is eight times more likely to be in prison on any given day than a European American individual is.

Perhaps most striking, of all the prisoners executed since 1930 in the United States, 2,375 have been European American and 2,385 have been African American; if you look just at executions for the crime of rape, only 48 European Americans have been executed compared with 405 African Americans (U.S. Bureau of the Census, 2000, 2004a). In 2004, African Americans made up nearly 42 percent of all prisoners living on death row (under sentence of death) (U.S. Department of Justice, 2003d). Such inequity was brought before the U.S. Supreme Court in 1986 in the case of *McCleskey v. Kemp*. The justices were further informed that any defendant who killed a European American was 4.3 times more likely to receive the death penalty than a defendant who killed an African American. The Supreme Court ruled in 1987 that the death penalty was constitutional anyway (U.S. Supreme Court Reports, 1987). Such a finding is of additional interest considering that there is little evidence that capital punishment has any effect on reducing acts of murder (see Bowers, Pierce, and McDevitt, 1984).

A further look at particular arrest statistics (U.S. Department of Justice, 2003a) shows that while African Americans accounted for over 27 percent of all arrests in 2002, they accounted for 40 percent of arrests for prostitution and vice and 68.3 percent of arrests for gambling. These arrests for victimless crimes may well indicate a certain amount of harassment on the part of the police. When was the last time you witnessed an upstanding European American member of your community hauled off to jail for betting on a football game? On the other hand, African Americans also dominate many of the FBI's index crimes—African American arrests account for 54.1 percent of robbery arrests, 50 percent of murder arrests, and 34 percent of forcible rape arrests (U.S. Department of Justice, 2003a).

An interesting arrest statistic is that African Americans make up 40.9 percent of all arrests for suspicion (U.S. Department of Justice, 2003a). One has to wonder if such individuals look suspicious because they walk around inside of black skin and are subject to stereotypical expectations of arresting officers. While there is some indication that police patrol more heavily in African American areas (and arrests tend to go up and down with the degree of police activity [Jernigan and Kronick, 1992]), African Americans almost certainly commit a much higher proportion of index crimes (based on their percentage in the population) than European Americans. And since we have already seen that index crimes result in the stiffest prison sentences, this fact could account for the high percentage of African Americans in prison.

How do we account for these statistics? Are the police and judges racists who discriminate in their treatment of African Americans? That's a possibility, although it's difficult to know for sure. The vast majority of American judges are European American, and the majority of American police are European American; the racial separation in the United States has created widespread distrust between European Americans and African Americans, and racism could well be a factor. The beating of Rodney King in Los Angeles coupled with police officer Mark Fuhrman's racist comments coming to light during the O. J. Simpson trial would both support such a conclusion. Police have at times been accused of **racial profiling**—the practice of singling out members of specific racial groups for more attention than they would otherwise warrant through their behavior (Withrow, 2004; Engel and Calnon, 2004). Most research, however, indicates that police bias, if any, is more likely to be based on the social class of the alleged criminal than on race or ethnicity; research results are mixed, however (Klinger, 1994; Lundman, 1994; Sheley, 1993).

Perhaps not surprisingly, the most accurate explanation for these statistics lies somewhere between criminal justice system discrimination and a high degree of African American criminal activity. In past years African Americans clearly faced massive discrimination, as the execution rates for rape point out. Much of this discrimination is no doubt still with us. On the other hand, African Americans probably do commit more than their share of index crime. Looking more closely, however, we see that most of these statistics concern lower-class African Americans as opposed to middle- and upper-class African Americans. Because African Americans

A bystander happened to film the savage beating inflicted upon Rodney King by the police. Mr. King had not committed any violent crime. When the news media showed the film, the public reacted in outrage. Would the beating have taken place if Mr. King were white? And how many such beatings take place where the only witnesses are the police?

are proportionately poorer than European Americans in the United States, their large numbers in the criminal justice system might indicate that the system discriminates not so much against African American people as against poor people (many of whom are African American). Who, then, are the European American people who are arrested and end up in prison?

Prisoners in the United States represent pretty much a cross-section of poor people in the United States. Part of this apparent discrimination against poor people may be a result of active discrimination by individuals in the criminal justice system; to middle-class judges and juries poor people just "look" more guilty, and poor families don't "seem" a proper environment for a juvenile offender to return to. Much of the discrimination against poor people, however, results from the general workings of the criminal justice institution itself. We've already seen that poor people tend to commit more index (as opposed to white-collar) crime and that index crime is viewed as being more serious and hence entails longer prison terms. Beyond that, we find the bail system.

The bail system in the United States provides a means for individuals to remain free between arrest and trial by posting bond (leaving a specified amount of money) with the court. If they do not appear for trial, this bond is forfeited; if they appear, it is returned. The amount is set by the judge according to the crime and its potential penalty, the theory being that an individual is more likely to skip town on a murder charge than a shoplifting offense. Individuals who own property are obviously better able to post bond than poor individuals. Wealthy individuals, in fact, are sometimes not even required to post bond; they are released on their "own recognizance" on the grounds that their property holdings in the area will ensure their presence. In addition, individuals able to make bail are also more likely to be acquitted when they do come to trial (Reiman, 1998). In short, the bail system benefits people with money and penalizes those without it.

One of the reasons individuals who can afford bail are more likely to be acquitted is that they can also afford lawyers. In the past, poor people simply did without legal representation. This practice was declared unconstitutional by the Supreme Court, and today in the United States anyone indicted for a felony crime has access to a public defender, a lawyer paid by the court. Public defenders are notoriously undertrained, underpaid, and overworked. Not surprisingly, the representation they provide is not usually the best. One of the reasons for inadequate representation (and one of the ways public defenders cut down on their work load) is the practice of plea bargaining.

Plea bargaining is the result of a bargaining session between the public defender (or any defense lawyer) and the prosecution. The prosecution agrees to lessen the charge against the defendant in exchange for a guilty plea. The vast majority of all American criminal proceedings operate with a plea of guilty achieved through plea bargaining. The courts, which are already overworked, could not function without this system, as jury trials are time consuming. The overwhelming majority of court cases begin with a guilty plea. In 2002 in the U.S. District Courts, 84 percent of all defendants charged with crimes pled guilty (U.S. Department of Justice, 2003d). The poorer defendant, threatened with the possibility of a long sentence at the end of a trial, may be pressured to accept the plea bargain even if the evidence for any criminal activity appears inconclusive. A paid lawyer is likely to weigh the evidence more than the work, since the amount of work will be paid for; the public defender earns the same income no matter how much work a case requires and has little free time to be creative.

The American criminal justice system responds most clearly to those acts commonly considered to be the most deviant. It also responds to those lawbreakers commonly considered to be the most dangerous: lower-class individuals. Although new kinds of rehabilitation programs are developed and tried from time to time, little funding is available for them; most taxpayers would rather see their tax dollars go elsewhere. Most of the people who end up in prison are poor, and they come out of prison the same way. As ex-offenders, they must face society's reaction to the label of their deviance—problems in finding jobs, housing, and friends. One alternative, of course, is to return to whatever lifestyle brought them to prison in the first place.

DEVIANCE AND SOCIAL CHANGE: WHEN DOES CREATIVITY BECOME DANGEROUS?

Deviance exists only because norms and values exist; if rules are made to be broken, deviance is the behavior that does it. We've looked thus far at some of the behavior labeled as deviant in the United States and at some responses to that behavior. It is important to keep in mind, however, that if deviance never occurred, norms and values would, by definition, never change, and we would have a pretty stagnant society. In this sense deviance is creative, as individuals try out alternatives to the status quo. Without deviance a society would be unable to adapt to changing circumstances. The question is: when do people find this creativity useful and when do they find it dangerous?

Unfortunately, there is no one answer to this question. Many of the greatest advances in the worlds of art, music, science, religion, literature, and certainly politics met extremely hostile responses in their day. It is almost tempting to suggest that the greater the level of genius, the greater the likelihood the genius will be labeled deviant. Creativity seems acceptable only when it moves slowly, giving others suitable time to get used to it. The paintings of van Gogh, unappreciated during his lifetime, now sell for record sums. The first doctor to suggest the possible presence of "germs" as a cause of disease died in a mental institution. And of course Christianity, like almost all religions, developed amid persecution and attacks upon its followers.

In part, then, deviance exists because of people's adherence to norms and values coupled with the need for social change that is always present in human societies. Creative behavior in response to those needs becomes deviance almost by the very nature of its creativity. Culture, in short, encourages creativity while simultaneously labeling that creativity deviant. The study of deviance rests on the fine line between cultural stability on the one hand and social change on the other. The relativity of deviance makes this study very difficult. We know that today's deviant may be tomorrow's savior. Today's deviant also may be tomorrow's deviant, however.

SUMMARY

Deviance is any behavior that breaks the norms and violates the values of a social group. Such behavior acquires the label of deviance when the social group in question possesses the power or authority to dominate those engaging in the deviance and to control their behavior.

Although the varieties of deviance are as boundless as the norms and values they violate, they may be divided into criminal and noncriminal forms. Criminal behavior is any behavior formally proscribed in a society by law or custom. The content of behavior has no relation to its label as deviant, as is indicated by the existence of victimless crimes—crimes in which the criminal is the only victim. Noncriminal behavior as deviance includes even the smallest violation of folkways, but major forms include alcoholism, mental retardation, and behavior considered to be irrational by societal authorities (labeled *mental illness* in the United States).

Theories explaining the existence of deviance may be separated into those that focus on the deviant individual (deviant-centered theories) and those that focus on society (society-centered theories). The former include theories that view biological and personality disorders as causes for individuals to vary from established norms. The latter include theories that point out the encouragement individuals receive from society for deviance (differential association theory and anomie theory) and others that find the source of deviance in the authorities that label it as such (labeling theory and the radical theories).

Behavior considered to be deviant could not exist without the authorities in society that have acquired the right (in the eyes of most members of society) to determine deviance. Such authorities often respond with a label of deviance when the behavior in question not only breaks norms but also attacks their right to label. As ongoing parts of social institutions, authorities are in an excellent position to present their labels and to have them accepted as part of social reality by most members of society. These "social definitions" are taken for granted, along with the legitimacy of the authority. One particular function of these definitions is to set boundaries between social groups, separating those who adhere to the social definition from those who are labeled by it as deviants.

Deviant behavior that is considered extreme by authorities is commonly responded to formally. Criminal behavior is responded to through the criminal justice system, which in the United States tends to focus almost entirely on poor people. Noncriminal deviant behavior is responded to in appropriate institutions; "irrational" behavior may be dealt with by mental health authorities, while unusual intellectual behavior may be labeled retardation by educational institutions.

Finally, deviance is an important source of social change. Deviance is often, in effect, creative behavior—some of which is necessary for adaptation to changing circumstances.

GLOSSARY

Anomie A state of normlessness in a society, when many people are unclear about what is expected of them.

Anomie theory A theory of deviance that explains varieties of deviant acts as responses to the socially produced strain of anomie.

Authority The right to control the behavior of others.

Boundary maintenance Any behavior that reminds the members of a social group of the boundaries between their group and others, distinguishing between "us" and "them." Boundary maintenance increases group solidarity.

Definition of the situation As defined by W. I. Thomas, the concept that social reality is a matter of definition; if members of a social group agree to the reality of anything, then it will be real in its consequences.

Deviance Behavior that violates the norms of a social group.

Deviant subculture A subculture viewed by both its members and outsiders as having norms and values fundamentally, and often threateningly, different from those of the general culture.

Differential association theory A theory of deviance that explains deviant acts as involving a change in attitudes of the deviant acquired through association with other deviants.

Index crime Crime considered as major by the FBI, including murder, forcible rape, robbery, aggravated assault, burglary, larceny/theft, and motor vehicle theft.

Juvenile delinquency Illegal behavior committed by individuals who are legally minors (usually under age eighteen).

Labeling theory A theory of deviance that views deviance as a label assigned to behavior and individuals by particular figures of authority.

Plea bargaining The result of a bargaining session between the public defender (or any defense lawyer) and the prosecution, in which the prosecution agrees to lessen the charge against the defendant in exchange for a guilty plea.

Power The probability for control over the behavior of others.

Primary deviance The commission of a deviant act without the knowledge of others, particularly those with the authority to label deviance. The primary deviant is not treated as a deviant.

Racial profiling The practice of singling out members of specific racial groups for more attention than they would otherwise warrant through their behavior.

Radical theory As applied to deviance, a theory that sees social control as an attempt by the ruling class of society to maintain its dominance. A criminal justice system, for example, is viewed as both protecting the current distribution of property in society and focusing the attentions of the middle class on lower-class lawbreakers and away from upper-class lawbreakers.

Secondary deviance Deviance that is labeled as such; the individual is treated as a deviant.

Social control theory A theory of deviance that explains deviant behavior as either a breakdown in the socialization process (as constraints on behavior are not internalized) or a loosening of ties within social groups to the point that others do not constrain the acts of the deviant individual.

Social reality The social norms, values, knowledge, and so on that define a given situation.

Status crimes Behavior considered criminal only when performed by members of a particular social status (for example, only a minor can be a runaway).

Subculture A social group or collection of social groups that exists within a larger culture yet has distinctive norms and values that set it off from the larger culture.

Victimless crimes Crimes in which there is no victim but the criminal, including prostitution, drug use, gambling, and homosexual acts.

White-collar crime Crime committed by middle-class and upper-class people in the course of an otherwise legal occupation, including fraud, tax evasion, and antitrust violations.

STUDY QUESTIONS
1. How do definitions of deviance change from one social group to the next? How does variation in norms produce varying definitions of deviance? Why is the concept of authority so central in understanding all these variations?
2. What is the relationship between deviant behavior and illegal behavior? When does the former become the latter?
3. Compare index crime and white-collar crime. Why is index crime much more severely punished?
4. What are victimless crimes? How do they differ from most other types of crime? How does the perspective of boundary maintenance provide some explanation for why victimless crimes are crimes?
5. What are the similarities and differences between differential association theory and subcultural theory?
6. What perspective does labeling theory take on deviance? How does labeling theory utilize the concept of authority? What is the difference between primary deviance and secondary deviance?

7. What is anomie? How does anomie theory view deviance? What are the typical types of deviant and conforming responses to anomie?

8. How does radical theory view authority in the creation of deviance? How would it explain the difference between index crime and white-collar crime? How does it view corporate crime?

9. How does Thomas's definition of the situation help us understand definitions of deviance? What makes those definitions "legitimate"?

10. What kinds of people are arrested and go to prison in the United States? What are their crimes? How wealthy are they? What color are they? How can these results be explained by studying the criminal justice system?

Myra Isaacs Pearson

DEVIL'S CHILD DOIN' TIME: THE SOCIALIZATION OF AN AMERICAN DEVIANT

"Where do deviants come from?" As you have seen from this chapter, sociologists differ in their answers to that question. A common thread running through many theories, however, is that deviants are produced through socialization, just like everyone else. They differ only in the form and content of that socialization.

Myra Isaacs Pearson offers the following autobiographical sketch as evidence. A combination of early childhood neglect and "doin' time" at an orphanage (and later at a reform school) resulted in her facing American society as an essentially clueless young adult. What everyone else knew, she did not. Values that others held sacred were missing from her experience; if anything, her upbringing made an adult deviant lifestyle seem more in tune with what she already knew.

Do not expect to have a particularly good time while reading the following story. But if you find Pearson's life story hard to read, consider that it was much harder to live.

I am a genuine, dyed-in-the-wool, irretrievable American deviant. I've been that way pretty much my whole life. There have been times when I've worn it all like a badge of honor; other times I've wanted nothing more than to just be "normal." Now, at the age of forty-six, having finally realized how little choice I had in the matter, I've arrived at a Zen-like approach to the whole situation: that's just the way it is.

I was born in the summer of 1952 to a mentally ill mother and an alcoholic father. According to a story my mother told me in her later years, I was actually labeled a deviant even before I was born. It seems that, although she had been raised a Baptist, by the time she became pregnant with me, she had converted to Pentecostalism. One night, a woman who was a "prophet" in the church she attended came to her and told her that

© 1998 by Myra Isaacs Pearson. Ms. Pearson would like to acknowledge the work of Erving Goffman in shaping her ideas. She encourages others who have experienced childhood institutionalization to contact her at 1225 Dodd Rd., Richmond, KY 40475.

the child she was carrying was "black." Because both of my parents were what has always been labeled "white," my mother made the logical assumption: the child she was carrying was the Devil's child.

Since I have no memories of interacting with other humans before the age of four, I cannot say how, or even if, this event affected her treatment of me as an infant and small child. Based on a few stories I've heard as an adult, however, I can loosely conjecture as to how things were for me in those earliest years of my life. I've been told, for instance, that the symptoms of my mother's illness included paranoia, hallucinations, hysterical paralysis, and outright catatonia. Because of the diversity and severity of these symptoms, she was periodically institutionalized during these years, and on at least one occasion even given shock treatments. I've also been told that during this period my father, who had picked up tuberculosis while serving in the Navy in Korea, actually spent more time living at the VA hospital than at home. By the time I was a year or a year-and-a-half old, the state had intervened in the situation and taken my three older siblings away. For some reason, however, it was decided that I would remain at home with my mother for the time being.

I have only heard a few stories about experiences I had after my father and siblings were out of the picture. One came from a man who had been our neighbor during that time. He told me that once, on his way home from work, he found me wandering alone several blocks from where I lived. He picked me up and took me home, only to discover that my mother was catatonic. A similar story came from one of my uncles, who told me how he once arrived from out-of-state for a visit, and again, found my mother catatonic. He didn't know how long she'd been that way, he said, but there was evidence that it had been long enough for her menstrual period to come and go. During this time, I had apparently been on my own. Whenever incidents like these occurred, either my mother and I would go to stay with some relative, or she would be hospitalized and I

would go alone to a relative's house. At any rate, as soon as she "got to feeling better," the two of us would return home.

The only other story I have heard from this period of my life came from my mother herself, and it's the single "happy" story in the bunch. It seems that during those times when she was "feeling better," one of her favorite activities was to take me down to the local drugstore. She knew both the employees and the regular customers there, and often the two of us were the recipients of treats or small gifts. As far as I can tell, it was also during these outings that others (outside my family) first began to remark on how "smart" I was—not only in terms of how fast and well I could learn, but in terms of "having a mind of my own." According to my mother, I became something of a minor celebrity among the folks down at the drugstore.

Although, as I have said, I have no memories of such interactions with others during these years, I do remember, in fair-to-middling detail, the small one-room apartment that my mother and I lived in. I also have one vague memory of pushing a small chair over to the refrigerator in order to gain access to a roll of bologna—which I promptly sat down and ate from with a spoon.

When these memory fragments are considered together with the stories I have related, it all seems to suggest at least two things about my earliest years which may not have firmly planted my feet on the path to deviance, but almost certainly helped point me in that direction. The first is that during this time I apparently did a lot of bouncing back and forth between extremes—that is, between periods of profound social isolation and periods of being the center of attention. Second, it also seems that I would have had to achieve—especially during those periods of profound social isolation—an unusually high level of independence for a child between the ages of one and four.

If these situations did indeed point me in the direction of deviance, the event which undeniably—and irrevocably—hurled me onto that path occurred shortly after my fourth birthday. It was then (with my father near death and my mother permanently institutionalized) that the state finally claimed me for its own and I was sent to join my brother and sisters in prison. Yes, prison.

THE ORPHANAGE AS PRISON

The name of the place was The Ohio Soldiers' and Sailors' Orphans' Home, but in reality it was everything that makes a prison a prison. First of all, the physical structure was designed to keep us in and the rest of the world out. Since we were children and escape was thus not a significant concern, the objective was not to make free movement across the institution's boundaries impossible, just unnecessary. This was accomplished with a physical plant that included two schools (one regular and one trade), a hospital, a produce and dairy farm, a church, a theater, a laundry, a barber shop, clothing "stores," repair shops, administrative office buildings, and housing for employees. We even had our own power plant and water tower.

A second prisonlike characteristic of the orphanage was the fact that the structure of its internal environment enabled staff members to keep an eye on us at all times. More importantly, it also maximized the general scope of their power over us. To begin with, we were forced to do everything in large groups. Each of the thirty-four "cottages" housed roughly eighteen to twenty children of the same age and sex, and all cottage mates were additionally required to attend school, church, the theater, and the dining hall together. There was also a proper time and a rule for everything. This meant that, along with being forced to do everything in large groups, we were additionally forced to do everything alike.

While the first of these two strategies maximized the staff's capacity for surveillance, the second made even minor infractions stand out like a sore thumb. And when that happened, the severest of consequences could follow. For instance, according to schedule and rule, we were required to wash our faces before breakfast. One morning I neglected to do this, and although I raced to the bathroom immediately after break-

fast to rectify the situation, I was too late. The cottage parent had arrived there before me, and my lone dry wash cloth had stood out in stark contrast to everyone else's wet ones. As punishment, she forced me to strip and get in the tub, where she proceeded to scrub me with a brush until I was covered with welts and scratches. Since this forced me to be late for school, she was obliged to write an explanatory note to my teacher. In this note—which she had ordered me to read aloud to the whole class—she described in detail what she had done to me, citing not my failure to wash my face at the proper time as her reason for doing it, but my "extreme filthiness."

Another aspect of the orphanage's internal environment—the one that maximized the general scope of the staff's power over us—was its system of authority. In this system, any staff member could punish any inmate, for any (real or fabricated) infraction, any time he or she saw fit, and often in any way he or she saw fit. I remember one day, for example, when a small group of about a half-dozen girls got punished for "sneaking out" of their cottage the night before. It was not their cottage "parent" who punished them, but the burly school principal and his equally burly sister, the girls' gym teacher. The girls were forced to roll up the legs of their pants and crawl—not on their hands and knees, but on their knees alone—up and down the sidewalk between their cottage and the chapel (a distance of about a quarter of a mile). It was a hot day, and several hours into their punishment, one of the girls passed out from heat exhaustion. The principal and his sister managed to bring her around—and then promptly beat her back into unconsciousness.

In addition to a highly inclusive physical plant and an internal environment that maximized the staff's capacity for surveillance and the general scope of its power, a third prisonlike characteristic of the orphanage was its privilege system. The standard privileges we were offered included being allowed to watch TV, engage in physical recreation, and attend the movie that was shown in the theater every Saturday night. Obviously, in addition to being few in number, these standard privileges were not really true indulgences, but merely a matter of not being deprived. Moreover, when push came to shove, almost anything could wind up being labeled a privilege: visiting with our families, making phone calls, even talking, eating, and being with other people. Any action or attitude that deviated from expectations—no matter how slightly—could result in the withdrawal of privileges. In this Spartan environment, that was serious enough. However, as this essay will continue to illustrate, punishments could be much more severe.

Finally, a fourth (and for me, the most) prisonlike characteristic of the orphanage was the fact that, from the day we entered the place, constant humiliation was a daily reality. The admissions procedures alone were rife with humiliating experiences. For the first week or two, we were isolated in the hospital. While we were there we experienced being undressed, bathed, and disinfected. We also underwent a series of medical exams and procedures, and were given standard haircuts and uniform-style clothing. As small children, being suddenly thrown into an environment that did not remotely resemble anything we had ever known and where everyone was a stranger was terrifying enough. These admissions procedures only added insult to injury. Yet if we balked at anything that was done to us, we were quickly and sharply reprimanded—and sometimes even physically assaulted. I myself do not remember this initial period of my incarceration, but my oldest sister has told me that when she started crying at the prospect of being vaccinated, she was slapped and told to "quit being such a baby."

Once we were released from the hospital, we quickly discovered that humiliating experiences were to be an integral part of our daily lives. Many such experiences simply accrued to standard practices which collectively served to rob us of privacy. These included toilet stalls without doors, dormitory-style sleeping arrangements, locker rooms for dressing, having to stand in line naked at shower time, having our mail cen-

sored, and being forced to undergo periodic and often unannounced searches of ourselves and our quarters.

However, the experiences which were far and away the most humiliating were those which were part and parcel of the general way in which the staff related to the children. It was not unusual for us to be called names, cursed at, made fun of, and treated like nonentities. And if a child responded defensively to some humiliating experience, that response itself was often used to justify not only the original experience, but an additional one as well. For instance, it was not uncommon for accidents and uncontrollable behaviors such as bedwetting, belching, breaking wind, and vomiting to be labeled deliberate actions. As such, they were all subject to punishment. It was also not uncommon, when an infraction had been committed and the culprit was unknown, for a child to be arbitrarily chosen as the culprit. Whenever a child got caught in one of these situations, the worst thing he or she could do was to assert innocence and protest punishment—because this was likely to result in either a more severe punishment or an additional one.

Being unusually gifted or talented in some way could also be a source of humiliation, albeit a more indirect one. This point was driven home to me countless times throughout my years as a child inmate. For in addition to the intellectual ability that had manifested itself so early, it became apparent while I was still quite young that I possessed unusual musical and artistic abilities as well. In later years this "multi-giftedness" would prove to be of great assistance in my enormous—and still ongoing—struggle to overcome the psychosocial legacy of my childhood. During my childhood itself, however, it generated quite a different set of consequences. For not only did it make it virtually impossible for me to adjust to institutional life anywhere near as well as most of the other children did, it tended to elicit resentment from the staff.

This latter situation makes sense when one considers that state-run institutions do not exactly tend to attract the cream of the crop as employees. The pay is usually lousy, and many institutional jobs require that one become what basically amounts to a voluntary inmate. This was the case for all of our cottage parents as well as a number of other employees. In addition, many employees who were not required to live on the grounds chose to do so anyway. It should come as no surprise, then, that a not insignificant number of these people were social isolates themselves. And it should also come as no surprise that they would consequently tend to resent unusually gifted or talented children and target them for humiliation. I could not even begin to remember all the times when my humiliating treatment at the hands of some staff member was preceded by statements like, "You think you're so smart," or, "You act like you're so special."

Of all the experiences which were part and parcel of the general way the staff related to the children, the ones which were far and away the most humiliating were those in which we were forced to humiliate ourselves. We were forced, for instance, to call our cottage parents "mommy"— even though there was precious little among the whole lot of them that was even remotely maternalistic. We were also forced to stand at attention in the presence of certain staff members, request permission to perform minor activities and receive minor supplies, witness the punishments of other children, and eat all of our food no matter how unpalatable we found it.

By now, you are no doubt wondering why the orphanage would possess such a prison-like character. The most logical and readily apparent answer to this question is simply that it shared some essential structural needs with prisons. To begin with, the need to minimize operating costs resulted in a double-edged situation that is also common to prisons: the inmates vastly outnumbered the staff members, and, as previously mentioned, the staff members tended to be somewhat less than ideally competent. In addition, the inmates at the orphanage, like the inmates in prisons, were there involuntarily.

Under such conditions, an institution would logically be obliged to establish a system for controlling the inmates that is both as effective and as efficient as possible. The most effectively controlled people are those who are completely obedient in both action and attitude, and the use of force is the most efficient means of producing such people. The optimal use of force, in turn, calls for an environment in which barriers to surveillance and constraints on the power of authority figures are both minimal, and barriers to outside influences are maximal.

REBELLION

By now you should be beginning to see why being forced to grow up in this environment was virtually destined to hurl me onto the path of deviance. For on the one hand, what we have in this story is a gifted child with a mind of her own who has, by the age of four, already been forced to see to her own survival. On the other hand is a totally encompassing, highly Spartan, and extremely homogeneous environment where daily life is profoundly monotonous, and nothing is expected of those who are forced to live there but to obey. It is only logical to expect that there would be some mutual—and serious—problems with adjustment here.

It should come as no surprise, then, that my oldest memory of interacting with others is one in which I was being dragged, screaming and fighting for all I was worth, up the stairs of the orphanage school to my first day of kindergarten (yes, even the four-year-olds had to attend school). While oppressive social environments can produce many different kinds of deviants, obviously I was destined to be a rebel.

For the first eight and a half years of my incarceration, my rebellion was purely situational and enacted only in my own behalf. The primary problem was that it was extremely difficult for me to keep my mouth shut whenever I was faced with punishment either for doing something I couldn't help, or for something I hadn't done in the first place. I didn't rebel every single time one of these things happened; in fact, more often than not, I managed to abstain. But when I did rebel, it was with unrestrained vehemence. Getting me back under control on these occasions tended to take a lot of time and energy—sometimes on the part of several staff members.

Besides being a rebel virtually from the word "go," sometime during my early years at the orphanage I became another sort of deviant— one of the worst kinds an institutionalized child can be. I became a bedwetter. Although this was obviously an uncontrollable reaction to the profound stress which institutional life induced in me, it was, as I have previously noted, labeled intentional deviance. For several years, however, I was lucky enough that it only happened occasionally, and that when it did, my punishment was usually the withdrawal of a privilege.

But all that changed the summer of my ninth birthday—when I was unlucky enough to be transferred into the cottage of a woman who quickly decided that she simply didn't like me. Although I was transferred to another cottage two years later, incredibly, she was also transferred to that same cottage a short time later. Altogether, I remained under her care for three and a half of the four years between my ninth and thirteenth birthdays—a situation that would culminate in my rebelliousness undergoing a major "growth spurt."

From the very beginning, this woman was constantly looking for excuses to punish or humiliate me, and my bedwetting gave her an opportunity to combine the two in what would ultimately be one of the most traumatic experiences of my entire childhood. For while she delighted in administering public paddlings whenever I wet the bed, her favorite punishment was to make me wear "the diaper." This was a one-piece plastic covered contraption that laced up both sides and was extremely bulky. It was impossible not to detect under one's clothing, and sometimes she did not even permit me to wear clothing over it. Normally, this punishment was of short duration because there was only one diaper, and usually

several bedwetters, per cottage. However, for the whole time I was under this woman's care, my bedwetting cottage mates rarely had to wear the diaper—because she pretty much kept me in it. In fact, at one point she even borrowed another cottage's diaper just to make sure that I'd have one to wear at all times.

Of course, all of this only increased the stress I was under, and my bedwetting thus occurred with ever greater frequency. Eventually it became pretty much a nightly occurrence. And throughout it all, my hatred of this woman kept growing, edging ever nearer to the boiling point.

That point came one day early in the summer of my thirteenth birthday. I had just returned to my cottage from band practice and gone out to the playground—where I found my best friend sobbing behind a tree. It took a few minutes, but I soon discovered the reason for her devastation: my friend, who had been given the extremely rare opportunity of allowing her hair to grow long, had just been informed by that witch of a cottage parent that she was going to cut it all off. She was not doing this because my friend had failed to take care of her hair or had committed some other infraction; the wretched woman just wanted to see how she would look with short hair.

Now, in case any readers fail to understand why the child was so utterly devastated, let me remind you that this was an environment where everyone was expected to look, act, and even think alike. In such an environment, even the smallest of allowed differences can become central bases of self-identity. Of course, at the time my understanding of the situation wasn't nearly so sophisticated. But I understood it well enough to know that it was a hell of a lot more than just my friend's hair that this woman was amusing herself with.

At any rate, my boiling point had finally been reached and I exploded. I flew back into my cottage and flew into that woman. Trembling and sobbing in my fury, I cursed at her, called her obscene names, and told her that she was not fit to be anybody's "mommy" and that I would never call her that again. And then I ripped off the diaper and flung it at her—with a choicely worded warning that wearing it was something else I would never do again. For several weeks after this, the confrontations between us came fast and furious. Then, for some reason, she just gave up and left me alone. And by this point, another remarkable thing had happened: I had stopped wetting the bed altogether.

It was only a month or two later that I was finally transferred out of this woman's cottage—and straight into the cottage of a woman who had such a reputation for being an ogre that, although her last name was Heckathorn, our version of it was Hellathorn. With my own reputation preceding me, it didn't take long for this woman to make me her favorite target. But by now the die had been cast, and so it also didn't take long for me to let her know that I was not going to be an easy target.

For a little while, my rebelliousness remained situational, but now it was also enacted in behalf of other children and was often imbued with unmitigated rage. Round and round we went, me and old Hellathorn, with neither of us giving or gaining an inch. But all that—and vastly more—changed one night when I was taking a shower and suddenly there she was, jerking the shower curtain back and starting in on me about something. I don't recall what it was, and I don't even recall if I said anything back to her. All I remember is suddenly grabbing her by the hair of her head and yanking her into the shower with me.

It was the first time I had ever actually physically assaulted a staff member—and it was my moment of emancipation. Suddenly I was able to comprehend, with exhilarating clarity, the difference between having the authority to control someone and having the power to control someone. For me, their jig was up, and what followed from that night on was utterly unstoppable. Within a year, my rebelliousness had become a full-blown lifestyle, and the institution had lost complete control of me. I did whatever I pleased—roaming the grounds at will, attending required activities only when it suited me, running away, initiating verbal and physical confrontations with the staff whenever I could, and openly laughing at them throughout it all. And, together with a little band of accomplices I had acquired by this time, I was constantly trying to stir up mass rebellion among the other children.

Shortly before my fifteenth birthday, I was finally isolated in the hospital while they tried to figure out what to do with me. Since I didn't mind lounging around all day, I settled down a bit during this period. Besides, I wasn't completely isolated—there was one other unrepentant deviant locked up with me. Because the two of us had never been in a cottage together, and had engaged in different types of deviance (she liked to visit the boys' cottages in the middle of the night), we hadn't really known each other before this point. However, in the month or two that we spent isolated together, I came to feel close enough to her that, in later years, she would be the only member of my childhood cohort (other than my siblings) whom I would attempt to locate. Her name was Althea Leisure, and she would one day become the wife of Larry Flynt, the flamboyantly deviant publisher of *Hustler* magazine.

NEXT STOP: REFORM SCHOOL

By the end of September, it had been decided that I would be expelled from the orphanage. After a few months in a small juvenile detention center (where I was sexually molested by the man who worked the night shift), I was sent to a "reform school" just north of Columbus. Once there, I quickly discovered that I had jumped from the frying pan into the fire. Everything that had characterized life at the orphanage was also present in this place—only to a much greater degree (this was, after all, an acknowledged prison). In addition, this was a whole different population of inmates I suddenly found myself enclosed with—streetwise inner city girls whom I could not possibly identify with. I felt alone and scared, and for a little while, then, was a model inmate.

But that all changed about a month or so into my incarceration. For some reason that was never explained to me, it had been decided that it was in my best interest to have no contact with anyone from my past—no letters, no phone calls, and no visitors. One day I was sitting at a window, wondering how my old friends and my siblings were doing, and I started to cry. Suddenly I found myself surrounded by several large men who proceeded to pick me up and carry me off to an isolation cell. By the time we got there, I was putting up a pretty good fight, and so after they got me in the cell, I was placed in "the straps." This set of "restraints" consisted of four leather ankle and wrist cuffs, and two straps that were used to tie them all together so that my hands were bound to my feet behind my back. Once they had me trussed up like a calf at a rodeo, they gave me a shot of Thorazine to knock me out.

After this experience, my rebelliousness returned with a vengeance. It also got increasingly creative. On one occasion, for instance, I carefully removed the stitching twine and cobbler's nails from a pair of old loafers and used them, along with a pencil, to construct a small spiked weapon. I didn't do this because I actually needed a weapon; I just wanted to show the staff that I could do it.

On another occasion, a friend of mine and I managed to force our way into the wing of the building where the social workers' offices were. Once inside that "invitation only" hallway, we quickly found the women's bathroom and, after divesting it of one very frightened social worker, barricaded ourselves in. In my whole career as a rebel inmate, this stunt turned out to be my "personal best"—because a local police squad armed with tear gas had to be called into the situation. We pretended to have a few demands, but again, this was really only about showing the staff that we could do it. After holding out for several more hours, it became apparent that they were actually going to gas us, and so we came out—and laughed all the way to our isolation cells.

It took more than a month, but I finally broke, and per the rules, requested an audience with a supervisor so that I could agree to her terms of release. But the other girl had broken sometime earlier, and so, to teach me a lesson about stubbornness, my request was ignored for nearly a week. As luck would have it, I was in a cell where I had stashed a sharpened pallet knife behind a wall grating several months earlier, and it had not been discovered. I managed to retrieve it, and when one of the girls was sent in with my supper that evening, she found me covered in blood from where I had slashed both arms in several places. I immediately got out of isolation—and without having to agree to any terms of release. More important, for the first time in all my years as a child inmate, the general reaction from the staff was one of genuine concern.

Obviously, I was hell-bent on letting the staff know that they might have the *authority* to control me, but they would never have the *power* to control me. They, in turn, were hell-bent on letting me know that I was wrong. Over my two-year stay in this place (the average stay was well under a year), I spent innumerable and often lengthy periods of time locked in an isolation cell with no human contact and nothing but a plastic mat to sleep on and a plastic bucket to use as a toilet. Whenever my stay was longer than a day or two, the bucket would start to smell so bad that I would cover it with the mat and sleep on the bare cement floor. And much, if not most, of the time, these periods of isolation would also include time spent in the straps.

But nothing they did, including eventually putting me on two daily doses of Thorazine, could stop me—until one spring day when they came to me with an offer I couldn't refuse. Although I had only attended school for a total of a few weeks that year, their offer was to graduate me come summer if I stayed out of isolation until then. This was a significant offer because, according to the rules, any girl who graduated from high school while in this place had to be released as soon as placement for her could be found. But the real reason it worked was that, again for the first time in all my years as an inmate, I had been treated as if I were someone who had the both the capability and the right to have at least some say-so regarding the course of my own life. And so that summer, just weeks before my seventeenth birthday, I received my sham diploma. Four-and-a-half months later, after more than thirteen years as a child inmate, I was finally paroled.

THE OUTSIDE WORLD

Although I was now (technically) a high school graduate, I was still a minor, and so I was sent to a foster home. I remember that I mostly just watched the scenery go by on the three-hour bus ride to my new home, because I didn't really have much to think about. I didn't know enough about the outside world to even begin to imagine what might lie ahead of me. I had no expectations and no plans for what I would do with my life. And except for a vague sense of apprehension, I didn't even really have any fear—because I had no idea what might be "out there" to fear.

Had I been able, at that point, to even begin to comprehend what I was facing, I would have been paralyzed with fear. To begin with, I had been thrown into the outside world at an age when I was expected to go to work and provide for myself rather than depending on others to do so. But I had not been given any of the "tools" I needed to do this. I couldn't drive a car, and I had no marketable skills or practical knowledge of how to go about even getting a job. In addition, the only motivation for working I had acquired was to avoid punishment. And what I understood of authority figures wasn't exactly conducive to a good relationship with workplace superiors.

But the work world was far and away not the only area of social life in the outside world in which I was unprepared to participate. In the environment where I had grown up, such things as intimate relationships, marriage, family, and home life did not exist. For all practical purposes, neither did money or economic concerns. Even birth and death were such rarities that, in my

thirteen years as an inmate in two different institutions, neither one occurred a single time. Because of this, I had no working understanding of these most basic of social realities. My ideas about what they meant to people and how they were dealt with or carried out were extremely vague and tenuous at best.

In addition, the environment where I had grown up had not exactly been conducive to the development of certain "internal capacities" which enable humans to function autonomously and to achieve a sense of "satisfaction" or "happiness" in life. These capacities—which include self-awareness, self-esteem, love, morality, will, intellect, humor, and artistry—are what "humanize" humans. But how much self-awareness can children develop in an environment where everyone is required to look, act, and think alike? How can they develop self-esteem in the face of constant humiliation? What can they learn about love and how to express it in a social landscape that depends on pervasive fear for its very survival, and where their "teachers" are emotionally bankrupt themselves? How can they develop morality and free will in a place where power is exercised arbitrarily and brutally? And how do their capacities for intellect, humor, and artistry grow in a drab and Spartan environment where every aspect of every daily activity is dictated in detail, and these capacities tend to elicit resentment?

Of course, my rebellion had probably functioned to protect me from the worst effects of the "dehumanizing" environment in which I was raised. But if my childhood deviance is viewed as a fierce struggle against the dehumanizing forces which pervaded the orphanage, then my deviance as an adult can only be viewed as evidence that those forces were simply too strong to be prevailed against. For the better part of the next two decades after my release, my life was one long downward spiral into psychosocial chaos. My long and hard struggle against those who would completely control me may have been over, but an even longer and harder struggle to assume that control myself still lay ahead of me.

While my first several years in the outside world were relatively uneventful compared to what would happen later on, they were not without their significant developments. A couple of brief forays into the work world showed me not only how profoundly naive I was, but that I could expect less than understanding responses to this naivete. After overhearing others making fun of me at one place I worked, and being sexually molested by my boss at another, I retreated into my foster parents' home, and never really went anywhere without them after that. I also converted to Catholicism during this period, beginning a long quest for a "spiritual" worldview that made sense to me. In addition, while both of my foster parents were very good to me, they detested each other. My introduction to intimate relationships, marriage, family, and home life was thus somewhat less than ideal.

It should come as no surprise, then, that at the age of nineteen I agreed to marry a man I had only known for less than a week. Not only was I a virgin, but I had never even been out on a date—with him or anyone else. In retrospect, the extent to which this man and I were intellectually and emotionally mismatched was almost comical. In addition, he was an alcoholic who could become abusive when he was drinking. The only thing we really had in common was that he had spent seven years of his childhood in an orphanage also. But, as has been the case with my siblings and myself, this was something we only rarely and superficially discussed.

Two years into this marriage I returned to my foster parents. After a brief affair with the priest who had baptized me into Catholicism (and who had helped me "escape" from my husband), I met a man who was handsome, smart, passionate, and an in-your-face deviant. At the age of twenty-four, he had already ridden with the Hell's Angels in California, been involved with the Mafia in Chicago, and done a year in prison in Ohio. He was a wholly unrepentant rebel, and as such, was the first person I had met since my release that I felt a sense of "connection" with. I was immediately and completely smitten. Dur-

ing the two-and-a-half years I lived with him, I became a member of a pagan cult, a drug addict, and a prostitute—and in the process, managed to get myself arrested several times. I also became a mother, and it was this that finally drove me from his life. With the police and social workers constantly hot on our trail, I knew that I could not let my son fall into the hands of "the system"— I could not let him go through what I had gone through.

With an intravenous drug habit to kick, I returned to my husband (whom I'd never bothered to divorce), intending to stay only until I got well. But I quickly became pregnant with a second and then a third child, and it was ultimately more than three years before I left and finally divorced him. My oldest son's father had just died (as outrageously as he had lived), and I moved in with his parents. I got on welfare and had a brief affair with a married cop. A year-and-a-half later, I moved into government subsidized housing and began an affair with a professional gambler.

"DARK NIGHT OF THE SOUL"
By now I was twenty-eight years old and, for the first time in my life, living on my own. The house I had moved into was in the poorest—and thus the roughest—neighborhood in town, and it didn't take long for me to become addicted to drugs again. After being arrested a couple of times in one week (once for assaulting a police officer, and once for trying to shoot the gambler after I caught him cheating on me), I was committed to a psychiatric facility for three months in order to undergo drug rehabilitation. My oldest son's grandparents had by now become deeply attached to all of my children, and took them in during this period.

After learning my history and becoming aware of my giftedness, the staff at the psychiatric facility decided that I was not just another street addict who simply needed to be cleaned up and sent home. With a genuine desire to help me realize my capabilities, they gave me their best efforts. But three months was not nearly long enough to sort out all the causes of the enormous gap between what I was and what I was so obviously capable of being. In the end, they sent me home completely clean, but only marginally enlightened. Within the first few days of my stay in this facility, I had developed a metaphorical understanding of my situation. The way I saw it, I had been thrown into the river of life without having been taught to swim or even being told that there was such a thing as swimming. Consequently, as soon as I had hit the water, I had begun to sink. As dead-on as this insight was, however, they failed to take it and run with it. Instead, they simply used it as a springboard to a conclusion that I immediately knew was way off base: they thought that I deeply resented my mother for "allowing" this to happen to me. I tried to tell them that this was ridiculous, that no one who knew my poor pitiful mother could have resented or blamed her. But they just thought that I was entrenched in denial, and kept encouraging me to try and vent my rage in some "healthy" way.

This failure to help me develop my seminal insight into the basic nature of my problems pretty much insured that my downward spiral into psychosocial chaos would continue. Within weeks after my release from the psychiatric facility, I was involved in an affair with another married man. This man made it clear from the start that all he wanted was sex. Since by now I had come to the conclusion that this was all men were good for anyway, it seemed like the perfect match. And it was—for the whole three months that it took me to get pregnant again.

In addition to all of the obvious problems with this situation, there was the fact that this new baby's father was not white. Because of my inability to feel a sense of connection with others and my profound psychosocial instability, I had never been able to build much of a "support system" in the first place, and now what little I had began to crumble fast. Except for a police officer and his family who took me in until the baby was born, everyone else I knew suddenly wanted nothing more to do with me.

As it turned out, my daughter was born with very few physical indications of her African heritage—she could "pass" for white any day of the week (although she has largely chosen not to). Not surprisingly, everyone was suddenly "all right" with the situation again. But for me, the damage had been done. Shortly after her birth, I moved back out on my own, and within a year I was living in virtual seclusion with my children. I was thoroughly disenchanted with the world and utterly disillusioned with people. Even my quest for a spiritual worldview that made sense—which had involved years of investigating a wide variety of religious beliefs—had yielded nothing.

With nothing left to believe in, I had entered the period of my life that would prove to be my "dark night of the soul." There were moments during this period when I thought that perhaps my children and I would all be better off dead, but whatever it takes for people to act on such ideas, I didn't have it. Instead, I entered such a deep state of depression that eventually I was sleeping all but a couple of hours every day. Naturally, it didn't take long for the local Department of Social Services to get wind of the situation. I was ordered into therapy, and when I resisted, my children were temporarily removed from my custody and sent to live with my oldest son's grandparents.

To me, this situation represented the reappearance of authority figures in my life who would utterly deprive me in order to completely control me. A profound sense of rage and helplessness totally engulfed me, and in an attempt to express this inexpressible state I was in, I began to engage heavily in self-mutilation. Consequently, over the course of the next year, I was hospitalized in psychiatric facilities a half-dozen times, and in between these periods of hospitalization, I was forced to undergo intensive therapy with a local public mental health agency. But for me, the mental health workers at both the hospitals and the agency were simply part and parcel of the whole system that was trying to control me. And so the more they tried to help me, the more I tried to deliberately thwart their efforts. I began drinking heavily, and doing drugs again, and both the frequency and severity of my bouts of self-mutilation increased—and all for no other reason than that I knew that these were precisely the behaviors they were trying to save me from. In other words, at this point, these behaviors were neither "escape mechanisms" or "cries for help," but were purely acts of rebellion—my way of telling these people that I would rather self-destruct than let them control me.

All of this only prompted the Department of Social Services to initiate legal proceedings to permanently strip me of custody of my children. However, the team of clinicians who had been attempting to work with me at the public mental health agency were vehemently opposed to this. By now they had become aware of—and impressed with—both my giftedness and my fierce love for my children. They were convinced that if they could just get me to trust them, they could help me become not only a capable parent, but much more. And so they went to bat for me and took on the Department of Social Services in a heated court battle. In the end, they were so successful at convincing the judge of their point of view, that she not only returned my children to me, but reprimanded the Department of Social Services for the way they had handled my case.

RESOCIALIZATION

Their efforts in my behalf also yielded the trust they had hoped for, and slowly but surely we began to make some real progress in my therapy sessions. Knowing that the last thing I needed at this point was to worry about how to provide support for myself and my children, they diagnosed me as having "borderline personality disorder with anti-social tendencies" and got a disability check coming in for me. Eventually this team of mental health workers was able to successfully identify the root of my problems. It was they who first introduced me to the concept of "socialization," explaining that in my case, this process had gone terribly awry. When I

asked them what they meant by this, the answer they gave me was really extremely reductionistic, but it was a start. What had happened, they told me, was that the ways of behaving I had learned while growing up may have been appropriate for the environment that I was raised in, but not for the larger society outside that environment. What I needed, they concluded, was to be "resocialized."

Their first idea was to accomplish this by "re-parenting" me, but I quickly proved unable to handle the emotional bonding this required on my part. Eventually, someone on the team came up with the idea of sending me to college as a means of resocializing me. This would not require a lot of emotional involvement on my part, they reasoned, and there was no doubt that I had the intellectual capacity for it. When they put this idea to me, however, I immediately and vehemently balked. There was simply no way that I was going to voluntarily enter another institutional environment—not in this lifetime. After trying in vain to reason with me, they ended up deciding that, in my own best interest, they were going to have to play hard ball with me. They issued me an ultimatum: I had six months to get myself enrolled in college, or they would turn me back over to the Department of Social Services, and let them have their way with me.

Grudgingly, I acquiesced. I never really got angry because, after several years of working intensely with these people, I knew that their hearts were in the right place where I was concerned. I just believed with everything in me that they were wrong, that there was absolutely no way I could flourish in any sort of institutional environment. Nevertheless, I was determined to give this thing my very best effort—not only because I felt that I owed it to them, but also because I believed that this was the only way they could ever know how wrong they were.

By the end of my very first semester, I had changed my mind. I was still unconvinced about this resocialization thing, but I did know that I had not had this much fun for a long time—

perhaps in my whole lifetime. Not only had I just spent four months doing something I was good at for a change, but I had also quickly discovered, to my amazement, that my unusual life experiences, and the unique insights and independent ways of thinking which these experiences had imbued me with, were actually *valued* in this new environment. I had no idea where this adventure would ultimately take me. All I knew was that, for as long as it continued to be this much fun, I was going to keep doing it.

By the end of my fourth semester I was still having fun, and I still had no idea where all of this was going to take me. In addition, some seminal resocialization had indeed occurred. But it was mostly in terms of the growth of self-esteem and self-confidence. I still did not have a significantly improved understanding of my social universe in general, but I did feel that I had finally found one small niche in it where I could flourish.

Then, in my fifth semester, I took an introductory-level sociology course. By the end of the semester, I was convinced that the insights and conceptual tools which this discipline had to offer could help me put together the working understanding of my social universe that had thus far so thoroughly eluded me. I declared sociology as my major, and by the time I graduated (magna cum laude, and well within the top 5 percent of my graduating class), I had taken nearly every sociology course the university offered. By this point, my initial expectations of the discipline had proven well founded, and so I applied to graduate school. Not only was I immediately accepted, but I was also offered a position as a teaching assistant.

THE MEANING OF BEING "DEVIANT"

After two years as a graduate student, ill health forced me to withdraw from school. However, by then my initial expectations of sociology had been vastly exceeded; I had gained a cohesive and comprehensive understanding not only of both my social universe and my personal biography, but of the connections between the two as well. I had come to realize, for instance, that in spite of my dual statuses as both a gifted child and an orphan of an individual who had offered up what Abraham Lincoln called "the last full measure of devotion" to this society, it had nevertheless been my status as a *poor* child which had determined my fate. This realization led to the understanding that there is some inherent and significant conflict among the basic sets of ideals which ostensibly drive this society—that those humanitarian values which underlie both democracy and Christianity stand in stark and undeniable contrast to the values which underlie our economic system. And, contrary to what Americans are socialized to believe in their schools and churches, in the "real" America these opposing sets of values do not—indeed, *cannot*—hold anywhere near equal sway. That this is a society where children are imprisoned for being poor not only clearly indicates which set of values dominates, but the horrific extent to which it dominates. No society that does this can legitimately claim to be even remotely driven by humanitarian ideals.

In short, then, the "working understanding" I had derived from my years as a student of sociology was I was not the only one who had been poorly socialized; the vast majority of Americans have also been "malsocialized," through the limitations in their experiences. For as traumatic as my childhood socialization and its legacy had been, it had still ultimately allowed me see "the truth" about the society into which I had been born. This, in turn, has allowed me to understand that being a "deviant" American does not have to necessarily amount to being a "dysfunctional" American, that I can make significant contributions—not in spite of my permanent status as a deviant, but because of it. Like many sociologists, I believe that Americans in general operate under many misguided assumptions and misperceptions about their society and that one of the primary "missions" of the discipline should be to "debunk" those assumptions and perceptions. I also believe that my personal history renders me uniquely qualified to aid in this mission. While I undertook the writing of this, my first published work, for many reasons, above all it was with the hope I have taken my first real step in that direction.

DISCUSSION QUESTIONS

1. What role do you think Pearson's early childhood neglect might have had in her reactions to socialization within the orphanage?

2. What would an institution such as an orphanage have to gain by prohibiting any exhibition of individualism from its charges? Do you think Pearson's "gifts" in intellectual and artistic pursuits made her a more ready target for abuse?

3. Deviance is clearly in the eye of the beholder. How would Pearson's early experiences have made standard American deviance look so normal when she first entered mainstream American life?

PART 3

SOCIAL
INEQUALITY

C H A P T E R

6

SOCIAL DIFFERENTIATION AND SOCIAL GROUPS

In the United States today it is possible to be born in New York City, grow up there, move to Los Angeles as an adult, and meet a native of that city with whom you have much in common. You may find, for example, that you enjoy the same movies or television programs, that you have the same attitudes toward religion and politics, that you enjoy the same music, and that in general you understand each other very well. Meeting someone with whom you share so many things is an exciting experience in communication, and it is all the more exciting when it occurs in an unlikely place. Strangely enough, the more "likely" places may be full of people you don't understand and can't stand; there are probably people who grew up a few blocks away from you with whom you have nothing in common and whose tastes and interests may be very different from yours. These two situations could be written off as coincidence. With so many people in American society, it stands to reason that many of them would be different from you (even if they live nearby) and some would be very much like you (even if they grew up far away). The coordination of society leaves little to chance, however, and these two occurrences are not exceptions.

As we have seen in previous chapters, individuals grow up as social creatures and are to a large extent shaped by their social experiences. The norms you follow, the roles you play, the knowledge you acquire, and the values you hold are all products of the experiences you have. Through socialization you come to internalize all of this and accept it as part of yourself. When you meet someone else who seems to share a lot of your behaviors, ideas, and values, it is undoubtedly because that individual had many of the same social experiences you did. Two individuals who like caviar, for example, must have grown up around or associated with other people who also liked caviar and introduced them to it. Two individuals who crack safes for a living must both have had associations with safecrackers. These similar social experiences can occur in very different places—such as New York City and Los Angeles. Of even more interest to sociologists is the fact that clusters of experiences tend to happen to the same individuals. Eaters of caviar are likely to be highly educated, to listen to classical music, and to be employed as lawyers or corporate executives, for example. Safecrackers, on the other hand, are more likely to be less educated, to prefer country-western music, and to be more fond of hamburgers than of caviar. Two individuals who share one important experience with each other usually also share just such a cluster of experiences. That clustering is part of the coordination in society.

This chapter explores some of the ways that clusters of experiences occur in the lives of members of society. Such an exploration would be interesting in its own right since it would tell us something about why people turn out as they do. But there is an added dimension to this study that is of particular importance to the sociologist: individuals who share clusters of experiences often note the things they have in common and form *social groups* around those points of similarity. Individuals with the same hobby may form a club. Individuals with the same religious beliefs may form a church. Individuals with the same problems may form a political party to do something about those problems. We tend to feel that our association with such social groups is voluntary and the result of individual decision. The sociological outlook, however, suggests that our previous experiences have primed us to be attracted to certain people and repulsed by certain other people. Just as our clusters of experiences are part of the coordination of society, so, too, are the social groups we form. Sociologists refer to this overall variation in society as *social differentiation*.

As we look at social differentiation in society, we pay particular attention to how differences among us influence the social groups within which we interact. We also look at the variety of forms those groups may take, finishing the chapter with a close examination of a particularly modern form of social group—the formal organization.

SOCIAL DIFFERENTIATION: CATEGORIES AND GROUPS

Social differentiation refers to the general process by which differences are created between individuals as a result of the different experiences they have as members of society. Because these experiences come in clusters, individuals turn out being different in a great many ways. In modern American society people are differentiated, for example, by the amount of wealth they possess. Rich people have a wide variety of experiences that only rich people have, and poor people have a wide variety of experiences that only poor people have. Depending on your level of wealth, you will likely eat different food, live in a different neighborhood, enjoy different music, go to different schools, speak and think differently, spend your leisure time differently, work at a different occupation, and have different kinds of everyday problems than people at other levels of wealth. You will have these experiences not because you choose to have them but because American society is structured so that you will be thrust into them. In any society, social differentiation exists when different sets of experiences occur in the lives of different collections of individuals. Although wealth is one of the more important such differences in many societies, it is only one of the many attributes that lead individuals into different sets of experiences. Sociologists refer to these attributes as social categories.

THE CATEGORY AND THE GROUP

A **social category** is a collection of individuals who have something in common. Technically, that something could be anything that an outside observer, such as a social scientist, might emphasize—for example, being left-handed and blue-eyed. The point of categories, however, is to call attention to some significant similarity among individuals that is useful in understanding other things about those individuals, and the category of being left-handed and blue-eyed does not particularly do that. If the category were instead all black women in the United States, its usefulness would be more apparent. Being black and being female are both factors that shape the experience of the individuals who are so defined. In fact, we could say that individuals in the category of black females encounter certain situations and experiences that no one outside the category could ever share. (For a view of the situation that many educated black females face, see the reading by Ellis Cose and Allison Samuels at the end of this chapter.) Thus, the idea of the category helps us understand how collections of individuals both share experiences with each other and differ in their experiences from other collections (or categories) of individuals. Perhaps most important, the idea of the category emphasizes that individuals share common experiences not because they go out of their way to share them but because society, by its structure, "sees to it" that they share them. The category calls attention to the ways that society shapes our experiences.

Although individuals who share a category may have much in common, there are two things they do not share. First, they do not usually know each other or even necessarily care to know each other. Second, they may not share the observer's enthusiasm for the category itself. They may, in fact, think that they share nothing with the other individuals with whom the observer has grouped them. This disagreement does not matter because the concept of the category belongs to the observer, not to the observed.

Unlike a category, a **social group**, in the usage of social science, is a collection of people who (1) know each other (or know of each other), (2) agree that they share something (at least their groupness and the goals of their group), and (3) have continuing interactions with each other. A group exists in the hearts and minds of its members; if it does not exist there, it does not exist. When groups do exist, their actions can change the course of human societies—a result that a lone individual can never hope to attain. It is not surprising, therefore, that one of the primary questions in social science is how the idea of groupness develops simultaneously in a collection of individual minds.

Members of a group feel that they have much in common. Members of a category also have at least one very important thing in common. If the category is a significant one in a given society, the individuals' common membership in that category will lead them to a number of common experiences in their everyday life. It is just such common experiences that can form the basis of a group. All that is needed is for the individuals in the category (or some of them, at any rate) to recognize their shared situation. In a circular way, the nature of a society itself (which forms the categories) can lead to the formation of social groups, which, through their actions, can change the nature of society.

In most complex societies a great many categories work at cross-purposes. For instance, one important category in the United States consists of all people who are poor—obviously a significant shared feature of their lives. But within the category of poverty are other, conflicting categories. Some poor people are white and others are black, for instance. A poor white person may not want to form a group with all other white people, since many of them do not share the common experience of poverty; equally, he or she may not want to form a group with all other poor people, since many of them do not share the common experience of being white. That example only begins to explore the contradictions and conflicts between and among categories.

TYPES OF SOCIAL GROUPS

Once categories of individuals decide that their points of common experience are important enough to warrant further interactions and they form groups, the kinds of social groups they form may vary considerably. One of the most important distinctions is between primary and secondary groups. **Primary groups** are typically small and are characterized by a great deal of face-to-face interaction and extremely strong emotional ties among the members. The family is perhaps the best example of a primary group (although kin relationships are not the only way to achieve the strong emotional ties; a group of close friends is another). Primary groups are very important in any society because of the tremendous impact they have on the lives of their members (Cooley, 1902). Socialization and social control within the primary group are generally more effective than similar social pressures coming from any other source; a loved one's threat to withhold affection may change your behavior more quickly and more completely than a formal law and the threat of imprisonment. Because our roles within primary groups are usually the most important ones we play, our dominant view of ourselves tends to come from these groups on the basis of those roles. Others may think you are a worthless individual, but the love of family members can counteract that judgment to a large extent and help you maintain self-respect.

Secondary groups are basically any social groups that are not primary groups. Secondary groups are typically larger than primary groups and are characterized by less intense emotional ties among the members and by more specific roles as a rule. Examples of secondary groups would include political parties, clubs or associations, the people you work with or play with, collections of acquaintances, and so on. Your emotional commitment to a secondary group will generally be less than to your primary groups. In addition, your secondary group roles will usually be more specific than those found in primary groups; you may be a precinct worker in your political party, a secretary for your club, a fellow office worker within your occupational

The family is probably the best example of a primary group. Our membership in such groups is generally more important and fundamental to who we are than our secondary group memberships.

group, a member on a bowling team, and a friend to your neighbors. In each case you are in a specific role in which only a part of yourself will be involved.

Social groups vary in a number of other ways:

1. Groups can be either **formal** or **informal.** Any bureaucratic organization (such as the military) would be extremely formal; a group of friends or your family would be far more flexible and informal. The formal organization, a social group with a clear structure of roles and norms consciously designed for the achievement of particular goals, is discussed in detail in the last section of this chapter.
2. Groups can be **voluntary** or **involuntary.** Some groups are a little hard to classify in this way; a family, for example, can be either, depending on whether you married into it or were born into it. A group of friends formed from inmates within a prison would be a group voluntarily entered into by individuals who were involuntarily placed in a common environment.
3. Groups can be **open** or **closed.** Open groups are those open to new members; closed groups accept no new members. Many groups are a little bit of both, being open to some individuals while closed to others. The Ku Klux Klan, for example, is a group that seeks new members but is closed to Jews and African Americans.
4. Groups can be **horizontal** or **vertical.** Horizontal groups contain members who all occupy the same social class; vertical groups contain representatives from a variety of social classes. In American society voluntary or informal vertical groups are rare. Some reasons for this rarity will be examined later in this chapter as well as in Chapter 7.
5. Groups can be **in-groups** or **out-groups.** In-groups are social groups in which the individual feels at home or with which he or she identifies. The out-group, on the other hand, is any group to which the individual does not belong. The out-group is perceived as "they" by the individual; the in-group is perceived as "we." One person's in-group is therefore another person's out-group, and vice versa.
6. Groups can be **reference groups** for their members or even for their nonmembers. Reference groups provide standards against which individuals may measure themselves and their accomplishments. Ultimately, individuals develop a self-image from their reference groups; we come to know more clearly who we are when we identify ourselves with specific norms and values found in specific social groups. Your circle of intimate friends may be a reference group for you; members of an occupational group to which you aspire may also provide a reference, acting as models for what you hope to see in yourself one day.

These classifications of social groups do not exhaust all the ways groups can differ, but they do call attention to some of the more important variations. Social

Social control by the group has an iron grip on young Americans. What chance would there be for a boy who couldn't skateboard to join this group?

groups are ultimately the product of human sociability, but the decisions people make about exercising that sociability have a lot to do with the social categories created within a society. Social groups are often the product of experiences shared by individuals who occupy the same category.

HOW INDIVIDUALS RECOGNIZE THEIR CATEGORY MEMBERSHIP (WITH A LITTLE HELP FROM THEIR FRIENDS)

As we saw earlier, in a complex society such as the United States any individual belongs to many social categories simultaneously. One individual might be a white, middle-income, Jewish male who works in an office and is confined to a wheelchair. Each of these characteristics is significant in the United States; the individual in question will have different kinds of experiences as a result of each. Whites have different experiences from people of other races; middle-income people live different lives than people of greater or lesser income; Jews are distinguished from other religious and ethnic groups; men are treated differently from women; office workers have experiences unique to office workers; and people in wheelchairs experience a world unknown to those who can walk. This individual will share at least some experiences with other people who share even one of his categories. He will, for example, have something in common with all other American men, since many experiences are parceled out by sex in American society. He will also, however, have many common experiences with women who are confined to wheelchairs—an experience most American men do not have. This sort of contrast raises a basic question for the sociologist: under what conditions does a given category membership become important enough to individuals that they are drawn together into a social group?

Most individuals become convinced that one category is more important than another with a little help from their friends. That is, other people with whom they share the category in question will maintain that that category is more fundamental than others. If our hypothetical individual knows other Jewish people, they will likely attempt to convince him that he has more in common with them than he does with middle-class non-Jews who work in an office. His Jewish friends can call upon the long Jewish tradition and the importance of religion to everyday life. They can also point to the large number of existing Jewish groups and organizations; if other members of the category feel that it is important enough to warrant grouping together, who is our hypothetical individual to object?

The informal pressure from friends to maintain loyalty to a category becomes most effective when already existing social groups and organizations back them up. The existence of synagogues, Jewish social clubs, Yiddish-language newspapers, weddings, funerals, religious holidays, and so on all serve to reinforce the importance of the social category for our Jewish individual. In the case of many such organizations (religions, political groups, labor unions, and the like) it will be in the interest of the organization to attract as many category members as possible into the group. Our hypothetical individual will find himself being systematically bombarded with the importance of his religious and ethnic background.

While our "friends" help call attention to social categories, events and life experiences can be just as important. Our individual in the wheelchair will have a variety of important experiences that only people in wheelchairs have. Some of these experiences may be physical (the difficulty in getting from here to there), and some may be social (job discrimination based on the disability, for example). The importance and vividness of these experiences cannot help but call attention to the category of the physically disabled, leading individuals in that category to recognize their similarity to other members of the category. In fact, these very kinds of experiences led many disabled Americans to organize politically; their efforts resulted in the passage of the Architectural Barriers Act of 1968 and the Rehabilitation Act of 1973. These pieces of legislation require, among other things, that public buildings be accessible to people in wheelchairs. The Americans with Disabilities Act of 1990 strengthened that category by prohibiting discrimination in the workplace.

Other events such as disasters or economic depressions play major roles in calling attention to social categories. A hurricane calls attention to geographical categories, separating people in its path from those who live safely distant. An economic depression will likely affect some economic categories more than others and will call attention to economic differences in a society. Inflation affects the poor and people on fixed incomes more than it does others. A war coupled with a draft calls attention to age categories, separating those of draft age from those who are younger or older. If only men are drafted, it also calls attention to gender categories. Events such as these all play a part in making certain social categories more or less important to their members at different times. The points of similarity among members of the category may be present all the time, but certain events may call attention to those points of similarity and lead people to act in groups based on the category.

SOCIAL GROUP PROCESSES

Social Groups and Boundary Maintenance **Boundary maintenance** refers to efforts by group members to keep track of who is in the group and who is not in the group—or, more basically, to keep "them" separate from "us." The most obvious and pervasive example of boundary maintenance occurs with family "titles" (son, daughter-in-law, cousin, and so on), which specify not only that you are a group member but what kind of group member you are. The family is an important group to its members, and membership requirements are generally quite strict. New members can join through marriage, and a great deal of attention is generally paid to the prospective new member before the ceremony. Other groups and organizations accomplish the same boundary maintenance through initiation ceremonies, membership cards, and group or organizational titles.

Boundary maintenance thrives on less formal techniques as well. Every family, for example, has traditional family stories, jokes, and ways of doing things that exist only within the family unit. When outsiders encounter these activities, they are reminded of the fact that they are outsiders. Groups or organizations can also have secret handshakes, distinctive clothing, specific mannerisms, or even a separate and distinctive vocabulary or style of speaking. All of these activities or attributes serve as constant reminders to both insiders and outsiders of exactly where the group boundary is located.

Social Groups and Social Control As a rule, group members don't need rational reasons for insisting on conformity to their norms. Humans are social animals and everything they do is in some way related to their sociability. A number of studies by sociologists and psychologists have demonstrated this aspect of human behavior quite clearly.

An experiment by Solomon Asch (1958) provides a striking illustration of group pressure. Asch constructed a test consisting of a set of lines of three lengths (lines 1, 2, and 3 in Figure 6.1) coupled with an additional, single line (A) that obviously corresponded in length to line 2. When he asked subjects individually which line in the set corresponded to line A, no one had any difficulty answering the question correctly. He then moved his experiment into a group setting in which a number of

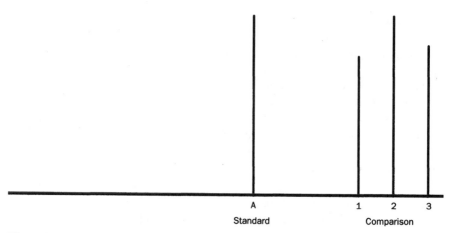

Figure 6.1 Sandard and comparison lines in the Asch experiment. (Adapted from Asch, 1958)

people had been instructed to answer the question incorrectly; these accomplices gave their answers aloud before the subject was asked the same question. In this group situation a significant number of subjects agreed with the group rather than trust their own eyes. Thus, we either keep our differences from the group to ourselves or, just as likely, we come to see things differently over time because of our desire to be part of the group.

Social control by the group appears just as strikingly in the world of everyday life. Where do fads come from? How can we explain large numbers of people simultaneously deciding to buy hula hoops, collect Beanie Babies, or add colors and spikes to their hair? Perhaps hula hoops are fun and Beanie Babies are cute, but that still doesn't explain why so many people first discover and then forget those facts simultaneously. One of the most fascinating aspects of fads is the power they exert on individuals during the fad's lifespan and how quickly fads can become out of date. Fads and fashions are clearly an example of group pressure and the desire of many individuals to do whatever the rest of the group is doing.

Social Groups: Conflict and Cooperation Individuals generally feel that their acts of conflict and cooperation are motivated by their own feelings and attitudes. Anger and hostility can lead to conflict, while warm and friendly feelings lead to cooperation. But where do the feelings and attitudes come from? As our social groups give us norms, encourage us to color our hair, and alter our perceptions, they also influence our feelings and attitudes toward others.

Georg Simmel, a German sociologist who wrote at the turn of the last century, focused a good deal of attention on the ways that social groups generate conflict and cooperation among individuals. His primary insight was that increasing conflict *between* two groups leads to increasing cooperation *within* each group (Simmel, 1955). A social group torn by internal differences can immediately be unified in the face of an outside threat. This principle can be witnessed in either small or large groups. A sports team builds unity through the experience of meeting other teams that seek to defeat it. A nation-state becomes more unified when attacked by the military forces of another country. The Japanese attack on Pearl Harbor in 1941 and the terrorist attacks of September 11, 2001, both served to generate intense feelings of patriotism among Americans.

An outside threat to a group can be real or imagined. A leader faced with dissension can manipulate the group by convincing members they face some outside threat. One of the most graphic examples is Adolf Hitler's attempt to unify the German people by convincing them that their problems were the result of an international Jewish conspiracy. Similarly, American politicians rally the electorate around their policies with pledges to counter the threat to the United States from Saddam Hussein and Iraq. If a social group can be convinced of an outside threat, they are likely to forget their individual differences in the name of group solidarity and follow their leader. Under such circumstances individuals in the group will experience feelings of friendship and warmth for other group members along with feelings of hostility toward individuals in the group that threatens them.

AGE DIFFERENTIATION IN AMERICAN SOCIETY

Age and gender are two ways that humans can vary. Almost all human societies provide different life experiences for men and women and for people of different ages. Most commonly, different roles are assigned to people on the basis of their sex and age. In most societies (including the United States) the most highly rewarded and influential roles are occupied by middle-aged men. Some societies provide better roles for women, and still more societies treat the aged better than they are treated in American society, but the generalization holds.

The assignment of different roles according to age is necessary to some extent. Humans mature very slowly; younger members of society must necessarily occupy dependent roles for quite a number of years. Most age and gender differentiation reflects general cultural values, however, rather than such practical considerations. People of both sexes and a variety of ages could fill far more roles than most societies permit. In American society a woman could easily fill the role of president, and a man could be a fine homemaker. Similarly, old people could continue to do a great many jobs beyond the age of retirement, and young people could no doubt handle more responsibility than they are usually given. If such situations existed, age and gender would be far less important social categories, and an individual's everyday life experience would not vary greatly on the basis of either sex or age. As it is, however, men and women grow up and live in different worlds with differing role expectations, and people of different ages are thrust into very different experiences and often live in isolation from each other. Not surprisingly, Americans often feel most comfortable in social groups containing others of their own sex and age. Considering that individuals are placed in age and sex categories involuntarily, these categories provide a fundamental starting point for the understanding of social differentiation. Let's look first at age differentiation.

AGE AS A SOCIAL CATEGORY

Biology requires that in any society the very young occupy somewhat different roles than older members. Even this basic statement must be qualified, however. Only in industrial societies such as the United States is "childhood" a fairly lengthy stage of life. In most nonindustrial societies children enter adult roles (especially work roles) quite early in life. American prohibitions against child labor may look much more humane, but the fact is that we have few jobs for unskilled child labor. Our industrial economy provides more skilled and fewer unskilled jobs with each passing year. It is important, therefore, to extend the period of childhood to keep young people out of the economy and in training programs (such as formal education) as long as possible. As the institution of education grows in response to this need, children are increasingly oriented away from their families and toward their peer group at school. The emphasis on their being children and not adults further serves to separate young people from older people. The "generation gap"—a popular concept in the 1960s—reflects the consciousness of both generations of this increasing isolation.

An industrial society also promotes rapid social change, which has many important repercussions at the top end of the age spectrum. In nonindustrial societies older people often receive respect because of their accumulation of knowledge and experience. In a rapidly changing industrial society, however, their knowledge may well be out of date and their experience may be considered irrelevant. And since values change at a similar pace, the young and the old wind up miles apart and often distrustful of each other. It is instructive that old people are often looked upon as being similar to children and are often treated as such; like children, old people are commonly out of the workforce and lack many of the skills and knowledge common to the wage-earning generation.

Between young and old is the wage-earning generation—the age group most actively tied into the economy. The demands of a modern industrial economy make children an expense and older people a nuisance to this middle, responsible category. Industrial employment requires the middle generation either to limit the number of children they have or to cease having children and to look outside the family if the grandparents need additional care. Not surprisingly, industrial employment leads to smaller families, plus an increased number of day-care centers, formal institutions of education, and nursing homes. In addition, the geographical mobility required of employees in an industrial economy tends to separate generations within a family as each new generation faces the possibility of having to move to find work.

One of the most basic characteristics of industrial societies is rapid social change in all aspects of culture. Beyond making the knowledge and experience of the aged irrelevant, rapid social change means that each generation will "come of age" in an environment fundamentally different from that of the previous generation. Norms and values favored by parents may only partially apply to the world facing their children. Because each generation's culture is unique in certain respects, age as a social category gains importance.

AGE AS A BASIS FOR GROUP FORMATION

The importance of age as a social category in modern American society is reflected in the growing number of social groups that form around the common experience of age. The term *youth culture,* for example, was popularized in the 1960s, but its roots go back several decades before that. The setting apart of youth as a "culture" can perhaps be seen most clearly in the world of popular music. Popular music used to be ageless in its audience; Bing Crosby appealed to a variety of age groups. In the 1940s, however, Frank Sinatra began his career amid the screams of teenage girls. By the 1950s and the rise of rock and roll, certain kinds of music were clearly directed at audiences of specific ages. Today you need only look at a tape or CD collection to know the age of the collector, no matter what his or her social position.

As younger people cluster together at one end of the age spectrum, so older people cluster together at the other end. All cities have senior citizen centers, and all

Many of our social roles depend on the age groups we belong to. In American society, most older people experience a restriction in social roles, as they have left the workforce and have fewer family responsibilities.

states have varieties of retirement communities and apartment complexes that specialize in housing for the aged. Special magazines, such as *50 Plus,* are directed specifically at older Americans, just as *Rolling Stone* is directed at younger Americans. Mandatory retirement places the aged in a relationship to the world of work similar to that of young people. Magazines like *50 Plus* devote considerable space to articles on how to fill the hours of the day, how to deal with loneliness, and how to have fun on a reduced income. The underlying thread behind many of these experiences common to the aged in the United States is *ageism.*

Ageism is prejudice toward the aged as well as acts of discrimination against them on the basis of age (Barrow and Smith, 1979). The United States has become a youth-oriented society in which baldness, gray hair, and wrinkles are feared as if they were diseases. Looking, acting, and thinking young have become highly valued and form the basis of a prejudice against the aged simply because they are old. This prejudice is often coupled with discrimination, particularly in the area of employment. Unemployed older workers find work very hard to come by when facing younger competition, and in spite of seniority systems older workers are often the first to be laid off (McVittie et al., 2003).

Contrary to popular stereotypes, however, old people are not uniformly poor; better retirement programs coupled with Social Security have produced economic stability for older Americans and have insulated them from some of the economic changes that have thrust younger Americans into economic hardships (O'Hare, 1985).

The various manifestations of ageism have called attention to the category of old age and have stimulated the formation of political groups organized to protect the rights of the aged. One of the earliest political organizations of the aged was the Townsend movement of the 1930s, the main program of which was to provide $200 a month for elderly Americans from federal government funds. The plan was never instituted, but parts of it were not much different from the provisions of the Social Security Act (passed shortly thereafter), which provided incomes for most aged Americans. Of the more modern political organizations for the aged, the largest is the coalition of the National Retired Teachers Association (NRTA) and the American Association of Retired Persons (AARP). A more radical and more loosely organized group is the Gray Panthers, founded by Maggie Kuhn. These and other organizations were instrumental in the passage of the 1967 Age Discrimination Act and recent amendments to that act, which, among other things, broke the iron rule of mandatory retirement in many sectors of the economy. The growth of these organizations in recent years reflects the increasing importance of age as a social category and the need of the aged to have their interests represented.

Age is a social category in the United States today because the modes of coordination we live by constantly call attention to our age. The roles we play and the norms we are expected to live by vary considerably as we grow older, and our attention is drawn to others who are also aging. We are apt to feel most comfortable with these people and to have interests in common with them, so we are also apt to form social groups with them. Human biology requires some of this differentiation, but much of it is forced upon us by the nature of our society. Gender differentiation operates similarly.

GENDER DIFFERENTIATION IN AMERICAN SOCIETY

The ever-popular "battle of the sexes" is probably fought in every human society in one form or another. The differing biological makeups of men and women are certainly responsible for some of the behaviors and interests that differentiate the sexes. But, as with age differentiation in society, the biological basis of the differentiation cannot come close to explaining the experiences and expectations we confront depending on our gender.

The vast majority of human societies—and certainly American society—place a great importance on gender differences. Boys and girls are raised in very different manners in order to make them suitable occupants for the gender-specific roles they will encounter later on. In American society it has traditionally been thought that women should be kind and nurturing so they will make better wives, mothers, nurses, and kindergarten teachers, while men should be aggressive and rational to become better corporation executives, football players, brain surgeons, and college professors.

GENDER-ROLE SOCIALIZATION

Johnny finds a truck, a football, and a six-gun under the Christmas tree, while Mary receives a doll, a frilly pink dress, and a set of play pots and pans—even Santa Claus believes that little boys and little girls are fundamentally different. Children in American society receive a clear message practically from birth as to just which sorts of thoughts, beliefs, and actions are appropriate for their sex. Adults even treat newborns differently depending on their sex; thus, to some degree gender roles have an impact in even the first few weeks of life (Condry and Condry, 1976). Parents, relatives, teachers, other children, and even total strangers appear to conspire in gender-role socialization. A boy cannot cry in front of any of these people without running the risk of being labeled a "sissy"; a girl should not climb trees or start fights unless she's willing to face taunts of "tomboy." By the time boys and girls are old enough to reflect on what's happening to them, they are already very different kinds of people.

The growing child and young adult becomes increasingly aware of the outside world, and much of what he or she encounters there supports the earlier messages. Men are generally portrayed in movies, fiction, and television as strong, independent, and self-confident; they are also usually the most important characters. Women, on the other hand, have usually been portrayed as weak, fearful, and dependent on some male figure. The six o'clock network news contains information about the activities of important men in the world and has generally been reported by men.

Men paint great paintings, write great books, invent important things, introduce great religions, and lead great revolutions; they exist everywhere as models for role behavior for the growing boy. Little girls, on the other hand, must hunt for such role models.

The results of all these socializing forces appear throughout the developing years of boys and girls. With adolescents, for example, girls are much more likely than boys to focus attention on social relationships and to seek support from social groups (Bakken and Romig, 1992; Frydenberg and Lewis, 1991). Boys are much more likely to exhibit behavior focused on control over others as opposed to seeking support from them (Bakken and Romig, 1992). While these differences might suggest that adolescent girls are more caring and giving, part of their group orientation appears to stem from lower self-esteem when compared with adolescent boys (McRae, 1991). Additionally, this lowered self-esteem affects the goal orientations of adolescent girls; the lower their self-esteem, the more limited futures they foresee for themselves, while boys, in general, aim their sights at more challenging futures (Levy and Baumgardner, 1991).

Just as with any form of socialization, gender-role socialization does not end with childhood. Adults are subject to much of the same socialization through the media, and they also spend a good portion of their time socializing each other. The "American date" is a classic situation in which gender-role expectations become reinforced through the established roles that are played. A woman can easily test this expectation not only by requesting the "date" in the first place (which is becoming acceptable) but also by continuing to play the "male" role throughout—driving the car, selecting the entertainment, paying for everything, and then aggressively seeking a sexual reward in return for the money she has spent on the evening. She would most likely receive a negative response to this dating behavior. Roles must be followed, with men and women staying on their own sides of the fence.

"DOING GENDER" IN SOCIETY: AFFIRMING GENDER ROLES IN INTERACTION

When men and women follow traditional gender roles in their everyday lives, they re-create and reaffirm the meaning of gender. The "meaning" of gender is the result of how gender is connected to those ongoing roles. If women, for example, traditionally play nurturing roles, then nurturing comes to be associated with the female gender. As a woman plays that nurturing role and thinks of herself "as a woman" in doing so, she is "doing gender" in the sense that her sense of gender is strengthened.

The sociological perspective on "doing gender" comes to us from the theoretical perspective of symbolic interactionism (see Chapter 3). It places the creation and affirmation of gender into the meanings that attach to ongoing social interactions in society (see West and Zimmerman, 1987; West and Fenstermaker, 1995). Gender is viewed not as inherently part of being male or female or as inherently part of certain social roles. Instead, gender is viewed as an ongoing process that people keep alive through their regular connection of certain behaviors with one or the other gender. And because these connections live through their everyday maintenance, they can be altered by changing the ways that the two genders behave and interact.

Consider the role of surgeon. Men have traditionally dominated the occupation. In addition, many behaviors characteristic of surgeons are also traditionally associated with the male gender. Surgeons are in command in the operating room, making decisions and giving orders to others. What happens when a woman becomes a surgeon? In many cases, she may face objections from other role players in the operating room if she follows the behaviors typical of male surgeons (Cassell, 1996).

SEX DISCRIMINATION AND SEXISM

As with age differentiation, more than simply role differences makes gender an important social category. Women clearly face discrimination in the United States. When we look at the economic marketplace, we find that women have been largely kept out of occupations thought unsuitable for them. Some job discrimination is tied closely to the stereotypes that guide gender-role socialization. Women have, for example, generally been kept out of the sciences because they are stereotyped as "not good at that kind of thing." If parents and teachers pass on the stereotype to little girls, who then come to believe it, the girls will, in fact, not do well in science and will not go on to seek careers in scientific fields. (Sociologists call this circular process a **self-fulfilling prophecy,** in which a belief that something will happen makes it happen.)

Other forms of job discrimination are more blatant. Several leading American religions refuse to allow women to occupy the dominant roles within their organizations. The Catholic Church, for example, has long insisted that only men may fill the role of priest. Other jobs have been closed to women by male employers simply choosing not to hire them. Even on the job, discrimination exists in the form of *sexual harassment,* when women are expected to provide sexual favors in exchange for advancement or even to keep the job they have.

In the past, women were largely limited to such occupations as grade-school teaching, semiskilled factory work, nursing, secretarial work, clerking, and household work. Defined as "women's work," most of these occupations have traditionally been poorly paid. This kind of double standard, in which traditionally female-dominated occupations are by and large lower paying than male-dominated occupations, has led to demands for comparable worth laws. These laws would provide comparisons between male and female occupations in terms of years of training required, difficulty of the work, and amount of responsibility inherent in the occupation. Occupations deemed similar by such standards would then be required by law to provide equal pay (Feldberg, 1984). The segregation of women into low-paying jobs coupled with hiring discrimination has maintained a considerable income gap between men and women, which has improved slightly over the last two decades.

Discrimination against women on the job reveals itself in sexual harassment, which is sometimes blatant, sometimes fairly subtle. This boss might appear to be simply discussing the work on the drawing board, but his arm is enclosing and pressing the young woman, who does not appear to welcome such attention. If she tells him to back off, however, how likely is it that she will get the next promotion that comes up?

Sexism refers to stereotyping on the basis of sex and to the prejudice and discrimination that are directed by sex. It's a useful concept to the sociologist for it weaves together the various aspects of gender differentiation. As with age, people experience their gender category in all walks of their existence; the experiences we have as children on the playground or around the Christmas tree are reflected later in life when we look for jobs. To argue that the United States is a sexist society is to argue that the male experience in this society is fundamentally different from—and more positive than—the female experience. Not surprisingly, the individuals involved notice these differences and group together accordingly.

What happens when gender is combined with other significant categories? An African American woman, for example, faces sexism because of her gender and racism because of her ancestry. Collins (1986, 1990, 1998) refers to this overlap as *intersectionality*. She views women of color as double outsiders who are bound together by their knowledge that oppression is multidimensional. A reduction of sexism will not alleviate these women's overall problems, for they will still be left facing racism. This experience prevents them from ever feeling totally connected with European American women or African American men (see also hooks, 1981, 1984; Hurtado, 1989).

GENDER AS A BASIS FOR GROUP FORMATION

As we saw with age differentiation, an important social category usually becomes a basis for the formation of social groups. The social category of gender is particularly interesting in this regard for, unlike different generations, people of both sexes must get together to some extent if the society is to continue beyond the current generation. This tie between the sexes is obviously a strong one; marriages and families are probably the strongest social groups that individuals form in any society. Yet different experiences based on gender work somewhat at cross-purposes. A man and a woman may be drawn together in marriage, yet both may actually have more experiences in common with members of their own gender than with their spouse. Years of gender-specific experiences can make understanding within a marriage very difficult. The early separation into Boy Scouts and Girl Scouts appears later in life in the husband's nights out with "the guys" and the wife's shopping trips with her friends—the social category of gender apparently makes us not want to go scouting or shopping with members of the opposite sex. We also see some of these differences in the ways men and women react to occupational stress. Johnson (1991) noted gender-specific reactions to the strains of being a police officer: while men learned to depersonalize the population they served (which is likely the source of some cases of police brutality), women officers were likely to turn the stress inward, experiencing "emotional burnout." Old habits are hard to break. When parties of married couples dissolve into a men's group in the living room and a women's group in the kitchen, it is clear that social categories are at work. Box 6.1 illustrates something of the sexual isolation in American society. When and if gender-role specification breaks down in the way we learn our appropriate roles, men's and women's interests should be more similar, and the voluntary social segregations depicted in Box 6.1 should be less likely to occur.

A great many of the voluntary social groups in American society are gender-specific. Many churches, which contain members of both sexes, have gender-specific social groups within the membership. Men's organizations such as the Masons, Elks, or Knights of Columbus are still very strong, and many maintain parallel organizations for women (such as the Eastern Star for the Masons and Emblem Club for the Elks) rather than permit female membership in the organization itself. On a less organized scale, Americans also belong to many gender-specific groups such as bowling leagues, softball teams, poker parties, cooking clubs, and so on; while many of these associations are increasingly becoming co-ed, for the most part the sexual separation is still there. Perhaps the most interesting example comes to us from the world of warfare. Traditionally, only American men have gone to war, and they have followed that experience by forming veterans' organizations such as the American

---

BOX 6.1

Confessions of a Female Chauvinist Sow

American society differentiates greatly on the basis of sex. Males and females are treated differently from birth and face a variety of expectations specific to their sex as they grow older. This differentiation isolates men and women, giving them experiences they find difficult to share and creating communication problems should they try. Moreover, men have traditionally received most of the advantages in this differentiation, leading many women to feel envious and bitter.

The following extract presents a few childhood memories and a few thoughts on this issue from writer Anne Roiphe (1972):

> I remember coming home from school one day to find my mother's card game dissolved in hysterical laughter. The cards were floating in black rivers of running mascara. What was so funny? A woman named Helen was lying on a couch pretending to be her husband with a cold. She was issuing demands for orange juice, aspirin, suggesting a call to a specialist, complaining of neglect, of fate's cruel finger, of heat, of cold, of sharp pains on the bridge of the nose that might indicate brain involvement. What was so funny? The ladies explained to me that all men behave just like that with colds, they are reduced to temper tantrums by simple nasal congestion, men cannot stand any little physical discomfort—on and on the laughter went.
>
> The point of this vignette is the nature of the laughter—us laughing at them, feeling superior to them, us ridiculing them behind their backs. If they were doing it to us we'd call it male chauvinist pigness; if we do it to them, it is inescapably female chauvinist sowness and, whatever its roots, it leads to the same isolation. Boys are messy; boys are mean; boys are rough; boys are stupid and have sloppy handwriting. A cacophony of childhood memories rushes through my head, balanced, of course, by all the well-documented feelings of inferiority and envy.

Legion and the Veterans of Foreign Wars. When the question of drafting women arose in 1980, most members of these organizations were opposed, suggesting a desire to keep a male domain male. The rapid gender shift in the American military after 1980 as more women joined has forced changes in attitudes. The American military is no longer a men's club.

The gender differentiation that has encouraged men to form men-only groups has had a similar effect on women, particularly in recent years. The separation of men and women over the right to vote led directly to the women's suffrage movement.

Throughout life in American culture, individuals find themselves in many same sex social groups.

Other forms of discrimination against women have led to the formation of a wide range of women's groups and organizations pursuing feminist issues. These groups have taken direct aim at economic discrimination against women as well as at the prejudices and stereotypes that define a woman's place as in the home, playing second fiddle to her husband. The effects of this movement have been far-reaching. Rigid gender-role socialization is less prevalent today than it was only ten years ago. Women can now be found playing strong roles in movies and on TV, reporting the news, and—perhaps most important—making the news.

We cannot choose our sex at conception, nor can we keep ourselves from growing older (although we spend millions every year trying). Both gender and age, however, are human attributes that are integrated into the coordination of most societies in such a way that the roles open to us and the norms that govern us will vary depending on age and gender.

Just as gender and age separate people, differences in wealth, prestige, and ancestry create walls between people in American society. We turn now to a brief examination of these aspects of social differentiation in American society, looking first at social class and social status differentiation and finally at racial and ethnic differentiation. These topics are covered in fuller detail in Chapters 7 and 8, for which these short sections will serve as an introduction.

SOCIAL CLASS AND SOCIAL STATUS DIFFERENTIATION

Unlike gender and age, social class and social status have nothing to do with human biology; they are both purely creations of society. In a modern society such as the United States both exist within the more general structure of social stratification. Although these concepts have been introduced in earlier chapters, it might be useful at this point to review them. **Social stratification** refers to the arrangement of various activities (or roles) into a hierarchy in which activities ranked high are highly rewarded and activities ranked low are poorly rewarded. The rewards generally consist of money, prestige, and influence over others. **Social class** refers to collections of individuals whose activities (or roles) are similar in terms of the rewards they bring to their participants. **Social status** refers to an individual's social position, particularly with respect to prestige. In some societies social status might be entirely determined by how others regard your parents. Although this is an important part of social status in any society, a modern society generally also associates high or low social status with roles (particularly occupational roles) and is therefore something an individual can achieve (or not achieve). Your occupational role within the system of social stratification generally has a major impact on your social class (your occupation is generally the source of most of your "rewards") and on your social status (people often think well or ill of you depending on "what you do"). In short, these three concepts are highly interrelated.

The introduction of a social stratification system makes social differentiation more organized and quite a bit more rigid. In an agricultural society, for example, farmers with fifty acres might not only be better thought of than those with 10 acres, but very likely will have more wealth. If their society is such that their children are able to inherit this wealth, a system of social stratification is born; social status then becomes more closely associated with "what you do" and the wealth that activity brings you (your social class). As new generations are born into this society, they will likely step into the shoes waiting for them, becoming high or low in both social class and social status as they inherit their parents' wealth and "good name" (or poverty and "bad name") simultaneously. Note the similarity between this form of differentiation and gender differentiation. You cannot choose your sex, nor can you choose the wealth or prestige of your parents; in both cases, the differentiation is there waiting for you and will place you into a specific social category. Just as being born a male leads you into experiences different from those of individuals born female, so being born into the upper classes leads you into experiences different from those of people born into the lower classes.

In comparison with age and gender, social class and social status would seem to be far more flexible. Social status, in particular, is basically a matter of how well you are thought of by other members of your society; such opinions should be more easily changed than the aging process. Similarly, social class is largely determined by where you tie into the economy, and people have been known to change jobs, make fortunes, and lose fortunes during a lifetime. The sociological idea that social groups will form out of social categories assumes that the categories will remain somewhat constant. Only then can a collection of individuals share a common body of experiences over time that might lead them to group together. If social class and social status are social categories, our first question must relate to their stability. How common is it for people to change in class and status?

For most societies (including American society) this question can be answered in a straightforward manner. It is in fact quite uncommon for people to change very much in social class or social status, not only during one lifetime but even from one generation to the next. This fact runs contrary to the American "rags to riches" ideal and the belief that "anyone can make it" by working hard enough. Obviously, some individuals do move from rags to riches; we are very aware, in particular, of professional athletes and movie stars who make this jump. We also read stories of little-known inventors who make millions through one of their creations. But keep in mind that these people are in the news because they are unusual. The individual who wins the state lottery is written about only because most of us do not win it. The same is true for movie stars and athletes. For every individual who makes it, a great many more try and fail. Most of us in fact wind up in a social class very similar to that of our parents. For reasons we'll look at in more detail in Chapter 7, a social stratification system generally makes it fairly easy to avoid falling much below your family's rank and fairly difficult to move much above it. Because social status has become so closely tied to social class in the United States, both status and class tend to remain constant for most of us, just like our gender.

We have looked previously at how the coordination of American society is such that people are thrust into very different experiences depending on their age and gender. The same is true for social class and social status. Just as men and women are to some extent isolated from each other, so people from different social classes and statuses are isolated from each other—and to an even greater extent. Social interaction across class lines tends to be sporadic and superficial. The reason is partly the financial differences between one class and the next. Large, expensive homes are effectively prohibited to the lower classes. This means that lower- and upper-class neighborhoods will be separated, which in turn means that children of different classes will not meet and play with each other. To the extent that schools serve particular neighborhoods or that wealthier children attend private schools, children will continue to be separated by class during their school years. Should they meet through a device such as busing, they will still not necessarily socialize beyond the superficial level required by attending the same school. Their parents will, by definition, be engaged in different kinds of work, so they, as well, are not likely to meet. All of these people are separated; they will be living, working, and playing with very little input from other classes. In short, all aspects of their lives, from the most important to the most trivial, will develop in relative isolation and, therefore, in different directions. And whatever that development is, it will be passed from one generation to the next. A growing child learns to play stickball, go bowling, or play polo because that activity is prevalent in his or her social environment. The same is true of modes of speaking, ways of worshipping, attitudes toward education, and so on. As differences develop through isolation, so they persist through isolation.

When individuals do meet each other across social class lines, usually they either follow rigid roles (such as master and servant or, to some extent, as employer and employee), or they become uncomfortable. Without those roles, people of different social classes discover how little they have in common and how their expectations for behavior (which had always worked well within their own social class) don't seem to be working. This kind of experience tends to make people return to the more comfortable realm of their own social class, usually bringing with them negative stereotypes such as "Poor people are rude, ungrateful, and slovenly," or "People with lots of money are snobs who'll step on anyone just to make a few bucks." The communication difficulties that often exist between men and women occur between members of different social classes as well, and for exactly the same reasons— different experiences make people different.

RACIAL AND ETHNIC DIFFERENTIATION

Ethnicity is cultural; an **ethnic group** is a group of people who share a common culture, claim to share a common culture, or are defined by others as sharing a common culture. Race, on the other hand, refers to biological similarity; a **racial group** is supposedly a group of people who share a biological heritage that is specific to them and distinct from that of other groups. The use of "supposedly" is necessary because not all biologists agree that race is a useful biological concept. People obviously inherit different genes and, among other results, look different. The question is, do they inherit different genes in groups? Can we argue, for example, that all black people are genetically more like each other than any of them is genetically like white people? No, we can't, for it's not true.

Whatever the biological questions involved in race, however, it has a quite particular social definition: a racial group is a group of people who are generally believed to share a biological heritage that is specific to them and distinct from other groups. In short, a race exists whenever a lot of people think it exists. This addition to the biological definition is important for, as we will see in Chapter 8, *race* is a term that has been used very loosely throughout history; a group believed racially distinct this year might not be thought of that way next year. Conveniently, groups that are labeled as racial groups at any point in time are also typically ethnically different from whichever group is doing the labeling; hence, racial groups either are or contain ethnic groups.

The United States has grown tremendously in its two hundred-year history, and massive numbers of people have come to its territory from other places. Sometimes called the "nation of immigrants," the United States is a unique society for the ethnic diversity within it as well as for the way this diversity occurred.

Groups of immigrants have set up tightly knit communities in cities all over the United States. Here, Chinese New Year is celebrated in Boston's Chinatown.

There is nothing like meeting someone from another culture to make you become aware of your own. Normally, people take their cultures for granted, but when they meet people whose diet consists mainly of raw fish, unleavened bread, tortillas, rice, or pasta, it makes them look at their own typical meals in a new light. Because people from any culture will be ethnocentric, the coming together of different ethnic groups makes ethnicity a natural characteristic with which to differentiate. As the United States grew and as its ethnic diversity increased, ethnic differences came to be seen as increasingly important; encountering all that ethnic diversity out on the street might make you want to get home to your family, where you felt warm and secure. This experience was especially strong for immigrant groups to the United States, who felt totally overwhelmed by the new culture they had entered and almost always formed tight immigrant communities where much of their old culture was maintained. The experience of immigration made the category of ethnicity stand out.

The immigrant brought not only a new culture to the United States but job competition as well. Particularly in times of economic recession, the immigrant was viewed with fear and distrust by those already here, who saw the newcomers as threats to their economic security. One response to this kind of threat is the prejudice and discrimination that always seem so common between racial and ethnic groups. Acts of discrimination, such as a refusal to allow members of the immigrant group to live in certain areas or work at certain jobs, makes your neighborhood and job all the more secure. Prejudice and stereotypes point out the supposed shortcomings of the immigrant group and their culture, thus justifying the discrimination against them.

Slavery in the United States is a good example of this process. It helped whites in that (1) white slave owners gained wealth through the labor of black slaves, and (2) all whites were spared having to compete with blacks for jobs since slavery kept blacks out of the job market. After the emancipation of slaves many other forms of discrimination against blacks were developed to serve the same purpose. Along with the discrimination went a variety of forms of prejudice and stereotypes, not the least of which was the basic belief in racial superiority that justified (in the minds of white people) a domination of black people.

Both setting up discriminatory processes against an ethnic group and facing those discriminatory processes call attention to ethnic differences. Slavery, for example, made whites very aware of being white and blacks very aware of being black. As a mode of social coordination, slavery served to differentiate people on the basis of skin color, thus making skin color an extremely important human characteristic. Although slavery is probably the most extreme example in American history (matched only by the near extermination of Native Americans), most ethnically distinct immigrant groups faced some forms of prejudice and discrimination in the United States. And prejudice and discrimination added to cultural difference makes race or ethnicity an important social category.

FORMAL ORGANIZATIONS AND BUREAUCRACIES

As we've seen, social groups vary in a great many ways; they can be large or small, primary or secondary, and varied in the kinds of people who form them. One of the most important variations in social groups is the degree to which they are formal or informal. A group of you and your friends, for example, is informal in that you do different things at different times and places and probably permit a wide range of behavior among yourselves. If your social group decided to form a charity, produce a salable product, or elect a political candidate, however, you would very soon discover a need for more organization. Who would do what and when? Who would make decisions? Who would be responsible for getting things done? In short, you would need to transform the informal organization of your social group into a formal organization. The formal organization is one of the clearest cases of a social group that reflects the coordination of society; informal groups take their social organization for granted, but formal organizations approach the question of coordination in a very self-conscious and conspicuous manner.

A **formal organization** is a social group with a clear structure of roles and norms consciously designed for the achievement of particular goals. It is characterized by a division of labor and a hierarchical chain of command. Formal organizations can be small and relatively simple, such as a local election campaign committee, or they can be large and extremely complex, such as Exxon or Microsoft. The more industrial and complex a society becomes, the more informal social groups will be replaced by formal organizations. If you are currently going to school or working, you have almost daily dealings with formal organizations. Because formal organizations are obviously much larger and more powerful than individuals, you will necessarily have to adapt your behavior to the organizations' demands. If you disagree with those demands, you might try fighting by forming your own formal organization; labor unions were formed for just that purpose. But the folk wisdom that "you can't fight city hall" indicates something of the difficulties you will have.

BUREAUCRACIES

Most modern formal organizations contain some elements of bureaucratic organization. A **bureaucracy** is a formal organization characterized by a set of positions arranged in a hierarchy of authority and governed by specific procedural rules designed to accomplish specific tasks. Because it is often claimed that bureaucracies work better on paper than in practice, it would be useful to begin this examination by looking at the ideal form of the bureaucracy presented by sociologist Max Weber.

According to Weber (1946), the ideal bureaucracy (or a bureaucracy as it might logically function) would have the following characteristics:

1. The bureaucracy should be based on a body of laws or rules intentionally constructed and specifically designed to meet the goals of the organization. This body of laws or rules should represent an impersonal order to which all

members of the bureaucracy should be subject. This means, in short, that rules should operate consistently on a day-to-day basis and that no one in the bureaucracy would be "above the laws." The successful working of the U.S. Constitution during the Watergate episode, the Iran-Contra affair, the impeachment of President Clinton, and the 2000 presidential election all suggest approximations of the ideal implementation of a bureaucracy's rules.

2. The offices of the bureaucracy should be organized according to a division of labor in which there is clear hierarchy of authority. Specific tasks should be assigned to specific offices to provide maximum efficiency of operation, and there should be no doubt as to which offices have the authority to give orders to the occupants of other offices. In a university, for example, a professor has the authority to assign certain kinds of educational tasks to students and to test the completion of those tasks according to acceptable testing procedures. That same professor does not have the authority, however, to assign killing as an educational task or to schedule tests on Sunday morning.

3. Individuals should exercise authority or be subject to authority according to the position they occupy within the bureaucracy. In a bureaucracy no one "owns" his or her position and the authority that comes with it. This is the basis of Weber's legal/rational authority type (Chapter 3), in which authority is clearly attached to positions and not to individuals. As we've seen, individuals very easily forget this as they commonly get caught up in their positions and come to identify with them.

4. Individuals should have specialized training for the particular tasks involved in their offices and should be appointed to those offices only on the basis of their technical qualifications. The specialized training is designed to provide for qualified bureaucratic officers. Appointment on any other basis (such as family relations or political connections) would make the bureaucracy less efficient.

5. There should be a separation between ownership of the bureaucracy (its property or profits, for example) and the offices within it. Bureaucratic officers should receive fixed salaries for the work they do and not have their decisions motivated by personal profit.

Weber's ideally efficient bureaucracy has some shortcomings even beyond frequent human unwillingness or inability to abide by it; indeed, Weber did not intend his ideal type to be a bureaucracy as it actually exists but as an extreme case. The most important shortcoming lies in the nature of the tasks performed by the bureaucracy. A bureaucratic organization is at its peak of efficiency when the tasks at hand are repetitive and do not require creative responses on a day-to-day basis. If specific tasks are assigned to specific offices whose occupants have specialized training, the introduction of new and different tasks can toss a monkey wrench into the workings of the organization. As we'll see shortly, bureaucratic structure often varies from Weber's ideal type in anticipation of such needs for flexibility (see Astley and Zajac, 1991).

Two semi-humorous criticisms of bureaucracies attempt to explain why bureau-cratic actions fall short of Weber's ideal conception. The Peter Principle states, "In a hierarchy every employee tends to rise to his level of incompetence" (Peter and Hull, 1969, 25). The explanation of this principle is that an employee who does well at a particular level of the bureaucracy will receive a promotion when a vacancy opens up above. (Note how this violates Weber's rule concerning specialized training.) Individuals who don't do well, on the other hand, will not receive promotions but will not be fired. The logical result of this practice, say Peter and Hull, is that every employee will ultimately arrive at a position beyond his or her level of competence—the level of incompetence—and will stay there forever, doing an inadequate job.

A second criticism of bureaucracies is Parkinson's Law: "Work expands to fill the time available for its completion" (Parkinson, 1957). If true, Parkinson's Law would result in waste and inefficiency instead of the hoped-for efficiency of the bureaucracy. The source of this observation lies in the tendency of all bureaucracies to continue over time and to grow in size. It is not in the interest of bureaucrats either to terminate their activities or to reduce the size of their staffs. It is, in fact, in their interest to increase the size of their staffs, as that adds prestige to their positions. Whatever work there is to do must be expanded to fill the time of the current staff in order to justify a later increase. One way to fill this time is to increase the amount of paperwork—a noted characteristic of all bureaucracies.

Finally, at the individual level, we come to one of the most basic problems con-fronted by all bureaucracies: individuals in the offices may choose not to follow the rational organization of the bureaucracy. Individual officers may ignore or circum-vent rules, may refuse to do the work in their job description (and then cover up that fact), or may form alliances with other officers of the bureaucracy to expand their section at the expense of another (and perhaps vital) section. In short, individuals may choose not to comply with the rules or the goals of the bureaucracy.

ORGANIZATIONAL ALIENATION AND COMPLIANCE

Alienation, a concept popularized by Karl Marx, refers to an individual's inability to control the forces that affect his or her own life. The individual consequently experiences these forces as "alien." In the world of work (and formal organiza-tions) alienation occurs when individual members of the organization, usually those at the bottom of the bureaucratic hierarchy, cease to feel any connection to the work they do. One result is that they may choose not to comply with the rules of the organization.

The hierarchy of authority that exists in any bureaucracy rests on its members' acceptance of its legitimacy. Authority is differentiated from power by the willing-ness with which people take orders. Weber's notion of legal/rational authority (which exists in bureaucracies) depends on this sense of legitimacy. If individual workers come to feel alienated from the organization as a whole, they will lose this sense of legitimate authority.

Are modern offices with their individual cubicles sources of workplace alienation?

The idea of worker compliance entered the discussions of American sociologists in the 1920s, largely as the result of a famous study of workers at the Hawthorne Western Electric plant in Cicero, Illinois (Roethlisberger and Dickson, 1964). The goal of the researchers was to find ways to increase worker productivity. Their findings were not at all what they expected. First, they separated two groups of workers into an experimental and a control group (see Chapter 2). In keeping with the rules of the formal experiment, they left the control group alone in one room and tried raising the level of lighting for the experimental group. The result? Productivity went up in both groups. After many more similar studies they came to the conclusion that the very fact of being studied (or the presence of the experimenters) was creating the differences in levels of productivity; unlike plants and single-celled animals, people know when they're being watched. This effect of the social scientific investigator on the object of study has come to be called the *Hawthorne effect,* after this study. It should also be noted that the reliability of the original data has been called into question by subsequent research (Jones, 1992).

The Western Electric investigators were in for a few other surprises as well. They found, for example, that informal groups of workers conspired to hold down production so that assembly-line rates would not be increased or piece rates changed. In short, the Western Electric investigators concluded that worker productivity had a lot to do with the workers' attitudes about the work they were doing. This conclusion largely founded the perspective on formal organizations known as the *human relations school.*

Some students of formal organizations have criticized the human relations school on the grounds that it makes value judgments biased toward management: that is, workers who comply are viewed as good, whereas those who don't are viewed as bad. These critics point out that a bureaucracy that is efficient and rational from management's point of view may result in worker layoffs. To workers, an efficient bureaucracy is one that maintains their jobs and may require an informal restriction of output.

David Mechanic (1962) continued this criticism of the human relations school in his study of the "lower participants" (or lower-level workers) in bureaucracies. Lower participants have, he pointed out, certain kinds of control for influencing the higher-ups. Secretaries, for example, can withhold administrative information from higher-ups in an office situation, or they can even slow down their work in order to change the way they are treated. Even prisoners have some control over guards. A guard who reports too many rule infractions will appear not to be doing a good job as a guard. It is in the interest of guards, therefore, to exchange a few favors with prisoners in return for their general cooperation in not breaking rules. In short, lower participants can often control persons, information, or behavior to which those higher up require access. Bureaucracies often operate on just such a system of negotiation (see Strauss et al., 1964). If lower participants lack this control or, worse from their standpoint, the freedom to express grievances, worker satisfaction drops significantly (Gorden and Infante, 1991; Infante and Gorden, 1991).

Although lower participants have some control over those above them in the authority hierarchy, a number of factors make them comply with that authority. Amitai Etzioni (1961) pointed out that, beyond the lower participant's belief in the "rightness" of the authority structure, he or she may be forced or may be induced with rewards to comply. If the lower participant believes in the authority hierarchy, the power of the formal organization is *normative;* that is, lower participants comply because they adhere to norms of compliance. Failing such norms, power can be *coercive;* that is, the lower participants are forced against their will to comply. Finally, organizations can be *utilitarian:* lower participants may not love their work or their boss, but they may need the job and will comply to keep it.

A close look at any utilitarian organization will reveal a wide variety of worker subcultures within the bureaucracy, each representing informal sets of values that may well contradict the official positions of the organization (Jermier et al., 1991). Coercive organizations include concentration camps, prisons, prisoner-of-war camps, and some mental institutions; utilitarian organizations include most unions, most occupational organizations, and the peacetime military; normative organizations include religious organizations, colleges and universities, hospitals, some fraternal organizations, and some political organizations (Etzioni, 1961).

Etzioni gave some attention to the lower participant in his analysis of various formal organizations. A coercive organization, he argues, leads to alienation among the lower participants; prisoners may follow orders, but they certainly have no extra love for their guards or the warden. Utilitarian organizations produce calculating workers; if you comply only for the money, every act of compliance will be figured out carefully in terms of "what's in it for me." Workers are often more concerned with their job and income than they are with the financial health of their employer. Finally, normative organizations produce moral compliance; members of religious or extreme political organizations may act according to a strict moral code inherent in their organization. As with all social groups, individuals who value the norms highly will also have a high level of loyalty to the group.

ORGANIZATIONAL STRUCTURE

Figure 6.2 illustrates schematically a typical bureaucratic hierarchy of authority. The levels of the hierarchy represent different levels of authority, the boxes represent different offices, and the lines between the boxes follow the paths by which orders are given and received. Although most real bureaucracies would be much larger, consider the effect this structure would have on the people who filled the offices. The lower participants, for example, would find themselves divided into five sets, or work groups, and would probably have very little interaction across those groups. The middle-level officers would (perhaps) have to keep a close eye on their underlings while being careful to "look good" to the boss at the top. In addition, the middle-level officers might (1) not know each other, (2) not understand each other because of the different kinds of work they do, or (3) be locked in intense competition, each trying to prove that his or her arm of the organization is the most important.

Consider the differences you might find in an organizational hierarchy like that in Figure 6.3. This organization has a head officer, as Figure 6.2 had, but beyond

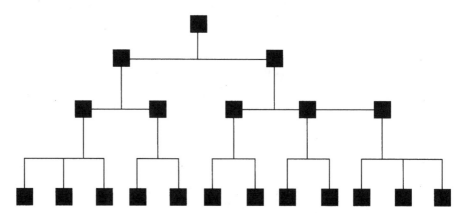

Figure 6.2 Bureaucratic hierarchy of authority.

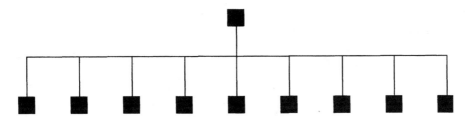

Figure 6.3 An organization of professionals.

that there is little similarity. All of the lower participants (if they can be called that) in Figure 6.3 are on an equal footing with one another. They may be doing totally different kinds of work, or, more likely, different versions or aspects of the same work. The fact that they cannot give orders to each other might encourage them to cooperate rather than compete (although other factors might be equally important in determining cooperation versus competition). Perhaps more important, the organization in Figure 6.3 would probably be less methodical but more flexible than the organization in Figure 6.2 (Ancoma and Caldwell, 1992). The Figure 6.3 organization would be able to adapt easily to changing circumstances and different work because of its simple structure, whereas the organization in Figure 6.2 would require more time changing its structure to adapt. But even though its structure might be more rigid, its employees are more interchangeable; a high turnover in personnel would not present difficult problems (Carley, 1992). When rigid organizational structures are asked to perform new tasks in a creative fashion, position occupants typically create new lines of communication informally, allowing the organization to adapt (Wilson, 1992). Figure 6.2 is a standard kind of bureaucratic structure, used, for example, in routine office work; Figure 6.3 is the kind of organization found, for example, in a university department, where each professor is equal and under the authority of the department chair. Professors and office workers do different kinds of work; the organizations that hire them can help or hinder that work by their very structure.

The need for flexibility and creativity in a formal organization can perhaps best be seen in the role of the doctor in the modern hospital. The problem is made even more complicated by the fact that the hospital requires large amounts of routine work completed and, in addition, is often administered by an officer who lacks medical training; doctors may feel that they should not be given orders by an individual who doesn't understand their work (a feeling doctors share with a great many other occupations) (Perrow, 1986). One solution to this problem is to create a hospital organization that combines Figures 6.2 and 6.3. With such a combination business officials, nurses, janitors, cooks, and receptionists can be placed in a Figure 6.2 structure for their routine work, while doctors can be placed in a Figure 6.3 structure, existing parallel to and separate from the rest of the hospital staff. This setup allows doctors to have considerable control over their work. Meanwhile, routine tasks are carried out, and the hospital runs efficiently.

ORGANIZATIONS AND THEIR ENVIRONMENTS

Formal organizations do not exist in vacuums. They operate in an environment that includes natural forces, technology, people, and, perhaps most important, other formal organizations. In the early twentieth century, formal organizations that mass-produced automobiles had a major impact on other formal organizations that refined gasoline, paved roads, engineered bridges, and designed roadside restaurants. People can affect formal organizations through such basic things as their ages, their numbers, or their concentrations. Formal organizations are commonly located in cities where large numbers of people are concentrated. If men go off to war, women will have to fill different positions (as during the World War II movement of housewives into factories). Americans today are having fewer babies and living longer, which means that soon the majority of Americans will be quite old. Such a change places considerable pressure on the Social Security Administration. We look at some of these changes in more detail in Chapter 9.

Probably the most significant environmental element for the formal organization on a day-to-day basis is the **organizational set**—the collection of other formal organizations with which the organization in question interacts (Evans, 1966). Consider the position of an urban police department. It is a public formal organization with specified tasks assigned to it, but it operates within a complex organizational set that affects everything it does. In the public sector alone, a police department must interact with other city organizations, both elected and civil service. In addition, the police department must interact with state and federal organizations. This connection is most obvious with regard to state and federal legal proceedings. But beyond the public sector of organizations, a police department must also cope with private organizations. A community organization, for example, might criticize the level or quality of police protection it receives. An organization of city business people might have similar concerns. And professional organizations, such as the American Bar Association, would clearly also have an interest in police activities. Because all of these organizations in the organizational set have different agendas, the police department faces the challenge of mapping a complex course through conflicted waters (Davenport, 2000; Edelman and Suchman, 1997).

As organizations are affected by their organizational set, so do they affect it. Formal business organizations, in particular, look out for their own interests and attempt to change their environment to further those interests when possible. Corporations give money to political candidates (sometimes illegally), hire lobbyists to promote their interests in Congress, engage in industrial espionage, bribe local and international officials, and attempt to control the markets for their goods. Large modern governmental bureaucracies tend to become permanent figures on the social landscape as their functionaries work to maintain the official structure of the organization, come what may. Labor unions—which once were small, radical bands of workers with socialistic goals—are now commonly much larger and more interested in maintaining a secure institutional place for their members. The growth of multinational corporations in recent years has made these possibilities for environment shaping more feasible and a little more frightening. Formal organizations that are larger than most countries and practically beyond the legal jurisdiction of any one country are in an excellent position to structure their corner of the world to make it as comfortable as possible for themselves.

SUMMARY

The coordination involved in any human society involves patterns of activities in which different people often fulfill extremely different functions. Engaging in different activities provides for different kinds of experiences and, consequently, makes people different from each other. This overall process is referred to as social differentiation. When differentiation occurs in a society, sociologists speak of the differentiated parts as social categories; individuals find themselves categorized according to the specific characteristics that make up the basis for the differentiation. Because being similarly categorized provides for similar experiences, people in the same social category are often much like each other and/or have similar interests; these points in common often lead them to form social groups.

Both the importance and the power of social groups become apparent through studying boundary maintenance and social control. Through the unlimited number of social interactions that produce boundary maintenance, group members remind one another about the distinction between group members and nonmembers. Social control becomes apparent through the need many group members have to conform to group standards, even at considerable personal cost, so as to not jeopardize their membership. This attachment to the group becomes stronger whenever the group is threatened from the outside.

While any human characteristic could conceivably become the basis for social differentiation, each society contains only a few categories that its members think significant. In the United States the major social categories are formed around social differentiation of age, gender, social class, social status, race, and ethnicity. We examined these important social categories in terms of (1) how American society creates them as categories, and (2) how individuals respond to sharing these categories by forming social groups.

Formal organizations are social groups with a clear structure of roles and norms consciously designed for the achievement of particular goals. If the organization contains offices arranged in a hierarchy of authority, it may be described as following the principles of bureaucratic organization. Organizations typically face problems in obtaining the compliance of lower participants, creating a structure that is conducive to organizational goals, and defending themselves (or furthering their interests) in an environment of other potentially competitive formal organizations.

GLOSSARY

Ageism Prejudice toward the aged as well as acts of discrimination against them on the basis of age.

Alienation A worker's lack of interest in and identification with his or her job and a feeling of powerlessness in general over the conditions that affect his or her life.

Boundary maintenance Efforts by social group members to separate one group (typically their own) from another by focusing on differences in group members or typical group behavior.

Bureaucracy A formal organization characterized by a set of positions arranged in a hierarchy of authority and governed by specific procedural rules designed to accomplish specific tasks.

Closed group A social group that allows no expansion in membership.

Ethnic group A social group whose members share a common culture, claim to share a common culture, or are defined by others as sharing a common culture.

Formal organization (formal group) A social group with a clear structure of roles and norms consciously designed for the achievement of particular goals. It is characterized by a division of labor and a hierarchical chain of command.

Horizontal group A social group whose members share a common social class.

Informal group A social group in which norms, roles, values, and goals are agreed to tacitly and have some flexibility.

In-group A social group that an individual feels "at home" with or identifies with.

Involuntary group A social group to which members belong involuntarily (for example, the family you are born into, a group of prison inmates).

Open group A social group open to new members.

Organizational set The collection of formal organizations with which a particular formal organization interacts.

Out-group Any social group that a particular individual does not belong to or identify with.

Primary groups Social groups that are small and characterized by considerable face-to-face interaction and strong emotional ties (for example, a family or a group of close friends).

Racial group A collection of individuals who define themselves or are defined by others as sharing a particular and distinctive biological heritage.

Reference group A social group against whose standards a particular individual measures himself or herself and his or her accomplishments.

Secondary groups Social groups that are typically larger and less emotionally based than primary groups. The individual's tie to the secondary group is generally through a specific role played within the group.

Self-fulfilling prophecy A social occurrence in which the belief that something will happen helps make it happen.

Sexism Stereotyping on the basis of sex, and prejudice and discrimination based on sex.

Social category A collection of individuals who have something (characteristics, attributes, abilities, etc.) in common.

Social class A collection of individuals whose activities or roles are similar in terms of the rewards these activities or roles bring to their participants.

Social differentiation The process by which differences are created among individuals as a result of the different experiences they have as members of society. The differentiation occurs along the lines of socially important attributes such as (in American society) gender, race, income, occupation, and so on.

Social group A collection of people who (1) know each other (or know of each other), (2) agree that they share something (at least their groupness and the goals of the group), and (3) have continuing interactions with each other, resulting in patterned behavior.

Social status An individual's social position within the social group, particularly with respect to his or her prestige.

Social stratification The arrangement of different activities or roles into a hierarchy whereby activities ranked high are highly rewarded and activities ranked low are poorly rewarded. The rewards generally consist of money, prestige, and influence over others.

Vertical group A social group whose members occupy a variety of social classes.

Voluntary group A social group to which members belong voluntarily.

Study Questions

1. How do categories and groups differ? Why are social categories often the basis for group formation?
2. What are the differences and similarities between the following: (1) primary and secondary groups, (2) formal and informal groups, (3) voluntary and involuntary groups, (4) open and closed groups, (5) horizontal and vertical groups, and (6) in-groups and out-groups?
3. Which groups make up an individual's reference groups?
4. Why are social group boundaries important to group members? What social processes serve to maintain those boundaries? How do social groups act as powerful agents of social control?

5. How does conflict with another group affect a group's internal level of cooperation?
6. How are age and gender both social categories in the contemporary United States? Explain both ageism and sexism in your discussion.
7. How does gender-role socialization produce major differences between men and women? How can that socialization operate as a self-fulfilling prophecy?
8. How are social classes formed? In what sense is social class a social category?
9. What is the difference between a racial group and an ethnic group?
10. What are the formal elements of a bureaucratic organization? How and why do real bureaucracies vary from that ideal form?
11. How does the structure of a bureaucracy determine the kinds of work that can be accomplished within it?

Ellis Cose and Allison Samuels

THE BLACK GENDER GAP

Of all the social categories explored in this chapter, two of the most significant are gender and race. These two categories have an enormous impact on our lives, thrusting different kinds of life experiences upon us and forcing us to react. In this reading, Cose and Samuels compare the different experiences and different responses of African American men and women. Their task is to explain why only African American *women* are achieving success in education and the job market while African American *men* are largely failing in both arenas. As we saw in the previous chapter, African American men are more likely to wind up in prison than any other group. But that observation does not explain the differences described below.

"I know what every colored woman in this country is doing . . . Dying. Just like me. But the difference is they dying like a stump. Me, I'm going down like one of those redwoods." America was in a very different place in 1973, when novelist Toni Morrison put those words in the mouth of the doomed yet defiant Sula, whose triumph lay solely in the fact that she could meet death on her own terms. Who then could have imagined that an African-American female would one day stand atop the nation's foreign-policy pyramid? Who could have predicted that black women would, educationally, so outstrip black men? Who could have dreamed the day would come when black women would lay claim to "white men's" jobs—the phrase used by banking executive Malia Fort's former boss as he reminded her of the

time when "the only thing a black woman could have done in a bank is clean up"? Today a black woman can be anything from an astronaut to a talk-show host, run anything from a corporation to an Ivy League university. Once consigned to mostly menial work, black women (24 percent of them, compared with 17 percent of black men) have ascended to the professional-managerial class.

This is not to say that black women have climbed the storied crystal stair. They remain "in the proving stage," observes Alabama Power executive Alice Gordon. Nearly 14 percent of working black women remain below the poverty level. And women don't yet out-earn black men. But the growing educational-achievement gap portends a monumental shifting of the sands.

From *Reason*, August/September 2001, pp. 36–43. Reprinted by permission of *Reason*, © 2001. All rights reserved.

College-educated black women already earn more than the median for all black working men—or, for that matter, for all women. And as women in general move up the corporate pyramid, black women, increasingly, are part of the parade. In 1995 women held less than 9 percent of corporate-officer positions in Fortune 500 companies, according to Catalyst, a New York-based organization that promotes the interests of women in business. Last year they held close to 16 percent, a significant step up. Of those 2,140 women, 163 were black—a minuscule proportion, but one that is certain to grow.

These days, few black women are willing to settle for Sula's life. There is a search not only for recognition but for "models of happiness," in the words of Veronica Chambers, author of a new book called "Having It All." But that quest brings with it a host of questions—some whispered, some loudly (even anxiously) debated. Is this new black woman finally crashing through the double ceiling of race and gender? Or is she leaping into treacherous waters that will leave her stranded, unfulfilled, childless and alone? Can she thrive if her brother does not, if the black man succumbs, as hundreds of thousands already have, to the hopelessness of prison and the streets? Can she—dare she—thrive without the black man, finding happiness across the racial aisle? Or will she, out of compassion, loneliness or racial loyalty "settle" for men who—educationally, economically, professionally—are several steps beneath her?

Such questions are now being debated because black men and women are, increasingly, following different paths. As choreographer Fatima Robinson put it: "I love brothers . . . But there is such a gap that I think I may not end up with a black man." In 1970 the numbers of black males and females in college (though much smaller than they are now) were essentially equivalent. There were only 6 percent more black women than black men enrolled. But in the aftermath of the women's liberation movement, females of all colors moved into the academy and the professions. In 1970 America's college population was predominantly male. Today it is 56 percent female.

Twenty-five percent of young black males go to college; 35 percent of women do. Only 13.5 percent of young black females are high-school dropouts; more than 17 percent of young black men are. The notion that college was a place to find a man has slowly given way to the conviction that decent, educated black men are rarer, to borrow Shakespeare's words, than pearls in beauteous ladies' eyes.

Daven Jackson, a 25-year-old veterinary student at Alabama's predominantly black Tuskegee University, thinks she understands why. In her high school in Thomasville, Ga., recalls Jackson, "most black males were encouraged to be athletes," not scholars. None made it big as jocks; instead, "over half of the males who graduated with me are in jail." Tametria Brown, a student at Meharry Medical College, remembers being singled out for leadership roles in high school. That rarely happened with the boys. Not just teachers but the entire educational support system now favors girls over boys, argues Monette Evans, a Tuskegee vice president. There is also the powerful drive of the women themselves. "Oftentimes women go into higher education and beyond because they can't depend on anyone else to support them or their children," Evans points out. And whereas boys typically lack focus, girls show up with a sense of purpose. "Females had no excuses about anything," says Kevin Cook, an administrator at Arizona State University. They arrive with an attitude that quietly announces, "We're here. It's tough. We're black. We're alone."

As they graduate and move into the work world, many black women stay just as tough-minded. "I never had this expectation that someone would reach down and pat me on the head," says Laura Murphy, head of the Washington office of the ACLU. "In order to advance, I had to change jobs." For many black women, that professional struggle never ends. "Nobody reaches out to [black women] . . . And when they reach out, the door gets slammed in their face," says Ella L. J. Bell, a professor at Dartmouth's Tuck School of Business and coauthor of "Our Separate Ways," a study of black and white women in corporations. Indeed, despite all the progress they have made, black women "are the least satisfied [of all groups of women] and overall least likely to stay in their current jobs," says Sheila Wellington, president of Catalyst.

Still, for significant numbers the atmosphere in corporate America is changing. In a recently released study of corporate women of color, Catalyst found that 57 percent had been promoted between 1998 and 2001. According to that study, 62 percent of black women reported having mentors, up dramatically from three years earlier, when the number was 35 percent. Although the updated survey drew from a much smaller sample, it indicates something extremely encouraging—that black women may be starting to overcome one of the most significant barriers to career advancement: connecting with influential people in the work hierarchy. Corporate types may still not see black women as members of the club, but they "don't feel threatened by us," notes Gwen DeRu, vice president of a black-owned consulting firm in Birmingham, Ala.

In fact, if watering-hole conversation is any criterion, the most difficult challenge black women face today may lie closer to home. Go any Friday night to Lola's Cajun eatery in Los Angeles and you'll find a weekly gathering of what could easily be dubbed "the black, beautiful, accomplished but can't find a mate club." In bars, colleges and other gathering spots across America, the question is much the same: where are the decent, desirable black men? "When I left high school, I had a boyfriend, but that went down the drain," confides Tametria Brown, 23. As an undergraduate at the University of Virginia, she found " a lot of people dating the same guy . . . The dating scene was not good." The marriage scene may be worse. According to the 2000 Census, 47 percent of black women in the 30-to-34 age range have never married, compared with 10 percent of white women. "I figured that as I made more money and got the

education that's required to get a good job, that that would automatically make it easier for me to find someone," said Lana Coleman, a Pasadena, Calif., attorney. "But it's really been the opposite."

For M. Belinda Tucker, a psychologist at UCLA and co-editor of "The Decline in Marriage Among African Americans," such comments evoke memories of her own experience as a graduate student at the University of Chicago some three decades ago. A fancy education, her black female friends had concluded, came at a significant price. "You were essentially consigning yourself to being unmarried . . . That's what we said to each other and that's what we were told." Tucker is quick to add that, for many, the prophecy proved false. But the sentiment resonates much more strongly today—if only because the numbers are so much more daunting.

Gwen McKinney considers herself among the blessed in being married to a black man (a systems engineer) who is unthreatened by her success as a Washington public-relations-firm owner. "I just consider myself like the Marines— the few, the proud—in terms of being so fortunate that I have a spouse who is supportive." McKinney believes her husband's comfort level stems from the fact that they got involved before her business took off. "Most of the time it doesn't work unless those relationships are forged before the woman's ascendancy," she says. That many black men seem threatened by successful women is a development that Michael Eric Dyson, author of "Why I Love Black Women," finds ironic. "I call it femphobia—the fear of black women. The same strength that was used to save black men is now being used against them."

Underappreciated by black men, many black women are looking elsewhere. Connie Rice, a Los Angeles civil-rights attorney and Radcliffe graduate, puts it plainly: "If you have to have the same race, your choices are limited." For years, there has been a general assumption that while black men were comfortable dating white women, black women (for many reasons, some having to do with exploitation dating back to the time of slavery) generally steered clear of white men.

Certainly, statistics show that interracial black-white unions, while relatively rare, have been much more common between black men and white women. But the marriage statistics are shifting. And if unpublished research by Tucker and her colleagues is any indication, the dating wall of Jericho is tumbling. In a survey of residents of 21 cities, Tucker & Co. found that 78 percent of black men (average age: 32) had dated interracially at least once, as had 53 percent of black women (average age: 34).

Those emerging trends represent a new promise of racial integration to some—and a threat of lost racial identity to others. Actor Samuel Jackson was caught a bit off guard when his only daughter, Zoe, began dating white boys in high school. "It was a little weird because you really always think of black couples being together and want that for your child, too," recalls Jackson's wife, Latanya Richardson. Last year the couple sent Zoe to Spelman College, a predominantly black all-female school in Atlanta. She now has a black boyfriend. "It made her father very happy," said Richardson. "I just think he wanted her to see the different side of things. To have the option of both, really."

Instead of crossing the racial line, others are trying to navigate the currents of interclass romance. Ellen Lewis, 32, a product manager for Oscar Mayer in Phoenix, Ariz., is married to a trucker. With a marketing degree and business experience, Lewis makes more than double her husband's salary. When they began dating, she hid all evidence of her success. "After a while, I could see he could probably handle it." But even now, says Lewis, "it's hard not to sense his resentment and his attitude that black women have it easier." Birmingham banker Malia Fort, who had a child (and is in a long-term relationship) with a laborer, has found the going somewhat smoother—in part because her expectations were brutally realistic. "He doesn't fit into my professional world, but he doesn't have to," she says.

In analyzing data collected from graduates of 28 selective colleges and universities, sociologist Donna Franklin found evidence of serious trouble with marriages where the wife was the dominant wage earner. The black women surveyed were much more likely than white women to have husbands who earned less; those who had been married were also more than twice as likely to have gotten divorced. The facts are not coincidental, says Franklin, author of "What's Love Got to Do With It?"—a probing look at relationships between black women and men. The higher divorce rate among highly educated black women was due, she believes, to the fact that they generally made more money than their mates.

Youtha Hardman-Cromwell, a Washington minister and associate professor at Wesley Theological Seminary, is hopeful that society is just going through a period of adjustment—that in the end, black women will not be penalized for marrying less successful men. "Look at how fragile interracial marriages once were," she says. But even among the most optimistic, there is an underlying sense of concern. Ella Bell, professor and soon-to-be Essence career-advice columnist, is far more successful than she ever dreamed she would be. Yet the never-married Bell is not exactly content. "I've come not to expect a traditional black husband," says Bell. "You can get a dog, keep yourself busy ... keep yourself tired ... You don't have to have a relationship," she says. Still, she wonders—neither morbidly nor excessively—if she "will die in a room all by myself."

Cassaundra Cain prepared her two daughters (now college-age) early on for the possibility of being alone. A divorced postal worker living in Atlanta, Cain says she "always stressed the Prince Charming thing wasn't our reality." She warned her daughters against getting "caught in what they saw young mainstream girls do ... I tell them they're young black girls—that they may end up on their own and alone." Even for women in "mainstream" white America, says Franklin, hard times may lie ahead. Black women may be the leaders in the trend of marrying less successful men, but white women are surely following. And, argues Franklin, they will reap the same

INTERRACIAL MARRIAGES
IN THOUSANDS

Year	Black husband/ white wife	White husband/ black wife
1980	122	45
1985	117	47
1990	150	61
1995	206	122
1998	210	120

consequences—more domestic tension and higher divorce rates. Professor Bell agrees: "Nothing lies in isolation in a culture this fluid. So what happens to us will happen to them." But what exactly will happen to "us"? Bell concedes that black women, particularly young, black, educated women, are journeying into uncharted waters. "They have a degree of liberty no other group of black women have had . . . It'll be interesting to see what they do with it."

Interesting, indeed. There are several competing visions. In the most bleak, more and more black women will lead lives of success but also of isolation, as poorer, less well-prepared black women raise the community's children and perpetuate the existence of the "underclass." Then

there is another view, one closer to that of Hardman-Cromwell's, the Washington minister. In that vision, black women are weathering a period of transition, after which they will find a way to balance happiness and success—and perhaps even serve as an inspiration for their sisters across the color line. It is, admittedly, the rosier view; but it is not necessarily less realistic. Given the history of black women on this planet, one would have to be supremely foolish to believe that there is any challenge they cannot overcome.

DISCUSSION QUESTIONS

1. Over the last thirty years, the proportion of women in American higher education has been steadily growing. This has been true for all Americans but the gap is more pronounced among African Americans. Why do you think men are now less successful in education? And why do you think that is especially true for African American men?

2. The authors relate stories of African American women who find difficulty in finding an African American spouse at their same level of education and occupation. Do you think this is the cause of the increasing numbers of black women-white men marriages described in the reading?

SOCIAL STRATIFICATION: SOCIAL DOMINANCE AND SUBORDINATION

T he supposedly unsinkable British ocean liner *Titanic* sank rapidly after colliding with an iceberg in 1912. Like most luxury liners, the *Titanic* was divided into different "classes": passengers could purchase the amount of luxury they wanted in their accommodations. And these "choices" proved to be fateful. Among women passengers, only 3 percent of those in first class died, compared with 14 percent in second class and 54 percent in third class. Although women and children were supposed to be first into the lifeboats, more third-class women died than first-class men, even though there were more first-class men on board (His Majesty's Stationery Office, 1912). Consumers are frequently lectured that "you get what you pay for"; the statistics on *Titanic* survivors are just one case in point. Even survival can be purchased.

Almost a century later, in August of 2005, Hurricane Katrina hit the Gulf Coast of the United States, inundating lower Louisiana and Mississippi with a thirty-foot wall of water. That surge ruptured the levee on the 17th Street Canal in New Orleans, flooding much of the city. Those parts of the city with the lowest elevations suffered the greatest damage. Those neighborhoods also contained the poorest residents of New Orleans. Areas like the Lower Ninth Ward were the least desirable locations in the city because they were the most dangerous; hence, only the poorest moved there. A similar pattern evolved in Biloxi, Mississippi, based on neighborhood elevation. Low elevation in the path of a hurricane is much like third-class passage on the *Titanic*. Again, survival can be purchased.

The separation of people into rich and poor through a system of social stratification permeates every aspect of life in a modern society such as the United States. It is one of the most distinctive features of such societies; it is also one of the most important features in the everyday lives of their members, including those who are sociologists. Sociologists spend a great deal of time pondering the nature of social class differences. That subject has run as a common thread throughout every chapter of this book so far. In this chapter we pause to hold it down for examination.

Let us recall once again that **social stratification** refers to the arrangement of various activities of a society into a hierarchy in which activities ranked high are highly rewarded and activities ranked low are poorly rewarded. Individual people perform those activities and receive any rewards as long as they occupy the position. In a manner of speaking, social stratification is a vast game board (not unlike Monopoly) on which people are forced to play. Corporation executives are more important than janitors, just as Boardwalk is more important than Baltic Avenue; the game board is there, and you must do what you can according to the rules of the game. If you don't happen to land in the executive's position (or on Boardwalk), you will have to take orders from those who do.

Our system of social stratification has almost as much impact on our lives as the game board and rules of Monopoly have on Monopoly players, constantly offering us reminders of our place and coordinating our behavior. This chapter examines the "game board" of social stratification, paying particular attention to the effects of the game on the players. We look first at the basic features of the social stratification hierarchy, emphasizing the arrangements of the positions and the degree to which it is possible for individuals to move among them. Second, we examine some of the theories offered by sociologists that attempt to explain why social stratification exists and who its beneficiaries are. Finally, we take a close look at social class differences as they exist today in the United States; as with the sinking of the *Titanic* in 1912, it is still true that being upper class adds years to your life. The sociological outlook on social stratification allows you to place yourself within this competitive situation and shows you some of the forces beyond your control that affect your life chances.

BASIC FEATURES OF SOCIAL STRATIFICATION

The separation of rich and poor in the United States is immediately obvious to any observer of society who opens either eye slightly. The United States does not have the extreme social class divisions found in some countries, yet the differences in living conditions between rich and poor in our country are nevertheless dramatic. Many fine lines separate the positions in the hierarchy, however, making it difficult to tell just which social classes contain which positions. "Rewards" also come in many different packages: money or property is clearly a reward, but so is the respect you receive from others. Which is more important? If you give up your job as a traveling salesperson to become a college teacher, you will probably make less money but receive more respect. Are you now in a different social class or the same one? This section of the chapter introduces the basic concepts sociologists use to answer these and other confusing questions about social stratification. By the end of this section we should at least be able to organize our confusion.

CLASS, STATUS, AND POWER

The rewards positions in a social stratification hierarchy are generally separated by sociologists into economic rewards (**social class**), social rewards (**social status,** or prestige), and political rewards (**social power,** or the ability to influence the behavior of others). Positions and activities in a society can be ranked in terms of how much of each kind of reward they produce for their occupants. Positions at the very top of the hierarchy will, by definition, bring their occupants large amounts of money, prestige, and influence over others; positions at the very bottom will also, by definition, bring their occupants poverty, ridicule, and the privilege of taking orders. The positions in the middle of the hierarchy (which most of us occupy) will bring their occupants varying amounts of each kind of reward. Traveling salespeople, for example, rank a little higher economically but proportionately lower socially than college teachers.

Class, status, and power are three dimensions of social stratification—or parallel hierarchies within the overall hierarchy—along which any given position might be ranked. Sociologists disagree, however, as to how these dimensions should be measured. They also disagree about how independent the dimensions are. Are they three separate aspects of social stratification, or are they just three different ways of measuring the same thing? Money, after all, usually generates respect and certainly can be used to purchase influence over others. In looking more closely at different positions on this question, we will discover that these concepts change meaning depending on the side of the dispute being argued.

Karl Marx: A Theory of Social Class Karl Marx was one of the first sociologists to single out social stratification as a fundamental and important feature of human

Karl Marx (1818–1883). Marx is best remembered for his ideas on revolution, but most of his time was spent analyzing economic relations in industrial society. His views on social stratification and social class provided many insights into the power relationships that govern social order.

society—in fact, to Marx it was the most important feature. Marx saw the forms of coordination in any society as reflections of the economic arrangements employed in that society. Social stratification, as a form of coordination, is the most direct reflection of the economy since it organizes people by their economic roles (or their social class).

Marx studied class within the framework of **capitalism,** an economic system in which most of the wealth is the private property of individuals. This wealth (or capital) can be invested and can be increased through profit—the difference between the cost of production of a marketable item and what it can be sold for. The most distinctive feature of capitalism for Marx was that it is a system in which wealth can accumulate in a few hands—in short, a system that produces and maintains social inequality (see Marx, 1956, 1976).

Marx defined social class in terms of the degree of inequality that exists within the economic system. Capitalist societies contain business enterprises that produce and distribute goods and services (the means of production and distribution, in Marx's terms). Individuals either own these enterprises or work for those who do. Those who own the enterprises are the **bourgeoisie** (or ruling class), while those who work for them are the **proletariat** (or working class).

Marx's concept of social class was clearly an economic one. He was aware of differences in prestige and power within societies, but he believed these differences to be determined by social class. In his view, the control of capital by the employer leads directly to power over the worker. Marx thought that social class also determines prestige, although in a less direct manner. The ruling class of a capitalist society not only controls the economy but also controls the government, the arts, the sciences, religion, philosophy, education, and practically every other aspect of social life. Those in the ruling class are in a position to define themselves as important and convince others (the proletariat) to accept that social definition. (We've already seen one example of this idea in the study of deviance: those in authority in a society are in a position to define deviance and convince others to accept their definition.) The proletariat is trained to accept the status quo under capitalism and to believe that those who rule should rule, by virtue of their social superiority. If social status and social power are the direct results of social class, there is no need to study them as separate aspects of social stratification. Thus, according to Marx, once you understand social class, you will understand the other two as well.

Max Weber: Class, Status, and Party Max Weber (1946) was almost as interested in social stratification as Karl Marx was. Whereas Marx placed all his eggs in the economic basket, however, Weber took a more general approach. With his concepts of class, status, and party, Weber began the three-dimensional approach to social stratification that dominates American sociology today.

Like Marx, Weber felt that social class is the most important dimension of social stratification; unlike Marx, Weber did not see it as the only dimension. Whereas

Max Weber (1854–1920). Weber's wide-ranging interests in sociology included a particular focus on social stratification. In opposition to Marx's view, Weber suggested a three-dimensional approach in which an individual's social position consists of social class, social status, and political influence.

Marx thought that social status would automatically follow social class (either up or down), Weber suggested that status might have a life of its own. There are some wealthy people, he said, who do not command the respect in their communities that some of their less wealthy neighbors do. Although these two aspects of social coordination—the economic and social—are highly related and affect each other, they do not totally determine each other.

The dividing line Weber perceived between social class and status runs parallel to the line between the everyday norms of social exchange and the rich life of cultural values. The economy operates more or less rationally (as individuals figure their advantages and disadvantages), but culture operates according to its own logic. A successful individual in the world of economic give-and-take might not exemplify cultural standards of honor and therefore not receive respect. Shared lifestyles, geography, ancestry, or a variety of other attributes can bind together those with property and those without. Weber suggested, in fact, that such points in common would be much more likely to attract people into groups or communities than a common relation to wealth (social class). On the other hand, Weber admitted, two individuals with the same relation to wealth (two rich people, for instance) would be more likely to share common lifestyles, geography, or ancestry with each other than either would with a poorer person. Status can live a life of its own, but it also tends to vary along with social class. Weber's conception is less rigid than Marx's but not all that different.

Weber referred to social power in terms of political parties, using the term **party** to refer to political action or interest groups of any size in any social arena. In the United States this would include traditional political parties as well as special-interest political pressure groups such as the National Rifle Association (which opposes gun control), the Right to Life movement (which opposes abortion), and Amnesty International (which fights to protect civil liberties around the world and publicizes violations). The purpose of the political party is to concentrate power and direct it to represent the interests of members of the party. Who are the party's members? Most of the time they will share social class, social status, or both with each other; it is common, he says, for people with a common social class to have common political interests and to form a party to represent those interests. A labor union would be a case in point. However, says Weber, this is not always the case, which is the reason for discussing party and power separately from class. Parties are not always mere reflections of social class or of social status; people can come together for a variety of reasons to exert political pressure.

Socioeconomic Status In the 1930s Weber's notion of class, status, and party was borrowed and put to work by American sociological researchers who wanted to measure these dimensions in the lives of the people they studied. They came up with the measure of socioeconomic status. **Socioeconomic status** (or SES as it is commonly abbreviated) is an average score assigned to an individual on the basis of (1) income level, (2) level of education, and (3) occupational prestige. Such a measure doesn't reflect the dimension of social power too accurately, but it does include a measure of wealth (income) and social status (occupational prestige). Educational level usually is an index of both, since education often leads to better-paying, more prestigious jobs and, in addition, by itself increases social status. We might note in passing that a measure such as SES is much farther away from Marx than Weber ever intended to be. Using income as a measure of social class, for instance, takes into account the amount but ignores the source of the income, which was for Marx of central importance.

Income and education are pretty straightforward attributes to measure, but how do you measure occupational prestige? The easiest way is to ask people to rank lists of occupations from those they most respect to those they least respect. If you ask enough people to do this, you can produce an average ranking that reflects a social consensus on occupational prestige (Davis and Smith, 1984). As Weber suggested, more than just occupational income produces occupational prestige. How else could college professors be ranked above dentists and plumbers (Merton, 1968)?

Status Inconsistency How do you average all the measures that come together to form an SES score? Does an individual who makes $40,000 a year with a third-grade

The way of life of many Native Americans who live on reservations is often very different from the surrounding culture as illustrated by this picture of life in the Taos pueblo.

education average out the same as an individual who makes $20,000 with two years of college? Once you accept the different dimensions of social stratification, it is possible to talk about an individual's consistency across all the dimensions (see Lenski, 1956). Sociologists call this status consistency.

Status inconsistency describes individuals who are not consistently high, medium, or low across all the dimensions of social stratification. A janitor with a Ph.D. would be status inconsistent, as would an impoverished dentist or a Nobel Prize winner with a grade-school education. The idea behind status inconsistency is that being different from most of the people with whom you associate would put a strain on you. If you were a janitor with a Ph.D., for example, the janitors you worked with wouldn't share your educational background and interests and the people who shared your educational background would not share your occupational experiences; you would be a marginal member of both groups. Greater degrees of status inconsistency can often lead to fewer opportunities for economic advancement (Lorber, 1984).

Many research studies have attempted to test hypotheses relating status inconsistency to a great variety of factors, including psychological stress (Rossides, 1976).

The results are inconclusive. Part of the problem is that many social circumstances can result in apparent status inconsistency, with very different attitudes and feelings among the individuals affected. Whatever its effects, however, status inconsistency is strongly related to industrial societies. A simple stratification hierarchy characteristic of agricultural societies is generally highly consistent; even where different dimensions of stratification develop in these societies, they ultimately diverge from a single ranking system. But even the existence of these different dimensions would probably not produce status inconsistency if it were not possible for individuals to move up and down within them.

SOCIAL MOBILITY

Social mobility is the movement of groups or individuals within the ranking systems of social stratification. Just as geographical mobility represents a change in physical space, social mobility represents a change in social "space" whereby someone becomes a changed social creature in the eyes of other social group members (Abrahamson, Mizruchi, and Harnung, 1976). **Vertical social mobility** is mobility up or down the stratification hierarchy; to achieve it you must move from an activity or position at one social class level to an activity or position at another social class level. Going from "rags to riches," or, less dramatically, from office clerk to head of the accounting department, illustrates upward vertical social mobility. Going from "riches to rags" would be downward mobility. **Horizontal social mobility** is a change from one activity to another within the same social class. A clerk/typist who becomes a keypunch operator is moving horizontally, as is a drugstore clerk who gets a job as a waitress in a coffee shop. The vast majority of activity changes are of the horizontal variety; it is much easier to change jobs within one social class than to move upward in social class.

Vertical social mobility is the most important kind of social mobility for the study of social stratification. Horizontal mobility represents relatively minor changes in society ("You wash the dishes and I'll dry tonight for a change"), but the existence of vertical mobility suggests a stratification system in which the rulers and the ruled change places. This one-sided emphasis is so strong that many sociologists leave out the word *vertical* in their writings without fear of being misunderstood; unless otherwise specified, social mobility means vertical social mobility.

Vertical social mobility can be either intragenerational or intergenerational. **Intragenerational vertical social mobility** is a change in social class that occurs within the lifetime of one individual (or within one generation). If you start your occupational career as an office clerk and work your way up to the top of the company, your mobility is intragenerational. **Intergenerational vertical social mobility** is a change in social class that occurs across generations. For example, your father might have worked a lifetime as a mail carrier, and you might have gone straight through law school to a position as a successful corporate lawyer. Within your experience no mobility has occurred, yet a definite change has occurred from one generation to the next; your social class is very different from your father's social class. As discussed in the final section of this chapter, both of these types of vertical social mobility are difficult to achieve.

Problems in Measuring Vertical Social Mobility Unfortunately, vertical social mobility is difficult to measure. One reason is that sociologists lack agreement as to just how many different social classes exist or exactly where the boundaries between them should be drawn. We look at this dispute in more detail when we turn to the class structure of American society in the final section of this chapter, but consider the differences we've already seen between Marx and Weber. Marx states that there are two social classes, determined by their relation to capital. Weber isn't as specific, but it's clear he has a more general conception of relation to wealth. For Marx, professional baseball players haven't changed classes even if they triple their income from one year to the next; for Weber (and for most American sociologists), such a change would be a clear-cut example of upward social mobility.

Measuring intragenerational vertical social mobility is difficult without knowing quite about the individual cases being measured. Consider the following two examples:

1. Jim drops out of Harvard in his freshman year after a fight with his parents and frustrating experiences with school requirements. He works for two years as a construction worker doing unskilled work. Tiring of this, he returns to Harvard, finishes law school, and goes to work for a prestigious Wall Street firm.
2. Jeanne goes to work as an office clerk after receiving her high school diploma. Her supervisor notes the attention she pays to her work and is impressed. Jeanne makes some suggestions for making the office run more smoothly that turn out to work very well. She is promoted. After observing her new work environment and doing a little reading on business administration, she makes more suggestions, which successfully revolutionize the organizational structure of the business. She is soon a vice president.

Are Jim and Jeanne equal? Obviously not, for Jeanne has worked much harder and started with much less. But on paper they both appear to be examples of dramatic upward intragenerational mobility.

How do you compare the occupations of parents and children? A child may take a job that didn't exist in the parents' generation, so how can you tell whether it represents a movement upward or downward? This problem becomes increasingly difficult when you look at overall occupational changes that have occurred in the United States over time. Most significantly, every year sees a decreasing number of unskilled and manual jobs and greater numbers of white-collar office and service occupations; the changes that occur in industry and technology make such occupational changes necessary. A white-collar offspring of a blue-collar worker would normally be considered a case of intergenerational upward mobility, but when you consider the historical shift in occupations, the change does not appear so great. A similar problem has occurred in measuring educational levels: each generation goes to school longer than the one before, so the younger you are, the more likely you are to have a higher level of education. Have you moved up from your parents, or have you simply flowed with the currents of your generation? Your college degree will probably get you a job at the same level your parents achieved with a high school diploma. Degrees inflate right along with dollars.

In short, vertical social mobility is difficult to measure, much less explain. Nevertheless, sociologists have tried their best. We look at some of those attempts in the final section of this chapter.

Class and Caste Societies: Social Mobility and Group Formation Class societies and caste societies are largely products of the sociologist's imagination (or "ideal types," such as Weber's conception of bureaucracy described in Chapter 6). A **class society** is a society that permits widescale vertical social mobility; positions in the social stratification hierarchy are open to all and achieved through an open competition process. A **caste society** is based entirely on ascribed status and permits no vertical social mobility; social positions are inherited as a right of birth. Neither of these two descriptions provides a good fit for any real society, although it's possible to find fair approximations of caste societies in the real world. The term *caste*, which refers to a totally closed social level, comes to us from India, where the population used to be rigidly separated into specific groups of social roles; the Brahmin caste was at the top of the hierarchy and the "untouchables" were at the bottom, with no possibility of change. The American system of slavery came close to a caste system since children born to a slave mother were automatically slaves. A similar caste system operated in South Africa throughout most the twentieth century.

True class societies are much harder to find in the real world. Modern industrial societies such as the United States have just about as much vertical social mobility as you'll find anywhere, yet access to positions is clearly limited. Even though many positions (or jobs) are technically open to anyone, it still often helps to "know somebody." Less obvious but perhaps more important advantages come as an accident of your birth. Your parents automatically pass on to you certain skills, abilities, resources, and knowledge. If your parents are upper class, that "inheritance" will get you admission to good schools, the abilities and skills to get through those schools, the confidence to get ahead, the social skills for leaving a good impression on employers at interviews, and a great many other advantages too numerous to mention. If your parents are lower class, you will receive an "inheritance" of equal size but you will find its content less useful for attacking dominant American institutions and becoming successful; those institutions are largely under the control of the upper classes. To form a true class society, you would have to remove children from their parents at birth, give them all an equal background at a state-run orphanage, and then fill jobs through a competition that would be truly open.

Sociologists use the concepts of class and caste in order to better understand the range of vertical social mobility that occurs between the two extremes. Different societies can be placed at different points between the extremes and compared accordingly. The same society can also change location between these extremes over time, as occurred with the emancipation of slaves in the United States. Class and caste societies provide some insight into the ways people form social groups.

Consider first a caste society. How would such a stratification system affect the individual? First of all, the individual would become extremely aware of his or her caste. Most individuals would probably accept the caste system as a basic and unchangeable fact of existence since they would have no experience with alternatives. Members of the bottom castes might feel a lot of hatred toward and envy of the castes above, but they probably wouldn't try to do much about it. The possibility of change might not even occur to them since they had never witnessed it. This description fits the American system of slavery fairly well, even though those slaves born in Africa had a clear picture of an alternative society. Slaves were extremely aware of the color line (as are most Americans still today), but they rarely attempted to do much about it. Slave revolts were very unusual, as most slaves apparently felt there was little hope for success. Such a response is characteristic of a caste system.

An ideal class society would produce very different kinds of individual thoughts and behavior. The rapidity with which individuals moved into and out of social positions would prevent groups of individuals from becoming aware of a shared situation, and, unlike in the caste system, there would not be strong senses of group identity. In fact, members of a class society would be engaged in constant acts of individual competition. The openness of the stratification system would encourage individuals to do something about their current positions but would discourage them from acting as groups. Your best shot at getting ahead would come from working alone. It's harder to find a real-world illustration of this case, but a classroom of students graded on the curve provides a rough approximation. A "grading curve" means that certain percentages of the class will receive certain grades, regardless of the quality of the work they do. Their work must only be equal in quality to the best work in the class for them to receive high grades; if that best work is of poor quality, then poor quality will receive top grades. This system is designed to encourage individual competition. What would you do if you found the answer sheet to a final examination in a class graded on the curve? Assuming you would be unscrupulous enough to use it at all, the most rational course would be to share the answers with no one; the lower the other grades, the better yours will look by comparison. You might want to share the answers with a few close friends (thereby competing as a group), but consider that the more people you help, the worse your grade will be by comparison. If you share the answers with the entire class, it will help you not at all.

A class system, like a grading curve, encourages individual competition but discourages people from competing in groups.

The United States falls somewhere between a caste system and a class system. These extreme ideal types help us understand the kinds of competition and group formation that come from such stratification systems. Because vertical mobility is possible to some extent in the United States, many Americans are competitive; where there is great potential for vertical mobility, they are even competitive as individuals. But American society is not all that open. As we've seen, the children of the upper classes enter the competition with advantages that children of the lower classes don't have. This inequality tends to keep the same families at the top or at the bottom, a castelike situation that makes individuals aware of others who share the boat with them and leads to strong feelings of group identity (see Chapter 6). When you combine the competition characteristic of mobility with the group formation characteristic of a caste system, you find the compromise characteristic of American society—group competition.

Americans have the idea and see the possibility of advancement, but they also see the hurdles set in front of their particular group. The labor union is a typical response to such a situation, as individuals seek to advance by improving the overall status of the group to which they belong. If social stratification were in fact turned into a board game like Monopoly, social mobility would be one of the strategies you could use to change the play of the game. When we look later at the effects of social class membership on the individual, this variable will become extremely important.

WHY STRATIFICATION, AND WHO BENEFITS?
OPPOSING THEORIES

Not all human societies are stratified, but most of them are. Some small societies don't even have an organized division of labor, and since social stratification organizes labor activities into a hierarchy, the division of labor must come first. In attempts to explain why stratification exists, these facts are hard to interpret. Apparently, social stratification is not absolutely essential to all human societies, as some of them get along quite well without it. On the other hand, the vast majority of human societies have some kind of social stratification hierarchy in their social organization; most human societies, in short, thrive on inequality. Stratification thus appears essential, for all practical purposes.

Why does social stratification exist in so many human societies? Does it benefit all members of the society or just those who occupy the top rungs? Sociologists are divided in the way they answer these questions. The *structural-functionalist*, or "order," theorists believe that social stratification is necessary for the existence of human society and, for that reason, benefits all members of society. The *conflict theorists*, on the other hand, argue that social stratification is an organized system of thievery in which one segment of the population benefits at the expense of

Davis and Moore would argue that hand picking agricultural produce is both less important to society than more highly rewarded jobs and is more easily replaced labor given the lack of specialized training involved.

another. While we looked at both of these perspectives in Chapter 2, this section will compare these two opposing perspectives on social stratification.

STRUCTURAL-FUNCTIONALISM: THE ORDER THEORISTS

Many general theories of society are derived from the school of structural-functionalism; it was a particularly popular perspective among American sociologists between the 1930s and 1950s, when it was largely unchallenged. During that period structural-functionalism was specifically applied to the question of social stratification. If all parts of society have developed because they fulfill some specific function and are important for the functioning of the whole, then mustn't social stratification be necessary and have a specific function? Two American sociologists, Kingsley Davis and Wilbert Moore, set out to answer that question.

According to Davis and Moore (1945), social stratification is necessary for getting the right people into the right jobs. Because different parts of society fulfill different functions, it stands to reason that different jobs fulfill different functions. It also stands to reason that some jobs must fulfill more important functions than others, just as your heart is more vital than your gallbladder and both are more useful than your appendix. Davis and Moore suggested that jobs that fulfill the most important functions for society are likely to be highly regarded in the social stratification hierarchy. Furthermore, because these jobs are the most important, it is essential that they be filled by competent members of society. One way to ensure competence is to provide more rewards for these more necessary jobs. These rewards encourage the most competent members of society to seek them. These individuals would be willing to undergo whatever training might be necessary for the job since the future rewards will make up for whatever deprivations they experience in the present.

Thus, for Davis and Moore, stratification exists for two basic reasons. First, some positions in society are more important than others. Second, personnel may be scarce to fill these important positions (since most important positions require a lot of training). Simpson (1956) raised the question of garbage collectors, whose work is essential to the health of society's members yet is poorly rewarded. Davis and Moore would point out the lack of specialized training involved in the occupation—important jobs that anyone can do may not be highly rewarded. Because almost all societies with a division of labor face differences in functional importance and the scarcity of personnel for many of those important positions, social stratification is necessary.

The structural-functionalists are sometimes called *order theorists*. This label suggests that the perspective of structural-functionalism focuses attention on maintaining social order and the status quo at the expense of understanding social change. The structural-functionalists have been accused of looking at social change as a sickness in society rather than as a common process. Particularly in looking at social stratification, the structural-functionalists tend to accept the current state of affairs as being "right" or natural. The functional importance of a position in society is at least partially determined by how highly rewarded it is; thus, functional importance is the same as success in convincing others of the importance of your position. The structural-functionalists are accused of not appreciating that success can vary from time to time. These accusations come from a perspective on society known as conflict theory.

THE CONFLICT THEORISTS

The general perspective on society known as conflict theory is traced from the theories of Karl Marx. As an overall perspective, conflict theory suggests that conflict, rather than order or consensus, is the usual state of affairs in society because of the inequality imposed by social stratification. Because the hierarchy of social stratification gives more to some people than to others, it is natural that individuals at one level of the hierarchy should be in competition and conflict with individuals at other levels. That conflict, when it occurs, can lead to social change.

Modern methods of sanitation have saved more lives than physicians could ever hope to do, yet garbage collectors receive relatively little respect for the work they do. They also receive much less financial reward than doctors—and incomparably less than professional athletes, who are not expected to save any lives. The order theorists argue that this sort of discrepancy is the result of the minimal specialized training needed for garbage collecting; conflict theorists argue that garbage collectors suffer from a lack of political clout.

Conflict theorists tend to view social stratification as an organized way for certain members of society to gain wealth at the expense of certain others. In the stratification system of the United States, for example, garbage collectors have to give up a larger portion of their earnings for medical care than physicians must give up for garbage collection (in addition to the different incomes they have in the first place). The system therefore benefits physicians at the expense of garbage collectors. Benefiting garbage collectors more would involve benefiting physicians less. The stratification system works this way not because there is consensus (even among garbage collectors) over the arrangement but because those who benefit are in a powerful enough position to keep the system going.

Where structural-functionalists see consensus and agreement over basic norms and values, conflict theorists see social power coercing those at the bottom into obedience. Power is one of the critical factors in the stratification hierarchy from any perspective; the conflict theorists emphasize its existence and the way it is used. One of its primary uses, according to this position, is to cover its own tracks as much as possible. Those at the top of the hierarchy prefer to have those at the bottom in as much agreement as possible with the status quo; they may therefore use their power to socialize those at the bottom into that acceptance through their control over schools ("Stand in straight lines and don't talk back to the teacher"), religion ("Blessed are the meek for they shall inherit the earth"), and general folklore ("The head of the sales department has so many worries and responsibilities, I'm just as glad I didn't get the promotion"). If the socialization fails, there is always military might to fall back upon (Verba, Oren, and Ferree, 1985).

Karl Marx: The Father of Conflict Theory We've already looked at Marx's theory of social class, but it is better understood within the context of his theory of social stratification, from which it came. As we saw, Marx viewed social stratification within a capitalist society as consisting of two social classes: the ruling class and the working class. Marx viewed capitalism as the latest stage in a long history of economic development in which a ruling class exploited a lower class according to whatever economic arrangements were currently in practice. Under feudalism, for instance, the serf was tied to the lord's land.

Exploitation, in Marx's terms, refers to the unequal manner in which the ruling class benefits from the working class. Under feudalism the lord becomes wealthy while the serf toils on the land; under capitalism the capitalist becomes wealthy through profit while the worker creates all the value in the product from which the profit comes. Since the serfs or the workers do not receive the value of their labor, they are exploited. A system of social stratification, therefore, is nothing more than organized exploitation; it has no other purpose, says Marx.

The ruling class is in a position to exercise great control over all aspects of society. Marx claimed that most of the forms of social organization we live by were constructed by the ruling class to maintain its position in society. A government, for example, is constructed to enforce the status quo and to punish those who seek to change it. Laws, such as those regulating the right to private property, benefit those who currently own property (the ruling class) while working against individuals who own none or very little (the working class). Even though much of society is organized for this purpose, many members of the working class don't understand their disadvantage and accept what they are told. What they are told, according to Marx, are ideologies of the ruling class.

An **ideology** is an idea or set of ideas that represents a particular interest of a particular social group; for Marx it is a set of beliefs that specifically represents the interests of the ruling class in a society. The American belief that private property is a good thing, for example, is an ideology of the ruling class; it is an idea that reflects the interests of the ruling class but not the interests of the working class. You may feel that the laws protecting private property are in your interest because you own a TV and a car that you would rather I not steal. You would be better off, says Marx, giving up your right to your TV and car to gain access to the billions and billions of dollars of private property currently closed to you in the hands of the ruling class. If you don't agree, says Marx, you are suffering from false consciousness.

False consciousness occurs when individuals in a particular social class are not aware of the true interests inherent in their class position. (If they are so aware, they have a **class consciousness**.) False consciousness occurs primarily among members of the working class when they accept the ideologies of the ruling class. If, for example, you are currently a member of what is generally called the middle class in America and believe you benefit from the current system of stratification, you have a false consciousness. The ruling class, says Marx, does everything in its power to perpetuate false consciousness, as it is in its interest to have willing obedience from the working class. Racial or religious hatred, for instance, keeps members of the working class from grouping together; thus it is useful to the ruling class, which will attempt to keep such divisions alive (see Box 7.1). Perhaps most important in false consciousness are all the income levels and status symbols that exist in a society. People who drive Cadillacs feel superior to those who drive Fords; people who wear expensive clothes feel superior to those who wear less expensive clothes; people who make $50,000 a year feel superior to those who make $25,000, who feel superior to those who make $10,000, and so on. From the point of view of the ruling class, all these differences are trivial, but the members of the working class are trained to believe them significant. They come to believe that they live in a great many different social classes instead of just the one large class that Marx claims they occupy. If the differences continue, they will prevent class consciousness and, ultimately, class action.

We come finally to Marx's idea of revolution, the part of his theory most roundly criticized today because his predictions have not come true. According to Marx, class action by the working class would ultimately take shape as revolutionary action when the working class came to recognize their exploitation. This recognition would be bound to occur, according to Marx, for it is in the nature of capitalism for

BOX 7.1

U.S. Steel versus the Unions: The Story of Gary, Indiana

Gary, Indiana, is a company town. Before 1905 it wasn't there; it was constructed by U.S. Steel Corporation right at the foot of Lake Michigan as an ideal location for steel mills. Between 1905 and 1907 $40 million was invested in the construction of Gary. All it needed then was workers. The initial methods used by U.S. Steel to locate workers for Gary might have come directly from a page written by Karl Marx. How does the ruling class control the working class? By making sure that the working class stays divided among itself. As Edward Greer (1971, 31) describes it:

> The corporation planned more than the physical nature of the city. It also had agents advertise in Europe and the South to bring in workers from as many different backgrounds as possible to build the mills and work in them. Today over 50 ethnic groups are represented in the population.
>
> This imported labor was cheap, and it was hoped that cultural differences and language barriers would curtail the growth of a socialist labor movement. The tough, pioneer character of the city and the fact that many of the immigrant workers' families had not yet joined them in this country combined to create a lawless and vice-ridden atmosphere which the corporation did little to curtail. Gary is indelibly stamped in the mold of its corporate creators.

According to Greer, U.S. Steel Corporation fostered ethnic hatreds and rivalries among its workers in hopes of preventing labor organization. But that is only chapter one of the story. As the labor unions inevitably came to Gary, as to the rest of the country, U.S. Steel used racial hatred to help control the union.

African Americans did not come to work in Gary until the labor shortages of World War I; most did not get there until the 1920s. By 1970 about a third of the steel mill employees were African Americans, although most of these workers were kept in the lowest jobs. Although the foremen were hired directly from the line workers, only 2 percent of the foremen were African American (Greer, 1971). According to Greer, U.S. Steel used its influence in Gary to maintain housing segregation and minimize the political power of African Americans. Such practices polarized the black and white populations of Gary. When Democrat Richard Hatcher was elected mayor in 1968 (Gary's first black mayor), 87 percent of the city's white Democratic voters switched to the Republican Party.

Marx argued that the ruling class will encourage or create divisions within the working class to keep the workers from realizing their true condition. Racism in Gary may not have needed much encouragement, but the hiring practices of

U.S. Steel in 1905 are most instructive. That was a period in American history when industry hoped it could prevent the growth of unions, especially in the heavy industries like steel. The year 1905 was also one of very high immigrations rates (see Figure 8.1). U.S. Steel's use of employment agents to provide a mix of fifty different ethnic groups is clearly manipulation by the ruling class.

---

wealth to become increasingly concentrated in fewer and fewer hands. This concentration would limit the ability of the ruling class to spread false consciousness around, which would force more and more members of the previous "middle class" into the poverty of the working class. In Marx's terms capitalism contains the "seeds of its own destruction" as it would force the working class ultimately to rise up against the ruling class, overthrow the capitalist system, and finally substitute a system Marx called *communism*. Ironically, Marx barely spoke about communism, as he claimed he was in no position to truly understand what it might be. All he knew for sure was that it would have no exploitation, no social classes, and, in consequence, no system of social stratification (see Marx, 1956).

Marx predicted that revolution would occur first in the most industrialized nations of the world. As it happened, the revolutions that have carried his name have occurred in nonindustrial nations and, in fact, have not led to classless societies in spite of some claims to the contrary. This apparent failing in Marx's theory should not, however, lead us to ignore the bulk of his work. His emphasis on power and conflict in society and, in particular, his theory of ideology have had a major impact on political and sociological theory.

Modern Conflict Theory Most of the modern conflict theorists (although not all) ignore Marx's predictions of revolution in favor of advancing his other ideas. One of the most influential in this effort is Ralf Dahrendorf (1959), who shifted focus somewhat from Marx's idea of economic class to the idea of social power. Modern industrial society, says Dahrendorf, is no longer as clear-cut with regard to class as it was in Marx's day. Marx witnessed the early days of the Industrial Revolution, when workers lived in abject poverty and the members of the ruling class who placed them in that situation owned the factories in which they worked. Today corporate enterprises are owned by stockholders and run by managers hired by the corporation. The managers don't own the means of production, but they are often in conflict with workers because they have authority over the workers.

Dahrendorf has focused his attention on the ways authority is exercised and maintained in modern society. Individuals are not limited to one social class, as Marx maintained, but are in fact involved in a wide variety of authority relations in many social arenas. A corporate executive, for example, may have authority in a work arena but lack authority in a political arena such as a court of law. The executive can give orders in one arena but must take them in another. The "boats" that people see themselves sharing, therefore, will be determined by the way authority operates in all these different arenas. Being on the same side of an authority relation gives you something in common, but only with others in that particular arena of society. If individuals form social groups based on these points in common and become involved in conflict, that conflict will be largely limited to the arena in question. Marx's theory is approximated only by the very top and very bottom of the stratification hierarchy; the very rich may give orders in every social arena, while the very poor find themselves taking orders every time they turn around.

Other modern theorists in the conflict tradition have directed their analyses closely to the Davis and Moore argument and to the world of work in general. Melvin Tumin, who made a career of attacking Davis and Moore, pointed out that, within the logic of structural-functionalism, social stratification could even be shown as a dysfunctional (or nonfunctional) system. Because social stratification has such limited routes of upward mobility, Tumin (1953) argued, very talented members of the lower and working classes will never be recognized and made use of by the society; they will, in fact, remain in their social classes while less talented members of the upper class compete for medical school and other high-status training programs. Bucher and Stelling (1969) pointed out that highly rewarded occupations may not necessarily be more important; rather, their members have simply "played their cards right." Professional status, they argue, has more to do with political processes through which the occupation gains prestige than with the nature of the work itself. Physicians, for example, have been much more successful in creating a positive image than chiropractors (Verba, Oren, and Ferree, 1985).

In general, modern conflict theory accepts Marx's notion of exploitation and the inherent nature of power and conflict within social stratification. Social stratification is viewed as a tempting form of social organization that occurs whenever a society can produce more than it requires for survival; in such a situation some members will surely attempt to appropriate the surplus for their own use. When such appropriation becomes institutionalized over time, social stratification is born. This structured inequality is accepted much of the time by many of the participants, but conflict is always a potential beneath the surface of the smooth interactions of everyday life.

ORDER AND CONFLICT THEORIES: A FINAL LOOK

An interesting philosophical difference between order and conflict theories may be a key to the way each interprets the world (Hamilton, 1990). That philosophical difference lies in the contrasting ways they view humans in their societies. The order theories, such as structural-functionalism, tend to view humans as inherently bad or disruptive creatures who are held in check by social norms and social power. Within this perspective society becomes a vast civilizing force that is necessary to prevent animal selfishness from taking hold. The conflict theories, on the other hand, tend to view humans as inherently good creatures who become surly and competitive only in societies that encourage such behavior. To the order theorists social stratification is necessary to motivate people to work and to keep the society functioning in some sort of orderly fashion; inequality is the necessary price we must pay for that service. To the conflict theorists social stratification is the cause of many of the less redeeming human qualities we see every day; a more orderly society might be possible if we removed the causes of hatred and conflict that currently keep us at each other's throats.

SOCIAL CLASS IN THE UNITED STATES

All modern industrial nations have elaborate systems of social stratification, and the United States is no exception. The activities we engage in every day are firmly embedded in a class hierarchy. Social class is a very real factor in the life of every American. It is probably the single most important social factor in explaining the differences among Americans—people in different social classes are different from each other in almost every way imaginable. This section explores some of those differences and the reasons for them: inequalities in wealth distribution and barriers to upward social mobility.

INEQUALITY IN THE UNITED STATES

Systems of social stratification introduce structured inequality into any society. By *structured*, sociologists mean that the inequality is not just the result of individual differences in talent or ability but is built into the roles people play and the rewards they receive. Any stratification system therefore produces inequality in that those at the top receive more rewards than those at the bottom. One question to be answered in regard to any particular stratification system is the degree of inequality. How much difference is there from top to bottom, and just how unequal is the distribution of rewards?

Figure 7.1 shows how income was distributed among citizens of the United States in 2001. It arbitrarily divides the population into five equal segments, ranging from the top 20 percent of the population in income level to the poorest 20 percent. The top 20 percent received 47.7 percent of all the income earned, while the bottom 20 percent received 4.2 percent of the available income.

Table 7.1 presents income distribution statistics for the years 1950–2001. Comparing this table with Figure 7.1 may tell you something you did not know: the distribution of income in the United States has changed only slightly since 1950. The top 20 percent grew from 42.7 percent of the income in 1950 to 47.7 percent in 2001; the bottom 20 percent changed even less during this period. Table 7.1 also provides a closer look at the very top of the stratification hierarchy: the top 5 percent in income earned. In 2001, the top 5 percent earned 21 percent of all income earned in the United States (up from 17.3 percent in 1950). In the last forty-five years, the only change in American income has been toward increasing inequality,

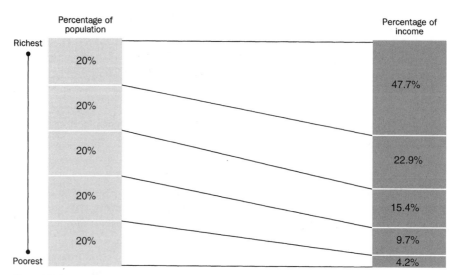

Figure 7.1 Percent of income received by fifths of population in the United States, 2001. (Data from U.S. Bureau of the Census, 2004a)

TABLE 7.1

HOUSEHOLD INCOME AS PERCENTAGE OF INCOME IN THE UNITED STATES BY FIFTHS OF THE POPULATIONS, 1950–2001

Year	Lowest Fifth	Second Fifth	Middle Fifth	Fourth Fifth	Highest Fifth	Top 5 Percent
2001	4.2	9.7	15.4	22.9	47.7	21.0
1997	4.2	9.9	15.7	23.0	47.2	20.7
1991	4.5	10.7	16.6	24.1	44.2	17.1
1980	5.2	11.5	17.5	24.3	41.5	15.3
1970	5.4	12.2	17.6	23.8	40.9	15.6
1965	5.2	12.2	17.8	23.9	40.9	15.5
1960	4.8	12.2	17.8	24.0	41.3	15.9
1955	4.8	12.2	17.7	23.4	41.8	16.8
1950	4.5	11.9	17.4	23.6	42.7	17.3

Source: U.S. Bureau of the Census, 2004a.

and that change has happened only in the last several years. Different people are certainly involved in the stratification system today than in 1950, but the system itself is only slightly different; the same percentages of rewards are still dispersed to the same segments of the population.

To say the least, social stratification in the United States has created a structured inequality. But how is it structured? Income distribution can be arbitrarily examined across five equal segments of the population, but that does not necessarily mean there are five social classes of equal size. Some sociologists who focus on the very top of the stratification system argue that 0.3 percent of the population makes up one social class (see Domhoff, 1983). There have to be at least two social classes, but beyond that, sociologists are in disagreement as to exactly how many there are.

SOCIAL CLASSES IN THE UNITED STATES: HOW MANY?

In 1949 Richard Centers asked people to label themselves as to their social class. From that group of labels, which Centers had provided, people organized themselves as follows:

Upper class	3%
Middle class	43%
Working class	51%
Lower class	1%
Don't know	2%

In 1976, the National Opinion Research Center received the following responses to the same question:

Upper class	1.5%
Middle class	47.7%
Working class	46.4%
Lower class	4.4%

One possible conclusion is that one generation answers the question in much the same way as the generation before. Can other conclusions be drawn?

One of the problems with such research is that it forces people to use the labels provided by the sociologist. Some people, for example, like to think of themselves as upper middle class. A more serious problem, however, is that the research doesn't tell us how important or how real most of the respondents consider their own social class to be. The concept *social class* is a social category, not a social group. It is a concept sociologists employ to understand or explain other things about people; it is therefore not absolutely necessary that the people themselves recognize the importance of the category. Unfortunately, sociologists are as confused and divided over the meaning of social class as the people to whom the concept is applied.

Thus far we've looked at social class through the eyes of Karl Marx and Max Weber. Marx left little doubt as to the meaning of the term. Weber spoke of social class in terms of "life chances": the higher the social class, the more life chances (or opportunities) one would have to acquire possessions and to control one's existence. He didn't specify how many social classes there might be. Some sociologists—Cuber and Kenkel (1954), for instance—have argued that social classes don't have boundaries and therefore can't be counted; they should instead be measured as temperature is measured by a thermometer. With Cuber and Kenkel at one extreme and Marx at the other, it is not surprising that most sociologists slide into the middle ground. If there is any consensus at all, it is that the number of social classes varies from community to community and, perhaps more important, that the sociologist might want to assume different numbers of social classes for different kinds of research. For some research questions you might care only about approximate social class divisions; for other questions (such as social mobility research), you might want to focus more closely on class boundaries. American sociologists have had a variety of research concerns related to social class and, as a result, have used a variety of ways to measure it.

One approach to social class is the *community study,* which involves in-depth interviewing and observation to determine how members of the community see themselves and each other. W. Lloyd Warner and Paul Lunt (1941) pioneered this work in a small New England community they called Yankee City, concluding there were six social classes: the upper upper class, the lower upper class, the upper middle class, the lower middle class, the upper lower class, and the lower class. Warner described his classes as follows:

Upper upper class: This class was very small (about one percent of Yankee City), was very wealthy, and thrived on strong family traditions; proper ancestry was necessary for membership. The members of this class did not need to work and were oriented toward the proper pursuit of leisure.

Lower upper class: This class was distinguished from the upper upper class primarily by the absence of prestigious family background. Sometimes referred to by other community members as the "new rich" or as having "new money," this class contained many doctors, lawyers, and businessmen, many of whom tried to emulate the members of the upper upper class.

Upper middle class: One of Warner's mind-bending terms that found a firm home in the American vocabulary, the upper middle class contained about 10 percent of the Yankee City population. This class included many professionals, but they clearly differed in lifestyle and amount of money from the members of the lower upper class. This class also included many wholesale and retail businessmen.

Lower middle class: The lower middle class contained a variety of white-collar workers such as clerks and a number of skilled workers. This class differed from the one above in both income and lifestyle; its members valued hard work, morality, and regular church attendance.

Upper lower class: The largest class in Yankee City, the upper lower class contained unskilled or semiskilled workers involved primarily in construction and factory work. Many of them were foreign born. They made up the "poor but honest" population of Yankee City.

Lower class: Finally, we come to the unemployed and poorly thought of members of Yankee City. Members of this class were believed to be lazy and responsible for their own condition.

The most interesting aspect of Warner and Lunt's research is the emphasis on noneconomic factors in social class. Warner's distinction between the upper upper class and the lower upper class, for example, has turned up time after time in sociological research as being significant in most American communities. The only difference between the two classes is social status, not economic standing; in other words, it's not how much money you have but where you got it and the style with which you spend it. This old rich new rich distinction lends support to Weber's multiple-dimension approach of class, status, and power.

THE MYTH OF THE CLASSLESS SOCIETY

American culture contains strong values regarding equality and democracy. Even though there are numerous exceptions to both, one consequence of these values is that many Americans prefer not to think of the United States in terms of class structure (Bartlett, 2000). It is more pleasant to think that some people accomplish more with the opportunity America offers and that economic success or failure need not separate people in terms of their more human concerns. One of our favorite movie plots, for example, is the romance between the rich boy and poor girl (or vice versa), in which love always triumphs over lifestyle differences and family objections. Actually, only rarely do people marry outside of their social class. Dating is only one of the many activities that most people confine to their own social class.

If a sociologist is asked to predict some human behavior and is allowed only one question about the people involved, the sociologist will want to know something about their social class. Beginning with birth, the classes are different. Lower-class women have more babies than upper-class women. The reason for this difference is that lower-class women are less likely to have detailed knowledge of birth control techniques and are more likely to have a cultural bias toward large families. Upper-class women, on the other hand, have access to birth control, may prefer to have careers, are more likely to view children as an economic drain on the family, and are less likely to value large families.

Once born, the children of the different social classes will be raised differently. Urie Bronfenbrenner (1958) found that lower- and working-class parents used repressive forms of socialization in which child obedience was highly valued and discipline was harsh. Middle- and upper-class parents, on the other hand, were much more likely to spare the rod and to deal verbally with their children over differences of opinion regarding behavior. Children in the latter families were treated much more democratically and given considerably more freedom. Kohn and Schooler (1983) explain these differences in socialization in terms of the occupational circumstances of the different classes. Middle-class people have more autonomy on the job and pass this independence along to their children; working-class jobs, on the other hand, are more likely to stress obedience on the part of the employee. Because people tend to marry within their social class, methods of raising children continue across generations as parents raise their children in the same way they were raised.

Bellair and Roscigno (2000) noted the high incidence of lower-class children arrested for acts of delinquency. We've already seen the relationship between social class and the American criminal justice system in Chapter 5 (see particularly Box 5.1). Whatever the explanations offered, your parents' social class has a major impact on the number of your encounters with the police and the courts.

On the whole, social class is the greatest single predictor of educational success, IQ scores, and anything else associated with educational expectations. George Farkas (2000) found that lower-class children did much more poorly in school than middle- and upper-class children, typically reading below grade level. As a result, lower-class children are more likely to have lower grades and be much less likely to attend college. Lower-class children are less likely to be prepared for teacher expectations when they enter school and less likely to become responsive to those expectations as they continue, falling farther and farther behind their middle-class peers.

Education seems to have a double relationship to social class. We have already seen that there is a definite relation between an individual's education level and subsequent earnings. As with childrearing techniques, class patterns in relation to education tend to continue across generations because lack of education limits social class, which will limit education in the next generation (Desimone, 1999; Kubitschek and Hallinan, 1996; Serwatka et al., 1995).

Social class also affects a wide variety of social behavior in adults. In such everyday matters as whom one chooses to invite into one's home, middle-class people are more likely to socialize with an assortment of friends (many of them work or business relations) than are lower-class people, who are more likely to confine their socializing to relatives, often being uncomfortable socializing with members of other social classes (Gorman, 2000). The upper classes are much more likely to belong to voluntary associations than are the lower classes (Oliver, 1999). There is also a difference in the kinds of associations that receive the participation of different classes; the upper classes are more likely to be involved in professional or charitable organizations, while the middle and working classes are more likely to belong to fraternal organizations (such as the Masons or the Knights of Columbus). A similar pattern of participation occurs in the world of politics; the higher the social class, the more likely the individual is to vote and the more likely he or she will vote Republican, as we will see in Chapter 13.

Social class is highly related to race or ethnic status. When racial or ethnic groups face discrimination, one of the many results is that routes of upward social mobility are cut off for their members; in other words, discrimination locks members of affected groups into the lower classes. Figure 7.2 presents the income levels of white

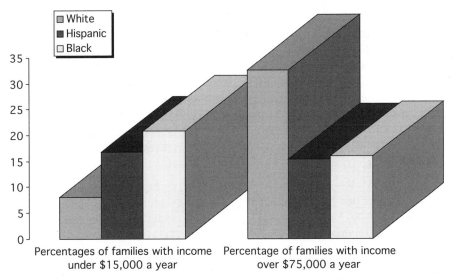

Figure 7.2 Family income in the United States, 2001. (Data from U.S. Bureau of the Census, 2004)

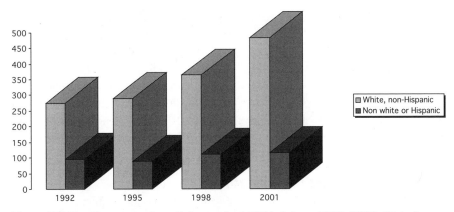

Figure 7.3 Family mean net worth in constant 2001 dollars, 1992–2001. (Data from U.S. Bureau of the Census, 2004a)

families, blacks, and Hispanics in 2001. If we look at net worth as opposed to income, the differences become even more striking. Figure 7.3 shows the mean net worth of American families between 1992 and 2001 with those families divided between white, non-Hispanic, and everyone else. The gap in net worth, which includes all assets, is clearly more extreme than the gap in income. In addition, Figure 7.3 also shows the increasing gap in net worth in the United States over the last decade. Non-Hispanic whites have clearly benefited from that period of considerable economic growth. By contrast, all other Americans made only modest gains (U.S. Bureau of the Census, 2004a). This vast difference is caused by the fact that many minority families owe more than they own; over 30 percent of black households and almost 24 percent of Hispanic households fall into that category, as compared with around 8 percent of non-Hispanic white households. The disproportionate presence of racial and ethnic groups in the lower social classes is a major cause of many of their problems, as well as the conflicts they become involved in with others. This distribution of racial and ethnic groups within social stratification is called **ethnic stratification.** It is a key concept in Chapter 8, on racial and ethnic groups.

Apparently, social class also affects people's happiness. The higher an individual's social class, the more likely he or she will report general satisfaction with the elements of his or her life (Bartlett, 2000). Individuals in higher social classes will also be happier for longer; being in the lower classes takes six to eight years off one's life because of higher infant mortality, poorer nutrition, higher rates of homicide, poorer sanitation, and poorer medical care in general (Luhman, 2002; Backlund and Sorlie, 1999). From start to finish, low social class can be hazardous to your health.

This brief discussion only scratches the surface of the differences among people that sociologists attribute to social class. The research included was selected for its range, particularly with respect to the different stages of life affected. One basic point is apparent: if people have so many differences due to social class, a great many individual experiences must be shaped by social class. For that to occur, however, the social classes must be relatively stable. The implication of the research we have looked at is that social classes differ from each other culturally as well as financially. Such cultural differences would not exist if people did not stay in social classes over generations for the most part, or if people in different classes had more social contact with each other—which brings us back to social mobility and the way social class shapes individual experience.

AVENUES AND BARRIERS TO SOCIAL MOBILITY

As near as most researchers can tell, American society contains quite a bit of both inter- and intragenerational mobility compared to other countries. Yet, as mentioned, it also appears that few individuals move very far (Vanfossen, 1979). There is enough movement to provide for some social change but apparently not enough to alter the basic class differences in American life.

As we saw earlier in this chapter, social mobility refers to an overall change in social class, but one that is very difficult to measure. As a result, most sociological research on social mobility focuses on occupational change and, in particular, the prestige of occupations. The most famous study of social mobility by American sociologists is American Occupational Structure, a 1967 study by Peter Blau and Otis Duncan. Working closely with census data, Blau and Duncan sought to determine just how much mobility occurred in the American occupational structure and, just as important, what caused it. They discovered, as we have noted, a fair amount of social mobility but most of it somewhat limited; both inter- and intra-generational mobility occurred, but generally the improvements were slight. Hauser and Featherman (1976) found a relation between father's occupational prestige and son's occupational prestige during the 1960s and 1970s; the most common occurrence was for white-collar fathers to have white-collar sons and for manual-working fathers to have manual-working sons.

The father's occupation appears to have a definite effect on the son's occupation, but Blau and Duncan wanted a more complete explanation. Using sophisticated statistical techniques designed to unearth such relationships, Blau and Duncan concluded that a variety of factors determined the son's occupation. The most important direct factor was the son's education. More education led to better jobs. But what determined the son's education? The more education and the higher the occupational level of the father, the more education the son would get. Similar results have been found by other researchers. Jencks et al. (1979) found that an individual's income and occupational status are best explained by looking at the educational level of the individual's family and, in particular, the skills and values for achievement acquired from the family. In short, social mobility is possible, but a variety of factors in family background have a strong impact on keeping the same kinds of jobs in the same kinds of families.

More recent research has increased our knowledge of this process. In particular, sociologists have searched for the factors in life that pass between generations, making mobility more or less difficult. Not surprisingly, educational attainment is critical to social mobility (Checchi, 1997). But while parent's educational attainment is a great predictor of the child's educational attainment, other factors also weigh in. Living in a low-poverty neighborhood, for example, increases mobility potential (Fauth et al., 2004). Parents' lack of money and the ability to borrow money decreases their ability to maximize their child's potential (Gaviria, 2002). And if assets are available to parents, the length of time they have been available strongly promotes the child's mobility (Caputo, 2003). If we sum up these findings, we note that being successful promotes being successful. The rates of intergenerational social mobility are not increasing in the United States (Rytina, 2000).

The avenues and barriers to social mobility have complex and intertwined roots that trail back into the overall workings of the social stratification system. Why, for example, should the father's level of education affect the son's level of education? Part of the answer, no doubt, is that a father who went to college might be more apt to encourage the same behavior from the son, but the full explanation is more complicated. Fathers who went to college will make more money and will be more able to send their sons to college. Fathers who went to college have acquired certain skills necessary to doing well in school that they will pass on to their sons. Fathers who went to college will probably have jobs that require a college degree and have friends with similar jobs; the sons will grow up in this environment, become aware of those kinds of occupations, and probably want to work in one themselves (for which college will be necessary). Fathers who went to college may belong to alumni associations and have some pull in getting their sons accepted; this is particularly true with high-prestige universities. Such explanations could continue indefinitely. The coordination of life within social stratification tends to keep values, skills, abilities, personal contacts, general information, and individual motivations passed on as a cluster from one generation to the next. This coordination is loose enough to allow for some social mobility but tight enough to prevent very much. Overall, the barriers to social mobility are high enough to give the United States clear differences in social class that persist over generations. As a result, individuals in different classes are very different from each other.

CHANGING OPPORTUNITIES IN THE UNITED STATES

As we've seen, many aspects of the social stratification system in the United States have changed little in many years. The rich and poor will always be with us and in approximately the same proportions. The rich have usually found it more comfortable to blame the poor for their poverty by pointing to behaviors of poor people that appear counterproductive for improving their economic status. (This perspective, sometimes termed the "culture of poverty" perspective, is reviewed by Banton, 1990.) On the other hand, there have been some major changes in both the U.S. economy and in the world economy over the past twenty years that have brought about profound changes in the experiences of American workers and their families. We have fewer jobs in the steel industry and more jobs in the computer industry. Another part of that change comes from economic competition from abroad. The trade deficit (the difference between what we export and import) grew steadily throughout the 1980s to the point where Americans were consuming far more foreign products than American products were being exported. Such a deficit threatened the value of the dollar and played a major role in the elimination of jobs in the United States.

Many of these changes were described by Bluestone and Harrison (1982) as the "deindustrialization" of America. The United States now has far fewer jobs available in the semiskilled and nonskilled categories; there are now fewer places to "start out" if one lacks basic occupational skills. Many assembly-line jobs are now performed by robots. In addition, much of America's basic heavy industry cannot compete with the lower prices and, in many cases, superior products from abroad. Hence many of the traditional blue-collar occupations, such as in the steel and automobile industries, are turning into dead-end careers. Given these changes, economic recessions now affect different Americans than they used to. In the recession of the early 1980s, for example, a new kind of poor emerged. Most notably, perhaps, they were young (Harrington, 1984; O'Hare, 1985). Older Americans were either well situated within the American economy or were retired with income such as Social

The growth of single-parent families headed by women has led to what some sociologists term the "feminization" of poverty.

Security that has built-in protections from economic changes. It was young workers just starting out who found few opportunities. Another change has been termed the "feminization" of poverty. More and more American families have become female headed, and since female occupations tend to be more poorly paid and women tend to be underemployed relative to their job skills, a growing number of the poor (and of the homeless) have been women and their children (Dabelko and Sheak, 1992). During the recession of the early 1980s, however, men slipped into poverty at a greater rate than women. Changes in the American economy may be more important in the long run than demographic changes in the American family (O'Hare, 1985).

We noted earlier in this chapter that racial and ethnic minorities tend to be clustered toward the bottom of the social stratification system. Not surprisingly, we find that blacks and other minorities also disproportionately occupy poverty status in the United States. Whereas most poor in the United States are white (due to the fact that most Americans are white), the percentage of African American families and Hispanic American families below the poverty line is almost three times that of European American families (U.S. Bureau of the Census, 2004a). These figures have changed little over the last twenty-five years. Industrial restructuring has had a major impact on inner-city African Americans (Singh, 1991). The loss of jobs coupled with residential segregation has created an almost insurmountable barrier (Massey,

BOX 7.2

The Homeless in the United States:
A Growing and Changing Group

The homeless in the United States have been much in the news in recent years. The attention they have received is generated by two fundamental changes in this group, which exists at the lower end of the stratification system. First, the homeless appear to be a growing group, particularly in the last two decades. Second, the kinds of people who have become homeless in the last decade also appear to be different. The word *appear* is necessary in the preceding two sentences because the homeless are a hard group to know; they are hard to count and, once counted, they are often hard to categorize because many of them seem to be without housing as the result of a combination of factors.

Until recently, the popular image of the homeless person was the skid-row, single, middle-aged male with an alcohol problem. Men and alcohol still create a potent combination in producing homelessness, but definite changes have occurred among the homeless. Today's homeless person is much more likely to be younger (low to mid-thirties) and female; there are also more likely to be children involved; at least 10 percent of homeless adults care for children (Baum and Burnes, 1993; Caton, 1990). While approximately 80 percent of the homeless are still single males, these changes in the homeless population clearly indicate new factors at work in creating homelessness.

Marcuse (1990) points to the lack of housing for low-income people in the United States. While housing is normally considered to be about 25 percent of one's cost of living, low-income people (earning under $5,000 a year) are more likely to be paying 50 percent of their earnings for housing. Gentrification (in which old neighborhoods are refurbished for upper-middle-class people returning to the cities) removes low-cost housing and replaces it with expensive housing. As Marcuse points out, there has been no corresponding growth in low-income or public housing to make up for the loss. Public housing that does exist often maintains long waiting lists. Bohanon (1991) also notes the importance of high rental prices, which, coupled with high levels of unemployment, figure prominently in predicting high levels of homelessness.

Baum and Burnes (1993) focus attention on a variety of factors beyond housing to account for some of the changes in the homeless population. They emphasize the multiple causes of homelessness, in which alcohol and drug abuse are often mixed with poverty, unstable families, and mental illness. They argue that alcohol problems afflict some 40 percent of the homeless, while 30 to 50 percent suffer from some form of chronic psychiatric disorder. Part of the mental illness problem stems from changes in institutionalization patterns of the mentally ill. Between 1955 and

1985, there was an 80 percent decline in the populations of state mental hospitals (Baum and Burnes, 1993). The real problem, researchers argue, is that the last decade has put individuals with the worst psychiatric disorders on the streets as funds for state institutions have been cut; similar increases in the numbers of homeless mentally ill have been noted in Canada (Herman, 1992). Their overall conclusion is that between 65 and 85 percent of the homeless population suffers from some combination of chronic alcoholism, drug dependency, and psychiatric problems (Baum and Burnes, 1993).

This brief discussion of homelessness only scratches the surface of the issue's complexity. As we've already seen in this chapter, the last decade has witnessed an overall growth in the percentage of the U.S. population living below the poverty level; this change, along with increased housing costs, has obviously played a significant role in the growing homeless population, particularly for women and women with children. Baum and Burnes, on the other hand, tend to emphasize individual characteristics of the homeless, which, among other things, make them less appealing and thus less deserving of help in the eyes of most Americans. This issue not only illustrates the complexity of basic sociological research but it also highlights the political implications of that research.

1991). The unskilled and semiskilled industrial jobs that allowed so many European immigrants to climb out of poverty early in the twentieth century are no longer available. For many of those immigrants, better jobs for one generation led to better education for the next generation and still better jobs for the third generation. African Americans and Hispanic Americans appear to be locked into a cycle of inadequate training and thus limited opportunities.

THE INDIVIDUAL EXPERIENCE OF SOCIAL CLASS

We come finally to the individual's perspective on social stratification. How exactly does social stratification make us so different from each other? This important question is unfortunately difficult to answer through any kind of systematic research. Your social class is a part of your life that affects every aspect from the moment you are born. Because of it, every day you will have slightly different experiences from those of people in other social classes. You will see different places and people, acquire different skills and abilities, be treated differently by others, learn different norms, and acquire different values. By the time you are an adult, this accumulation of experience adds up to making you a different kind of person, just as the accumulation of experience if you were growing up in London would make you different from those who call New York home. How do you then go back through research to determine just which of those experiences played the major role in making you

Social classes in the United States live in different worlds in all senses of the word. A poor family living in a two-room shack in rural West Virginia might as well be on a different planet from the one in which upper class folk in white flannels play croquet on wide expanses of manicured lawn.

the person you are today? Social class is a general concept. Because it is so general, it is difficult to nail down. Its generality also makes it very important.

Even if we don't know all we need to about the exact causes of social class differences, we can see many of the effects. Some of these were examined earlier in this chapter, but many are not easily expressed as research results. For example, people of different social classes are generally uncomfortable around each other in social situations. Of course, there are social settings where people of different classes commonly meet, but most of them are formal. Interactions between an employer and employee, for example, are necessary to get on with the business at hand, but do the two individuals ever really come to know each other very well? Most such settings have fairly strict rules as to how each person should talk and the kinds of topics that may be discussed. If the employer were to invite the employee to a party (or vice versa), both would probably be uncomfortable. The different classes have different kinds of parties, for one thing, but they also have different kinds of interests and different styles of expressing those interests. There is often not enough common ground for such interactions to occur easily.

Most of us don't consciously see our experience as shaped by our social class. We encounter people and situations, some of which we like and some of which we don't. We rarely say, "I'm comfortable with these people in this situation because both are part of my social class." Instead we say, "They are good people and a lot of fun." Part of the reason they are "good" and "fun," however, is that they fit in with the way we see the world and the people in it. And we acquired that worldview as part of our social class. Left to our own devices, we will organize our life so that we can spend as much time as possible with the people and situations we prefer. Considering that the people we like are doing the same thing, it's not surprising that people cluster together within social classes, rarely venturing out into the chaos and uncertainty that lies beyond.

The tendency for people to group according to social class has been a primary concern of sociological research on social stratification from the very beginning. Marx was waiting for the day when class consciousness would replace false consciousness, leading the working class into the revolution he predicted. Weber thought this wouldn't happen because people would form groups based on similarities of power or social status as well as on economic concerns. But even Weber recognized that class, status, and power operate together more often than they operate independently; most of us are ranked at more or less the same point on each hierarchy. Nevertheless, people may often group according to class similarities without being aware of it; a neighborhood association, a labor union, or a fraternal organization may represent more common interests than its members realize. This is one of the most confusing yet most interesting questions raised by the study of social stratification: how do individuals perceive their place in the system? These perceptions can change drastically, and sociologists are still searching for the reasons why.

SUMMARY

Social stratification refers to the arrangement of activities of a society into a hierarchy whereby activities ranked high in the hierarchy are highly rewarded and activities ranked low are poorly rewarded. These rewards consist of economic privilege (social class), respect from others (social status), and influence over others (social power). These three dimensions overlap considerably, as activities that receive economic rewards generally also receive respect and are allowed to influence others. Individuals acquire these rewards by virtue of their engaging in one of the activities and only as long as they engage in it.

The movement of individuals from one activity to another is called social mobility. If the activities are within the same social class, the social mobility is horizontal; if the activities are in different social classes, the mobility is vertical. Societies that permit no vertical social mobility are called caste societies, while societies that permit open vertical mobility are called class societies. The former encourage the formation of large social groups based on caste, while the latter encourage individual competition. Societies located somewhere between the two extremes, such as the United States, are characterized by group competition and conflict.

The structural-functional theory of social stratification maintains that stratification is necessary to place competent individuals in the activities most important to the society. This theory maintains that highly ranked activities are by definition more necessary to society and that high levels of rewards will encourage individuals to compete for those activities. The conflict theory maintains that social stratification is a form of social organization designed to benefit certain members of society through the organized exploitation of other members. This theory maintains that social stratification forces competition and inequality on the society and benefits only those who occupy the top positions of the hierarchy.

The United States has a clear system of social stratification in which a small percentage of members in a society control most of the wealth and power. There is consistent social mobility of individuals over one social class boundary. To the extent that barriers to social mobility exist, individuals tend to remain in given social classes across generations, living in social and spatial isolation from each other. This class isolation creates distinctive class cultures or lifestyles, which further serve to separate the members of different social classes. As a general and important sociological concept, social class defines a wide variety of social experiences that people have. No social category has as great an impact on separating individuals as social class.

GLOSSARY

Bourgeoisie As defined by Karl Marx, the social class that owns the means of production and distribution in a capitalist economy (the ruling class).

Capitalism An economic system in which most of the wealth is the private property of individuals. This wealth (capital) can be invested and can be increased through profit.

Caste society A society with a social stratification hierarchy in which no vertical social mobility occurs.

Class consciousness As defined by Karl Marx, the ability of individuals in a particular social class to recognize the true interests of that class.

Class society A society with a social stratification hierarchy in which vertical social mobility occurs.

Ethnic stratification The clustering of ethnic group members at certain class levels of social stratification, with the result that members of certain ethnic groups will be found disproportionately in certain social classes.

Exploitation As defined by Karl Marx, the unequal manner in which the ruling class in society benefits from the working class.

False consciousness As defined by Karl Marx, the inability of individuals in a particular social class to recognize the true interests of that class.

Horizontal social mobility The movement of groups or individuals from one activity to another within the same social class level.

Ideology An idea or set of ideas that represents a particular interest of a particular social group. As defined by Karl Marx, it refers specifically to the set of beliefs that supports the interests of the ruling class in society.

Intergenerational vertical social mobility Vertical social mobility occurring between generations (results in differences between the social class levels of parent and child).

Intragenerational vertical social mobility Vertical social mobility occurring within the lifetime of one individual (or within one generation).

Party As defined by Max Weber, a political action or political interest group.

Proletariat As defined by Karl Marx, the social class that does not own the means of production and distribution in a capitalist economy but works for those who do.

Social class A collection of individuals whose economic activities (or roles) are similar in terms of the rewards they bring to their participants.

Social mobility The movement of groups or individuals within the ranking system of social stratification. (See also vertical and horizontal social mobility.)

Social power The ability to influence the behavior of others.

Social status An individual's social position within the social group, particularly with respect to his or her prestige.

Social stratification The arrangement of various activities (or roles) into a hierarchy whereby activities ranked high are highly rewarded and activities ranked low are poorly rewarded. The rewards generally consist of money, prestige, and influence over others.

Socioeconomic status A sociological measure of social class, representing a combination of income, education, and occupational prestige.

Status inconsistency A social situation in which an individual is not consistently high, medium, or low across all the dimensions of social stratification.

Vertical social mobility The movement of groups or individuals up or down the stratification hierarchy, from one social class level to another.

STUDY QUESTIONS

1. What is a social stratification system? How do individuals come to occupy positions within it?
2. Positions within a social stratification system may be ranked according to class, status, or power. How do these three dimensions of stratification vary? Why are many positions similarly ranked along all three? What is status inconsistency?
3. How do Karl Marx and Max Weber differ in their analyses of social stratification? Which comes closer to American society and why?
4. What promotes and what inhibits vertical social mobility? How are class and caste societies defined by their relative levels of social mobility? Which kind of society is the United States?
5. How do the structural-functionalists and conflict theorists differ in their analyses of social stratification? How differently might they view exploitation?
6. To what degree does the United States have inequality in income and wealth?
7. How and why are people different in a cultural sense depending upon their social classes?
8. Why do the very poor find upward mobility so difficult in the United States?

James B. Twitchell   **READING**

NEEDING THE UNNECESSARY:
THE DEMOCRATIZATION OF LUXURY

As we saw in this chapter, social classes in the United States vary not only in wealth and power but also in the way they live their lives. Members of different social classes typically grow up in different neighborhoods, attend different schools, acquire different occupations, and pursue different leisure activities. In the following reading, James B. Twitchell focuses on what and how people consume as one of the most critical differences among us. He revisits the work of Thorstein Veblen (discussed in Chapter 3) and shows how our interests in consuming both reflect our lives and, in some ways, are our lives.

If you want to understand material culture at the beginning of the 21st century, you must understand the overwhelming importance of unnecessary material. If you are looking for the one unambiguous result of modern capitalism, of the industrial revolution, and of marketing, here it is. In the way we live now, you are not what you make. You are what you consume. And most of what you consume is totally unnecessary yet remarkably well made.

The most interesting of those superfluous objects belong in a socially constructed and ever-shifting class called *luxury*. Consuming those objects, objects as rich in meaning as they are low in utility, causes lots of happiness and distress. As well they should. For one can make the argument

that until all necessities are had by all members of a community, no one should have luxury. More complex still is that, since the 1980s, the bulk consumers of luxury have not been the wealthy but the middle class, your next-door neighbors and their kids. And this is happening not just in the West but in many parts of the world.

When I was growing up in the middle class of the 1950s, luxury objects were lightly tainted with shame. You had to be a little cautious if you drove a Cadillac, wore a Rolex, or lived in a house with more than two columns out front. The rich could drip with diamonds, but you should stay dry. Movie stars could drive convertibles; you should keep your top up. If you've got it, don't flaunt it. Remember, the people surrounding you had lived through the Depression, a time that forever lit the bright lines between have-to-have, don't-need-to-have, and have-in-order-to-show-off.

The best definition of this old-style off-limits luxury came to me from my dad. I was just a kid, and it was my first trip to a cafeteria: Morrison's Cafeteria in Pompano Beach, Florida, February 1955. When I got to the desserts, I removed the main course from my tray and loaded up on cake and JELL-O. My dad told me to put all the desserts back but one. I said that wasn't fair. To me the whole idea of cafeteria was to have as much as you want of what you want. My dad said no, that was not the idea of cafeteria. The idea of cafeteria is that you can have just one of many choices.

LUXURIFICATION

Look around American culture, and you will see how wrong he was. Almost every set of consumables has a dessert at the top. And you can have as much of it as you can get on your tray or as much of it as your credit card will allow. This is true not just for expensive products like town cars and McMansions but for everyday objects. In bottled water, for instance, there is Evian, advertised as if it were a liquor. In coffee, there's Starbucks; in ice cream, Häagen-Dazs; in sneakers, Nike; in whiskey, Johnnie Walker Blue; in credit cards, American Express Centurian; in wine, Chateau Margaux; in cigars, Arturo Fuente Hemingway; and, well, you know the rest.

Name the category, no matter how mundane, and you'll find a premium or, better yet, a super-premium brand at the top. And having more than you can conceivably use of such objects is not met with opprobrium but with genial acceptance. This pattern persists regardless of class: The average number of branded sneakers for adolescent males? It's 4.8 pairs. And regardless of culture.

A favorite consumer product in China? Chanel lipstick dispensers sans lipstick.

Basil Englis and Michael Solomon, professors of marketing in the School of Business at Rutgers University, have studied the effects of brand consumption, particularly how college students

cluster around top-brand knowledge. They drew guinea pigs from undergraduate business majors at their institution and presented them with 40 cards, each containing a description of a different cluster of consumers.

The professors sifted the clusters to make four groups—lifestyles, if you will—representative of undergraduate society. They were Young Suburbia, Money & Brains, Smalltown Downtown, and Middle America. Then Englis and Solomon gathered images of objects from four product categories (automobiles, magazines/newspapers, toiletries, and alcoholic beverages) that fit into each group. The students were asked to put the various images together into coherent groups; they were also to state their current proximity to, or desire to be part of, each group in the future.

As might be expected, the Money & Brains cluster was the most popular aspirational niche. What Englis and Solomon did not expect was how specific and knowledgeable the students were about the possessions that they did not have but knew that members of that cluster needed.

When asked what brand of automobile they would drive, here's what they said: BMWs (53.6 percent), Mercedes (50.7), Cadillacs (30.4), Volvos (23.2), Porsches (21.7), Acuras (17.4), and Jaguars (15.9). They knew what they wanted to read: travel magazines (21.7 percent), *Vogue* (21.7), *Business Week* (20.3), *Fortune* (17.9), and *GQ* (15.9). Again, this is not what they did read but what they took to be the reading material of the desired group. What they were actually reading (or so they said) were *Forbes*, *Barron's*, *The New Yorker*, and *Gourmet*. No mention of *Rolling Stone*, *Playboy*, *Spin*, or *Maxim* for this group. They certainly knew what to drink: Heineken beer (33.3 percent), expensive wines (26.1), scotch (18.8), champagne (17.4), and Beck's beer (15). They also knew what to sprinkle on their bodies: Polo (27.5 percent), Obsession (15.9), and Drakkar (15.9).

What the professors found was not just that birds of a feather had started to flock together, but that these young birds already knew what flock to shy away from. They were not ashamed of smoking, for instance, but of smoking the wrong brand. Their prime avoidance group corresponded to the Smalltown Downtown cluster.

The Money & Brainers knew a lot about the Smalltowners. They knew about favored pickup trucks, Chevys (23.2 percent) and Fords (18.8). They knew that this group reads *People* (30.4), *Sports Illustrated* (26.1), *TV Guide* (24.6), *Wrestling* (21.7), fishing magazines (20.3), and *The National Enquirer* (18.8). They assumed that Smalltowners preferred Budweiser (59.4), followed by Miller (24.6) and Coors (18.8). Essentially, the Money & Brainers had learned not just what to buy but what to avoid (or at least what to say to avoid).

Such shared knowledge is the basis of culture. This insight was, after all, the rationale behind a liberal arts education. John Henry Newman and Matthew Arnold argued for state-supported education in the 19th century precisely because cultural literacy meant social cohesion. No one argued that it was important to know algebraic functions or Latin etymologies or what constitutes a sonnet because such knowledge allows us to solve important social problems. We learn such matters because it is the basis of how to speak to each other, how we develop a bond of shared history and commonality. This is the secular religion of the liberal arts and sciences, what French sociologist Pierre Bourdieu calls cultural capital.

In our postmodern world we have, it seems, exchanged knowledge of history and science (a knowledge of production) for knowledge of products and how such products interlock to form coherent social patterns (a knowledge of consumption). Buy this and don't buy that has replaced make/learn this, don't make/learn that. After all, in the way we live now, everyone is a consumer, but not everyone is a worker. As Marcel Duchamp, sly observer of the changing scene, said, "Living is more a question of what one spends than what one makes." Thus a new denomination of cultural capital.

A shift in currency has clear ramifications. A producer culture focuses on the independent self of the worker: self-help, self-discipline, self-respect, self-control, self-reliance, self-interest. Responsibility is situated in the individual: Can she get work? A consumer culture, however, focuses on community: Fit in, don't stand out. Be cool. The standard of judgment becomes the ability to interact effectively with others, to win their affection and admiration—to merge with others of the same lifestyle. Can he consume the right brands?

INVENTING PASHMINA

The powerful desire to associate with recognized objects of little intrinsic but high positional value is at the heart of Luxe Americana. It is what Martha Stewart is doing down at Kmart introducing her Silver Label goods. Of her many endorsed products, one is of special interest: her line of matelassé coverlets and shams—really, just bedcovers. They are available in yellow, white, and multicolored stripes and come in silk, linen, crushed velvet, Egyptian cotton, cotton sateens, and even cashmere. Remember three things: This is Kmart, a bedspread is something you buy not to show off to others but to please yourself, and cashmere is supposed to be something really special.

So here is the Cashmere Company hawking something it calls pashmina. The word is a linguistic trick. Cashmere is goat hair from Kashmir, an area between India and Pakistan, whereas pashmina is simply the Persian word for the same goat in the same area. In other words, it's the same stuff. But that's not what is interesting. It is that pashmina has been introduced precisely because places like Kmart have too much cashmere. So what we have is a top-of-the-line product topped because too many people were in the checkout line.

But then again, what of Michael Graves designed toasters for Target, Ralph Lauren house paint, and Ernest Hemingway and Cole Porter brand furniture at Ethan Allen Furniture stores? This tectonic shift in consumption is why the designer Lynette Jennings, host of the Discovery Channel's *Lynette Jennings Design* and *House-Smart,* is peddling doorknobs at Home Depot.

If you want to see how varied the consumers of the new luxuries are, just take a tour of your local Costco or Sam's Club parking lot. Observe the shiny new imported sedans and SUVs alongside aging subcompacts. Or spend an hour watching what is being sold on the Home Shopping Network, a televised flea market for impulse buyers. The system now has 23,000 incoming phone lines capable of handling up to 20,000 calls a minute. Home Shopping no longer sells just cubic zirconium rings. Not when the real money is in designer handbags.

In the older culture, my dad's culture, the limited production capacity of the economy sharply reduced aspirations to material comfort. In the modern world, my culture, much greater material satisfactions lie within the reach of even those of modest means. Thus a producer culture becomes a consumer culture, a hoarding culture becomes a surplus culture, a work culture becomes a therapeutic culture. Because what you buy becomes more important than what you make, luxury is not a goal; for many it is a necessity.

LUXURY CREEP

Michael J. Apter, a psychologist at Northwestern University, has studied why we do things and, by extension, why we buy things. In *The Experience of Motivation: The Theory of Psychological Reversals,* he divides general orientations into telic (arousal reducing) and paratelic (arousal seeking). A telic motivation starts with isolating a need and then feeling anxious about resolving it. The experience ends, if successful, with a feeling of relaxation. If the ending does not satisfy the need (postdecision dissonance), the anxiety continues, and the process is repeated until it abates. A paratelic tendency, however, begins in a state of well-being that edges over into boredom. The person seeks excitement and judges the act by the experience. Does it resolve boredom? Not to put too fine a point on it, but consuming luxury for many Americans has gone from telic to paratelic, from product to process, from problem resolution to emotion seeking, from object to experience.

The one characteristic of modern luxe is its profound oxymoronic nature: If everyone can have it, is it still luxury? If you want to see the difference that a generation makes in downshifting luxury, just look at how top-of-the-line domestic automobiles are advertised. Compare Cadillac in the early part of the 20th century with Lincoln at the end of the century, and you'll get the idea.

Cadillac's pitch in a 1915 advertisement was that luxury comes at a price and that price includes humility, even mild mortification. You buy this car and you take responsibility for sharing excellence. The true price of luxury is not cheap. In fact, you will be reviled, assailed, and envied. This car is a laurel. Be careful how you wear it. The real headline is not just "The Penalty of Leadership," it is "The Penalty of Luxury."

By contrast, Lincoln's current pitch is pure indulgence: Buy this object and let your lust for comfort run wild. Lincoln is "what a luxury object should be." And after all you've been through, you deserve it. If not to own, then to lease.

Needless to say, as the 20th century faded into oblivion, Cadillac, which had a history of "owning" the luxury category, lost its vaunted place as the best-selling domestic luxury car to Lincoln. The Lincoln division of the Ford Motor Car Company has a single-word advertising motto: "Luxury."

Perhaps the best example of what I call luxury creep, in which a down-market product comes uptown solely on the basis of advertising, is the Buick Century. Buick has had a history of being a car for strivers who have not quite made it. Just look back on Buick advertising in the '60s, and you can see the company's typical reticence. In 1965 Buick advertising carried the tag line, "Wouldn't you really rather have a Buick?," which survived through the 1980s. In 1980 the company added a second theme: "The great American road belongs to Buick." Then in 1986 the McCann-Erickson ad agency positioned Buicks as "premium American motorcars."

Now Buick does have a luxury car, the Park Avenue. But the Century is an underling, now positioned as "a luxury car for everyone." Never mind that the tag line is an oxymoron. The problem is more fundamental. This car is just a standard Buick, which is just a jazzed-up Chevy, which is just a dumbed-down Cadillac, which is just an Oldsmobile, which is just like tons of Fords and Chryslers, as well as most Japanese midrange cars. The only luxury about it is the pretension of saying this is luxurious.

PUNK LUXE?

In the last few years I have spent hours flipping through a new genre of magazine—*The Robb Report, Millionaire, Indulgence, Flaunt, Luxe, Icon, Self: The Best of Everything, Ornament: The Art of Personal Adornment*—as well as standard glossy pulp from Condé Nast like *GQ, Vogue, Vanity Fair,* and, most recently, *Lucky.* I have trolled Rodeo Drive, Worth Avenue, and upper Madison Avenue and traveled to Las Vegas, where I stood agog for hours in the Bellagio and Venetian hotels.

I admit from the start that you could argue that this is not real luxury but a kind of ersatz variety, punk luxe, and maybe you would be correct. My father would have argued that real luxury is characterized not by shine but by patina, that its allure comes from inborn aesthetics, not from glitzy advertising, that it is passed from generation to generation and cannot be bought at the mall, and, most of all, that its consumption is private, not conspicuous. His words for modern luxury would have included *gauche, vulgar, nouveau, tasteless,* and, most interestingly, *offensive.*

In fact, maybe the rich have only two genuine luxury items left: time and philanthropy. The rest of us are having a go at all their stuff, albeit for a knockoff to be held only a short time. I can't afford a casita on Bermuda, but my timeshare can get it for me at least for a week. I can't own a limo, but I can rent one. If I can't fly on the Concorde, I can upgrade to first class with the miles I "earn" by using my American Express card. I can lease a Lexus.

In a sense luxury objects don't exist anymore as they used to because "real" luxury used to be for the "happy few," and in the world of the jubilant Dow there is no more "happy few." The world that we live in, as John Seabrook recently argued in *Nobrow: The Marketing of Culture and the Culture of Marketing,* and as David Brooks explored in *Bobos in Paradise: The New Upper Class and How They Got There,* no longer easily fits into intellectual classes. It now fits into consumption communities. So, for instance, we don't talk about high class, upper middle class, and middle class. Instead we talk about boomers, yuppies, Generation X, echo-boomers, nobrows, bobos (short for bourgeois bohemians), and the rest, who show what they are buying for themselves, not what they do for a living. And that's why each of these groups has its own luxury markers—positional goods, in marketing jargon—to be bought, not made.

HIGH BROW TO NOBROW

In a way, the new luxury is the ineluctable result of a market economy and a democratic political system. As journalist Thomas Beer wrote, "Money does not rule democracy. Money is democracy." Back in the late 1940s Russell Lynes, editor of *Harper's,* concocted a taxonomy of taste: highbrow, upper middle-brow, lower middle-brow, and low-brow. His system, as gleefully celebrated in the April 11, 1949, issue of *Life* magazine, was scandalous when published, the topic of much cocktail party concern.

Lynes knew even then that Americans were no longer divided by "wealth, birth, or political eminence" but by consumption. These material distinctions were further explored in the 1980s in Paul Fussell's *Class: A Guide Through the American Status System.* Tongue almost in cheek, Fussell even proposed a new class, what he called "category X people," to be based not on material consumption but on a shared taste for the better life. Fussell got the phenomenon of the "massification" of the upper class correct, and he certainly understood how the democratizing of luxury was a mixed blessing, but he missed the materiality of this confluence. Instead of superfluous stuff being pushed aside, it became even more central. You had to buy your way out, one Volvo, one glass of merlot, one bow tie, one Sub-Zero refrigerator, one granite countertop at a time.

From time to time in Western history there is vociferous antipathy toward high-end consumption. From Plato to the early Christians to the Renaissance, luxury was thought to effeminize and weaken. But this was hardly a pressing problem, because just getting to the necessities of life was a full-time job for most.

With increasing affluence this view shifted. Luxury became dangerous not because of debasement but because it was a sign of overreaching, of getting out of place. An interesting transformation shows how fluid this category can be. In the Renaissance, luxury objects became those things thought worthy of being painted. Such objects were called *objets d'art*. Now, of course, the luxury object is the painting itself. But you can see that even before the industrial revolution there was a growing desire to show stuff off, to use the material world as marker of social dominance, to strut, to flaunt.

By the 18th century, social critics like Bernard Mandeville and economists like Adam Smith were beginning to suggest that, for improving the weal of humanity, the promise of consuming luxury might be a better carrot than the stick of shame. Yet there was still deep resentment for consuming out of your class, beyond your means.

This suspicion about consuming beyond your class continued well into the 19th century. In fact, ancient sumptuary laws, explaining exactly what objects were forbidden by church and state, were read from the Anglican pulpit until the 1860s. Reading these laws took two hours of church time to complete, and the laws kept people in their places, if only to have to listen to them.

Clerics, clearly supported by the aristocracy, were not alone in stiff-arming luxury. With the onset of industrial surpluses, secular pundits like Henry David Thoreau railed against what they took to be the excesses of mass production. "Most of the luxuries, and many of the so-called com-

forts of life are not only not indispensable, but positive hindrances to the elevation of mankind," he pointed out in *Walden*.

By the *fin de siècle* this view of high-end consumption had so exploded that Thorstein Veblen unloosed the first modern sustained attack on luxury in his thoroughly entertaining *Theory of the Leisure Class* (1899). Coining all manner of nifty concepts like conspicuous consumption, invidious comparison, bandwagon effect, symbolic pantomime, vicarious leisure, and parodic display, Veblen had at the excesses of robber-baron shopping.

THE LEISURE CLASSIC

In fact, one might say that Veblen enjoyed it rather too much and succeeded only too well. When he formulated his theory of the leisure class at the turn of the century, ostentation in dress was at its full plumage, not least because new money was desperate to prove that it had made it to high society. Veblen's argument was so simple that it cut like Occam's razor. It has proved so powerful that it has achieved the status of unquestioned truism.

Here is Veblen's argument: As wealth spreads, what drives consumers' behavior is increasingly neither subsistence nor comfort but the attainment of "the esteem and envy of fellow men." Because male wage earners are too circumspect to indulge themselves, they deposit consumption on surrogates, on loved ones. Vicarious ostentation—the way that plainly dressed Victorian men encouraged their wives and daughters to wear complicated trappings of wealth—is how this unfolds. Ditto their servants, horses, and even house pets.

In retrospect, Veblen was too successful, too neat, too sharp. Veblen thought that the purpose of acquisition was public consumption of esteem, status anxiety resolved by material display. Not much more. Wealth, he argued, confers honor; it suggests prowess and achievement. But wealth would have no social meaning were it simply consumed or possessed. "In order to gain and to hold the esteem of men," he wrote, "it is not sufficient merely to possess wealth or power. The wealth or power must be put in evidence, for esteem is awarded only on evidence."

Thus the absolute centrality of conspicuous consumption. In what Veblen called "barbarian culture," trophies such as property or slaves were signs of successful aggression. In modern societies luxury is a sign of status and class. It's what we have for harems. But only certain sorts of goods work this magic. There is no rational system. The only constant is that consumers seek the luxurious object for two reasons: to show that they are members of the classes above and to distinguish themselves from those below. Veblen calls the first motive "pecuniary emulation"; the second, "invidious comparison."

From this comes the economic irrationality of the Veblen effect, namely, that the value of a luxury object is in direct proportion to its cost. Raise the price of certain luxe objects and you increase their value. The Veblen effect is why a T-shirt sold at Sears costs less than the same T-shirt at the Gap, which costs less than the same T-shirt at Hugo Boss, and so forth. Could you sell Evian water if it were priced below a generic? What about Ben & Jerry's ice cream? *The Robb Report?* A Lexus? An Ivy League education? It is not enough for me to know what I paid for opuluxe. *You* have to know.

Today these products, which are no more (and maybe less) useful than their functional equivalents, are sometimes called "positional goods," goods that are valued not despite their expense but because of it. Indeed, Veblen argued that since the reasons for buying such goods are "pecuniary emulation" and "invidious comparison," their utility rises as their prices go up. With insights like this, Veblen proved himself to be too strong a critic to dismiss. You don't need to have read a word he wrote to know him. He set the tone of modern criticism.

ECONOMIC MORALISM

The second modern attack on luxury came in the 1950s with John Kenneth Galbraith's *The Affluent Society* and, to a lesser degree, the pop-

ularizing work of Vance Packard in *The Hidden Persuaders, The Status Seekers,* and *The Pyramid Climbers.* Veblenism is all over these books. Galbraith had read Veblen, if not wisely, then too well. In fact, he had edited *Theory of the Leisure Class* with all kinds of approving nods and winks. Packard and his snappy titles went along for the ride. To these critics high-end consumption is against our "better nature"; we are duped into consuming by advertisers; consumers are dolts who should be doing other things; luxury is consumption run amok.

The usual suspects for Galbraith had changed from the captains of industry to the Joneses across the street. Keeping up with them was every bit as dangerous as it had been for a Carnegie to keep up with a Vanderbilt, a Morgan with a Gould. Perhaps even more dangerous because these Joneses now are so numerous. And, as opposed to the robber barons who were outfitting family members, this new solipsistic breed of showoff was outfitting himself.

Veblen's descendants are still at it. Following in the footsteps of Galbraith have been two moralists passing as economists: Juliet Schor, a professor now at Boston College, who has published *The Overspent American: Why We Want What We Don't Need,* and Robert Frank, a professor at Cornell, who contributed *Luxury Fever: Why Money Fails to Satisfy in an Era of Excess.* Just read the subtitles.

The modern attack usually centers around a specific object as an exemplum. While Galbraith disliked Cadillac tail fins, Schor disdains granite countertops in the kitchen, and Frank holds up expensive watches as symptomatic of bad habits. On the surface they have such good points: How do those fins help the car move, are those stone countertops better than Formica, does a Lucian Picard keep better time than a Timex?

But here's the problem. The 1958 Cadillac has been featured in the Museum of Modern Art's retrospective show celebrating industrial design as art, and if you now want to buy one in mint condition, you'll pay about 20 times the purchase price. The granite countertop really makes more sense as a cutting surface than as a slab to lay down over the dead body of Uncle Louie, and—who knows?—it might even be passed from generation to generation, while the sensible Formica is carted out to the dump. And had Frank invested in Lucian Picard watches at the beginning of the bull market, he would have made more on his watch investment than on the S&P 500. Drats! That this stuff could have increased in value tells us how slippery these slopes can be.

No matter. Critics of consumption love to point out that people with these things are no happier than people without them. Ergo, why buy extra stuff? But people who can't buy unnecessary opuluxe are definitely unhappier for not being let into the cycle; buying this notational stuff and having such stuff are different experiences; consumers move in definite stages, from adolescence, where consumption is central, to middle age, where it ceases to be so important, to old age, where having things is positively a hindrance. Religious fanatics invariably rank highest on happiness scales, irrespective of culture or religion. Let's give happiness a rest. Consumption of the new luxury is about far more interesting sensations.

Whereas Veblen contended that male aggression caused the crazed consumption of deluxe items at the end of his century, these modern critics are more au courant in putting forth their etiology. They medicalize consumption, in large part because the bulk consumers of luxe are now young women. The diagnosis, although they would never use this precise term, is addiction. We are addicted to luxury. That's what causes the fever. That's why we yearn for what we don't want. Diagnosis from the National Public Radio crowd: not just Sudden Wealth Syndrome but the dreaded "affluenza."

OVER THE TOP

I must say that I found most of the luxury objects that I've looked at, from Patek Philippe watches to Porsche Turbos to the men's room of the Bellagio Hotel, to be a little over the top. But I am not so oblivious to the world around me that I

can't appreciate how important the new luxury has become. And I can't overlook how high-end consumption promises to do exactly what critics of the stuff have always yearned for, namely, to bring us together, often traumatically. Yes, indeed, the transgenerational poor are excluded, as the bottom fifth of our population has not budged an inch in the luxe explosion. Yet more people than ever are entering the much-vaunted global village because of consumption, not despite it.

In fact, one could argue, as Dinesh D'Souza, Virginia Postrel, and W. Michael Cox and Richard Alm have recently done, that the aspiration of the poor to get at these unnecessary goods has done more than any social program to motivate some of the disenchanted to become enfranchised. While one may be distressed at seeing a dish antenna atop a ramshackle house or a Caddie out front, the yearning to have superfluous badges of affluence may promise a more lasting peace around the world than any religion or political system has ever delivered. I don't mean to overlook the complexities here.

This is not a universal phenomenon, as the al-Qaeda have wickedly demonstrated. Some of the world's poor are most certainly not becoming better off in absolute or relative terms. I only want to say that, given a choice between being mugged for your sneakers or having your ethnic or religious heritage cleansed, the lust for sneakers may prove a more lasting way to improve the general lot of humanity.

Let's face it. In the world that I grew up in, your religion, your family name, the color of your skin, your language skills, your gender, where you went to school, your accent, and your marriage partner were doing the work that luxury consumption does now. My dad went to Exeter, Williams, and Harvard Med, and he never drove anything fancier than a Plymouth. He never had to. Today I wouldn't go to a doctor who drove a Plymouth. I would figure that if she doesn't drive a Lexus, she is having trouble with her practice.

So I admit the ugly truth. After spending the last few years trying to understand the pull of the material world, I am far more sympathetic to its blandishments and far more forgiving of its excesses. The democratization of luxury has been the single most important marketing phenomenon of modern times. And it has profound political implications. It may not be as bad as some lifestyle scolds make it out to be. In its own way it is a fair, albeit often wasteful, system, not just of objects but of meaning. Don't get me wrong: It's not that I came to mock and stayed to pray, but I do feel that getting and spending has some actual worth. Nobody checks the number of vowels in your name, or the color of your skin, or whether you know the difference between *like* and *as* when you are buying your Prada parka—that's got to mean something.

Although luxury has become a mallet with which one pounds the taste of others, this misses some essential points. One is that humans are consumers by nature. We are tool users because we like to use what tool using can produce. In other words, tools are not the ends but the means. So too materialism does not crowd out spiritualism; spiritualism is more likely a substitute when objects are scarce. When we have few things, we make the next world luxurious. When we have plenty, we enchant the objects around us.

Second, consumers are rational. They are often fully aware that they are more interested in consuming aura than objects, sizzle than steak, meaning than material. In fact, if you ask them—as academic critics are usually loath to do—they are quite candid in explaining that the Nike swoosh, the Polo pony, the Guess? label, the DKNY logo are what they are after. They are not duped by advertising, packaging, branding, fashion, and merchandising. They actively seek and enjoy the status that surrounds the object, especially when they are young.

Third, we need to question the standard argument that consumption of opuluxe almost always leads to disappointment. Admittedly, the circular route from desire to purchase to disappointment to renewed desire is never-ending, but we may follow it because the other route—from melancholy to angst—is worse. In other words, in a world emptied of inherited values, consuming what looks to be overpriced fripperies may be preferable to consuming nothing.

Finally, we need to rethink the separation between production and consumption, for they are more alike than separate and occur not at different times and places but simultaneously. Instead of wanting less luxury, we might find that just the opposite—the paradoxical luxury for all—is a suitable goal of communal aspiration. After all, luxury before all else is a social construction, and understanding its social ramifications may pave the way for a new appreciation of what has become a characteristic contradiction of our time, the necessary consumption of the unnecessary.

DISCUSSION QUESTIONS

1. Twitchell describes his father as someone who never wanted to own an object that might be described as "luxury," even if the money needed to purchase it was not an issue. Why does Twitchell think his father felt this way? And how does Twitchell think people have changed?

2. Borrowing some ideas from Thorstein Veblen, Twitchell argues that the value of consumable goods goes up when their prices increases. He argues that no upgrade in the quality of the consumable item is necessary for this to occur. Why would people spend more money for something that is not higher in quality?

3. Twitchell speaks of the democratization of luxury, referring to the ability of middle-class individuals to purchase things they previously could not afford. Does money buy happiness?

CHAPTER 8

RACIAL AND ETHNIC RELATIONS

I magine a scene somewhere in the country. A farmer is standing on a country road looking fondly at his most prized possession—several hundred acres of good farm land. A stranger comes walking down the road and strikes up a conversation.

"That's a mighty nice piece of land there," says the stranger.

"Yup," replies the farmer.

"Belongs to you?" asks the stranger.

"Yup," replies the farmer.

"How did you come by it?" asks the stranger.

"Well," replies the farmer, "I got it from my father, who worked it all his life and left it to me."

"Well, how did he get it?"

"From my grandfather."

"But how did he get it?"

"From his father before him."

"But how did he get it?"

"Well," replies the farmer, "he fought for it."

"That's fine," counters the stranger, "I'll fight you for it."

Why doesn't the stranger have a right to fight for the land? No piece of land on the face of the earth is occupied by its original owner or even the descendants of the original owner. All ownership is initially or subsequently fought for. At some point following the fight, the state takes over to maintain the status quo. In the case of the story above, the farmer's great-grandfather took the land by force, but he subsequently received a legal deed to the property from the state. That deed means that the next person who wants to fight for the land will have to fight the state as well as the farmer. Like a vast game of musical chairs, the state has the power to stop the music and award the chairs to whomever it chooses. Throughout American history, for instance, most land was awarded to European immigrants, while very little was awarded to Native Americans. Box 8.1 provides an example of similar loss of land by Spanish settlers in New Mexico in 1848 following the Mexican War.

As this example suggests, the study of racial and ethnic groups in any society is also the study of power. This chapter focuses on the racial and ethnic groups in the

BOX 8.1

Minority Status and Property Ownership:
Land Grabs in New Mexico after the Mexican War

The parable that opens this chapter is designed to show the relationship between power and property ownership. Ultimately, the group in power gets to make the rules, which typically favor itself. But while that parable is fictional, there are many historical cases that provide clear illustrations of the principle in practice. One such case occurred in the state of New Mexico in the last half of the nineteenth century, as land ownership moved from Spanish settlers to Anglo speculators.

Prior to the 1846 war between Mexico and the United States, northern New Mexico represented the largest Spanish settlement in what was then northern Mexico. Some sixty thousand people lived there. The much weaker Mexico was easily defeated and was forced to turn over its northern provinces to the United States according to the terms of the Treaty of Guadalupe Hidalgo signed in 1848. (Incidentally, the United States had less claim to this land than Iraq had to Kuwait in 1990, but the victors do get to write the histories.) The interesting aspect of the treaty is that it pledged to respect the land-ownership rights of current settlers even though they would now be living in American territory instead of Mexican territory. The U.S. government was under no constraint to be so gracious, but, as it turned out, the pledges were not honored in any case.

Between 1848 and 1900, approximately four-fifths of land formerly owned by Spanish citizens passed into Anglo hands (Barrera, 1979). The methods used were as varied as the human imagination. Many Spanish settlers could not prove specific land ownership because of differences in surveying methods between the two countries (Westphall, 1965). Much land was held as communal grants by settlers, so no one person owned the land; American courts recognized no such form of land ownership (Knowlton, 1967). When land ownership was challenged, Spanish settlers were required to hire lawyers; having little money but much land, the settlers were forced to pay lawyers with land, so even a successful court outcome resulted in land loss (Knowlton, 1967). Property taxes were introduced. Since most land owners did not operate on a cash economy, they had little money to pay such taxes; in some cases, they were not even told about the existence of taxes until their land had been taken for nonpayment (Swadesh, 1974). And finally, records were forged, government officials were bribed, and an assortment of other clearly illegal methods were employed when none of the above "legal" methods was successful. Some Spanish resistance was stimulated by all of this. Most notable was *Las Gorras Blancas*—a secret society that operated near Las Vegas and Santa Fe in northern New Mexico around 1890 and that specialized in destroying fences and railroad property (Larson, 1975). Nevertheless, the economic and legal clout of Anglos (coupled with their growing numbers as the Old West was settled) proved too strong an enemy. Today, the descendants of those early Spanish settlers still live in northern New Mexico but most in minority status and most without their land.

United States, paying particular attention to the power relations among them. As we will see, those power relations are organized within a system of ethnic stratification in which different racial and ethnic groups disproportionately occupy certain class levels in the stratification hierarchy. A major focus of this chapter is thus the way ethnic stratification encourages the formation of stereotypes, prejudice, and discrimination. We also examine the cultures that ethnic groups bring to a society and what happens when those cultures meet. Finally, we take a more specific look at some of the racial and ethnic groups that make up the population of the United States. Racial and ethnic diversity in any society adds an important wrinkle to its basic social coordination. Our ideas about racial and ethnic groups change the meanings we have about specific forms of social interaction and specific roles; a black policeman, for example, is somehow different from a white policeman in both black and white community perceptions. The sociological outlook will help you understand why those perceptions are different.

Key Issues and Concepts in Race and Ethnic Relations

The sociological study of racial and ethnic groups is typical of the sociological outlook in general. Though racial and ethnic groups are social groups that adhere to different norms and values, much like social groups anywhere, a few distinctive aspects to this study have led sociologists to create some specific concepts to explain them. It's not always clear, for example, just what difference might exist between the concepts of racial group and ethnic group. And what makes either a minority group or a majority group? Perhaps the most important concept is ethnic stratification, which explains much of the hatred and conflict we're so used to seeing between racial and ethnic groups.

RACIAL AND ETHNIC GROUPS

As we saw in Chapter 6, an **ethnic group** is a group of people who share a common culture, who think of themselves as sharing a common culture, or who are defined by others as sharing a common culture. Another way of putting it is to say that they share common ethnicity. Ethnicity is not a complicated concept to apply, since culture is observable and that observation is often agreed on by both the observer and the observed. The concept of a racial group, however, is not so easily defined.

Because an ethnic group is a group of people who share a common cultural heritage, we might suggest that a **racial group** is a group of people who are socially defined as sharing a common genetic heritage. Genetic heritage could be roughly defined as a cluster of genetic information that differs from other clusters of genetic information. Thus, a given individual in one racial group might have the same shape of nose or the same blood type as an individual from another racial group, but, on the whole and as groups, they would have different characteristics. This seemingly simple definition appears to make sense in everyday observation. Most people think they can distinguish between white people and black people, for instance, by looking for a cluster of physical characteristics that are supposed to separate the races. White people are supposed to have lighter skin, finer hair, thinner noses, and so on. If a particular individual happens to have somewhat darker skin, he or she might still be classified as white because of the presence of other "white race" characteristics. The problem, however, is that parents who are classified as black could have children who might be classified as white (as long as the children do not challenge the new classification). Conversely, "white" parents might have children classified as black purely on the basis of appearance.

The real problem with the concept of race is that, although we think of it as a biological term, its meaning derives from the social interactions of nonbiologists. When people become convinced that two or more races exist, then those races do, in fact, exist in the everyday lives of the people who are labeled accordingly (Trillin, 1986). We thus have at least two possible definitions of race: a scientific definition and a social definition. With regard to the scientific definition, biologists do not unanimously agree on the meaning or even the existence of race. As interesting as that dispute is, it does not directly affect us, for our concern forces us to the second, or social, definition of race. We must be concerned with what nonbiologists think of race, for it is their decisions that affect individual lives in society.

A brief look at history suggests that nonbiologists are more confused by the concept of race than biologists are. For example, some Americans of northwest European ancestry suggested in the early twentieth century that they belonged to a different (and, of course, superior) race than that of the Poles, Italians, Greeks, and other southeast Europeans. The latter group they thought to be, at best, feeble-minded. This idea, which seems ridiculous today, is little more than eighty years old; one wonders how our ideas of race will stack up fifty years from now.

Consider a tentative solution to this confusion. Returning to our original concept of ethnic group, we find that groups of people who are said to differ racially usually also differ ethnically from whoever is doing the labeling. Thus, racial groups are also usually ethnic groups. This is true for a remarkably simple reason: the term *race* is usually used as justification for doing something unpleasant to someone else. It becomes less upsetting to do that unpleasant thing if the victim can first be defined as unworthy or in some way unequal. It is much easier, for instance, to enslave someone who is defined as ignorant by reason of belonging to an inferior race. This makes it easier to give human beings the status of farm animals; like the black slave, farm animals are not thought capable of handling a more independent situation. In a strange twist of logic the slave owner can even conjure up the belief that he is doing the slave a favor. In short, people do not face discriminatory treatment because they are racially different; rather, they are defined as racially different to justify discriminatory treatment. The function of these kinds of social situations is to keep people separate from each other. If the people did not enter such a situation already ethnically different, a relatively short stay would create that difference.

MINORITY AND MAJORITY STATUS: A QUESTION OF DOMINANCE AND SUBORDINATION

The terms *minority group* and *majority group* are used for reasons having more to do with tradition than with science. Traditionally, a **minority group** was a relatively small ethnic group living within the country of a much larger ethnic group. The minority often found itself getting the short end of the stick because the majority group would help itself to whatever was valued in the society before giving the minority group a chance. The majority group's ability to dominate the minority appeared at first glance to be the result of its larger size; hence the names *minority* and *majority*. The problem, however, is that although power can come with larger group size, it can be achieved in other ways as well. Smaller groups can dominate larger groups if they are more powerful. That power is more important than group size leads to the following definitions. A **majority group** is a social group that controls the organization and distribution of rewards in a society. A minority group is a relatively powerless social group that is subject to the decisions of the majority group. The general term *rewards* here refers to the wide range of possessions and activities within a society that its members might value, such as jobs, prestige, and power. Access to rewards in any society is always a matter of utmost concern, and control over that access is perhaps the ultimate measure of power. A majority group, by definition, is the ethnic group that has that power. A minority group, by definition, is one that does not. More accurately, then, we should perhaps call a majority group a dominant group and a minority group a subordinate group. If that dominance becomes structured into the society in an ongoing manner, the result is a system of ethnic stratification.

ETHNIC STRATIFICATION: THE EXPLOITATION OF MINORITY GROUPS

Ethnic stratification refers to a specific arrangement of ethnic groups within an already established system of social stratification; it is therefore a special type of social stratification. The "specific arrangement" of the ethnic groups refers to the location of a disproportionate number of people from a given ethnic group in particular social classes. For example, in the United States we have never had a black president, nor are you likely to find many blacks running major corporations; there is, in fact, a definite lack of black people occupying upper-class positions in American society. (When individual black Americans do move into high-level positions, their race seems to come to the forefront and to overshadow their other accomplishments; when Jesse Jackson ran for the Democratic presidential nomination he was viewed as a black candidate by both black and white voters.) If you look at the other extreme, however, you will find that black Americans make up more than their share of people below the poverty level in the United States. That is ethnic stratification.

We have already looked at social stratification in general and the routes (or barriers) to social mobility within it (see Chapter 7). Lower-class people in general find it difficult to move up in social class; lower-class nonwhite people find such barriers even more insurmountable. Certain ethnic groups have been placed into specific jobs at certain levels of the stratification hierarchy and tend to remain there across generations.

The upper classes in the United States have long been dominated by white Protestant Americans descended from northwest European immigrants (popularly called white Anglo-Saxon Protestants, or WASPs). When you think of a typical upper-class American, such a person immediately springs to mind, as our system of ethnic stratification continues to place such people (and their offspring) in those top positions. When you think of a household servant or a garbage collector, on the other hand, a very different image will spring to mind. Depending on where you live, that image may very likely be of a nonwhite person.

Ethnic stratification is a useful system for those at the top (the dominant group). Its primary use is that it structures exploitation into the everyday business of society. **Exploitation** is a concept with many definitions, but it generally describes a situation in which an individual does not receive the full value for his or her labor. Such situations occur when individuals have few options in their lives. If, for example, your choice is to starve or to take a difficult or dangerous job at low pay, you will probably take the job. Historically, that is what most people have done. Those individuals doing the hiring (again, members of the dominant group) are therefore in a position to benefit, as their employees have no choice but to work on their terms. Ethnic stratification exists when routes to upward social mobility are cut off for particular ethnic groups. This situation leaves them little choice but to work at the jobs left over (see Box 8.2).

The most obvious example of exploitation through a system of ethnic stratification is the American system of slavery. Under slavery blacks were legally locked into their economic position; having no other choice, they worked. White slave owners, of course, benefited greatly from this system. As a more recent example, many American employers today specialize in hiring illegal aliens, individuals who dare not object to working conditions or pay scales for fear of being deported. Exploitation depends on the exploited individuals' having limited options, and ethnic stratification provides that situation by keeping those individuals locked into the lower classes through some means of discrimination.

Discrimination appears in society in many manifestations. Individuals may be denied housing, forced to ride at the back of the bus, refused employment, denied the vote, or deprived of their land. In each case there is a common core that defines the concept. **Discrimination** is any action that shows a bias against an individual on the basis of his or her group membership; it is typically designed to hinder the competitive abilities of individuals in that group. Discrimination, in short, closes routes of upward social mobility and allows ethnic stratification to survive from one generation to the next. Instances of discrimination that do not appear to hinder competitive abilities directly (such as requiring blacks to ride at the back of the bus) tend to serve this purpose indirectly: the act of discrimination may do psychological

Migrant farm workers coming from Mexico to harvest crops in the United States have no rights as citizens and so are prime candidates for exploitation. The wages they receive may be extremely low by American standards, but the money is still more than the workers can earn in Mexico.

damage to members of the affected group, and, furthermore, segregated buses are usually accompanied by segregated employment.

As one of the central concepts in the sociological study of race and ethnic relations, discrimination reappears throughout this chapter. For now, it is important to grasp the relationship between the system of ethnic stratification within which we live and the discriminatory actions with which we respond to that system. As we will see, discrimination is not the result of a bigoted person blindly striking out at members of other ethnic groups; it is rather a coldly rational and highly effective weapon for achieving success. Ethnic stratification encourages the use of many such weapons.

STEREOTYPES, PREJUDICE, AND DISCRIMINATION: RESPONSES TO ETHNIC STRATIFICATION

STEREOTYPES

A **stereotype** is a piece of knowledge (an idea or a belief) about a piece of the social world. The phrase "piece of the social world" refers to the way in which we subdivide

BOX 8.2

American Ethnic Minorities and the World of Professional Boxing

Occupying the bottom rung of a stratification system generally means you have to do the work that no one else wants to do for whatever they want to pay you; lower-class jobs are typically poorly paid and unpleasant. One unusual example of a lower-class job that fits that description generally is professional boxing. It does not fit the description perfectly, however. Although most boxers make little money, there is always the possibility of "making it." In addition, the obvious physical unpleasant-ness of the job is lessened somewhat by the necessary skill and social status involved. Nevertheless, boxing is and always has been an occupation of the lower classes.

S. Kitson Weinberg and Henry Arond (1952) studied the ethnic groups that were professional boxers in America between 1909 and 1948. Their findings offer some interesting insights into the interplay between social class and cultural differences that occur within ethnic stratification. Some ethnic groups, for example, seem to have a cultural bias against boxing. The Irish became boxers but not the Scandinavians; Filipinos became boxers but not the Chinese or Japanese. Of the ethnic groups that did favor boxing, their members went in for the sport only during the time their particular group occupied the lowest classes of American society. The year 1909 saw boxing dominated by the Irish, and by Germans; 1909 was the middle of the south-eastern European immigrant influx, and these new groups had yet to settle into the occupational world of boxing. By 1928, however, two southeastern European groups, the Jews and Italians, had displaced the Irish and Germans in boxing as well as in the lower classes in American society in general. By 1948 black Americans and Mexican Americans came to dominate the sport—a trend that is still with us today.

Like most lower-class jobs, boxing is an occupation shunned by those with other (and presumably better) options. As one 1950 statement from a boxing promoter suggests,

> They say that too much education softens a man and that is why the college graduates are not good fighters. They fight emotionally on the gridiron and they fight bravely and well in our wars, but their contributions in our rings have been insignificant. The ring has been described as the refuge of the underprivileged. Out of the down-trodden have come our greatest fighters. . . . An education is an escape, and that is what they are saying when they shake their heads—those who know the fight game—as you mention the name of a college fighter. Once the bell rings, they want their fighters to have no retreat, and a fighter with an education is a fighter who does not have to fight to live and he knows it. Only for the hungry fighter is it a decent gamble. (Weinberg and Arond, 1952, 461–462)

an otherwise overwhelming confusion of human beings into manageable pieces, such as black or white, men or women, rich or poor. A term such as *African American* refers to many different human beings who share one trait that is important to the user of the term, who ignores differences in favor of calling attention to similarities the user thinks important. In this sense any descriptive term does damage to the thing it describes by only partially describing it, but this kind of mental organization is necessary so that the vast variety of experience can be made manageable (for example, see Levin, 1975; Schutz, 1970).

Now we can return to the first part of our definition of stereotype: a stereotype is a "piece of knowledge." A piece of knowledge is simply an idea or belief that the holder of that piece of knowledge finds convincing. The "knowledge" is usually nothing more than a collection of adjectives that the user of the stereotype believes is an accurate description of some group of people. Most stereotypes can in fact be reduced to the following simple form: "(insert name of human group here) are (insert adjective here)." For example, blacks are lazy, women are illogical, Poles are dumb, Jews are cheap. Enough of these statements will tell you all you think you need to know about some group of people. If their group is in the way of your group or threatens your group, you can make sure that all of the adjectives are negative, as in these examples. In practice, therefore, a stereotype becomes a generalized description (usually negative) of a specific social group, also applied to its individual members (see Luhman, 1990).

THE PSYCHOLOGY OF PREJUDICE

Prejudice is a negative attitude toward a group of people. It is built on stereotypes, which specify the boundaries between groups of people (enabling you to find the people you dislike) and which provide a handy set of reasons for your negative attitudes. A dislike of African Americans can be rationalized with the stereotype, "They are lazy and stupid"; a dislike of Asian people can be justified with the stereotype, "They are ambitious, clever, and inscrutable." Almost any adjective can fuel a negative stereotype if it is thought of and said in just the right manner. As Gordon Allport pointed out, Abraham Lincoln is admired for being thrifty, hard-working, ambitious, and devoted to the rights of the average person. Jews, on the other hand, are hated for being tight-fisted, overambitious, pushy, and radical (Allport, 1954).

The Prejudiced Personality Because prejudice is an attitude or belief, it seems to fall at least as much within the province of psychology as of sociology. Not surprisingly, therefore, much research has attempted to determine the nature of prejudice and its psychological roots. One direction this research has taken is a search for what might be called the prejudiced personality. Two assumptions behind this research are (1) that prejudice is a general orientation toward the world rather than a specific set of ideas or beliefs regarding particular groups of people, and (2) that prejudice is somehow pathological and indicates an emotional disturbance in the prejudiced

individual. The most famous research on the prejudiced personality was done by
T. W. Adorno and his associates (see also Conrad, 1992).

The years immediately following World War II saw considerable reflection on
the fascism and anti-Semitism that had characterized Nazi Germany. Adorno and
his colleagues (1950) concluded that there existed a group of personality characteristics that, as a set, might be described as "potentially fascistic" and that might further be linked to prejudice. They came to label this potentially fascistic personality
as the *authoritarian personality,* and they explained it as the result of particularly
harsh and restricted childhood socialization.

A supporting piece of research within this tradition is E. L. Hartley's (1946) study
of prejudiced attitudes. Hartley found that individuals prejudiced against ethnic or
racial groups showed the same prejudices when confronted with questions about
fictional ethnic groups such as Wallonians, Pirenians, and Danerians. The implication is that an individual who displays prejudice against even a nonexistent group
(which precludes having rational reasons for the dislike) must be considered as
having a prejudiced orientation toward the world.

Maintaining Self-esteem **Self-esteem** is an individual's subjective evaluation of his
or her worth. That worth can be measured against some objective standard (such as
success in following the Ten Commandments) or against the performance of others
in the individual's immediate environment. In the first case the individual's self-
esteem can rise only through personal achievements; in the second case self-esteem
can rise either through personal achievements or through the failure of others: when
others fail, one's own performance looks superior. Individuals whose self-worth is
measured relative to others therefore may choose between expending their energy
on succeeding themselves or on helping others fail. For those who choose to help
others fail, prejudice is an excellent tool; it downgrades others, making the prejudiced individual feel superior by comparison. The important point is thus not so
much the maintenance of self-esteem (since everyone must do that) but the extent to
which individuals measure it through comparison with others.

Jack Levin (1975) related this line of research directly to questions of prejudice.
He first separated his subjects into "self-evaluators," who tended to evaluate
themselves against fixed standards, and "relative evaluators," who relied more on
the immediate competition. Levin exposed the subjects to situations in which their
performances and abilities were questioned and then tested their prejudice against
Puerto Ricans. He found that the individuals labeled as relative evaluators responded
to attacks on their abilities with increased prejudice, but the self-evaluators showed
no such increase. Thus, it appears that prejudice can be a way to increase self-esteem
if the individual involved measures that self-esteem against the performances and
abilities of others rather than against a fixed standard. But even relative evaluators
must first feel a threat to their self-esteem before they will defend themselves with
prejudice.

Prejudice gets passed along from generation to generation in a culture.

THE SOCIOLOGY OF PREJUDICE

Prejudice can also be used as a social weapon within a system of ethnic stratification. Prejudice, and the stereotypes that accompany it, discredits whole groups of people who might otherwise be a social threat. If you are a white person and an African American is competing for your job, you may be able to save your job by convincing others (especially your employer) that African Americans are lazy and irresponsible. Losing your job (or even the threat of losing it) can lower self-esteem and create frustration. If your employer is too strong to be the object of your aggression, prejudice becomes all the more useful as a weapon in fighting the secondary source of the frustration. In more general terms, prejudice is the natural outcome of the competition inherent in social stratification; prejudice helps maintain a social position when the potential social mobility of others threatens that position.

Prejudice produced by social competition becomes most noticeable when the individuals or groups involved are of similar rank. This puts those individuals or groups into competition for the same jobs, housing, education, and any other rewards that people get more or less of, depending on their class level. It is therefore not surprising that most prejudice against African Americans in the United States is found among working-class whites, for they are in direct competition with these individuals (who are similarly ranked, for the most part) and feel threatened by them (Levin, 1975).

Prejudice can also become part of the culture of a group, passed from parents to children along with the rest of their culture. The worldview, as transmitted, takes an "us versus them" form, making each individual feel even more distant from the opposing group and, at the same time, more firmly rooted in his or her own group.

DISCRIMINATION

Attempts by groups either to improve their class position or to defend it from another group usually extend well beyond the realm of ideas to acts of discrimination. As we've seen, such acts are designed to hinder the competitive abilities of individuals in another group, thus giving the group doing the discriminating a competitive advantage within some arena (or arenas) of the stratification system (Bonacich, 1972). The appeal of discrimination stems from an interesting fact: competition can encourage excellence, but it requires only being "better than." One can be better either through excellence or through hindering the opponent. Discrimination, of course, does the latter. It can operate directly, as in refusing employment to members of certain groups, or indirectly, as in constructing biased employment tests that require information not present in the culture of certain groups.

Discrimination is basically an attempt to control social mobility by introducing elements of a caste society into a class society. Rather than allowing individuals to compete for mobility as individuals, it forces them to compete as groups. Discrimination separates those groups so that members of higher-ranked groups can achieve and hold their position against intruders. Those who discriminate give in to the temptation to load the dice. The higher a group is ranked, the more power it has; therefore, its ability to enforce its brand of discrimination is increased. The lower-ranked groups are forced to play with the dice provided for them.

Just as prejudice and stereotypes can become part of a group's culture, thereby keeping that group apart from others, so discrimination can maintain group separation and lead to further conflict. At the outset, discrimination maintains groups on separate ranks in the stratification system, which tends to keep groups separate. But, in addition, discrimination rubs salt into the wound. The we-they orientation that is begun by prejudice is nourished by the continued experience of discrimination. Recognizing that another group has loaded the dice to ensure your loss tends to solidify your group; discrimination convinces the affected group that the only hope for improvement is group action rather than individual effort.

INSTITUTIONAL (COVERT) DISCRIMINATION

Institutional discrimination consists of the indirect forms of discrimination that affect a certain group because of certain attributes or abilities most of that group's members have (or lack). More often than not, institutional discrimination operates through the situation already provided by ethnic stratification: because minority group members are disproportionately poor, institutional forms of discrimination that affect the poor disproportionately affect minorities. In this case poverty becomes the "attribute" possessed by the minority that leads to its members being affected by discrimination. To the extent that they are culturally different from the dominant group, minorities often have different kinds of skills and abilities from the dominant group. Should the dominant group decide to discriminate on the basis of certain abilities, the minority group might easily be disproportionately affected.

Institutional discrimination that affects minorities because of their cultural background can be intentional or unintentional. The dominant group employer, for instance, may insist that a prospective employee have certain abilities because the employer knows that a given minority is not likely to possess them. On the other hand, the employer might simply value those abilities for their own sake, with no intention of discriminating. Unlike overt discrimination, intent is not inherent in the act of institutional discrimination, and it cannot be proved by the existence of the discrimination. For that reason it is a tempting alternative for members of the dominant group who wish to discriminate in the face of laws prohibiting such actions.

Dominant groups are in a position to organize social relations; not surprisingly, they tend to shape social relations to their benefit. Thus, social institutions develop along lines that emphasize and reward the values and abilities of dominant group members; simultaneously, those institutions deemphasize and do not reward the values and abilities of other ethnic groups that share the society. For example, all major institutions in the United States today operate in (and reward the speakers of) Standard American English. Individuals who speak other languages or other dialects of English are at a disadvantage, whether they are going to school, to court, to work, or to vote or are attempting to fill out an income tax return.

African Americans encounter overt forms of discrimination in employment, education, and housing that intensify their problems in overcoming poverty. But institutional discrimination by itself (which we might call the cycle of poverty) accounts for a good number of the barriers against them. Box 8.3 discusses one social response to this situation.

RACIAL AND ETHNIC GROUPS IN CONTACT: SOCIAL AND POLITICAL ARRANGEMENTS

So far I've emphasized the competition between ethnic groups brought about by ethnic stratification. This emphasis offers a picture of people using every social trick in the book as they attempt to maintain or better their social position. This approach is useful in the study of racial and ethnic relations, as competition certainly plays a major role, but it does not present the whole story. In fact, it emphasizes the *group* of ethnic group while glossing over the *ethnic*. Ethnic groups are culturally distinct entities beyond their different economic interests. The cultural changes that occur when two ethnic groups meet are highly related to the economic arrangements they hammer out. As you read on, keep that relationship in mind.

BOX 8.3

Employment Discrimination and Affirmative Action

Of all the forms discrimination may take, one of the most far-reaching is discrimination in employment. Jobs are basic to quality of life for most of us, and being denied access to them directly affects the way we live. For many years, certain occupations have been closed to certain social categories. African Americans have been kept out of many labor unions and training programs over the years, while women have met a similar fate in the male-dominated occupations. Affirmative action programs were designed to change all that.

Affirmative action refers to any program designed to bring more members of a previously discriminated-against group into a job or training program. Because African Americans have traditionally been kept out of the craft unions and apprenticeship programs for craft occupations, an effort to train more African Americans for craft occupations would be an affirmative action program. There is a certain degree of political resistance to such programs, however. Getting more African Americans or women into an occupation, for example, is simultaneously not getting more whites or men. Members of the latter social categories sometimes charge that affirmative action is actually reverse discrimination—the same kind of treatment previously given to minorities but now directed in reverse. And the Civil Rights Act of 1964 made occupational discrimination on the basis of sex, race, or ethnicity illegal.

One of the first challenges to affirmative action came from Allan Bakke, a white male whose application had been turned down by the University of California (Davis) Medical School. The medical school allowed 100 new students to enter their program every year; of those 100, 10 slots were set aside for the most qualified minority applicants. As it turned out, Bakke was not qualified enough for the top 90 slots, but his grades and test scores were superior to those of the 10 minority students. Bakke went to court, charging illegal discrimination. The U.S. Supreme Court finally decided that (1) the extreme quota system employed by the medical school was unfair and that Bakke should be admitted, and (2) affirmative action was still a good idea in some form if not in this one.

The implications of affirmative action programs affect all aspects of the world of work. For example, what about seniority? Unionized workers are commonly laid off in order of seniority, and plants with affirmative action programs will have many women and ethnic minority employees with little seniority. The Supreme Court has argued that seniority should come along with the affirmative action program, with new workers being given credit for several years of work (when, presumably, they would have been working had not discrimination kept them out of work) (*Time*, 1976). This would mean that a white male worker with several years' experience would find himself out of a job in a recession, while more recently hired women and minority workers would be kept on. Such actions have created considerable conflict within America's labor force.

Affirmative action programs represent an attempt to alter the structure of ethnic stratification in American society. It is hard to say at this point what their long-term effects will be, but they certainly illustrate an important lesson about ethnic and social stratification: there is only so much to go around, and your gain will be my loss. The conflict is built in. And ongoing changes in the structure of the American economy leave all workers increasingly worried and watchful over their competitive advantages and disadvantages (Garrison-Wade and Lewis, 2004; Joseph, 1991; Meyer, 2004).

In recent years, the Supreme Court has withdrawn support from some affirmative action programs through imposing limitations on discrimination suits; other affirmative action programs have received support. In 1989, for example, the case of *Wards Cove Packing Co., Inc. v. Atonio* changed the burden of proof regarding discriminatory policies, requiring that proof to be documented by employees. Such changes in the court were accompanied by congressional action such as the Civil Rights Act of 1991, which essentially reversed five previous Supreme Court decisions.

More recently, the Supreme Court gave out mixed messages to the University of Michigan. In *Grutter v. Bollinger* (2003), the Court allowed the University of Michigan Law School to retain its affirmative action program for selecting new students to its program. At the same time, the Court decided in *Gratz v. Regents* (2003) that the use of adding "points" to racial and ethnic minorities for undergraduate admissions was not constitutional.

And voters have also become involved. In the California election of 1996, Proposition 209 passed, requiring the state to *not* use race, sex, color, ethnicity, or national origin in decisions of public employment, public education, or public contracting. The future of affirmative action is cloudy indeed.

The results of culture contacts between ethnic groups are as varied as the ethnic groups themselves. For convenience sociologists have divided the primary types of culture contacts into a few basic categories. In this section they are grouped under three basic headings: first, the melting pot, presented here as largely a myth (for reasons to be explained shortly); second, the dominant group's response to culture contact (those cultural results generally preferred by the stronger of the two groups); and third, the subordinate group's response (those cultural results sometimes fought for by minority groups).

THE MYTH OF THE MELTING POT
The **melting pot** refers to the mixing and blending of cultures through intermarriage (see Gordon, 1964a; Newman, 1973). While the melting pot depends on

Very little of the "melting pot" effect can be seen in the Miami, Florida, area where great numbers of Cuban immigrants have settled. The neighborhood shown here is, in fact, known as "Little Havana."

intermarriage to mix people from different ethnic groups, intermarriage by itself does not result in a melting pot. The cultural elements, when blended, must produce a new culture. For example, two languages could combine vocabulary and grammar to form a new language; two religions could combine their beliefs and rituals to form a new religion; two styles of dress could merge into one new style; and two styles of cooking could combine to form one. Though they do not begin to catalog the many facets of culture, these examples provide some idea of the give and take involved in blending different cultures into one. The result would be a totally new culture, composed of equal parts of the individual cultures that blended to form it.

The key words are *equal* and *give and take*. The problem with the melting pot is that the meeting of ethnic groups usually results in more taking than giving, and whatever cultural mixing occurs is usually anything but equal. It is an advantage to any ethnic group in any society to have its culture dominate that society's institutions. When ethnic groups come together, each will generally attempt such a domination. A melting pot situation can therefore occur only when no single group is able to dominate—a situation that usually occurs only when the groups involved are remarkably similar in power and no one group can get the upper hand. The odds of such similarity are not great, so the melting pot is a rare occurrence.

THE RESPONSE OF THE DOMINANT GROUP

We turn now to less mythical descriptions of cultures in contact—specifically, to a variety of descriptions that are either promoted by or generally acceptable to the dominant ethnic group in the society. One could argue that any variety of cultural contact must be more or less acceptable to the dominant group; if it were not, they could probably alter the situation. That argument has a great deal of merit, but I prefer to emphasize degrees of acceptability. This section deals with situations either promoted by the dominant group or generating at least the tacit acceptance of the dominant group. The next section examines situations that usually achieve, at best, the grudging acceptance of the dominant group and that are never promoted by them.

Genocide and Expulsion **Genocide** is actions by the dominant group that cause the deaths of most or all members of a given subordinate group. These actions might be systematic and intentional, as they were in Nazi extermination camps; they might also be largely unintentional, as was the spread of smallpox among Native Americans after the arrival of the Europeans. We focus here only on intentional genocide.

Expulsion refers to the physical removal of most or all members of a subordinate group from within the boundaries of a nation-state. Under this heading we might include the removal of eastern Native American tribes to reservations west of the Mississippi before that land was part of the United States.

Segregation **Segregation** is the dominant group's decision to separate itself, either socially or physically, from a given minority group. When that separation occurs, the minority group may be described as segregated. Note that the term *segregation* refers only to group separation instigated by the dominant group; when separation is the minority group's choice, it is separatism, which is discussed later. The two are very different.

Social segregation is a situation in which two ethnic groups live near each other and interact with each other regularly but only on a highly formalized basis. For example, in a master-slave relationship there is considerable interaction, but all interaction follows rigid cultural norms of formality. Master and slave interact in terms of limited social roles and not as individuals who might aspire to a more well-rounded relationship. They are not and cannot be friends in any sense of the word. In such a situation, people can talk to each other every day without ever knowing each other. This situation occurs between many African Americans and whites in the United States today.

Physical segregation is a situation in which two ethnic groups live spatially apart from each other within the same political boundaries. For example, the decision of the dominant group has placed Native Americans in reservations. By its very nature, physical segregation includes social segregation; for this reason it is a more extreme measure on the part of the dominant group. In fact, there is only a fine line between physical segregation and expulsion.

Throughout the first half of the twentieth century, segregation by race in the United States was both legal and commonplace.

Until the 1960s, education in the United States was essentially conducted as two separate systems, one for European Americans (the dominant group) and one for African Americans (a subordinate group). When the Supreme Court declared these "separate but equal" schools illegal, busing was instituted in an attempt to integrate schools. Some members of the dominant group reacted violently to busing. This convoy of school buses had to be accompanied by armed police to protect the children aboard.

Assimilation **Assimilation** is the incorporation of one ethnic group into the continuing culture of another ethnic group. For example, one ethnic group (usually a relatively weak one) intermarries with members of another ethnic group, losing or giving up its cultural distinctiveness in favor of the culture provided by the stronger group. In a less extreme form of assimilation, the weaker ethnic group might not intermarry with the stronger, but after several generations it takes on most of the culture of the stronger. The original culture of the assimilated ethnic group is no longer recognizable or distinct. None of its component parts (its members) have been lost; they have simply become part of a powerful system through taking on its culture.

Assimilation in one form or another is one of the most common outcomes when two cultures come into contact. This is particularly true in the history of the United States, in which a basically English culture has become the dominant way of life to which all newcomers must conform.

It is always in the interest of any ethnic group to promote its culture when it comes into contact with other ethnic groups. The more its culture comes to dominate a society, the more competitive advantage its members will have in that society. In the United States people of English descent had the power to promote their culture as the dominant one in the early days of the nation, and the English culture has not lost that domination since; over two hundred years later, it is still people of basically English descent who hold a competitive advantage in the United States. Social assimilation is a long process requiring a series of stages (Gordon, 1964a, 1978).

THE RESPONSE OF THE MINORITY GROUP:
CULTURAL PLURALISM AND SEPARATISM

Members of minority groups may be quite happy with a cultural arrangement like assimilation, which was the stated goal of many immigrants to the United States. Assimilation destroys the ethnic group by requiring conformity to the host culture, however. It may not be unpleasant overall, but it certainly occurs beyond the control of the minority group. Nevertheless, it is an option usually taken, if available.

Ethnic groups locked into the bottom of the ethnic stratification system have created other options, the two main (and related) ones being separatism and cultural pluralism. **Separatism** requires the political separation of land occupied by members of the minority ethnic group so that they may govern themselves. A number of French Canadians in Quebec became interested in separatism for Quebec in the mid-1970s and advocated that the province should leave Canada to become a separate French-speaking country. Separatism changes a minority ethnic group into the only ethnic group and ends the minority group–dominant group relationship. Box 8.4 discusses Marcus Garvey, an advocate of black separatism.

Cultural pluralism is a similar but less extreme route for the minority group. As it is much more common than separatism, especially in the United States, we focus on it in this section. **Cultural pluralism** describes a social situation in which two or more ethnic groups share one society in which (1) each ethnic group maintains its

BOX 8.4

Marcus Garvey: Early Separatism in Black America

Marcus Garvey was an extremely controversial political leader of African Americans in the years following World War I. Speaking largely to the new urban African Americans of the 1920s, Garvey advocated racial separation and a return to Africa. His organization, the Universal Negro Improvement Association, grew rapidly, publishing a newspaper and selling shares in the Black Star Steamship Line, which would one day make the trip back to Africa. Garvey's politics worried white political leaders. He was imprisoned in 1925 for using the mail to defraud (by selling steamship tickets) and was finally deported to his native Jamaica in 1927. Perhaps Garvey was a con man, but, considering that African Americans were never prosecuted in the 1920s for victimizing other African Americans, his legal problems were no doubt motivated by feelings other than a love of justice among white political leaders.

Garvey may have been personally unsuccessful, but his ideas survived in one form or another. Though few African Americans advocate a return to Africa today, the following statement made by Garvey in 1923 sounds much like the ideas of cultural pluralism now common in the black community:

> Some Negro leaders have advanced the belief that in another few years the white people will make up their minds to assimilate their black populations, thereby sinking all racial prejudice in the welcoming of the black race into the social companionship of the white. Such leaders further believe that by the amalgamation of black and white, a new type will spring up, and that type will become the American and West Indian of the future.
>
> This belief is preposterous. I believe that white men should be white, yellow men should be yellow, and black men should be black in the great panorama of races, until each and every race by its own initiative lifts itself up to the common standard of humanity, as to compel the respect and appreciation of all, and so make it possible for each one to stretch out the hand of welcome without being able to be prejudiced against the other because of any inferior and unfortunate condition.
>
> The white man of America will not, to any organized extent, assimilate the Negro, because in so doing, he feels that he will be committing racial suicide. This he is not prepared to do. It is true he illegitimately carries on a system of assimilation; but such assimilation, as practiced, is one that he is not prepared to support because he becomes prejudiced against his own offspring, if that offspring is the product of black and white; hence, to the white man the question of racial differences is eternal. So long as Negroes occupy an inferior position among the races

and nations of the world, just so long will others be prejudiced against them, because it will be profitable for them to keep up their system of superiority. But when the Negro by his own initiative lifts himself from his low state to the highest human standard he will be in a position to stop begging and praying, and demand a place that no individual, race or nation will be able to deny him (Garvey, 1968, 26).

separate cultural distinctiveness, and (2) no one ethnic group dominates the other(s). In a society such as the United States, which is already ethnically stratified, cultural pluralism becomes a political movement in which the minority group attempts to maintain its ethnicity while gaining power for the group. Its success as a political and cultural goal can be viewed through ethnic groups such as the Amish (Kephart, 1987) or Hasidic Jews (Harris, 1985)—two distinct groups that have managed to maintain clear cultural separation between themselves and the outside dominant society.

As an ideology, cultural pluralism has found varying popularity with almost every ethnic group in the United States in recent years. Native Americans have organized and begun fighting for tribal land; Hispanics have fought for bilingual education; Japanese Americans recall the years of internment during World War II as they learn to speak Japanese in night school; and, perhaps most interesting, some European ethnic groups, such as Polish Americans and Italian Americans, are rediscovering roots well covered by years of assimilation. In terms of ethnic identity and goals, cultural pluralism was clearly the most visible if not the dominant ideology of the 1970s and 1980s (Bukowczyk and Faires, 1991; Lyman, 1992).

If further evidence is needed for pluralism as a trend, we can look outside the world of ethnic politics. The variety of movements making up feminism and women's liberation all suggest a pluralistic basis. There are separate magazines intended for women only and women's legal and social services (rape counseling centers and organizations to help abused wives, for example). Similarly, many organizations that seek gay rights have a pluralistic emphasis. Many homosexuals in the past chose to keep their lifestyles as private as possible while "passing" as heterosexuals. But it is more common today for homosexuality to be stated openly, coupled with the demand that homosexuals be accorded all the rights that heterosexuals enjoy. One important goal of gay liberation is to convince everyone (especially homosexuals) that homosexuality is perfectly normal and that individuals have a right to that lifestyle. Efforts beginning in the late 1990s to legalize gay marriage are clearly an example of pluralism. And the opposition to those efforts from many other Americans is just as characteristic of pluralism in terms of the conflict it often produces.

Along with "gay power" (not to mention the earlier white, black, brown, red, and yellow forms) we now have "gray power." This minority is made up of old

Gays and lesbians in the United States demand the right to be different and recognition of those differences under the law. Such movements illustrate cultural pluralism.

people who feel that American society has a negative stereotype about the nature and abilities of old people and constantly discriminates against them. Probably the most colorful of the political organizations that represent the interests of old people is the Gray Panthers, organized by the late Maggie Kuhn (see Hessel, 1977). The Gray Panthers condemn American society for putting its old people out to pasture and emphasize the virtues of being old and the right of old people to be free from discrimination based on their age. Those organizations that come under the label *gray power* or *the gray lobby* have taken on the task of protecting the special interests of older people, working against discrimination ranging from individual acts to the acts of Congress. Once again, we see political organizations defending the right to be different, while insisting that American society be altered so as not to abridge those rights.

Organizations of those with physical disabilities also use pluralism as the basis for their political action. Such groups initially formed to eliminate the kinds of discrimination their members faced because of particular disabilities. People confined to wheelchairs, for example, could not engage in activities that took place in buildings with stairs. The Architectural Barriers Act of 1968, the Rehabilitation Act of

1973, and the Americans with Disabilities Act of 1990 were passed in response to those needs; federal funds can now be withheld if structural accommodations are not made for those with physical disabilities. The Rehabilitation Act of 1973 mandated the creation of affirmative action programs for their benefit. The Americans with Disabilities Act of 1990 provided widescale protection against job discrimination for workers with disabilities. These successes were the direct result of group organization.

Such programs often run up against the sense of pride in difference that is characteristic of pluralism, however. Among those with physical disabilities, the most striking parallel with ethnic pluralistic politics is found among the deaf. In the past deaf people were encouraged to learn lip reading, which can be considered an effort at assimilation by conforming to the mode of communication favored by hearing people. Today, however, many deaf people favor the use of sign language and take pride in its use. Institutions such as Gallaudet College in Washington, D.C., which accepts only students with serious hearing impairment, have become centers for the development of group pride. This pride erupted in early 1988 when a hearing president was appointed at Gallaudet over a popular deaf candidate. The students went on strike, closing down the campus until their demands were met (Brand, 1988). The touring National Theater of the Deaf (in which the actors communicate in sign language, coupled with spoken "subtitles" for people with communication impairment in understanding sign language) has helped turn sign language into an art. In short, there is a growing pride among the deaf based on the strengths inherent in their difference from those who can hear.

Such examples of organizations that form to build group pride and to work for the right of the group to be different, in whatever way, suggest a reevaluation of conformity among Americans. Instead of viewing differences in sex, sexual preference, age, ethnicity, or physical ability as unfortunate, many Americans now call attention to those differences and challenge the rest of society to accept them.

RACIAL AND ETHNIC GROUPS IN THE UNITED STATES

The United States is often called the "nation of immigrants." This is a more fitting title than you might think, for even our "native" Native Americans were themselves immigrants, coming from Asia some twenty thousand to forty thousand years ago. As human history goes, that's relatively recent, but compared to the other people who moved to what is now the United States, they are clearly the "native" old-timers of the area. The first non-Native American immigrants (responsible for calling the inhabitants Indians) were the Spanish explorers. The Spanish were followed in short order by the English, Dutch, French, and Portuguese. The English soon gained control over the eastern coast of what is now the United States and were joined over the next several centuries by one of the wildest mixes of ethnic groups the world has ever seen. But as diverse as that ethnic mix became, descendants of those original English colonists maintained control over the basic coordination of social life that characterizes the United States today. Everyday life in the United States today is largely an experience of an Americanized English culture.

THE GROWTH OF RACISM

When the English Pilgrims arrived in Massachusetts in 1620, they had been beaten by one year by the first African arrivals in the colonies: twenty Africans who were sold from a Dutch freighter in Jamestown, Virginia, as indentured servants. The Africans weren't yet permanent slaves, and ideas of racism were still very much in their infancy in the new land, but both slavery and racism were already on the horizon.

Racism can describe either a belief or a way of life. As a belief, it represents the social separation of people into two or more races coupled with the idea that different races are biologically inferior or superior to each other. As a way of life, racism describes the individual experience of living within a system of ethnic stratification in which the groups at the bottom of the hierarchy are defined as racially inferior.

Racism is an idea peculiar to the minds of Europeans over the last several centuries; previously humans had been guilty of all kinds of atrocities against each other, but they never defined their victims as biologically inferior while having them drawn and quartered. Europeans became increasingly attracted to the ideas of racism that were popularized throughout the 1700s and 1800s. The central idea (later to be dusted off by Adolf Hitler) was that northwestern Europeans ("Aryans") were a separate race and superior to all others; southeastern Europeans (such as Slavs, Italians, and so on) were thought to be of a clearly inferior race. With such fine distinctions in operation among types of Europeans, it's no wonder that the peoples of the rest of the world soon found themselves the possessors of increasingly derogatory labels. Asians were in one race, Native Americans in another, and Africans in still another. No finer idea than racism could ever be found to justify exploitation.

EUROPEAN IMMIGRATION

The English and Africans were not the only immigrants to the New World in the 1600s; ever since the beginning of colonization in North America, a variety of European ethnic groups made up the immigrants (even though those of English descent generally were the most influential). Of these early non-English immigrants, probably the most prominent were the Germans and the Scotch-Irish. It is noteworthy that all the early European immigrants were both Protestant and from countries in the northwest of Europe. Their cultural differences, in short, were not really very great.

The first major non-Protestant immigrant group was the Catholic Irish, who fled the potato famine in Ireland in the late 1840s. These Irish faced some of the most vicious prejudice and discrimination ever to appear on the American scene. (African Americans faced worse discrimination through slavery, but in that case the white Americans had such complete control that they were not moved through fear into angry acts of protest and hatred.) Almost any northern American newspaper of the

1850s would include a cartoon portraying the Irishman as an ape with interests only in drinking and fighting. Many neighborhoods and occupations were closed to the Irish. Such discrimination led them to work on the canals and railroads, where cheap labor was needed. While African Americans were being exploited in the South through slavery, Irish Americans were being exploited in the North through less organized means of discrimination.

If the Irish looked culturally different to white Protestant Americans in the 1850s, imagine the shock touched off by the coming of the southeastern Europeans in the 1880s. As we saw, racist ideas of the day placed southeastern Europeans in a separate race from northwestern Europeans. Moreover, southeastern Europeans were either Jewish or Catholic—never Protestant. But probably most important was the manner in which they came: huge numbers of southeastern European immigrants poured into the eastern cities, especially New York City, and formed ethnic communities. Figure 8.1 illustrates this change in the source as well as the volume of immigration beginning in the late 1800s.

The surge of southeastern European immigrants into the United States altered the society greatly; suddenly the Irish didn't look so bad. The early 1900s saw increasing racism directed against the newcomers from Europe. Early IQ tests determined that most Jews and Italians were "feebleminded." Popular books were written about the ruining of good old Yankee stock with the entrance of inferior genes into the population. The result was a 1924 law that essentially cut off immigration to the United States from anywhere except northwestern Europe.

The descendants of most European immigrants cannot properly be termed minority groups in the United States today. The Irish, who were locked into labor exploitation in their early years, are today largely in the middle and working classes of American society. The Italians and Poles present a similar picture. On the whole, however, the descendants of northwestern European immigrants dominate the upper classes of American society, reflecting their domination of a hundred years ago.

ASIAN IMMIGRATION

Just as the northeastern United States was becoming home to waves of European immigrants, the West Coast was becoming the focal point of Asian immigration. The largest group were the Chinese, who began to enter the United States in 1850. The vast majority of the Chinese immigrants were men from southern China who perceived the move more as a temporary expedition than as permanent immigration. Their goal was to accumulate wealth and then return to their families in their native land. As unskilled laborers, they were immediately useful to the railroad companies in building the transcontinental railroad. They soon became the object of racist attacks from non-Asian Westerners who, among other things, did not appreciate the competition for jobs. In an 1871 Los Angeles riot twenty-two Chinese were hanged, and the 1885 Rock Springs, Wyoming, massacre claimed twenty-nine Chinese (Kitano, 1976). Less physical attacks took the form of attempts to end Chinese

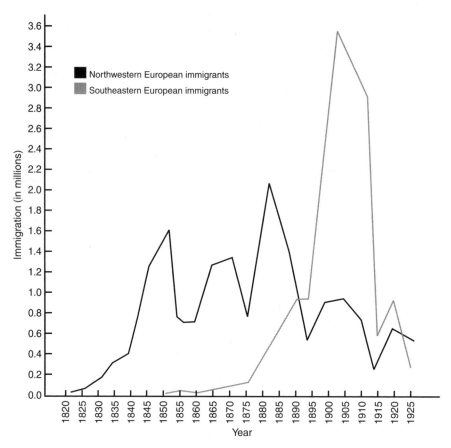

Figure 8.1 European immigration to the United States, 1810–1930. (U.S. Bureau of the Census)

immigration, which bore fruit in 1882, when the door from China was closed. In the meantime the "Chinatown" pattern in western cities had begun, as Chinese male immigrants banded together for mutual support, protection, and pleasure. The lack of families greatly hindered the establishment of an ongoing Chinese community.

The second largest Asian immigrant group, the Japanese, began to arrive soon after Chinese immigration ended. They found anti-Asian sentiment already established and readily transferable to them. The Japanese emperor had not permitted emigration until 1885, when increasing population density on the islands plus favorable earlier Western contacts made the idea more appealing. Between 1885 and 1898 Japanese immigrated to Hawaii, and, around 1900, Japanese began coming to the West Coast states. California, the most popular destination, had little over 1,000 Japanese in 1890, but their numbers increased to over 10,000 by 1900 and over

The 1942 "relocation" of West Coast Japanese Americans from their homes into guarded camps in the interior of the country was a dark moment in American history. Anti-Asian racism at the time led many to view all of Japanese decent as threats to security after the bombing of Pearl Harbor. This Japanese American family has been tagged and waits for transportation to a camp for the duration of the war.

40,000 by 1910 (Kitano, 1976). Unlike the Chinese, many Japanese immigrated as families; in other cases families selected wives in Japan and sent them over to join waiting grooms. In either case the early Japanese communities were family centered and industrious. Though industriousness was as American as apple pie, in this case it incited racist attacks on the Japanese from those sectors of the non-Asian population that feared competition. As the Japanese became successful at truck farming, such fears led to the passage of the California Alien Land Law of 1913, which prohibited aliens (which is to say, Japanese) from owning land. Although this law could be circumvented by Japanese fathers who could transfer ownership to their

American-born children, it indicates the building resentment and racism that would erupt at the outbreak of World War II.

The entrance of the United States into World War II, and in particular the Japanese attack on Pearl Harbor in Hawaii, resulted in widespread fear and distrust of the Japanese American communities in the western United States. Ironically, there was no such fear in Hawaii itself (which then and now has the largest Japanese American population of any state), because there had been so much cross-cultural contact. Nevertheless, the western states convinced the federal government to "relocate" the Japanese American population through the auspices of the U.S. Army. Beginning in early 1942, all persons of Japanese descent (who, of course, included a great many American citizens) were sent for the duration of the war to what can only be called concentration camps (see Tsukamoto and Pinkerton, 1987). An important exception to this rule were the young men in the camps who volunteered for military service. They were combined with Hawaiian Japanese Americans to form an all-Japanese American army unit. Sent to Europe, this unit—the 442nd—compiled one of the finest records in the history of the American military. After the war these men, along with relocation camp inmates, returned to their former communities, where they faced much of the same racism they had left four years before and went to work to overcome the setback of lost property and time.

With the passage of the Immigration Act of 1965, the door to Asian immigration was once again open. New Chinese immigrants arrived along with Koreans, Filipinos, and, with the ending of the Vietnam War, Vietnamese and Laotians. During the 1970s, Asians made up 34 percent of the total legal U.S. immigration and since 1980 have accounted for a full 48 percent of the total. There are currently just over 11.5 million Asian Americans and Pacific Islanders in the United States (U.S. Bureau of the Census, 2004a). Of this number, Chinese account for over 22 percent and Filipinos just under 20 percent; Japanese, Koreans, and Asian Indians each comprise around 11 percent; and Vietnamese make up over 8 percent. Some groups, such as the Vietnamese and Koreans, are largely immigrants, while other groups, such as the Japanese, are largely native born.

It is difficult to make generalities about many of the Asian groups, as there are many internal divisions within each group. A Chinese American, for example, may be descended from many generations of American citizens or may have arrived just last week. Nevertheless, most statistics regarding Asian success in the United States are impressive. Consider high school graduation. A high school diploma is achieved by 87 percent of the white population, 75 percent of the black population, and 59 percent of the Hispanic population; by contrast, the same achievement is accomplished by 96 percent of Japanese, 88 percent of Chinese, 90 percent of Asian Indians, and 87 percent of Filipinos (Gardner, Robey, and Smith, 1985). In addition, family income for Asian Americans is higher than for Americans as a whole.

Of course, not all Asians are wealthy; positive stereotypes can be just as inaccurate as negative stereotypes. On the other hand, the history of Asian immigration to the United States suggests that much can be accomplished, even in the face of racism and discrimination. Asian cultural orientations, such as strong family ties and positive values toward work, have aided Asians considerably in the competitive struggle that all immigrant groups face. Continued immigration should enlarge the Asian community in the United States in coming years.

AFRICAN AMERICANS

The institution of slavery in North America began inconspicuously in 1619 and grew steadily larger and more oppressive before its demise during the Civil War. Slavery in the United States was unusually cruel because the captured Africans were systematically separated from members of their families or tribes when they were sold. The slave owners' purpose was to break down native cultures more quickly and to replace them with a slave culture more suitable for the work and lifestyle demanded by the system. All children born to slaves were automatically slaves, and families thus formed could be broken up if the owner had economic or punitive reasons for doing so. In short, slaves were not legal persons in the United States except

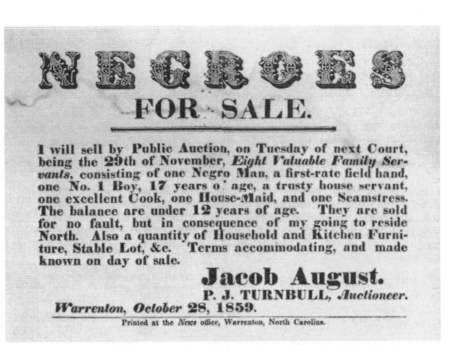

This 1859 handbill offers property for sale, human as well as "household and kitchen furniture." Three of the slaves offered for sale were "under 12 years of age." One may assume that these were children of the "Negro Man" or "excellent Cook" or the other slaves mentioned, but if it suited the owner, all could have been sold separately so that parents and children would never see each other again.

for the strange way they were counted (one slave equaled three-fifths of a man) to help the slave owners increase their numbers in the House of Representatives. Slaves could not own property, they could not enter into a contract of any kind, and they had no legal recourse whatsoever. They were pieces of property and could be used and disposed of as their owners saw fit. The one small advantage the slaves did have was that they were relatively expensive property, which provided them protection from some grosser abuses.

Beyond the legal restrictions, African Americans were also limited socially. The most notable restriction concerned education: it was generally against the law to teach a slave either reading or writing. Once again, the rationale behind the law was that slaves could thus be more easily controlled. The law certainly served this purpose. It also placed African Americans at an extreme disadvantage upon emancipation, when they had few skills to use to improve their situation. The inferior education most African Americans have received since emancipation has not made their task any easier.

The end of slavery did little to improve the situation of African Americans in the United States. While it was a necessary condition for improvement, many other obstacles stood in the way. The vast majority of African Americans had been slaves; therefore the vast majority of free African Americans after the Civil War found themselves unskilled and living in the rural South. The relatively short period of Reconstruction was of temporary benefit to them, but the end of Reconstruction and the return of political control to white southerners placed African Americans once again in a situation of powerlessness. With options severely limited, the only viable alternative to starvation appeared to be sharecropping.

As practiced in the South at the end of the nineteenth century, the system of share-cropping kept African Americans with almost as little power as slavery had. Typically, a sharecropper farmed land belonging to someone else and shared the profits from the crop with the owner. The sharecropper took the risks, however, and was responsible for buying such necessities as seed and farm tools. Because former slaves had no available capital, they purchased on credit, with the understanding that they would pay debts out of their profits from the expected crop. Food and clothing were purchased the same way. More often than not, all these purchases were made from the land owner himself, who arranged prices so that the sharecropper's profit would never be enough to pay back the debt. When the crop came in, the sharecropper's remaining debt was listed against the next year's crop. In the process of producing the next year's crop, however, more debt was incurred. In short, to sharecrop was to be forever and increasingly in debt. Furthermore, it was against the law to attempt to leave the area while in debt. Sharecroppers were almost as effectively tied to the land as slaves, but now no one cared whether they starved to death in the process (Daniel, 1972). As immigrants from southeastern Europe moved into the northern cities and gained footholds in the industrial economy, 90 percent of African Americans were still living in the South, many locked into the sharecropping system (Pinkney, 1975).

The same period of American history that witnessed the legal slavery of share-cropping also saw the final institutionalization of racial segregation through what have come to be called the Jim Crow laws. These laws, as a group, forced racial separation in practically all aspects of life, from separate drinking fountains and washrooms to separate schools and neighborhoods. Perhaps ironically, such laws originated in the North before the Civil War in response to growing numbers of free African Americans. These blacks, although free from the bonds of slavery, faced severe restrictions on their activities in almost every northern state. With the emancipation of the southern African American population, southern whites began looking for alternative means of domination. They found those means in the Jim Crow laws. During the later years of the nineteenth century the southern states enacted a vast collection of such laws, and by the turn of the century African Americans found themselves once again firmly and legally placed in a situation of subordination. In the legal sense this subordination lasted until 1965.

The turn of the last century also brought high levels of violence into the lives of African Americans along with the Jim Crow laws. The murder of African Americans through lynching almost became ritualized in the American South. At times, the European Americans responsible for the murder would pose for a group picture in front of bodies hanging from trees in the background, much as a hunter would pose with prey. These high levels of violence in the South coupled with labor shortages in the North during World War I motivated large numbers of African Americans to migrate to northern cities (Tolnay and Beck, 1992).

There are now over 36 million African Americans (U.S. Bureau of the Census, 2004a). The Jim Crow laws are no longer with us, but those political changes have not been matched by economic changes in the black-white relationship. As the statistics show, African Americans are much more likely than European Americans to live in the central cities, be poorly educated, be unemployed, work at blue-collar jobs, make less money, and wind up below the poverty level (Boyd, 1991; Eggers and Massey, 1991; Wilson, 1992). Perhaps even more significant is the lack of change over time in many of these areas. The gap in income between the races, for example, has remained about the same since 1950 and has even worsened somewhat in recent years. In 1970, African Americans earned 61 percent of European American earnings; by 1998, that percentage had risen to only 62 percent (U.S. Bureau of the Census, 2004a). The gap in unemployment rates has also remained the same during the same period, while the gap in life expectancy between African Americans and European Americans has actually widened since 1930. As of 2001, being born an African American male in the United States took 6.8 years off your life as compared with European American males; African American women could expect to live 4.7 fewer years than European American women (U.S. Bureau of the Census, 2004a).

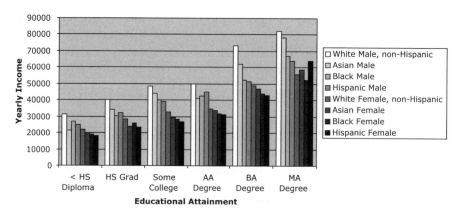

Figure 8.2 Mean income by educational attainment for year-round, full-time workers 18 years or older, March 2002. (Data from U.S. Bureau of the Census, 2004b)

The picture of African Americans that emerges is clearly one of ethnic stratification. African Americans face discrimination in all of the dominant American institutions; past widespread and built-in discrimination is reflected in the range of problems that African Americans face today. For instance, over 80 percent of African American students in the major cities of California, Michigan, Illinois, and New Jersey attend segregated schools; this suggests similar patterns of housing segregation (Miller, 1995). Additionally, African Americans are much less likely to be homeowners, wherever they live, than European Americans (Horton, 1992).

As Figure 8.2 shows, African American and Hispanic men lag behind European American men in yearly (mean) income at all educational levels. They also generally trail Asian American men, particularly at the higher educational levels. As these figures only apply to full-time, year-round workers, the results are all the more striking in that African Americans and Hispanics are more likely than European Americans to work part-time and to be laid off more frequently. The income gap at each educational level suggests a factor of discrimination that is still very much with us, as presumably qualified African American and Hispanic workers are either not getting the jobs or not getting the promotions that European American workers get. While differences between European American and Asian American men are not as striking at each educational level, the gap is nevertheless consistent.

The data on females in Figure 8.2 are interesting on two levels. On the one hand, there appears to be less discrimination against African American and Hispanic women than against their male counterparts; at each educational level, the mean income levels are similar. In particular, improved occupational opportunities for African American women are attributed more to changes in discriminatory practices than to changes in skills (Cunningham and Zalokar, 1992). On the other hand, sexism in the American economy is very clear here: no women of any ethnic or racial group can compete with similarly qualified male employees in terms of earnings. We will examine the gender gap in American education and the economy in fuller detail in Chapter 11.

Figure 8.2 includes all workers in the United States. You might wonder what would happen if we limited our focus to only younger workers. We could imagine two arguments for doing so. First, European American men are more likely than any other group to have been in the workforce longer and therefore to have received extra compensation for seniority or promotion; indeed, this is generally true for all men in relation to women. Second, workers under the age of thirty-four have spent their entire lives in higher education and the workforce during the period of affirmative action. If European American males had faced any problems in recent years (or if others had faced hurdles), it would show up with this age cohort. As it turns out, the relationships depicted in Figure 8.2 are virtually identical to those that exist among younger workers (U.S. Bureau of the Census, 2004b). If we cannot find equality even when stacking the information to reveal it, we can only conclude that it just is not there.

Within the African American community, other changes are at work. O'Hare et al. (1991) report that the widening gap between rich and poor in the United States that occurred in the 1980s hit the African American community especially hard. After making some gains in the 1960s and 1970s, poorer, unskilled African Americans faced a particularly bleak decade in the 1980s, with no hope of improvement in the near future. At the same time, middle-class African Americans with skills and education have benefited from changes in the economy and, to some extent, from affirmative action policies. Among African Americans, it is the middle class that is most supportive of federal government efforts to advance affirmative action; their support is likely the result of their beginning with easily acquired entry-level jobs but then facing minimal promotion (sometimes termed a "glass ceiling") as a result of discrimination (Fine, 1992). It is also interesting that middle-class African Americans tend to have dropping levels of life satisfaction in general when compared to lower-class African Americans, presumably the result of coming face to face with the barriers of everyday discrimination after higher expectations (Austin and Dodge, 1992).

With middle-class African Americans moving up and lower-class African Americans moving down, the African American community in the United States today is looking increasingly polarized. The middle-class African American experience is typified by higher education, two family wage earners, delayed childbearing, and ultimately fewer children (Lewin, 1991). In short, middle-class African Americans look remarkably like middle-class European Americans in many respects. The economic growth and low unemployment during the 1990s greatly benefited middle-class African Americans. The remarkable unity that has characterized African American politics over the years, particularly in party affiliation, may well be threatened by the growing disunity in African American economic positions (Evans,

1992). In spite of these changes, however, the 2004 presidential election found African American voters firmly in the Democratic column.

HISPANIC AMERICANS

Hispanic Americans (or Americans of Spanish origin) is a category that includes a wide variety of people. Altogether, there are over 38 million Hispanic Americans. Of that number, almost 67 percent are Mexican Americans, 8.6 percent are Puerto Rican, 3.7 percent are Cuban, and 14.3 percent are Central and South American (U.S. Bureau of the Census, 2003a, 2004a). Most Mexican Americans live in the Southwest, about two-thirds of the Puerto Ricans live in New York City, and most Cubans live in Florida. Thus, these people vary in geography as well as culture, home country, time of immigration, and reason for immigration. In the case of Mexican Americans some are not even U.S. immigrants—their ancestors already occupied the territory when the United States came to them. Hispanic Americans are, as a category, a minority group in the United States today. In many areas, especially education, they are behind African Americans and far behind European Americans. We look at the history of Mexican Americans in the United States as representative of Hispanics; not only are they the largest ethnic group within this overall category, but they illustrate typical patterns of discrimination faced by minority ethnic groups in the United States.

Mexican Americans originally joined the United States under the terms of the peace treaty that followed the war with Mexico in the 1840s. Before that war the area that is now the entire southwestern United States was controlled by Mexico, which had been a colony of Spain. Spanish settlement of the area began around 1600. As happened with other Spanish settlements, the original settlers soon found themselves in varying degrees of isolation. When Spanish control passed to Mexico, the isolation continued; few Mexicans could be convinced to move north and strengthen the Mexican hold over the land. As the Mexican government watched European settlers pour into what is now the state of Texas, it became obvious that Mexico would soon lose control over the northern provinces. Heroics of the Alamo aside, the result of the war with Mexico was a largely foregone conclusion at the outset.

At the end of the war there were about 60,000 Mexicans in New Mexico, 5,000 in Texas, 7,500 in California, 1,000 in Arizona, and a few settlements in what is now Colorado (Moore, 1976). Each of these areas entered the United States somewhat differently. In New Mexico, for example, the basic activities of the people remained relatively stable although considerable changes in power and the economy took place (see Box 8.1). Texas, on the other hand, was the scene of much of the conflict of the war. Even though many Texas Mexicans had favored the formation of the Texas Republic, they were soon very far from the seats of power and commerce as Texas entered the Union. California, of course, became engulfed in the gold rush. The old Mexican ranchos could not survive the rush of the forty-niners to the gold fields and the rush of merchants to the forty-niners. However different the various situations, there was one important point in common: in no territory did the Mexican population really maintain political control. It did for a while in New Mexico, but even then the Spanish language passed out of use in the legislature, and control over land and power slowly slipped from Mexican hands. The same transfer occurred more quickly and more completely in each of the other territories. Only recently has any political power whatsoever been in the hands of Mexican Americans.

There is an important second chapter in the history of Mexican Americans in the United States, the story of immigration from Mexico after the treaty of 1848. This immigration of primarily poor and rural northern Mexican peasants did not occur on a large scale until the early 1900s. In the half century between the end of the war with Mexico and the beginning of large-scale migration from Mexico, European dominance was established throughout the Southwest. Only New Mexico still had a numerical majority of Mexicans, but even that advantage was no match for incoming settlers or, more important, for the power of the U.S. government, which had firm ideas on how the territory should operate. By the time Mexican immigrants began arriving, the minority status of Mexican Americans was well established in the area. The newcomers, almost entirely unskilled, found work, when it was available, primarily on railroads and in agriculture. When work was less available, during the Great Depression, for instance, the familiar pattern of ethnic group competition over employment repeated itself, and Mexicans joined the ranks of so many other ethnic groups pronounced racially different from Europeans. Such clashes followed the ups and downs of the economy, major flare-ups occurring in the 1930s (when more than four hundred thousand Hispanics were deported) and again in the 1950s (Davis, Haub, and Willette, 1983).

In both periods many Mexicans were deported to Mexico under the charge of being illegal aliens. Many no doubt were, but welfare and immigration officials were not concerned with absolute accuracy on that point. In times of prosperity, on the other hand, Mexicans were more than welcome as industrial and agricultural workers. In short, Mexican Americans fell into the familiar pattern of the involuntary immigrant. Even though many were technically voluntary, their low status had already been established in the course of conquest, and their lives were very much at the mercy of the dominant European Americans, who alternately used them and discarded them as the situation required.

Today, Hispanic Americans make up varied components of the ethnic scene in the United States. Cubans, who are concentrated in Florida, are economically better off than other Hispanics and have also been more successful in maintaining a thriving Spanish cultural community as an island within English culture. Mexican Americans, who are also becoming increasingly urbanized, have maintained strong cultural ties, particularly with regard to family loyalty (Keefe and Padilla, 1987). Nevertheless, most Hispanics trail non-Hispanic white Americans in economic, educational, and occupational indicators. In 2002, 21.4 percent of Hispanics lived below the poverty level, compared with 7.8 percent of non-Hispanic whites; mean family income was less than 64 percent of non-Hispanic white family income—a percentage that has improved only slightly since the 1970s (Davis, Haub, and Willette, 1983; U.S. Bureau of the Census, 2003a, 2004a). The pattern of discrimination with regard to Hispanic men is similar to that with regard to black men; at every educational level, Hispanic men earn less than their non-Hispanic white counterparts (see Verdugo, 1992). Perhaps the worst socioeconomic gap between non-Hispanic whites and Hispanics comes in the field of education. In 2002, only 57 percent of the Hispanic population over age 25 had achieved a high school diploma or more, compared with 88.7 percent of the non-Hispanic white population and 79 percent of the African American population (U.S. Bureau of the Census, 2003a, 2003b).

These statistics are all the more important when demographic predictions for the Hispanic population are considered. A high birth rate coupled with growing immigration have led to predictions that Hispanics will greatly increase their percentage of the overall U.S. population. If these population predictions are accurate, Hispanics will become the largest minority group in the United States, surpassing African Americans. Projections for the year 2050 foresee a Hispanic American population up to 24.5 percent of the overall population, while African Americans will be only 14.6 percent (U.S. Bureau of the Census, 2004a).

NATIVE AMERICANS

A complete history of Native Americans would have to be long and complex to capture the uniqueness of each tribe. Despite their uniqueness, however, they have seldom been in a position to express it in the face of the overwhelming power of the European Americans, who exercised their domination in a manner highly standardized for all tribes. That power was used to place almost all Native Americans in a common situation, and it is that common situation that concerns us.

From the point of view of European Americans, Native Americans have always had two grave drawbacks. First, they could never be successfully exploited as a labor force. Attempts in the early days failed because tribal cultures proved to be too strong an obstacle, and returning to the tribe was too easy. The latter problem was not, of course, a factor in the control of African Americans, which made them far more desirable as laborers (Noel, 1968). Second, Native Americans were in the way as European American settlement expanded westward. In light of these two facts, European Americans had the choice of either killing Native Americans or moving them to undesirable land. Both solutions were adequate from the European American point of view. The magnitude of their domination is perhaps best expressed by statistics. Today there are 2.7 million American Indians and Alaskan Natives living in the United States, making up less than one percent of the overall population (U.S. Bureau of the Census, 2004a). Estimates are that by the year 2050, this number will increase to 4.4 million, which will still represent only one percent of the overall population (U.S. Bureau of the Census, 2004a).

Note, however, that 2.7 million is a considerable drop from the estimated 5 million Native Americans who were living in what is now the continental United States in 1492. Contact with Europeans left many tribes extinct, and the overall numbers of Native Americans in general reached near extinction around 1900. Since that time, there has been a rapid population growth among Native Americans as the death rate has decreased. The greatest killer of Native Americans through European American contact was disease, particularly smallpox, typhus, and cholera, against which Native Americans had no natural defenses. While smallpox killed around 10 percent of a European population in the early days, it could completely eliminate a Native American tribe (Thornton, 1987). There are even documented reports that European Americans intentionally spread the disease through donating infected blankets to Native Americans (McNeill, 1976; Thornton, 1987). While the disease needed little such help, such actions indicate something of the total disregard for Native Americans common to many European Americans.

The Native Americans who were moved (and many tribes were moved more than once) found themselves in the curious limbo of the U.S. government created reservation. The reservation was and is a no-man's-land between two cultures. It is organized along the lines of tribal autonomy and group activity that made up so many Native American tribes. The tribe has no real political control, however; the U.S. government has taken up the position of legal guardian, supposedly acting in the interests of the tribe. More often than not, government actions were and are designed to make the Native American as European as possible, imposing European forms of education and political processes from without. The result was that many Native Americans became non-Native Americans, but very few became Europeans.

Since 1924 Native Americans have been legal citizens of the United States, yet they are still caught between two worlds. On the reservation all control is in the hands of the Bureau of Indian Affairs, part of the executive branch of the federal government. There is no legislative recourse to actions by the bureau. Off the reservation Native Americans have the rights of a U.S. citizen—but legal freedom is only part of the battle. The non-Native American, non-European culture of the reservation, coupled with the lack of political control by Native Americans, gives the contemporary Native American little future on or off the reservation. Native Americans have no power in either place and cannot compete economically in the modern industrial world. The use of political pressure as a group, with which other cultural groups have achieved so much, is, for Native Americans, nonexistent. Their group has been defused by the powerless institution of the reservation. Off the reservation, they are largely on their own.

Today, less than half of the Native American population remains on reservations. Those who leave tend to have higher levels of education and higher incomes, but, as a group, Native Americans have the lowest median income of all the ethnic groups discussed in this chapter. Alcoholism and suicide are chronic problems, infant mortality rates are high (although improving rapidly relative to those of whites), life expectancy is low, and diseases such as tuberculosis that specialize in lower-class victims have extremely high rates (Thornton, 1987).

The one shining light that may be on the horizon for Native Americans beams from political processes. The U.S. government has, over the years, signed a great many treaties with Native American tribes and has subsequently broken almost all of them. Many of these treaties granted land to Native Americans, land that was later taken back for other uses. Today the federal government faces a barrage of legal claims from various tribes over old treaties. A number of cases have been settled in the Native Americans' favor, resulting in payments of large sums of money from the government to the tribes in question. It is perhaps ironic that the government's reservation system helped keep tribes intact, making these court cases possible today.

That same government reservation system has also resulted in a somewhat higher-profile change in Native American reservations and on the American landscape as a whole—casino gambling. The relative independence of reservations in setting laws has allowed many tribes to legalize casino gambling in states that otherwise prohibit such activity. When tribes set up such gambling industries, they are directed specifically at the non-Native American population. The lack of gambling competition in such states has given many tribes a "corner on the market" that has attracted considerable patronage from enthusiastic gamblers. The success of such efforts has brought new income into many tribes, enabling them to improve their socioeconomic status significantly.

SUMMARY

Ethnic groups are social groups whose members share a culture, think of themselves as sharing a culture, or are defined by others as sharing a culture. If two or more ethnic groups share a society and one ethnic group controls the distribution of rewards so as to benefit itself with upper-class membership, a system of ethnic stratification exists. Within this system the ethnic groups with power are majority (or dominant) groups, and the ethnic groups without power are minority (or subordinate) groups. A system of ethnic stratification is maintained through discrimination, which may operate either overtly or covertly (institutional discrimination). Whichever form it takes, discrimination closes routes to upward social mobility for the ethnic groups it is directed against.

Social stratification in general and ethnic stratification in particular produce competition between individuals and among groups in society. This competition is potentially threatening to all members of society. Prejudice, or a negative attitude toward a group of people, is a natural outcome of this threatening situation as individuals seek to support their sense of individual worth and their social position. Prejudice generally contains stereotypes—generalizations (negative in this case) about the group that is the recipient of the prejudice.

When ethnic groups come together, a variety of social arrangements and cultural outcomes are possible. One American dream has always been the "melting pot," in which individuals would intermarry and intermingle their cultures so as to produce new people with a new culture. Closer to reality are some alternatives such as genocide (the physical extermination of an ethnic group) and expulsion (the physical removal of an ethnic group from a society). Segregation may also be employed as a means for keeping two ethnic groups culturally separate (on the dominant group's terms) while sharing the same society. Separatism is separation of a minority group by their own choice.

Assimilation, one of the most common outcomes, occurs when the minority group's culture fades away, and simultaneously, the dominant group accepts the minority group's individual members into dominant group activities and, ultimately, families. A social and cultural alternative generally proposed by minority groups is cultural pluralism. Cultural pluralism is the peaceful coexistence of two or more ethnic groups within the same society in which (1) they maintain their cultural differences and (2) all ethnic groups share in the power and rewards of the society.

The United States has been a center of immigration for centuries. The dominant ethnic group today is made up of descendants from northwestern European immigrants. Although a great many different ethnic groups have faced racist situations and discrimination at varying times in American history, the three ethnic groups currently facing the most difficulties are African Americans, Hispanic Americans, and Native Americans. Each of these groups is defined as racially different, occupies the lower classes disproportionately, and faces discrimination as a part of everyday life.

GLOSSARY

Affirmative action Any program designed to alter the racial, ethnic, or sexual composition of a social group (students, employees, etc.) by actively seeking minority group members.

Assimilation The incorporation of one ethnic group into the continuing culture of another ethnic group.

Cultural pluralism A social situation where two or more ethnic groups share one society; each ethnic group maintains its separate cultural distinctiveness, and no one ethnic group dominates the other(s).

Discrimination Any action that shows a bias against an individual on the basis of his or her group membership; it is typically designed to hinder the competitive abilities of individuals in that group.

Ethnic group A group of people who share a common culture, think of themselves as sharing a common culture, or are defined by others as sharing a common culture.

Ethnic stratification The disproportionate location of ethnic group members in particular social classes of a social stratification system.

Exploitation The situation of an individual who does not receive full value for his or her labor.

Expulsion The physical removal of most or all members of a subordinate group from within the boundaries of a nation-state.

Genocide Actions that result in the deaths of most or all members of a given subordinate group.

Institutional (covert) discrimination Indirect forms of discrimination (intentional or unintentional) that affect a certain social group because of certain attributes or abilities most of that group's members have (or lack).

Majority group (dominant group) A social group that controls the organization and distribution of rewards in a society.

Melting pot The mixing and blending of two or more cultures through the intermarriage of their members.

Minority group (subordinate group) A relatively powerless social group that is subject to the decisions of a majority (dominant) group.

Prejudice A negative attitude toward a group of people.

Racial group A group of people socially defined as sharing a common genetic heritage.

Racism (1) The belief that people are separated into different races and that those races are biologically inferior or superior to each other. (2) The individual experience of living within a system of ethnic stratification in which the groups at the bottom of the hierarchy are defined as racially inferior.

Segregation The dominant group's decision to separate itself, either socially or physically, from a given minority group.

Self-esteem An individual's subjective evaluation of his or her worth.

Separatism The physical and political separation of a minority group, by their own choice, from a dominant group.

Stereotype A generalized description (usually negative) of a specific social group, also applied to its members.

STUDY QUESTIONS
1. What determines whether a racial or ethnic group has minority or dominant status in a society? Be sure to explain ethnic (or racial) stratification in your answer.
2. Explain how discrimination maintains the minority status of an ethnic group while also making it vulnerable to labor exploitation.

3. How do stereotypes support prejudiced attitudes?
4. What psychological states and social circumstances promote prejudiced attitudes in individuals?
5. How does institutional (or covert) discrimination differ from overt discrimination?
6. What are affirmative action programs, and which types of discrimination to they address?
7. Why does the melting pot seldom occur when ethnic groups encounter each other?
8. What is the difference between genocide and expulsion? Which more accurately describes the history of Native Americans?
9. Which ethnic groups benefit from segregation and why? What is the difference between physical and social segregation?
10. How does assimilation differ from either cultural pluralism or separatism? What is the result for the minority group in each of the three cases?
11. What role has religion played in the history of American immigration?
12. What forms of discrimination have Asian immigrants faced throughout American history?
13. Why did slavery arise in the United States? What lasting damage has it done to African Americans?
14. Describe the variation among Hispanic Americans today. How many ethnic groups might exist within that overall category?
15. Why did Native Americans suffer so much from their first encounters with Europeans? What problems do they currently face?

Gene Callahan and William Anderson   **R E A D I N G**

THE ROOTS OF RACIAL PROFILING

Racial profiling is the practice of targeting members of certain racial or ethnic groups on the grounds that members of their groups commit more crimes. Callahan and Anderson examine this practice in American law enforcement, comparing arguments from police against complaints from suspects.

WHY ARE POLICE TARGETING MINORITIES FOR TRAFFIC STOPS?

It is early in the morning, and the well-dressed young African-American man driving his Ford Explorer on I-75 sees the blue lights of the Georgia State Patrol car behind him. The officer pulls behind the sport utility vehicle and the young man's heart begins to sink.

He is on his way to Atlanta for a job interview. The stop, ostensibly for speeding, should not take long, he reasons, as the highway patrol officer walks cautiously toward the Explorer. But instead of simply asking for a driver's license and writing a speeding ticket, the trooper calls for backup. Another trooper soon arrives, his blue lights flashing as well.

The young man is told to leave his vehicle, as the troopers announce their intention to search it. "Hey, where did you get the money for something like this?" one trooper asks mockingly while he starts the process of going through every inch of the Explorer. Soon, an officer pulls off an inside door panel. More dismantling of the vehicle follows. They say they are looking for drugs, but in the end find nothing. After ticketing the driver for speeding, the two officers casually drive off. Sitting in his now-trashed SUV, the young man weeps in his anger and humiliation.

Unmotivated searches like this are daily occurrences on our nation's highways, and blacks and white liberals have been decrying the situation for several years. Many conservatives, on the other hand, dismiss such complaints as the exaggerations of hypersensitive minorities. Or they say that if traffic cops do in fact pull over and search the vehicles of African Americans disproportionately, then such "racial profiling" is an unfortunate but necessary component of modern crime fighting.

The incident described above should give pause to those who think that racial profiling is simply a bogus issue cooked up by black leaders

---

From *Newsweek,* March 3, 2003, vol. 141 Issue 9. Reprinted by permission of *Newsweek,* © 2003. All rights reserved.

such as Al Sharpton and Jesse Jackson to use as another publicity tool. One of us teaches in an MBA program that enrolls a fairly large number of African Americans, and the story comes from one of our students. Indeed, during class discussions, all of the black men and many of the black women told stories of having their late-model cars pulled over and searched for drugs.

While incidents of racial profiling are widely deplored today, there is little said about the actual root cause of the phenomenon. The standard explanations for racial profiling focus on institutional racism, but that idea runs contrary to the sea change in social attitudes that has taken place over the last four decades. On the contrary, the practice of racial profiling grows from a trio of very tangible sources, all attributable to the War on Drugs, that $37 billion annual effort on the part of local, state, and federal lawmakers and cops to stop the sale and use of "illicit" substances. The sources include the difficulty in policing victimless crimes in general and the resulting need for intrusive police techniques; the greater relevancy of this difficulty given the intensification of the drug war since the 1980s; and the additional incentive that asset forfeiture laws give police forces to seize money and property from suspects. Since the notion of scaling back, let alone stopping, the drug war is too controversial for most politicians to handle, it's hardly surprising that its role in racial profiling should go largely unacknowledged.

THE PRACTICE OF RACIAL PROFILING

Although there is no single, universally accepted definition of "racial profiling," we're using the term to designate the practice of stopping and inspecting people who are passing through public places—such as drivers on public highways or pedestrians in airports or urban areas—where the reason for the stop is a statistical profile of the detainee's race or ethnicity.

The practice of racial profiling has been a prominent topic for the past several years. In his February address to Congress, President George W. Bush reported that he'd asked Attorney General John Ashcroft "to develop specific recommendations to end racial profiling. It's wrong, and we will end it in America." The nomination of former New Jersey Gov. Christine Todd Whitman as head of the Environmental Protection Agency was challenged on the basis of her alleged complicity in racial profiling practices in the Garden State. Whitman had pioneered her own unique form of "minority outreach" when she was photographed frisking a black crime suspect in 1996. Copies of the photo were circulated to senators prior to her confirmation vote. (By the same token, in February 1999, Whitman fired State Police Superintendent Carl A. Williams after he gave a newspaper interview in which he justified racial profiling and linked minority groups to drug trafficking.) More recently, Eleanor Holmes Norton, the District of Columbia's nonvoting member of Congress, has tried to introduce legislation that would withhold federal highway dollars from states that have not explicitly banned racial profiling.

Although some observers claim that racial profiling doesn't exist, there is an abundance of stories and statistics that document the practice. One case where law enforcement officers were particularly bold in their declaration of intent involved U.S. Forest Service officers in California's Mendocino National Forest last year. In an attempt to stop marijuana growing, forest rangers were told to question all Hispanics whose cars were stopped, regardless of whether pot was actually found in their vehicles. Tim Crews, the publisher of the *Sacramento Valley Mirror*, a biweekly newspaper, published a memo he'd gotten from a federal law enforcement officer. The memo told park rangers "to develop probable cause for stop . . . if a vehicle stop is conducted and no marijuana is located and the vehicle has Hispanics inside, at a minimum we would like all individuals FI'd [field interrogated]." A spokeswoman for Mendocino National Forest called the directive an "unfortunate use of words."

The statistics are equally telling. Consider *Crises of the Anti-Drug Effort, 1999*, a report by Chad Thevenot of the Criminal Justice Policy

Foundation, a group that monitors abuses of the American legal system. Thevenot writes: "76 percent of the motorists stopped along a 50-mile stretch of I-95 by Maryland's Special Traffic Interdiction Force (STIF) were black, according to an Associated Press computer analysis of car searches from January through September 1995. . . . Blacks constitute 25 percent of Maryland's population, and 20 percent of Marylanders with driver's licenses." As this story was being written, New Jersey was holding hearings on racial profiling, and one state police investigator testified that 94 percent of the motorists stopped in one town were minorities.

Minorities are not only more likely to be stopped than whites, but they are also often pressured to allow searches of their vehicles, and they are more likely to allow such searches. In March, *The New York Times* reported that a 1997 investigation by New Jersey police of their own practices found that "turnpike drivers who agreed to have their cars searched by the state police were overwhelmingly black and Hispanic."

Some commentators, such as John Derbyshire in *National Review,* have defended racial profiling as nothing more than sensible police technique, where police employ the laws of probability to make the best use of their scarce resources in attacking crime. As Derbyshire put it in his story, "In Defense of Racial Profiling," the police engage in the practice for reasons of simple efficiency: "A policeman who concentrates a disproportionate amount of his limited time and resources on young black men is going to uncover far more crimes—and therefore be far more successful in his career—than one who biases his attention toward, say, middle-aged Asian women."

George Will, in a *Washington Post* column, contends that the use of race as a criterion in traffic stops is fine, as long as it is just "one factor among others in estimating criminal suspiciousness." Similarly, Jackson Toby, a professor of sociology at Rutgers, argued in a 1999 Wall Street Journal op-ed that, "If drug traffickers are disproportionately black or Hispanic, the police don't need to be racist to stop many minority

motorists; they simply have to be efficient in targeting potential drug traffickers."

Clayton Searle, president of The International Narcotics Interdiction Association, writes in a report, *Profiling in Law Enforcement,* "Those who purport to be shocked that ethnic groups are overrepresented in the population arrested for drug courier activities must have been in a coma for the last twenty years. The fact is that ethnic groups control the majority of the drug trade in the United States. They also tend to hire as their underlings and couriers others of their same group." (Searle's report is available at www.inia.org/whats-new.htm#Profiling.)

CASE PROBABILITY VERSUS CLASS PROBABILITY

The stories and statistics that draw outrage tend to share two common elements: They involve a search for drugs and the prospect of asset forfeiture. These types of investigations have led police from the solid ground of "case probability" to the shifting sands of "class probability" in their quest for probable cause. Once police are operating on the basis of class probability, there is a strong claim that certain groups of people are being denied equal protection under the law.

Case probability describes situations where we comprehend some factors relevant to a particular event, but not all such factors. It is used when a doctor tells a patient, "Given your lifestyle, you'll probably be dead in five years." Class probability refers to situations where we know enough about a class of events to describe it using statistics, but nothing about a particular event other than the fact that it belongs to the class in question. Class probability is being used when an insurance company estimates that a man who is 40 today will probably live to be, on average, about 80. The insurance company is not making any statement about the particular circumstances of any particular man, but merely generalizing about the class of 40-year-old men.

This distinction helps us to differentiate two ways of using information about race or ethnicity in a police investigation. As an example of the first type, employing case probability, consider a mugging victim who has told the police that her mugger was a young Asian man. Here, it is quite understandable that the group of suspects investigated will not "look like America." There is no sense in forcing the police to drag in proportional numbers of whites, blacks, women, and so on, proving that they have interrogated a representative population sample of their city, before they can arrest an Asian fellow. No, their investigation should clearly focus on young Asian men.

It's not at all impossible that a prevalence of some type of criminal activity in some ethnic group will lead to many investigations that focus on members of that group. As long as this is based on evidence gathered from particular crimes, there is nothing untoward here. If it turns out, for instance, that Bulgarians are especially numerous among purse-snatchers in some city, then a summary of police interrogations might discover evidence of "Bulgarian profiling" in the investigation of purse-snatching. But this may be a statistical mirage if it turns out that no one in the police force set out to focus on Bulgarians as potential purse-snatchers. The emergent result is an unintended outcome of policemen following an entirely valid principle of crime investigation: Concentrate on suspects who fit the description you have of the suspect.

But when we turn our attention to the type of racial profiling that occurred on the highways of Maryland and New Jersey, or that is described in the Forest Service memo, we find a very different phenomenon, one where investigations proceeded on the basis of class probability. Here, before having evidence of a particular crime, police set out intending to investigate a high proportion of people of some particular race, ethnic group, age group, or so on. Their only justification is that by doing so, they increase their chances of discovering some crimes.

Additionally, there is a fundamental difference between the type of crime, such as the mugging example above, that is usually investigated by gathering evidence about a known crime, and narrowing the search based on such evidence,

and the type investigated by looking in as many places as possible to see if one can find a crime. The first type of crime generally has a victim, and the police are aware of a specific crime that has been committed. The crime is brought to the attention of the police by a complainant, even if the complainant is a corpse.

George Will, in his defense of current police practice, points out: "Police have intelligence that in the Northeast drug-shipping corridor many traffickers are Jamaicans favoring Nissan Pathfinders." This is quite a different situation than having intelligence that a particular Jamaican robbed a store and escaped in a Pathfinder. If you are a law-abiding Jamaican who by chance owns a Pathfinder, you frequently will find yourself under police surveillance, even though the police have no evidence about any particular crime involving any particular Jamaican in a Pathfinder.

We could not have any effective law enforcement without allowing some scope for case probability. If your twin brother robs a bank in your hometown, it does not seem to be a civil rights issue if the police stop you on the street for questioning. When the police discover their mistake, they should apologize and make you whole for any damages you have suffered. Such an event, while unfortunate, is simply a byproduct of attempting to enforce laws in a world of error-prone human beings possessing less-than-perfect knowledge. It will be a rare event in law-abiding citizens' lives, and it is highly unlikely that such people will come to feel that they are being targeted.

However, the use of class probability in police investigations is correctly regarded with extreme suspicion, as it violates a basic principle of justice: The legal system should treat all citizens equally, until there is specific, credible evidence that they have committed a crime. In the cases we've been discussing, we can say that the odds that any particular young black or Hispanic man will be hassled by the police are much higher than for a white man who, aside from his race, is demographically indistinguishable from him. These minority men, no matter how law-abiding they are, know that they will be investigated by the police significantly more often than other citizens who are not members of their racial group. The social cost of the alienation produced by this situation cannot, of course, be measured, but common sense tells us that it must be great.

As important, in the majority of "crimes" that such stops discover, there is no third party whose rights have been violated, who can step forward and bring the crime to the attention of the police. To discover victimless crimes, investigators must become intrusive and simply poke around wherever they can, trying to see if they can uncover such a crime. When someone drives a few pounds of marijuana up I-95 from seller to buyer, who will come forward and complain? It's not merely that, as in the cases of robbery or murder, the perpetrator may try to hide his identity, but that the "crime" has no victim.

DRUG WAR PROFILING PRACTICES

Both statistical studies and anecdotal evidence support the view that drug crimes are the almost exclusive focus of investigation in racial profiling cases. Hence, *The New York Times* reported that, "The New Jersey State Police said last week that the number of drug arrests on the Garden State Parkway and the New Jersey Turnpike fell last year, after the department came under scrutiny for racial profiling. The number of drug charges resulting from stops on the turnpike were 370 last year, compared with 494 drug charges in 1999. There were 1,269 charges filed in 1998. On the parkway, troopers reported 350 drug charges last year compared with 783 in 1999 and 1,279 in 1998."

The Record, a Bergen, New Jersey, newspaper, obtained state police documents last fall. One document, used for training, teaches troopers to zero in on minorities when scanning state roadways for possible drug traffickers. Titled "Occupant Identifiers for a Possible Drug Courier," the document instructs troopers to look out for "Colombian males, Hispanic males, Hispanic and a black male together, Hispanic male and female posing as a couple." (One's mind

boggles at how the police are able to detect that two Hispanics are "posing" as a couple as they zip by at 60 miles per hour.) The undated document also teaches troopers how to use supposed traffic violations, such as "speeding" and "failure to drive within a single lane," as a pretext to pull over suspected drug couriers.

If police have a goal of maximizing drug arrests, they may indeed find that they can achieve this most easily by focusing on minorities. Blacks on I-95 in Maryland, for instance, had a significantly higher initial propensity to carry drugs in the car than did whites. "Racial Bias in Motor Vehicle Searches: Theory and Evidence," a 1999 study by University of Pennsylvania professors John Knowles, Nicola Persico, and Petra Todd, shows that despite the fact that blacks were stopped three-and-a-half times more than whites, they were as likely to be carrying drugs. But this doesn't mean their propensity to carry is the same. If we assume that the high likelihood of being stopped reduces some blacks' willingness to carry drugs, then if not for the stops, they would have been carrying proportionally much more than whites. The Penn professors conclude they are displaying what they call "statistical discrimination" (i.e., the police are operating on the basis of class probability) rather than racial prejudice. Perhaps more to the point, they conclude that the police are primarily motivated by a desire to maximize drug arrests.

Some racial profiling defenders agree that the drug war bears a large part of the blame for racial profiling. "Many of the stop-and-search cases that brought this matter into the headlines were part of the so-called war on drugs," writes Derbyshire. "The police procedures behind them were ratified by court decisions of the 1980s, themselves mostly responding to the rising tide of illegal narcotics." But Derbyshire dismisses the argument that racial profiling is chiefly a byproduct of the drug war. He contends that even if drugs were legalized tomorrow, the practice would continue.

He is confusing the two forms of police procedure we have outlined above. The practice of laying out broad dragnets to see what turns up would almost entirely disappear but for the attempt to stamp out drug trafficking and use. Derbyshire, to bolster his case, cites the fact that in 1997, "Blacks, who are 13 percent of the U.S. population, comprised 35 percent of those arrested for embezzlement." This statistic would be useful if he were defending the fact that 35 percent of those investigated for embezzling that year were black. But does Derbyshire believe that stopping random blacks on an interstate highway is catching very many embezzlers? Or that, absent the drug war, cops would start searching cars they pull over for embezzled funds?

HOW ASSET FORFEITURE FUELS PROFILING

In the 1980s, state legislatures and Congress were frustrated with their inability to arrest and convict "drug kingpins." So they passed laws that gave police the power to seize the property of suspected dealers. The dubious rationale: The "pushers'" property had been purchased through ill-gotten gains and hence didn't rightly belong to them. (Questions about establishing actual guilt were brushed aside as counterproductive.) The federal Comprehensive Crime Act of 1984 was the most important of these measures, as it allowed local police agencies that cooperated in a drug investigation to keep the vast majority of the assets seized.

In addition, the Department of Justice decided that police in states that did not allow their agencies to keep asset forfeiture proceeds could have the feds "adopt" their seizures. The *Kansas City Star*'s Karen Dillon has done extensive investigative reporting on asset forfeiture over the past three years. She writes: "Wisconsin law mandates that forfeiture money goes to public schools, but only $16,906 went into Wisconsin's education fund during the year ending in June 1999, according to the state treasury department. During just six months of the same period, local law enforcement gave the federal government $1.5 million in seizures."

In a paper published in the September 2000 issue of the economics journal *Public Choice,*

"Entrepreneurial Police and Drug Enforcement Policy," Brent D. Mast, Bruce L. Benson, and David W. Rasmussen report that forfeiture receipts roughly doubled every year for several years after the passage of the Comprehensive Crime Act. According to the *Sourcebook of Criminal Justice Statistics,* the total value of Drug Enforcement Administration seizures reached nearly $1 billion in 1992. A large amount of that revenue flows back from the federal government to state and local police departments. Dillon notes: "In 1997 and 1998, the St. Louis Metropolitan Police Department received back more than $2.5 million. In 1998 alone, the Georgia Bureau of Investigation took back $1.7 million."

A letter to the International Narcotics Interdiction Association (INIA) from the Richmond Metro Interdiction Unit, posted on INIA's Web site, is accompanied by a photo of two cops in front of a pile of $298,440. The letter says: "We took this money off a guy coming from NY to Miami on Amtrak about two weeks after returning from SKY NARC [an INIA training session] in Anaheim. It was a great school and as you can see it paid off."

The U.S. Department of Justice reports: "Collectively, local police departments received $490 million worth of cash, goods, and property from drug asset forfeiture programs during fiscal 1997. Sheriffs' departments had total receipts of $158 million."

This kind of money adds a major incentive to police efforts to discover drug crimes. The study by Mast, Benson, and Rasmussen concludes: "The results for the impact of asset seizure laws are robust. . . . Police focus relatively more effort on drug control when they can enhance their budgets by retaining seized assets. Legislation permitting police to keep a portion of seized assets raises drug arrests as a portion of total arrests by about 20 percent and drug arrest rates by about 18 percent."

Of course, if the police begin harassing all motorists in a particular locale, support for their activities will soon evaporate. However, if they can identify a minority group that is somewhat more likely to commit a particular drug crime—and if they know that members of that group are not politically powerful—then the police can focus on those people in order to enhance their departmental revenue.

The usual supposition, that the accused is innocent until proven guilty, has been explicitly reversed in asset forfeiture cases. The authorities are not required to prove that a crime, involving the goods in question, has been committed. Instead, they must merely have "probable cause" for the seizure; the burden of proof is on the defendant trying to recover his property. The Schaffer Library of Drug Policy (druglibrary.org/schaffer) has found that 80 percent of those who have had assets seized are never charged with a crime, let alone convicted of one. Federal law provides for up to five years in prison for attempting to prevent one's own property from being grabbed.

It did not take long for those in law enforcement to conclude that their best haul would come from seizing goods from citizens who lack the resources to win them back. In one highly publicized case that occurred in 1991, federal authorities at the Nashville airport took more than $9,000 in cash from Willie Jones, a black landscaper who was flying to Houston in order to purchase shrubs. According to the police, that money could have been used to purchase drugs. After spending thousands of dollars and two years on the case, the landscaper was able to convince the courts to return most of the seized cash.

Sam Thach, a Vietnamese immigrant, found himself in a similar situation last year. He was relieved of $147,000 by the DEA while traveling on Amtrak. Thach was investigated because the details of his ticket purchase, which Amtrak shared with the DEA, "fit the profile" of a drug courier. He was not charged with any crime and is now fighting to retrieve his money in federal court. (See "Railway Bandits," *Citings,* July 2000.)

When the University of Pennsylvania study and the study by Mast, Benson, and Rasmussen are considered in tandem, the implication is clear. The possibility of rich pickings through asset forfeiture, combined with the higher propensity for black motorists to carry drugs, provides police departments with a tremendous incentive to engage in racial profiling. It is hardly surprising, then, that police take the bait, even at the cost of racial bias accusations and investigations.

Last year, in reaction to high-profile cases of abuse, Congress passed legislation that changed the standard in federal civil asset forfeiture cases. Rather than showing "probable cause" that property was connected to a crime, the feds must now demonstrate "by a preponderance of the evidence" that the property was used in or is the product of a crime, a significantly higher legal standard. The revised law also awards legal fees to defendants who successfully challenge property seizures and gives judges more latitude to return seized property. Exactly what effect the law will have on federal agents, or on state and local cops, is not yet clear.

THIS IS YOUR LAW ENFORCEMENT ON DRUGS
In the panic created by the drug war, our traditional liberties have been eroded. Rather than regarding case probability as a necessary component of probable cause for searches or seizures, the American law enforcement system has now come to accept class probability as sufficient justification for many intrusions.

Unfortunately, the current protests against racial profiling are not addressing the root causes of the practice. Politicians, eager to please voters, have created potentially greater problems by trying to suppress the symptoms. As John Derbyshire points out, the laws rushed onto the books to end racial profiling result in severe obstacles to police officers attempting to investigate serious crimes. He notes, "In Philadelphia, a federal court order now requires police to fill out both sides of an 8-1/2-by-11 sheet on every citizen contact." Unless our solution to this problem addresses its cause, we will be faced with the choice of either hindering important police work or treating some of our citizens, based on characteristics (race, age, and so on) completely beyond their control, in a manner that is patently unfair.

If we really wish to end the scourge of racial profiling, we must address its roots: drug laws that encourage police to consider members of broad groups as probable criminals. We must redirect law enforcement toward solving specific, known crimes using the particular evidence available to them about that crime. Whatever one's opinion on drug legalization may be, it's easy to agree that the state of seizure law in America is reprehensible, even given last year's minor federal reforms. It should be obvious that there's something nutty about a legal system that assumes suspects in murder, robbery, and rape cases are innocent until a trial proves otherwise, but assumes that a landscaper carrying some cash is guilty of drug trafficking.

Drugs, prohibitionists commonly point out, can damage a user's mind. They apparently can have the same effect on the minds of law enforcement officials.

DISCUSSION QUESTIONS

1. How could profiling by group aid law enforcement? What arguments can be made for allowing such practices by weighing the public good against the rights of individuals?

2. Why do you think the racial and ethnic minorities are more likely to allow police to search their automobiles during routine traffic stops when compared with other motorists?

3. The authors distinguish between "case probability" and "class probability" in their discussion. What is the difference between them, and how does that difference affect racial profiling?

PART 4   SOCIAL INSTITUTIONS

SOCIAL CHANGE AND INDUSTRIALIZATION: THE GROWTH OF SOCIAL INSTITUTIONS

S ociologists look at societies in terms of the way human behavior is coordinated. Societies produce this coordinated behavior in endlessly creative and often complicated ways. A society can consist of twenty people who agree to share a specific place to gather berries or it can consist of a vast industrial giant like the United States. This chapter explores some of the variation to be found in human societies, with a particular focus on the elaborate separation of various social activities into what sociologists refer to as *institutions*.

Types of Human Societies (and Types of Humans)

So far we have looked at the ways humans coordinate their activities into the social patterns of society. We have also looked at the ways people become socialized into those patterns so that their thinking and their behavior are appropriate for the particular patterns by which they live. Sociologists examine this interplay between societies and people, paying particular attention to the different kinds of people that result from different kinds of societies. Comparing society to playing a game can help you understand how this happens. The game of Monopoly makes people competitive, methodical, envious, anxious, and alert—you may well wind up hating your best friend before the game ends. By contrast, playing catch with a Frisbee on a sunny afternoon makes people noncompetitive and relaxed. Societies differ just as games do. Some, like modern American society, require competition; because of their socialization, Americans tend to be competitive people (and may find the casual tossing about of a Frisbee somewhat unfulfilling as a result). Other societies, such as some American Indian tribes, require cooperation among their patterned activities, and their members thus tend to be less competitive (and likely to favor more cooperative games). Observations of such differences have led sociologists to examine the range of human societies.

TECHNOLOGICAL CHANGE IN SOCIETY

Of modern sociologists, Gerhard Lenski has examined the range of human societies in the most detail (Lenski, 1966; Lenski and Lenski, 1974). He separated societies into types according to the dominant forms of technology. One advantage of using technology as the organizational principle is that it reminds us that the basic problem of any society is survival; a society's technology is a key to survival and thus affects all other elements. Lenski organized the types of societies into a hierarchy ranging from those with the simplest forms of technology to those with the most complex forms. As a result, two interesting relationships appeared. First, as technology becomes more complex, the social division of labor becomes more complex. This development is not too surprising, since a complex technology would require a complex organization of labor, and a division of labor is fairly efficient. The second relationship, however, is not as obviously necessary and is in many ways more interesting. As technology becomes more complex, a gap opens between the "haves" and the "have nots" in society.

Let us simplify Lenski's typology down to its four most basic types. We first encounter the *hunting and gathering society,* the extreme of rudimentary technology, in which relatively small nomadic groups are constantly on the move in search of food. This type of society is usually characterized by group cooperation, as the difficulty of life requires that the group work together if its members are to survive. If there is any division of labor at all in the hunting and gathering society, it is a basic one based on sex, in which men specialize in hunting activities and women specialize in gathering activities. The amount of time spent in procuring food coupled with the need to keep on the move limit both the physical and social development of culture. (More recent researchers, such as Richard Lee [1979] have studied modern hunting and gathering societies such as the !Kung bushmen and have noted that less than full-time attention is paid to food procurement, leaving the people with considerable leisure. Lee explains their lack of accumulated wealth by the need for constant mobility.)

Moving up one step in technology, we encounter the *horticultural society.* The primary technological difference between the hunting and gathering society and the horticultural society is an extremely important one: the horticultural society produces its own food rather than depending solely on the environment for it. The horticultural society can stay put, grow larger (as more people can be fed by the same amount of work), and develop other forms of technology, all of which further increase the division of labor. In addition, the horticultural society is advanced enough to produce a surplus of goods, more than needed for the immediate survival of group members. It is this surplus, says Lenski, that first opens the gap between the haves and have nots. It becomes possible for some members of the society to take more than their fair share without starving the remainder of the society. As acquired goods, land, and so on are passed along in families, ongoing patterns of social inequality are intensified and perpetuated.

The third basic type is the *agrarian society.* In most ways the agrarian society is an extension of the social patterns begun in the horticultural society. The agrarian society is characterized by introduction of the plow. Still more people can be fed with

Example of a nontechnology modern-day hunting and gathering group.

less work, leading to larger societies (and governments), more leisure, more technology, an increasing division of labor, greater surpluses, and an increasing gap between the haves and the have nots.

The fourth basic type of society is the *industrial society.* The industrial society still produces food through farming, but the overall society is characterized by manufacturing, complex technology, large cities, elaborate and highly organized divisions of labor (such as the modern bureaucracy), large and powerful governments, and a continuing gap between the haves and the have nots (although not as rigid a gap as in some of the other types of society, according to Lenski).

Modern American society could be considered a prime example of Lenski's industrial society. Some sociologists, however, feel that industrial societies have changed so much that a new category—the *postindustrial society*—is needed. A postindustrial society is one in which workers primarily produce information and services. A staple of that information is technological knowledge, which can be used to increase profits in local industry as well as to export for foreign industry. Such a new focus in industrial activity relegates much of the heavy industrial activity to other countries (which often provide cheaper labor) and changes the labor needs of the society; unskilled workers are no longer in demand (see Wacquant and Wilson, 1993; Caputo, 1995).

The auto assembly line, where the work is done almost entirely by robots, is a perfect illustration of the postindustrial society. Computer-driven machine tools like these replaced many thousands of industrial workers, whose jobs disappeared forever.

The parallel development of the increasing division of labor and the gap between the haves and have nots in Lenski's scheme points to one of the fundamental concepts used by sociologists in understanding modern society and the people in it: **social stratification.** As Lenski observed about the beginnings of the gap between the haves and have nots, for the most part these activities run in families; the children of large stockholders tend to have many options in society and can generally find their way into a highly rewarded activity, while the children of welfare recipients are more likely to become welfare recipients.

Social stratification makes people competitive. The hope of moving to a more highly ranked activity and the fear of moving down in the hierarchy make people highly conscious of how they're doing in relation to others; they watch out for their own interests in order to succeed. We give our children grades when they begin school and give them Monopoly games to play in order to prepare them for competition later in life. If we turn our attention to the kind of cooperation necessary for the survival of a hunting and gathering society, we can see how societies differ and, ultimately, how people differ from one society to the next.

GEMEINSCHAFT AND *GESELLSCHAFT:*
TRADITIONAL AND INDUSTRIAL SOCIETIES

Ferdinand Tönnies, a German sociologist writing around the turn of the last century, looked at the same variation in human societies that would later interest Lenski, but from a slightly different perspective. Rather than emphasize the variations in technology, as Lenski did, Tönnies focused more on changes in the basic ways people relate to each other. He organized this focus by isolating two extremes in human societies, which he labeled *Gemeinschaft* and *Gesellschaft* (Tönnies, 1957).

German sociologist Ferdinand Tönnies (1885–1936). Tönnies was an important figure in the early growth of sociology but is best remembered today for his twin concepts of *Gemeinschaft* and *Gesellschaft,* which compare small communities with large modern societies.

Gemeinschaft is best translated into English as a traditional or communal society. It is characterized by small size and little division of labor. In addition, the activities are in one way or another tied to family or kin relationships; families tend to be quite large, and they stay together not only because they pray together but because they work together, fight together, learn together, raise children together, and settle personal disputes together. Individuals have a variety of highly personal encounters with the same people on an everyday basis. As a result of this close interaction and the simple division of labor, *Gemeinschaft* individuals tend to be relatively similar to each other. When people constantly do the same things with the same people and group cooperation is strongly emphasized, people tend to turn out pretty much the same. In a *Gemeinschaft,* the group comes first and the individual second.

At the other extreme is **Gesellschaft,** best translated as an industrial society. More specifically, the German word *Gesellschaft* refers to commercial activities (as opposed to personal or non-money-related activities), and it is that business relationship that Tönnies wished to emphasize. In an industrial society the family becomes far less important as more and more of the individual's activities occur with nonrelatives. The personal and emotional basis of human interaction that characterizes *Gemeinschaft* is replaced by impersonal and formal relationships in *Gesellschaft.* These new relationships develop as the society becomes larger and develops a complex division of labor involving a wide variety of activities. The diversity of activities in the society leads to a diversity of individuals, who follow different norms and hold different values. In a *Gesellschaft* the individual places himself or herself first; the group comes second.

No society is ever likely to be 100 percent *Gemeinschaft* or 100 percent *Gesellschaft;* the two concepts represent extremes in the organization of human societies. Even the most basic hunting and gathering societies would probably have some kind of division of labor, the beginnings of social stratification, and nonfamily relationships conducted on a formal basis. At the other extreme, a *Gesellschaft* society such as the United States has many *Gemeinschaft* features, particularly in the more traditional or rural corners of the society. (The Amish in the United States form just such a corner. Their community life is described in more detail in the reading following this chapter.) The terms are designed to call attention to general features of society and, most important, to help us understand something about social change. Whereas Lenski directed our focus to technological change, Tönnies concentrated on the growing complexity of the division of labor in society as we move from *Gemeinschaft* to *Gesellschaft.*

In *Gemeinschaft,* the same people (usually your relatives) take care of all your needs; in *Gesellschaft,* the complex division of labor means that a wide variety of people (usually not your relatives) take care of your needs, and different groups of these people specialize in different needs (Harrigan, 1992). For example, in *Gemeinschaft* socialization occurs within the family. In *Gesellschaft,* on the other hand, the process of socialization happens in the family, in school, with friends and acquaintances, from the media, at church, on the job, and so on. Even more significantly, these various spheres of activities may be populated by very different people, who are not necessarily in agreement as to what you should be learning. In order to make some sense of this complexity, sociologists attempt to look at these spheres of activities, or institutions, one at a time. Complex societies such as the United States contain elaborate social institutions that provide a specific kind of social organization for the society. As we encounter institutions in everyday life, we may feel that we are in fact living everyday lives (as opposed to one single life) as our experience becomes separated into different arenas.

THE DEVELOPMENT OF SOCIAL INSTITUTIONS

Most people think of an institution as a mental hospital or, perhaps, a prison. That meaning of the term has nothing whatever to do with the way sociologists use it. To a sociologist, an **institution** is a cluster (or sphere) of interrelated activities within a society, coupled with the knowledge, beliefs, and objects that relate to those activities. Institutions are typically stable configurations of social forms that meet social needs in specific areas. For example, the family (though not a particular family) is an institution in modern American society. Within that institution are included mothers, fathers, brothers, sisters, aunts, uncles, cousins, beliefs about family togetherness, attitudes toward divorce, family reunions, marriage ceremonies, in-law jokes, family Bibles, genealogy tracing, and Thanksgiving dinner (even the turkey). For all its variety, this list just scratches the surface of the family. Understanding any one item on the list requires understanding the other items as well; because they are all part of the same institution, they are all interrelated. Brother cannot be defined without sister; divorce must be defined with marriage; and the Thanksgiving turkey sacrifices all in the name of family togetherness.

Of all the activities, ideas, and objects that cluster within institutions, one element that is not limited within the institution is the individuals who act out the activities, think the ideas, and use the objects. A woman who is a mother/daughter/wife/sister in a family can think thoughts of family togetherness and cook a Thanksgiving turkey, but she can also attend church, hold a job, join the PTA, and run for political office. These activities take her outside the institution of the family and into the institutions of religion, the economy, education, and politics, respectively. Each time she moves into an activity in a different institution, she confronts the other activities, ideas, and objects that cluster within that new institution; just as mothers, fathers, and Thanksgiving dinners exist within the family institution, teachers, students, examinations, and classrooms exist within the educational institution.

The major difference between an institution and a society is that a society takes care of a wide variety of human needs, whereas institutions (as parts of larger societies) take care of just a few needs. The institution of education, for example, specializes in socialization and does little along the lines of providing food, shelter, and protection to members of society. Those needs are taken care of by other institutions.

As societies change from *Gemeinschaft* to *Gesellschaft,* the development and separation of institutions become evident. Figure 9.1 illustrates how a *Gemeinschaft* might take care of the variety of human needs. A *Gemeinschaft* is structurally a fairly simple society; if it can be said to have institutions, it has only one—the family. But imagining any modern meaning for the term *family* as applied to *Gemeinschaft* will cloud the real functions of the family in such a society. As suggested by Figure 9.1, the *Gemeinschaft* "family" satisfies the needs of religion, protection, survival, and socialization at the same time that it provides companionship and oversees the raising of children. We might call it a government as well as a family for, in the modern sense of those words, it has the functions of both. In *Gemeinschaft,* all needs are met by the same people.

At the other extreme a *Gesellschaft* might be represented by Figure 9.2. The institutional separation characteristic of *Gesellschaft* can be viewed as a kind of gradual "eating away" of the importance of kin relationships. As the institutions develop into separate spheres of activities, they come to specialize in taking care of certain needs, and as they specialize, the family provides less and less for the individual. It is important to realize, however, that individuals do not necessarily choose to relieve their families of importance in these areas. As the overall society changes, it becomes

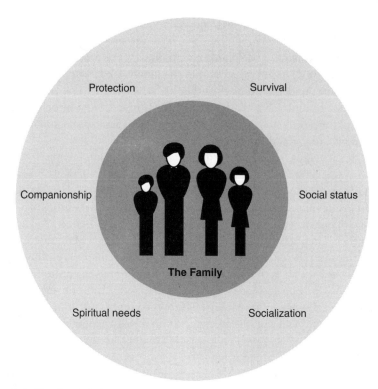

Figure 9.1 Meeting individual needs in *Gemeinschaft:* the multifunctional family.

increasingly impossible for individuals to depend on their families for everything; institutions take over the business of caring for human needs. These personal changes stemming from global social changes continue to consume the interests of sociologists. In his 1992 Presidential Address to the American Sociological Association, James S. Coleman (1993) reflected on such changes, noting the decreasing importance of the family in shaping our lives coupled with the inability of other forms of social organizations to fill this gap.

Social change often forces changes in the lives of many individuals who are unable to withstand them. The spread of *Gesellschaft* around the world prevents third world people from living in their traditional ways, yet the speed with which it is occurring makes the transition extremely difficult; old opportunities evaporate, with few alternatives provided to make the transition bearable (see Clinton-Davis and Fassil, 1992; Copeland, 1992). Part of the explanation for this dilemma comes from the growing complexity of society as industrial development occurs. We can perhaps best understand this development by looking individually at the major institutions that develop: education, economics, politics, religion, and the family in its

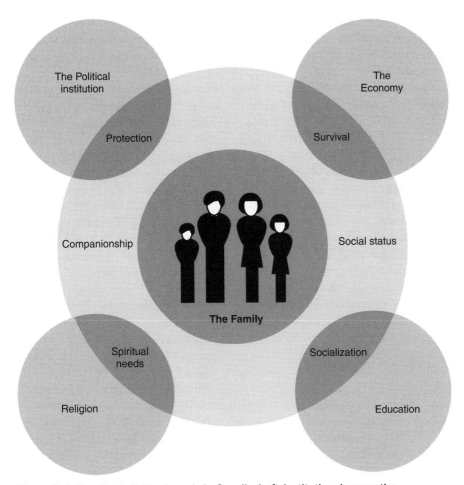

Figure 9.2 Meeting individual needs in *Gesellschaft:* institutional separation.

modern sense. These institutions are discussed briefly in the rest of this chapter. Each is then examined in greater detail in Chapters 10–13.

EDUCATION

Industrial societies require literate and skilled employees to cope with the technological sophistication on which they depend. Relatives may do well at teaching the young how to farm and manage simple crafts, but they fall short when the society needs fewer farmers and more computer technicians. The efficient way to meet this need is to relieve relatives of their educational duties and to encourage the young to consult the specialists of education, who, presumably, know more about the things that need to be learned. The modern institution of education in a typical industrial society consists of teachers, students, classrooms, books, ideas and beliefs concerning the whys and hows of learning, and many more such elements. As it exists today in the United States, the institution of education has become a vast enterprise (both public and private) that is structurally separate from families.

As with all institutions, the separation is not complete. Schools are ultimately controlled by local school boards, the members of which are elected by the public. In addition, parents may opt for a variety of forms of private education (if they can afford it) that may add religion to the curriculum or even alter the basic curriculum itself. In 1974 parents in Charleston, West Virginia, organized a protest over the religious and political content of school textbooks. A similar event occurred in Cobb County, Georgia, in 2002, when the school board decided to place stickers on science textbooks that read, "This textbook contains material on evolution. Evolution is a theory, not a fact, regarding the origin of living things. This material should be approached with an open mind, studied carefully and critically considered." In 2005, a federal judge in Atlanta ruled that the stickers had to be removed as they violated the constitutionally required separation of church and state (CNN, 2005). But such rulings do not erase the conflict.

As the institution of education physically removes children from family settings, it places them into educational settings with other children of their own age. The old one-room schoolhouse with all ages mixed together closely approached a family-style arrangement; modern education, however, uses larger facilities and organizes children by age. As a result of this age segregation, children focus their attention on others of their own age and away from individuals of different ages. Modern education could thus be seen as largely responsible for the growth of the "youth culture" in the United States since World War II. Young people come to develop distinctive lifestyles, habits, and tastes through their age isolation, becoming a distinctive market for certain music, clothes, movies, and other products (both legal and illegal). The more young people focus their interests and activities on their own age group, the less dependent they will be on their families, not only for socialization but for affection and companionship. Needs that once were solidly within the family domain are now partly, if not largely, satisfied by the institution of education and social groups associated with that institution.

THE ECONOMY

Physical survival is clearly a fundamental human need. If a society cannot provide survival for its members, its existence will soon be a faint memory. Recognizing this fact, Lenski organized his society types according to the dominant means used for survival. Whether humans hunt, gather, grow, raise, or manufacture their food, they still must have the means to stay alive. Traditionally, the real strength and necessity of the family lay in providing for the survival of its members. Families may or may not have been sources of love and affection for their members, but they were always work units.

Perhaps the ultimate ideal of the family work unit is the family farm characteristic of an agricultural society. In a society where everyone is responsible for his or her food needs, the family becomes a workable organization for producing that food. It is not so large that the organization of work and the distribution of food become complicated, yet it is not so small that the work cannot be done. The family is not as useful a work unit in an industrial society. As every year goes by in the United States, fewer and fewer people are engaged in agricultural work as the family farm becomes replaced by the agricultural corporation. People do not necessarily leave the family farm out of choice but because their changing society forces that choice upon them; the small-scale family farm is simply not economically competitive (Heck, 1991; Ikerd, 2001).

The problems of the family farm in an industrial society represent more than just a change in agriculture; they represent a fundamental change in the way people survive. The family has ceased to be an effective work unit in all areas of industrial society. In the United States today the "mom and pop" grocery store cannot compete with the supermarket; in general, the family-run business cannot compete with the corporation. As a result, most modern American families have no direct role in the productive economy at all. Income within the family comes from outside the family unit as its members enter the institution of the economy, most typically in a job.

As an institution, the economy is made up of a vast variety of "work" activities, both public and private, and a vastly complicated system of capital that controls investment, credit, interest rates, profits, and wage scales. Even more clearly than with education, to enter the world of the economy is to leave the family behind. The emotions and loyalties that characterize family relations seem out of place in the world of work. Corporations may fire an individual with little thought of the effects of unemployment on that individual's family. They may also subject the individual to hazardous work conditions or insist on a transfer across the country if it serves the interests of the corporation. The world of the economy seems to follow its own momentum; individuals may get on or off at their own risk.

Perhaps the greatest irony in comparing the family with the institution of the economy comes from the needs of the economy itself. Whereas the family used to be an economic necessity for an individual, it is now actually a hindrance. Children on a family farm were necessary for getting the work done, but children in an industrial society become a large expense for their wage-earning parents. Not surprisingly, industrial societies, wherever they are found, result in smaller families. In addition, the flexibility demanded by the economy in an industrial society can be a problem to the marriage relationship, particularly if both partners work. Consider the problems, for example, if one spouse is transferred when the other isn't. Beyond being a source of new workers, the family is not highly important in keeping the economy alive; instead of producing goods, the modern family relates to the modern economy more by consuming goods.

In highly industrialized societies, the division of labor gives rise to highly specialized jobs. These groundskeepers, for instance, know exactly what is required to maintain a baseball field and to build a pitcher's mound to exact specifications.

GOVERNMENT AND POLITICS

Next to survival—perhaps a fundamental part of it—protection is a basic human need. Food was probably the first necessity of early humans, but having a sheltered place to eat it probably came second. Considering that we need shelter from both the elements and other humans, protection can be seen as a fundamental human need for society to fill.

In a hunting and gathering (or *Gemeinschaft*) type of society one of the basic tasks of the family unit is to provide protection for its members. Very large extended families often attain their size for the same reason societies raise large armies—the more soldiers you have, the more protection you can provide. Individuals can live through the day relatively safely knowing that a great many other individuals will be at their side should they need help. The loyal ties characteristic of family relations make that help particularly valuable since it is dependable. In particular, the large family provides protection against the worst foe that humans have—other humans. A potential enemy will be less likely to attack knowing that an attack on one person will bring about the retaliation of a great many relatives.

The protective aspect of the family can be most clearly seen in the institution of marriage, and many such aspects still remain (at least symbolically) in marriage in modern industrial societies. Some societies require their members to select a spouse from a neighboring community. Such rules keep families large by constantly bringing in new relatives. This function of marriage can be seen today in the traditional marriage ceremony, where the groom's family sits on one side of the aisle and the bride's family on the other side; as the bride and groom are joined, the two parts of the community are joined together. In the past, the marriage partner's family was really of more importance than the marriage partner himself or herself. In the United States today we leave marriage largely up to the bride and groom. One reason we do is that the family is no longer important for protection.

In an industrial society the political institution provides official protection for the individuals. The political institution in such a society consists of any activities, beliefs, or ideas that relate to what we generally call government. Thus, we would include police, laws, jails, judges, constitutions, elections, prisoners, and, to some extent, feelings of patriotism. Like every other institution, it also limits the rights of persons or other institutions to fulfill its function. If you have a complaint against another individual in the United States, your only legal recourse is to turn your complaint over to some official in the political institution. Taking care of the problem yourself (taking the law into your own hands) will result in your society having a complaint against you, no matter how justified you might be. Your government does not see fit to allow you to make that decision without its help. If you have been robbed, its representatives will catch and punish the culprit (if they wish), but you may not.

As with education and the economy, government specializes in fulfilling a few basic needs and developing a whole sphere of activities and ideas that are separate from those of other spheres. The simplicity of turning to your uncle for help has been replaced by elaborate systems of laws and legal procedures that specify the ways individuals and groups of individuals may legally relate. As is typical of *Gesellschaft*, your help now comes from strangers.

RELIGION

Whereas the institutions we have looked at so far respond largely to the physical and practical needs of humans, religion responds to people's spiritual needs. In an industrial society such as the United States the institution of religion would include religious functionaries (priests, ministers, rabbis, and the like), laypeople, churches, beliefs, Bibles, hymns, parochial schools, and church socials, to name just a few elements. The United States offers a variety of religious activities and beliefs, but they are all remarkably similar in the way they provide their activities and beliefs as a separate sphere outside the family.

In the United States, religion is more closely tied to the institution of the family than are education, the economy, or government (although it is tied to all). Religions generally support (while attempting to influence) the family structure and are in turn dependent on families for their support. Many significant family activities and events occur through or with the aid of religious functions, including baptisms, Bar Mitzvahs, marriage ceremonies, and funerals. Nevertheless, a fundamental boundary separates family activities and religious activities in our society. When the family blends its activities into religious activities, it must adhere to the rules and regulations of the religion it follows; like other institutions, religion provides "specialists" who presumably know what's best.

In a *Gemeinschaft*-type society without institutional separation, religious activities and beliefs are integrated through the daily lives of the people who adhere to them. By contrast, it is possible in the United States, for example, to preach charity

Even though the religious institution in modern times is embodied in large organizations, it still depends on families to make up its congregations and give it strength. Shown here is a Catholic church filled to overflowing for a blessing of the animals.

on Sunday and then return to cutthroat business dealing the other six days; institutional separation makes this possible and even reasonable to the individuals concerned. In *Gemeinschaft,* religion is inseparable from everyday life, as part of an agricultural endeavor or basic to a social gathering.

If religious specialists developed in a *Gemeinschaft,* the first such specialists might typically be certain family members. For example, the religion might specify that a father, an aunt, or an uncle be in charge of religious education. The family individual in charge of economic and protection decisions (likely an elder) might also be in charge of religious decisions. In fact, these three decisions would probably be seen as one, for it is only our institutional separation in the United States that makes us see such things as separate. Today, religions generally request that religious decisions be made by religious people who specialize in such decisions. The family looks outside itself for religious leadership.

THE CHANGING FAMILY

We come finally to the *family,* the last of the five basic social institutions. Although the needs it fulfills have steadily dwindled, the family is still the most basic institution and probably still the most important. Before the school sees the child, the basic work of socialization (whether good or ill) has been accomplished within the family. Even with the increasing use of day care, the family unit is still the greatest force in socialization.

Families provide for the creation as well as the raising of children; however, they are not necessary for either. For instance, there have always been children born out of wedlock, and in the United States today illegitimacy is far from the social stigma it once was. Furthermore, single-parent families are increasing continually as divorce rates rise. As remarriage occurs, complex multiple families are constructed, frequently including one or two sets of stepparents and stepsiblings. Although this may sound confusing, it is hardly as complicated as some of the extended families characteristic of *Gemeinschaft*-type societies. Clearly, our traditional definition of a family as mom, dad, and the kids is in for some change.

In the United States today we generally treat children in relation to the status of their parents. Thus, the children of rich parents are often seen as more valuable and important than the children of poor parents. (These conceptions are particularly important when teachers hold them.) Although the family determines the entering (or beginning) status of the child, the child may be able to change status during his or her lifetime through achievement; industrial societies are typically less rigid in this regard than more traditional societies, where no one ever forgets your roots.

Families are also still an important source of affection and companionship. Although they are no longer the only such source, the growth of voluntary associations and singles apartments doesn't appear to be capable of replacing the family. This function of the family seems all the more apparent today with the rise in the number of childless marriages in the United States; individuals presumably enter such marriages for the sole purpose of companionship.

Finally, the family also fulfills part of a wide variety of needs, although it sometimes creates as many problems as it solves. When no one will lend you a dollar, not even the friendly loan company on TV, perhaps a relative will. On the other hand, a relative may want to borrow from you and never pay you back. When your physical well-being is threatened by a fellow citizen, perhaps a family member will give you a hand before the police arrive. Family members may also, however, be responsible for threatening you in the first place. Many homicides and assaults are committed by relatives; increasing child abuse is often cited as responsible for the millions of teenage runaways each year, along with a high level of juvenile delinquency (Kaufman and Widom, 1999; Tyler et al., 2000).

When your teacher has neither the time nor the interest (or maybe even the skill) to teach you something, perhaps a wise relation will share some knowledge or a skill. And when you doubt the meaning of it all, the caring of your family may have more impact on you than the ministrations of an organized religion. As Figure 9.2 suggests, the family may have lost primary control over the satisfaction of many needs, but it has not lost total control over any of them. The family is perhaps the only institution still searching for its area of specialization and willing to do a little of everything in the meantime.

UNDERSTANDING SOCIETY THROUGH INSTITUTIONS

Institutions provide the sociologist with units of manageable size for analysis. The complex division of labor that characterizes any *Gesellschaft*-type society complicates the sociologist's job. We know something about how people are affected by their group affiliations, but how do we trace those effects when the individual seems lost in the sea of affiliations? The wife and mother who works, prays, joins the PTA, and runs for political office, along with cleaning house and cooking the Thanksgiving turkey, is an increasingly common phenomenon in the United States. The concept of institution directs the sociologist to separate the spheres of those activities along their natural boundaries, allowing for a clearer perspective on the division of labor as well as providing some insight into the effects on individuals of each institution. If the wife and mother becomes obsessed with political injustice, for example, the concept of institution would suggest not only where she probably got those ideas but also the arenas of her life in which she is likely to express them.

Chapters 10 through 13 take us through an exploration of the five major institutions of American society, providing a more detailed picture of how those institutions function and the problems that occur within them. As we explore them, the interrelations among them will also become more apparent. Chapter 10 takes us back to the family for a closer look and is followed by an examination of education in Chapter 11. Chapter 12 examines religion, and Chapter 13 completes the series with an analysis of the economy and the political institution. Taken together, these chapters will give you a view of sociology "at work" on understanding social problems within their institutional contexts.

SUMMARY

Technology plays a major role in the kinds of organization found in a society. Societies that live by hunting and gathering are typically small because of the physical mobility required by their technology. Horticultural and agrarian societies—those that produce their own food—typically grow much larger and develop more elaborate forms of social organization based on an increased division of labor. The greater efficiency of food production that characterizes them permits the growth of social differences, as certain members of the society gain control over the surplus produced. Industrial societies are characterized by urban life, an extremely complex division of labor, large size, powerful governments, and elaborate technology.

As technology changes, so do forms of social organization. The smaller, less technologically developed societies may be classified as *Gemeinschaft;* the larger, more technologically developed societies may be classified as *Gesellschaft.* The change from the former to the latter results in an increase in purely economic social arrangements and impersonal social relationships.

Gesellschaft-type societies are characterized by institutional separation. Institutions are spheres of interrelated activities within a society that focus on the satisfaction of specific human needs. The five basic institutions in a modern industrial society are education, religion, the economy, politics, and the family. Each contains a separate body of activities, ideas, values, and physical objects that differentiate it from other institutions. The modern individual acts within all institutions. At the same time that institutions are separate, however, definite interrelations obviously occur among them, so that changes in one result in changes in the others.

GLOSSARY

Gemeinschaft As defined by Ferdinand Tönnies, a traditional or communal society characterized by small size, a simple division of labor, and a strong sense of shared values.

Gesellschaft As defined by Ferdinand Tönnies, a society characterized by an emphasis on economic interests, considerable group diversity, and impersonal social relationships.

Institution A cluster (or sphere) of interrelated activities within a society coupled with the knowledge, beliefs, and objects that relate to those activities. Institutions are typically stable configurations of social forms that meet social needs in specific areas.

Social stratification The arrangement of different activities (or roles) into a hierarchy whereby activities ranked high are highly rewarded and activities ranked low are poorly rewarded. The rewards generally consist of money, prestige, and influence over others.

STUDY QUESTIONS

1. What historical changes does Lenski see as having developed in societies as a result of technological change? In particular, what argument does he make for the relationship among technology, the production of surplus, and the growth of social stratification?

2. Describe the differences between Tönnies's *Gemeinschaft* and *Gesellschaft*. How do they compare to Lenski's society types?

3. What is a social institution? Why are they characteristic of *Gesellschaft* (or industrial) societies but not the other types?

4. Explain in detail how industrial societies require the growth and separation of institutions such as education, the political institution, religion, and the economy.

5. How has the role of the family changed from *Gemeinschaft* (or agricultural) societies to *Gesellschaft* (or industrial) societies?

Eric Brende

TECHNOLOGY AMISH STYLE

As we've seen in this chapter, industrialization brings about society-wide changes as it changes our technology and our economic systems. It changes the scope of knowledge, the division of labor, and the functions of the family. But even within a classic *Gesellschaft* society like the United States, you can still find small *Gemeinschaft* islands here and there where many outside changes are kept out. One such island is the Amish communities in the eastern United States, where a small religious minority still follows many old ways of life just as strictly as they follow their religion. In the following reading, Eric Brende shares his firsthand experience with one Amish community. Some of what he will tell you will come as no surprise to anyone who has even a small knowledge of the Amish; other Brende observations will probably be very surprising. As the title suggests, the Amish don't totally ignore technology just because they choose to ignore most of the industrial world's technology.

When it comes to technology, the Amish aren't really close-minded, just choosy. And given the success of their way of life, we might want to take some lessons from them.

We were busily working, the Amish crew and I, dismantling an old house to gather a cheap lumber supply. The wood would be used for a new dwelling now partially completed on the southeast slope of my recently purchased property. After a year and a half living amongst the Amish, my wife Mary and I have decided to stay, and although we have declined to join the Amish church, our "advisory board"—a plain-dressed widower and his four grown children—has ex-

ceeded what we thought possible in their friendliness and eagerness to assist.

"Eric . . . !" someone was calling to me. "Maybe you could come over here and do this for us." What special task have they singled out for me? I wondered. I tiptoed across the exposed floor joists and looked. On the floor below, one of my new Amish friends gazed up plaintively and pointed to an overhead light fixture near my feet. "Could you please take those lights down?" he asked. I suppressed a giggle. I no more knew how to take apart an electric light than how to tie a double halfhitch. Did he actually suppose that because I had grown up in an electrified environment I knew how electric lights were put together?

In fact, he might well have made such an assumption. In many or most Amish settlements, everyone does know how to do everything. Many women know carpentry, including the daughter in the family that was helping me tear down the old house and build the new one. The other day I happened upon an Amish wife sawing boards for a piece of furniture she was building. Cabinetry is her hobby. Simply speaking, most work demands that have been broken down into innumerable fields of specialization in modern technological culture have remained whole among the Amish. Families will fail to make ends meet unless all household members know how to do sundry inter-connected tasks—among them growing, preserving, and preparing for the table most of their food; constructing and maintaining homes; making clothes; and often even medicating themselves.

Underlying the reluctance to specialize is an awareness of how well shared know-how helps keep Amish society stable. Without it, how could Amish neighbors so readily join together in under-takings such as tearing down or building a house? Or threshing wheat? This is not to say the Amish are necessarily experts in each of the tasks to which they aspire. "I don't do anything long enough to get good at it," an Amish fellow once told me with a self-effacing chuckle. Still, the extent of their mastery is considerable. A glance at their efforts reveals beautiful, well-maintained farms thriving in an age when many others can-not even survive. Inhabitants of what seems to be a provincial backwater, the Amish turn out to be surprisingly enlightened, at least with regard to the material conditions of their life. Next to them I feel sheltered from the world around me.

I feel oddly ungrounded as well. Life in a fast-paced society is next to impossible without nar-rowing one's focus—few of us have the time to learn the inner workings of such conveniences-cum-necessities as cars and computers—and it is axiomatic that in narrowing one's focus one can lose sight of the larger picture. But that's not the only problem. New developments continu-ally evolve in the myriad areas that this narrowed focus excludes. The result is that people are often plagued by what seems like uncontrollable change.

The Amish, by contrast, consciously steer their cultural course in the sea of alternatives opened by technological advance, accepting only those that enhance their way of life. If the Amish plead ignorant on the subject of electrical wiring, for instance, it is because they have made an active decision not to avail themselves of the technology. Installing electricity would only permit them to plug in clever contraptions that could, at the push of a button, shift much skilled work away from them, reducing the need for shared know-how and the opportunities for community building.

Word of how successful the Amish way of life can be is spreading, and for not a few, curiosity has enkindled conversion. In the community near us, I can think of at least 10 separate parties, either individuals or families, who have initiated the process of baptism into the Amish church. But I doubt that it is necessary to embrace the Amish religion to attain their community cohe-sion or their sense of connection to the material world.

A TRADITION OF INNOVATING

The full extent of the differences between Amish society and mainstream America becomes clear every time the Amish council near us meets. Mem-bers present are allowed to speak their minds on any matter before the community: since everyone has intimate knowledge of how the whole of Amish life works, everyone is considered compe-tent to volunteer insights and ideas as well as assist in decisions. If anyone has clout, it's prin-cipally because of experience—first speaking rights go to older members. The practice of draw-ing lots for central Amish leadership positions underscores people's confidence in their mutual abilities.

Interestingly, one of the recurring items on the agenda is technology. Unlike mainstream technol-ogists, who never test the social impact of their products but unscientifically presume a beneficial effect, the Amish often adopt new technologies only after a trial period in which they assess the effects. For example, when members of the local community began using a nearby pay phone to facilitate sales of produce to regional grocery-store chains, a council was called to discuss the possible ramifications. Participants pointed out that lightning-fast communication across the miles was undermining the face-to-face intimacy so important to their community. But they also observed that without the phone they would be at a competitive disadvantage among suppliers to grocery stores, which prefer up-to-the-minute information on shipments. Out of this dilemma came the decision to urge only sparing use of the phone.

At times the Amish actually promote technological development. After all, some technologies help perpetuate a tight-knit community. The Pioneer Maid wood cookstove is a case in point: conceived by two Amish brothers, Elmo and Mark Stoll of Aylmer, Ontario, and now produced by an Amish factory, it was the first wood cookstove in North America to employ an airtight combustion compartment. The only significant advance in household wood-fired stoves in 300 years, it efficiently cooks food, heats a water supply, raises bread dough, dries vegetables, and warms 2,000 square feet of living space all at the same time. The stove does require a sizable repertoire of domestic skills and knowledge to operate, but because everyone needs to operate it, vital resources and activities remain in the purview of the community and help hold it together.

Similarly, an Amish blacksmith in Indiana has refitted the motor-driven John Deere 24-T hay baler with a slick assemblage of gears, drive-chains, and a steel wheel from the 1940 vintage W-30 International Tractor. Unlike the balers used by the Amish everywhere else, which are drawn along by horses but use fuel-powered engines for the actual task of baling, this one is powered entirely by horses. And in the community next to us, Amish farmers have resurrected an old stationary threshing machine. They salvaged the transmission of a junked cement truck and fitted it with wooden shafts that fanned out from the hub. Five teams of two horses each are hitched to the shafts, and when they move forward, horse-power is redirected along a rubber belt that connects the transmission with the threshing machine. Having threshed with the innovative Amish crew two summers in a row, I can avow that the contraption leaves ample work to bond together a gang of laborers.

Indeed, the Amish were, from their beginnings in seventeenth-century Europe, leaders and innovators in agricultural techniques. While most Alsatian peasants were still using the sickle, the Amish had moved to the more efficient scythe, which allowed a greater range of motion and required less stooping. They were also forerunners in practices like rotating crops, irrigating meadows, and using clover and alfalfa to build up the soil. Hoping to improve the productivity of the land in their jurisdictions, progressive eighteenth-century noblemen enticed the Amish to settle in Poland and Russia, while more recently Mexico, Belize, and Paraguay have welcomed Amish immigrants with open arms.

Even though traditionalism may prevail among the Amish, often the tradition itself is one of tinkering, adaptation, and innovation. Ivan Glick, a farmer and writer especially interested in agricultural history, points to the large number of surprisingly competent self-taught engineers in the Amish settlement of Lancaster County, Pa. And in some cases where the Amish have resisted technology, history has vindicated them. For instance, they have been the living cornerstone for a nation-wide return to horse farming, which they have proven is "much more profitable than tractor farming if done correctly," according to agricultural industry observer Baron Taylor of Lancaster County. Though feasible only if the scale is not too large, the practice keeps capital costs low and promotes sustainable soil management, enhancing land value and use. The number of non-Amish horse farmers has tripled over the last 20 years and now exceeds that of the Amish.

More striking than Amish technical command, however, is Amish emotional health. According to a study by psychiatrist Janice Egeland, Amish people suffer nonorganically based depression at a small fraction of the national rate. And then there's the strong Amish family. The Amish divorce rate is next to nil, and only about one in four Amish offspring leaves the community.

While there are doubtless a variety of reasons for such impressive statistics, my firsthand acquaintance with the Amish leads me to believe that copossession of vital know-how is certainly one of them. It helps unite spouses by giving women a fuller sense of partnership in the overall household enterprise and a more visible, respected place in the community. I suspect that it also puts parents in an excellent position to be parents—to instill emotional stability and adult responsibility in their progeny. Amish parents are their children's primary educators, employers, and financiers—a position that would hardly be possible if they had not acquired the lion's share of the society's knowledge.

The work of child psychologist Urie Bronfenbrenner reinforces this notion. In his book *Two Worlds of Childhood* comparing child-rearing practices in the United States and the Soviet Union, Bronfenbrenner asserts that children who can meaningfully participate in the world of adult work enjoy far greater psychological well-being than children deprived of such participation—and so do the adults those children become.

BRAVE NEW BOUNDARIES

Unusual as the Amish may seem, their roots are not very much different from those of mainstream society, which may help explain why some conversions to their way of life succeed. Sociologist Max Weber employed the term "Protestant ethic" to account for the meticulous industry widely in evidence among Calvinists and their cultural descendants, including white Anglo-Saxon Protestants. It could be argued that this industry has been duplicated by the Amish in agriculture. Historically, both Calvinism and the Amish church have sparked behavior that suggests a close psychological tie between earthly works and personal salvation. Perhaps the key

difference between the two religions is the greater Amish emphasis on membership in Christian community, which they see as a prerequisite for redemption. Amish theology, far more than Calvinist, provides religious incentives for channeling industry into social solidarity.

Conversion is an uphill battle, however. One youth I know who was about 22 when he entered the local Amish church became dismayed at the amount of catching up he had to do, and not just in the area of knowhow and skill. His Amish friends received help and money from their parents, enabling them to buy buggies and save up for marriage and a farm. Without similar support from his own parents, who lived several hundred miles away and had none of the same resources, he languished. He finally left—but not without heartache, for he had grown attached to the community and its ideals.

The Amish stress on religious dogma is another reason why converts may leave. The list of possible complaints, to be sure, can be daunting: that Amish religious indoctrination of the young generally leaves little room for critical or creative thought; that the traditionalism informing every sphere of Amish activity can inhibit even common sense; that the practice of shunning adult backsliders is unduly harsh; that baptism into the Amish faith, while ostensibly voluntary, is expected by parents when a child comes of age and virtually foreordained; and that, in short, the survival of Amish culture can be attributed less to anything positive than to inertia and the fear of change and reprisal. Amish expert John Hostetler, quoting a formerly Amish woman, notes that "in Amish society one is always conscious of keeping as many rules as one can, and each person tends to feel an obligation to see that other members of the family also keep these rules."

On the other hand, it is worth remembering that it was the Amish themselves who set up the rules, and that their efforts have borne fruit in a flourishing handicraft civilization and an oasis of religious sentiment. As Hostetler himself remarks, "conformity implies that persons are committed to the goals and means of their culture, voluntarily accept them, and live in a state of commitment to the appropriate rewards."

Yet while religion is inextricably interwoven with Amish practice for the Amish themselves, for the rest of us such issues can be kept more distinct. My wife and I are in the midst of an attempt to initiate an alternative to Amish community that is less enmeshed with dogma. Chary of religious codes of technological enforcement, we nonetheless appreciate the need such measures address: that of conscious boundary setting, backed by some kind of clout. Without some such boundaries, seekers of alternative lifestyles could easily drift and re-merge with the practices they have set out to avoid. Several other communities already in existence in this country employ one or another method of common discipline: land trust or coop or commune. For our part, we are trying to translate the Amish religious codes into deed restrictions, aiming for a kind of low-technology zoning. By legally limiting electric and telephone lines, as well as motorized farming and woodcutting devices, we aim to help establish on a circumscribed space nonsectarian guideposts for the kind of social stability the Amish enjoy.

In other words, we hope for the best of both worlds: a reliable structure for neighborly solidarity without the pincers of theological sanction. This is not to say that we have disallowed religion. In fact, we are practicing Catholics ourselves. But we do not wish to make religious belief the basis of technological norms. We welcome anyone who shares a desire for technological simplicity.

Other ways to further the same ends might include a summer internship program in homesteading for college students, or a school for homesteading apprentices that would complement the conventional liberal arts curriculum. Plunging into the nitty-gritty versatility our ancestors once shared, students would pick up new skills, enhancing, shall we say, their career options. The Cabin Fever University at Celo, N.C., the Shelter Institute of Bath, Maine, and the Christ-

ian Homesteading Movement of Oxford, N.Y., are already pursuing this idea. I hope one day to inaugurate something similar here on our own homestead—if I ever know enough to do it.

But even in the absence of such opportunities, the mere example of Amish settlements is instructive. In a world whose rapid changes give credence to the notion of unstoppable "progress," the Amish remind us of what may have helped to propel much of that progress: Francis Bacon's dictum that knowledge is power. Amish successes are an index of what we can achieve by attempting to integrate practical knowledge and social intimacy. They teach us not that the modern world can or should somehow be ignored, but that within it—even as part of its own program—something vital from the past may persist. And perhaps even nose ahead of the present.

DISCUSSION QUESTIONS

1. Brende notes that most members of an Amish community know virtually all the information and skills that other members know; there is no division of labor in the modern society sense, where individuals specialize in one area of work or knowledge and have little experience outside their world. Brende suggests that this lack of division of labor (and knowledge) helps hold the Amish community together. What do you think of his argument?

2. The Amish people accept some American technology, reject much of it, and improve on some of it. What tests must technology pass before it becomes acceptable to the Amish?

3. Brende notes that many people consider the strict rules of the Amish community harsh and sometimes unforgiving. Yet he also credits those rules with helping to hold the community together. Is it possible to have one without the other?

THE FAMILY

S ociologists study the family as an institution to better understand how its structure and the changing activities that occur within it affect its members' lives. As with all institutions, the family does not exist in a vacuum. At the same time the family affects members' lives, it is affected in turn by the wider society and must change in response to those more general social forces. As just one example (which we examine further), changes in the economy can make it necessary for women to spend more and more of their time outside the home in the labor force. Such changes in role affect not only the women directly involved but their husbands and children as well. In its approach to the modern family as an institution, sociology attempts to provide a better understanding of why families change and how those changes affect individuals.

ELEMENTS OF FAMILY LIFE

No two family structures are ever exactly alike, but their variation seems to occur along certain dimensions rather than randomly. Among other things, families vary in size, authority relations, numbers of spouses involved, and the way spouses are selected. We first discuss some general patterns that appear cross-culturally in family structures, then examine the centerpiece relationship of the family: marriage.

PATTERNS OF FAMILY LIFE

Variation in size is perhaps the most basic dimension of family life encountered in cultures around the world. In the smallest unit, the **nuclear family** contains only two spouses and their immature offspring. An increasingly common variation on the nuclear family is the single-parent family, in which one of the parents (usually the father) is missing. Although nuclear family members typically note and give importance to other kin relationships, the primary focus of attention is on the marriage relationship and the parent-child relationship. Another form of family structure is the **extended family**, which includes a number of related nuclear families that live together as one unit. Extended families can become quite large. Some cultures, such as that of the United States, lean toward the nuclear family as the common unit,

Family patterns vary greatly from culture to culture. In the United States and most Western cultures, the basic pattern is the nuclear family—parents and children.

whereas other cultures contain more extended families. In general, nuclear families are more typical of industrial societies; extended families provide many services for their members (such as economic support and protection) that are provided by other sources in industrial society. Moreover, the urban life and high geographical mobility characteristic of industrial societies make stable extended families difficult to maintain. It should be remembered, however, that kin ties outside the nuclear family can be important in even the most industrialized societies (we explore this importance later in this chapter).

Individuals alter their relationship to the family unit as they age, whether they reside in a culture that emphasizes the nuclear family or one that favors the extended family. The child is a member of a **family of orientation:** parents and siblings provide for the child's basic socialization, thereby "orienting" him or her to life in the wider society. Although the family of orientation becomes less important as the child grows into maturity, its early central role in shaping the individual gives it a critical importance throughout the life course of that individual. For example, child abuse in the family of orientation can lead that child to grow into a parent who in turn abuses children. The family of orientation is often complemented later in life by the **family of procreation,** in which the individual raises children; this parental role is typically (although by no means always) coupled with the role of spouse.

Authority within the family unit is of critical importance and varies cross-culturally. In a **patriarchal family,** men (sometimes the oldest male) have the authority; in a **matriarchal family,** women govern; and in an **egalitarian family,** men and women share the decision making. The patriarchal family is by far the most common across cultures. Matriarchies are rare in that few if any cultures provide women with such regularized institutional authority. They can arise when male authority figures are absent. The egalitarian family is found most typically in industrial or postindustrial societies where new economic roles have been extended to women. Economic independence for women tends to weaken the monopoly on authority characteristic of a patriarchy. American families have traditionally been patriarchal but are becoming increasingly egalitarian.

Tracing descent within the family varies from one culture to another. In cultures that practice a **patrilineal descent,** one's identity is defined entirely through the father's line, and, perhaps more important, inheritance is passed along only through the father's side. Such systems are fundamental for the status-bestowing function of the family. By contrast, a system of **matrilineal descent** bestows identity and wealth through the mother's side. While it might appear that matrilineal tracing of descent would be coupled with matriarchal authority in the family, there is no necessary connection. In a matrilineal system, wealth may always be in the hands of men but simply passed along through the woman's line. For example, a boy might inherit from his mother's brother. Finally, in **bilineal descent** both lines are used for tracing identity and bestowing inheritance. Typically, the American family uses the bilineal system, even though our surnames come to us in a patrilineal fashion because most women change their names upon marriage. A woman who keeps her maiden name (her father's surname) simply moves the process back one generation without fundamentally altering it. Naming is symbolic of descent tracing, but bilineal naming can become extremely cumbersome.

The residence of newly married individuals varies cross-culturally from **patrilocal residence** (in which the newlyweds move in with or near the husband's family) to **matrilocal residence** (in which the happy couple locates with or near the wife's family). **Neolocal residence** patterns find the bride and groom in a new place of residence separate from either of their families. The norm in American culture is neolocal residence for newlyweds whenever possible.

Social changes in the United States over the last fifty years have created larger numbers of alternative family structures. Increased divorce rates coupled with remarriage have produced larger numbers of **step families** in which one or both of the parents are not the biological parents of the children. Those same divorce rates, coupled with sexual relations out of wedlock, have produced **single-parent families** in which children are raised by only one parent. Currently, 82 percent of those families are headed by women (U.S. Bureau of the Census, 2004a). When neither parent is available for raising children, **grandparent families** often fill the vacuum. These family types can also be combined in virtually any combination. A family of four might consist of a grandparent and a single parent of one child who is also a stepparent of another child.

In addition to families linked by biology and marriage, the United States has also seen an increase in **foster care families.** Foster care families are designed to protect children who have been abused, neglected, or abandoned; they also provide temporary protection of children whose parents are temporarily unable to care for them. Foster parents work for and with the state to provide either temporary or long-term care of children. In some cases, foster parents permanently adopt their foster children.

PATTERNS OF MARRIAGE AND MATE SELECTION

Perhaps the most fundamental variation found cross-culturally in marriage is in the number of spouses involved. **Monogamy** is a marriage between one man and one woman. Extra participants produce **polygyny** (the marriage of one man and two or more women) or **polyandry** (the marriage of one woman and two or more men). Of the three, polygyny is by far the most common. One study found that polygyny was permitted in 83 percent of the cultures surveyed, while monogamy was the ideal in fewer than 20 percent (Murdock, 1967). It should be noted, however, that permitting polygyny does not necessarily mean that it will be the most prevalent form of marriage in a given culture; typically, only the wealthiest men have more than one wife. At the other extreme, polyandry is rare, even in those societies in which it is permissible. And when it does appear, it is not typically in a matriarchy. In polyandry it is more common for women to be shared among men who, more often than not, have kin ties to one another. Finally, monogamy makes up for its lack of historical and cross-cultural popularity by being the dominant marriage form found in industrial societies.

All cultures regulate mate selection to some degree. Rules of **exogamy** specify the group outside of which an individual must choose a mate. In American society, these rules coincide with cultural norms concerning incest (see Chapter 3); that is, the rules name individuals deemed too closely related for consideration as marriage partners. An American is supposed to look beyond his or her first cousin for a prospective spouse. Rules of exogamy in other cultures are often more extensive; in fact, one's whole community may be declared off-limits for marriage. Such rules, which force individuals to look elsewhere, can create important economic and political ties for the community through its members' marriages.

Rules of **endogamy** specify the group inside of which an individual must choose a mate. In American society, it was once illegal in most states to marry anyone not in one's racial group. While such laws are no longer around, many of the same cultural expectations remain. In 2002, for example, only 1,674,000 of 57,919,000 married couples in America were interracial, making up only 2.9 percent of the total couples. That figure represents a significant increase since 1970, however, when only 310,000 (or 0.7 percent) of the then 44,597,000 total married couples were interracial (U.S. Bureau of the Census, 1995, 2004a). While the rules of endogamy prohibiting interracial marriage in the United States are weakening, they are still clearly in force for most people. We also find rules of endogamy specifying marriage inside of one's religious group and even within one's social class. In short, any expectation that you marry someone "like yourself" represents a rule of endogamy.

Marriage between people with the same social characteristics is termed **homogamy.** In American society, we tend to focus more on achieved status than on ascribed status when we define "homogamy" for ourselves; we are more likely to marry someone of equal educational background, for example, than we are to marry someone whose parents' social status matches our own parents' status (Kalmijn, 1991). Rules of endogamy, along with the structure of American society (such as the isolation of social classes described in Chapter 7), tend to place most of us in homogamous marriages. Cupid is apparently quite selective about the destinations of his arrows. Figure 10.1 provides a graphic representation of how the rules of exogamy and endogamy structure the social world of spouse selection.

In many cultures, mate selection is deemed far too important to be left in the hands of the prospective mates. As we have seen, the family is an institution with many functions, and when parents select spouses for their children, they keep many of those functions in mind. Whether or not mate selection is in the hands of the prospective mates, not all cultures accept the notion of romantic love that dominates mate selection in the United States. Romance is hardly new to the world, but its spread as a value to all social classes (not just the elite with time to write sonnets) plus its connection with mate selection is a modern phenomenon, arising in industrial society. Romantic love is probably not the best basis on which to build a marriage, because it seldom lasts in face of the fundamental day-to-day demands of family life. In any case, society's hand tends to point Cupid's arrow at "suitable" partners. People very different from ourselves more often irritate than fascinate us, making romance and marriage an unlikely outcome.

SOCIAL CHANGE AND THE AMERICAN FAMILY

Social change in American society directly affects the American family. Most notably, changes in the economy have created new opportunities for (and demands on) American women. And as women have changed, so have the men to whom they are married. Sociologists of the family have been extremely interested in tracing some of these changes in an attempt to understand the new family patterns that have resulted and the changing values that accompany them. In this section, we examine some of the effects of social change on sex roles within the family and changes in the value placed on children.

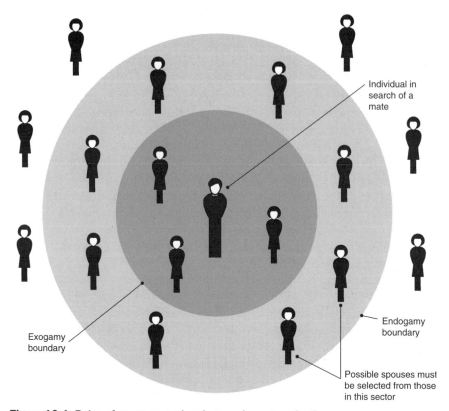

Figure 10.1 Rules of exogamy and endogamy in mate selection.

CHANGING ROLES IN THE AMERICAN FAMILY

The average age of Americans at their first marriage has been steadily rising since the mid-1960s. In 1994, the median age at first marriage was 26.7 for men and 24.5 for women—higher than any previously recorded level (U.S. Bureau of the Census, 1996b). Between 1990 and 2002, the percentage of never-married Americans rose from 22.2 percent to 24.4 percent (U.S. Bureau of the Census, 2004a). This increase has been greater for women than for men, which suggests that some of the social forces creating this change are focused on women. One of the sex-specific forces that has caused women to delay or avoid marriage is greater economic opportunity (Gottfried and Gottfried, 1988; Oppenheimer, 1988; Teachman and Schollaert, 1989).

The same opportunities that encourage women to delay marriage for education and career advancement also encourage them to remain in the labor market after marriage. Today, close to 70 percent of all American married couples have both members in the labor force. Nevertheless, women typically earn 74 percent of what their husbands earn. Initially, these two-income families were couples who lived with the assumption that the husband's work is more important when priorities come into conflict (McRae, 1991). Today, more married men and women are coming to alter their traditional views regarding the gender role of the family breadwinner (Zuo and Tang, 2000).

Family values relating to gender roles both at home and at work have changed, offering support for the new roles required by a changing society. In television programs that depict family life, for example, the homemaker mothers that dominated those programs in the 1950s have now been largely replaced with more independent women's roles. On the other hand, such values change slowly, often bringing up the rear of social change; Bridges and Orza (1992) found that college students disapproved of mothers of infants going out to work, particularly if those mothers' reason for working was personal growth rather than financial necessity. The traditional woman's role of nurturing infants is clearly ingrained in our American value system.

Women who spend more time at work have less time to spend on the home activities of the traditional women's role. Because women have traditionally had primary responsibility for childrearing, their unavailability has created a near-crisis

Changing women's roles in the workplace have brought about significant changes in women's family roles.

socially—at least in the United States. The United States is distinctive among indus-trial nations for the exceptionally small role the federal government plays in provid-ing child-care facilities or subsidizing their costs. Regulations to ensure the quality of such facilities are also minimal, and some psychologists were concerned that chil-dren's social and intellectual development might suffer. In spite of these obstacles, however, all indications are that the children of working mothers develop with few differences from the children of mothers who stay at home; the key factor in pro-ducing normal development in such families appears to be a combination of ade-quate funds in the family plus a parent's spending of "quality time" with the child (Gottfried and Gottfried, 1988). Although some of that "quality time" is provided by fathers, many fathers are selective in the form of their involvement; they prefer to specialize in the less routine aspects of child care—a trip to the zoo rather than changing diapers (Pleck, 1985). Fathers are also likely to become involved in chil-dren's sports activities. Such activities sometimes *decrease* the likelihood that the father will become involved in more routine child care, however (Coltrane and Adams, 2001).

If the husbands of working women have a somewhat checkered record with regard to child care, their efforts at housework are even less impressive. One of the most common findings of research on the two-breadwinner family is that women still do most of the housework (Godwin, 1991). An interesting study of this issue discovered that men who help the most with housework are those whose income is the closest to their wife's (Ross, 1987). And when men do become involved with housework, they are less likely than their wives to take over chores that carry the stress of being fixed in time (such as preparing meals); they are more likely to spe-cialize in activities that can wait (Milkie and Peltola, 1999). Coltrane and Adams (2001) found that when fathers do become involved in routine child care (driving, helping with homework, having private talks, and so on), they are more likely to also help with housework. Nevertheless, women still do about twice as much house-work as men (Coltrane, 2000a).

Jesse Bernard (1982) argues that, for many of the reasons outlined above, mod-ern marriage is beneficial for men but detrimental to women. Ross, Mirowsky, and Huber (1983) pursued that question in an interesting piece of research relating types of marriage to levels of depression experienced by the participants. Figure 10.2 summarizes their findings. At first glance, it seems apparent that marriage in any form is associated with higher levels of depression in women than in men, with the lone exception of the husband who would prefer his working wife to remain at home. Bernard's assertion seems to have some basis in fact. For women, working outside the home has little association with depression regardless of whether the working woman herself prefers being employed to remaining at home. The highest levels of female depression are associated with confinement to the home when the woman would prefer to be employed. When a husband's support with housework

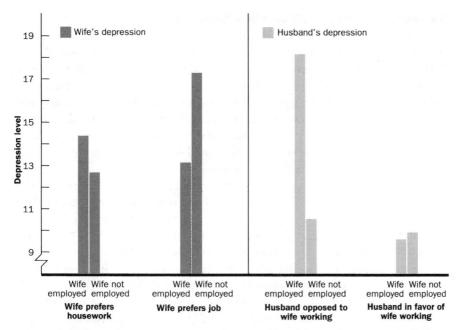

Figure 10.2 The interactive effects of preferences for wife's employment and wife's actual employment on the depression levels of husbands and wives. (Data from Ross, Mirowsky, and Huber, 1983)

for a working wife was examined, high support produced (not surprisingly) the lowest levels of female depression. Since such male support with housework is still a rare occurrence, the marriage relationship seems in need of additional change before it functions as well for women as it does for men.

Gender changes in the home and gender changes in the workplace go hand in hand. American values concerning career dedication and long hours in the workplace conflict with the ideal of the nurturing home with an ever-present parent dedicated to childrearing (Gerson, 2004a, 2004b). Sociological research in this area has focused on how parents alter (or attempt to alter) their job responsibilities with the need for family time. And all of this must occur with alterations in both male and female interpretations of gender roles. Gerson and Jacobs (2001) note the desire of full-time workers to see more family-supportive workplace options, allowing them the potential to strengthen their family activities. But those same workers also recognize the high costs involved when family demands confront job expectations. In their interviews with married couples conducted between 1981 and 1997, Rogers and Amato (2000) report higher levels of marital discord than found prior to 1981. In addition, that discord was higher with increases in the wife's conflict between home and work pressures.

THE VALUE OF CHILDREN: CHILDLESS MARRIAGES

In the preindustrial world, children were an economic asset, but industrialization removed their economic potential and replaced it with additional costs (Zelizer, 1985). Children also place considerable stress on the marriage relationship. Sociological research has shown that couples without children are happier than those with children and that those whose children are grown are happier than those with younger children (Morgan, Lye, and Condran, 1988). It is not surprising, then, that attitudes about ideal family size have changed over the years. Currently, the majority of Americans consider two or fewer children to be ideal. Most couples now carefully consider the costs before having children.

In fact, the number of couples choosing to remain childless has increased notably in American society. In most cases, these are dual-career couples with higher-than-average income and education and lower-than-average affiliation with organized religion; the connection between these attributes and childlessness is particularly true when they apply to women (Jacobson and Heaton, 1991). Because couples foresee that childrearing would interfere with their careers, many couples delay having children or eliminate having them altogether (White and Rogers, 2000). These decisions become all the more important with the growing number of adult children returning to live with their parents (although in many cases the returning adult child aids the parent's economic circumstance) (Grigsby, 1989; Hartnung and Sweeney, 1991). The same forces that affect general attitudes about the ideal number of children have helped support decisions to remain childless. As the expense of raising children continues to increase, voluntary childlessness should become increasingly common.

THE FAMILY AND INEQUALITY

An individual's entering status into society is determined solely by his or her family. You can alter your status during your lifetime through your own efforts, but your first status will be that of your family. If your family is of low social status and is looked down on by others, it follows that those same observers will not expect much of you. If such observers are teachers or police officers or judges, their prejudgments can have a significant impact on your life. Because your family's income level will determine what options are open to you, your family can also have a fundamental effect on your economic well-being as an adult.

Sociologists are interested in the issue of economic inequality—in particular, the increase in the number of children in the United States being raised by a single parent. Figure 10.3 shows the growth in the percentages of children being raised by a single parent from 1960 to 2002, comparing European American, African American, and Hispanic populations. If we view trends over the years of childhood for individual children, we find that 40 percent of European American children and 85 percent of African American children spend at least some years with a single parent (Rawlings, 1989). Because almost all single parents are women, these children are more likely to live in poverty than children with two parents. In 2001, the median income for families with two parents present was $60,335, compared to a figure of $25,745 for families headed by single women. Only 9.2 percent of the two-parent families lived below the poverty level, while 26.5 percent of the families headed by women did so (U.S. Bureau of the Census, 2004a). Part of the reason for the large gap in income is the presence of two wage earners in many of the two-parent families. Another part of the reason, however, is the lower pay that American women receive relative to men. If we compare the 2001 families headed by single women with those headed by single men, we find that the median yearly income of the families headed by single fathers was $36,590 as compared to a median yearly income of $25,745 for families headed by single mothers (U.S. Bureau of the Census, 2004a). The yearly income for male-headed families is still well below that earned by two-parent families but significantly higher than that earned by women.

Another concern sociologists have with single-parent families headed by women is the disproportionate number of nonwhite women involved. As Figure 10.3 shows, in 2002 only 25.5 percent of European American children lived with one parent, compared to 61.5 percent of African American children and 34.9 percent of Hispanic children. If we combine ethnic differences with the income differences noted

It is much easier to maintain a higher socioeconomic position for a family when two parents are present.

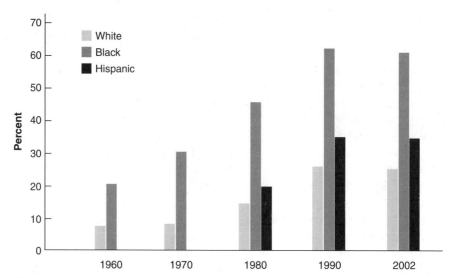

Figure 10.3 Percent of children raised by a single parent, 1960–1998. (Data from U.S. Bureau of the Census, 1992b; 2000; 2003c)

above (displayed graphically in Figure 10.4), the relationship stands out clearly. While families headed by single women tend to be poorer, that situation is even more true of African American and Hispanic families than of European American families. There are clear patterns of interaction among family structure, race, and income in the United States (see Eggebeen and Lichter, 1991).

The growth in single-parent families, especially in nonwhite populations, has been explained in a variety of ways by sociologists. One of the more controversial was a 1965 study by Daniel Patrick Moynihan titled *The Negro Family*. Pointing to some of the statistics cited above (which were far less pronounced in 1965), Moynihan concluded that the rise of the female-headed family in the African American community indicated a cultural breakdown within that community and would, in itself, be a cause of poverty for the upcoming generation of African Americans because of a lack of proper male role models. The implication of this study was that African Americans would have to clean up their own act before they could expect anything better from life.

Critics of Moynihan's study (and subsequent restatements of the conclusions in various forms) have argued that the lack of two-parent families is a product of poverty rather than a cause. The pressures of low-income jobs and frequent unemployment make stable family life difficult, to say the least. Moynihan traced these aspects of the African American family to the disruptions of family life caused by slavery, but other observers have noted that the rise of the female-headed family has been more a response to the problems of poverty in an urban environment than a

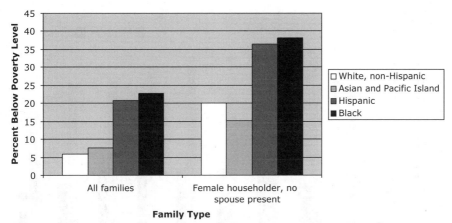

Figure 10.4 Poverty status by family relationship, race, and Hispanic origin, 2002. (Data from U.S. Bureau of the Census, 2003d)

result of history (Wilson, 1987). There is also considerable debate as to whether the African American family is indeed weak (see Stack, 1975). Fathers may be absent, but ties to other relatives in an extended family sense are quite strong. In 2002, for example, 8.2 percent of African American children were being raised by someone other than either parent, as compared to 3.1 percent for European Americans and 4.9 percent for Hispanics (U.S. Bureau of the Census, 2003c). In almost all cases, these caretakers are other relatives of the children, who have stepped in to help (Ford et al., 1990–1991), especially grandparents, who find themselves once again raising a family. Forsyth et al. (1992) note growing changes in the grandparent role in all ethnic groups in the United States, leading them to suggest a "new grandparent" role emerging in response to the growing divorce rate.

In addition to family members, black families also find support from unrelated members of their communities who maintain long-term relationships with family members. Such people, termed "fictive kin," take on many of the responsibilities and social relationships typically associated with family members. In many ways, fictive kin are the result of creatively filling the family gaps when they occur.

The bottom line of Moynihan's critics, however, is that poverty must be ended if the nuclear family is to grow. And even economic change may not be enough, given the many factors that have combined to increase divorce rates in the United States. (The reading by Thompson following this chapter explores the African American family in much greater detail.)

MARRIAGE AND DIVORCE

The relationship between marriage and divorce in the United States is a curious one. Divorce rates have risen noticeably since the 1950s and 1960s (see Figure 10.5), to

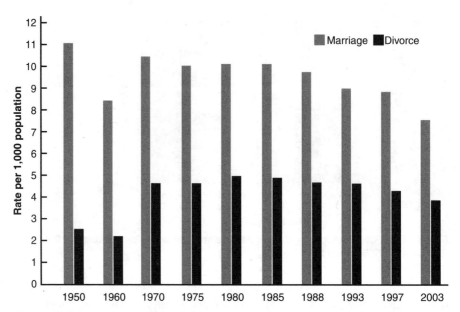

Figure 10.5 Marriage and divorce rates in the United States, 1950–1997. (Data from U.S. Bureau of the Census, 1993c; 2000; U.S. Centers for Disease Control and Prevention, 2004)

the point that there is now a ratio of about one divorce for every two marriages. One estimate is that half of all marriages occurring now will not last beyond thirty years (Weed, 1989). We have already seen that Americans who do marry are marrying at older ages now than at any recorded time. We have also seen an increase in the number of Americans who choose not to marry at all. Figure 10.6 shows the changes from 1970 to 1998 for three age groups for both men and women. Nevertheless, 90 percent of all Americans marry at some time in their lives. The higher divorce rates seem to indicate a greater ease and willingness to terminate a marriage relationship but not a widespread disenchantment with marriage itself. We have already seen evidence that suggests the marriage relationship is more beneficial to men than to women. On the other hand, both suicide rates and overall death rates are higher for divorced people than for married people (Emery et al., 1984; Kessler, Borges, and Walters, 1999).

The higher divorce rate in itself is not easily explained, but certain changes in American society seem to have played an important role. As noted earlier, the marriage relationship and the family are no longer the practical necessity for life they once were. Individuals can earn a living outside of the marriage relationship; increasing occupational opportunities for women, in particular, mean that they are much less likely to be trapped economically in an unpleasant marriage. Further-

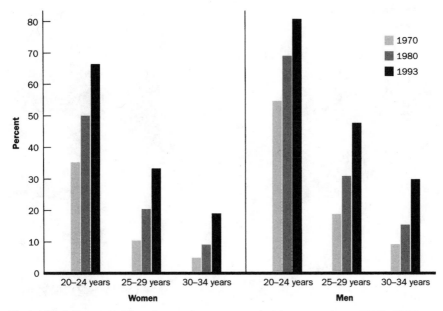

Figure 10.6 Percent of Americans who never married, by age and sex: 1970, 1980, and 1993. (Data from U.S. Bureau of the Census, 1994)

more, because children have changed from an economic asset to an economic drain, there may be fewer of them—or none—so "staying together for the children" loses its force. Remarriage introduces stepchildren, and the presence of stepchildren on both sides in a remarriage increases the likelihood of divorce (White and Booth, 1985). Stresses of modern life and, in particular, the problems faced by lower social classes play a role; unemployment, frequent moving, low levels of education, and low income are all linked with high probabilities of divorce (Raschke, 1987). Finally—and perhaps as a result of these other changes—divorce no longer carries the social stigma it once had or presents the legal difficulties formerly involved. When we contemplate divorce, our friends are less likely to discourage us than they were a generation ago. Almost all states now have no-fault divorce laws (originated in California in 1970), which ease the legal process. Divorce is now generally accepted as a rational and often beneficial way to cope with an unpleasant marriage relationship.

While the ease of divorce today may save some individuals from an unhappy life married to the wrong person, it also creates significant economic problems, particularly for women. Sociologist Lenore Weitzman (1985) studied the effects of California's no-fault law and found that most women face severe financial problems following a divorce. One year after a typical divorce, a woman's standard of living

The living standard of single mothers decreases drastically after divorce. A few bad breaks—an illness, a company downsizing that eliminates a job, an unexpected raise in rent—can send a woman, and her children, into the homeless ranks.

decreases by 73 percent, while her ex-husband's standard of living increases by 42 percent. Part of the reason for this change is that most women are awarded custody of children following a divorce. Fathers typically move on (and away from) their former families following divorce (Logan et al., 2003); Arendell (1992) found that many fathers see this moving as a conscious tactic in dealing with divorce-related conflict.

Even if the ex-husband pays court-ordered child support (and many do not), the average amount of child support is generally not enough to cover the costs of raising a child. Probably a more important cause of women's financial problems following a divorce is that women generally have fewer job skills or have a less solid career history from which to become self-supporting. Courts are currently evaluating findings such as these in order to make divorce settlements more equitable.

Another interesting question about no-fault divorce concerns its impact, if any, on the divorce rate. Rodgers, Nakonezny, and Shell (1999) compared states that were early adopters of no-fault divorce with states that changed their laws later. Their conclusion is that higher divorce rates in many of the early-adopter states can be attributed, in part, to changes in the divorce law, making divorce easier to accomplish. On the other hand, divorce rates were climbing before the introduction of no-fault divorce; the change in the law can in fact be viewed as a legal response to those rising rates.

GAY AND LESBIAN FAMILIES

Between 6 and 9 million children in the United States live in a home with either one or 2 gay or lesbian parents (Stein, Perrin, and Potter, 2004). Those figures account for about 10 percent of all American children. And the presence of children in the homes of gay and lesbian couples is a common phenomenon: 33 percent of lesbian/bisexual couples are raising children, along with 22 percent of gay/bisexual couples (Gomes, 2003).

Gay and lesbian families look remarkably like heterosexual families. While gender roles may be more creative and less traditional, it is common to find one partner focused on housework and childrearing while the other is more connected to the workplace (Carrington, 1999). The needs of running a household and raising a child apparently take precedence over all else. Distinctive features within the gay and lesbian communities, however, do produce some interesting differences. Family support is often provided through community-wide networks where nonfamily members take on some of the characteristics of an extended family (Rose and Brave-womon, 1998). In many ways, such networks are similar to the fictive kin found in African American families. And as with the African American communities, such networks for gay and lesbian families are in part a response to a minority setting in which creative alternatives become necessary.

As we have seen, heterosexual families come into being in a wide variety of ways. Gay and lesbian families have a similar wide range of origins. Because many gays and lesbians spend parts of their lives in heterosexual relationships, children in gay and lesbian families are often the natural child of one partner and the stepchild of the other. In the absence of a partner, such families can also be single parent. Gay and lesbian families also form through surrogate parenthood and adoption. Only a few states prohibit the adoption of children by gays or lesbians (Gomes, 2003). And the growth of international adoption has also had a significant impact on gay and lesbian adoption. As with heterosexual families, the mode of formation in gay and lesbian families leads to different strengths and weaknesses (van Dam, 2004).

Gay and lesbian families often face specific problems as a result of the stigma placed on their sexual orientation by the heterosexual community. Facing such negative attitudes can be a particular problem for children, adding yet more obstacles to the difficult problems of growing up (Stein et al., 2004; van Dam, 2004). Some research suggests that coming from a gay or lesbian family may be less of a problem for children and teens than other factors of family life. For example, Wainright et al. (2004) found that school adjustment by children had more to do with the closeness of parent-child relationships than with the sexual orientations of the parents. Beyond the social stigma issues, most research suggests that the sexual orientation of parents, by itself, has little to do with the normal processes of child development (James, 2002; Stacey and Biblarz, 2001; Tasker, 1999).

Of all the similarities between gay and lesbian families as compared with heterosexual families, an obvious missing component is legal marriage. In 1996, the U.S. Congress passed the Defense of Marriage Act, which stated that a "spouse" is a person of the opposite sex. It also stipulated that no state must accept definitions of marriage passed by another state (this coming shortly after Hawaii temporarily legalized gay marriage). Since then, Vermont created "civil unions" for gay and lesbian couples in 2000, the Massachusetts Supreme Court decided in 2004 that only full marriage rights for gays and lesbians were constitutional, and many states in the 2004 election passed amendments banning same-sex marriage. The issue of gay and lesbian marriage is clearly of critical importance within both the gay and lesbian and the heterosexual communities. But whether or not the legal protections (and responsibilities) of marriage become options for gay and lesbian couples, the gay and lesbian family will continue to play a significant role in the upbringing of American children.

FAMILY VIOLENCE

At the same time that the family is the source of warmth and affection, it is also sometimes a setting for incredible violence. Some violence against relatives may be misdirected; people may really want to strike out at individuals who are the source of their frustration—a boss, a tax collector, a policeman—but it is family members who are nearby and relatively defenseless. Nevertheless, the family also promotes some of the frustration that explodes as family violence. The family deals with matters of utmost importance to its members, where intense emotions may be combined with economic relationships. It is not surprising, therefore, that members often come into conflict over the obligations and responsibilities they have to each other (Hutchings, 1992; Shupe et al., 1987).

Spouse abuse is typically the abuse of women by men (although the opposite does occur). It has been estimated that 1.6 million wives are beaten each year in the United States (Straus and Gelles, 1986). Andrews (1984) estimated that 25 percent of all wives have been slapped; 15 percent have had sex forced on them by husbands; and 10 percent have been beaten. Hasday (2000) traces the history of this violence, noting that male dominance within the family was once supported by both church and law. While that latter support has dropped away, male dominance continues largely through economic dominance. In her study of battered women in a spouse-abuse center who returned to their husbands, Johnson (1992) notes that women are more likely to return when they are unemployed but their husband's income is relatively high.

Child abuse involves either the physical or sexual abuse of children by adults. Estimates are that 27 percent of girls and 16 percent of boys experience sexual abuse; estimates of physical abuse are considerably higher (Neugebauer, 2000). Physical abusers are about 90 percent men, and sexual abusers are almost entirely men. Evidence indicates that most child abusers were themselves abused as children (Elam and Kleist, 1999; Tyler et al., 2000).

While this violence occurs in all social classes (particularly sexual abuse of children), it appears to be more common in the lower social classes (Gelles and Straus, 1988). Once again, the stresses of poverty are generally blamed for the added tensions they create among family members. It should be kept in mind, however, that all the figures and estimates available reflect only those cases that come to the attention of authorities. Spouse abuse is commonly hidden by women who are unable or unwilling to stand up to their husbands. (The rapid growth of battered women's shelters is an attempt to make this kind of reporting easier for women.) Families also conceal physical child abuse and, of course, the sexual abuse of children. The child victims of sexual abuse (who are almost always female) often feel shame, and the adult female members of the family are typically fearful or passive; the result is that the crime goes unreported. Family violence incidents in the lower social classes are more likely to come to the attention of police and social workers than similar incidents in the middle or upper classes; we should therefore use the available figures with some caution.

The rape of an acquaintance ("date rape") has only recently received the attention it deserves from the media, the law, and social scientists. More specifically, date rape includes any situations in which verbal or physical means are used to gain sexual activity against consent (Adams-Curtis and Forbes, 2004). By college age, approximately 20 percent of women report having been victimized at least once (Johnson and Sigler, 2000). Not surprisingly, college-age men hold a much narrower view of what constitutes date rape than college-age women do; behavior viewed as rape by a woman may well be viewed as normal sex by a man (McDonald and Kline, 2004; Osman, 2003). As with spouse abuse, date rape is generally not reported, although media attention has helped to increase the report rate through increased awareness (Bogal-Allbritten and Allbritten, 1992).

The rape of one's spouse has now come to be recognized as a crime independent of other forms of spouse abuse. The fact that many legislators traditionally held that a husband's "rights" precluded any question of rape indicates something of male insensitivity to the rights of women, which is reflected in many laws governing family violence.

THE FAMILY: A LAST LOOK

Increases in the divorce rate plus rising numbers of Americans avoiding marriage do not indicate a "death of the family," as some observers fear, but rather reflect changes in other social institutions. As we have seen, institutions are always in the process of change, and changes in one inevitably lead to changes in the others. The future of the family will no doubt involve increasing attention to issues such as artificial insemination, in vitro fertilization, surrogate mothers, and homosexual marriages. One of the most striking events of the last two decades for the American family may well be the rapid growth of AIDS and the threat of its spread into the heterosexual community. All indications are that fear of AIDS has produced the best public relations that monogamy has seen for some time in the United States. The modern American family may be a new creature in many ways, but it is far from extinct.

SUMMARY

As an ongoing form of social organization based on kin ties, the family is a universal social phenomenon, although its structure varies considerably from one culture to another. This variation includes differences in size, decision-making power, lineage tracing, and number of spouses involved in the marriage relationship. Spouse selection is always restricted to some degree, so as to ensure selection from the appropriate group. In the United States, the traditional family structure is undergoing change in response to other social changes that affect the institution. Important among these is changing roles for women in the wider society, which have led to important changes in women's roles within the family. Changes in the industrial world have also led to fewer (or no) children, higher divorce rates, increases in the number of people who choose not to marry, and a significant rise in the number of single-parent families, most headed by women. Such families, which are particularly common among some minority groups, are associated with lower income levels and fewer opportunities for the children involved. Family violence is also apparently on the increase in the forms of spouse abuse and child abuse.

GLOSSARY

Bilineal descent A system of descent tracing that combines both the mother's and the father's line for descent purposes.

Egalitarian family A family unit in which men and women share the decision making.

Endogamy Cultural norms that specify the group inside of which an individual must choose a mate.

Exogamy Cultural norms that specify the group outside of which an individual must choose a mate, those norms often coinciding with cultural rules regarding incest.

Extended family A family unit consisting of a number of nuclear families that live together as one unit.

Family of orientation The family into which an individual is born and which provides the basic socialization for that individual.

Family of procreation The family in which an individual raises children.

Foster care family A family unit designed to protect children who have been abused, neglected, or abandoned; they also provide temporary protection of children whose parents are temporarily unable to care for them. Foster parents work for and with the state to provide either temporary or long-term care of children.

Grandparent family A family consisting of at least one dependent child who is raised by one or both grandparents.

Homogamy Marriage between two people with the same basic social characteristics.

Matriarchal family A family in which women have the authority and are responsible for most of the decision making.

Matrilineal descent The tracing of family lineage through the mother's family as opposed to the father's family.

Matrilocal residence The practice through which newly married individuals reside with the wife's family.

Monogamy A marriage between one man and one woman.

Neolocal residence The practice through which newly married individuals reside in a location apart from both husband's and wife's families.

Nuclear family A basic family unit consisting of only two spouses and their immature offspring.

Patriarchal family A family in which men have the authority and are responsible for most of the decision making.

Patrilineal descent The tracing of family lineage through the father's family as opposed to the mother's family.

Patrilocal residence The practice through which newly married individuals reside with the husband's family.

Polyandry The marriage of one woman with two or more men.

Polygyny The marriage of one man with two or more women.

Single-parent family A family consisting of at least one dependent child who is raised by only one biological parent.

Step family A family consisting at least one dependent child who resides with a parent who is not a biological parent.

STUDY QUESTIONS

1. What are some of the ways in which nuclear families differ from extended families?
2. Gender is often important in family structure and decision making. How are families affected by whether they are matriarchal, patriarchal, or egalitarian? How are living patterns affected by whether newlyweds follow matrilocal, patrilocal, or neolocal residence? What is the importance of matrilineal, patrilineal, or bilineal tracing of descent? Which of all of these is typical of the United States?

3. Cultures vary depending on whether marriages follow patterns of monogamy, polygyny, or polyandry. Even cultures that permit multiple mates tend to have mostly monogamous marriages. Why?

4. What are the most important factors determining rules of endogamy and exogamy in the United States?

5. What have been the most important changes in the American family during the last half century? What has caused those changes?

6. How are gay and lesbian families the same as and different from heterosexual families? Why do you think same-sex marriage is such an important issue for many Americans?

7. Why is the study of families important for the understanding of inequality in society?

Aaron Thompson

BOY, YOU BETTER LEARN HOW TO COUNT YOUR MONEY

Aaron Thompson is an African American sociologist whose research, in part, focuses on educational attainment among African Americans. He wrote the following article shortly before receiving his Ph.D. degree. Such times of transition are often times to reflect. In the first section of this article, Thompson describes his early childhood, focusing on the importance of his family in influencing him to work hard and to be successful in a newly integrated school system that was often less than hospitable to him. "Little Aaron" responded to those influences and succeeded, but his story is not the story of all African Americans in the American educational institution. In the second part of the article, Thompson examines some of the differences between black and white families, tracing those differences to the history of discrimination, particularly job discrimination, faced by blacks. His overriding message is clear: social institutions are connected to one another in significant ways. Here we see how the economic institution affects the family, which, in turn, influences the success of children in the educational institution.

The closer I got to the pinnacle of educational achievements, the Ph.D., the more I heard the remark, "Your family must really be proud of you." That remark always brought me pause because the word "pride" did not adequately accommodate the range of feelings that accompanied my approach to the Ph.D. You see, this guy had extremely humble roots, and it is precisely the family institution that made my academic success possible.

Two words best describe my childhood days: poverty and discipline. Love played a major role in our household, but at times other things needed to come first, such as food. Being African American and living in southeastern Kentucky, the heart of Appalachia, did not provide for the grandest of living styles. Even though my father worked twelve hours a day in the coal mines, he earned only enough pay to supply staples for the table; our family also worked as tenant farmers to have enough vegetables for my mother to can for the winter and to provide a roof over our heads.

My father, Aaron Senior, was born in October 1901 in Clay County, Kentucky, with just enough African ancestry to be considered black. My mother, on the other hand, was a direct descendent of slaves and moved with her parents from the deep south at the age of seventeen. My father lived in an all-black coal mining camp, into which my mother and her family moved in January 1938. It wasn't long before the dark, beautiful lady met the tall, light-skinned, handsome man and married him. At age thirty-seven this was my father's first marriage, and he was marrying a woman half his age. I remember asking him why he waited so long and why he chose to marry my mother. He answered, "How many eligible black women who are not your kin do you know?" I said, "Very few" and he replied, "There were even less then."

My father always seemed an extremely logical person; he was also quiet, reserved, and somewhat shy. I'm not sure my mother ever really appreciated these attributes in him. The one thing I remember the most about my father was his ability not to let anything or anyone antagonize him to the point of interrupting him in the pursuit of his goals. He often tried to pass this attitude along to his children. He would say to me, "Son, you will have opportunities that I never had. Many people, white and black alike, will tell you that you are no good and that education can never help you. Don't listen to them because soon they will not be able to keep you from getting an education like they did me. Just remember, when you do get that education, you'll never have to go in those coal mines and have them break your back. You can choose what you want to do, and then you can be a free man."

In early adolescence, I did not truly understand what he meant, but now I believe that I can finally grasp what he was trying to tell me. My father lived through a time when freedom was something he dreamed his children might enjoy someday, because before the civil rights movement succeeded in changing the laws African Americans were considerably limited in educational opportunities, job opportunities, and much else in what is definitely a racist society. My father

remained illiterate because he was not allowed to attend public schools in eastern Kentucky. The eight brothers and sisters who preceded me also had many barriers to attaining a higher level of education, and many did not exceed the level of my father.

In the early 1960s my brother, my sister, and I were integrated into the white public schools. Since there were so few blacks in our small community, we three seemed to get the brunt of the aggression that so many whites felt toward a race they considered inferior. Physical violence and constant verbal harassment caused many other blacks to forgo their education and opt for jobs in the coal mines at an early age. But my father remained constant in his advice to me: "It doesn't matter if they call you nigger; it doesn't matter if they hate you with all their might; they probably will never know how to be your friend anyway. What really matters is that you are the hope of this family to achieve something better than breaking your back in these coal mines. If it gets too unbearable, get one of them alone and beat the shit out of him, but don't you ever let them beat you by walking out on your education."

My father died at the age of 77, after I had finished my undergraduate degree. He was truly proud that I had made it beyond the coal mines. Now, my mother is another story. You see, my mother's method for motivating me was vastly different from my father's. My father was a calm, wise man who conscientiously searched for the right things to say and do. My mother, on the other hand, had no verbal or physical reticence. I can still hear her voice, "Boy, I'm gonna get your ass when we get home." My mother was fire and brimstone, and now in her 70s, her ardor has cooled very little. Mother was the true academic in our house, with an eighth grade education, which made her truly proud. An eighth grade education represented quite an achievement in the 1930s to a southern black woman.

My mother would tell me stories of how blacks were treated in the "old South" and what to watch out for with the white man. She would say,

"They don't want you to have an education because then you would have a way to get money; they definitely don't want you to have money." This attitude was part of my mother's philosophy, and it colored mine, since she started my childhood education early. In my preschool years she taught me writing, reading, and, most importantly, how to count money. By the time I was 4 years old, I could walk to the little country store to buy small amounts of groceries, and I knew to the penny how much change was due me. This feat was not so much a credit to my learning abilities but rather a credit to my mother's belief that people will take your money if you don't watch them closely.

When I was ready to start school, the representative from the three-room, all-black school came by our house to talk to my mother. I was five years old and listened closely to the conversation. The representative said, "Mrs. Thompson, we would like to start Aaron in school early because we think that in the next several years the schools will be integrated, and we want him to be able to have enough skills to perform with the little white children."

I vividly remember my mother's classic response to this person. She said, "Shit, my son can read and write better than you can and will someday make a whole lot more money than you. You don't need to get him ready, just don't hold him back." So I started school that year and from then on "Little Aaron" could do no wrong academically in his mother's mind. If I ever had any problems, it was someone else's fault because she made sure I did my homework, attended school every day, and did everything the "No-Goods" down the hollow didn't do.

When I graduated from college, my mother was present and very happy. She often said, "He made it through school without our help. We had no money to help him, but he worked hard and made it. Reckon how much money he's going to make with this degree." My mother definitely appreciates my educational achievements, and the more she can empirically measure it monetarily, the prouder she becomes. She has always been my biggest cheerleader, and my achievements could not have happened without those cheers.

These circumstances help explain why I have trouble using adjectives like "proud" to express how my family truly felt about my education. I believe that most families are proud of their own, but it takes a truly special family to overcome such monumental social obstacles and continue to see hope in the future of their offspring. I look at the negative conditions that my brothers and sisters lived through, knowing how my mother and father wanted opportunities for them, and I understand the frustrations and sadness my folks experienced when the opportunities were not there and some did not achieve. But I lived in my own little world when my parents were giving me those motivational encouragements.

Many black families throughout the United States face seemingly insurmountable obstacles, and the future seems to be a shadow rather than a reality. Many live in conditions of poverty and many in one-parent households. But as my mother always said, "If you listen to the morals that are being taught to you, throw out the ones with hatred, and just learn how to count your money; then you will do okay in life." My mother seems to have the perfect answer to many of the problems of our society in this one statement. But as we all know, when many of us were growing up, there was very little money to count. Today, with both mother and father doing paid labor, it is harder for parents to give the direct attention to children that my mother showered on me. This issue could become problematic since socializing our children to understand that education is the important route to success usually starts in the family at an early age. Economics can be the culprit in the successes and failures of our children in this society. With education, success is not assured, but without education, failure seems imminent. Being poor, black, and Appalachian did not offer me great odds for success, but constant reminders from my parents that I was a good and valuable person helped me to see beyond my deterrents to the true importance of education. My parents, who could never provide me with monetary wealth, truly made me proud of them by giving me the gift of insight and an aspiration for achievement.

Insight and knowledge are the paths for success in people of all races and classes. The family is where these paths begin. The black family is a family of strengths and diversity. Growth and success can take place within our institution regardless of the structural make up. To make this growth and success possible, we need to know the truth of our history, a knowledge of the structure, the courage to seek assistance, and the strength to lend assistance.

To be located in the professional ranks inside most organizations, candidates need to have attained certain levels of academic credentials, at least a four-year degree. Many other organizations require a higher level of academic achievement. For example, a Ph.D. represents the minimum requirement to be a professor in a university. Black Ph.D.'s are at their lowest level since 1975 (Bunzel, 1990:46). African Americans are finding it difficult getting into major colleges and graduating from them. In 1984, 617,000 blacks were enrolled in four-year colleges and universities. By 1986 this figure had dropped by 2,000 and continues to drop. Blacks are the only demographic category affected to this degree (Bunzel, 1990:50). By 1990, approximately 29 percent of European Americans had completed four years or more of college compared to approximately 16 percent of African Americans (Pinkney, 1993).

When African Americans are admitted to elite universities, issues of reverse discrimination seem to loom in the background (Bunzel, 1989). Even if blacks are strong academically, research shows that because they are more disadvantaged economically, there is a greater chance of their not pursuing and continuing an education. This is in contrast to white students who might have lower academic skills but have the finances to pursue college (DeMott, 1991). Elite universities are having trouble in both gaining and retaining African

American students (Exum, 1983). Many of these problems' roots lie in the legacy of slavery and the power of racism; the impediments to gaining these necessary skills are rooted in the history of black America (Dill, 1979).

Black Americans and their families have faced segregation, discrimination, and inequalities throughout the history of industrial America. When compared to whites, blacks were more often faced with discriminatory laws, individually and in the family structure. Under slave law, black women, black men, and their children were the property of slave owners. Although during the slave period there were many freed married blacks, family units under slavery existed at the slavemaster's discretion. People could marry, but property could not, and slaves were considered property. Although many slaves defied this law and were married within their own community, slave owners could destroy this bond at any time they saw a need to do so by merely selling one or both of the partners to different slave owners.

After slavery, whites created formal and informal laws for the domination of black labor, a labor they once owned. These "Jim Crow" laws were enacted after Reconstruction. These laws as much as anything else fostered an ideology of blacks as subordinate and whites as superordinate. These laws also contributed to a division of labor by sexes in the black family, as well as placing barriers to the formation of black two-parent households. For example, if a black woman married a black man, then the property she owned would go to him. Since the laws stated that property could only be owned by males, women did not relish the idea of working to give property to a male, so many decided to remain unmarried. If the black husband did not have a job, then the state could take his property. Of course, there was a good chance that the black male would not have a job, so many marriages did not take place. Thus, with the barriers to the black family being an intact family unit, there was a greater chance for poverty in the black community. Black women faced a dismal prospect for survival above the poverty level because they needed to find a job that could support them and, in many cases, their children. The state made laws saying that if black parents could not afford to care for their children, then the children could be apprenticed out as free labor. When girls were apprenticed out, most went to white households as domestic help. When boys were apprenticed out, they went as outside manual laborers such as blacksmiths. These divisions reflected a wider labor market distinction between men and women as well as the distinctions made in the African American community (Boris and Bardaglio, 1987).

Historically, there is a difference between the family structures of black Americans and white Americans. The work roles inside and outside the households seem to be one of the major differences. American plantation slavery did not make a distinction between the work performed by black men and that done by black women. Both worked in the fields and both worked within the household doing domestic labor. Gender role expectations were very different for black and white women. Black women were not seen as weak: in fact, they were seen as being able to work in the fields, have a baby in the evening, and cook breakfast the next day. (White women, on the other hand, were viewed as weaker than black women, unable to deal with the normal stresses of the day-to-day activities of the plantation. A woman's duties centered on pleasing her husband, whatever his wishes might be.) Black men also experienced different gender role expectations than did white men. Under slavery, the black male understood that both he and his family (whatever family could exist at this point) were at the service of the white family.

In the late 1800s when there was a need for more females in the work force, laws were loosened to include this need. These laws had a significant effect on the white family but very little effect on the black family. Later, when black family members moved into industrialization, they went into the paid labor market at a different pace and level than the white family. Black women most often were paid less than black men or white women, and they always maintained

jobs in the paid labor market as servants, seamstresses, laundresses, and other domestic positions. Black women were not allowed to serve as salesclerks, cashiers, bookkeepers, etc., which were jobs filled by many white women in the labor market. In 1900, black women constituted approximately 20 percent of the female population and were 23 percent of the servant population. By 1920 they were 40 percent of the servant population. As the twentieth century got older, the black female servant proportionally grew compared to other demographic populations (Kessler-Harris, 1981:83).

Black men who had job skills in many cases could not practice those skills. For example, blacks were not allowed to join many of the trade unions in the South, where most blacks lived. The United Mine Workers Union in the South used blacks as strikebreakers but had many problems getting black members accepted as regular union members. Thus, in many cases blacks who worked as miners remained outside the union, with inadequate pay compared to the white union members (Gutman, 1975). The black family, because of a history of discriminatory laws undermining family structure, did not have a support system going into the paid labor market. Often there were no husbands in the family. Black women could not depend economically on their men because many did not have husbands or their husbands faced an economic market that discriminated against them. This lack of labor force participation by the black male led the black female to see him as a liability to her and her children, which further undermined the black family structure. To survive in the labor market, black women would accept any job to support their family, but the jobs that were available were the traditionally "female-specific" domestic jobs, such as house cleaners, cooks, nannies, etc. The few jobs that were available to black men were also jobs that were of a domestic nature. These jobs tended to pay less than jobs that were reserved for the white male.

Early in industrialization, a family wage system was enacted. A family wage system is one that is designed to pay enough money to the male in the paid labor force to support him and his family. This system allowed the female to stay in the household and the male to stay in the paid labor force with the title of "head of household." Although laws stated that men were heads of households, black men could not assert themselves as the undeniable heads of their households if they did not have the economic ability to back their claims. Thus, a pattern of single female-headed households started in the black family. Black men clearly did not and could not make a family wage for their family, and so black women continued to work. Since black men did not have the political or economic power structure on their side to help keep their families intact, the patriarchal father was not as dominant in the black household as he was in the white family.

White women and black women shared the burden of being forced to be in domestic positions in the home, and when they had to get paying jobs, they were forced to occupy sex-typed jobs in the labor market. The difference here is that the family wage white women depended upon was considerably higher than the wage black women enjoyed or expected. Without a doubt, black women from the beginning have not been able to depend on a constant family wage; thus, they never have.

Black women have headed their households for most of this century and have been accustomed to accepting all kinds of jobs throughout their lives to support their families. Black men are still experiencing unemployment and underemployment, and when they do get jobs, the majority of jobs are in the secondary labor market or in work that many white men would not accept. Black female-headed households comprise approximately 54 percent of all black families with children. This percentage is almost as high as the total black male paid labor force participation. Though it is harder for a black woman to obtain enough education to increase her chances in the labor market, she still surpasses the black male in gaining these necessary resources. With the black male's inability to break the barriers

of institutional racism, the ideal of a dual-career black family as the norm is not in the foreseeable future.

Women as a whole are getting more education, and dual-earner marriages are the norm in America now instead of single-earner marriages. Children expect to see their mothers as well as their fathers working outside the household and supporting the family financially. This change will likely bring about a change in the structure of the family. Hopefully, more egalitarian conditions for males and females will emerge. However, the black family, in general, still is not financially stable when compared to the white family. Black women are not experiencing the same level of new-found freedom in the paid labor market that white women are beginning to find. Black men are still underemployed or unemployed when compared to their white counterparts. Until black workers reach a point in our society where they are operating on the same footing as the white workers (equal education, equal employment, equal pay), blacks will be hard pressed to move into the twenty-first century with an egalitarian balance in the family and work.

In conclusion, labor market participation, low wages for both sexes, and discriminatory laws have affected the black family structure, producing the large number of households headed by a female. The family is the primary institution for socialization in our society, and this is where we should start looking for answers and providing solutions. Although I have no instant solutions to any problems suggested in this paper, as a sociologist I do believe there are some directions we can follow, and they can be stated in three simple steps: (1) We should teach our children the importance of education for the sake of knowledge as well as for economic survival. (2) We should set forth a pattern of appreciating cultural and economic diversity (understanding that race and class are social mechanisms for prejudice and discrimination). (3) We should teach our children to look beyond the limitations that society might have placed on them so as to build on steps one and two.

REFERENCES

Boris, Eileen, and Peter Bardaglio. "Gender, Race, and Class." In *Families and Work,* edited by Naomi Gerstel and Harriet E. Gross. Philadelphia: Temple University Press, 1987.

Bunzel, John H. "Affirmative Action Must Not Result in Lower Standards or Discrimination Against the Most Competent Students." *The Chronicle of Higher Education,* March 1, 1989, B1(2).

———. "Minority Faculty Hiring." *American Scholar* 59 (Winter, 1990):39–52.

Dill, Bonnie T. "The Dialectics of Black Womanhood." *Journal of Women in Culture and Society* 31 (1979):543–555.

Exum, William H. "Climbing the Crystal Stair: Values, Affirmative Action, and Minority Faculty." *Social Problems* 30 (1983):383–399.

Gutman, Herbert G. *Work, Culture & Society.* New York: Vintage, 1975.

Kessler-Harris, Alice. *Women Have Always Worked.* Old Westbury, N.Y.: The Feminist Press, 1981.

Pinkney, Alphonso. *Black Americans* (4th edition). Englewood Cliffs, N.J.: Prentice Hall, 1993.

DISCUSSION QUESTIONS

1. Thompson argues that gender role expectations have traditionally been different for white and black Americans. How are these expectations connected to economic and family roles in both the white and black family?

2. Single-parent families make up a greater proportion of black families than of white families. How does Thompson explain this difference?

3. Thompson describes the economic and social forces that have created a lack of stability within the black family. Did his family reflect this lack of stability? Why or why not?

EDUCATION

In industrial societies such as the United States, the institution of education provides children with their first major step outside the family. From the child's point of view, whole new sets of human relationships await in new physical settings called schools. From the sociologist's point of view, however, education represents one of the separate social institutions that warrant an individual look in the process of understanding the structure of an industrial society. As with all institutions, it operates with some degree of isolation, carried along by its own logic, as teachers, students, and school administrators go through their respective motions in their respective roles. But as with all institutions, the institution of education has important connections with other institutions. Its connection with the family is obvious as it removes children from one set of caretakers and socializers to place them in the hands of others. Its forceful intervention into the family, however, stems primarily from other important institutional forces that help shape education's goals and functions. Specifically, the institution of education responds to the political institution, which, in turn, is highly responsive to the needs of the economy (two institutions we will look at in more detail in Chapter 13). In this section, we begin by looking at the goals and functions of education (as influenced by politics and the economy); this discussion provides a basis for understanding some of the important outcomes of this institution, such as its effect on social inequality and its effectiveness in reaching its stated goals.

EDUCATION AND SOCIETY: GOALS AND FUNCTIONS

Some overlap certainly occurs in the stated goals of education and the sociologically observed functions of education. Goals that are achieved represent functions that the institution fulfills. Education attempts to make Americans literate, for example, which is a skill the economy requires in the workforce. Although schools are not completely successful in accomplishing this goal (see Box 11.1), they achieve at least a modest success with most of us. This goal is part of the function of imparting knowledge to each generation, a topic we explore in just a moment. On the other hand, schools sometimes achieve ends for which they not only do not strive but perhaps might prefer to avoid (such as thrusting together large numbers of youths the same age who subsequently form a youth culture in which drug use and gangs may be

BOX 11.1

Literacy in the United States

Can you pass this test? Read the following advertisement for a rental house and then answer the questions.

Attractive house in excellent condition. Three floors. Full basement. Large living room. Backyard with garden. Two-car garage.

1. Would you tell me how the ad describes the living room of the house?
2. How does the ad describe the backyard?
3. How does the ad describe the basement?

If you have read ten chapters in this book with no problem, this test is unlikely to be much of a challenge, but many Americans would have difficulty with it. Since literacy is a fundamental skill for most jobs in an industrial society, the idea that some 20 to 30 percent of the American population might have trouble with such a simple reading task makes one wonder how work ever gets done (Stedman and Kaestle, 1991; Kozol, 1985).

Literacy is the ability to extract meaning from the written word. Our schools teach this skill and then teach other skills that require literacy. This kind of "school literacy" requires even higher-level skills than the preceding test of "functional literacy," which measures the ability to read in an everyday life context. As Kozol (1985, 4) points out, "Twenty-five million American adults cannot read the poison warnings on a can of pesticide, a letter from their child's teacher, or the front page of a daily paper. An additional 35 million read only at a level which is less than equal to the full survival needs of our society."

The initial inclination of most Americans is to blame the school system. Bumper stickers that read, "If you can read this, thank a teacher," also invite the public to blame teachers for those who cannot read. Over one-third of the member nations of the United Nations have higher literacy rates than the United States (Kozol, 1985). Many of those same countries also require more months in the school year and more homework. Some think they have more dedicated teachers and students. But such statistics and surmises do not necessarily give us a complete picture. Spending more money and time on formal education cannot hurt our literacy statistics but neither does it offer a guarantee of a magic solution (see Bishop, 1991). Most illiterates are found among the poor and minorities, who have never been well served by the American system of formal education. While some of the difference between African American and European American literacy rates in the United States can be accounted for by economic differences alone, some of those differences seem to be connected to more general causes, such as prejudice and alienation (Stedman and Kaestle, 1991).

Kozol (1985) believes that the best cure for illiteracy is to employ less formal, community-based programs. The poor and minorities have had too many negative experiences with formal bureaucracies, argues Kozol, to be responsive to programs housed in such environments. Yet recent decades have not seen periods of excess funds for domestic programs in the United States. The adult illiterate described by Kozol, who, from embarrassment, attempts to navigate through life while hiding a lack of reading ability is likely to be a large and often invisible portion of the American workforce for some years to come.

promoted). Such nongoals are functions nonetheless (often called *latent* functions) in that the institution produces them on an ongoing basis. A first step in understanding this institution is to explore its impact on those who pass through it and its functions for the wider society.

AMERICANIZATION OF IMMIGRANTS

In the early nineteenth century, education was privately provided, and generally only the rich could afford it. Most occupations did not require any of the fine points of learning, and most workers did not have the leisure to pursue education, no matter what its cost. In the nineteenth century, industrialization began its spread in the United States and created demands for basic literacy. The nineteenth century also brought large numbers of immigrants to the United States and they brought considerable cultural diversity (see Chapter 8). Power in the United States, then and now, was held largely by Protestant Americans of European descent; this power elite felt that their values were threatened by these new arrivals. Compulsory public education appeared to be a solution: teach the new arrivals American values.

If you saluted the flag in elementary school, you were participating in a ritual that had its roots in the Americanization concerns of the nineteenth century. That pledge of loyalty was originally designed to teach the children of foreign immigrants that they could no longer have any allegiance to a political entity other than the United States. In addition, the schools were also viewed as a method for promoting the basic Protestant values that were seen as central to all other American values. Public schools were structured as a way to counteract the force of other religions whose memberships were growing rapidly through immigration, especially Catholicism (see Soltaw and Stevens, 1981). The goals behind the public school movement in the late nineteenth century were not lost on the newcomers; one major response came from the Catholic Church, which placed a major emphasis on the growth of parochial schools so as to isolate the children of Catholic Americans from the anti-Catholic forces behind the public school movement (Gabriel, 1948). Less powerful groups, most notably American Indians, were unable to structure alternative schools and found themselves at the mercy of imported public education, which ignored or downgraded their cultures while promoting mainstream American culture. Today public education continues to promote American culture to new immigrants.

CULTURAL AND POLITICAL INTEGRATION

An area in which education's goals and functions clearly overlap is cultural and political integration. Such integration means that a state's citizens are enough alike for the state to function as a unit. This does not mean that they have to be cultural clones of one another but that they are able to communicate with one another and share both a political loyalty to and knowledge of their government. As with the Americanization of immigrant children, education also provides this function for each generation. In the United States, for example, all public schools teach classes in English or use other languages (as in the case of bilingual schools) only to pave the way for children to master English at some point in their student career. Courses in government are also generally required so that no child can leave the system without encountering the U.S. Constitution and learning some of the basics of the political structure that has grown from it. This process of education does not eliminate cultural differences among Americans, but it does give them common ground at some level. Even industrial nations with minimal cultural diversity (such as Japan) use the institution of education to maintain a higher level of cultural and political integration.

IMPARTING AND CREATING KNOWLEDGE

The most obvious goal of education is also probably its most obvious function. As we saw in Chapter 9, there are many ways to acquire knowledge besides the formal process of education, but industrial societies have found formal education to have a number of advantages. The most important is that compulsory education produces literacy. As we have seen, an industrial economy cannot function without most of its citizens having at least some basic skills. Beyond that, the wide range of skills that characterizes the occupations in a society with a high division of labor are generally beyond the capabilities of most parents or other family members to teach. Finally, the institution of education also plays a major role in the creation of new knowledge. A primary goal of the modern American university is professorial research designed to expand the various disciplines represented.

SCREENING

In the process of providing knowledge, the institution of education also evaluates those who seek it, separating the successful from the unsuccessful. Education can be viewed as a series of hurdles that must be jumped en route to the finish line of graduation. A missed hurdle at any point can produce a nonfinisher; some students drop out of high school while others acquire a diploma. Some stop with that diploma while others enroll in a college or university. And some of those who enroll will fail or quit while others receive degrees. Of those, the elite will pursue still more education in search of advanced degrees. The farther along the hurdles, the fewer the number of students who will still be in the running. Employers therefore have their applicants already screened for them. Simply placing an educational requirement on a given occupation will automatically eliminate certain kinds of people who missed the hurdles prior to that requirement. Sociologists examine the institution of education carefully to understand this screening process and, most important, to understand just why some kinds of people falter at hurdles so easily jumped by others (see the reading by Murai following this chapter). A common observation is that education tends to preserve the system of social stratification from one generation to the next (see Colclough and Beck, 1986; Mingle, 1987). We examine this process more closely in the next section of this chapter.

SOCIALIZATION (AND THE HIDDEN CURRICULUM)

When the topic of discussion is socialization, we normally think of the family, but the institution of education plays a significant part in the socialization of all who pass through it. Socialization includes the imparting of knowledge discussed earlier, but schools provide a much more wide-ranging experience to students than simply the opportunity to acquire knowledge and skills. They create social arenas within which children have their first major encounters with both adults and peers outside the family. The child's ability to develop social relationships thereby grows. The school experience also imparts more general cultural values, as students are encouraged to admire and dislike specific cultural objects, people, lifestyles, forms of government, and so on. Children who spend considerable classroom time studying the Founding Fathers but little time on the history of nonwhite Americans, for example, acquire a clear picture as to what is important and what is not.

Instruction in values is an intended goal of education, but the institution imparts many values that are not found in textbooks or teacher training programs. Rather, these values are built into the basic structure of school systems and have been termed the **hidden curriculum** (Jackson, 1968). For example, one of the most notable aspects of the educational system is the competition it requires of students. The grading system is only the obvious sign of the competitive pressures that exist everywhere in school. When a child fails to answer a teacher's question correctly, for example, other children who know the answer cannot contain their enthusiasm in their desire to show up their fallen comrade. Schools cannot take all the credit for the student desire to be "better than," however, as competition colors all aspects of life in an industrial society. As part of that society, the institution of education is consistent with the dominant values. The emphasis it places on competition makes it an important factor in the socialization of children. Being a student is learning to compete—a lesson for later life that may be more important than much of the specific subject matter of education.

In American society the school has become one of the most important socializers in the early life of its members. Children learn to sit quietly, walk in straight lines,

Along with reading, writing, and arithmetic, children learn all sorts of things in school. One of the most obvious is competition—which is not surprising, since the American culture is a very competitive one. The vigor of some hand-raising in elementary school is saying, "Call on me so I can show off and give the right answer and get one up on my classmates."

salute the flag. They learn to "get along" with each other in socially approved ways, following norms typically different for boys and girls. Boys, for example, learn to act more aggressively on the playground and dominate in math, science, and social studies in the classroom; girls, on the other hand, do better in writing, reading, and literature. Children become adults during the school years. The kinds of adults they become can be traced in large part to the impact of their many years spent in the classroom, playing the student role.

EQUALITY OF EDUCATIONAL OPPORTUNITY

As we saw earlier, one of the major reasons public education grew in the United States in the nineteenth century was to respond to the growing cultural diversity brought about by immigration. Schools face that same situation going into the twenty-first century as immigration continues and as ethnic and racial groups of long standing in the United States still bring cultural diversity to the classroom. In addition, lifestyle differences from one social class to the next are profound enough (see Chapter 7) that lower-class and middle-class students from the same ethnic or racial group bring strikingly different backgrounds to school (Rossides, 2004).

Beyond school, levels of education have traditionally been connected to the level of occupational advancement an individual later achieves (Blau and Duncan, 1967). But as diplomas and degrees have become increasingly tied to specific kinds of work in the economy, jobs that individuals once could "work into" are now formally connected to particular educational expectations and credentials; workers who lack that education cannot even be considered (Lowe, 2000).

With education such an important route to success in the economy, the ability of schools to provide that opportunity to their diverse student population becomes increasingly important. In general, American schools have not provided that opportunity on a large scale. The schools are there, but most students who have significant cultural differences from the school curriculum do not succeed. As noted in the reading by Murai following this chapter, these students usually have so much catching up to do that the task becomes insurmountable. In looking at how schools respond to group differences, sociologists have given us a much more complete picture of how the education institution responds to them.

TEACHER STEREOTYPES AND EXPECTATIONS

Most elementary school and secondary schoolteachers come from the middle classes of American society. Predictably, they hold many middle-class values and stereotypes about people who are significantly different from themselves. While most teacher training programs attempt to sensitize prospective teachers to the cultural differences they will encounter in the classroom, such sensitizing can only go so far. As with most of us, teachers respond more favorably to students who are culturally more like themselves, and teachers have higher academic expectations of them. They respond less favorably to students who differ from them in social class, race, or ethnicity (Alexander et al., 1987; Farkas et al., 1990). Such differences in responses and expectations are not lost on the children who receive that different treatment.

Much of the concern with teacher expectations was generated by a 1968 study by Robert Rosenthal and Lenore Jacobson. They told the teachers involved in the study they had a test that would predict "late bloomers"—students who might or might not have done well in the past but who should do exceptionally well during the coming year. Then the researchers randomly selected some students from the classrooms and gave their names to the teachers as the individuals from whom big things should be expected. Returning at the end of the year, the researchers discovered that the children randomly selected had done significantly better than other children in the classroom. The only plausible explanation for this outcome was a change in the teachers' behavior; a teacher who conveys to a child that more is expected may well behave in ways that cause the child to fulfill that expectation. Efforts to replicate this study of positive teacher expectations have not produced identical results (see Boocock, 1978), but researchers have been able to show clearly that negative teacher expectations can hinder the academic progress of students (Dusek, 1985).

TRACKING (ABILITY GROUPING)

The school experience communicates a definite message to children about their individual abilities and inabilities, good points and bad points. When elementary school reading groups are separated into the "bluebirds" and "robins," for example, children in the robin reading group soon discover that they are moving through their reading book much more slowly than the bluebirds. Later, in high school, those same slow readers may be placed into classes not designed to prepare them for college. This process of placing different students into different classes according to a measure of their ability is called **tracking,** or ability grouping. It is used in over half of all American elementary schools and is a common element in most high school programs. The idea behind it is that students learn best in classes whose content is geared to their abilities and in which other students have similar abilities; advocates say that the higher-achieving students will not be held back by slower learners, while those with less ability will not face frustration. While tracking is clearly useful to schools and teachers, there is mixed evidence as to whether advanced students advance more quickly when segregated (Leonard, 2001; Rogers, 2002). There is more evidence as to whether the same segregation damages less successful students (Leonard, 2001; Ollerton, 2001).

Tracking affects a student's achievement in two ways. First, students on the lower track receive a different course content, which, over the years, will give them a substantially different education. Students who do not receive college preparatory classes, for example, will have less background in necessary subjects should they ever decide to venture into the ivory tower. Second, students in all tracks respond to the expectation that their track placement communicates. Students on the high track will presumably think well of themselves (since school officials obviously do) while those tracked in slower programs will get that message as well (Ollerton, 2001; Oakes, 1985). In short, tracking affects both the quality and, ultimately, the amount of education that students receive (Henze, 2001; Venkatakrishnan and Wiliam, 2001; Gamoran and Mare, 1989).

Which students are placed in which tracks? Students whose parents have a high level of education are much more likely to be placed in the higher tracks, aiming toward the same educational level as their parents (Kerbo, 1983). Minorities and students from low-income families are much more likely to be found in the lower tracks than would follow from their proportion of the school population (Boocock, 1978). And, as we saw in Chapter 5, minorities are also likely to be overrepresented in the ultimate of low tracks—classes for the mentally retarded (Mercer, 1973). Students who are placed at higher levels are often those whose cultural and verbal behavior most closely approximates the individuals making class assignments—an outcome that calls into question the accuracy of the process (Ireson et al., 2002).

Students are initially separated through tracking, and tracking fosters continued separation. Ironically, tracking also affects the friendships of students. Because most students draw their friends from their classes, tracking assures that most students will select their friends from a pool of students much like themselves (Hallinan and Williams, 1989). Even schools that contain considerable diversity in social class, race, or ethnicity may experience little socializing across those boundaries if students never meet in classes. Tracking is clearly one of the ways in which the institution of education helps to maintain the current system of inequality in the United States: poor students are placed in low tracks, which lead to more poorly paid jobs, which make them poor adults, soon to be parents of poor students as the cycle begins again.

INEQUALITY IN SCHOOL FUNDING

Public schools in the United States have traditionally served the neighborhoods surrounding them. Because schools receive a large share of their funding from property taxes and because the value of property varies considerably from neighborhood to neighborhood, some school districts receive considerably more money than others. And since neighborhoods often contain many representatives from one racial or ethnic group, schools have traditionally reflected little diversity in social class, race, or ethnicity. This was one of the first observations made by sociologist James Coleman and a team of researchers in 1966, when they were seeking answers to questions about educational inequality in the United States. Although schools were not segregated by law in the United States by 1966, most of them experienced de facto segregation; that is, ethnic neighborhoods coupled with neighborhood schools produced segregated schools.

Coleman and his colleagues were primarily interested in finding out why good students excelled. They concluded that the most important factor in student success was not the amount of money spent in the school district but rather a student's attitude toward school, work habits, and socioeconomic background. Furthermore, they found higher test scores among African American students who attended schools with high levels of racial and economic diversity, as compared to African American students in largely segregated schools. Their overall conclusion was that unequal school funding was not the primary cause of educational inequality; the blocks to success were poor school attitudes coupled with a poor cultural background among segregated African American students. The logical solution seemed to be compensatory education and busing.

Compensatory education assumes that certain students come from cultural backgrounds that ill prepare them for the demands of the public school system; compensatory education is designed to fill in the gaps in that background so that those students will be able to compete on an equal footing with other students. The best-known such program is Head Start, which attempts to prepare preschool children for the demands of first grade and beyond. Early studies on the efficacy of Head Start were somewhat inconclusive; the program obviously helped students in the short run, but findings are less clear on how much it helped in the long run. Such questions are difficult to answer because so many factors affect school achievement. Nevertheless, other studies suggest that Head Start graduates do make long-term gains (Barnett and Hustedt, 2005; Brown, 1985).

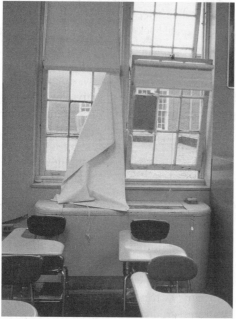

Public primary and secondary schools in the United States vary considerably in quality.

Busing is the attempt to create student bodies with diversity in race, ethnicity, and social class through the movement of students within and across school district lines. Busing within a district may produce few results if all schools within the district contain mostly poor nonwhite students. In fact, many American cities today lack diversity as increasing numbers of middle-class families have moved from cities to suburbs. When busing plans cross district lines between city and suburb, the goals of diversity become possible to achieve. Although busing created considerable political conflict when it was first introduced, there was less conflict in the 1990s, partly because other approaches to integration, such as magnet schools, had been introduced. Busing does help minority students achieve higher grades and test scores when buses bring them to schools containing European American students from a higher socioeconomic background (Mahard and Crain, 1983). The fact that efforts such as busing are dependent on increasing contact among students from different classes suggests that much of the inequality we see in student performance stems from inequality outside the classroom and probably cannot be removed through even the most innovative educational experiments. It may be asking too much of our schools that they do more than mirror the society that created them.

THE STRUCTURE OF AMERICAN PRIMARY AND SECONDARY EDUCATION

Primary and secondary education comprise grades one through twelve, commonly with kindergarten at the outset. For most American children, this process begins at the age of five or six and continues until eighteen. Although many children spend more hours watching television than attending classes during these years, it is still easy to make a case for the tremendous impact of the educational institution on the child. We have already looked at some of those effects, but we should also remember that not all schools (and school experiences) are the same. Parents are given a number of traditional options for how their children will spend those twelve years—especially the choice between private or public education. Recent times have produced new choices within the public system. In this section of the chapter, we first look at the differences between public and private education, then take a look at new programs in public education, such as magnet schools, bilingual and multicultural education, and the mainstreaming of students with disabilities.

PUBLIC AND PRIVATE SCHOOLS

More than 93,000 public schools currently offer primary and secondary education in the United States; they educate over 86 percent of American children enrolled in schools. The remaining 14 percent primarily attend over 27,000 private schools, of which over 21,000 are run by religious institutions. More than 8,000 of those religious schools are run by the American Catholic Church (U.S. Bureau of the Census, 2004a).

While it might appear at first glance that the relatively large number of private schools enrolling so few students would result in many fewer students per teacher,

In public schools, especially schools in big cities, classes may consist of thirty to forty students. With so many children in a classroom, it is usually necessary to arrange desks or tables in rows and make fairly rigid rules of conduct, just to keep some semblance of order. A number of private schools can offer smaller class sizes, some small enough so that students can sit around casually and discuss things with each other as well as with the teacher.

class sizes in private schools are only slightly smaller than those in public schools. Private schools tend to be much smaller than public institutions and to have smaller staffs. But while the student-teacher ratios are similar, the results of student achievement vary considerably. Private schools are doing a better job. The figures in Table 11.1 suggest something of the differences in student achievement between these primary and secondary schools in the United States.

A higher percentage of private school students attend college than the graduates of public schools (Falsey and Heyns, 1984). A logical explanation for this difference might seem to be the difference in costs between the two forms of education. Because private education creates direct costs for parents, the students would be economically screened, producing far fewer lower-class children in the private school classrooms. That economic explanation certainly accounts for some of the differences in educational achievement, but it does not explain all the differences. If we compare private and public school students whose parents are similar in social class and education, students in the private schools still achieve more than their matched comrades in the public schools (Coleman et al., 1982; Coleman and Hoffer, 1987). If we narrow that comparison down to just Catholic schools and just minority students, the private school again appears to be doing a superior job of both educating and

TABLE 11.1
AVERAGE MATHEMATICS AND SCIENCE PROFICIENCY BY SCHOOL TYPE, 1999

| | Type of School | | | | | |
| | Public | | | Private | | |
	9-year-olds	13-year-olds	17-year-olds	9-year-olds	13-year-olds	17-year-olds
Mathematics	230.6	274.2	306.7	242.0	285.8	320.6
Science	228.0	254.0	293.4	238.9	269.3	311.4

Source: U.S. Department of Education, 2003.

motivating students (Greeley, 1982). As we have seen, no major differences exist in student-teacher ratios between public and private schools, but differences do exist in other areas. Catholic schools tend to have both stricter discipline and higher educational standards for their students than public schools; presumably, their students are willing and capable of responding (Jensen, 1986).

Public schools are unlikely to make major economic inroads on private education. Public schools now receive about half their funding from state sources and the other half from local property taxes. The latter source produces school inequality, as we have seen, and public schools' overall dependence on the American taxpayer (who has not been inclined lately to favor higher taxes) suggests that their economic difficulties will continue. And the lack of money to purchase educational resources clearly has an impact on student success (Page, 2002).

The less tangible factors that seem to favor private education are more difficult to assess. Could, for example, public schools effectively raise both academic standards and standards for discipline to create an environment approximating that of Catholic schools? Other factors may be involved as well. Even inner-city Catholic schools with predominantly nonwhite students may be able to create higher motivation because of their distinctiveness amid a public school environment. Private schools may also be attracting students from those parents who are most committed to and supportive of their children's education. We do know that parental involvement in a child's education pays dividends down the road for that child's educational success (Barnard, 2004). Nevertheless, the relative success of private schools suggests what is possible in education. Even though a child's socioeconomic background has a major impact on school success, educators are not completely helpless in counteracting that impact.

MAGNET SCHOOLS

Magnet schools are secondary public schools that specialize in a particular area of the curriculum, providing students with focused (and presumably excellent) instruction in classes with other students who share their interests. A school might specialize in the humanities, science, the performing arts, or foreign language and culture. A school might even choose traditional studies, emphasizing the basics of education in a highly disciplined environment. By providing such a focus, the schools attract not only the best and most highly motivated students but also dedicated teachers to whom that educational environment is appealing. In general, magnet schools have been successful in attracting European American students back to the inner city. In some cases, they have been perhaps too successful, as inner-city nonwhites have had some difficulty in competing for enrollment space. In spite of their value, magnet schools are only a partial answer to the problems of unequal and segregated public schools in the United States, since there is not enough funding to provide such facilities for all students.

MULTICULTURAL AND BILINGUAL EDUCATION

Although public schools have generally been under local control, the form of instruction and curriculum content has been largely standardized, so children throughout the country have received a remarkably similar experience. The schools, not surprisingly, have reflected the predominantly English culture that characterizes American life, with an emphasis on English language and literature couched within a generally Eurocentric view of the world.

In the past, students who brought non-English or non-European cultures with them to school faced a large gap between who they were and what their teachers wanted them to become. Traditionally, public schools have been less than tolerant about such student problems, sometimes punishing students for speaking languages other than English in class or even on the playground. Such treatment has helped to eliminate certain non-English cultural traits from the American landscape, but it has not always been successful at replacing those traits with the skills promoted by the school curriculum (Lee, 1992). Minority children often fail to learn what schools teach, and a significant number drop out before receiving a diploma. An assumption made by many educators is that this lack of attention to the cultural diversity of students lessens their achievements through lowering their self-esteem (Hymowitz, 1992; McCarthy, 1990). Since the 1960s, American schools have tried to respond to these shortcomings through bilingual schools and multicultural programs.

Programs providing bilingual or multicultural education vary both in form and in degree. Some provide additional course content designed to match the cultures children bring to school, while others devote a significant portion of the curriculum to non-English content and to classes taught in a language other than English. The official goal of such programs is to provide children with an easier route to traditional American educational objectives. For example, children who do not speak English are first taught to read in their native language while simultaneously learning to speak English; once they have accomplished both these ends, learning to read in English should be easier. Such programs have been geared primarily to Spanish-speaking children in the Northeast, Florida, and the Southwest, and to Asian children who have immigrated to the United States over the last twenty-five years (see

Chapter 8). An unofficial goal of such programs, particularly with regard to Spanish-speaking populations, has been to maintain some of the elements of Spanish culture through the institutional support of the educational system.

Although the programs and schools have been in place for a number of years, it is difficult to assess fully their success in achieving either goal. Factors beyond school curriculum also have a major impact on students' attitudes toward school achievement and toward mainstream American culture. Under the circumstances, it is difficult either to credit such programs with success or to blame them for failure. Nevertheless, they do reflect a fundamental change (if they remain permanently in place) in how open the educational institution is to other cultures.

MAINSTREAMING STUDENTS WITH DISABILITIES

American public education has theoretically been open to all since its inception, but not all students have had equal access. As we saw in Chapter 8, certain ethnic and racial groups have been singled out for special (and unequal) treatment at various times in American history. In addition, individual students thought to be incapable of handling the standard school curriculum because of mental or physical disabilities have either been denied access to public education or been relegated to separate classes. In 1975, Congress passed the Education of the Handicapped Act, which provided for a "free and appropriate public education" to all children with handicapping conditions.

Between 1977 (when the law was implemented) and 2000, the number of special education students rose from 3.7 to 5.6 million, primarily as a result of an increase in the number of students classified as "learning disabled." Learning disabled students now make up over 50 percent of all special education students; the other major categories include speech-impaired students (19 percent), mentally retarded students (11 percent), and emotionally disturbed students (8 percent). Special education students as a whole make up more than 11 percent of all students enrolled in the United States (U.S. Bureau of the Census, 2004a).

Traditionally, special education students were handled in segregated classes or facilities. In recent years, however, efforts have been made to mainstream these students—that is, to integrate them in normal public school classes whenever possible. One goal of **mainstreaming** is to undermine the stigma connected with segregated "special" classes. In addition, educators hope that integration will benefit students with disabilities educationally through their increased contact with a wider variety of students; they also hope that "normal" students will gain a wider perspective. Such efforts are of particular importance considering that close to half of all special education students have been labeled as "learning disabled" and that this label has been criticized as being subjectively applied (Carrier, 1986). The fact that poor and minority children are more likely to acquire this label lends credence to the argument that these children should not be isolated from the more general school curriculum and population.

SCHOOL EFFECTIVENESS

In April 1983, the National Commission on Excellence in Education presented its findings as to the effectiveness of public education in the United States. The members concluded that America's schools were failing in their mission to educate America's youth with the skills necessary for dealing with a technological society. They cited such facts as the 23 million American adults who were functionally illiterate, the drop in student scores on standardized achievement tests, and the poor showing of American students on tests relative to scores achieved by students in other industrialized societies. The commission concluded that if such an educational system had been imposed on us by a foreign power, we would have viewed it as an act of war (National Commission on Excellence in Education, 1983).

In 2001, Congress passed the Elementary and Secondary Education Act, better known as the No Child Left Behind Act. Its focus was on holding public schools accountable, particularly in students' mathematics and reading scores. After testing students, schools would be expected to show Adequate Yearly Progress toward reaching a goal of 100 percent of students reaching proficiency. Schools failing to show such progress would ultimately be restructured, and students would have the option of requesting transfer to another school.

Table 11.2 shows some of the differences in student abilities in various industrial nations. In international tests of mathematics and science literacy among fifteen-year-old students in 2000, American students scored at or close to the bottom on both. Part of this difference is explained by improvements in education achieved by other countries. It is interesting to note, for example, that teachers in Japan are in the top 10 percent of all wage earners in that country, whereas in the United States, teachers rate about average with regard to other occupations; such differences suggest the relative importance placed on education by the two countries. But part of the difference between American students and those of other countries appears to be the result of changes in American education over time as well. American students today may not be the equals of American students a generation ago.

Secondary school educational outcomes clearly vary for different students in the United States. Table 11.3 compares the achievement test scores of twelfth-grade students on history, writing, and geography. The most striking differences appear in relation to parents' educational attainment and race/ethnicity. For parents' education, test scores line up neatly from less-educated parents to more-educated parents. Parents' education is generally the most important family predictor of student success, particularly with regard to the mother's educational attainment (Thompson and Luhman, 1997). For race and ethnic differences, the most successful students are either white or Asian; African American, American Indian, and Hispanic students all lag behind. Keep in mind, however, that those three groups are also more likely to come from families in which parents have less education. It is difficult to know from raw figures such as these just what is causing the variation. We do know that high values on educational success are widespread in American society, regardless of social class or race (Tedin and Weiher, 2004).

TABLE 11.2

AVERAGE READING, MATHEMATICS, AND SCIENCE LITERACY SCORES OF
15-YEAR-OLDS, 2000

Country	Reading Literacy	Mathematics Literacy	Science Literacy
Canada	534	533	529
Japan	522	557	550
United Kingdom	523	529	532
Republic of Korea	525	547	552
Australia	528	533	528
Finland	546	536	538
Sweden	516	510	512
France	505	517	500
United States	504	493	499
Germany	484	490	487

Source: U.S. Department of Education, 2003.

TABLE 11.3

TWELFTH-GRADE STUDENT ACHIEVEMENT PROFICIENCY PERCENTAGES ON HISTORY,
WRITING, AND GEOGRAPHY, 1998–2001.

	Sex		Race/ethnicity					Parents' Education		
	Male	Female	White	Black	Hispanic	American Indian	Asian	<HS	HS	College
History*	12	10	13	3	5	1	21	2	4	18
Writing**	14	29	26	8	10	9	24	5	13	30
Geography*	28	21	31	4	10	–	26	10	12	36

* Percent rated at or above proficient, 2001.
** Percent rated at or above proficient, 1998.
Source: U.S. Department of Education, 2003.

A few pages ago, we looked at tracking in the American school system, whereby students are placed in courses according to the expectations school administrators have of them. At times, tracking simply means placing students into the same general classes but varying the level of difficulty. A higher-tracked English class might have more reading assigned, for example. At other times, the classes themselves may differ. Table 11.4 shows some of the variation in the students who take particular mathematics and science classes in American high schools. Many of the classes tend to be cumulative (you have to take algebra before you can take calculus), and some of the classes are Advanced Placement (AP) or Honors classes. Moving down the list, you will note the increasing disappearance of African American, Native American, and Hispanic students. Much of the difference in twelfth-grade achievement

TABLE 11.4

PERCENTAGE OF HIGH SCHOOL GRADUATES TAKING SELECTED MATHEMATICS AND SCIENCE
COURSES IN HIGH SCHOOL, BY SEX AND RACE/ETHNICITY, 1987 TO 2000

					2000						
								Race/ethnicity			
Courses	1987	1990	1994	1998	Sex		White	Black	Hispanic	Asian/ Pacific Islander	American Indian/ Alaskan Native
					Men	Women					
Mathematics											
Any mathematics	98.9	99.6	99.8	99.8	99.8	99.9	99.8	99.8	99.8	100.0	100.0
Algebra I	64.0	64.2	65.8	62.8	60.0	63.4	60.5	66.5	69.5	48.8	65.2
Geometry	59.7	63.4	70.0	75.1	74.9	81.4	79.2	77.9	72.8	80.6	65.0
Algebra II	48.6	51.7	61.1	61.7	64.8	70.5	68.9	64.8	59.8	80.4	60.3
Trigonometry	18.6	18.2	11.7	8.9	7.3	7.7	8.5	4.1	2.9	14.5	4.3
Analysis/ pre-calculus	12.6	13.4	17.3	23.1	25.4	27.9	28.2	16.2	19.3	48.8	12.6
Statistics/ probability	1.3	1.0	2.0	3.7	5.8	5.6	6.1	3.8	2.3	11.5	2.1
Calculus	6.0	6.5	9.3	11.0	12.2	11.1	12.5	4.7	5.6	30.8	2.4
AP calculus	3.2	4.1	7.0	6.7	8.5	7.3	8.4	2.6	3.6	24.0	1.7
Science											
Any science	98.7	99.4	99.5	99.5	99.3	99.7	99.6	99.5	99.1	99.7	99.6
Biology	86.0	91.0	693.2	92.7	89.0	93.3	91.8	92.3	89.7	88.3	88.4
AP/honors/ biology	9.4	10.1	11.9	16.2	13.8	18.5	17.9	10.8	10.8	25.9	8.0
Chemistry	44.2	48.9	55.8	60.4	58.0	65.7	63.0	59.9	52.4	75.4	43.6
AP/honors chemistry	3.5	3.5	3.9	4.7	5.8	5.7	6.1	2.8	3.4	16.2	1.7
Physics	20.0	21.6	24.5	28.8	34.2	29.0	32.4	25.2	23.2	54.0	17.5
AP/honors/ physics	1.8	2.0	2.7	3.0	5.4	2.5	4.0	2.2	2.0	11.0	0.5
Engineering	2.6	4.2	4.5	6.7	4.3	3.5	4.2	2.7	2.4	3.1	1.8
Astronomy	1.0	1.2	1.7	1.9	3.0	2.6	2.8	1.8	3.7	2.0	3.8
Geology/ earth science	13.4	24.7	22.9	20.7	18.4	16.6	17.5	18.8	15.9	11.1	16.0
Biology and chemistry	41.4	47.5	53.7	59.0	54.5	63.8	60.3	58.0	50.4	71.1	39.4
Biology, chemistry, and physics	16.6	18.8	21.4	25.4	26.4	24.0	25.7	20.1	17.6	47.2	11.9

Source: U.S. Department of Education, 2003.

TABLE 11.5

SAT SCORES BY SELECTED AMERICAN ETHNIC GROUPS, 2001–02

Ethnic Group	Verbal	Mathematics
White	527	533
Asian	501	569
Mexican American	446	457
American Indian	479	483
Puerto Rican	455	451
African American	430	427

Source: U.S. Department of Education, 2003.

test scores stems from the tracking systems used in most high schools. Students are unlikely to score high in subjects they have not taken. Not surprisingly, we also see these differences reflected in the racial and ethnic breakdowns of SAT scores (see Table 11.5).

In response to charges of failure from critics, some public schools in the United States have turned to minimum-competency tests for high school graduates. The purpose of such tests is to require high school graduates to have acquired at least a minimum level of competency in certain skills. Students who fail that exam will be denied their diploma until they are able to pass the test. The proponents of such tests argue that schools will no longer have incentives to give "social promotion" without course mastery, since a diploma is not guaranteed. Those who oppose such mandatory testing for diplomas argue that (1) tests are not always the best measure of one's knowledge but also measure other things (such as cultural background or test-taking skills), and (2) ethnic minorities in the United States will be unfairly affected and rejected by such tests, thereby blocking them from moving forward in their educational pursuits.

It is difficult to measure academic accomplishment by students or, when measured, to assess blame or credit for the results. As we saw earlier in this chapter, schools in the United States vary considerably from district to district. Poorly funded schools tend to be filled with lower-class students who, on any measure, tend to exhibit poor academic accomplishments regardless of their racial or ethnic background. Beyond that, American students today may lack the levels of dedication of previous generations, and that change may be reflected in changing standards at public schools. It is difficult for a teacher to keep his or her attention on nouns or verbs if students are bringing violence or drug sales into the classroom.

HIGHER EDUCATION IN THE UNITED STATES

Postsecondary education in the United States currently faces a declining population of eighteen-year-old high school graduates but benefits from a higher percentage of

those graduates enrolling in college, plus increasing numbers of older students returning to college after years in the labor market. More and more jobs require specific
college degrees; also, a number of jobs have come to require more advanced degrees
than they once did. This "degree inflation" (sometimes termed *credentialism*) occurs
as the employment sector comes to evaluate individual qualifications more on the
amount of training than on demonstrable skills and abilities. In short, higher education in the United States is healthy, but the interest of sociologists in its structure and
processes stems from its connection to the labor market. As higher education becomes
increasingly the route to occupational advancement, sociologists want to know which
Americans benefit from it and which do not. In this section, we take a brief look at
the structure of higher education and then examine who has access to it.

HIGHER EDUCATION: PUBLIC AND PRIVATE

There are currently over 2,450 4-year institutions of higher learning in the United
States, along with over 1,700 2-year institutions. Current enrollment stands at
15.3 million students. (As recently as 1967, only half that number was enrolled.) Of
that 15.3 million, approximately 77 percent are enrolled in public institutions; the
remainder attend private institutions. Currently, 61.7 percent of high school graduates enroll in college within the next year. That figure has been dropping gradually
in recent years from a high of 67 percent since 1997 (U.S. Bureau of the Census,
2004a). In short, higher education is a major enterprise in the United States that
touches many of our lives in one way or another.

Institutions of higher learning in the United States vary in more ways than their
public or private status. Universities offer four-year degrees but also provide graduate education in a variety of liberal arts and professional programs. Some universities are research oriented; that means that their primary aim is the production of
new knowledge and technology through the efforts of their faculty, who are required
to contribute toward that end. In such institutions, some faculty members become
so engrossed in research that they rarely, if ever, see the inside of a classroom. Research
is supported in part by the universities themselves but primarily through grants provided by outside agencies, often those of the federal government. These institutions
are typically the homes of doctoral programs, through which new generations of
researchers and faculty members are produced. By contrast, other universities and
almost all four-year colleges are teaching oriented. That means that research may or
may not occur, but the primary aim of the institution is to provide a complete and
stimulating educational environment for students.

Two-year colleges include a wide variety of private colleges to complement an
ever-growing community college system through which low-cost education is provided. These schools provide for the enrollment of over 38 percent of American
undergraduate students (U.S. Bureau of the Census, 2004a). Their low cost, availability, and open admissions policies make them the logical choice of many Americans who lack the income or the educational skills to attend more prestigious (and

more expensive) institutions. While community colleges were initially viewed as a stepping stone to four-year colleges, the majority of their students do not take that step but rather enter the labor force after completing two-year programs. According to some research, community college education is perceived as less valuable in the occupational marketplace (Monk-Turner, 1990).

ACCESS TO HIGHER EDUCATION

While educational degrees provide the credentials essential for occupational advancement, it is also true that the absence of educational degrees effectively blocks occupational advancement. Education clearly has a pivotal role in modern American society. Therefore, an important sociological quest is to find who has access to the institutions that bestow these valued goods. In particular, sociologists are interested in the availability of education to those most in need of advancement—poor Americans in general, and racial and ethnic minorities in particular.

The first step toward higher education is high school graduation. In 2004, over 84 percent of European Americans over age 25 had at least graduated from high school; by comparison, in 1960 only 43 percent of this group held a diploma in hand. For African Americans, the same span of time has seen an increase from 20 percent to 78 percent. And that improvement has been largely the result of greater academic success among African American girls; African American boys have clearly been falling behind (Cohen and Nee, 2000; Downey and Ainsworth-Darnell, 2002).

For Hispanic Americans, their 57 percent graduation rate in 2002 (up from 32.1 in 1970) suggests a less successful experience with public education. Looking just at Mexican Americans, their 2002 graduation rate of 50.6 percent improved from 24.2 percent in 1970 (U.S. Bureau of the Census, 2004a). Figure 11.1 sheds more light on this experience by comparing these American ethnic groups of all ages in 2002 by the percentage of each group failing to finish high school. All the major Hispanic groups have higher failure rates than either European or African Americans; the largest Hispanic group—Mexican Americans—have the most difficulty, almost half of them failing to gain a diploma. Evidence suggests that Hispanic educational failure stems from a combination of lower social class status coupled with significant cultural differences from the schools (Janinski, 2000). For many African Americans and Hispanic Americans, therefore, access to higher education is cut off before they can even get to the admissions door.

Of all Americans who received high school diplomas in 2001, over 61 percent enrolled in a college or university in the following year. If we break that figure down into its ethnic components, we find that 64.2 percent of European American high school graduates continued their education immediately, as compared to 54.6 percent of African Americans and 51.7 percent of Hispanic Americans. They did not all enroll in the same schools, however. While African Americans make up 11.3 percent of all college students nationwide, they make up 10.6 percent in 4-year institutions as compared to 12.4 percent in 2-year institutions. For Hispanic Americans, those

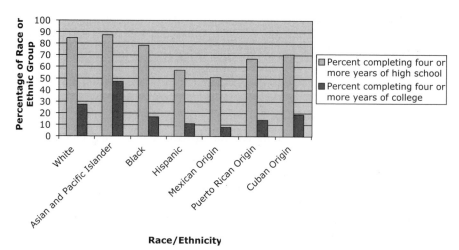

Figure 11.1 Educational attainment by race/ethnicity, 2002. (Data from U.S. Bureau of the Census, 2004a)

same figures are 6.6 and 14.2 percent (U.S. Department of Education, 2003). Unless they graduate and transfer, therefore, both African Americans and Hispanic Americans are less likely to achieve a 4-year college degree than European Americans. Figure 11.1 also shows the differences in 2002 in the percentage of American ethnic groups of all ages who had received a 4-year college degree or more. African Americans graduated at a rate only 63 percent that of European Americans, while Mexican Americans fared less well, graduating at 28 percent of the same rate.

Lack of success with higher education by ethnic minorities in the United States has many causes. A good part of the problem is simply money. Ethnic stratification in the United States guarantees that ethnic minorities will be disproportionately poor (see Chapter 8). Money buys higher education directly but it also buys experiences and environments throughout life that add to success later in higher education. Table 11.5 shows SAT scores for American ethnic groups in 2001–2002. Only Asian Americans outdistance European Americans, and they do so only in mathematics. High SAT scores, which open doors to colleges and scholarships, also indicate something about the familiarity that members of different groups have with the skills expected for college education. Individuals with lower scores will be in the situation of Murai in the reading following this chapter: facing frustration in the classroom because the vocabulary and course material are unfamiliar.

Ethnic minorities have less access to higher education because they have less income, but poorer European Americans face many of the same limitations. Hodgkinson (1986) found that wealthier young people with only medium scholastic abilities were more likely to enroll in college than were lower-income young people with high scholastic ability. When poorer European American students do enroll in college,

BOX 11.2

"Political Correctness" versus Multiculturalism: Issues in American Higher Education

The issues of multicultural and bilingual education in the primary and secondary areas discussed in this chapter have also entered the world of higher education. The traditional Eurocentric curriculum of American higher education has come under attack for ignoring the cultural diversity of students. Proponents of multicultural education argue that minority students are deprived of the opportunity to explore their cultural roots and are simultaneously denied rewards for the non-European cultural strengths they bring with them to higher education. At the same time, it is argued that dominant group students are deprived of a curriculum that would provide them a greater sensitivity to cultural diversity in general and to culturally diverse students with whom they share their classrooms.

The most widely publicized opposing view to multicultural education is Allan Bloom's 1987 book, *The Closing of the American Mind*. Bloom characterizes (and often caricatures) multiculturalism as an educational fad that marches to the drumbeat of "political correctness" (for fear of offending anyone) while denigrating the cultural achievements of the Western world. He defends the traditional curriculum while ridiculing multicultural alternatives as second-rate at best. Others also observe that politically correct speech (particularly with regard to what different minority groups are called) tends to limit free speech as students and faculty alike feel compelled to follow the politically correct path (Hentoff, 1991).

Education has always been a political issue. As we've seen in this and earlier chapters, the control over culture equals a control over society. Knowledge defined as "valuable" by major societal institutions rewards those who have that knowledge while simultaneously penalizing those who don't. The issue of multiculturalism in American universities is more properly seen as part of a larger power struggle in which those previously left out now wish to have their strengths validated by major institutions. And to the extent that they are successful, those who have previously held power will be forced to give a little. Jokes about political correctness aside, the issue of multiculturalism in higher education raises serious questions about the distribution of power in American society and should not be taken lightly (see Bell-Villada, 1991; Daniels, 1991).

they are likely to enroll in two-year institutions, as are ethnic minority students. While the public two-year institutions enroll large numbers of all students, their specialization in lower-income students is obvious. As with ethnic minorities, poorer students in general are less likely to be in four-year institutions or in institutions with graduate programs. They are also most likely to be students in private, for-profit schools, such as business schools.

Education is not the only determinant of economic success in American society. Nevertheless, as education becomes increasingly formalized in the United States and as degrees become increasingly connected to routes of economic mobility, education becomes a significant institution in determining the quality of life for most of us. As the data presented above suggest, education may be available in the United States, but it is not accessible equally to all. To the extent that poor Americans and minorities do not benefit from education, it can be argued that formalized education justifies the current system of social stratification by convincing those whom it fails that the responsibility for failure is theirs and not the institution's.

SUMMARY

The growth of the educational institution has occurred in large part as a response to the changing needs of an industrial economy. In addition to passing along knowledge and skills needed in that economy, schools also serve to provide social and cultural integration (through both intended and less obvious forms of socialization that accompany the school experience) and to "screen" the population in the allocation of certain people to certain areas of employment. Research on the educational institution indicates that the social class of incoming children is the strongest predictor of educational success; this relationship is produced through a variety of influences, including teacher expectations, tracking, and cultural differences among incoming students. In addition, inequality of funding from one school district to another has provided fewer resources for poor children than for middle-class children. Compensatory education and busing have both been tried in the last few decades to minimize the results of such inequality.

Besides public education in the United States, there are private educational institutions (some independent, some sponsored by religious organizations), which, on the whole, appear to be more effective in reaching their educational goals, as measured by standardized tests of student achievement. The public school system has responded to critics with new approaches, such as magnet schools (in which individual schools offer a specialized curriculum) and bilingual education (in response to the growing numbers of new immigrants who are not English speaking). Efforts have also been made to "mainstream" those with disabilities so as to end their segregation from the general school population.

Many other industrial nations appear to be surpassing American schools in their success, as measured by student achievement. Also, American students appear to be less well prepared than in the past, again as measured by standardized tests.

Higher education has become increasingly necessary because American occupations are demanding better training for entry-level positions. Growth in higher education, both public and private, has been considerable in response to this change; in particular, enrollment in two-year institutions has increased. As with primary and secondary education, social class is the best predictor of student success in college. Nonwhite students compete even less effectively among their white college counterparts than they do in the earlier grades, and this gap in achievement in higher education appears to have been growing in recent years.

GLOSSARY

Busing The attempt to create school populations with diversity in race, ethnicity, and social class through the movement of students within and across school district lines.

Compensatory education Programs, such as Head Start, that aim to give children from "deprived" backgrounds the same skills that middle-class children start school with.

Hidden curriculum Basic cultural values imparted indirectly to students through the school experience; generally acquired through the requirements of the role of student.

Magnet schools Secondary public schools that specialize in a particular area of the curriculum, providing students with focused instruction in classes with other students who share their interests.

Mainstreaming The integration of physically, mentally, or emotionally disabled students in normal public school classes.

Tracking The process of placing students into different classes according to their measured ability.

STUDY QUESTIONS

1. Why does an industrial society require a separate institution of education?
2. What have been the traditional goals or functions of the educational institution during the last century in the United States?
3. What is the relationship between educational inequality and (1) teacher expectations, (2) tracking programs, (3) access to advanced placement courses, and (4) traditional methods of school funding? What changes have occurred in this equality due to busing, multicultural (and/or bilingual) education, magnet schools, and compensatory education?
4. How does American education compare with education around the world?
5. How does the American school system interact with the racial and ethnic diversity of American society?

H. M. Murai

No Can Geeve Up:
Crossing Institutional Barriers

Institutional discrimination is discrimination that affects particular racial or ethnic groups not because of their group membership but because of skills or abilities that tend to distinguish them from dominant group members. When our institutions discriminate on the basis of such skills or abilities, particular racial or ethnic groups may be adversely affected just as surely as if their group had been singled out for unequal treatment. In the following article, H. M. Murai tells the story of his childhood and his experiences as a university freshman. Growing up in a distinctive Japanese American community in Hawaii, he differed in many ways from the dominant group, which conceived and operates the University of Hawaii. Of those many differences, Murai focuses on his language. He grew up speaking a form of language known as a pidgin (which combines and simplifies elements of two or more other languages). A pidgin language accomplishes the task of communication (which is all a language really need do), but Murai found it less than acceptable to his freshman English teacher at the university; to Murai, freshman English might as well have been freshman Greek. Since he was able to write the following article, he must have succeeded, but many in his place wouldn't have.

I grew up in a sugar plantation community near Hilo on the "Big Island" of Hawaii. In spite of its size, it is still considered to be one of the "outer islands" of Hawaii; i.e., not the center of industry and especially the tourist industry, which thrives on the island of Oahu and more recently, Maui and Kauai. Growing up in a plantation community one was considered to be "from the country(side)." People from the country are often considered lower class and lower in "class."

Plantation language, which was my first language, was closer to the pidgin spoken by the original immigrant workers, somewhere between a Creole and a dialect of English. You were likely to find interaction between ethnic groups in the plantation camps in spite of management's attempts to keep the groups separate and ununited. The integration of ethnic groups contributed to the perpetuation of the original pidgin created for communication across languages. On any given Sunday you would find Filipinos, Japanese, and Portuguese gathering at the local cockpit and billiard hall. Growing up in this environment made it difficult to identify the sources of words borrowed from Filipino, Japanese, Portuguese, Hawaiian, and so on in the local dialect.

I believe that the majority of the children coming from the camps were proud of their roots. Being proud of our backgrounds I believe further contributed to our maintenance of the language and culture of the camps. Life in the camp was rarely dull. One could always go "pick cane" from the cane fields or "catch cane" from the flumes delivering the cut sugar cane stalks to the mill. There was also "poking crayfish" and opu (mudfish) in the rivah (river), catching opal (river shrimp), picking wild guava and rose apple, or just following the rivah. In my case there was also body surfing with scraps of board at one of dah bes beaches in the islands. During the summer months, baseball and the Japanese bon dances (commemorating the deceased) provided more weekend recreation and entertainment. Entrance into the middle and secondary schools located in the city provided for a broadening of one's cultural-linguistic circle, however; the foundation of the personalities of the kids from the camps was formed in the camps, and Hilo, Hawaii, is indeed a country town when compared to Honolulu.

Leaving the warmth and security of home for the first time to venture off to school in the big city, Honolulu, provided as much cultural-linguistic conflict as I could handle. The institutional barriers to being successful in college were many.

I had heard about how one-third of the freshman class failed English composition at the University of Hawaii and how failure in composition usually led to flunking out of school. English comp. was known as the screening class for those who could and those who couldn't. This was especially true of students with my background; i.e., students who were from the rural areas of the islands and who spoke "pidgin" English (actually a dialect of English). I was from one of the "outer islands" (islands other than Oahu, where Honolulu, the capital, is located). Adding to my fears was the self-doubt that haunted me throughout my first year—self-doubt that was set in motion by my almost total failure during my final two years in high school and by a counselor who thought I would be "wasting time and money" by pursuing a university degree. I am quite sure that my father had the same sense of doubt when he waved me off at the airport with the somewhat ambiguous, "No can come home" (may be interpreted as "You can't come home" or the intended, I believed, "If you can't make it, come home"). In fact, till this very moment it is still not clear to me how I was able to attend the university out of high school. I had taken college preparatory courses such as chemistry, geometry, and a second year of algebra, but I would have been the first to admit that I had no demonstrable proof that I had learned anything in these classes. Nearly straight D grades were an accurate reflection of my near total neglect of academics. Attitudinally, I learned that I was not capable of anything beyond the usual requirements for high school graduation. I definitely felt much more comfortable playing for extra spending money in the pool room or drinking beer "wid dah boys" than in any classroom.

Perhaps my greatest fear during the first semester was that someone would discover that I was mistakenly admitted to the university and that yes, my high school counselor was correct in suggesting that it was a waste of time and money for me to pursue a university education. This led to more than a bit of paranoia. I felt that I was being watched and could not afford to attract any attention through failure. Failure on any examination and definitely failure in any class I was sure would lead to immediate discovery. Visiting the office of any instructor was thus out of the question. My inability to speak "good English" would surely lead to my being spotted as an imposter. Much to my relief none of my professors required individual meetings. In fact, I do not recall any professor mentioning office hours, much less inviting students with problems to come in for consultation.

I can still recall, after 25 years, what my first semester freshman schedule was like. I know I felt compelled to enroll for 18 units, which was the maximum allowed. I thought (incorrectly) that I had to do this in order to graduate in four years, just as the catalog had illustrated. I recall speech class, where I was obviously in deep trouble trying to pronounce the "th," "ed," short "i" and "schwa" sounds and vainly attempting to speak "like one haole" (anglo). Western civilization class was at 7:30 A.M., Tuesday, Thursday, and Saturday and freshman English was Monday, Wednesday, and Friday at 2:00 P.M. Western civ. was a memorable class not simply because of the time and the 300 or so students packed in an auditorium, seat numbers assigned, but because of the difficulty I had in note taking. Note taking was a skill I had never acquired in high school. I assumed that my notes had to be accurate and thought that someone might ask to read them. I wrote in pencil, filling every line and margin as though I had spent my last penny on the notebook. I also erased words while desperately trying to record lectures verbatim. Someone forgot to tell me that I was only supposed to capture the main points (assuming I could determine what they were). Needless to say, when it came time to review my notes I had difficulty deciphering my own handwriting and could barely make sense of the little that I was able to decipher. I received a well-earned D in the first semester of Western civilization. But ah, English composition, there was the ultimate challenge.

The instructor for English 101 was, I learned later, a former high school English teacher. She had what may be referred to as a "no nonsense" approach with an emphasis on actually writing rather than grammar or the how-to of writing. In correcting papers, my papers at least, Mrs. C. tried to interpret what I, more frequently than not, was unable to clearly express. She was a risk taker. She was not afraid to substitute words or rewrite sentences in attempting to clarify my compositions. Throughout the first half of the semester, Mrs. C. came close to totally rewriting my compositions. More often than not, she was,

as far as I could ascertain, on the money. I was impressed, amazed, astonished even, to see how clearly she could represent my deepest thoughts and feelings without ever consulting with me. Nevertheless, I managed to receive straight F's on my first six compositions. We were at mid-term and I thought, "You in real trouble bruddha. How you going do dis!" There were no remedial classes offered. It was the prototype of the "sink or swims," "give up or geev um!" (show what you can do) situation.

Receiving graded papers, due on Monday and returned on Friday, was the most demoralizing and embarrassing part of that first semester. In high school I could laugh at the fact that I did not try to do well and thus expected poor grades, but this was the big time and I was indeed trying my utmost to succeed. Thus when I received my straight F's, I simply slid my papers into my notebook so they would not be revealed to my classmates. I also avoided looking at any of my classmates who spoke aloud about their disappointment in receiving B's or C's and even A minuses! Even the gal with the friendly smile sitting next to me who did not say anything about the straight A's she was receiving was a threat to my ego. Surely these people realized that I did not belong in the same room, much less the same university. Surveying the class of twenty-five or so students, it was difficult not to conclude that I was the one of three who were destined for failure: "I just gotta show um (them)" (that I could do it).

As soon as we were given the topic for the next composition on Friday, I headed for the library. Thanks to the good advice of two older students, I had left time after each of my classes to review notes or conduct the research necessary to clarify points in doubt. Although it was extremely painful, and partly because it was required, I immediately began the rewrite of my paper. Because of the detailed correcting by Mrs. C., this was not a terribly difficult task. During the first few weeks, library work included looking up words that were part of the assigned topics. After the very first class, the first word I had to look up was "composition." I was not sure what was being required. I also looked up "plagiarize" (I knew the "Don't" part of the phrase). Although my dictionary never left my side, I frequently found it necessary to look up more detailed descriptions of words in the encyclopedia or unabridged dictionaries in the library. Then began the writing process, outlining, and starting the rough draft. Because the composition class was my last class on Friday, I could spend two to three hours in the library before heading back to my apartment for dinner. My goal was to write the exact number of words required for the composition.

The writing continued immediately after dinner and ended sometime around midnight. As reward for my hard work, I would often treat myself to a bowl of crisp kau chee mein (Chinese noodles with vegetables) and several cups of tea in a restaurant sparsely patronized mainly by people who had closed the local bars. This was a treasured time for meditation and contemplating my world view. Friday evening or early morning at the Golden Duck and martial arts practice during the week were the few breaks in my daily academic routine. I was always happy to get out of the studio apartment I shared with two working brothers. Although only fifteen minutes from Waikiki, I never spent time on the beach that first year in school. Saturdays were devoted to Western civilization, so the final draft on the composition was not completed until Sunday. Until my teacher hinted that it would not be a bad idea to either write the composition with a pen rather than a pencil or even type the final draft, I did not have to spend a lot of time producing the final draft. In spite of the usual ten to fifteen hours of writing spread over three days, I seemed to make little progress during the first six weeks. None of my classmates seemed to be experiencing any difficulty in the class.

I vividly recall standing outside the classroom a half hour before class began, listening to students who were actually completing their compositions before class! These were students who were receiving A's and B's. All I could think of was "You in beeg trouble bruddha!" There were

many days of loneliness and discouragement during which times, for some reason, I refused to accept failure, thinking that all I had to do was work ten times as long and hard as my classmates, a hundred times if necessary. "No can geev up!" was always my final thought.

Then, alas, during the seventh week of class, I was asked to read my paper to the class, an honor given to the chosen few each week. I panicked and hesitated. I was also having serious problems in my speech class at that time. In addition, I had been turned down as a volunteer reader for a blind student because of my inability to read English fluently, and I was not at all confident about getting up in front of the class. The kind teacher obliged by reading my composition for me while I listened with ambivalent feelings of pride and shame: I made it through English composition with a C grade the first semester and a B for the second semester.

I often wonder how and why I persisted during that first semester, especially during the first half of that first semester. I had no one to turn to except myself and a sister-in-law who sometimes read my papers for obvious flaws. I can think of some obvious reasons, such as the fact that I was able to survive without a great deal of effort in my Spanish and psychology classes and of course, P.E. and the required ROTC. However, it was also clear to me that by any combination of grades that I could expect, failing English composition would definitely lead to disenrollment from the university. Reflecting back into that time, I can see numerous reasons for my survival.

I come from a family background where it was assumed that anything could be achieved through effort. I think I felt that failure in school was worse than death. "No can come home" was an ever-present thought throughout my four years as an undergraduate. Hereditary limitations in intellect were not considered important. My father, who I greatly admired, had himself risen from the ranks of a plantation laborer to a supervisorial position. During my junior year in high school he had been selected to join a team of engineers and horticulturists to help modernize sugar mills in a third-world country. Daddy, though extremely strict in discipline, always provided a loving arm around the shoulders in a timely manner, and obviously put the needs of his children over and above his personal needs. He had an eighth-grade education. My mother I admired for her determination to provide for the family through hard work and persistence under difficult economic, sociocultural, and oftentimes highly stressful psychological conditions. She was the model of the nurturing mother, always there in times of need and never punitive. She, too, put her children's needs ahead of her own. Relatives, especially Uncle and Aunty Y, Roy and Kay, also impressed upon me the importance to success of hard work and the willingness to suffer through hard times. These values were reinforced by participation in the martial arts from an early age and by Japanese samurai films that my aunt and uncle introduced to me early on.

Participation in sports must have had some influence on my attitude about persistence in the face of difficult odds. Although never an outstanding athlete, I had experienced some success in baseball, track, and football and even tried swimming and amateur boxing during my junior year when I was injured and unable to participate in football. I had the experience of competing under teachers and coaches who were, for better or for worse, sometimes sadistic in their training methods. Being able to run the last wind sprint and stand up for the final tackle drill and experiencing some success throughout all of the trials I am sure contributed somewhat to my belief that hard work could conquer all.

Although academic successes were few and far between throughout my early school years, I recall reminding myself that I had had some moments of success achieved through hard work. I had vague memories of being fairly successful in challenging social studies, science, and English classes during my junior high school days just prior to being initiated into one of the local gangs. I also had memories of being able to learn Spanish without too much effort and elementary algebra, which did not seem to come too easily

for some of my classmates who I thought were higher achievers. It is funny how a few successful experiences can be so meaningful in times of doubt and carry you over hurdles.

I have always attributed some of my success to a cousin whose intelligence I respected although he had not completed his college work. He had told me that I would never fail if I attended classes faithfully and kept up with my daily work. For the first two years I took his words to heart, never missing a class even though I suffered through several bouts of illness during that time period. I could think of absolutely nothing that could keep me from attending classes, an extreme contrast with my attitude during my high school days when I missed more classes than I attended. This was all in spite of the fact that attendance was never applied as a factor in grading in any of my classes.

My financial situation must be included as a factor that encouraged me to persist and survive. It was my feeling that I would have no second chances in any of my classes; my financial situation, I believed, did not allow for second chances. Although my parents were able to help me with cost of room and board during my first year, I had saved from my part-time job in high school and from several summer jobs, including work with a trucking company and in a fertilizer factory.

There is little doubt that the teacher of my composition class was of primary importance in helping me persist. Although the grades she gave me were not encouraging, the fact that she obviously took the time to correct my errors gave me hope that I could improve if I could learn to self-correct as she had been modeling for me. In fact, I think I spent time committing most of the corrections she modeled for me to long-term memory. I was determined never to make the same error more than once, and though I was not always successful, I knew that I was improving by my fourth or fifth failure. I wonder if Mrs. C knew how her comments and grading of my papers affected me. She gave me no indication that she did, yet she must have surely wondered how I ever managed to get into the university and why I kept coming back for more punishment.

Any one of the reasons discussed above could account for my persistence in English composition. I am of the opinion that, as with most of human behavior, only a complex combination of many reasons, including but not limited to the above, must be considered. Nevertheless, today, as I relate my experience to my students who seem to be in similar situations, I emphasize that one can only fail if one lacks the desire to succeed, the willingness to sacrifice for one's goals. No can geeve up.

DISCUSSION QUESTIONS

1. Do you think that Murai's problems in his freshman year were due to his cultural differences from the university or his lack of attention to school during high school? Are the requirements of freshman composition just to learn to communicate effectively, or do they also include that one do so in a certain approved language? What would have happened if Murai had written clearly but in pidgin?

2. Murai describes his frustration and embarrassment in getting such low grades during his freshman year. How is failure made more difficult to bear when you are surrounded by others to whom success comes so easily?

3. Murai's story is one of surmounting the barriers of institutional discrimination. If he could do it, why can't everyone? How high a barrier is institutional discrimination when we broaden our vision from one person's story to large numbers of people who have important cultural differences from dominant societal institutions?

RELIGION

Human societies around the world have created almost infinite variations on the theme of survival. Although every society, for example, must care for and socialize its young if it is to last, what constitutes the "family" varies widely from culture to culture. Families can be large or small, authoritarian or equalitarian, and so on. Even so, the universal presence of families of some description points to the family as being basic for survival. But is religion basic to survival? Virtually all human cultures contain shared beliefs concerning a supernatural realm, along with some expression of those beliefs in their everyday behaviors. We commonly think of those shared beliefs as religions and of those behaviors as religious ritual.

Specifically, **religion** includes those shared beliefs, associated behavior patterns, and forms of social organization that are oriented toward the supernatural. We find such beliefs, behaviors, and social organizations in practically all human cultures. In industrial societies, religion takes on the characteristics of a separate institution as its social organizations become formalized into churches; religious ritual comes to be closely associated with church doctrine and church settings. In this chapter, we examine the growth of the religious institution. First, we look briefly at some of the basic varieties of religious belief and behavior. Then we examine some theories of religion offered by sociologists, each providing a different perspective on why religions come into existence and how they affect other aspects of society. Finally, we turn to the role of religion in the United States, focusing on the interplay between religions and family behaviors, political attitudes, economic position, and a variety of other aspects of social life on which religion leaves its mark.

RELIGIOUS BELIEFS AND ORGANIZATIONS

In dealing with the supernatural world, religious beliefs integrate human consciousness with forces clearly outside the individual. Other beliefs also fill this function. Patriotic beliefs, for example, integrate the individual with others who share his or her nation or state. When such beliefs are intensely held, they take on many of the characteristics of religious beliefs. Nineteenth-century French sociologist Emile Durkheim (1858–1917) identified this fundamental characteristic as the **sacred,** referring to those elements of human experience that inspire awe, fear, or reverence.

In Western society, for example, a Bible is a sacred object as compared to an atlas. The atlas belongs to the other realm of human experience, which Durkheim called the **profane,** including all elements of experience that are commonplace or everyday. In comparing religious beliefs with patriotism, we can see some similarities; a flag, for example, in standing for a belief held in reverence (patriotism), takes on sacred qualities. Yet political beliefs and behaviors should not be confused with religious beliefs, however interesting the similarities may be. Religious beliefs occupy the world of the sacred, but they also take us into the realm of the supernatural, providing meaning for and explanations of human existence that come clearly from beyond the scope of human dealings (such as governments).

VARIETIES OF RELIGIOUS BELIEFS

Animism refers to religious belief systems that impute supernatural forces to natural objects. For example, an animal, a river, or a mountain could be viewed as a sacred object, possessing supernatural forces that will be reflected in the lives of humans. A sacred animal might offer protection; an aspect of the environment—ground considered sacred—might seek revenge if it has been mistreated. For example, the Sioux of the American plains viewed the Black Hills of the Dakotas as sacred. When gold was discovered and pressure from miners led the U.S. government to appropriate considerable territory in the Black Hills from the Sioux, their displeasure obviously involved far more than just a distaste for losing land. Indeed, their religion had been attacked, and negative repercussions for the tribe could well be expected.

Whether Muslim, Jewish, or Protestant, a religion's rituals serve to create social cohesion for the participants. The rituals also mark and maintain boundaries between groups.

By contrast, **theism** is the belief that supernatural forces are controlled by a number of gods or a single god interested in and responsive to human affairs. **Monotheism** is the belief in one god, and **polytheism** is the belief in more than one god. Of major world religions, Christianity, Judaism, and Islam are all monotheistic, while Hinduism (which is the oldest) is polytheistic (see Winther's reading following Chapter 3). Theistic belief systems hinge on the power of their god or gods, relating that power to a religious worldview that connects human behavior to religiously provided meanings. A given god, for example, might require particular kinds of ongoing human behavior (such as religious ritual) if those humans are to achieve particular kinds of religiously defined ends (such as salvation). Included within the belief system is the recognition that the god or gods have the power to intervene in human affairs for good or ill, depending on the behavior of the believers.

Some major religions are not theistically oriented at all; their supernatural worldview provides goals for human behavior and encourages particular behaviors as being best suited to meeting those goals. For example, Buddhism (which originated in India) shares a belief in reincarnation (or rebirth) with Hinduism but omits the gods of that religion, turning instead to a belief in the possibility of attaining a state of enlightenment and understanding through the redirection of one's personal actions toward that end. An even clearer example of a nontheistic religion is Confucianism, which originated in China more than two thousand years ago. Confucius recommended a life of loyalty to and concern for others in place of self-interest. Confucianism thus appears to be more of a moral code than a supernaturally oriented religion.

Religious rituals consist of behaviors that are defined and promoted by particular religious belief systems. All religions make demands on the actions as well as the beliefs of their adherents. We normally think of such rituals in terms of rigidly defined repetitive acts of religious significance (such as saying the same grace before every meal), yet all behaviors that carry religious significance fall under this heading. In Confucianism, for example, displaying loyalty for one's family would constitute a religious ritual, while in Christianity church attendance itself can be viewed as a ritual, independent of (but necessary for) the other rituals that occur after one arrives at the church. In making such demands on what people do as well as what they believe, religious beliefs affect society in a tangible way. Rituals require one's time, they often entail some degree of sacrifice, and, perhaps most important, they make one's beliefs visible to others. To other people with whom one shares those beliefs, rituals serve to create a form of social cohesion through a shared activity. To those who do not share beliefs, rituals serve to mark and maintain boundaries between groups who believe and those who do not. Rituals thus simultaneously hold social groups together and create distance between one social group and another. The more public, frequent, and distinctive the rituals, the more this is true.

FORMS OF RELIGIOUS ORGANIZATION

Social organizations that grow up around religious belief systems vary almost as much as the belief systems themselves. Sociologists typically categorize those organizations under a few broad headings. Critical factors highlighted by those headings include (1) differences in organization size, (2) degree of independence of the associated belief system from other religions, and (3) the type of relationship between the religious organization and political forces that control the society within which it exists.

An **ecclesia** is a religious organization that is essentially one with the state, enjoying the support of the government and claiming all citizens of that state as members. More often than not, the need for unity between the church and state will be a central part of the religious doctrine, as in the religion of Islam. The Islamic states in Iran and Saudi Arabia are examples of ecclesia in which all governmental action occurs in accordance with the rules of Islam. Islamic beliefs concerning the consumption of alcohol, for example, become reflected in official prohibition of alcohol for all citizens and even visitors. Within Islam, behavior is seen to be governed by holy law (or *shari'a*) which supersedes secular government law. Such beliefs can make the establishment of Western-style democracies in the Middle East highly problematic (Scruton, 2002). Iraq, following the 2005 election, may well become a natural laboratory for watching this process in action.

Iran is currently an ecclesia in which political leaders and religious leaders are the same individuals.

A somewhat less extensive form of religious organization is the **denomination.** A denomination is a large and formally organized religious organization that enjoys a harmonious relationship with the state but shares the religious sector of society with other denominations, all of which benefit from relatively high levels of social respectability. In the United States, the Roman Catholic Church, the Episcopal Church, and the Presbyterian Church are all denominations. Denominations tend to be large and have at least a minimum amount of tradition to draw on to augment their authority (see Chapter 3). Members come and go according to their acceptance or rejection of denomination doctrine. That doctrine is formulated and promoted through the activities of a formal bureaucratic organization with paid employees.

One of the major sources of change in the religious world happens when a split (or schism) occurs in the membership of a denomination and some members leave to form a new religious organization. These new organizations, called **sects,** are small, informally organized groups that follow a doctrine derived from that of the denomination that gave them birth. In general, the largest religious organizations give birth to the most sects (Liebman, Sutton, and Wuthnow, 1988). The most common scenario for such a split is for a minority within the denomination to accuse the denomination of losing sight of its original goals in the course of striving to achieve growth and respectability; those "original goals," transformed somewhat in response to changes in society, then become the basis of the sect's doctrine. Although the sect's doctrine may be to some degree responsive to changes in society since the inception of the original denomination, it does not typically reflect the dominant values of the social order within which it arises; it is indeed a sect characteristic to stand against many of those dominant values. Sects therefore do not usually enjoy anywhere near the level of respectability that characterizes denominations. If the sects persist over time and grow, however, they turn into denominations themselves with amazing regularity, thereby giving birth to new sects as members again become disgruntled. During the time of Martin Luther in the Reformation, the Lutheran Church was a sect; today, it is clearly a denomination.

The final category of religious organization is the **cult.** Sharing many characteristics with the sect, the cult is a small, usually informally organized group with a generally low level of respectability in the wider society; unlike the sect, the cult's religious doctrine is not a reformulation of some established denomination's doctrine but represents a distinctively different religious orientation. In the United States, some recent cults include Scientology, Heaven's Gate, and the Unification Church (see Chapter 4). A less easily classified organization is the Church of Jesus Christ of Latter Day Saints (or Mormons). This religious organization contains many elements of Christianity (which would suggest a sect) yet so many variations on that theme as to suggest a cult. Other organizations such as the Unification Church also contain elements of Christianity yet with enough contradictory doctrine (such as suggesting divinity for their Korean-born leader) that they are never confused with sects. The Church of Jesus Christ of Latter Day Saints clearly had cultlike beginnings, yet today it is well down the road to recognition as a denomination in the United States, particularly in Utah. It also reflects many of the changes that moving toward denomination status brings about, such as the elimination of polygamy in order to better match dominant American values. Church members opposed to such changes toward moderation have formed splinter groups in response, thus showing how a cult can become a denomination while producing sects along the way.

SOCIOLOGICAL THEORIES OF RELIGION: ORIGINS AND FUNCTIONS

Sociologists have traditionally been interested in religion as a social phenomenon, focusing on the effects that certain religious beliefs have on social groups or on the variety of ways that people organize their religious activities. Religions provide meaning to life. Although they may locate the source of those meanings in another world, they apply the meanings very much in this world.

Emile Durkheim was very interested in the relation between religion and what today we would call social values. Society is possible, said Durkheim (1954), because its members feel bound together by sharing common values. Because they are shared, these values exist outside the individual, thriving in the everyday interactions among the group members who share them. The more we engage in those interactions, the stronger the hold these values will have over us, and we will experience that hold as coming from an outside source. Our religious experience, said Durkheim, reflects that experience of group values. In other words, we experience the source of religious meaning, such as a deity, as existing outside ourselves; in worshipping a deity, we actually worship the social forces that bind our group together in common purpose. Religion, in short, functions to hold social groups together.

Karl Marx (1818–1883) focused more on the ways religion separates individuals in society. Religion, Marx argued, is often used to justify social inequality. Christianity, for example, states that the meek are blessed, that the other cheek should be turned, and that the poor will find a just reward in heaven. These ideas make the poor less likely to attack the rich and more likely to make the best of their current situation.

Max Weber (1864–1920) emphasized the role of religious ideas in directing other activities. In his famous work *The Protestant Ethic and the Spirit of Capitalism*, he argued that early Protestantism (Calvinism in particular) glorified hard work as its followers sought proof through their worldly success that they were in God's grace (Weber, 1958). This glorification of hard work, which Weber named the *Protestant ethic*, played a major role in promoting the growth of capitalistic enterprise during the early days of industrialization. Protestant capitalists poured their profits back into their businesses to make them grow still bigger to obtain even more secure proof of their state of grace. According to Weber, the religious basis for this activity largely passed away, but the work ethic remained very much alive as a social value. As we saw earlier, Americans still value work in itself as an activity.

These early theories of religion have played a major role in directing more modern sociological research. Durkheim's observation of the connection between religion and group solidarity has been both supported and extended. Sociologists today emphasize the group cohesion function of religious beliefs and rituals. Shared beliefs and, probably more important, shared patterns of behavior associated with religious ritual provide constant reminders of group membership to those who participate. When certain evangelical religious groups in the United States speak of holding "revivals" during group worship, they are focusing clearly on the potential role of group ritual in providing a boost to group solidarity through strengthening the attitudes of individuals in a group setting. Rituals conducted in such group settings are probably the most important in this regard, but even private rituals conducted in one's home provide reminders of the larger group with which one is associated.

The religious affiliations that provide people with ties to social groups make that group a source of social control over individuals' actions. As we saw in Chapter 4, individuals and groups to which we are most closely and most emotionally attached can exert considerable influence through the threat of removal of their attention and affection. An ultimate threat is expulsion from the group. Connections to religious social groups are some of the most intense ties that exist, and this intensity makes religious groups an effective source of social control. Both the beliefs and the attachment to the group that shares those beliefs give people motivation to choose or avoid certain behaviors. Weber's work on how the Protestant ethic influences behavior falls within this general perspective.

Marx's work on the connection between religion and inequality has also been extended. Sociologists have examined the role of religion spread by missionaries during the period of Europe's colonization in Asia, Africa, and the Americas. While the missionaries' goals were no doubt religious, the expansion of Christianity played a major role in spreading Western culture in general, making people in colonies more receptive to their rulers. An even clearer example comes from the use of Christianity during the period of slavery in the United States. The "turn the other cheek" aspects of Christianity were emphasized, while the more violent and revolutionary aspects of the religion were kept carefully hidden from the slaves; since slaves were prevented by law from learning to read, most had no direct access to the Bible (see Chapter 8).

RELIGION IN THE UNITED STATES

An important aspect of both Christianity and Judaism is their acceptance of the separation of church and state. The Judeo-Christian heritage that dominates American culture is in harmony with the democratic form of government structured by the U.S. Constitution, which prohibits religion from directly controlling the political institution while simultaneously protecting the rights of citizens to practice their religions without interference from either the government or other citizens who may not approve. While there have been exceptions to this generalization, most notably the oppression of several Native American religions, the United States for the most part has been fertile ground for religious diversity, participation in religious organizations, and religious change. In this section, we examine some of the ways that religious beliefs and organizations affect other social institutions and how the organizations reflect the variation among members of American society.

ORGANIZATION

A full 90 percent of Americans report a preference for a particular religious organization when asked if they have such a preference (Gallup, 2004b). While all world religions are represented in the United States, the vast majority of American religious affiliation is with Christian and Jewish organizations. Of the 90 percent with a preference, 49.4 percent report a preference for Protestant Christian religious organizations; 23.7 percent report a Roman Catholic preference; and 2.2 percent report a Jewish preference (Gallup, 2004b). In addition, 0.5 percent of Americans describe themselves as Muslim, 0.5 percent as Buddhist, and 0.4 percent as Hindu (Kosmin et al., 2001).

American Protestants are dominated by a few major denominations, including Baptists (17 percent), Methodists (7 percent), Lutherans (5 percent), Presbyterians (4 percent), Episcopalians (2 percent), and the United Church of Christ (3 percent); the remainder consists of a wide variety of Protestant denominations and sects. During the last twenty years, these percentages have been relatively stable (Gallup, 2004c). Jewish identification is somewhat more complicated, since Jews are both an ethnic and a religious group; those who identify a preference for Judaism in response to a poll question may exhibit few religious behaviors otherwise. Of those Jews who do identify themselves as religious (which includes converts to Judaism), approximately 8 percent identify with Orthodox Judaism, 24 percent with Conservative Judaism, and 30 percent with Reform Judaism (Mayer et al., 2002). Table 12.1 provides more complete information about membership of the larger American denominations.

While the major religious organizations are found to some extent throughout the United States, some interesting geographical concentrations have resulted from earlier ethnic migrations. The Catholic Church, for example, dominates in the northeast and north central United States, where so many southeastern European immigrants settled. It is also strong in southern Florida (home to Cuban refugees) and in the southwestern United States, with its large Hispanic population (see Casanova, 1992). The Baptists dominate the southern states up to the Ohio River and west through Missouri, Oklahoma, and Texas. Lutherans dominate the Dakotas, Minnesota, and some areas of Montana and Iowa, where so many German and Scandinavian groups settled. Methodists, while found in large numbers in many locations, show particular dominance in Delaware, Maryland, Ohio, West Virginia, Iowa, Nebraska, and Kansas. Finally, the Church of Jesus Christ of Latter Day Saints dominates Utah and southern Idaho, the result of Mormons' nineteenth-century search for a land free from persecution.

TABLE 12.1

CHURCH MEMBERSHIP FOR SELECTED DENOMINATIONS, 2003

The Roman Catholic Church	65,270,000
Southern Baptist Convention	16,053,000
The United Methodist Church	8,298,000
The Church of God in Christ	5,500,000
The Church of Jesus Christ of Latter-day Saints	5,311,000
Evangelical Lutheran Church in America	5,100,000
National Baptist Convention, U.S.A., Inc.	5,000,000
National Baptist Convention of America, Inc.	3,500,000
Presbyterian Church (U.S.A.)	3,456,000
The Lutheran Church—Missouri Synod (LCMS)	2,540,000
African Methodist Episcopal Church	2,500,000
National Missionary Baptist Convention of America	2,500,000
Progressive National Baptist Convention, Inc.	2,500,000
Episcopal Church	2,333,000
Churches of Christ	1,500,000
Greek Orthodox Archdiocese of America	1,500,000
Pentecostal Assemblies of the World, Inc.	1,500,000
African Methodist Episcopal Zion Church	1,448,000
American Baptist Churches in the U.S.A.	1,443,000
United Church of Christ	1,359,000
Baptist Bible Fellowship International	1,200,000
Christian Churches and Churches of Christ	1,072,000
The Orthodox Church in America	1,000,000
Jehovah's Witnesses	989,000
Church of God (Cleveland, Tennessee)	932,000
Seventh-Day Adventist Church	901,000
Christian Methodist Episcopal Church	850,000
Christian Church (Disciples of Christ) in the U.S. and Canada	805,000

Note: Includes the self-reported membership of religious bodies with 650,000 or more as reported to the *Yearbook of American and Canadian Churches.* Groups may be excluded if they do not supply information. The data are not standardized so comparisons between groups are difficult. The definition of "church member" is determined by the religious body.

Source: Yearbook of American and Canadian Churches, 2003.

Although 90 percent of Americans feel comfortable stating a particular religious preference, only 68 percent report themselves as actual members of a particular religious organization, and 43 percent state that they attended a church or synagogue during the preceding seven days. During the last half century, these figures have shown some consistency. There have been only minor long-term drops in church membership and virtually no change in the percentage of Americans who attended services during the week before they were interviewed (Gallup, 2004c). Considering that over the same half century, church attendance in Europe has dropped considerably (particularly among the young), one might conclude that organized religion in the United States is at least holding its own (Greeley, 1989).

THE CORRELATES OF RELIGIOUS AFFILIATION: ORGANIZATIONS, BELIEFS, AND SOCIAL ATTITUDES

In this section, we look at the variation in religious beliefs and social attitudes that exists across religious organizations, along with differences in the social backgrounds of their members. Differences in beliefs should, of course, be expected. But sociologists have found variations not included in the official theologies of dominant American religions. Also, beyond religious beliefs, there are significant differences among members of different religious organizations in their attitudes on such secular (or nonreligious) topics as civil liberties, race relations, women's rights, and the appropriateness of various personal behaviors. Religious affiliations obviously have an impact on many aspects of their members' lives.

Table 12.2 shows some of the variation in religious belief across some of the major denominations in the United States. A prime example of this variation is found with the next to last question, concerning the existence of God. In a Gallup survey, 95 percent or more of the American public claims a belief in God or a universal spirit (Gallup, 2004b). In the Table 12.2 survey (which includes different wording), that percentage drops to 69 percent. But Episcopalians drop even lower than that. By contrast, members of the Pentecostal Church and Assembly of God are close to unanimous in their positive response to this question. Interestingly, these numbers have changed little since the 1960s (see Stark and Glock, 1968). Even larger differences appear when it comes to accuracy of the Bible and the existence of Satan. These data certainly suggest that individuals might wish to investigate various denominations in order to find one that is convivial to them, but an equally important fact is the variation within each religious organization. With the exception of percentages close to zero or a hundred, these data suggest that most major American religious organizations contain members who have fundamental disagreements among themselves as to religious doctrine. If 40 percent of Presbyterians believe that the Bible is totally accurate, that means that 60 percent of Presbyterians harbor doubts about it. In each organization, irrespective of official church doctrine, members vary in their degree of acceptance of that doctrine. The religious diversity in American life apparently goes beyond even the number of organizations available.

TABLE 12.2.
VARIATION IN RELIGIOUS BELIEFS IN THE UNITED STATES BY DENOMINATION, 2001

	A. Bible is totally accurate	B. Must tell faith to others	C. Relig. faith is important	D. Satan is real	E. Works don't earn Heaven	F. Christ was sinless	G. God: all-powerful Creator	H. Absolutely committed to christianity
All adults	41%	32%	68%	27%	30%	40%	69%	41%
Adventist	64	42	73	37	32	45	76	53
Assemblies of God	77	61	86	56	64	70	96	66
Baptist (any type)	66	51	81	34	43	55	85	58
Catholics	26	17	68	17	9	33	70	43
Church of Christ	57	51	81	36	42	54	80	59
Episcopal	22	12	60	20	26	28	59	46
Lutheran (any type)	34	27	63	21	27	33	72	55
Methodist (any)	38	28	74	18	24	33	73	47
Mormon/Latter Day Saints	29	55	90	59	15	70	84	NA
Christian nondenominational	70	59	86	48	60	63	89	67
Pentecostal/Foursquare	81	73	94	47	62	73	90	66
Presbyterian (any)	40	33	71	22	31	45	76	60

A = strongly agrees that the Bible is totally accurate in all that it teaches
B = strongly agrees that they have a personal responsibility to tell others about their religious beliefs
C = strongly agrees that their religious faith is very important
D = strongly disagrees that Satan is just a symbol of evil
E = strongly disagrees that if a person is generally good, or does enough good things for others they will earn a place in Heaven
F = strongly disagrees that Jesus Christ committed sins while on earth
G = believes that God is the all-powerful, all-knowing perfect Creator of the universe who rules the world today
H = says that they are absolutely committed to Christianity
NA = not asked
Source: http://www.adherents.com/misc/BarnaPoll.html

Religious organizations in the United States also vary considerably in the social backgrounds of their members. Table 12.3 provides an overview of this variation. For example, the decreases in membership experienced by the Methodist and Presbyterian denominations are reflected in the age distribution of their respective memberships: more of their members are over fifty, while relatively few are under thirty. These data suggest some difficulty in keeping the children of current members within the fold plus low birth rates, perhaps, among the members. By contrast, Baptists have a large number of young members, which reflects their growing membership. Another young organization is the Roman Catholic Church, but the explanation here comes from the large Hispanic proportion of their membership (see Table 12.4). Both birth rates and immigration rates are high within the Hispanic population (see Chapter 8), which translates to a growing population of new members. High birth rates within the African American population of the United States also play a role in the vitality of the Baptist Church (see Table 12.4).

Variations in income and education across religious organizations are particularly interesting and help explain some of the basic differences we have seen in religious practice and belief. Income and education are basic measures of socioeconomic status (see Chapter 7) and give us some indication of social class differences across organizations. The best educated and wealthiest organizations in Table 12.3 are Episcopalians and adherents of Judaism. It is rare to find a high school dropout in either group. Lutherans and Presbyterians are also both relatively high on both variables. By contrast, Baptist organizations represent the other extreme, with poorer, less educated members. While Table 12.3 does not include the more fundamentalist Protestant denominations and sects, their memberships share these characteristics with the Baptist Church. In short, the more liberal and less strict organizations are also the wealthiest, best educated, and slowest growing (or declining); the more fundamentalist organizations are the poorest, least educated, and fastest growing. Although Table 12.3 does not distinguish among the different forms of American Judaism, the least strict (Reform Judaism) contains the wealthiest members while the most strict (Orthodox Judaism) contains the poorest (Lazerwitz and Harrison, 1979). This connection among the variables of social class, form of religious belief, and vitality of organizational membership makes up one of the most interesting areas for contemporary sociological research in religion.

Table 12.4 depicts the racial and ethnic variation among American religious groups. Asian Americans are most highly represented in Buddhism and Islam— religions they brought (and are bringing) to the United States as immigrants. Overall, they have not been ready converts to other religions. That lack of conversion may be the result of their low levels of religiosity in general (Kosmin et al., 2001; Gallup and Lindsay, 1999). At the other extreme of religiosity are African Americans, who report the highest levels of religious beliefs of all groups represented in this table (Kosmin et al., 2001; Gallup and Lindsay, 1999). Such reports are supported by the data in Table 12.4, which show high levels of African American interest in

TABLE 12.3

VARIATIONS IN AGE, EDUCATION, AND INCOME AMONG MAJOR CHURCHES IN THE UNITED STATES (PERCENTAGES)

	Catholic	Jewish	Total Protestant	Baptist	Methodist	Lutheran	Presbyterian	Episcopalian
Age								
Under 30	30	19	23	28	17	20	16	17
30–49 years	38	41	37	38	35	39	32	40
50 and older	31	39	39	34	48	41	51	42
Education								
College graduates	17	44	18	10	19	29	29	44
College incomplete	26	25	24	20	24	29	30	27
High school graduates	34	24	33	37	36	32	25	21
High school incomplete	22	7	25	32	20	15	16	8
Household income								
$40,000 and over	23	36	19	14	21	25	29	39
$25,000–39,999	25	24	22	20	24	27	22	20
$15,000–24,999	21	16	22	23	22	22	22	15
Under $15,000	25	17	31	39	28	22	22	18

Source: Religion in America 1990, Princeton Religion Research Center, Princeton, NJ, 1990.

TABLE 12.4

RACE AND/OR ETHNIC MAKE-UP OF SELECTED RELIGIOUS GROUPS, 2001
(WEIGHTED ESTIMATE)

Name of Group	Number of Adults	Non-Hispanic Percent White	Percent Black	Percent Asian	Percent Hispanic	Percent Other	Total
Catholic	50,873,000	64	3	3	29	2	100
Baptist	33,830,000	64	29	1	3	2	100
No religion	29,481,000	73	8	5	11	4	100
Christian	14,190,000	67	12	3	14	3	100
Methodist	14,140,000	86	11	1	1	1	100
Lutheran	9,580,000	96	1	0	1	1	100
Presbyterian	5,596,000	91	3	2	3	1	100
Protestant	4,647,000	87	4	0	6	3	100
Pentecostal	4,407,000	58	22	0	17	3	100
Episcopalian/Anglican	3,451,000	89	9	1	0	1	100
Jewish*	2,831,000	92	1	1	5	1	100
Mormon	2,787,000	91	0	0	8	1	100
Churches of Christ	2,503,000	89	6	1	2	2	100
Non-denominational	2,489,000	73	11	1	13	2	100
Congregational/UCC	1,378,000	93	0	0	5	2	100
Jehovah's Witnesses	1,331,000	46	37	0	14	3	100
Assemblies of God	1,105,000	80	5	5	8	2	100
Muslim/Islamic	1,104,000	15	27	34	10	14	100
Buddhist	1,082,000	32	4	61	2	1	100
Evangelical/Born Again	1,032,000	77	3	0	20	0	100
Church of God	944,000	84	12	0	4	0	100
Seventh-Day Adventist	724,000	67	26	0	7	0	100
Total U.S. Adults	208,000,000	70	10	3	12	5	100

*Note: This category refers only to Jews by religion.
Source: Kosmin et al., 2001.

some of the most fundamental Protestant denominations such as Jehovah's Witnesses, Pentecostal, and Seventh-Day Adventist. They also still maintain their historically strong showing among Baptists and Muslims. Hispanic Americans are
traditionally thought of as Catholic, and they do make up a significant percentage
of that religion. But they also show high levels within a wide variety of Protestant
denominations, particularly some of the stricter, most fundamental denominations.

Finally, European Americans strongly dominate many of the older Protestant denominations but are found in percentages beyond those of the research sample in a wide variety of groups. Their prevalence within the older denominations is due to the inability of those churches to attract new members as rapidly as the more fundamentalist groups (Gallup and Lindsay, 1999).

Members of different religious organizations also vary in their political affiliation. Table 12.5 shows political party preferences among major American religious groups. The Democratic Party gains its strength from Jews, Catholics, and Baptists. The source of this strength, as well as its expression, varies considerably, however. Catholic affiliation with the Democratic Party results from the early days of Catholic immigration, when poor, urban Catholic neighborhoods at the turn of the last century were organized by the Democratic Party in its efforts to build a power base to combat the stronger Republican Party, which had dominated American politics following the Civil War. Jews became Democrats for similar reasons, but also because the Democratic Party came to be viewed as the party of social reform, minority rights, and organized labor, all of which fit into the major political concerns of many Jews. The Baptist Church gains much of its Democratic Party strength from the large numbers of African Americans in the membership. But white Baptists, along with many of the stricter Protestant organizations, are moving increasingly to the Republican Party—a trend we examine more closely in the next section.

Historically, the Republican Party has gained its traditional strength from the world of Protestant America in general and from the wealthiest denominations within that world in particular. Part of that connection is most certainly related to social class. On economic issues, the Republican Party generally takes conservative stands that tend to appeal to those who have benefited most within the economic sector. Additionally, the religious specialization in the political parties, which began in the last century, has strengthened Protestant membership within the Republican Party. In more recent years, the Republican Party has become increasingly conservative on social issues such as abortion, gay marriage, and prayer in school—stands that have strengthened its appeal to the stricter denominations within Protestantism. Current high percentages of Republican Party preference within Assemblies of God and Evangelical Christians suggest this trend.

Social variation such as those reflected in Tables 12.3 through 12.5 explains some of the ways that religious organizations are perceived by nonmembers and ways that members of organizations perceive themselves. The beliefs and styles of worship of the wealthier churches, for example, tend to be harmonious with the beliefs and behaviors of Americans of a higher social class, in general. In addition, when individuals attend a particular church, they respond not just to the theology of that organization but also to the current membership. An individual from a lower social class, for example, would probably feel uncomfortable attending a church whose membership came largely from the wealthier side of the tracks (and, of course, vice versa). As we saw in Chapter 7, social classes in American society vary in a great

TABLE 12.5

POLITICAL PARTY PREFERENCE BY SELECTED RELIGIOUS GROUPS, 2001
(WEIGHTED ESTIMATE)

Name of Group	Number of Adults	Percent Republican	Percent Democrat	Percent Independent	Other/ None	Total
Catholic	50,873,000	28	36	30	4	100
Baptist	33,830,000	33	39	22	6	100
No religion	29,481,000	17	30	43	10	100
Christian	14,190,000	34	28	31	7	100
Methodist	14,140,000	36	32	27	5	100
Lutheran	9,580,000	39	26	31	4	100
Presbyterian	5,596,000	46	25	26	3	100
Protestant	4,647,000	37	22	32	9	100
Pentecostal	4,407,000	32	34	27	1	100
Episcopalian/Anglican	3,451,000	35	35	26	4	100
Jewish*	2,831,000	13	56	26	5	100
Mormon	2,787,000	55	14	26	5	100
Churches of Christ	2,503,000	41	27	26	6	100
Non-denominational	2,489,000	46	16	30	8	100
Congregational/UCC	1,378,000	34	28	33	5	100
Jehovah's Witnesses	1,331,000	2	10	34	54	100
Assemblies of God	1,105,000	59	16	19	6	100
Muslim/Islamic	1,104,000	19	35	39	7	100
Buddhist	1,082,000	9	31	48	12	100
Evangelical/Born Again	1,032,000	58	12	20	10	100
Church of God	944,000	38	28	25	9	100
Seventh-Day Adventist	724,000	38	28	31	13	100
Total U.S. Adults	208,000,000	31	31	30	8	100

*Note: This category refers only to Jews by religion.
Source: Kosmin et al., 2001.

many cultural or lifestyle ways. People's interest in surrounding themselves with other members of their social class does not stop at the church door.

TRENDS IN RELIGIOUS CHANGE

What is the role of religion in everyday American life, and how might that role be changing? Sociologists have offered different analyses at different times. Robert Bellah (1970) argued that America was headed toward being dominated by a "civil

**The Ten Commandments
join the American flag in
adorning the Capitol in
Jackson, Mississippi.
Since 2005, it has been
legal in that state to post
religious documents on
public property.**

religion," a watered-down compromise of all religions that presumably would offend
no one. American money carries the motto, "In God We Trust," without specifying
which God from which religion is receiving that trust. In the 1950s, the Pledge of
Allegiance to the flag had its patriotism augmented with religion as "under God"
was added to the "one nation" receiving that pledge. Many of our public functions
involve prayers as part of the ceremony, including locker-room prayers before football games in hopes that God might throw that last block for the winning touch-
down. Such a civil religion would express Americans' desire to keep religion alive,
but it also would suggest a weakening of strict religious commitment.

Some sociologists predicted a growing secularization in American life (Berger,
1961; Cox, 1971). **Secularization** is a weakening of religious tradition as people
turn away from otherworldly, religious concerns and focus their attention on this-
worldly, secular issues. Many theorists predicted a continuing move in this direction
in industrial society as a result of the increasing prominence of science and scientific
method in society. Indeed, many everyday human behaviors or problems are no

longer explained by most Americans in religious terms but in social scientific terms; bank robbers are not possessed by the devil but are simply brought up improperly, having had no appropriate moral code ingrained in them. Alternately, they may suffer from chemical imbalances or have been rejected by their mothers at a tender age. When science takes over the basic business of getting us through the turmoil of life, it would seem logical that religion might be on the way out.

In addition, some of the other social changes that were brought about by industrialization seem to be at odds with traditional religious behavior. High rates of geographical mobility have tended to follow industrialization, for example, and people who move are less likely to attend religious services than those who do not migrate (Wuthnow and Christiano, 1979). As a result, certain areas of the United States with high rates of geographical mobility tend to have lower rates of church attendance. The western region of the United States, including Alaska, Washington, Oregon, Nevada, and California, has been termed the "unchurched belt" (as opposed to the traditional "Bible belt") because it has the lowest rates of attendance in the country. Interestingly, residents of these states report having the same level of religious belief as other Americans, but those beliefs are not reflected in organizational participation; this finding gives support to the migration hypothesis, as migration rates are higher in those states than in others (Stark and Bainbridge, 1985). Despite all these changes, however, most indications are that religion in the United States is holding its own and, in some ways, is even growing organizationally stronger.

As we saw earlier, 90 percent of Americans still identify themselves with a particular religion, and church attendance has been relatively steady over recent years. Most Americans still report that they believe in God. But the most interesting support for a religious revival in the United States comes from research identifying which religions are most responsible for maintaining this support. Trends in church membership indicate that the sects and denominations growing the fastest are those with the strictest adherence to religious doctrine (Bromley and Shupe, 1984; Flake, 1984; Hout and Greeley, 1987; Hunter, 1985). In addition, Protestant and Jewish denominations that have traditionally been more liberal are becoming more traditional in their doctrine and practices (Steinfels, 1989). The mainstream Protestant denominations are no doubt responding to growth among the more fundamentalist Protestant groups (to which we turn in a moment). The Jewish groups have noted a resurgence among younger Jews in their observance of more traditional aspects of their religion. The most strict of all American Jewish religious groups—the Hasidic Jews of the northeastern United States—have been attracting more liberal Jews (Danzger, 1989). The intermarriage of Jews with non-Jews, which used to result in lost members of the Jewish religion, is now producing growing numbers of conversions from among the non-Jewish spouses, who become very committed religious Jews (Roof and McKinney, 1987). Interestingly, the forms of mainstream religion in the United States that might be viewed as most closely tied to the secular world are the very ones facing a decline in popularity.

Perhaps no aspect of the religious revival in the United States more clearly characterizes the trend than the growth of fundamentalism. **Fundamentalism** includes those forms of religion characterized by a strict and unquestioned adherence to religious doctrine and sacred writings. In the United States, fundamentalism has been a powerful force within the Protestant religious sector. The growth of fundamentalist organizations is not easily explained. Sociological theories have focused on the appeal of both the belief systems and the organizational attractiveness. The high rate of social change in other aspects of life is often cited as enhancing the attraction of the stricter fundamentalist beliefs. Among other things, social change can include alterations in an individual's social status; such change can result in higher levels of anxiety among those affected. One might therefore expect to find that people suffering from such "status anxiety" might be those most attracted to fundamentalism (Lipset and Raab, 1981). Some support for this hypothesis comes from the fact that the most conservative Protestant sects tend to have converts with a lower socioeconomic status than the status of families that were already members (Stark and Bainbridge, 1985).

Other research indicates that belief systems may be secondary to more personal considerations for people who convert. Converts are most likely to have personal relationships with current sect members. Those relationships may well be as important as religious beliefs in promoting organizational growth (Stark and Bainbridge, 1985). In keeping with that perspective, Roof and McKinney (1987) point out that both liberal and conservative churches exhibit considerable stability in the United States today. The important factor is not their doctrine but the communal stability of their membership.

Certainly the most colorful aspect of the growth in fundamentalism has been the booming business in religious television, which has made household names of such religious leaders as Oral Roberts, Jimmy Swaggart, Jim and Tammy Bakker, Jerry Falwell, and Pat Robertson. In spite of legal and ethical problems of some television evangelists, religious television continues to be a major force in American religion. Over two hundred television stations are owned by religious groups, and the growth of cable TV has increased the viewership of such programs tremendously. Much of this growth stems from technological advancements in the medium, but it should also be noted that religious television programs were once largely managed by the mainstream denominations (Hadden, 1987). The change in popularity of religion over the airwaves for viewers thus parallels the change in orientation we see in community-based religious participation.

The impact of fundamental Christianity in the United States is felt well beyond the world of the religious institution. Many fundamentalists derive a particular political agenda from their beliefs, and this agenda has resulted in some of the more hotly debated political conflicts in recent years. Public schools have been attacked for teaching evolution in science classes. An alternative has been proposed, *creationism,* which attempts to make scientific data conform to the contents of Genesis in the Old Testament of the Bible. Textbook companies have also been attacked, not only for the evolution content of their material but also for what fundamentalists perceive as a general approach (termed *secular humanism*) that promotes relativity in values. But the ultimate conflict is undoubtedly the ongoing argument over prayer in public schools. In 1960, the U.S. Supreme Court ruled that religious observances in public schools violated the separation of church and state mandated in the Constitution. The fundamental wing of American Protestantism is uniformly in favor of changing that ruling and has actively (although unsuccessfully) worked toward that end for many years.

The clearest movement on the American political scene by fundamentalists was the formation of the Moral Majority in the 1980s by Jerry Falwell. During that decade, Falwell attempted to create a political agenda based on fundamentalist Protestant beliefs that might unify and mobilize followers toward common political ends. This agenda included opposition to the Equal Rights Amendment, pornography, abortion rights, and homosexual rights. Efforts were made to identify politicians who supported these issues and to work toward their defeat, either through direct political attacks or through the backing of alternative candidates whose positions were acceptable. The culmination of this effort was the candidacy of Pat Robertson for president in 1988. While Robertson was unsuccessful and the Moral Majority is no longer an active force, the political issues of fundamentalist Protestantism remain central areas of conflict in American political life. The resurgence of evangelical Protestantism during the 2004 presidential election (see Chapter 13) shows the growing strength of the more fundamentalist strains within American religious groups. The growth of fundamentalist Protestant sects and denominations along with growing membership in the Catholic Church and a resurgence of interest in Judaism among American Jews suggests that the secular side of American life will soon have considerable company from religious organizations.

SUMMARY

Religion includes those shared beliefs, associated behavior patterns, and forms of social organization that are oriented toward the supernatural. In industrial societies, such organizations operate within a separate institution. They vary in form from the ecclesia (which is a religion closely associated with a state) to denominations (which are highly organized but independent of the state) to sects or cults (which are small and represent new trends in religious practice and belief). Some religious organizations function as ideologists for traditional authorities within society, while others may act as agents of social change. Within the United States, religion is organized in a wide variety of independent denominations, sects, and cults, most of which stem from the Judeo-Christian tradition. These organizations vary in terms of beliefs and practices but also in terms of the social characteristics of their members. Americans profess high levels of religious belief and exhibit high levels of religious participation as compared with citizens of other industrialized nations. In recent years, the United States has seen an increase in secularization in some sectors of society, along with a growth of interest in the most fundamental forms of religious belief in other sectors of society.

GLOSSARY

Animism Those religious belief systems that impute supernatural forces to natural objects.

Cult A small, usually informally organized religious group, generally with a low level of respectability in the wider society, whose doctrine represents a distinctively different religious orientation.

Denomination A large and formally organized religious organization that enjoys a harmonious relationship with the state but shares the religious sector of society with other denominations, all of which benefit from relatively high levels of social respectability.

Ecclesia A religious organization that is essentially one with the state, enjoying the support of the government and claiming citizens of the state as members.

Fundamentalism Those forms of religion characterized by a strict and unquestioned adherence to religious doctrine and sacred writings.

Monotheism The belief in one god.

Polytheism The belief in more than one god.

Profane All elements of human experience that are commonplace (see sacred).

Religion Those shared beliefs, associated behavior patterns, and forms of social organization that are oriented toward the supernatural.

Religious rituals Behaviors that are defined and promoted by particular religious belief systems.

Sacred Those elements of human experience that inspire awe, fear, or reverence.

Sect A small, informally organized religious group that follows a doctrine derived from that of the denomination which gave it birth.

Secularization A weakening of religious tradition as people turn away from other-worldly, religious concerns and focus their attention on worldly issues.

Theism The belief that supernatural forces are controlled by a single god or a number of gods that are interested in and responsive to human affairs.

STUDY QUESTIONS

1. What are the various types of religious beliefs? What role do rituals play in religion?
2. How do religious organizations vary in their structure and goals?
3. Discuss the theoretical perspectives taken on religion by Marx, Weber, and Durkheim.
4. What are the dominant religions in the United States? Which religions appeal the most to which Americans? What is the connection between religious affiliation and other social behaviors?

Gregg Easterbrook

FAITH HEALERS

The family that prays together may stay together, but do they also enjoy good health while they do so? We have become so used to linking health with biology (what we eat, pills we take) that perhaps other producers of good health are overlooked. Author Gregg Easterbrook takes us through the relation between religion and health, turning up links that may surprise you.

Traditionally, religion is viewed as a haven for the sick and afflicted; Jesus, when he walked the ancient Holy Land, often ministered first to the diseased. But what if the traditional view is wrong and belief actually promotes better health? To the exasperation of some academics, that is what a growing body of medical research is beginning to show.

Recent studies indicate that men and women who practice in any of the mainstream faiths have above-average longevity, fewer strokes, less heart disease, less clinical depression, better immune-system function, lower blood pressure, and fewer anxiety attacks, and they are much less likely to commit suicide than the population at large. These findings come from secular medical schools and schools of public health. The results seem to hold even when researchers control for such variables as believers' health histories, the self-selection effect (whether the kind of people who bound out of bed for a Sabbath service tend to be more able-bodied to begin with), and "social support" (the fact that religious groups offer care networks to those who fall ill). In the most striking finding, Dr. Harold Koenig of Duke University Medical Center has calculated that, with regard to any mainstream faith, "lack of religious involvement has an effect on mortality that is equivalent to 40 years of smoking one pack of cigarettes per day."

Koenig and a group of researchers affiliated with such schools as Duke, Harvard, and Yale recently reviewed some 1,100 health-effects studies involving religious practice and found that most, though not all, show statistically significant relationships between worship-service attendance and improved health. (Researchers use service attendance as their proxy because it is an objective data point, as opposed to trying to classify what people privately believe.) In one study, the blood of regular worshipers contained low levels of interleukin-6, a protein associated

From *The New Republic*, volume 221, July 19–26, 1999, pp. 20–23. Reprinted by permission of *The New Republic*, © 1999 The New Republic, Inc.

with immune problems (low is good for inter-leukin-6). Even subjects with the AIDS virus who regularly practiced a faith had reduced levels of this protein. Another study found that, in Jerusalem, secular Israeli adults "had a significantly higher risk" of heart disease than practicing religious adults.

A 28-year cohort study of approximately 5,000 Californians, conducted by the researcher William Strawbridge and published two years ago in the *American Journal of Public Health,* found that women who attended one worship service per week significantly extended their life spans, though benefits were not as clear for men. Strawbridge found that believers as a group were not initially healthier than average (that is, self-selecting and leaving the bedridden behind) but instead tended to start off in worse-than-average health and then gradually improve to superior outcomes. Another new study, conducted mainly by researchers at the University of Texas, found that those who regularly attended worship services lived an average of seven years longer than those who never attended.

Duke's Koenig says the association between religious participation and good health holds for almost all Christianity and Judaism, and he assumes it would hold for Islam as well, though studies have not included enough Muslim subjects to be sure. "The main distinction seems to be whether you are a regular practitioner," Koenig says. "Within Christianity there is very little difference in outcomes among the various denominations, except for nonmainstream denominations. Between Judaism and Christianity there is very little difference." Positive results can pass between generations, too. When parents regularly attend worship services, they increase the odds that their children will live longer, healthier lives.

For nonmainstream denominations, the story is different. Christian Scientists suffer some of the nation's worst longevity statistics, despite their denomination's claim to exalt health. The Faith Assembly, a Christian offshoot whose mem-

bers may shun medical care, has horrible mortality figures. And when people join cults their health indicators fall off the bottom of the curve—most catastrophically in Jonestown and Waco.

Some in the medical community are unhappy about the proliferation of studies suggesting a faith-health link or about the fact that 60 of the nation's 126 medical schools now have religion courses on their curricula, a much higher figure than a few years ago. Dr. Richard Sloan of Columbia University's medical school says, "The majority of these studies focus on Christians, suggesting a Christian political agenda behind the work." Even Dr. David Larson, the president of the National Institute for Healthcare Research and a leading exponent of faith-and-medicine—his letterhead proclaims, "Bridging the gap between spirituality and health"—notes, "There is a fair concern this research will be misused by the Christian right." But any U.S. research would have to focus on Christians, since they compose the country's predominant religious group. If there really is a faith-health link, patients deserve to know.

John Billings, the Civil War-era surgeon general of the Army and, later, the first librarian of the New York Public Library, wrote that religion appeared to reduce mortality in the groups he studied. But correlation never proves causation; the fact that people practice a faith and also improve their well-being doesn't establish that religion was the reason.

Medical research is replete with "confounders," complications that can never really be controlled out of studies, no matter how hard researchers try. To cite a mundane example, for decades studies of caffeine have landed all over the map—some find it dangerous, some beneficial, some neutral. Caffeine studies are confounded by the huge range of other influences to which every person is exposed: different diets, lifestyle habits, home and work circumstances, heredity. Researchers try to get confounders to "wash out" of studies by examining large cohorts and also by following subjects for long periods, on the theory that whatever persists is statistically strong. But, even so, it is not unusual for two equally well-done studies to reach widely differing conclusions. If medicine still can't be sure whether a cup of Starbucks helps or hurts, it can't be sure about church, mosque, or synagogue, either.

Why would practicing a faith improve your longevity and well-being? When studies first began to show a faith-health relationship, many assumed social support would be the explanation. It's clearly an important factor: people who regularly attend religious services are seen by concerned friends who will notice if something appears wrong, call to check up if a person suddenly stops attending, visit, and provide care and encouragement during illness. All these influences improve health and longevity. Merely having a support group that expresses concern if something seems wrong and encourages treatment can be a big plus, as early therapy is almost always most effective.

But studies tend to find a faith-health link even when social support is factored out. Some researchers thought the faith-health relationship might emanate from denominational bans against alcohol, caffeine, and smoking or from dietary standards such as the kosher laws. But confound those confounders—it now looks as if small amounts of alcohol might be good for you, while studies don't show much health-benefit distinction between self-denying Seventh Day Adventists and anything-goes Episcopalians.

Current thinking tends toward the assumption that spiritual practice confers its main health benefit by promoting a sensible lifestyle. Specifics differ, but every mainstream Western denomination encourages the flock to drink in moderation, shun drugs, stop smoking, live circumspectly, practice monogamy, get married, and stay married. (Bickering and skillet-throwing notwithstanding, as a group married adults have better health indicators than singles of comparable ages, in part because spouses serve as each other's "social support.") The lifestyle choices

encouraged by faith for reasons of theology aren't terribly different from the choices physicians encourage for reasons of playing the percentages. Of course, secular systems of life philosophy also encourage people to practice moderation and fidelity. But, encompassing millions of members and calling on an ultimate authority, religions may simply be doing a better job of advocating the circumspect life, thus conferring comparative health advantages on practitioners.

The believer's lifestyle might even have a historical foundation in the relationship between spiritual practice and longevity. Historians, for instance, are reasonably confident that the Jewish-Muslim prohibition against pork consumption had its origin in protecting believers from trichinosis. Perhaps self-preservation effects such as this extend across many aspects of religion. Those faiths that taught adherents to live circumspectly and care for one another were more likely to prosper, passing down their assumptions, and their health benefits, to the present day.

Jumping off from that, Dr. Herbert Benson of Harvard Medical School has proposed that one reason faith may be linked to better health—indeed, a reason faith and society are historically linked—is that natural selection favors religion. In Benson's theory, during prehistory those clans or groups that possessed the stirrings of religious belief would have developed better health habits and recognized a responsibility to care for family and neighbors. This would have increased "kin fitness," or the likelihood that the group overall would pass along its members' genes. Descendants were then raised with a disposition toward belief; the descendants increased their own survival fitness through faith-motivated health habits and altruistic care of others; they created new descendants and so on. In this way, Benson thinks, human beings became "wired for God," genetically predisposed to have faith. Obviously, religion did not confer a selection advantage in every case: sometimes it caused communities to become targets of war or to engage in internal repression. But, on the macroscale of evolution, those who believed were likelier to live long, healthy lives than those who did not believe. The same, Benson thinks, remains true today.

None of the respectable faith-and-health researchers proposes that religion extends longevity through supernatural agency. Some do, however, take seriously the utility of prayer. Studies of "intercessionary" prayer—Person A prays for the health of Person B—haven't turned up much. But studies do suggest that prayer favorably influences health outcomes for the person who does the praying.

The nonsectarian form of prayer that is akin to meditation has long been recognized by clinicians to improve composure and the sense of well-being; anyone can benefit from a period of meditative prayer each day. Studies at Duke University and elsewhere have recently found that traditional religious "petitionary" prayer, or silently addressing God, also favors health. In one study, subjects who both attended worship services and regularly prayed had lower blood pressure than the control group. Researchers assume that traditional prayer can confer health benefits through the psychological effects of equanimity. Benson's studies, for instance, suggest that a calm state of mind improves the body's self-healing abilities.

Camps in the medical community were displeased when the American Cancer Society recently declared, "Sometimes answers come from prayer when medical science has none." On one level the statement is inarguable; reverence for higher purpose might comfort the victim of illness in ways that no drug or technology ever could. But conventional medicine is comfortable only with the sociological notion that the sick may console themselves by addressing a Maker, real or speculative. The idea that there is an actual reply, that "answers come from prayer," is one that makes much of the medical establishment uneasy, even if the source of the "answer" is no more than the person's own contemplative understanding.

Yet one of the modern era's little secrets is that it is hardly only the Bible-thumpers who pray.

John Houghton, among the world's foremost atmospheric physicists and a leading proponent of global-warming theory, regularly prays and has written articles on the value of prayer. The Nobel Prizewinning physicist Charles Townes, principal inventor of the laser beam, says that he prays daily. Pundits might snicker, but, if regular prayer composes the mind and confers health benefits, the person who prays is following the intelligent course, regardless of the verity of any religion.

Another possibility for the link between longevity and faith turns on mental health. Koenig suspects that many physical benefits of religious practice originate with the sense of well-being or purposefulness that believers report: he finds it revealing that the faithful experience fewer bouts of clinical depression than the population at large and that, when depression does strike, they recover faster. In this view, faith doesn't merely have an agreeable placebo effect on the mind but helps believers acquire coping mechanisms that ward off stress and anxiety, lower stress in turn being favorable for physical health. Dr. Esther Sternberg, a researcher at the National Institute of Mental Health, devotes a fine new book, *A Delicate Balance,* to the evidence that health and quality of life are improved by possessing an affirmative emotional sense, including the belief that existence is worthwhile and has purpose.

The mental health point isn't just a detached observation. Sternberg's premise, after all, is not much different from saying that postmodernism is bad for your health. Many in the academic establishment are uncomfortable with evidence that belief promotes mental health, as this implies that faith ought to be the normative condition, compared to unbelief.

Here faith-and-health treads some of the same ground as the emerging "good life" movement in psychology. Postwar psychology and social science have emphasized dysfunction, studying what causes people to become alienated or antisocial. The good-life movement seeks instead to emphasize what causes people to become high-minded and altruistic. "Good life" in this sense means the admirable path, not wine and roses; Eleanor Roosevelt is a favorite topic of good-life proponents. Martin Seligman of the University of Pennsylvania, recently president of the American Psychological Association, is a leader in this evolving discipline, having said that scholars ought to "turn their eyes to the best in life."

The regnant intellectual view is that the awful truth about society is revealed when people are driven to madness; the good-life movement asserts, instead, that the shining truth is revealed when people become selfless. But academia is today much more comfortable with lamenting ugliness than endorsing virtue. To hold up Eleanor Roosevelt—or anyone else—as a psychological archetype goes against the current vogue for radical nonjudgmentalism.

There's an obvious corollary here between good-life psychology and the faith-and-health question. If psychology ought to be focusing on what causes morality, and mainstream religions promote morality and mental health, we have a new argument for taking faith seriously. The cynical view of religion was so deeply ingrained in postwar intellectual thought that, until 1994, the American Psychiatric Association classified strong spiritual belief as a "disorder." Now faith is looking like a health boon. Quite a switcheroo.

And, speaking of fun twists, it's established that physicians have an obligation to advise patients to take steps that research shows to be associated with longevity, such as not smoking. It's also established that doctors may counsel patients on highly personal subjects, such as sexual behavior. So, if faith increases your odds of good health, does this mean your physician has an obligation to advise you to become religious?

Sloan, of Columbia, says he fears doctors may soon be pressured to dispense such advice and counters that, although research has shown that being married correlates with better health, this does not cause physicians to advise patients to rush to the chapel. The trouble with this reasoning is that counseling patients to wed is not utilitarian: there's no guarantee you'll find a compatible partner. Recommending religion, on the other hand, is quite pragmatic advice. Anyone can join a faith; attending services is a lot easier than quitting smoking.

Nevertheless, "Even if the research shows that religion is good for health, that doesn't mean doctors should prescribe it like antibiotics," says Larson, the faith-and-health advocate. Koenig thinks the research only demonstrates that physicians should "ask the patient if he or she practices a religion and, if so, what the physician can do to offer support. At this point, we have enough research to say that is good clinical medicine."

Spiritual awareness may indeed be good for you, but it's just as well that your doctor not double as clergy. If faith ever became a formal adjunct of medicine, HMOs could end up publishing lists of preferred-provider churches, mosques, and synagogues, requiring a precertification number before the priest can perform last rites, and—well, you can guess the rest.

DISCUSSION QUESTIONS

1. What part of faith or religious observance seems the most strongly connected with good health?
2. What conflict exists between religion and the scientific community over the connection between religion and health? Why does that conflict exist?

C H A P T E R

13

THE ECONOMY AND THE POLITICAL INSTITUTION

When we compare the modern industrial society with agricultural and less complex societies, the family is one of the most recognizable holdovers, despite the many changes it has experienced in the name of progress. As we've seen, relying on kin for our survival is no longer feasible; it is not that the kin are necessarily unwilling but that the institutional changes in society serve to thwart the best intentions in the world. In looking only at the development of the educational institution (as we did in Chapter 11), we saw that knowledge transmission and much of basic socialization has moved from stories at grandfather's knee to mass-produced, culturally approved "knowledge" served up in structured classroom situations. In Chapter 12, we focused on the institution of religion and how it lives both connected to but separate from both the family and education. But those three institutions cannot be viewed in isolation. As we've already seen, the relationships among the family, education, and religion are firmly connected to other major institutions in society. We cannot understand the educational institution, for example, without also understanding the politics that control its operation and the economy into which its graduates leap (or are pushed). This chapter explores two other major institutions in society in order to complete the story begun in the previous three chapters. If the family, education, and religion represent the first three major institutions we confront in the life cycle, the economy and the political institution shape our experiences as adults.

THE ECONOMY

Societies satisfy many basic needs of their members, but perhaps the most basic need is survival. If that need is not met, little else matters. Some sort of coordinated system is necessary to create and distribute the essential means of survival so that members of society can live long enough to accomplish other ends. As we saw in Chapter 9, hunting and gathering societies typically have a fairly loose (although still coordinated) system. At the other extreme, industrial societies use a complex system that requires elaborate forms of coordination and extreme specialization of tasks (a high division of labor). If farmers, truck drivers, and grocers unknown to you don't do their jobs, you will find yourself without food. Sociologists refer to this complex form of coordination as the economic system. An **economic system** is the organization of social activities that produces and distributes goods and services within and between societies. All individuals in an industrial society have some connection to this institutional sector of activity, whether they live off occupational income, inherited wealth, or public assistance. Sociologists are interested in the various kinds of economic systems and how individual activities and social interactions are affected by them.

The economic system is typically divided into three sectors, to specify differences in goods and services produced. The **primary sector** of the economy encompasses activities associated with the production of raw materials. These activities include farming, fishing, mining, harvesting timber, and so on. The **secondary sector** of the economy comprises manufacturing activities that transform raw materials into usable goods, such as food, clothing, fuel, lumber, machines, and all consumer goods. The **tertiary sector** consists of the production and distribution of services— such activities as law making, house cleaning, teaching, running a grocery store, and frying potatoes at the local fast-food outlet.

All three sectors must be active and coordinated with one another for the economic system to function properly, but coordination can be complex. When economic systems operate between societies (international trade), it becomes possible for one society to engage in largely primary sector activities while other societies emphasize secondary or tertiary sector activities. Changes in such relationships affect the overall wealth of societies and consequently the quality of individual life within a society as people respond to changes in the economic system.

TYPES OF ECONOMIC SYSTEMS

While all economic systems produce and distribute goods and services, the system can be organized in a variety of ways. Different systems create differences in such basic areas as who does what job, how decisions are made as to what will be produced, and how benefits of the system are distributed to members of society. An important variable that affects all these areas is the degree to which a given society's political institution directs the economic system. Economic systems with lower levels of political direction are **capitalist economies,** which are characterized by private ownership of property and a form of coordination based on a market system of exchange; in the market system, the value of goods and services is determined by supply and demand. When economic systems are subject to high levels of political direction, they are referred to as **socialist economies.** In these economies property is owned by the state, and the state coordinates the production and distribution of goods and services. A **mixed economy** represents a compromise between capitalist and socialist types: some property is privately owned and some is controlled by the state. The privately owned property is coordinated through a market system in the capitalist mode, whereas the state-owned property is managed by the state as in the socialist mode. As we look at each type of economic system in more detail, it will become apparent that the structure of a society's economic system affects almost every aspect of life for the people who live and work within it. One of the changes we have witnessed in recent years is the turning of many socialist economies toward mixed economies. The political and economic changes in Europe with the fall of the Soviet Union will probably be overshadowed by more recent changes in China, whose economic growth in the early twenty-first century has been massive.

Capitalism The cornerstone of capitalism is capital. *Capital* is any kind of wealth or property that can become productive as income. A factory, for example, is capital because it can earn income for its owner through its products. Money in the bank is also capital in that it draws income through interest. It draws that income, of course, because it can be used elsewhere in the economy (through the bank's investment) to create other income (it might be borrowed by someone to start a business, for example). In this sense, all capital is interchangeable, as any form of it can be turned into any other form of it. The hallmark of capitalism is that capital is privately owned by individual members of society. Its value to those individuals is determined by the market, which coordinates its exchange.

The *free market* is the system of exchange through which the value of property is determined. As goods and services are exchanged, supply and demand will regulate their values. *Supply* is the amount of a given good or service available to those who might want it. *Demand* is the number of people who desire that good or service. If you are trying to sell shoes to an already well-shod population, you will probably find few buyers. Your response may be to lower prices on your shoes enough so that potential buyers might be induced to purchase a pair anyway, perhaps to save for later when their current footwear wears out. Full supply coupled with low demand acts to lower prices (or value) of the goods or services in question. At the other extreme, if you have the only supply of shoes in a market of desperate barefoot consumers, you will be free to raise prices on your goods considerably, as demand is high while supply is short. But if you raise prices beyond the ability of these consumers to pay, they will go without your product, even though they desire it. In a free market, the price (or value) of your product will level off at a point low enough that the shoes still sell but high enough so that they do not all sell out in the first hour of business. As other manufacturers notice your success, they will turn to shoe production themselves, hoping to cash in on this bonanza. As more of them do so, the supply of shoes will rise and slowly the price will begin to drop. This is how supply and demand determine value in an ever-changing balance in a market economy.

The driving force in capitalism is the motivation of individuals to use their capital to increase their wealth. The increase created through productive capital is called *profit*. The market's mechanisms offer the incentive to invest capital toward this end. An early observer of this economic system was Adam Smith (1723–1790), who published an explanation of capitalism in 1776 called *The Wealth of Nations*. He argued that the market system through which capitalism operated would balance itself naturally and encourage producers to fill demand in response to rising prices. In this way, he argued, all necessary goods and services would automatically be produced. Because the market is subject to a natural balance, he pointed out, it is important that no outside force (such as government) interfere; any such interference would artificially force producers to (for example) stop creating a product if a government prevented the product's prices from rising even though demand for the product was high. The principle of no government interference in the market is referred to as *laissez faire*.

The market's response to the forces of supply and demand sometimes causes it to respond inadequately to other social concerns. For example, high prices in the wake of low supply and high demand often put prices for goods or services out of the reach of many individuals. When medical care is priced by that means, the rich will tend to remain healthy and live while the poor are more likely to get ill and die. The high prices encourage great advancements in medicine but make its benefits less available throughout society. The free market ensures that goods and services will always be available, but some may be at a cost too high for many.

A second problem of the free market is that the fluctuations of supply and demand do not always fall into a state of equilibrium instantly. If demand falls too far for too long, producers will stop making a good. Factories will close, which creates unemployment, which gives consumers less money to spend, which lowers demand yet farther, which cuts down farther on production, and so on. Such downturns in business cycles are called recessions or depressions, depending on their degree and length. During such downturns, many investors lose their wealth and many members of society who depend on their labor for subsistence lose their income through unemployment. Perhaps not surprisingly, the growth of unemployment is strongly related to prison admissions and the overall size of the prison population (as unemployed workers presumably turn to alternative pursuits) (Chiricos and Delone, 1992). When the cycle ends and a business upturn occurs, those who withstood the downturn (usually the holders of relatively large amounts of capital) return to increasing their wealth through creating profit, and laborers return to the newly created jobs caused by expanding production.

No economic systems today could be characterized as purely capitalist. No industrial society is willing to follow Adam Smith's directions entirely by keeping government hands off the economy and away from productive ownership. Nevertheless, the United States comes close to this form, with a major part of its industrial wealth in private hands. Even in this society, however, government does run a number of enterprises, including the postal service, the military, education, various social services, and so on, employing approximately 15 percent of the labor force; it also interferes greatly in business cycles through its control of interest rates, tax rates, and the money supply, in an effort to manipulate the wide swings that would presumably otherwise take place.

Socialism Socialist economic systems place productive capacity in the hands of the government. This means that production of all major goods and services is state owned and controlled; individual members of society work for the state in some capacity, either through the administration of this elaborate system or through direct labor within it. The driving force in a socialist economy is intended to be the welfare of society's members. Decisions as to what goods and how much of them should be produced, as well as the prices of products, are made by government administrators rather than by market forces. Thus, demand cannot create supply unless the government approves. If prices are not allowed to rise as demand rises, consumers will continue to buy, supply will quickly run out, and shortages will occur. A typical government response in such a situation would be to introduce rationing of the good or service in low supply until government directives can create more of it. While capitalism may deprive low-income members of society of some goods and services through price rises when shortages start to occur, socialism spreads that deprivation around more evenly. Also, shortages in supply are more resistant to government directives than they are to market forces, which generate investment in that area of the economy. Shortages can thus become a common problem in socialist economic systems.

As with capitalism, there are no perfect examples of socialist economic systems in societies around the world, but countries such as North Korea, Cuba, and China have represented efforts to achieve this ideal. In socialist societies, most enterprises are state run. In general, socialist economic systems have been less successful than capitalist systems at achieving high levels of productivity. The huge governmental bureaucracies required to make economic decisions have been unsuccessful at responding efficiently to the economic needs of socialist societies, and the result has been less production and more shortages.

Mixed Economies Mixed economies represent the middle ground between capitalism and socialism. In mixed economies, the government wields considerable economic power, particularly with regard to major industries and social services; this government activity is coupled with a sizable private sector in which market forces operate. The goal of such mixed systems is to achieve the economic growth of a free market while also protecting workers, as in socialist economies. For example, medical care in the United States receives some government support, but the majority of medical bills are paid through private insurance companies. Individuals unable to afford such insurance are therefore likely to receive medical care of poorer quality. In countries such as Great Britain, France, and Sweden, which have mixed economies, basic medical care is subsidized by the government for all citizens regardless of income. Similarly, other services such as day care, basic utilities, and even transportation services may be government run. This kind of governmental support prevents the extremes of social inequality that result from an unrestricted

The Chinese economy, which had until recently been totally Communist, is now opening up to capitalism and international trade. Shown here is the General Motors stand at the Shanghai motor show. Vehicle sales are growing rapidly in China.

market economy—the rich are less rich and the poor are less poor. Of course, everyone pays high taxes in order to pay for all these services.

Mixed economies may well be the economic form of the future. Although the United States was clearly a capitalist economy at the turn of the last century, it has been moving steadily toward increasing the government's control over economic fluctuations and its support of basic social services. Programs such as social security, which seemed radical to Americans in the 1930s, are taken for granted today by most Americans, in spite of efforts from the conservative movement to replace it with private investment accounts. Government provision of basic medical care may not be far behind; in fact, the United States is one of the few industrialized nations in the West that does not provide it. And very few Americans would want the government to retreat from its economic regulatory function through such agencies as the Federal Reserve. At the other end of the continuum, the introduction of elements of the free market into Russia and China, coupled with the democratic and economic reforms in Eastern Europe, suggest a steady move away from the extremes of state socialism.

CORPORATIONS

A **corporation** is a legal entity that functions in the economic sector of a capitalist or mixed economy with rights of ownership and potential liabilities much like those of an individual; on the other hand, it is legally separate from the individuals who own it in the sense that they do not personally own what the corporation owns, nor are they personally liable for what the corporation does. Corporate ownership is typically through shares of stock, which may be held by a few individuals or a great many. The actual business operations of the corporation are conducted by various levels of managers, organized bureaucratically (see Chapter 6), who are answerable to the shareholders for their decisions.

Corporations were developed in the United States toward the end of the nineteenth century. By 1905, 74 percent of domestic production in the United States was corporate production (Roy, 1983). As the United States became a growing industrial power, corporations helped increase both the size and efficiency of business operations. The open ownership of corporate stock gives the illusion that American capital is in the hands of many rather than the hands of a few. Since 1980, the number of people in the United States who own shares of stock has been growing. In spite of this, however, approximately 30 percent of all corporate shares are still in the hands of the wealthiest one percent of American households (Weicher, 1997).

Monopolies and Oligopolies One of the assumptions of the free market is that business competition will maintain the supply-demand balance. For example, rising demand for a product forces prices to rise until supply also rises to meet the demand. If many independent producers are involved, that should happen, but a single producer could respond to that rising demand by not producing more on purpose so as to keep prices and profits high. It would then obviously be in the business interest of a corporation to minimize competition with its product or service. Corporations therefore often attempt to form monopolies or oligopolies.

A **monopoly** is the control over a given product or service by a single entity. An **oligopoly** exists when a few corporations dominate the production of a given product or service. In fact, with regard to most products, only a few corporations control the vast majority of the market. For example, Anheuser-Busch, Miller, and Coors control 77.8 percent of beer sales in the United States (with Anheuser-Busch enjoying 45.8 percent alone); General Motors, Ford, and DaimlerChrysler control 58.6 percent of the car and truck market in the United States. Similar oligopolies exist in such industries as automobile tires, soap, dairy products, drugs, and petroleum refining (Taub and Weissman, 1998). Outright monopolies usually face legal challenges under antitrust legislation that was designed to prevent such complete control over a given market. An oligopoly is conducive to price fixing—also illegal—whereby the few corporations involved agree informally not to compete in their product pricing but to maintain prices at a certain level, regardless of demand (see Chapter 5).

Conglomerates and Interlocking Directorates A **conglomerate** is a large corporation formed through the merger of many smaller corporations that operate in different sectors of the economy. For example, R. J. Reynolds Tobacco, which grew through the manufacture and sale of cigarettes, merged with Nabisco Brands (famous for crackers and other food products) to form RJR Nabisco. Beatrice Foods expanded in the early 1980s to form a conglomerate of fifty companies, which added, among other things, luggage and cosmetics to its line of food products. More recently, large Japanese firms have acquired numerous American business interests outside their primary product line. Conglomerates do not create monopolies per se, since they are so diversified, but their size gives them the edge when confronted by competition from smaller corporations in any of their lines.

Competition is also reduced through interlocking directorates. **Interlocking directorates** exist when the same individuals sit on the board of directors of a number of different corporations. In this way, corporations with different products but complementary interests can act in unison when making economic decisions or, more extensively, when moving into the political realm—for example, in backing political candidates. In general, such connections allow for the passage of considerable information and foster collusion. General Motors, for example, is connected to the boards of directors of twenty-nine other firms, including oil companies, banks, insurance companies, mining companies, and transportation companies. Because members on the boards of those firms sit on the boards of still other firms, General Motors is connected to some seven hundred other American corporations.

Multinational Corporations A **multinational corporation** is a corporation located in one country while owning companies based in other countries. Virtually all major corporations were multinational by the 1990s. These corporations without a country represent one way in which economic systems have outdistanced political systems. While political systems still operate within separate states, multinational corporations exist in the margins between those states, often answerable to no one state; from the point of view of any given state, much of the corporation's assets lie elsewhere, beyond taxation and control. When such corporations do interact with separate political systems, the results can have major international political repercussions. For example, the multinational ITT was able to convince the American government in the 1970s to help overthrow the Chilean government of President Allende. ITT's goal was to protect its assets in that country, which had promised to move to a socialist economy and would then have nationalized telecommunications.

Corporations become multinationals for the same reason they do most things: corporate managers are under constant pressure to increase profits. A major expense of any business is labor, and labor costs in the United States have grown steadily over the years as American workers have demanded a higher standard of living. Cheaper labor is available in the countries of the nonindustrialized world. It makes good economic sense, therefore, to shut down factories in the United States

Most major corporations are truly multinational with economic interests that span the globe.

in favor of factories overseas in Asia, South America, or Africa, where labor costs are a fraction of what they would be at home. An added benefit of such multinational connections is that if American workers fear factory closings, they may become willing to work for lower wages (Harrison and Bluestone, 1988).

The developing nations of the third world contain 75 percent of the world's population but only 20 percent of its wealth (Haub and Kent, 1987). That makes them ripe for development by multinationals. But what are the effects of such economic development? Some observers argue that bringing basically agricultural societies into the modern industrial world will ultimately have positive results by increasing the amount of wealth in those countries and helping promote the growth of democratic forms of government, which they see as logically connected to industrial development (Berger, 1986). Other observers focus on the degree to which traditional economic relationships are destroyed by such developments; industrialization may result in the end of subsistence agriculture, for example, which may force native people into the overcrowded slums of third world cities to compete for industrial employment. These observers also note that profits made by multinationals seldom find their way into third world economies (Wallerstein, 1979). Few observers disagree, however, on the amount of impact such industrial expansion has on third world cultures and on employment changes in the industrial world as the primary and secondary sectors of the economy become noncompetitive, which leads to growth in the tertiary sector.

Regardless of these changes, however, economic growth in countries such as India and China is having a huge impact on the economics of the older industrial nations. No longer pawns in the globalization game, India and China are already growing in their balance of trade with the rest of the world, increasing their exports with each passing year. In addition, modern communications have made possible the "outsourcing" of many jobs in fields such as information technology, marketing, and graphic arts. As industrialization spreads, nations such as these will clearly come to play dominant roles on the global scene.

THE WORLD OF WORK IN THE UNITED STATES: PROBLEMS AND TRENDS

How do individual workers fit into this picture? The forces that drive major corporations also drive the individual workers that produce their goods. An industrial society such as the United States contains fewer and fewer "traditional" occupational opportunities, and individual workers are pushed into the changing needs of the corporate economy. Since 1900 the percentage of agricultural workers and unskilled laborers has dropped notably, while the proportion of service workers has increased. The extent of this change can easily be seen by looking only at changes in the farm population in the United States. In 1900, over 39 percent of the American population lived on farms; by contrast, 1.8 percent live on farms today (U.S. Department of Agriculture, 2004). The needs of a modern manufacturing nation can be seen in the increasing numbers of professional and technical workers and substantial increases in the number of clerical workers. And all these changes (along with broader changes in the economic system) have caused changes in worker satisfaction, the rates and impact of unemployment, and the importance of labor unions in mediating between the individual worker and the employer. We examine these issues in this section as we change course in our examination of economic systems, focusing now on how American workers cope with changes in the economic institution.

Worker Satisfaction: The Work Ethic and Alienation Although their motives differ, both workers and management are concerned with worker alienation and job satisfaction. In this situation, **alienation** refers to a worker's lack of interest in and identification with the job, coupled with a general feeling of powerlessness over the conditions that affect his or her life (Seeman, 1972). The separateness of the economic institution from other activities often carries over into specific jobs, which the worker may see as a necessary but separate facet of existence, not connected to the things that "really matter." An individual who is extremely loyal to friends and family may care little about the corporation for which he or she works, wanting only to get the work done with as little effort as possible. Jobs such as assembly line work may increase alienation as the individual worker loses perspective on the overall product, concentrating instead on the three bolts that must be tightened every thirty-seven seconds on each item that moves down the line. Sociological research indicates that loss of job autonomy (such as happens on an assembly line) tends to increase levels of alienation (Kohn et al., 1990). Assembly line work is a far cry from the work of a craftsperson, who sees a task through from start to finish and can take pride in the product. But, then, the modern corporation is also a far cry from the small, intimate units within which people used to work. Japanese industry used to pride itself on having solved this problem. Japanese workers once had just that kind of intimate sense of loyalty to large multinational corporations (Naoi and Schooler, 1985). But times have changed. Still in the midst of a long recession, Japanese corporations today are cutting costs by cutting workers (Kin, 2003; Kakuchi, 1999). Worker loyalty apparently cannot surpass the bottom line.

In spite of any dissatisfaction American workers might feel, they want to work, having accepted the work ethic. The **work ethic** is the cultural value placed on work as an end in itself, independent of its products. If you ever feel guilty for "wasting" time even though you may not have much you really need to get done, you may well have internalized this value yourself; it is one of the more commonly held values in the United States. We are socialized to value activity over inactivity, and most of us find it quite difficult to do nothing for any extended period of time. In keeping with this pattern, older Americans have attacked mandatory retirement rules in hopes of working just a few more years. Part of this concern is undoubtedly purely economic, since retirement on a fixed income is frightening. But interest in prolonging the period of work also comes from the central place work has in most people's lives. Many of us acquire much of our self-identity as well as our identity in society from our jobs. Retirement can be a wrenching experience, a loss almost like a death in the family.

The level of attachment workers feel for their jobs and their employers plays a role in *industrial productivity,* the number of worker hours required to produce a given product. Because worker hours are a major expense for a corporation, low productivity is reflected in higher prices for the manufactured product and therefore a product that is less competitive than that of a more productive corporation. The productivity of American workers has been called into question in recent years because of the inability of American products to compete with foreign imports. One result of this poor competitiveness is that many industries are moving out of the United States. Simultaneously, the American economy has been moving toward an increasing specialization in service and information technologies. This change was the source of the 1990s economic growth, however hard it has been for manufacturing workers who lack the necessary skills to move with the changes.

Other reasons for low productivity, however, stem from more general structures in the economy. Robert Reich, while director of the Office of Policy Planning at the Federal Trade Commission, pointed out some fundamental differences between the United States and Japan. Of every 10,000 citizens in Japan, he notes, one is a lawyer, 3 are accountants, and 400 are engineers and scientists. Of every 10,000 American citizens, 20 are lawyers, 40 are accountants, and only 70 are engineers and scientists. The difference, he claims, is that the American economy rewards what he calls the "paper entrepreneurs" with money, job security, and high social status, while the truly productive occupations carry fewer rewards and attract fewer people (Fallows, 1980). According to Reich, Americans may be working hard, but they are working at the wrong things. Yet they work where they work because our economic system is structured that way.

Unemployment Unemployment is a permanent part of life in an economic system based on a free market. As business cycles fluctuate, the percentage of American workers employed rises and falls accordingly. During boom cycles, production is high and jobs are plentiful; during recessions or depressions, production drops from lack of demand, and jobs disappear. Individual workers may come to experience a certain feeling of helplessness, as their employment is clearly directed by forces beyond their control. It may make clear corporate sense to sell off parts of the corporation, close plants, and move operations overseas, but corporate priorities may seem misplaced from the perspective of the individual worker. Unemployment exists even during the most productive business cycles. The end of the 1990s economic boom (pre-9/11) dropped the unemployment rate to only 4.0 percent; by 2003, that figure had climbed back to 6.0 percent (U.S. Bureau of the Census, 2004a).

Unemployment rates affect the economy as much as they affect the individual workers who find themselves without jobs. When employment is high, a great many workers have money to spend, and—not surprisingly—they spend it. This situation increases demand, which increases prices. In short, high employment can fuel inflation. One way to stop inflation is to force a recession, which lowers employment, decreases disposable income, lowers demand, and ultimately lowers prices. The recession of the early 1980s effectively ended the runaway inflation of the late 1970s in the United States because it left many American workers without jobs. The implication of this examination of cycles is somewhat sobering. It suggests that a certain level of unemployment is necessary if our economic system is to function without inflation. The expression "The poor will always be with us" seems to have some sound economic basis to it.

Unemployment is measured by counting the number of people who are actively seeking work at any given time. Such a tally doesn't take into account many American workers who are not exactly thriving in their employment status. For example, many Americans are underemployed. *Underemployment* means that a worker is employed in a job that is different from (and also well below) his or her previous employment and that is unrelated to acquired job skills. A skilled machinist unable to find work in that field might drive a taxi to make ends meet; he or she would not therefore be counted in unemployment statistics. Since the 1980s, the American economy has changed drastically with the closing of many major manufacturing plants and steel mills and the growth of a service economy. Workers with skills for one kind of economy face either underemployment or job training in a different kind of economy.

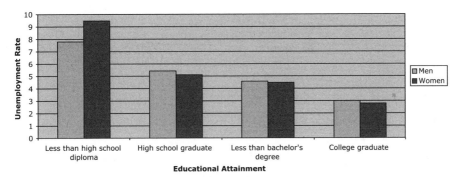

Figure 13.1 Unemployment rate for persons aged twenty-five and older by educational attainment and sex, 2002. (Data from U.S. Bureau of the Census, 2004a)

Another uncounted American worker would be a single mother living on public assistance. While she might prefer to work, the combined problems of paying for day care for her children plus losing the free medical coverage that comes from public assistance (but not from all jobs) would keep her on public assistance and off the unemployment rolls; she is not, after all, actively seeking work. Finally, many Americans have simply given up on finding employment. Inner-city black teenagers, for example, may search for work in an urban arena where there is little work for anyone and almost none for those without job skills. Even relatively low unemployment rates, therefore, miss many who are unemployed or poorly employed.

Figure 13.1 illustrates the ways that American workers are affected by unemployment. Individuals without a high school diploma clearly stand in the greatest danger of unemployment. Beyond that, the more education one has, the more likely that one's place in the economic system will be assured. As the American economy changes, with decreased opportunities in the primary and secondary sectors coupled with increases in the tertiary sector, fewer and fewer opportunities are available for the unskilled—with the exception of the most basic service jobs (such as cooking fast-food hamburgers or working as a hotel maid). We will examine this change in occupational opportunities shortly.

Another factor affecting unemployment is an individual's race or ethnicity. Figure 13.2 shows the difference between black and white unemployment over a number of years. Black unemployment is typically about twice that of white unemployment regardless of whether the economy is strong or weak. Black workers often describe themselves as last hired, first fired; these unemployment statistics suggest that there is considerable truth in that statement. More significantly, the gap between white and black unemployment has been increasing over the last twenty years rather than decreasing. Part of the explanation for this phenomenon lies in the lack of educational equality we saw in the previous chapter. African Americans, along with other minorities, have not achieved qualifications that equal those of European

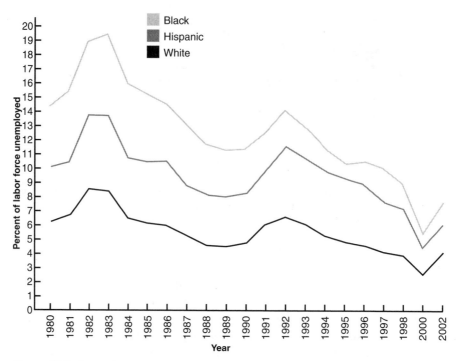

Figure 13.2 Unemployment rates of black, white, and Hispanic American workers aged twenty-five and over, 1980–2002. (Data from U.S. Bureau of the Census, 2004a)

Americans. But still, differences remain. As Figure 13.3 makes abundantly clear, more education does not guarantee either African Americans or Hispanics a place in the workforce.

The presence of more blacks in well-paid jobs previously denied them in American society leaves the impression that significant economic advances have occurred for blacks in general; but for most black workers, that impression is just not accurate. And these differences in unemployment are even greater if we add the factor of age. Workers under the age of twenty (many of whom obviously lack important job skills) typically have unemployment rates three times that of adults. Thus, if white unemployment is running about 5 percent, white youth unemployment rates will typically run 15 percent. More strikingly, black adult unemployment rates of 10 percent will result in 30 percent unemployment rates for black youths. Such statistics make it clear that the American dream of economic advancement is available only on a selective basis to American workers.

Labor Unions in the United States Labor unions have had their ups and downs in American economic history. In the early nineteenth century, most business leaders

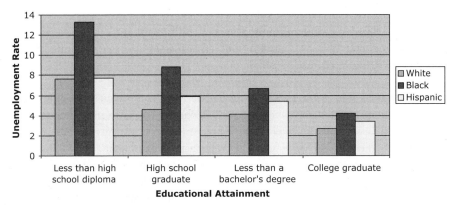

Figure 13.3 Unemployment rate for persons aged twenty-five and older by educational attainment and race/ethnicity, 2002. (Data from U.S. Bureau of the Census, 2004a)

viewed labor leaders as radicals intent on overthrowing the American government. Labor leaders were often denied employment (a procedure known as "blacklisting"), which denied them access to workers. Labor demonstrations were routinely put down with violence, as police were typically allied with employers. And employers found endlessly creative ways to prevent the growth of unions. Nevertheless, efforts by the American Federation of Labor and the newer Congress of Industrial Organizations culminated in federal legislation in the 1930s that guaranteed the right to organize, to bargain collectively, and to strike. Approximately 35 percent of the workforce belonged to unions by 1945; membership remained at that level until the early 1960s, when it began to drop, falling to 12.5 percent by 2004 (U.S Bureau of the Census, 2004a).

During their period of dominance, unions achieved many rights for American workers; the medical and pension programs they put in place, coupled with job security based on seniority, made employees feel less helpless. Of course, unions did not bring down the American way of life, as feared by many employers; in fact, they often added an element of predictability to labor costs and thus promoted more accurate planning by management. The drop in union membership over the last forty years probably has more to do with changes in the American workforce than it does with worker attitudes about unions—although the public image of unionism has clearly dropped over the last few decades (Delaney, 1991). Nevertheless, the change from manufacturing jobs to service jobs has moved unions into new realms as police officers, nurses, and schoolteachers form unions to protect their interests.

The strength of unions traditionally was in the secondary sector of the economy—in the major manufacturing industries such as steel and automobile production. Unions also made inroads in some areas of the primary sector, such as coal mining. The tertiary sector (which includes white-collar and professional occupations) has always been difficult to unionize but there has been steady growth in the 1990s and into the current century. Interestingly, however, similar economic changes in Europe have not produced the drastic drop in union membership seen in the United States (Blanchflower and Freeman, 1992).

Changes in the Labor Market: The Growth of Service Occupations The labor market in the United States underwent enormous change in the twentieth century. A massive decline in agricultural employment coupled with a steady decline in blue-collar employment was roughly balanced by a massive rise in white-collar jobs in the tertiary sector, which is predicted to rise even more over the coming years.

As we've seen, the exploitation of cheap labor in developing countries by multi-national corporations has eliminated considerable employment in the United States in the primary and secondary sectors of the economy. This change is forcing many American workers to seek job retraining as the need for their current skills disappears. It is almost impossible today to find American-made televisions, DVD players, or cameras; the label on the clothing you are wearing right now may inform you that it was stitched together in Korea, China, or perhaps the Caribbean; and every passing year increases the chances that your automobile either originated overseas or was produced in the United States by a foreign-owned corporation. While the United States imports so many of these goods, many of its exports involve the information technology (IT) that Americans still dominate (although the outsourcing of IT service jobs and new manufacturing overseas are both increasing rapidly). Growth in such new services provides strength to the American economy and sound opportunities for some skilled American workers, but not all new jobs in the service sector offer such a bright future.

For every new job in designing computer software in the United States, there is another new job handling routine tasks in the fast-food industry. Although both may be labeled as service jobs, the differences in which workers will get them and how the job will affect the worker are obvious. An important distinction that may help us understand some of these changes is that between the primary and secondary labor markets. The **primary labor market** includes those occupations that provide a range of employee benefits coupled with relatively high job status and at least some security. By contrast, the **secondary labor market** includes relatively low-skilled and poorly paid occupations that provide little if any employee benefits. Employee benefits include such essentials as medical insurance, retirement programs, and the like. But along with these benefits in the primary labor market come status, higher pay, greater security, and, most typically, greater autonomy and inherent interest in the work activity. Individuals entering the secondary labor market will lack these advantages and satisfactions; more important, they will probably be entering a world of employment from which escape may be difficult. With the exception of teenagers working summer jobs, these secondary labor market occupations may well represent dead ends in terms of upward mobility.

As the American economy comes more and more to consist of this split world of service occupations, there is some danger that our social stratification system may become even more rigid in terms of mobility than it has been in the past. Many of the occupations in the secondary labor market are becoming homes for nonwhite workers, while more affluent white workers live in the separate world of the primary labor market. As we have seen in this chapter and in Chapter 10, some routes for advancement have become less open than they had been. With fewer and fewer black and Hispanic youth achieving four-year college degrees relative to white youth and with the uselessness of job skills learned in the secondary labor market for advancement, it is hard to see new areas of opportunity in the American economy appearing in the coming decade.

THE POLITICAL INSTITUTION

If we focus on institutions in terms of the basic human needs they satisfy, the political institution specializes in the basic need for protection from other members of society (see Chapter 9). This need grows from the fact that people attempt to use power in their social relationships to further their own ends. As we turn to explore the operation of the political institution, we need to first examine the ways in which power and authority operate in modern societies; we pay special attention to the growth of the modern state. We also examine the various types of governments, ranging from democratic to authoritarian, that direct the political system within states. Following this introduction to political systems, we turn to politics in the United States, examining political participation in electoral politics and the role of interest groups and the media in determining who has power and how they use it. Finally, we look at various theories of political power, each providing a different perspective on who really has power in the United States.

POLITICAL SYSTEMS: ARRANGEMENTS OF POWER AND AUTHORITY

The **political system** represents the social organization in an industrial society that distributes power within a society and governs its use. The system determines what rights and obligations citizens have to each other and to government at various levels. Much political activity is highly structured and ongoing, involving legal decisions, law enforcement, and overall government functioning; however, it also includes a wide range of "unofficial" political activities. When communities or social groups organize to protest, for example, those activities exist within the political system, as the protest groups seek to bring about changes in who has power or how decisions regarding social rights or obligations are made. (We explore these types of protest groups fully in Chapter 15; in the meantime, Box 13.1 explores the world of terrorism.) To better understand political systems, we examine the institutionalization of power and authority in society and the various types of government within which it occurs.

BOX 13.1

Terrorism

Terrorism is the commission of real or threatened acts of violence, often involving random victims in order to achieve specific political goals. The point of terrorism is to achieve some combination of spreading fear (anyone could be a potential victim) and disrupting the everyday routines of a society. Most Americans first firmly focused their attention on terrorism on September 11, 2001. On that day, the United States joined much of the rest of the world in learning how to live with terrorism (Merari, 2005). A significant part of learning to live with it is to understand it better.

Perhaps most important, terrorism is a tactic, not a political goal. And it is not connected in any way with any particular goal. It can achieve a wide variety of them. And it is not limited to any particular group of people. It is usually not a tactic of first resort but, for certain kinds of situations, it may be seen as the only effective tactic available (Sedgwick, 2004).

Second, the level of violence resulting from conflict does not define terrorism. The greatest violence in human history has occurred in wars between countries, but those wars are not terrorism. Even guerrilla wars are not terrorism if the guerrillas are only attacking other soldiers. And even if civilians die in large numbers during warfare, it is still not terrorism. Civilians must be the *targets* of violence before we have terrorism.

While anyone can commit an act of terrorism for any reason, there are two basic types of terrorism we examine here, differentiated by the levels of authority held by those committing the acts. *State terrorism* refers to acts of terror committed or condoned by established governments. On November 9, 1938, thousands of Jewish businesses were destroyed throughout Germany and Austria in what has come to be called Krystal Nacht (the night of broken glass). It was an organized, state-supported beginning of the eventual arrests and genocide of the Jewish people under Nazi leadership. A similar example is found in the United States as state governments turned a blind eye for many years to the lynching of African Americans. More recently, genocide in Rwanda and the Darfur region of Sudan both occurred under government auspices (Fowler, 2004). State terrorism is most commonly connected to ethnic issues.

The second type of terrorism is connected to *ethnic nationalism*. This type is the opposite of state terrorism in the sense that those committing the acts have no state-connected authority but hope to achieve it from those who do. Ethnic nationalism stems from the hopes of an ethnic minority to achieve nationhood by creating a separate country that will reflect its culture. (See Chapter 8 for a more complete discussion.) When ethnic nationalism movements lack sufficient resources for a more traditional armed rebellion, terrorism often emerges as the tactic of choice.

The Basque separatist movement in Spain has long used terrorist tactics in the hopes of creating a Basque country separate from Spain. Similarly, terrorism from the insurgents in the 2002 Iraq War reflected the hopes of Sunni Muslims to retain their ethnic control over the government of Iraq.

In the modern world, terrorism gains effectiveness from modern weapons, improved transportation and communication, and input from the media. A very few people can easily move sophisticated weapons around the globe and have a huge impact. After striking, terror is increased by media coverage and Internet communication. Understandably, terrorism is increasing as the tactic becomes more effective. In addition, ethnic nationalism is on the rise, adding to the number of potential players in this game. It seems unlikely that September 11 will be the last occurrence within the United States.

Power, Authority, and the State The issues of power and authority became central issues in sociology through the work of Max Weber. As we saw in Chapter 3 (which includes a more complete discussion of these concepts), *power* is the ability to control the behavior of others regardless of their willingness to be dominated. By contrast, *authority* is a special kind of control in which the individuals who are dominated feel that the domination is legitimate in some sense. Weber identified three dimensions of the legitimation that characterizes authority: tradition, the charisma of individual leaders, and rational systems of law. Rational systems of law (such as the U.S. Constitution and the many laws enacted by Congress since) command respect through the acceptance of their usefulness by those who are governed by them.

Although charismatic authority is often the source of social change as charismatic leaders generate respect for themselves among protest movement followers, traditional authority, rational systems of law (or legal-rational authority), and raw power often become institutionalized within a state. A **state** is a form of social organization that controls the means of coercion (or force) over a territory with specified political (or international) boundaries. (A **nation-state** is a state with only one significant ethnic group within its boundaries.) The state defines citizenship within its jurisdiction, controls the use of force within its boundaries (setting and enforcing law), and defends its boundaries against other states that may wish to take control of them (see Enloe, 1981; Giddens, 1985). The state obviously controls power within its territory, but it generally attempts to generate authority among those it governs; no state can survive if it must hold its entire citizenship (or even a sizable portion of it) at gunpoint. Leaders of states develop traditional authority over time, but a more immediate source of authority is the acceptance among its citizens of the utility of its legal system plus its maintenance of a monopoly over the right to alter that system. In this sense, there is no difference between the acceptance by Americans of their rule of law and the acceptance by Germans of Hitler's decisions during

The authority found in any courtroom is Weber's legal/rational authority.

the early days of Nazi Germany. In both cases, the laws are perceived to be legitimate and this perception gives the state authority.

States have grown in territory as industrialization has progressed; they have also become more formalized. The large scale of commerce characteristic of industrialization becomes more efficient in a large state. One can produce goods in Oklahoma, for example, and market them throughout the other forty-nine states without fear of paying tariffs or having one's assets seized by a rival state government. In addition, the federal government of the United States facilitates the export of those same goods to foreign countries through its establishment of international economic and political relations. The formalization (or bureaucratization) of states provides even more efficiency. Whatever its shortcomings, bureaucratic organization provides consistency and predictability, which are crucial to anyone attempting to make long-term business decisions (see Chapter 6).

During the twentieth century, many states expanded their roles beyond the maintenance of boundaries, internal order, and economic relations. In particular, state concern for and action on behalf of the public welfare is now expected in all highly industrialized nations. In the United States, programs such as social security, Medicare, and Medicaid reflect the intervention of the state in the personal affairs of its citizens. In the case of social security, for example, most workers participate automatically, with or without their consent. In those industrialized states described earlier in this chapter as having mixed economies, it is typical to find a much wider range of public services than found in the United States. Great Britain and Sweden, for example, provide for the public welfare from cradle to grave; this state activity eliminates some of the economic inequality found in states with less welfare orientation, such as the United States.

Democratic Governments While all states share the same basic functions, they vary in the degree to which they permit citizens to participate in the affairs of government. A **democratic government** is a government in which citizens are permitted to participate, either directly or indirectly. A **direct democracy** occurs when each citizen has an equal voice and directly participates in governmental activities. By nature, direct democracies must be quite small; for example, some New England towns call meetings to which all members of the community are invited to discuss and vote on community actions. A **representative democracy** involves the election of representatives by groups of citizens; those representatives discuss and vote on governmental actions. The representatives may be organized in various governmental bodies. In a *democratic republic* such as the United States, some representatives are combined into legislative bodies (as in the House of Representatives and the Senate) while an executive (the president) is elected separately. A parliamentary system, such as that in Canada, Great Britain, Israel, and most democratic governments, elects a leader (a prime minister) from either the majority party in parliament or some coalition of political parties in parliament who agree to form a government.

As human history goes, democracies are both new and still relatively rare on the world scene; such governments have only become common since the onset of the industrial revolution. As we saw in the previous section, the free market is the cornerstone of capitalist economies. A democratic government is clearly one way to facilitate the growth of such economic systems. In keeping with the famous quotation from President Calvin Coolidge, "The business of America is business." A clear connection cannot always be made between the nature of the economic system and the structure of the political system. Some observers have argued that free markets and democratic institutions are necessarily connected (Berger, 1986). Other observers have noted that free markets have prospered under quite authoritarian forms of government and that democratic governments are particularly rare when considerable economic inequality exists within the society or there is disagreement among elites as to the basic value of democratic institutions (Higley and Burton, 1989; Muller, 1988). Lipset and Schneider (1973) found that high levels of economic development in general helped maintain stable democracies.

Authoritarian Governments Whereas democratic governments are characterized by widespread political participation in and control over the state, an **authoritarian**

government is characterized by the concentration of political control within the hands of a few members of society. A **dictatorship** is the concentration of political power in the hands of one person; an **oligarchy** is the concentration of political power in the hands of a small group of people.

Authoritarian governments differ in the degree to which they exert control over their citizens. Most allow some freedom and control outside the scope of government as, for example, in permitting religious freedom and giving some autonomy to religious organizations. By contrast, a **totalitarian government** is an authoritarian government that seeks control over all aspects of communal and individual life within its boundaries. Nazi Germany provides a clear example, as does the Khmer Rouge regime in Cambodia in the 1970s, during which hundreds of thousands of people were executed and many were relocated to rural areas. The goal of leader Pol Pot was to completely wipe out all aspects of the previous culture so as to govern over a totally transformed society. Totalitarian regimes are typified by rigid ideologies (which justify the existence of the regime), complete control over the media, a single (and overwhelmingly strong) political party, considerable control over the economy, and extreme methods of social control in response to deviance. We see similar governments in the former regime of Saddam Hussein in Iraq and of Kim Jong-il in North Korea.

POLITICS IN THE UNITED STATES

The United States has been governed by a representative democracy since its formation following the Revolutionary War. The percentage of the population represented has grown considerably since that time, however, as initially only white male property holders were allowed to vote. The right to vote was extended to African Americans in 1870, to women in 1920, and to Native Americans in 1924. The political system within which they vote has changed very little in structure for over two hundred years. The three branches of the federal government have remained intact, with offices filled as specified in the U.S. Constitution. But while the structure of government has changed little, considerable change has occurred not only in who votes but in why they vote, their interest in voting, and the information that affects their voting. Similarly, many changes have occurred in how candidates are selected, advertised, funded, and influenced after election. The framers of the Constitution would recognize their work in the current political system but would be astounded at the forces that move it and the manner in which it is manipulated.

Political Participation: Voting Behavior and Apathy Individual citizens in the United States can become involved in the political institution in many ways, including, of course, actually running for office themselves. Short of that, they may work for candidates or become involved with special interest groups and lobbying. The vast majority of people, however, limit their direct participation to voting (and many choose not even to do that). Sociologists attempt to understand some of this variety in participation by studying **political socialization**—the process by which individuals acquire values and patterns of behavior with regard to the political institution. Not surprisingly, political socialization occurs in much the same way as more general forms of socialization. The strongest influence on the political socialization of most people is the views of their parents (Jennings and Niemi, 1981). Children not only learn political attitudes from parents, they also acquire behavior patterns: children who watch their parents go to the polls on election day are presented with a role model that they may accept for themselves in later life. Other important factors in political socialization include education (courses in government are often mandatory) and the media (which provide debates, interviews, political commentary, and endless political advertising around election time). During the 2004 presidential election, many voters claimed they received their political information and socialization from Jon Stewart's *Daily Show* or from Jay Leno's monologs. And weblogs are clearly in growth mode as a major factor in American politics.

Although the U.S. Constitution is not structured around the existence of political parties, a wide variety of political parties have entered the political arena since the early days of the Republic. By the Civil War, both the Democratic and Republican parties were in place, and the two-party dominance of the political system was soon established. The parties have both gone through many changes in the course of their respective histories. The Republican Party has traditionally been the party of business, but it was also the party of the North (until the 1960s) and of black voters (until the 1930s) because of its association with Lincoln and the Union forces in the Civil War. The Democratic Party gained strength in the second half of the nineteenth century as the party of immigrant voters, many of whom were Catholic or Jewish. It was also the party of the South (again, thanks to the Civil War). President Franklin Roosevelt altered some of these allegiances in the 1930s when he built a coalition of working-class, Jewish, Catholic, nonwhite, and southern voters, which lasted for over thirty years. The association of the Democratic Party with the civil rights movement of the 1950s and 1960s and with assorted other liberal causes has allowed the Republican Party to make inroads among southern voters and, to a lesser extent, among working-class, Jewish, and Catholic voters. Woven through all this history is a fundamental difference between the two parties with regard to government economic and public welfare policies. The Republican Party has retained its relation to American business through its support of conservative economic policies, which has included efforts to minimize the welfare role of government. The Democratic Party has generally favored more liberal economic policies and has promoted the welfare role of government.

Many of the differences between the two parties can be seen in the data provided by Table 13.1, which allow us to analyze where support has come from in the last four presidential elections in the United States. Turning first to income data, the support of Democratic candidates by poorer voters and the support of the Republican candidate by wealthier voters is clear in every election. Characteristics related to

TABLE 13.1
PORTRAIT OF THE AMERICAN ELECTORATE, 1992–2004

	Share of the 2004 vote	1992			1996			2000			2004		
		Clinton	Bush	Perot	Clinton	Dole	Perot	Gore	Bush	Nader	Kerry	Bush	Nader
Overall													
Total vote	100	43	38	19	49	41	8	48	48	2	48	51	—
Sex													
Men	46	41	38	21	43	44	10	42	53	3	44	55	—
Women	54	45	37	17	54	38	7	54	43	2	51	48	—
Race & ethnicity													
White	77	39	40	20	43	46	9	42	54	3	41	58	—
Black	11	83	10	7	84	12	4	90	8	1	88	11	—
Hispanic	6	61	25	14	72	21	6	67	31	2	58	43	—
Asian	2	31	55	15	43	48	8	54	41	4	56	44	—
Age													
18–29	17	43	34	22	53	34	10	48	46	5	54	45	—
30–44	29	41	38	21	48	41	9	48	49	2	46	53	—
45–59	30	41	40	19	48	41	9	48	49	2	48	51	—
60 and older	24	50	38	12	48	44	7	51	47	2	46	54	—

Religion													
All Protestants	54	36	45	18	41	50	8	40	58	1	40	59	—
White Protestants	41	33	47	21	36	53	10	34	63	2	32	67	—
Catholics	27	44	35	20	53	37	9	49	47	2	47	52	—
Jewish	3	80	11	9	78	16	3	79	19	1	74	25	—
Attend church at least once week	41	36	48	15				39	59	2	39	61	—
Family Income													
Under $15,000	8	58	23	19	59	28	11	57	37	4	63	36	—
$15,000–$29,999	15	45	35	20	53	36	9	54	41	3	57	42	—
$30,000–$49,999	22	41	38	21	48	40	10	49	48	2	50	49	—
$50,000–$74,999	23	40	41	18	47	45	7	46	51	2	43	56	—
$75,000–$99,999	14				44	48	7	45	52	2	45	55	—
$200,000 and over	3										35	63	—
$100,000 and over	18				38	54	6	43	54	2	41	58	—
$50,000 and over	55	39	44	17	45	48	7	44	52	2	43	56	—
Education													
Not a high school graduate	4	54	28	18	59	28	11	59	39	1	50	49	—
High school graduate	22	43	36	21	51	35	13	48	49	1	47	52	—
Some college education	32	41	37	21	48	40	10	45	51	3	46	54	—
College graduate or more	42	44	39	17	47	44	7	48	48	3	49	49	—
College graduate	26	39	41	20	44	46	8	45	51	3	46	52	—
Postgraduate education	16	50	36	14	52	40	5	52	44	3	55	44	—

Source: New York Times Sunday, November 7, 2004.

income, such as level of education and occupational status, show a similar relationship: the Democratic Party receives a majority of support from less-educated and low-status voters while better-educated and higher-status voters are more likely to lean toward the Republican Party—although education is not consistent at all levels.

The racial and ethnic breakdowns of voting trends show some continuities and some changes in the traditional allegiances of the two parties. Nonwhite voters still lean toward Democratic candidates to a wide degree while white voters are more likely to vote Republican. The traditional Jewish support of Democratic candidates has remained fairly steady, while Catholic voters, once staunch Democrats, have been moving steadily to the Republican Party. Protestant voters are a large diverse group, although they clearly lean toward the Republican Party; this is particularly true for more fundamentalist, "born again" Protestants who are attracted by the social conservatism of the Republican Party. In addition, regular church attenders, regardless of their religion, have become strong supporters of the Republican Party. Finally, a new wrinkle in American politics has appeared in the differences in support by gender for the two parties. In every election, men have favored the Republican candidate more than women. The most probable explanation for this is the continuing support for federally funded social programs by the Democratic Party—programs that are more likely to be favored by women than by men.

Although party loyalty is an important result of political socialization, an equally important result is voter apathy. In every presidential election since 1920, the winning candidate has received fewer votes than the number of Americans of voting age who chose not to vote. While men and women vote in almost equal numbers, most other social-category distinctions are reflected in different levels of voting. Whites, for example, are more likely to vote than blacks, and both groups are much more likely to vote than Hispanics. Because Hispanic Americans are one of the fastest-growing American minority groups, their current lack of political participation is of particular importance. Older Americans are much more likely to vote than younger Americans; this fundamental result of political socialization is reflected in continuing decreases over time in the percentages of voting-age Americans who vote. (Eighty percent of the voting-age population voted in 1896.)

Table 13.2 gives us a closer look at who votes and who doesn't, using data from the presidential election of 2000. Older age definitely brings people to the voting booths. Turning to an element of socioeconomic status, we find that Americans with more education are much more likely to vote than poorer or less educated Americans. In addition, African Americans and, in particular, Hispanic Americans are much less likely to vote than whites (see also Uhlaner, 1991). A statistic not included in Table 13.2 is the strong relationship between church participation and voting (Schwadel, 2005); those who are active in any organized religion are also more likely to be active in the political arena. While the people elected to political office parallel the voters in terms of church participation, their religious affiliation is not a reflection of the religious configuration of the voters; liberal Protestants, Jews, and

TABLE 13.2

PERCENTAGES OF THE VOTING AGE POPULATION WHO VOTED IN THE 2000
PRESIDENTIAL ELECTION

	Percentage Voting
Years of education	
Less than 8 years	26.8
9th–11th	33.6
High school: 4 years	49.4
College: 1–3 years	60.3
College: 4 years or more	72.0
Age	
18 to 20 years old	28.4
21 to 24 years old	35.4
25 to 34 years old	43.7
35 to 44 years old	55.0
45 to 64 years old	64.1
65 years old and over	67.6
Race/ethnicity	
White	56.4
Black	53.5
Hispanic	27.5

Source: U.S. Bureau of the Census, 2004a.

Mormons hold more seats in Congress than would be expected from the size of each group in the electorate (Banks, 2001).

Why are voter turnouts lower in the United States than in other industrialized countries, and why are particular categories of Americans more likely to vote than others? For one thing, most other industrialized countries make the registration process less complicated so that more voters find themselves eligible to vote when election day comes around (Glass, Squire, and Wolfinger, 1984). Kaempfer and Lowenberg (1993) suggest that voter turnout increases with the degree of political polarization in a society (with the United States perhaps having less than some other industrialized societies). Looking to differences among categories of voters within the United States, we find that voting is more likely to occur among individuals who have a clear personal sense of political efficacy (Orum, 1978). These are people who perceive that individuals can make a difference in influencing the factors that affect their lives. Individuals with lower socioeconomic status are much less likely to perceive politics as a solution to the problems in their lives (Teixeira, 1987).

Because low-status Americans are, by definition, going to have more problems by any objective measure, these differences are profoundly important. Perhaps their relative lack of problems provides higher-status Americans the illusion of individual efficacy, so they are more likely to attribute their success to their own efforts. Another possible explanation is that the political institution does in fact work better for higher-status people, who have the money and the influence to affect the system. Whatever the explanation, different levels of political participation can result in the continuation of the current inequalities in how the system works. Politicians are less likely to respond to the concerns of groups that do not vote; similarly, people whose concerns are not addressed by politicians may have less reason to think that the system can work for them and less motivation to participate.

Interest Groups: Politics and Money Candidates respond to constituents who vote, but they are likely to pay more attention to constituents who contribute to their campaigns. Private individuals do contribute, but the bulk of campaign contributions in the United States comes from special interest groups. **Interest groups** are social organizations that represent particular political interests and seek to influence the political institution to further those interests. Their actions may involve contributions or lobbying. **Lobbying** is the provision of special information to political leaders coupled with attempts to convince them to vote in accordance with the desires of the interest group. Interest groups may range from highly specialized interests of particular groups of Americans to much more general interests, which may have wide-ranging appeal. For example, the American Medical Association is an interest group that seeks to further the interests of physicians in the United States; nonphysicians would receive no direct benefits from such actions and could be negatively affected by the results of such lobbying. A somewhat more general example would be the National Rifle Association (NRA), which seeks to prevent legislation aimed at limiting access to firearms; hunters and gun enthusiasts (who belong to the NRA) benefit directly from such lobbying, but other Americans who have definite opinions on gun control also have a stake in the results. Finally, very general interest groups such as consumer protection organizations may seek to require manufacturers to provide additional product information or to increase safety levels in the use of their products. Such actions directly affect all consuming Americans to some degree. (Box 13.2 traces such issues by examining the political side of responses to AIDS in the United States.)

Interest groups are often organized as political action committees. A **political action committee** (or **PAC**) is an organization formed to raise and contribute money to support the political aims of a particular interest group. PACs may represent any interest group, but their most common form is the PAC that represents business or occupational interest groups. PACs typically provide ongoing sources of money for candidates so that the politician's ear may be available when particular pieces of legislation appear that have a direct bearing on the PAC's interests. Because large PACs

BOX 13.2

The Politics of AIDS

Sociologists take notice when human populations increase or decrease for whatever reason. Such changes can only occur as a result of changes in birth rates, death rates, and migration rates. While population size changes affect all aspects of society, the source of change often affects a specific portion of the society more than others. For example, the illegal migration of Mexican workers to the United States affects some states more than others and some members of the U.S. employment sector more than others because of resulting employment competition. Similarly, a rise in the birth rate among poor mothers adds members to the bottom rungs of the social stratification system while leaving other levels affected only indirectly. But the rising death rate in the United States due to AIDS (acquired immunodeficiency syndrome) not only affects distinct portions of the U.S. population, it also connects with some dominant American values and challenges American governmental political response.

AIDS first appeared on the American scene in 1981, when gay men began to die from rare diseases normally found only among people with deficient immune systems. AIDS received its name in 1982 and Congress appropriated funds for research. By 1984, the virus had been isolated and scientists began to understand the difficulty of its transmission—by blood or other bodily fluids—which tended to keep the disease from spreading rapidly throughout the population. In other words, if your degree of social contact with AIDS victims was limited, so too would be your danger of contracting the disease. While many African countries suffer from widespread distribution of the virus, transmitted through heterosexual contact, the virus in the United States was primarily limited to the homosexual and bisexual community and to those who share needles for the purpose of intravenous drug injection.

In the United States today, 61 percent of AIDS cases stem from male homosexual or bisexual contact, and 14.6 percent result from intravenous drug use. Another 5.7 percent result from the combination of those situations. Of the "respectable" ways to acquire AIDS, one percent is from such things as mother to child contact, contamination of blood, and organ or tissue transplants. The remaining 17.3 percent are from heterosexual contact with a high-risk partner. In this context, "high risk" means the partner is known to have HIV/AIDS, is a male who has had homosexual sex, is an intravenous drug user, or is a hemophiliac (U.S. Centers for Disease Control, 2004b).

These figures paint a picture of affected subpopulations in the United States that share deviations from mainstream American values. Homosexuals violate some basic

(continues)

BOX 13.2

The Politics of AIDS (continued)

American values, some religiously based and some not, while IV drug users receive the negative evaluation associated with drug use in the United States. In addition, most IV drug users tend to be both poor and nonwhite. For example, almost all women who acquire HIV/AIDS do so via "high risk" heterosexual sex. Black women are twenty-two times more likely to acquire HIV/AIDS than white women while Hispanic women are five times more likely. We find very similar figures for black and Hispanic children, who often contract the disease from their mothers (U.S. Centers for Disease Control, 2004b; Gayle et al., 1990). Turning to men, 76.6 percent of AIDS within the European American community is connected to the homosexual community. This is not true for African American and Hispanic men, for whom the percentage spread through homosexual contact is 48.5 percent and 60.9 percent, respectively; IV drug use plays a much more pivotal role within minority communities (U.S. Centers for Disease Control, 2004b).

All these figures have led to major political clashes in the United States in the 1990s and into the twenty-first century. AIDS victims and activists argue that government is not doing all that it could because the disease has left the mainstream population (and most politicians' constituents) relatively untouched. Unlike the situation in African countries, the disease has not yet moved into the middle-class heterosexual community with significant force. That same middle-class community often opposes the spread of information in the schools regarding safe sex or the dissemination of sterile needles to IV drug users. The recent advent of more effective drug treatment makes the social class differences all the more important since the drugs are expensive and poor people are less likely to have medical insurance. The expense of these drugs is also creating a new international pressure as the countries with the highest rates of the disease—primarily in Africa and Asia—are the countries with the least ability to pay.

may contribute millions of dollars in any given election, many political ears stay tuned to PAC interests. Most PACs contribute to politicians from both major parties and from various points on the political spectrum in hopes of maximizing the number of allies for important votes. The only kind of politician generally ignored by PACs is the one who is currently out of office and thus cannot vote. PACs are not so much interested in packing Congress with sympathetic politicians as they are in influencing those who are already there. That generalization is particularly true for business or occupationally related PACs, but it should be noted that interest groups often do become involved in the election process itself. Organizations such as Right to Life (which supports legal limitations on abortions in the United States) often contribute to out-of-office politicians who support their agenda.

The tendency for PACs in general to support incumbents has made it increasingly difficult for aspiring politicians to break into the political arena. Even when voter dissatisfaction is high (as measured by voter opinion polls), incumbents still win with overwhelming regularity. Although large amounts of money in a campaign chest have always been important in waging a successful campaign, money has become even more essential with the greater expense and spreading influence of the media in modern American political campaigns.

In 2002, Congress passed the McCain-Feingold bill, which limits various forms of campaign financing. The goal was to cap the influx of "soft money" that could be donated to political campaigns. The 2004 election highlighted a loophole in this law through which interest groups (often called "527 groups," named for the tax code that governs them), can spend their own money to influence elections. In 2004, the Swift Boat Veterans for Truth (anti-Kerry) and Moveon.org (anti-Bush) played major roles through their attacks in the media.

Politics and the Media The most important elements of the media for political socialization are television, radio, and newspapers. Of these, television has clearly become the most important, as it is the major source of news for most Americans. Both the inherent nature of television and its popularity with consumers have given it a major and distinctive influence on American political life.

By its nature, television cannot provide the depth and detail of political information that newspapers can provide. Time constraints on both network and local news programs force a condensation of material; newspapers have no such constraints. This lack of time affects political information in two ways. First, the details of political issues and positions cannot be reported, nor can the possible repercussions of those issues and positions. Voters receive the broad brush strokes but may be left unaware of other facets of the issues that might personally affect them and thus alter their positions and political behavior. Second, certain kinds of political issues are either too detailed or too narrow in focus to warrant the attention of television news. The news not shown represents important decisions made by news producers and directors with an eye toward general interest and higher viewer ratings.

The popularity of television with American consumers has fundamentally altered both the nature of political campaigning in general and political advertising in particular. Individuals who direct political campaigns are fully aware of the constraints on and desires of television news programs. As a result, campaigns are turning increasingly into a series of media events in which the politician finds himself or herself in photogenic (and often symbolically important) surroundings uttering neat sound bites that lend themselves to the close editing needed for the evening news. Viewers are thus confronted by politicians at flag factories or on military

Some things about politics never change. American political campaigns often seem more theater than politics.

bases repeating phrases that they hope will become ingrained in the political consciousness of American voters. The visual and brief nature of the medium forces campaigning to become picturesque and short, which tends to oversimplify complex political issues.

The amount of political advertising on television has grown enormously in recent years, paralleling the growing popularity of the medium with the public. The old-fashioned stump speeches of politicians who traveled from town to town are no longer an effective way to reach large numbers of voters; such speeches survive only if films of them can be "sold" to news program directors or can be included in professionally produced television advertisements. Campaigning on television isolates politicians from voters (who may have very real questions they wish to ask) and forces politicians to simplify their messages (because of time limitations). Perhaps most important, however, television advertising is extremely expensive; poorly funded candidates are therefore at an extreme disadvantage. We have already seen that incumbents have built-in advantages as a result of their increased levels of contributions. A dependence on television by both voters and politicians creates a situation in which the more poorly funded candidates may not even be able to achieve name recognition among voters. While lesser-known candidates have shown effective use of the Internet for fund-raising in recent years—Howard Dean in his bid for the 2004 Democratic presidential nomination comes to mind—there still is no substitute for the fund-raising opportunities available to incumbents.

THE SOURCES OF POWER: PLURALISM VERSUS ELITISM

In industrial societies, the role of power has spread to a wide range of social activities, particularly with regard to maintaining the built-in inequalities of social stratification. Power keeps the rich in control, enabling them to remain rich. Power also plays a role in attacks on the status quo as less-favored groups use their influence to restructure the bases of power. The diversity characteristic of industrial societies creates a great number of interests that often come into conflict; when that conflict occurs, power invariably plays a major role in determining the outcome. When there is no outright conflict, the sources of power in society are not so readily apparent. Sociologists do not agree as to just how power is distributed in society. A variety of theories have been suggested, but most fall under one of two general headings: pluralism or elitism.

Pluralism essentially sees power as relatively evenly distributed among the members of society. This perspective is most clearly in keeping with representative government as it is commonly assumed to work. Democratic political representation is supposed to place power in the hands of the people through the vote. In a pluralistic society, therefore, power would appear to be evenly distributed among the voters. The essence of pluralism is that just such a distribution exists.

Elitism assumes that a small group of individuals (an elite) in society holds the vast majority of power, leaving little for the mass of the population. Elitist theorists point out that elected representatives don't always vote as their constituents would wish, perhaps leaning more strongly toward satisfying their wealthier contributors. More important, however, elitist theorists question the degree to which power is directly in the hands of elected representatives. Corporate leaders, for example, may play a major behind-the-scenes role in shaping the decisions of an industrial society; elitist theorists search for just such leaders.

An example of the pluralist perspective can be found in Robert Dahl's 1961 book *Who Governs?* which traces the history of political control in the city of New Haven, Connecticut. According to Dahl, the early leaders were descendants of the Puritans who first settled the area. The industrialization of the nineteenth century brought businessmen into the circle of power, widening the distribution of power in the area. Finally, massive immigration of southeastern Europeans into the area in the early twentieth century added still another group to the picture, widening the distribution of power still further. According to Dahl, the early elitist power structure of New Haven has given way to a pluralistic power structure; a wide variety of groups share power and contest decision making. He sees similar pluralistic power distributions in other American cities (Dahl, 1982). Subsequently, Dahl (1989) modified his earlier pluralistic perspective, introducing some more radical perspectives (see also Held, 1991), but his earlier work is one of the clearest examples of political pluralism.

Another version of pluralism offered by David Riesman introduces the concept of the **veto group,** a political group that exercises sufficient power to prevent the actions of other political groups. According to Riesman, the sharing of power under pluralism does not allow a variety of groups enough power to change society directly into the form they would prefer. These groups do, however, have enough power to limit the excesses of other groups in their attempts to have their way. This limitation takes the form of a veto, in which power acts in a negative way. In Riesman's view, power is at least evenly enough distributed in American society for a variety of groups to defend themselves from others (Riesman, Glazer, and Denney, 1950).

A classic example of the elitist perspective is presented in C. Wright Mills's *The Power Elite* (1956). According to Mills, there are three major sources of power in American society: the executive branch of the government, business leaders, and the military. He sees these three spheres as acting in concert much of the time because of the interchangeability of their leaders; the same individuals can be found moving among major positions in the military, the government, and the business world. These "elites," according to Mills, make the decisions that govern our lives. As a unit, they form a "military-industrial complex," with elites in each area making decisions that will benefit all three. Ironically, Mills found a willing convert to this idea in President Dwight Eisenhower, who, in his farewell address to the nation in 1961, warned against just such a centralization of power in American society.

The elitist interpretation gained some additional support from the research of G. William Domhoff (2002). In his book *Who Rules America?* Domhoff searched for the actual individuals in the elites referred to by Mills. According to Domhoff, the "governing class" is a relatively small group of individuals (about one-half of one percent of the American population) who make most of the decisions that govern the lives of the whole population. Mostly rich businessmen and their families, they form quite a cohesive group. They seem to be interchangeable on the boards of directors of major corporations, and, perhaps more interestingly, they have clear social ties within their group, ranging from country club memberships to marriage ties. According to Domhoff, these people are not only a small ruling elite, they are also a social group conscious of themselves as a ruling elite. If their decisions appear to follow a pattern of providing mutual benefits within the group, it may be more than chance.

The complexities of a modern industrial society such as the United States create difficulties for sociologists in every area of study, but the number of decisions made in everyday life and the elaborate forms of social organization from which they emanate (such as bureaucracies) make the question of power truly one of the most difficult. Many Americans express the sense that they are losing control over the events that affect their lives. We seem to have a clear sense of where power isn't but a much less clear idea of just where it is.

SUMMARY

An economic system is the organization of social activities that produces and distributes goods and services within and between societies. In industrial societies (in which it is a clearly separate institution), it consists of three sectors: the production of raw materials, basic manufacturing, and the production and distribution of services. Modern economic systems vary in terms of ownership of property: largely private ownership occurs in capitalist economies, and largely public ownership of property in socialist economies. Within the former, a basic economic unit is the corporation, which operates with the rights of ownership and the liabilities of an individual but is typically owned by a number of individuals who are its shareholders. Corporations can be large (even multinational in scope) to the point where they may control whole sectors of the economy.

Modern economic systems run on the labor of workers whose efforts are obtained through contract with employers. The nature of this relationship (and, in particular, the level of satisfaction of workers) plays an important role in determining industrial productivity. Business cycles result in rising and falling levels of unemployment as demand for products rises and falls. In response to these and other uncertainties in the workplace, many workers have formed and joined labor unions in order to gain a more forceful voice in affecting their situation in the marketplace. In the United States, industrialization has changed over the years; there has been growth in the service sector of the economy coupled with declines in raw material production and basic manufacturing (much of which now occurs in newly industrializing nations with lower labor costs). The growth of the service sector has changed the occupational structure of American society, including the formation of highly skilled and well rewarded occupations (the primary labor market) and unskilled and poorly rewarded occupations (the secondary labor market).

A political system represents the social organization in a society that distributes power and governs its use. Modern industrial societies vest such power in a centralized organization called a state, which coordinates power and comes to hold considerable authority. Membership in state governments and forms of decision making range from democratic governments (controlled through popular election) to authoritarian governments (in which power is concentrated in the hands of a few leaders). Democratic participation in the United States, particularly with regard to electoral politics, has declined throughout the twentieth century. Of the more organized forms of participation, such as lobbying, a particularly important development is the growth of the political action committee, through which considerable money and influence are channeled. Equally important is the role of the media in politics as candidates must now finance and orchestrate their activities through media, especially television. As a result, candidates are encouraged to spend more money and to maintain campaigns emphasizing symbols and often considerable superficiality.

GLOSSARY

Alienation A worker's lack of interest in and identification with the job, coupled with a general feeling of powerlessness over the conditions that affect his or her life.

Authoritarian government A government characterized by the concentration of political control within the hands of relatively few members of society.

Capitalist economies Economic systems characterized by the private ownership of property and a form of coordination based on a market system of exchange through which goods and services are exchanged according to value determined by supply and demand.

Conglomerate A large corporation formed through the merger of many smaller corporations that operate in different sectors of the economy.

Corporation A legal entity that functions in the economic sector with rights of ownership and potential liabilities much like those of an individual but legally separate from the individuals who own it.

Democratic government A government in which citizens are permitted to participate, either directly or indirectly.

Dictatorship The concentration of political power in the hands of one person.

Direct democracy A democratic government in which each citizen has an equal voice and directly participates in governmental activities.

Economic system The organization of social activities that produces and distributes goods and services within and between societies.

Elitism The belief that a small group of people in a society inevitably holds power.

Interest group A social organization that represents particular political interests and seeks to influence the political institution to further those interests.

Interlocking directorate The appearance of the same individuals on the boards of directors of several corporations simultaneously.

Lobbying The provision of special information to political leaders by an interest group, coupled with attempts to convince them to vote in accordance with the desires of the interest group.

Mixed economies Economic systems characterized by a compromise between capitalist and socialist economic systems whereby some property is privately owned while other property is controlled by the state.

Monopoly The control over a given product or service by a single corporation.

Multinational corporation A corporation that is located in one country yet owns companies that are based in other countries.

Nation-state A state with only one significant ethnic group within its boundaries.

Oligarchy The concentration of political power in the hands of a small group of people.

Oligopoly The domination over the production of a given product or service by a relatively small number of corporations.

Pluralism The belief that power in a society is relatively evenly distributed.

Political action committee (PAC) An organization formed to raise and contribute money to support the aims of a particular interest group.

Political socialization The process by which individuals acquire values and patterns of behavior with regard to the political institution.

Political system The social organization in an industrial society that distributes power within the society and governs its use.

Primary labor market Those occupations that provide a range of employee benefits coupled with relatively high status and at least some security.

Primary sector That sector of the economy associated with the production of raw materials.

Representative democracy A democratic government involving the election of representatives by groups of citizens, after which those representatives discuss and vote on governmental actions.

Secondary labor market Those occupations that are relatively low-skilled and poorly paid and that provide few if any employee benefits.

Secondary sector That sector of the economy associated with manufacturing activities through which raw materials are transformed into usable goods.

Socialist economies Economic systems characterized by the public ownership of property and the state-run coordination of the production of goods and services.

State A form of social organization that controls the means of coercion (or force) over a given territory with specified political (or international) boundaries.

Terrorism The commission of real or threatened acts of violence often involving random victims in order to achieve specific political goals.

Tertiary sector That sector of the economy associated with the production and distribution of services.

Totalitarian government An authoritarian government that seeks control over all aspects of communal and individual life within its boundaries.

Veto group A version of pluralism in which distribution of power occurs because one group—a veto group—has enough power to limit any actions of another group that might result in that group's ascension.

Work ethic The cultural value placed on work as an end in itself, independent of its products.

STUDY QUESTIONS

1. Explain the variation among capitalist economies, socialist economies, and mixed economies. Which best describes the United States?
2. What distinguishes the corporation from other kinds of business organizations? How is economic competition affected when corporations are either monopolies or oligopolies? How is that competition affected when corporations become conglomerates or have interlocking directorates?
3. What is a multinational corporation? How does it interact with multiple governments in whose countries it does business?
4. Why is worker satisfaction a concern to both employers and employees? What makes it rise and fall?
5. Why do unemployment rates rise and fall over time in the United States? Which Americans are most affected by high unemployment and why?
6. What role have labor unions played throughout their history in the United States? What is their role today?
7. Why has the service sector grown so dramatically in the U.S. economy? What is the difference between the primary labor market and the secondary labor market?
8. What is the relationship between a political institution and authority?
9. How are direct democratic governments different from representative democracies? Which is characteristic of the United States? How are such governments different from authoritarian governments?
10. Who votes in the United States and who do they vote for? How have both of these changed over time?
11. What role do interest groups play in American politics? Be sure to discuss lobbying and political action committees.
12. How do the theoretical schools of pluralism and elitism differ in their perception of power and how it is exercised?

The Editors, Atlantic Monthly

AMERICA'S FORTUNES

The editors of *Atlantic Monthly* magazine paused in 2004 to examine America's economy and to make predictions about changes they believed were in store. They term America's current economic situation the "reverse-lottery economy" in which many workers have successful economic outcomes while others hit the reverse jackpot, facing layoffs or underemployment. They attribute all of this to growing labor productivity, which puts some workers out the door while simultaneously strengthening the overall economy. Who will be the winners and losers in America's economy down the road? And what can be done to lessen the pain of those losers? Read on to see *Atlantic Monthly*'s predictions and suggestions.

At any given moment the state of any nation—and especially the state of any stable industrial democracy, where a measure of political calm and social order can generally be taken for granted—is determined largely by the state of its economy. Wars, relative military strength, terrorist attacks, natural disasters, demographic changes, social trends, election outcomes, even the results of international sporting competitions, can all contribute significantly to a country's perception of its own well-being. At times, certainly, one or more of these factors can outweigh the economy in affecting the collective sense of how the country is faring. But as any presidential candidate will tell you, for the average American citizen the most basic measure of national well-being amounts one way or another to economics. Is my income higher or lower than it was last year? Is my job more or less secure? Across the spectrum of class or income well-being is measured to a considerable degree by the question "Can I afford . . . ?" Can I afford to put the kids through college? Buy a house? Put my mother in a nursing home? Pay for day care? Put food on the table? Buy a vacation home?

But as important as the economy is in determining the state of the union, it is also a problematic measure, because the "real" state of the economy does not match our collective perception of it. That is, although one could in theory deduce America's exact sense of its economic well-being at any given moment by extrapolating from each citizen's income and expenses a kind of aggregate national answer to the question, "Can

From *The Atlantic Monthly,* January/February 2004, pp. 110–120. Reprinted by permission of *The Atlantic Monthly,* © 2004.

I afford to . . . ?" that would provide only an indirect and backward-looking measure of the economy's real strength. The true condition of the economy is best seen not as a snapshot of individuals' circumstances but as the movement of deeper forces through time; economists look back for measures of what has already happened, and then use various logical assumptions to project what will happen in the future.

Obviously, the state of the economy is a somewhat relative thing; how we judge it depends greatly on what we use as a basis for comparison. Compared with 2001, for instance, last year was in some respects a good one for the economy. Compared with 1999, however, it was in many ways disappointing. And in fact the economy of 2003 was by several measures comparable to the economy of 1997. Does this mean the economy has regressed? Or that it has returned to its natural level after a period of aberration? And what, if anything, can these historical comparisons tell us about the coming years?

Although the essays in "State of the Union" cover a wide variety of topics—from the long-term federal budget deficit to the changing nature of the middle class, from the health-care-cost conundrum to the rising level of anger in American society—all these topics are ultimately bound up with (either as influences on or as derivatives of) the state of the economy. In this opening essay we aim to establish the broader context that underlies all these issues, and to provide a balanced view of the U.S. economy—not just of how it's doing today, or this year, but of the deeper structural forces that will determine our prosperity over the long term.

In retrospect, the late 1990s appear to have been a golden age produced in part by the serendipitous confluence of unsustainable factors such as the stock-market boom, the post–Cold War "peace dividend," and a consumer borrowing binge of historic proportions. (Today, three years after the stock-market bubble burst, we are still suffering something of a hangover from the excesses of that giddy era.) But as accidental as that brief golden age may in some ways have been, and as irrational as the exuberance that propelled it was, the underlying forces at work in the late 1990s were real, and they began to reshape the economy in fundamental ways. We can now begin to see the enduring effect of those forces.

In the short term—let's say the next couple of years—the majority of Americans can expect to keep improving their economic lot; however, a significant minority—mainly the newly jobless in certain old-line industries—will watch their already dim prospects darken even further. And over the longer term—let's say ten years or more—a much broader swath of the American population will have reason to be very concerned about the economic future.

THE REVERSE-LOTTERY ECONOMY

Recent media coverage of the economy has focused on the troubled state of the job market. We are told that proportionally fewer adults are working today than at any time in the past ten years; that not since the Great Depression have we failed to produce an increase in the number of jobs for such a long period of time; and that median household incomes have fallen.

All this is true. Yet the overall picture that emerges from these facts is largely false. The "jobless recovery" has hardly been jobless: the unemployment rate—which stood at 5.9 percent in November—is lower than the average for the past thirty years, and is right at the threshold that most economists as recently as the mid-1990s believed was the lowest it could go without triggering inflation. Although it is true that some jobless people have given up looking for work, and therefore no longer even counted in official unemployment statistics, about half these people are teenagers, many of whom have forsaken the part-time job market in order to focus on schoolwork—hardly the stuff of a national crisis. In fact only 5.4 percent of those who have left the work force fit the definition of "discouraged workers"—people who have given up looking for work principally because they don't believe they can find it.

Those workers who have kept their jobs have for the most part prospered, despite the slackening of the job market. Real hourly-wage growth has continued through the recession and the recovery, albeit at a slower pace than in the 1990s. And wage growth has been broadly distributed, meaning that most workers, including most of the middle class, have benefited. In fact, there is a wide gap between how most people feel the economy in general is faring (poorly) and how they feel they themselves are doing (quite well). A poll conducted by the Gallup Organization in August found that 75 percent of the respondents rated the financial well-being of "average Americans" as "poor" or "only fair," and that 89 percent considered the employment situation specifically to be either "poor" or "only fair." (Nearly 50 percent rated it as downright "poor.") Yet when asked about their personal experiences, only 19 percent of those currently working said they were worried about being laid off, and even fewer worried about having their hours or wages reduced—the same percentage that feared these things in 1997, when the economy was booming. Another recent poll, by the Pew Research Center, found that only 35 percent of Americans disagreed with the statement "I'm pretty well satisfied with the way things are going for me financially." The percentage of Americans disagreeing with that statement has been lower only three times out of twelve since Pew first began asking about it, in 1987. Similarly, the percentage of respondents agreeing with the statement "I often don't have enough money to make ends meet" has been lower only twice—in 2002 and in 1999.

None of this is to deny that the job market is weaker today than it was in 1999—and policymakers should be taking steps to strengthen it. But for most Americans things are still going pretty well.

The real problem is neither flagging income for the unemployed nor the sheer number of workers laid off but, rather, the economic prospects of those workers who do lose their jobs. In June the average duration of unemployment hit 20.1 weeks—the highest it's been since January of 1984. And 43 percent of workers who signed up for unemployment benefits in 2002 exhausted them. This may have been an unusually mild recession for most Americans, but it's been unusually harsh for those who have lost jobs.

The problems facing recently laid-off workers—those who are still unemployed and also those who have found new jobs at reduced pay—are not likely to disappear as the economy picks up; these problems lie deeper than the business cycle. Over the past ten years, through boom and bust, unanticipated job loss has become a more wrenching experience for many workers. In earlier decades the unemployment rate and the average number of weeks unemployed tended to move in tandem: out-of-work people had a harder time finding jobs during recessions and an easier time during recoveries. But by the early 1990s many unemployed workers had trouble finding new work even in a strong job market. In 1997, with the unemployment rate down to 4.7 percent, the average duration of unemployment stood at about sixteen weeks—higher than it had been in all but three years during the 1980s, when unemployment was much higher.

When unemployed workers did find new jobs during the 1980s and 1990s, they had to settle for wages that were on average 14 percent lower than those in their previous jobs. A 14 percent pay cut is financially painful enough—but it's even more painful when it occurs amid a widespread expectation of steadily rising income. And since the mid-1990s the situation has been getting worse. In fact, a 2003 analysis by Henry Farber, an economist at Princeton University, reveals that when workers who lost their jobs finally found new ones, the gap between their new wages and the wages they would have earned (had they been able to stay in their old jobs) was nearly triple what it would have been almost a decade ago. The gap is greatest for highly educated workers. According to Farber's analysis of the most recent Displaced Workers Survey from the Bureau of Labor Statistics, covering 1999 through 2001, shows that workers with more than sixteen years of education saw an average reduction in income of roughly 23 percent upon finding new jobs; in the mid-1990s the reduction averaged only 12 percent.

The worsening plight of the unemployed is closely related to changes in American business practice. As productivity has increased and global competition has intensified, firms have continually restructured their operations—not just by laying off workers in response to temporary downturns in demand but by eliminating positions, even whole classes of positions, altogether. The share of lost jobs owing to the abolition of positions rather than to slack work, plant closings, or other reasons has doubled since the early 1980s. Erica Groshen and Simon Potter, economists at the Federal Reserve Bank of New York, argue that the main reason higher unemployment has lingered so long into the current recovery is that most lost jobs have been restructured out of existence. Workers whose jobs have been eliminated outright often cannot find anything directly comparable, either because the work they do has become obsolete or because their skills are company- or industry-specific, and not easily transferable elsewhere. These displacements are still not exceedingly common, but they are quite damaging to individuals when they occur.

In short, we have entered what might be called a "reverse-lottery economy." The broad majority of American workers continue to do well; yet in any given year—even in boom times—a few workers hit the negative jackpot and must accept lengthy or even permanent reductions in living standards. Increasingly, these unfortunates hail from a variety of educational backgrounds and occupations. (One recent study found that U.S. financial-service firms are planning to move more than 500,000 jobs—or eight percent of the total work force in that sector—offshore within the next five years. These relocations will include higher-status, higher-income jobs than such transfers have typically included in the past; jobs in financial analysis, research, accounting, and

graphic design are among those expected to be moved offshore.)

In a society where many people buy on credit, counting on ever expanding good fortune, the decline in income from job displacement is especially hard to bear financially. It is hard to bear psychologically as well. As the anthropologist Katherine Newman observed in *Falling from Grace: Downward Mobility in the Age of Affluence* (1988), the downwardly mobile family "jealously guards its public face, even if this means that everyone must eat a dreary diet so that the children can have some stylish clothes for school." Displays of desperation by these families are presumably kept within the walls of homes they can no longer afford.

THE MIRACLE OF AMERICAN PRODUCTIVITY

But here's the rub: the force that has produced deepening problems for reverse-lottery winners is the same as the force that has produced good fortune for many more Americans: the sudden and continuing acceleration of labor-productivity growth over the past eight years. Rising productivity is driving much of the change in American society. Yet its role is often misunderstood.

As the economy has pushed through its second year of jobless recovery, the media have mistakenly cast rapid productivity growth as the villain in a simplistic contest between people and technology. If productivity rises, this story goes, fewer people can generate the same output, and (all else being equal) unemployment will go up; if four workers can produce as much as five could only eight years ago, why hire the fifth? In the short term this is true; rising productivity has almost certainly helped to suppress new hiring after the recession. But beyond the short term this story is simply wrong. And it misses the bigger picture entirely.

Productivity growth is the bedrock of a healthy economy over time. In fact, continued rapid growth in productivity is certainly the best—and arguably the most important—feature of the U.S. economy today. It is no accident that past eras of high productivity growth (such as the 1920s and the 1950s) coincided with a national climate of energy and optimism. An annual productivity growth rate of 1.4 percent (roughly the average from 1973 to 1995) causes real national income to double every fifty years; increase the rate to 2.8 percent (roughly the average in the 1950s and the 1960s), and real national income will double in just twenty-six years, and nearly quadruple in fifty years. Throughout the second half of the twentieth century unemployment was lowest and real wages grew fastest during eras of rapid productivity gains. In some individual years, of course, high productivity growth coincided with high unemployment or low wage growth; but over a longer period of time—say, five years or more—high productivity growth has consistently buoyed both incomes and employment.

Since the sudden acceleration in productivity growth eight years ago, economists have worried that it might prove ephemeral, or even illusory— the result of either a short-lived technology boom or an exceptionally strong (and unsustainable) increase in demand. But these concerns have diminished markedly over the past three years: demand has cooled, and the high-tech bubble has burst, yet productivity growth has continued unabated. In fact, from 1995 to 2002 labor productivity growth grew at an average rate of 2.8 percent a year, matching the rate of the post–World War II "golden era" that lasted from 1948 to 1973. That's almost double the rate of growth from 1973 to 1995, and nearly one percentage point more than the average for the twentieth century as a whole. There is even evidence that productivity growth may be continuing to accelerate; from 2001 through the first half of 2003 (a period that included a recession, which typically slows productivity growth) it averaged an annual rate of about 4.1 percent. In 2002, the most recent year for which complete data are available, productivity grew by 4.8 percent—the highest annual increase since 1950. (One must be careful in interpreting these last figures; productivity growth typically accelerates in the early stages of economic recovery, and figures are often revised downward over time, as more-

extensive data become available. Nonetheless, at an absolute minimum there is no sign of a falloff of growth.)

The lesson here is that the New Economy is real. Most economists now believe that productivity— and living standards—will continue to rise rapidly over the next five to ten years (according to many of the estimates productivity will rise by two to three percent a year). The advances in information technology—particularly in computer processing power—that helped launch the boom have not slowed. Meanwhile, productivity growth in nontechnology industries, which remained low through much of the mid-1990s, has accelerated, as managers begin to integrate cheaper, more powerful information technology into their businesses. (Indeed, the real exemplar of the New Economy may not be Kozmo.com— the Internet courier that burned through $280 million in venture capital before going bust—but Wal-Mart, the ubiquitous discount chain that has pioneered ways of using information technology advances to cut costs.) Interestingly, the pattern we are now witnessing—productivity growth rippling from industry to industry after the initial acceleration in computer production—is similar to the pattern that followed the development of another "transformative technology": the electric generator. In this case, the resulting boom in productivity lasted well over a decade.

High productivity growth in recent years has also allowed most Americans to enjoy wage growth even as unemployment has risen. And relatively high employment levels and continued wage growth most likely contributed to relatively strong consumer demand throughout the recession, mitigating its effects.

Over the longer term broad-based productivity gains should mean not only higher incomes for most Americans but also cheaper products and more-competitive U.S. industries. The widespread diffusion of new technology will probably continue to give rise to products and services that would have been neither technologically feasible nor widely affordable just a few years ago.

(Recent examples of such products include cell phones and iPods.) The combination of higher incomes and new products should spur both demand and production—and over the long run these will produce new jobs. Theoretically it's possible to conceive of a future in which productivity gains yield no new, widely adopted products; in which consumer confidence and consumer demand never rise despite rising incomes; and in which employment therefore remains stagnant or even in decline. But history suggests that such a future is quite unlikely.

WINNERS AND LOSERS

For all the good that rapid productivity growth has yielded, its benefits have not been felt equally by all Americans—even among those who have managed to avoid layoffs. Nor is productivity growth by any means the only factor shaping our fortunes; other forces, more sweeping and just as fundamental, have pushed and pulled the various socioeconomic classes in different directions. Which of these forces prevails will go a long way toward determining the depth of class division in the United States in the coming years.

Viewed through the lens of class politics, one of the most striking elements of the past quarter century has been what Gary Burtless, an economist at the Brookings Institution, calls "the slow erosion of bargaining power" among low-income and middle-income workers. Better information technology and more-sophisticated robotics have significantly reduced job opportunities for many types of "routine" laborers, such as factory workers and middle managers, especially as globalized production has allowed U.S. companies to move many jobs—particularly low- and middle-skilled jobs—to countries where wages are lower. Increased global competition and the aggressive expectations of the financial markets (mainly in the form of shareholders demanding increased earnings per share every quarter) have eroded traditional managerial notions of "fairness" in setting wages and benefits and replaced them with a relentless focus on reducing cost; many companies now refuse to pay workers more

than their immediate ability to contribute justifies, regardless of how old they are, how long they've worked for the company, or how much they've earned in the past. On top of all this, increased immigration of low-skilled workers since 1970 has disproportionately increased the labor supply at the lower end of the economy, probably depressing wages for less skilled workers.

This story—told repeatedly in recent years—is clearly reflected in the numbers. Between 1973 and 1995, while real wages for the top five percent of Americans rose (and while total income for the top five percent of American households increased by about 30 percent), the bottom half of the American work force experienced an outright decline in real wages. Median hourly wages declined from $12.54 to $10.44 per hour.

But the numbers—and the story they reflect—changed in the mid-1990s. Since then, the upward pressure on wages associated with rapid productivity growth has been stronger than the downward pressure on the pay of many low- and middle-skilled workers that automation and the decline of benign corporate paternalism generates. Thus even socioeconomic classes that should be made worse off by the *fact* of technological changes (because technology displaces them from their jobs) may be left better off by the rapid *pace* of it (because wages rise and the job market tightens.) This is basically the story of the late 1990s. Despite technological advances, continual corporate restructurings, and heavy job churning, the wages and incomes of workers of every socioeconomic status and education level increased, while the growth in income inequality slowed down. Globalization, immigration, and the substitution of machinery for labor have not stopped exerting powerful forces on the economy since 1995—but the effects of rapid productivity and economic growth have been even more powerful.

The poor have done well, relatively speaking, in this economic environment. Jobs in such sectors as retail sales, hotel services, and basic healthcare provision have proved tough to automate, and so haven't been substituted out of existence. Moreover, because jobs in the service sector—

where the most low-skilled jobs have been created in recent years—are less affected by recession
than are jobs in manufacturing, employment has
been remarkably stable for the poor. And real
wages for "McJobs," though still low in absolute
terms, rose during the late 1990s as rapid economic growth tightened the labor market. Job
growth and wage growth at the lower end of the
economy—along with welfare reform—helped
lift millions of people out of poverty since the
mid-1990s; and a large portion of them have
stayed out, even through the latest recession.

The middle class, too, has done well recently.
And although the New Economy has eliminated
certain kinds of middle-class jobs, it has created
others. Manufacturing, for instance, continues
its slow decline, but construction work and other
high-paying blue-collar fields have grown significantly since 1995; and technologically driven
"job destruction" in middle management is out-
weighed by strong growth overall in white-collar
fields. In short, concerns about an emerging job
market in which some jobs pay six figures, many
jobs pay minimum wages, and a few jobs exist in
between appear overwrought. As unemployment
began to rise in 2000, real median incomes did
falter somewhat—but at the end of 2002 they
were still six percent higher than in 1995, and
21 percent higher than in 1970.

The contradictory forces that pull the middle-
class and the poor up while simultaneously pushing them down have tended to push the wealthy
and well-educated in only one direction: upward.
Advances in information technology have complemented the skills of workers in analytic occupations (such as management consultants,
financial analysts, and marketing executives),
hence raising these workers' value. Globalization
has almost certainly created more opportunities
for this class of workers than it has eliminated;
white-collar U.S. workers are now able to manage, advise, or provide analysis for a growing
number of international plants and businesses.
The shift toward a "winner-take-all" society has
produced rapid pay increases for executives and
high-end professionals. (And large reductions in

the upper tax brackets have allowed high earners
to keep more of their pay.)

Though growth in inequality slowed in the
late 1990s, it did not stop; while incomes rose
at every socioeconomic level, they rose fastest for
the workers who were already earning the most
money. Without significant policy shifts—toward
much higher marginal income-tax rates for high
earners, for example, or an immigration policy
that strongly favors skilled immigrants over unskilled ones—the rich are likely to continue to
pull away economically (and perhaps culturally
and socially, as well) from the rest of society.

At the moment it appears to be an open question whether in the coming years the middle class
and the poor will advance quickly (as they did in
the late 1990s) or stagnate (as they did throughout much of the 1970s and 1980s). We're poised
on the cusp between broad-based wealth creation
and stagnation: while productivity growth has
helped keep wages rising for the employed, immigration and the continued movement of jobs to
offshore locations weakens the labor market
and depresses wages. Given the continuing rapid
pace of innovation and productivity growth, it
appears likely that broad-based income gains will
eventually resume, and that the prevailing conditions of the next several years will more closely
resemble those of the late 1990s than those of the
1970s. But for that to be assured of happening,
unemployment will need to drop significantly
below six percent. And however much the typical
middle- or working-class family sees its income
rise on an absolute basis, the incomes of the richest families will likely improve even faster.

SMOOTHING CAPITALISM'S ROUGH EDGES
Whether or not the fortunes of the various socioeconomic strata rise or fall together in the future,
the fortunes of individuals—regardless of what
class they hail from—are more volatile today.
For some workers rapid improvements in income
and socioeconomic status may be punctuated by
sudden and painful declines in both. This volatil-
ity has become one of the defining attributes of
the economy.

The flexibility of the American labor market—its ability to shift workers quickly from fading companies or industries to growing ones—is among the U.S. economy's greatest assets; but such rapid shifts are often bad for individual workers, at least temporarily. (For older workers, or for people who lack geographic mobility, these negative reversals are more likely to be permanent. A married worker, for example, may fare worse than other workers after being laid off, especially if a spouse's job has anchored the family to a particular community.) And many traditional remedies for worker displacement, such as protectionism and inflexible labor laws, are often rightly considered to hurt the nation's economic competitiveness.

But there may be ways to help displaced workers without harming the economy. In "Are We Still a Middle-Class Nation?" Michael Lind proposes that the federal government grant equity-market stakes to every citizen, so that all Americans, not just the richest, might draw extra income from investments.

For both political and practical reasons Lind's plan would take time to implement. For the shorter term Robert Litan, an economist at the Brookings Institution, and Lori Kletzer, an economist at the University of California at Santa Cruz, have proposed a fairly inexpensive extension of unemployment insurance to cover workers who find new jobs that pay much less than their old ones. "Wage insurance" would make up a portion of the difference between old and new incomes for up to two years, so that the transition to a lower-income lifestyle would be more gradual. (A pilot program already exists for workers displaced by the movement of jobs overseas.) But wage insurance has potential as more than just a safety net; if unemployed workers knew they could more easily afford to take lower-paying jobs, they might feel freer to jump into whole new industries or career tracks; this would help the economy grow faster (by increasing the speed at which new industries grow) and might also ultimately increase the long-term income prospects of individual workers.

A more radical variation on this concept comes from Robert Shiller, an economist at Yale, who believes that continuing financial-market innovations may soon enable private insurers to offer 'livelihood insurance" that could protect workers from potential declines in their occupations (though not against an individual worker's underperformance within a flourishing field). Similar products might insure against the eventual devaluation of specific academic degrees in the United States (such as those in software engineering or Russian language), or even against declines in the performance of the U.S. economy as a whole, relative to the rest of the world. (As Shiller notes, the fact that the past century was a good one for America does not necessarily mean that the next one will be.) Collectively, these products might lessen the large and arguably increasing risks inherent in the U.S. capitalist system.

These are bold ideas; it may be hard at first to wrap one's mind around them. And it is perhaps ironic that financial markets—which are regarded by many people as amoral if not immoral—might ultimately solve some of the problems that socialists and utopian thinkers have been trying for centuries to address. But as improbable as livelihood insurance may sound, advances in data collection, data analysis, and financial-risk theory are lowering the technical barriers to such a system. Government action could help the creation of livelihood insurance on a large scale. Part of the government's role would be technical—for instance setting the standards for the collection and sharing of personal income data that are necessary if livelihood insurance is to work. But two equally important tasks would be the articulation of a new vision of society—one where people are protected against the unexpected shocks that accompany rapid economic change—and the promotion of financial-services products that can sustain that vision. Without large markets covering a wide range of occupations, carriers offering livelihood insurance might have difficulty hedging their risk sufficiently.

Economists argue that the benefits of technological advance, freer trade, and greater competition are great enough that when—as inevitably happens—some people suffers as a result of these forces, those people can in theory be fully compensated for their losses. But in practice such workers are rarely, if ever, compensated—and the consequences of the setbacks they suffer are more severe in the New Economy than they were in the past. Our economic (and political) system can tolerate a certain level of inequality resulting from differences in ability and work ethic (though just how much is an open question). But too often inequality is gratuitous; many people's economic fortunes are buffeted by factors they cannot reasonably predict and over which they have no personal control. As a society we should seek to minimize the randomness of fortune that is inherent in democratic capitalism.

THE LONG TERM

It is hard to say at any given point in time what the exact best recipe for growth is; economic and business environments vary widely from boom to bust. Yet when they stand back from the vicissitudes of the business cycle and consider longer periods of time, most economists agree that three factors are crucial for rapid, sustainable economic growth: new ideas and the technologies they create; business investment in new technologies and equipment; and ample "human capital": the collective skills and knowledge of the work force.

In 2000, though expectations of what the stock market and the economy in general could produce were wildly unrealistic, there was genuine cause for optimism. Ideas and innovations were proliferating. Investment in these ideas and the technologies they created was considerable. And a flexible, highly educated work force stood ready to adopt new technologies quickly, and to generate still more innovations for the future.

Three years later these conditions—a decline in the level of business investment notwithstanding—remain largely in place. Moreover, technologies and business practices developed before the bust (and not yet fully exploited) have generated a momentum that should help the economy over the next several years.

The long-term picture, however, may be bleaker. Two key factors that have historically given the U.S. economy a competitive advantage—a superior education system and an attractive investment climate—now appear to be eroding.

To a substantial degree America's economic strength during the twentieth century was attributable to the quality of its education system, and in particular to the expansion of educational opportunity to a large proportion of its citizens. America began that century with the world's best-educated population, and spent much of the next hundred years further improving its standing. In 1940, 30 percent of American workers had graduated from high school and fewer than six percent had graduated from college. By 2000, 89 percent had graduated from high school and 28 percent had graduated from college.

Overall, Americans born in 1975 spent nearly twice as many years in school as Americans born a century earlier. Over the past twenty years, however, this trend has markedly slowed, and is expected to do so further in the coming decades. Whereas from 1980 through 2000 the proportion of the labor force with a college education increased by 8.6 percent, over the next twenty years that proportion is expected to increase by only 1.5 to five percent—despite the fact that the financial benefits of a college education have been increasing. In most other economically advanced countries the average number of years people stay in school is now growing faster than it is in the United States—and young adults in a handful of those counties are now more highly educated, on average, than their U.S. counterparts. Ever since the launch of *Sputnik*, in the late 1950s, Americans have been concerned—perhaps excessively so—with the *quality* of the education that U.S. citizens receive. But only more recently has the United States seen its relative advantage in *quantity* of education begin to decline.

The consequences of this stagnation must color any discussion of the future of the U.S. economy. As the rate at which we produce college graduates begins to slow the rate at which the U.S. economy creates and adopts new technologies and products will also slow. Income inequality will no doubt grow: the smaller the supply of college graduates, the higher the incomes they are likely to command. And the larger the supply of less-educated workers, the lower their wages will be. Indeed, every high school student who chooses not to attend college hurts not only his own income prospects but also (by adding to the pool of workers competing for low-skill jobs) those of other less-educated workers.

Just as our declining educational progress threatens the ability of the work force to absorb innovations quickly, so the deterioration of the government's fiscal position undermines the willingness of firms to invest in new technologies. The long-term fiscal problems of the federal government are covered in detail elsewhere in this feature. Suffice it to say here that the size of the budget deficit can have a real impact on the economy.

Whereas low levels of debt keep interest rates down and inspire the confidence of foreign investors, high levels of debt ultimately discourage private investment by raising interest rates. It is no coincidence that as the federal budget swung into surplus in the second half of the 1990s, after a period of annual deficits averaging almost four percent of GDP in the early part of the decade, domestic investment as a share of GDP rose, by 3.5 percent. And although the country has managed to survive periods of high and rising debt in the past without calamity (in the late 1980s, for example, and during World War II), we are embarked on a period of deepening annual deficits of unprecedented size, with no end in sight. According to the Congressional Budget Office, if the government does not make significant changes in spending or taxation, debt will mount rapidly over the next few years, reaching $10 trillion by 2010—and that's before it begins an exponential increase as the Baby Boom enters retirement.

The long-term fiscal crisis facing the United States comes primarily from a growing imbalance between what the government spends— primarily on Medicare and Social Security—and what it reaps in taxes, which were not high enough to sustain current entitlements even before the series of sharp tax cuts enacted since 2000. Today we're simply foisting the many costs of this imbalance—rising debt, slower growth, and ultimately either higher taxes or broken promises—onto future generations.

A reasonable observer might conclude that all these problems are the ingredients for national economic decline. Historically, America has been an adaptable, resilient nation; decline is not inevitable. But unless we devote more attention to education and fiscal imbalance, two issues that are absolutely central to long-term prosperity, the conditions that have produced widespread growth will dissipate. As weak as today's economy may look relative to that of 1999, at the rate we're going we may look back on 2003–2004 in ten or twenty years with wistful longing.

DISCUSSION QUESTIONS

1. Why do the authors blame and praise rising productivity in the American economy?
2. How do the authors believe different social classes will be affected by changes in productivity over time and why?
3. What connection do the authors see between the economy and education?

PART 5 SOCIAL CHANGE

HUMAN POPULATIONS AND DEMOGRAPHY

U nlike many of the areas that occupy the sociological outlook, human populations are easy to measure—all that's required is a head count. If the head count changes from time to time, there are only a few possible explanations. If you count more people this year than last, you had either more births than deaths or some immigration (movement into a country) or both; if you count fewer heads, there must have been more deaths than births or some emigration (movement out of a country) or both. A very large population may make the logistics of this head count somewhat difficult, but in principle it's a pretty basic process.

After the heads are counted, new babies tallied, deaths recorded, and overall migration noted, the discipline of demography takes over. **Demography** is the study of human populations. Demographers are particularly interested in the changes related to human populations, from two points of view.

First, demographers seek to explain the causes of population changes. Why did people have more babies this year than last? Why are fewer people dying now than in the past? Why do people move? Second, demographers attempt to trace the effects of population changes. What happens to the distribution of food when births go up and deaths go down? What happens to the social life of a country when large numbers of immigrants enter? Demography places human population in a pivotal position in relation to the other aspects of society.

This chapter explores some of the theories offered by demographers to explain many important recent and historical changes in the world's population. We compare population changes in the industrial and nonindustrial worlds, paying particular attention to the population explosion of recent years and its effects on natural resources. At the other extreme, we explore the possibility of zero population growth (a stable population) and look at the effects of a stable population on the rest of society. Finally, we examine human migration, with a focus on why people move and what happens when they get where they're going. This look at migration is coupled with a special section on the most important form that migration has taken over the last two centuries: the movement from farms to cities. The field of demography is an especially clear example of how the sociological outlook helps us understand our own lives in relation to society.

DEMOGRAPHY: CONCEPTS AND PERSPECTIVES

The concepts and perspectives of demography are largely shared with sociology. Demography represents an application of sociological ideas to questions of human population; its uniqueness comes from the object of its study rather than either its methods or its theories. Box 14.1 defines some of the special terms demographers use in their study of population changes. These terms describe numerical changes in the population but tell us little about the composition of the population. At the outset we will want to know at least something about the age range of the population and the gender of its members.

The *age-sex pyramid* is one of the demographer's most basic tools. For any given year it shows the percentage of the overall population to be found in any given age range and sex. Figure 14.1 depicts age-sex pyramids for four countries of the world: Sweden, the United States, Mexico, and Zimbabwe. For example, in Mexico over 20 percent of the population is under the age of four, while only 10 percent of the Swedish population falls in that age range. You can also see from these pyramids that, in most societies at most ages, the two sexes are roughly even. The major exception is among people over the age of seventy-five, where women make up a larger share of the population than men. Such exceptions to balanced sexes can also be found in societies at the close of major wars, which usually remove sizable portions of the men in the younger age groups.

Turning our attention to the United States, we see, in Figure 14.1, that one prominent feature of the population was a definite bulge between the ages of forty and fifty and a slight indentation after the age of sixty. The indentation is the result of lower birth rates during the Depression of the 1930s. The Depression created extreme hardships for many American families, which they chose not to increase with added children. The bulge in the population is the result of the famous "baby boom" in the United States following World War II (see Figure 14.2). World War II, like all major wars, was highly disruptive of family life. Beginning in 1946, the children that families had put off for so long entered the U.S. population like water through a broken dam. This baby boom was then followed by lowered birth rates through the 1960s, which reached a low point in the mid-1970s. In 1975 the baby boom babies were of childbearing age and should have created another bulge in the population just by the sheer number of women. Many changes in U.S. society, however, had created alternatives for those women, who apparently selected options other than motherhood. Some observers have suggested that these women simply delayed having babies (because of occupational options, for example) and started their families later, as is evidenced by the higher birth rates since 1975. All of these statistics receive a much closer inspection later in this chapter; for the time being they illustrate some of the social explanations offered by demographers for population changes.

The age-sex pyramids in Figure 14.1 illustrate some other population characteristics of interest to demographers. Mexico is an example of an expanding population. The extreme pyramid shape of Mexico indicates that a relatively small number

BOX 14.1

A Traveler's Phrase Book for the World of Demography

Like members of any specialized occupation, demographers have their own vocabulary for the matters they deal with. Many of these specialized terms relate to the measures demographers use; aside from those measures a demographer sounds pretty much like any garden-variety sociologist. Although the measures of demography are essentially basic counting, some of the numbers are transformed into other kinds of statistics, which have specific names.

Birth rate: The number of births for every thousand people in the population. The statistic is created as follows:

$$\frac{\text{number of live births in a given year}}{\text{population}} \times 1{,}000 = \text{birth rate}$$

General fertility rate: The number of births for every thousand women of child-bearing age. This statistic tells you more about individuals in the population. A society with a great many women of childbearing age would tend to have a high birth rate even if most of the women were not having that many children. Fertility rate is calculated like birth rate except for changing the "population" number to the number of "women of childbearing age."

Death rate: The number of deaths for every thousand people in the population. It is figured like the birth rate with the substitution of "number of deaths" for "number of live births."

Immigration rate: The number of immigrants for every thousand people in the population in a given year. It is figured like the birth rate with the substitution of "number of immigrants" for "number of live births."

Rate of natural increase (or decrease): The difference between the birth rate and the death rate. Because you are subtracting "rates," your answer will also be a "rate"; thus, the difference between the birth rate and the death rate will give you the natural (nonimmigrant) increase in the population for every thousand members of the population.

Growth rate: The rate of natural increase plus the immigration rate. Once again, you are adding rates and will end up with a rate. The growth rate tells you how many new people there are in a population for every thousand people already there. It tells you, in short, just how fast your population is growing no matter what the source. More births will make it grow, but so will fewer deaths, more immigrants, or fewer emigrants. The growth rate combines all this information.

(continues)

A Traveler's Phrase Book for the World of Demography (continued)

Keep in mind that a phrase book is for tourists. The vocabulary of demography goes far beyond this short list. These few terms will get you started and give you a clue as to the kinds of concerns demographers have. Consider the growth rate. A population of 100 could grow to 150 over a year, while another population of 10 could grow to 20. The first, larger population is more drastic due to all the new individuals, but the second society may be experiencing much greater social change. The growth rate focuses on such proportional changes and allows demographers to compare populations of very different sizes.

These rates can be summarized as follows:

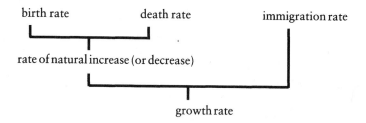

of women are having a relatively large number of babies. Most of the countries in the nonindustrial world today have age-sex pyramids similar to Mexico's. If the children currently under the age of ten in Mexico have the same fertility rates in the future as their parents have now, the pyramid will acquire an even more extreme shape and the population will expand even more rapidly.

The age-sex pyramid of the United States represents a slow-growth population. A key term here is **replacement level,** the number of babies necessary in a population for the parents to replace themselves, thus leading to a stable population, or **zero population growth,** as it is often called. Two parents having two babies (on average) provides for replacement, but the baby boom bulge in the U.S. population will still lead to later population bulges because of the large percentage of women of childbearing age. Population bulges exhaust themselves over time much like ripples in a pool of water, each ripple being smaller than the one before. A large number of women of childbearing years, each having two babies, will still produce a large number of children. And when all of those children reach childbearing age themselves, we will have

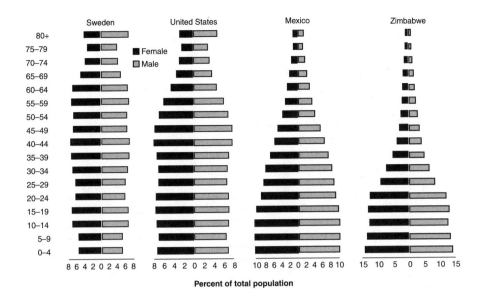

Figure 14.1 2005 population comparison by age and sex for Sweden, the United States, Mexico, and Zimbabwe. (Data from U.S. Bureau of the Census, 2004)

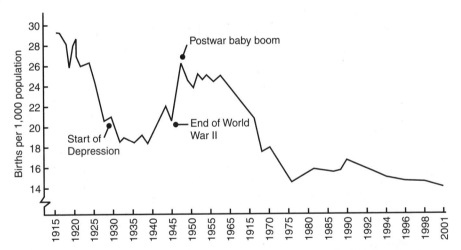

Figure 14.2 United States birth rates, 1954–2001. (Data from the U.S. Bureau of the Census, 1995a, 1998a, 2004a)

another (although smaller) spurt in population growth. A population that simply replaces itself in each generation will ultimately lead to zero population growth when the ripples disappear. In the meantime, the United States is still growing slowly. The age-sex pyramid for Sweden is fairly close to a negative growth population.

A variation on these population pyramids is seen in Zimbabwe. For a non-industrial country, we would expect to see large percentages of the population in the early years, reflecting a high birth rate. We do, in fact, see that. But we also see a definite drop in the population in the mid-twenties and continuing thereafter. Wars can produce such phenomena but typically only with the male side of the pyramid. The Zimbabwe pyramid is the result of AIDS, which takes the lives of the young adults in Zimbabwe and so many African countries.

When age-sex pyramids are combined with the other measures of population demographers use, an overall picture of population change emerges. The ages, sexes, and other characteristics of the population come to be viewed through measures of births, deaths, and migration into and out of the population. All of these changes occur within the fabric of society, and, in turn, they all change the society in which they occur. That is where the sociologist/demographer takes over.

POPULATION IN THE INDUSTRIAL WORLD

The world has a population of over 6 billion people and is growing at a rate of 1.5 to 2 percent a year; we should see an additional 2.3 billion people on this planet in the next 25 years (U.S. Bureau of the Census, 1994). The population of the United States in 1998 was over 270 million (U.S. Bureau of the Census, 2000). This relatively small population in comparison to livable area is characteristic of industrialized societies, such as Canada, Australia, and most European countries, which make up a minority of the world's population and only a fraction of its growth rate. The differences between the industrialized and nonindustrialized nations are far from chance. Industrialization fundamentally altered the societies in which it occurred and, consequently, it altered the human populations of those societies. Demographers refer to this set of changes as the **demographic transition.**

THE DEMOGRAPHIC TRANSITION

Before 1750 the world's population was under 800 million people. Perhaps more important, it was growing at no more than 0.1 percent a year. This low growth rate wasn't for lack of trying, but high death rates effectively counteracted high birth rates. This was stage one of the demographic transition. Infant and maternal mortality took a heavy toll, along with infectious disease; between 1346 and 1350 bubonic plague (the "black death") claimed 25 million lives—one-fourth of the world's population.

Starting around 1750, fundamental changes began to occur in the societies that now make up the industrialized nations. The most important change was in nutrition. New crops and agricultural techniques created an amount and a variety of foods that allowed more people to survive. For one example, the potato became the staple of the lower classes; it was nutritious, easy to grow, and easy to store. The population of Ireland increased 172 percent between 1780 and 1840, almost entirely as a result of the development of the potato and the lowered death rates to which it led.

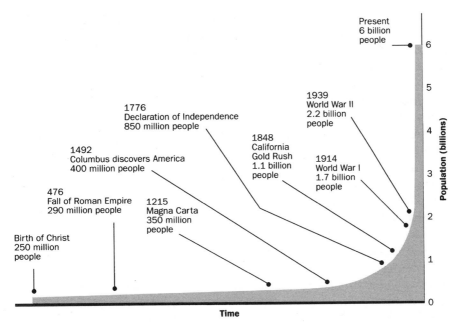

Figure 14.3 World population growth.

The resistance to disease brought about by better nutrition was aided by improved sanitation techniques, which helped lower the incidence of the diseases themselves. These changes ushered in the next stage of the demographic transition.

Stage two of the demographic transition was characterized by high birth rates coupled with rapidly declining death rates. The result, of course, was a population explosion. The case of Ireland was extreme but typical of many countries during this stage; as Figure 14.3 illustrates, the world's population began to grow at an unprecedented rate at this time.

The population continued to grow as death rates dropped still farther over time, but fertility rates finally began to drop as well; this was the beginning of stage three. Throughout the nineteenth century and into the twentieth century women of childbearing years began having fewer and fewer babies. Various explanations have been offered for this drop in fertility rates, but all the explanations are related to industrialization. Industrialization led to urbanization as people left the farms and headed for the factories (see the section on urbanization at the end of this chapter). Large families were both useful and inexpensive on the farm, but in the city they were neither. In addition, the industrial lifestyle lessened the individual's economic dependence on the family (see Chapter 9) and led to major changes in family roles (particularly women's roles) and values. People no longer wanted so many children. In the realm of technology, contraceptives entered the picture in the 1870s. Although the death rate continued to drop throughout stage three (and is still dropping), the birth rate began to drop at the same rate until it finally caught up in many industrial countries (Brown, 1973). The relative balance of birth and death rates makes stage three of the demographic transition a stable stage.

THE MODERN INDUSTRIAL WORLD: CHANGES IN WOMEN'S ROLES AND FAMILY VALUES

Pronatalism is the societal value of having children and large families. Included within this view, by necessity, is the value of the motherhood role for women. In stage one of the demographic transition pronatalism was clearly a necessary value for the survival of society; the high death rates of that period required spending considerable energy having children. Motherhood was a full-time job that was both essential and dangerous; pronatalism encouraged women to accept it.

Industrialization ended all of that. Children were no longer needed either to support the current generation in their old age or to stock the next generation. Simultaneously (and clearly related to this change), new doors were opening for women outside the home. Many industrial occupations opened to women, and with those occupations came a previously unknown sense of independence. Women's roles in industrial society have changed steadily over the last century and are still changing today with the growth of the women's movement. Early women's leaders, such as Margaret Sanger (who fought for birth control) and Susan B. Anthony (who fought for the vote), were clearly important to this change, but the real source of change came from growing industrialization.

Modifications of pronatalism have been occurring in the United States for some years. In just the brief span from 1967 to 1973 the number of women in their early twenties who wanted three or more children dropped from 55 percent to 30 percent (Griffith, 1973). Since then, as we see in Figure 14.2, birth rates climbed and then dropped back down again where they stand today. A more extreme illustration is the rise of the childless marriage. In direct opposition to pronatalism, younger Americans are carefully calculating the economic and social costs of children; those who have them are having fewer, and many are deciding against having any at all. It has become increasingly common for apartment complexes to bar children and to evict those residents who have them after moving in. While these changes horrify some Americans, others are becoming more and more vocal about their right to remain childless.

POPULATION IN THE NONINDUSTRIAL WORLD

Until as recently as World War II, the growth rate of the industrialized nations was still higher than that of the developing (then undeveloped) nations of the nonindustrial world. The industrialized world had not fully settled into stage three of the demographic transition, while the nonindustrialized world was still firmly locked into the high death rates of stage one. The story of the world's current population explosion is largely the story of how the industrialized nations dragged the non-

This view of the Mumbai, India, train station illustrates the result of population growth in developing nations. Even though the government is dedicated to controlling the birth rate, the number of women having babies is very large.

industrialized world (not always kicking and screaming) into stage two of the demographic transition.

The example of Sri Lanka (formerly Ceylon) provides a pointed illustration of this interference. Before World War II Ceylon had a very high death rate, due largely to the malaria-carrying mosquito. Between 1934 and 1935, for example, a hundred thousand people died of malaria. Following World War II DDT was sprayed in the swamps of Ceylon, killing the mosquitoes and producing a 34 percent drop in the death rate in a single year (Davis, 1956). Today, malaria is practically unknown in Sri Lanka, and the population is exploding.

The case of Sri Lanka is not unusual. Most of the developing nations are growing three times faster than the United States. In every case the populations are growing because of dropping death rates and stable (though still very high) birth rates. Insecticides provide an interesting example but, as with the history of the demographic transition in the industrial world, the dropping death rates are largely attributable to better nutrition and sanitation. This "interference" from the industrialized world appears humane, but the resulting population explosions in the nonindustrialized world have made it difficult for the developing nations to develop. In some cases, such as Ethiopia, an expanding population makes people more vulnerable to environmental problems (such as drought) or even creates environmental problems through an overexpansion of agriculture to feed the growing population. And as we've seen in Ethiopia, the results of such population changes can be tragic.

ECONOMIC DEVELOPMENT IN THE NONINDUSTRIAL WORLD

Part of the problem faced by the developing nations is the ratio of dependent young and old to mature adults in their populations. Demographers usually separate populations into three general groups on the basis of their age. Both the very young and the very old are dependent groups that require assistance from those in the middle if they are to survive. An age-sex pyramid such as Mexico's does not have too many dependent elderly, but close to half its population is under the age of fourteen. This kind of ratio between the dependent and active sectors of the population makes economic development extremely difficult. The society has more than it can handle just in feeding the present dependent portion of the population without directing its energies into economic expansion and the formation of a strong industrial base. A high birth rate in itself does not ensure long-term poverty for a country, but it clearly acts as a hindrance for economic growth (Merrick, 1986).

The absence of economic expansion in the nonindustrial world results in poverty and hunger. Death rates remain relatively low, while high birth rates make the populations larger and more bottom heavy all the time. The already-begun process of industrialization in these countries has forced people from the rural areas into the cities, where there is too little economic activity to support them. Almost all of the major cities in the nonindustrialized world today contain massive numbers of poor residents, many of whom have no shelter. Calcutta, India, is perhaps the best-known example, but similar poor populations can be found in Hong Kong, Mexico City, Cairo, and elsewhere. Meanwhile, the separation between the haves and the have-nots in these countries stays extreme or grows as industrialization advances.

RESPONSES TO POVERTY

The Marxist Position Modern-day Marxists (or socialists) see the solution to poverty in the developing nations as existing apart from the population explosion. In keeping with the theories of Karl Marx (see Chapter 7), modern socialists argue that poverty in the developing world is caused not by overpopulation but by the unequal distribution of wealth characteristic of capitalism. Some argue that the ruling classes in the industrialized nations have put off revolutions in their own countries by making the nonindustrialized nations poorer in order to support the middle classes at home. Others focus more on levels of exploitation within the developing nations. In either case the solution to poverty is seen as a revolution that will bring about a fundamental redistribution of wealth.

Marx predicted that revolutions would occur first in the most industrialized nations. As it has turned out, however, the socialist revolutions have occurred in the least industrialized nations, such as China, Cuba, Vietnam, Cambodia, and Angola. These countries may not be in the throes of capitalism, but they are certainly good illustrations of extreme poverty and gross inequalities in the distribution of wealth. While modern-day Marxists may argue that the population explosion is not the cause of poverty in these countries, it certainly doesn't help. It also, incidentally, provides large numbers of young people in the population, who are the most likely to become active revolutionaries.

The Green Revolution One way to feed more people is to produce more food. During the 1960s, a scientific effort (termed the Green Revolution) searched for new hybrid strains of wheat and rice in hopes of creating an easier-to-grow, faster-to-harvest, and more productive substitute for the crops in current use. Between 1965 and 1971 the amount of Asian land devoted to these new crops jumped from 200 acres to over 50 million (Brown, 1973).

Reviews of the Green Revolution are mixed. On the one hand, the new strains of rice and wheat have provided more food for the world; clearly, they do have a higher yield than the older varieties. On the other hand, it turns out that these new varieties are more easily grown by larger and wealthier farmers than smaller and poorer farmers; that is, anyone can grow them but the real advantage comes with access to credit, fertilizers, and irrigation. They also force farmers away from a subsistence form of living to producing a cash crop—a change that brings them into the twenty-first century and places them at the mercy of international markets. Thus the income differentials in the developing nations tend to become even larger than they were before (Brown, 1973). Furthermore, more and better food lowers the death rate, raises the birth rate, and makes the population problem worse in the long run.

Reducing Fertility The general consensus among demographers is that the population explosion must be stopped before poverty can be reduced in the developing nations (see Box 14.2). This consensus, which is shared by many government officials in the nonindustrial world, has led to the formation of fertility-control programs around the world. Through these programs governments try to convince the members of the population not to have so many babies; in addition, they provide means of birth control. The techniques of convincing have varied considerably.

Probably the most extreme attempt at fertility control occurred in India, where some states required sterilization of either the husband or the wife after the birth of two children. This was not a popular law in India—nor would it be elsewhere. Childbearing is generally considered a personal activity that should be decided on without government interference. Also, typically, enforced sterilization programs affect only the poor, and, if the poor happen to differ ethnically from the rich, as they do in many countries, the sterilization programs raise questions of genocide. No one seems to like the population explosion, but it's always someone else's babies that should be limited.

BOX 14.2

The Population Explosion:
Threatening the Third World's Future

ROBERT W. FOX

I was walking through the streets of Cartago, Costa Rica, some twenty years ago when the bells rang and the elementary schools let out. A thousand scrubbed and uniformed children flooded the streets. That Lilliputian world was a dramatic reminder that Costa Rica, like the rest of Central America, is a nation of children. Nearly half the population is under the age of fifteen.

Central America's population explosion—and the population explosion taking place throughout the Third World—was captured for me in that incident. Today, ever-larger numbers of children are pressing hard on small and, in some cases, shrinking economies. The 8 million Central American children under the age of 15 in 1970 represented a large increase from the 4 million children in 1950. There are 13 million Central American children under the age of 15 now. If projections hold true, there will be 19 million in 2025.

In one lifetime, Central America's population is not just doubling or tripling. It is rising by a factor of seven—if the ecology can support it. And growth will not stop in 2025.

The population explosion that began in the 1950s and continues today is arguably Central America's most significant historical event, overriding the importance of the Spanish conquest and the independence movement 270 years later. Never has the region experienced anything of this magnitude and force. Not only is the amount of growth of serious concern, but also the speed with which it is occurring.

Overwhelming population growth is wreaking havoc on the region's cultures, economies, social systems, and natural-resource base. Forget the failure of political systems and civil wars as the leading issue. Forget economic depression and unemployment, affecting as much as half the labor force. Forget old debates over land-holding systems where power is concentrated in the hands of a few export-crop producers. Forget low standards of living and miserable urban slums that appear occasionally to be clusters of smoking cardboard and tin boxes strung along the arroyos. Forget the exodus of tens and hundreds of thousands headed north to cross the porous Mexican-U.S. border in search of jobs.

Focus instead on the rise in population as the single basic issue. It has put an incredible burden on attempts to resolve old problems and has, meanwhile, created new ones. In Central America today, you truly must run faster and faster just to stay in place.

The concept of "economic development" has dominated, for the most part, the third world's view of its future since the 1960s. A fast pace of economic growth was expected to more than offset rapid population gains. Population growth was still considered a given. The idea of slowing it down offended many—for religious and political reasons—and grated deeply on personal convictions. But it was always recognized that economic growth had to keep pace with population growth. If the economies faltered, the continuing population gains would slip right by, producing lower and lower standards of living. This is precisely what has happened.

Central America offers a typical case of the demographic forces working in the third world. Demographers—not only in Central America, but in many developing nations around the world with rapidly growing populations—have informed politicians that they see a very major problem emerging for which there is no short-term solution. Further, the problem is guaranteed to continue to intensify for the next half century and longer.

Slowly but surely, the soundness of these alarming population projections is being recognized. These projections, accompanied by commonsense observations in the increasingly crowded streets outside, are convincing politicians that a serious and intractable problem has emerged.

The third world's demographic future contains hard messages that are difficult to swallow. But, with rapid population growth still accelerating, neither Central America nor other developing nations are likely to stabilize and take the pressures off their social, ecological, and economic systems—or those in the first world.

China has approached the problem somewhat differently. Given a huge population of approximately one billion, extreme measures seemed called for. The government responded in a variety of ways, but the most effective and the most controversial measure was the one child per family rule. If every two married people produce one offspring, that should slowly halt the population growth. While it makes sense on paper, it goes against the value of pronatalism that exists in China as elsewhere. Probably the most striking response by the Chinese people to this law has been the rise of abortions and the infanticide of female babies; Chinese parents have a strong preference for sons and, if they can have only one child, seem prepared to go to extreme lengths to have their wishes fulfilled (Johansson and Nygren, 1991; Merrick, 1986).

Most fertility-control programs direct their efforts toward changing values of pronatalism and providing information about birth control. Most American women use some form of contraception, but in other parts of the world such use may be rare, because of unavailability of birth control products or values that prohibit them. When you combine the values of pronatalism (which are almost universal around the world) with feelings of nationalism and ethnocentrism ("We're the best so we

These Chinese women are taking a birth control class. China's population problem is not unique in the nonindustrial world, nor is its effort to control population growth through reducing fertility. The hope is that classes like this will provide both the means and the desire to have smaller families.

should have more babies"), it's amazing that fertility ever goes down. On the more practical level, poorer families in the developing nations needed large numbers of children for survival. In India, for example, poor people are dependent on their children in old age. Furthermore, the traditional division of gender roles in most societies, with women locked into the wife and mother role, makes children almost essential if a woman is to have any social status in the community.

Government programs aside, the most effective way to lower fertility is economic development. The same industrial development that lowered the death rate in the developing nations will, if it continues, also lower the birth rate. This, you'll note, is basically what happened in Europe and the United States. One explanation for this predicted change is that economic development will automatically alter values of pronatalism. Demographer David Heer (1966) argues that the key factor in industrialization is the level of education that accompanies economic development. As Heer points out, educational levels must rise if economic development is to occur, and those developing nations that have emphasized education seem to have the most rapidly declining birth rates. Ehrlich et al. (1992) stress that the education of women is the critical factor (along with an entrance of women into the labor force). Whatever the case, there is something inherent in the process of industrialization that lowers birth rates. Merrick (1986) has predicted that most less-developed countries will stabilize by the year 2025, but considerable problems can develop before then. Nigeria, for example, currently has a population of 100 million; by the time it stabilizes in the year 2025, it will have a population of 532 million somehow packed into its relatively small area.

THE EFFECTS OF ZERO POPULATION GROWTH

Let us return to the age-sex pyramids in Figure 14.1. If the demographers had to predict, their prediction would be that Mexico's 2005 pyramid would be more likely to look like that of Sweden some day than vice versa, given the effect of industrialization on birth rate. The United States appears also to be approaching a situation of no growth.

But what are the effects on society of a stable population? We've already seen that an age-sex pyramid like Mexico's makes economic development difficult because of the large dependent portion of the population. What about the other extreme? Part of the answer to this question will consist of guesses as we project into the future. Before we get into the future, however, it might be useful to look at some of the past effects from various age-sex pyramids in the United States. Figure 14.4 illustrates some age-sex pyramids for the past and projected ones for the future in the United States, the latter presuming a relatively stable fertility rate.

In 1975 the United States had an expanding population with high percentages of the population under the age of nineteen. A large proportion of the population—the

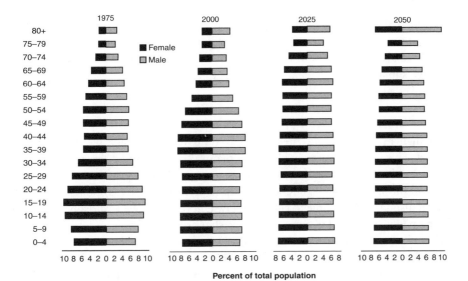

Figure 14.4 Population composition by age and sex, past and projected. (Data from U.S. Bureau of the Census, 2004)

baby boom babies—was in the late teens and early twenties. Also note the indentation after the age of thirty that reflects the low birth rates during the Depression of the 1930s (see Figure 14.2). In the 1960s, as the baby boom children grew older, a tremendous emphasis on youth developed in American society. Not only was this a large segment of the population, but, unlike young people of past generations, they had money and independence. Whole industries, such as segments of the clothing and record industries, grew up in response to this very large potential market. It was important during the 1960s for everyone to think, act, and look young. As this young age cohort organized politically, one slogan was "Don't trust anyone over thirty." The age-sex pyramids for this period suggest that it wasn't so easy to find someone over thirty.

The Vietnam War of the 1960s had a major impact on all of American society, but consider this impact with relation to the age characteristics of the American population. The potential warriors for that war were the baby boom males. There were certainly enough of them for the purpose, but there were also enough of them to hold some political clout in opposition to that war. The famous "generation gap" of the 1960s will probably never appear in American society in quite the same way, as the numbers of young people shrink in proportion to a population growing steadily older.

Moving ahead to 2000, we can see the baby boom babies in their forties and fifties. We see fewer people in the younger cohorts but, in spite of their smaller numbers, they may find fewer job opportunities until the baby boomers start to retire. We can also see more older people in 2000, suggesting that those younger people on the job market might do well to go into medical professions. The average age in the United States is getting older and older as the baby boomers move through the pyramid, and by their sheer numbers they will have a definite impact on society at each stage of their maturation. They will begin reaching retirement age in about 2010. And we should expect to see a greater impact on retirement programs and social security as a result.

What will be the impact of this "graying" of America? How will the social security system survive? Currently, people working provide the funds for those retired, but a higher proportion of retired people could put an unmanageable strain on the system. This issue has already become a major economic and political one. How about medical care? Now is the time to go into the medical professions, since the demand for medical care is bound to go up with the advancing age of the population. It also may be the time to get out of law enforcement. We've already seen that young people commit far more than their share of index crime. Who is going to commit those crimes when we run out of young people? Probably no one, which will put police officers out of work. On the other hand, the years ahead should see an increase in white-collar crime (which is more frequently committed by people of middle age), so if you do want to go into law enforcement, you probably should specialize in embezzlement, tax fraud, and price fixing.

The American family has already felt the effects of slower growth, and it will continue to feel those effects. Women are having fewer children and living longer after they have them. That leaves a lot of years for other things. The woman's role in the family is changing from an emphasis on motherhood to an emphasis on an economic role. Every year, more and more women enter the labor force; that trend should continue. Simultaneously, men in the future will have to take more of a role in child care to make up for this change. This also might be a good year to get into some aspect of child care. There may not be as many children out there, but larger and larger percentages of them are spending their early years in day care centers.

As we look ahead to 2050, the United States should be a very different place. It will be a no-growth society with a very large proportion of its population past retirement age, creating all the problems that an aging population does. And we may see labor shortages with such a small proportion of the population in the earning stages of life. If the past is any guide, we should be looking at fewer restrictions on immigration in an effort to ease this shortage.

The increasing age of the population has already had political and economic effects on American society. Older people have organized politically in order to have more clout in society. Just one of their successes has been the removal of many mandatory retirement rules. With more and more people older and healthier than ever before, it makes sense that people might want to work longer. What impact will this have on younger people coming along with hopes of promotions? There may be fewer occupational opportunities for younger people, and they may have to wait longer for the opportunities that do exist.

MIGRATION

Thus far we have been focusing on the comings and goings of warm bodies through birth and death. Humans are notorious movers, however, and populations can swell or shrink from the effects of migration, the physical movement of a population. Migration forms a particularly interesting aspect of population change; births and deaths bring (or take away) more of the same people, but migration brings cultural diversity into the population. For purposes of convenience, we can separate **migration** into international migration (movement that crosses national boundaries) and internal migration (movement within the same country).

INTERNATIONAL MIGRATION

International migration is the most extreme form of migration in that it creates legal problems (such as changing citizenship) and generally involves greater cultural clashes between the immigrant and the host culture, as typically, cultures vary more across than within national boundaries. International migration is a particularly fascinating study, as it must take a lot before an individual is willing to leave home for unknown problems elsewhere. Furthermore, until relatively recently most international migration was permanent because of the time and the cost of travel; those who left knew there was no coming home. People can have a variety of reasons for taking such a big step, but most of them fall under the headings of economics or politics.

Economic Reasons for International Migration   Historically, economic reasons have been the primary motivating force in all forms of migration. People leave home in hopes of enjoying a better standard of living elsewhere. This story is perhaps as old as human existence; wherever the first humans originated, they've done a lot of traveling since. In more recent history knowledge of other societies plus improved transportation technology has made possible migration on a scale not known before. This can be seen very clearly in the history of the United States.

The first immigrants to the United States were the ancestors of those people today known as Native Americans. They were followed by the Spanish, French, and English and later by people from the rest of Europe and much of Asia. In almost every case an economic factor emerged as the primary motivation. In Europe, for example, populations were growing rapidly as a result of a declining death rate. In addition, economic arrangements were in the process of changing to large-scale industry and agriculture, making existence increasingly difficult for the poor (Jones, 1960). In Asia economic concerns were also in the front of the emigrants' minds. The rigid social structure of nineteenth-century China could be broken by poor individuals only if they earned money in a foreign country; the early Chinese immigrants to the United States came here fully expecting to return home with great wealth to buy land (Lyman, 1975). The early Japanese immigrants to the United States were interested in the system of private enterprise that prevailed here and became very successful at it (Kitano, 1976). Until 1924, when the U.S. government finally closed most of the doors to foreign immigrants, millions of immigrants pulled up stakes to come here. In the early 1900s, particularly, the numbers of European immigrants were large enough to change the cultural landscape of America as well as add considerably to the population.

Of all the economic motivations for international migration, one of the most dramatic examples is the Irish potato famine. As we've seen, the potato improved nutrition throughout Europe and led to rapidly declining death rates and high growth rates. The population of Ireland, in particular, grew dramatically in the first part of the nineteenth century; in fact, Ireland had become the most densely populated country in Europe, almost entirely because of the potato. For most peasants in Ireland the potato was their only food. Starting in 1845, a blight attacked the Irish potato crop and continued for several years, leading to almost complete crop loss. As a consequence, 8 million Irish were literally without food, and starvation became a part of everyday life. Between 1846 and 1850, 870,000 Irish came to the United States to escape the famine, and by 1860 there were 1.6 million Irish in the United States (Duff, 1971). The histories of other immigrants are not always this extreme, but the story of the Irish suggests something of the economic reasons that lead people to take such chances.

Demographers generally look at all forms of migration in terms of push and pull (Bouvier and Gardner, 1986). On the one hand, there is often a "push" from the home region (such as the Irish potato famine) that encourages migration. On the other hand, there is also generally some kind of "pull" from the host region; after all, the Irish could have gone elsewhere, but in the nineteenth century America was viewed as the "land of opportunity" and attracted immigrants from all over. It is still attractive to many people around the world, as evidenced by the large numbers of Mexicans who enter the country illegally. The push and pull factors in migration make it impossible to characterize economically motivated immigrants as particular types of people, as some observers may want to do. A push from a home region generally has the greatest effect on the poorest and most unskilled members of the population since they are usually the most affected by bad times at home. On the other hand, the pull from the host region tends to select for the most enterprising immigrants who are interested in trying something new in hopes of bettering themselves. In looking at immigrants to the United States who came largely for economic reasons (which was most of them), it is often hard to separate the push factors from the pull factors. American society became home to many poor and unskilled immigrants but also gained a sturdy group of enterprising people who played a major role in the development of American society.

Political Reasons for International Migration Crossing national boundaries changes politics as well as economics. Political difficulties at home have always been a prime reason (or push) for people to submit to the upheaval and disruption of immigration. While political motivations are not as common as economic motivations (as they generally don't affect as large a percentage of the home population), they are nevertheless important motivations and certainly result in some colorful immigrants.

Political motivations for immigration to the United States have been more important because of the political and religious freedom that characterizes this society relative to others. The French Huguenots (Protestant French) came to the United States in the late 1600s to avoid persecution in their predominantly Catholic home country; in this sense they were much like the more famous Pilgrims who arrived here earlier. The first Jewish immigrants to the United States came in hopes of finding religious tolerance. European political upheavals and revolutions in the late 1840s brought a variety of Germans and Austrians to the United States. More recently, individuals fleeing from fascism in Europe in the 1930s and later from communist countries such as Hungary, Cuba, and Vietnam have come to the United States to avoid political problems at home.

Who are the political immigrants? There is no easy answer to this question. Those who were a problem to their home governments may be perceived the same way by the host government. Some radical European immigrants, for example, were important members of many of the early radical labor unions in the United States, and many were deported by the U.S. government. On the other hand, the scientists who created the atom bomb for the United States during World War II, Einstein and Fermi, for example, had fled their home countries to avoid fascism. Individuals who flee after communist revolutions tend to be the upper and professional classes, who have the most to lose under a socialist political regime. Push and pull are certainly both operative in political migration, but they yield no easy generalizations.

INTERNAL MIGRATION

People move around within their own countries far more freely than they cross national boundaries, but they move for many of the same reasons. Their primary reasons are economic (as politics would not change significantly), and very definite pushes and pulls are in operation.

Roughly 20 percent of the American population moves each year. Some move down the street, but many move from state to state or across the country. They move largely in response to occupational concerns and fluctuations in the economy. The increasing rate of occupational specialization in American society has increased the rate of internal migration as people must move to where the jobs are. American employers also have come to take migration for granted in their expectations that higher-level employees should be open to relocating in the interests of the company. The more new occupations that are created in the United States and the more that individuals go through specialized training programs for those occupations, the more internal migration we should see.

As jobs vary from place to place, so does the economy. In the early days of the industrial revolution in the United States the movement was from the farms to the cities as jobs changed from agricultural to industrial. This process of urbanization, which receives a closer look in the following section, required people to move if they wanted to survive. In the past few decades, some industry moved out of the cities, in particular to the West, South, and Southwest. Not surprisingly, employees once again moved to follow the employers; migration to the "Sunbelt" (as these areas are called) has been the dominant goal for most internal migrants in the United States in recent years.

Who are the internal migrants, why do they leave, and where do they move? In general, internal migrants in the United States tend to be younger and more educated than those who move not at all or less often. Their motivation is economic, more often than not. And the economies of both their current and future homes play a role. The states that have been losing population during the 1980s and 1990s have generally been those in the north and east—the old industrial states. Their economies have not been growing as fast as those in the south and west, particularly with regard to the "new technology" economic growth in areas such as computers. States with high growth rates from internal migration during the 1990s include Nevada, Arizona, Colorado, Florida, Georgia, Idaho, New Mexico, North Carolina, Oregon, Tennessee, Utah, and Washington. And do these moves prove fruitful for these internal immigrants? Generally, they do, particularly so for young, single women (Frey, 1995; Jacobsen and Levin, 2000; Suro, 2000; Yankow, 1999).

What is the social impact of internal migration? Part of the impact is caused by differences in population size. The area deserted will have to get by with fewer people, which means a lower tax base, fewer workers, empty buildings, vacant desks in the schools, fewer voters, fewer representatives in Congress, and a whole range of other changes. The area moved to will have opposite problems: a lack of housing, insufficient public services, overcrowded classrooms, perhaps too many workers, not enough hospital beds, and so on. Migration can change population size much more quickly than changes in fertility.

There is more to the social impact of internal migration than just change in population size, however. As we saw earlier, it is generally not a random sample of the population that moves but a specific part of it. The move to the Sunbelt by younger and better-educated members of the population will change not only population size but the age-sex pyramids in each place as well. Moreover, higher education levels among migrants probably mean that not just workers but different kinds of workers are moving, which will drastically change the nature of the labor force in each area. If the migrants are of a particular racial or ethnic group, racial and ethnic group relations will change in both locations (see Box 14.3). The possibilities are endless and will be different in each case of internal migration. As Will Rogers (a native Oklahoman) once said about the 1930s migration from Oklahoma to California, it raised the level of intelligence in both states.

URBANIZATION

Urbanization, the concentration of people in urban areas, results from the large-scale migration of people from rural to urban areas. The term is generally reserved for societies in which that migration remains steady over time. Although urbanization is a form of migration, it was not included in that section because of its own historical importance. The movement of a society toward industrialization requires urbanization, a relationship we examine momentarily. As a result, urbanization is far more than a lot of individuals deciding to make a move. It is the outcome of particular social pressures that force people to move, and it comes to play a major role in the kinds of lifestyles characteristic of a society. This section examines urbanization with an emphasis on cities in the United States. Particular attention is paid to the causes of urbanization, its effects on the lives of individuals, and the current situation of American cities.

WHY URBANIZATION?

The physical patterns of human settlements have always been related to the ways human beings earn their living. Hunting and gathering societies, for example, required their members to move constantly in search of new food supplies. Consequently, as

BOX 14.3

The Internal Migration of African Americans

African Americans have moved within the United States for some of the same reasons—primarily economic—that European Americans move. In addition, they have moved to escape discrimination, although many times such moves have taken them out of the frying pan and into the fire. Whatever their reasons for moving, the arrival of many African Americans in any section of the United States in any time of its history has been an event of considerable concern to the people already there.

Before the end of the Civil War approximately 90 percent of all African Americans were locked into the system of slavery in the American South. The other side of that statistic is that 10 percent of them were free, and many of these lived in the northern cities. During the 1800s African Americans were commonly used as strikebreakers in northern cities—when the immigrant workers went on strike, management would hire African Americans. Though the immigrants were angry at management, they were furious with African Americans; this was the beginning of much of the prejudice these new immigrant groups came to feel toward African Americans. The use of African Americans as strikebreakers continued well into the twentieth century. Edna Bonacich (1976) counted twenty-five separate strikes between 1916 and 1934 where African Americans were brought in to break the strike.

The end of slavery did not dramatically change the residence of most African Americans; 90 percent of them remained in the South as late as 1910. The big change was World War I, which ended immigration from Europe and created a labor shortage at home. Between 1914 and 1920 an estimated 400,000 to 1,000,000 African Americans left the South for work in northern industry (Pinkney, 1975). Though many of the jobs didn't last beyond the war, the migration changed the patterns of African American life tremendously. New York City developed a concentrated and highly talented African American community, with noted poets, composers, and historians, many of whom are being rediscovered today. New York was also the center of Marcus Garvey's "back to Africa" political movement in the 1920s (see Chapter 8), which preached racial separation and black nationalism. By 1924 Garvey had 100,000 dues-paying members—made possible by the concentration of African Americans into cities (Vander Zanden, 1972).

World War II again brought African Americans to northern cities for the same reasons that World War I did, but this time far more blacks made the move. They also moved to new locations, most notably the West Coast. The years following World War II provide a picture of social change through racial migration. Since World War I northern European Americans had been learning to discriminate against African Americans; there were no official antiblack laws on the books as in the South, but the practice in the North was every bit as effective: African Americans lived in separate neighborhoods, attended separate schools, and worked at the dirtiest and most poorly paid jobs. Bob Blauner (1975) argues that their late arrival in northern industrial occupations handicapped them greatly. The newly concentrated African American population was in a position to organize politically more effectively than it ever had before. The civil rights movement grew during the 1950s, followed by the more radical black power movement of the 1960s. Just as African American migration stimulated European American northerners to acts of discrimination, those acts coupled with the new physical environment of the cities allowed African Americans to make an effective political response to their situation.

In the 1970s (and for the first time since World War I) the direction of African American migration turned around; African Americans began moving from the northern cities back into the South, along with the rest of the Sunbelt migrators. Many of the forms of discrimination in the South that encouraged northern migration are now gone. Perhaps most important, there are economic opportunities for African Americans in the South today that were closed through discrimination yesterday. As the South and West respond to the influx of internal migrants in general, part of that response will no doubt include the changing African American communities and workforce brought about through the paths of migration.

we saw in Chapter 9, such societies had to remain small and without a good many of the creature comforts we take for granted today. The first horticultural societies allowed humans to sit and rest a little. Producing your own food allows you to produce more of it more efficiently and allows you to stay put while you do it. Horticulture led to some of the first permanent human communities. Typically small, those communities were geared to the farm life that permitted them to form.

Most of us in the United States have given up on hunting and gathering as a form of survival, but agriculture is still a basic necessity of life. We grow and raise more than ever before, in fact, but we do it differently. In 1900, some 39 percent of the American population (over 29 million people) lived on farms; by 1990, that percentage had dropped to 1.8 percent of the American population—fewer than 5 million people (U.S. Department of Agriculture, 2004). Who is doing the farming? Fewer people working more acres. Agribusiness has largely replaced the family farm, making it almost impossible for smaller operations to be profitable. Between 1900 and 1997 the average American farm grew from 146 acres to 487 acres (U.S. Department of Agriculture, 2004). Changes in the industrial economy of the United States forced these changes on the American farmer; just as hunting and gathering societies could not compete with agricultural societies, the family farm has not been able to compete with the new economic patterns in American society.

Those new economic patterns reflect the increasing dominance of industry and technology. The same economic and technological transformation that turned the

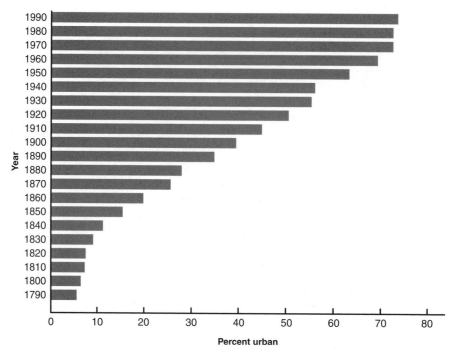

Figure 14.5 Percent of U.S. population living in urban areas, 1790–1990. (Data from U.S. Bureau of the Census, 1992d)

family farm into agribusiness has turned the "mom and pop" grocery store into the supermarket and the small manufacturing plant into the conglomerate corporation. The United States has been an industrial society for over a century, but the change is gradual and is still continuing. As economic life becomes more centralized, it also becomes necessary for the population to become more centralized. The American population has become centralized in the cities, as Figure 14.5 suggests.

Urbanization drives people to cities because it drives employers to cities. Big businesses need large labor forces that live in proximity to the office or factory. Just as important, big business needs to be near other big business. The division of labor that affects all aspects of American life is reflected in the business world as well. A steel mill needs to be near supplies of iron ore. Manufacturers who use steel must be near the steel mills. And all of these businesses must be near other businesses that supply paper, machinery, paper clips, transportation, work clothes, communication, and all of the many other items and services that must come together for an industrial economy to work. The centralization of business forces people to concentrate as they pursue the ends of their own survival in a society that offers progressively fewer options in rural areas and more in urban areas. And as people become concentrated, so too will the services and other businesses that people need in their everyday lives. Urbanization is therefore far more than just a movement of people; it is a concentration of all aspects of society into one physical setting called a city. As in all human societies, it reflects the way people earn a living.

THE EFFECTS OF URBANIZATION

In the early 1960s a New York City woman named Kitty Genovese was attacked and murdered on her street. The attack lasted more than thirty minutes. It was later discovered that thirty-eight people had heard her screams, but not one had come to her aid; no one even called the police because they "didn't want to get involved" (Rogers and Eftimiades, 1995). This story fits in with many of the stereotypes Americans hold about cities. Cities are jungles, large impersonal environments in which everyone looks out for number one. Cities are hotbeds of sin and crime in which traditional moral values are quickly forgotten. These stereotypes sit in contrast to a prevalent view of rural life in which we go over the river and through the woods to a nice wholesome dinner at Grandma's house. What, in fact, does city life do to people?

The negative stereotype of cities has been around as long as there have been cities. An early sociological view of cities comes from German sociologist Georg Simmel in his article "The Metropolis and Mental Life," written in the early 1900s (Simmel, 1950). In this article Simmel offers two of the dominant ideas regarding the effects of urban life on the individual. On the one hand, says Simmel, the city is an environment of intense nervous stimulation that would "short circuit" the personality of a rural person. To counteract this stimulation, the city dweller learns to respond "with his head instead of heart." As a result of urban intensity, the city dweller becomes somewhat blasé; other people and situations are viewed in terms of rational calculations much in the same way one would enter into a business relationship.

On the other hand, says Simmel, the city is the source of individual freedom. Small groups tend to be very restrictive of their members. They hold strongly to certain values and pay close attention to behavior to see that norms are adhered to. In contrast, the anonymity cities provide for their residents allows individual personalities to develop without the shackles of continual surveillance. Our modern ideal of individuality and individual rights is a creature of the city. And what of Kitty Genovese? Simmel would argue that individual freedom to not become involved goes hand in hand with the intellectual (as opposed to the emotional) response of the city dweller.

Louis Wirth, an American sociologist, offered a later but in some ways similar view of the city in his famous 1938 article, "Urbanism as a Way of Life." Wirth emphasized the diversity of city life and the effect of that diversity on its members. We deal with many strangers in cities, and most of the people we encounter we see only in very specialized roles. This situation contrasts with that in small communities, where we know the "whole person." This difference understandably would alter the nature of human relationships. In addition, says Wirth, the diversity of city life can be very confusing and can produce a state of anomie in its citizens.

The diversity of urban life is certainly one of its most striking characteristics. People move to cities from all over and bring their cultures with them. They usually try to live with others from their hometown (or state or country) when they get there. Herbert Gans (1962) emphasized this aspect of urban life, pointing out that cities may appear at first glance to be vast mixtures of people but are, in fact, joined-together communities in which people have many of the interpersonal contacts and emotions common to small towns. Meeting people from other cultures provides a new perspective on our own, perhaps calling attention to beliefs or behaviors to which we had never given a second thought. Thus, cities have the potential for reducing ethnocentrism as individuals can become more understanding of cultural differences. On the other hand, cities can also become a vast battleground in which people from different backgrounds discover just how much they hate each other.

Cities are fertile ground for politics. Urban life concentrates people and exposes them directly to outsiders and assorted other threats. If you have a gripe, there are probably a number of others around with the same gripe acquired in the same way. There is also probably a potential political leader around who will find the physical concentration of potential followers to be convenient for purposes of organization; a speaker can draw a much bigger crowd in downtown New York City than in the grasslands of west Texas. It is not surprising, therefore, that most American political movements—from labor unions and political machines to a variety of revolutionary movements—have grown in cities.

One of the most important changes brought about by urbanization occurs with the family. Migration of any kind tends to break up extended families as the members become scattered and lose touch. Moreover, urban life accompanies industrialization, which tends to reduce family size. All in all, families change quite a bit as a result of the urban move. And as families change, so, too, do many of the norms, roles, and values that are associated with families. Urbanization affects childrearing practices, gender roles within the family, religion, education, leisure-time activities, and friendship patterns, to name just a few.

Generalizations about urban impact should be taken with a grain of salt. A massive overall change in our way of life, the growth of cities has been a many-faceted phenomenon. Our responses to the urban environment have been just as varied. The urban experience is clearly a factor of change in all aspects of life, but sociologists have yet to discover exactly how that factor operates.

TRENDS IN URBANIZATION: CITIES TODAY AND TOMORROW

Since World War II American cities have become increasingly decentralized—larger in size and less dense in population. The popular term for this change is

Suburbia may offer space and quiet, but big-city life has its pluses, too. People spend more time out on the streets (weather permitting) and so have more social contacts. When there are hundreds of families on a block, there's often a group of children playing in the streets.

suburbanization—more and more people leaving the central cities for the dream house and lot in the suburbs. Once again, however, it is not only the people who are moving; jobs are moving with them. As that trend has continued, it has grown less and less necessary for businesses to locate in urban areas. The loss of people to the suburbs is hard enough on the city's tax base, but the loss of all those jobs can be backbreaking. A thriving city factory generates tax revenue in a variety of ways, while an empty shell of a building (especially one nobody wants) is worth little. And, as money leaves, the cities have to cut back on services, either temporarily or permanently. Some of the central areas of American cities are beginning to look more like wastelands than the centers of activity they once were. The South Bronx in New York City, for example, was largely deserted and left to the arsonists by 1980.

The people who leave for the suburbs are specifically middle-class people. Many suburbs control this immigration by zoning regulations that force certain kinds of structures (expensive) to be added to certain size lots (large). When middle-class people leave the cities, lower-class people are left behind. To the extent that the urban poor are nonwhite, the process of suburbanization in American society leads to racial segregation: Whites live out in suburbia while nonwhites struggle in the remains of the central cities. In addition, central cities are becoming the loci for increasing numbers of homeless Americans. Changes in the structure of the American family coupled with 1980s decreases in government spending on social programs have produced larger numbers of people who spend years without a permanent residence except a street corner or bus station. A study of homeless people in Chicago found that most tend to have the same education as the rest of the population (about twelve years) but are characterized by either mental or physical disabilities and by a lack of family ties; a full 50 percent of those in the sample had never married (Rossi et al., 1987).

Decentralization appears to be occurring in American society today even beyond the bounds of general metropolitan areas. The mass migration to the Sunbelt indicates a movement not only out of the central city but even away from the city altogether. Businesses are taking advantage of new advances in communication and transportation that permit them to enjoy the low tax rates and nonunion labor of smaller communities in the South and the West. Where businesses used to have to huddle together, usually near a major waterway, today they apparently feel they can spread out, connected only by computers, telephone lines, and highways. And where business goes, people follow.

One of the questions for the future of cities concerns their relation to the growing energy shortages we face, however. Suburbs grew along with railroad commuter lines and, more important, the automobile. Living far from work was no problem as the transportation costs were negligible. Today, however, cities appear in a new light. Expensive transportation makes centralized living patterns appear once again attractive. Some Americans are looking at cities as if for the first time, thinking how convenient it would be to have people living and working in close proximity—add a church, a school, and a corner grocery store, and folks would have everything they needed. Some American cities have in fact experienced something of a rebirth as people and business have moved back, bringing restored buildings and new tax revenues with them. It is certainly too early to speak of a centralization trend (countering the decentralization we've experienced for several decades), but American cities are clearly far from dead (see the reading by Owen following this chapter).

SUMMARY

Demography is the study of human populations, focusing on the social factors that affect populations and the effects of changes in those populations on the rest of society. Populations increase or decrease through the interplay of three fundamental processes: birth, death, and migration.

In the eighteenth century advances in nutrition and sanitation caused the death rate in Europe to drop, which resulted in a population explosion. The population continued to rise well into the industrial revolution, after which the birth rate began to drop, causing population growth to level out. This historical occurrence, today called the demographic transition, is thought by some demographers to be a general pattern for population change.

The nonindustrial world today appears to be in stage two of the demographic transition, as death rates have dropped but birth rates remain high. This situation creates a population explosion as well as a very high proportion of the population under the age of fourteen and in a state of dependency. Modern-day Marxists argue that poverty in the nonindustrial world is due to capitalism rather than to the population explosion. Some scientists have tried to aid the situation by creating more productive crops (the Green Revolution). Most demographers see fertility control as essential to ending poverty.

A stable population (zero population growth) has occurred in several industrial countries already, but its long-term effects are not known. One effect would be a change in the age distribution of the population—fewer young people and more older people. This change would certainly alter the economic structure of society.

Migration is the movement of people from one physical location to another. International migration crosses national political boundaries, whereas internal migration is movement within such boundaries. In both cases, the primary motivations for migration have been economic, although significant numbers of international migrants move for political reasons. Most demographers view migration from the dual perspective of the "push" the migrant feels from the home area and the "pull" from the host area.

Urbanization is the most extreme historical example of migration, but its importance goes beyond the mere movement of people. It refers to the ongoing concentration of people, things, and activities into relatively small geographical areas known as cities. This concentration has coincided with industrialization as the city has been a necessary physical setting for industrialization to occur. The physical concentration of people and their activities into cities, from the individual standpoint, tends to increase personal freedom while simultaneously loosening the individual's attachment to the social group. Recently, some trends toward decentralization have been noted in the United States and elsewhere through both the growth of suburbs and industrial movement to less urban settings.

GLOSSARY

Birth rate The number of births in a given year for every thousand people in the population.

Death rate The number of deaths in a given year for every thousand people in the population.

Demographic transition The set of population changes that occurs with industrialization, eventually resulting in a drop in both birth and death rates, leaving them in relative balance.

Demography The study of human populations, emphasizing the causes and effects of population changes.

General fertility rate The number of births in a given year for every thousand women of childbearing age.

Growth rate The rate of natural population increase plus the immigration rate.

Immigration rate The number of immigrants for every thousand people in the population in a given year.

Migration The physical movement of a population, either international (if it crosses national boundaries) or internal (if it does not).

Pronatalism The societal value of having children and large families.

Rate of natural increase (or decrease) The difference between the birth rate and the death rate in a given year.

Replacement level The number of babies necessary in a population for parents to replace themselves.

Suburbanization The movement of people to, and the growth of residential housing surrounding, a city.

Urbanization The physical concentration of people in urban areas resulting from the large-scale migration from rural areas.

Zero population growth A stable population in which each individual is replaced through a stable birth rate.

STUDY QUESTIONS

1. How and why do demographers study the age and sex characteristics of a population? Why does a population existing at the replacement level have

zero population growth? What types of countries are most likely to have that characteristic?

2. What is the demographic transition? To what extent are developing countries today going through it?

3. How did industrialization change population growth and family structure?

4. What are the various perspectives and solutions offered by demographers for the current poverty found in the nonindustrial world?

5. Consider the various baby booms and baby busts in the last half century of the United States. What effects have we seen from boom generations and bust generations? How could we predict the future with such information?

6. Why do people move internationally? How is such immigration affected by whether the immigrants are politically motivated or economically motivated?

7. What factors determine internal migration in the United States? Who moves and why?

8. Why do industrial societies become urbanized? How has urbanization affected how people live and how they feel? What social changes have produced suburbanization?

David Owen

Green Manhattan

Living "green" means to find a lifestyle that is environmentally friendly in every sense of the word. As we have seen in this chapter, population growth can, by itself, threaten the environment by overly stressing its resources. So how could a major city—in this case, the island of Manhattan in the heart of New York City—ever be described as "green"? In this look at modern urban life in the United States, David Owen comes to some interesting conclusions about how a green lifestyle might develop in some of the least likely settings.

My wife and I got married right out of college, in 1978. We were young and naïve and unashamedly idealistic, and we decided to make our first home in a utopian environmentalist community in New York State. For seven years, we lived, quite contentedly, in circumstances that would strike most Americans as austere in the extreme: our living space measured just seven hundred square feet, and we didn't have a dishwasher, a garbage disposal, a lawn, or a car. We did our grocery shopping on foot, and when we needed to travel longer distances we used public transportation. Because space at home was scarce, we seldom acquired new possessions of significant size. Our electric bills worked out to about a dollar a day.

The utopian community was Manhattan. (Our apartment was on Sixty-ninth Street, between Second and Third.) Most Americans, including most New Yorkers, think of New York City as an ecological nightmare, a wasteland of concrete and garbage and diesel fumes and traffic jams, but in comparison with the rest of America it's a model of environmental responsibility. By the most significant measures, New York is the greenest community in the United States, and one of the greenest cities in the world. The most devastating damage humans have done to the environment has arisen from the heedless burning of fossil fuels, a category in which New Yorkers are practically prehistoric. The average Manhattanite consumes gasoline at a rate that the country as a whole hasn't matched since the mid-nineteen-twenties, when the most widely owned car in the United States was the Ford Model T. Eighty-two percent of Manhattan residents travel to work by public transit, by bicycle, or on foot. That's ten times the rate for Ameri-

From *The New Yorker*, October 18, 2004. Reprinted by permission of *The New Yorker*, © 2004.

cans in general, and eight times the rate for residents of Los Angeles County. New York City is more populous than all but eleven states; if it were granted statehood, it would rank fifty-first in per-capita energy use.

"Anyplace that has such tall buildings and heavy traffic is obviously an environmental disaster—except that it isn't," John Holtzclaw, a transportation consultant for the Sierra Club and the Natural Resources Defense Council, told me. "If New Yorkers lived at the typical American sprawl density of three households per residential acre, they would require many times as much land. They'd be driving cars, and they'd have huge lawns and be using pesticides and fertilizers on them, and then they'd be over-watering their lawns, so that runoff would go into streams." The key to New York's relative environmental benignity is its extreme compactness. Manhattan's population density is more than eight hundred times that of the nation as a whole. Placing one and a half million people on a twenty-three-square-mile island sharply reduces their opportunities to be wasteful, and forces the majority to live in some of the most inherently energy efficient residential structures in the world: apartment buildings. It also frees huge tracts of land for the rest of America to sprawl into.

My wife and I had our first child in 1984. We had both grown up in suburbs, and we decided that we didn't want to raise our tiny daughter in a huge city. Shortly after she learned to walk, we moved to a small town in northwestern Connecticut, about ninety miles north of midtown Manhattan. Our house, which was built in the late seventeen hundreds, is across a dirt road from a nature preserve and is shaded by tall white-pine trees. After big rains, we can hear a swollen creek rushing by at the bottom of the hill.

Deer, wild turkeys, and the occasional black bear feed themselves in our yard. From the end of our driveway, I can walk several miles through woods to an abandoned nineteenth-century railway tunnel, while crossing only one paved road.

Yet our move was an ecological catastrophe. Our consumption of electricity went from roughly four thousand kilowatt-hours a year, toward the end of our time in New York, to almost thirty thousand kilowatt-hours in 2003—and our house doesn't even have central air-conditioning. We bought a car shortly before we moved, and another one soon after we arrived, and a third one ten years later. (If you live in the country and don't have a second car, you can't retrieve your first car from the mechanic after it's been repaired; the third car was the product of a mild midlife crisis, but soon evolved into a necessity.)

My wife and I both work at home, but we manage to drive thirty thousand miles a year between us, mostly doing ordinary errands. Nearly everything we do away from our house requires a car trip. Renting a movie and later returning it, for example, consumes almost two gallons of gasoline, since the nearest Blockbuster is ten miles away and each transaction involves two round trips. When we lived in New York, heat escaping from our apartment helped to heat the apartment above ours; nowadays, many of the Btus produced by our brand-new, extremely efficient oil-burning furnace leak through our two-hundred-year-old roof and into the dazzling star-filled winter sky above.

When most Americans think about environmentalism, they picture wild, unspoiled landscapes—the earth before it was transmogrified by human habitation. New York City is one of the most thoroughly altered landscapes imaginable, an almost wholly artificial environment, in which the terrain's primeval contours have long since been obliterated and most of the parts that resemble nature (the trees on side streets, the rocks in Central Park) are essentially decorations. Ecology-minded discussions of New York City often have a hopeless tone, and focus on ways in which the city might be made to seem somewhat less oppressively man-made: by increasing the area devoted to parks and greenery, by incorporating vegetation into buildings themselves, by reducing traffic congestion, by easing the intensity of development, by creating open space around structures. But most such changes would actually undermine the city's extraordinary energy efficiency, which arises from the characteristics that make it surreally synthetic.

Because densely populated urban centers concentrate human activity, we think of them as pollution crisis zones. Calculated by the square foot, New York City generates more greenhouse gases, uses more energy, and produces more solid waste than most other American regions of comparable size. On a map depicting negative environmental impacts in relation to surface area, therefore, Manhattan would look like an intense hot spot, surrounded, at varying distances, by belts of deepening green.

If you plotted the same negative impacts by resident or by household, however, the color scheme would be reversed. My little town has about four thousand residents, spread over 38.7 thickly wooded square miles, and there are many places within our town limits from which no sign of settlement is visible in any direction. But if you moved eight million people like us, along with our dwellings and possessions and current rates of energy use, into a space the size of New York City, our profligacy would be impossible to miss, because you'd have to stack our houses and cars and garages and lawn tractors and swimming pools and septic tanks higher than skyscrapers. (Conversely, if you made all eight million New Yorkers live at the density of my town, they would require a space equivalent to the land area of the six New England states plus Delaware and New Jersey.)

Spreading people out increases the damage they do to the environment, while making the problems harder to see and to address.

Of course, living in densely populated urban centers has many drawbacks. Even wealthy New Yorkers live in spaces that would seem cramped to Americans living almost anywhere else. A well-to-do friend of mine who grew up in a town house in Greenwich Village thought of his upbringing as privileged until, in prep school, he visited a classmate from the suburbs and was staggered by the house, the lawn, the cars, and the swimming pool, and thought, with despair, You mean I could live like this?

Manhattan is loud and dirty, and the subway is depressing, and the fumes from the cars and cabs and buses can make people sick. Presumably for environmental reasons, New York City has one of the highest childhood-asthma rates in the country, with an especially alarming concentration in East Harlem.

Nevertheless, barring an almost inconceivable reduction in the earth's population, dense urban centers offer one of the few plausible remedies for some of the world's most discouraging environmental ills. To borrow a term from the jargon of computer systems, dense cities are scalable, while sprawling suburbs are not. The environmental challenge we face, at the current stage of our assault on the world's non-renewable resources, is not how to make our teeming cities more like the pristine countryside. The true challenge is how to make other settled places more like Manhattan. This notion has yet to be widely embraced, partly because it is counterintuitive, and partly because most Americans, including most environmentalists, tend to view cities the way Thomas Jefferson did, as "pestilential to the morals, the health, and the liberties of man." New York is the place that's fun to visit but you wouldn't want to live there. What could it possibly teach anyone about being green?

New York's example, admittedly, is difficult for others to imitate, because the city's remarkable population density is the result not of conscientious planning but of a succession of serendipitous historical accidents. The most important of those accidents was geographic: New York arose on a smallish island rather than on the mainland edge of a river or a bay, and the surrounding water served as a physical constraint to outward expansion. Manhattan is like a typical seaport turned inside out—a city with a harbor around it, rather than a harbor with a city along its edge. Insularity gave Manhattan more shoreline per square mile than other ports, a major advantage in the days when one of the world's main commercial activities was moving cargoes between ships. It also drove early development inward and upward.

A second lucky accident was that Manhattan's street plan was created by merchants who were more interested in economic efficiency than in boulevards, parks, or empty spaces between buildings. The resulting crush of architecture is actually humanizing, because it brings the city's commercial, cultural, and other offerings closer together, thereby increasing their accessibility—a point made forty-three years ago by the brilliantly iconoclastic urban thinker Jane Jacobs, in her landmark book "The Death and Life of Great American Cities."

A third accident was the fact that by the early nineteen-hundreds most of Manhattan's lines had been filled in to the point where not even Robert Moses could easily redraw them to accommodate the great destroyer of American urban life, the automobile. Henry Ford thought of cars as tools for liberating humanity from the wretchedness of cities, which he viewed with as much distaste as Jefferson did. In 1932, John Nolen, a prominent Harvard-educated urban planner and landscape architect, said, "The future city will be spread out, it will be regional, it will be the natural product of the automobile, the good road, electricity, the telephone, and the radio, combined with the growing desire to live a more natural, biological life under pleasanter and more natural conditions." This is the idea behind suburbs, and it's still seductive. But it's also a prescription for sprawl and expressways and tremendous waste.

New York City's obvious urban antithesis, in terms of density and automobile use, is metropolitan Los Angeles, whose metastatic outward growth has been virtually unimpeded by the lay of the land, whose early settlers came to the area partly out of a desire to create space between themselves and others, and whose main development began late enough to be shaped by the needs of cars. But a more telling counterexample is Washington, D.C., whose basic layout was conceived at roughly the same time as Manhattan's, around the turn of the nineteenth century. The

District of Columbia's original plan was created by an eccentric French-born engineer and architect named Pierre-Charles L'Enfant, who befriended General Washington during the Revolutionary War and asked to be allowed to design the capital. Many of modern Washington's most striking features are his: the broad, radial avenues; the hublike traffic circles; the sweeping public lawns and ceremonial spaces.

Washington is commonly viewed as the most intelligently beautiful—the most European—of large American cities. Ecologically, though, it's a mess. L'Enfant's expansive avenues were easily adapted to automobiles, and the low, widely separated buildings (whose height is limited by law) stretched the distance between destinations.

There are many pleasant places in Washington to go for a walk, but the city is difficult to get around on foot: the wide avenues are hard to cross, the traffic circles are like obstacle courses, and the grandiloquent empty spaces thwart pedestrians, by acting as what Jane Jacobs calls "border vacuums." (One of Jacobs's many arresting observations is that parks and other open spaces can reduce urban vitality, by creating dead ends that prevent people from moving freely between neighborhoods and by decreasing activity along their edges.) Many parts of Washington, furthermore, are relentlessly homogeneous. There are plenty of dignified public buildings on Constitution Avenue, for example, but good luck finding a dry cleaner, a Chinese restaurant, or a grocery store. The city's horizontal, airy design has also pushed development into the surrounding countryside. The fastest growing county in the United States is Loudoun County, Virginia, at the rapidly receding western edge of the Washington metropolitan area.

The Sierra Club, an environmental organization that advocates the preservation of wilderness and wildlife, has a national campaign called Challenge to Sprawl. The aim of the program is to arrest the mindless conversion of undeveloped countryside into subdivisions, strip malls, and S.U.V.-clogged expressways. The Sierra Club's Web site features a slide-show-like demonstration that illustrates how various sprawling suburban intersections could be transformed into far more appealing and energy-efficient developments by implementing a few modifications, among them widening the sidewalks and narrowing the streets, mixing residential and commercial uses, moving buildings closer together and closer to the edges of sidewalks (to make them more accessible to pedestrians and to increase local density), and adding public transportation—all fundamental elements of the widely touted anti-sprawl strategy known as Smart Growth.

In a recent telephone conversation with a Sierra Club representative involved in Challenge to Sprawl, I said that the organization's anti-sprawl suggestions and the modified streetscapes in the slide show shared many significant features with Manhattan—whose most salient characteristics include wide sidewalks, narrow streets, mixed uses, densely packed buildings, and an extensive network of subways and buses.

The representative hesitated, then said that I was essentially correct, although he would prefer that the program not be described in such terms, since emulating New York City would not be considered an appealing goal by most of the people whom the Sierra Club is trying to persuade.

An obvious way to reduce consumption of fossil fuels is to shift more people out of cars and into public transit. In many parts of the country, though, public transit has been stagnant or in decline for years. New York City's Metropolitan Transportation Authority and Department of Transportation account for nearly a third of all the transit passenger miles traveled in the United States and for nearly four times as many passenger miles as the Washington Metropolitan Area Transit Authority and the Los Angeles County Metropolitan Transportation Authority combined.

New York City looks so little like other parts of America that urban planners and environmentalists tend to treat it as an exception rather than an example, and to act as though Manhattan occupied an idiosyncratic universe of its own.

But the underlying principles apply everywhere. "The basic point," Jeffrey Zupan, an economist with the Regional Planning Association, told me, "is that you need density to support public transit. In all cities, not just in New York, once you get above a certain density two things happen. First, you get less travel by mechanical means, which is another way of saying you get more people walking or biking; and, second, you get a decrease in the trips by auto and an increase in the trips by transit. That threshold tends to be around seven dwellings per acre. Once you cross that line, a bus company can put buses out there, because they know they're going to have enough passengers to support a reasonable frequency of service."

Phoenix is the sixth-largest city in the United States and one of the fastest growing among the top ten, yet its public transit system accounts for just one percent of the passenger miles that New York City's does. The reason is that Phoenix's burgeoning population has spread so far across the desert—greater Phoenix, whose population is a little more than twice that of Manhattan, covers more than two hundred times as much land—that no transit system could conceivably serve it. And no amount of browbeating, public-service advertising, or federal spending can change that.

Cities, states, and the federal government often negate their own efforts to nurture public transit by simultaneously spending huge sums to make it easier for people to get around in cars. When a city's automobile traffic becomes congested, the standard response has long been to provide additional capacity by building new roads or widening existing ones. This approach eventually makes the original problem worse, by generating what transportation planners call "induced traffic": every mile of new highway lures passengers from public transit and other more efficient modes of travel, and makes it possible for residential and commercial development to spread even farther from urban centers. And adding public transit in the hope of reducing automobile congestion is as self-defeating as building new highways, because unclogging roads, if successful, just makes driving seem more attractive, and the roads fill up again. A better strategy would be to eliminate existing traffic lanes and parking spaces gradually, thereby forcing more drivers to use less environmentally damaging alternatives—in effect, "induced transit."

One reason New Yorkers are the most dedicated transit users in America is that congestion on the city's streets makes driving extraordinarily disagreeable. The average speed of crosstown traffic in Manhattan is little more than that of a brisk walker, and in midtown at certain times of the day the cars on the side streets move so slowly that they appear almost to be parked. Congestion like that urges drivers into the subways, and it makes life easier for pedestrians and bicycle riders by slowing cars to a point where they constitute less of a physical threat.

Even in New York City, the relationship between traffic and transit is not well understood. A number of the city's most popular recent transportation-related projects and policy decisions may in the long run make the city a worse place to live in by luring passengers back into their cars and away from public transportation: the rebuilding and widening of the West Side Highway, the implementation of EZ-Pass on the city's toll bridges, the decision not to impose tolls on the East River bridges, and the current renovation of the F.D.R. Drive (along with the federally funded $139 million Outboard Detour Roadway, which is intended to prevent users of the F.D.R. from being inconvenienced while the work is under way).

Public transit itself can be bad for the environment if it facilitates rather than discourages sprawl. The Washington Metropolitan Area Transit Authority is considering extensions to some of the most distant branches of its system, and those extensions, if built, will allow people to live even farther from the city's center, creating new, nondense suburbs where all other travel will be by automobile, much of it to malls and schools and gas stations that will be built to accommodate them. Transit is best for the environment when it helps to concentrate people in dense urban cores. Building the proposed Second Avenue subway line would be environmentally sound, because it would increase New Yorkers' ability to live without cars; building a bullet train between Penn Station and the Catskills (for example) would not be sound, because it would enable the vast, fuel-squandering apparatus of suburbia to establish itself in a region that couldn't support it otherwise.

On the afternoon of August 14, 2003, I was working in my office, on the third floor of my house, when the lights blinked, my window air-conditioner sputtered, and my computer's backup battery kicked in briefly. This was the beginning of the great blackout of 2003, which halted electric service in parts of eight Northeastern and Midwestern states and in southeastern Canada. The immediate cause was eventually traced to Ohio, but public attention often focused on New York City, which had the largest concentration of affected power customers. Richard B. Miller, who resigned as the senior energy adviser for the city of New York six weeks before the blackout, reportedly over deep disagreements with the city's energy policy, told me, "When I was with the city, I attended a conference on global warming where somebody said, 'We really need to raise energy and electricity prices in New York City, so that people will consume less.' And my response at that conference was 'You know, if you're talking about raising energy prices in New York City only, then you're talking about something that's really bad for the environment. If you make energy prices so expensive in the city that a business relocates from Manhattan to New Jersey, what you're really talking about, in the simplest terms, is a business that's moving from a subway stop to a parking lot. And which of those do you think is worse for the environment?'"

People who live in cities use only about half as much electricity as people who don't, and people who live in New York City generally use less than the urban average. A truly enlightened energy policy would reward city dwellers and encourage others to follow their good example. Yet New

York City residents pay more per kilowatt-hour than almost any other American electricity customers; taxes and other government charges, most of which are not enumerated on electricity bills, can constitute close to twenty percent of the cost of power for residential and commercial users in New York. Richard Miller, after leaving his job with New York City, went to work as a lawyer in Consolidated Edison's regulatory affairs department, spurred by his thinking about the environment. He believes that state and local officials have historically taken unfair advantage of the fact that there is no political cost to attacking a big utility. ConEd pays more than six hundred million dollars a year in property taxes, making it by far the city's largest property-tax payer, and those charges inflate electric bills. Meanwhile, the cost of driving is kept artificially low. (Fifth Avenue and the West Side Highway don't pay property taxes, for example.) "In addition," Miller said, "the burden of improving the city's air has fallen far more heavily on power plants, which contribute only a small percentage of New York City's air pollution, than it has on cars—even though motor vehicles are a much bigger source."

Last year, the National Building Museum, in Washington, D.C., held a show called "Big & Green: Toward Sustainable Architecture in the 21st Century." A book of the same name was published in conjunction with the show, and on the book's dust jacket was a photograph of 4 Times Square, also known as the Condé Nast Building, a forty-eight-story glass-and-steel tower between Forty-second and Forty-third Streets, a few blocks west of Grand Central Terminal. (The New Yorker's offices occupy two floors in the building.) When 4 Times Square was built, in 1999, it was considered a major breakthrough in urban development. As Daniel Kaplan, a principal of Fox & Fowle Architects, the firm that designed it, wrote in an article in Environmental Design & Construction in 1997, "When thinking of green architecture, one usually associates smaller scale," and he cited as an example the headquarters of the Rocky Mountain Institute, a

nonprofit environmental research and consulting firm based in Snowmass, Colorado. The R.M.I. building is a four-thousand-square-foot, super-insulated, passive solar structure with curving sixteen-inch-thick walls, set into a hillside about fifteen miles north of Aspen. It was erected in the early eighties and serves partly as a showcase for green construction technology. (It is also the home of Amory Lovins, who is R.M.I.'s cofounder and chief executive officer.) R.M.I. contributed to the design of 4 Times Square, which has many innovative features, among them collection chutes for recyclable materials, photovoltaic panels incorporated into parts of its skin, and curtain-wall construction with exceptional shading and insulating properties.

These are all important innovations. In terms of the building's true ecological impact, though, they are distinctly secondary. (The power generated by the photovoltaic panels supplies less than one percent of the building's requirements.) The two greenest features of 4 Times Square are ones that most people never even mention: it is big, and it is situated in Manhattan.

Environmentalists have tended to treat big buildings as intrinsically wasteful, because large amounts of energy are expended in their construction, and because the buildings place intensely localized stresses on sewers, power lines, and water systems.

But density can create the same kinds of ecological benefits in individual structures that it does in entire communities. Tall buildings have much less exposed exterior surface per square foot of interior space than smaller buildings do, and that means they present relatively less of themselves to the elements, and their small roofs absorb less heat from the sun during cooling season and radiate less heat from inside during heating season. (The beneficial effects are greater still in Manhattan, where one building often directly abuts another.) A study by Michael Phillips and Robert Gnaizda, published in *CoEvolution Quarterly* in 1980, found that an ordinary apartment in a typical building near downtown San Francisco used just a fifth as much heating fuel as a new tract house in Davis, a little more than seventy miles away. Occupants of tall buildings also do a significant part of their daily coming and going in elevators, which, because they are counterweighted and thus require less motor horsepower, are among the most energy efficient passenger vehicles in the world.

Bruce Fowle, a founder of Fox & Fowle, told me, "The Condé Nast Building contains 1.6 million square feet of floor space, and it sits on one acre of land. If you divided it into forty-eight one-story suburban office buildings, each averaging thirty-three thousand square feet, and spread those one-story buildings around the countryside, and then added parking and some green space around each one, you'd end up consuming at least a hundred and fifty acres of land. And then you'd have to provide infrastructure, the highways and everything else." Like many other buildings in Manhattan, 4 Times Square doesn't even have a parking lot, because the vast majority of the six thousand people who work inside it don't need one. In most other parts of the country, big parking lots are not only necessary but are required by law. If my town's zoning regulations applied in Manhattan, 4 Times Square would have needed sixteen thousand parking spaces, one for every hundred square feet of office floor space. The Rocky Mountain Institute's showcase headquarters has double-paned krypton-filled windows, which admit seventy-five percent as much light as ordinary windows while allowing just ten percent as much heat to escape in cold weather. That's a wonderful feature, and one of many in the building which people ought to copy. In other ways, though, the R.M.I. building sets a very poor environmental example. It was built in a fragile location, on virgin land more than seven thousand feet above sea level. With just four thousand square feet of interior space, it can hold only six of R.M.I.'s eighteen full-time employees; the rest of them work in a larger building a mile away. Because the two buildings are in a thinly populated area, they force most employees to drive many miles—including trips between the two buildings—and

they necessitate extra fuel consumption by delivery trucks, snowplows, and other vehicles. If R.M.I.'s employees worked on a single floor of a big building in Manhattan (or in downtown Denver) and lived in apartments nearby, many of them would be able to give up their cars, and the thousands of visitors who drive to Snowmass each year to learn about environmentally responsible construction could travel by public transit instead.

Picking on R.M.I.—which is one of the world's most farsighted environmental organizations—may seem unfair, but R.M.I., along with many other farsighted environmental organizations, shares responsibility for perpetuating the powerful anti-city bias of American environmentalism. That bias is evident in the technical term that is widely used for sprawl: "urbanization." Thinking of freeways and strip malls as "urban" phenomena obscures the ecologically monumental difference between Phoenix and Manhattan, and fortifies the perception that population density is an environmental ill. It also prevents most people from recognizing that R.M.I.'s famous headquarters—which sits on an isolated parcel more than a hundred and eighty miles from the nearest significant public transit system—is sprawl.

When I told a friend recently that I thought New York City should be considered the greenest community in America, she looked puzzled, then asked, "Is it because they've started recycling again?" Her question reflected a central failure of the American environmental movement: that too many of us have been made to believe that the most important thing we can do to save the earth and ourselves is to remember each week to set our cans and bottles and newspapers on the curb. Recycling is popular because it enables people to relieve their gathering anxieties about the future without altering the way they live. But most current recycling has, at best, a neutral effect on the environment, and much of it is demonstrably harmful. As William McDonough and Michael Braungart point out in "Cradle to Cradle: Remaking the Way We Make Things," most of the materials we place on our curbs are merely "downcycled"—converted to a lower use, providing a pause in their inevitable journey to a landfill or an incinerator—often with a release of toxins and a net loss of fuel, among other undesirable effects.

By far the worst damage we Americans do to the planet arises not from the newspapers we throw away but from the eight hundred and fifty million or so gallons of oil we consume every day. We all know this at some level, yet we live like alcoholics in denial. How else can we explain that our cars have grown bigger, heavier, and less fuel efficient at the same time that scientists have become more certain and more specific about the consequences of our addiction to gasoline?

On a shelf in my office is a small pile of recent books about the environment which I plan to reread obsessively if I'm found to have a terminal illness, because they're so unsettling that they may make me less upset about being snatched from life in my prime. At the top of the pile is "Out of Gas: The End of the Age of Oil," by David Goodstein, a professor at the California Institute of Technology, which was published earlier this year. "The world will soon start to run out of conventionally produced, cheap oil," Goodstein begins. In succeeding pages, he lucidly explains that humans have consumed almost a trillion barrels of oil (that's forty-two trillion gallons), or about half of the earth's total supply; that a devastating global petroleum crisis will begin not when we have pumped the last barrel out of the ground but when we have reached the halfway point, because at that moment, for the first time in history, the line representing supply will fall through the line representing demand; that we will probably pass that point within the current decade, if we haven't passed it already; that various well-established laws of economics are about to assert themselves, with disastrous repercussions for almost everything; and that "civilization as we know it will come to an end sometime in this century unless we can find a way to live without fossil fuels."

Standing between us and any conceivable solution to our energy nightmare are our cars and the asphalt-latticed country we have built to oblige them. Those cars have defined our culture and our lives. A car is speed and sex and power and emancipation. It makes its driver a self-sufficient nation of one. It is everything a city is not.

Most of the car's most tantalizing charms are illusory, though. By helping us to live at greater distances from one another, driving has undermined the very benefits that it was meant to bestow. Ignacio San Martín, an architecture professor and the head of the graduate urban-design program at the University of Arizona, told me, "If you go out to the streets of Phoenix and are able to see anybody walking—which you likely won't—they are going to tell you that they love living in Phoenix because they have a beautiful house and three cars. In reality, though, once the conversation goes a little bit further, they are going to say that they spend most of their time at home watching TV, because there is absolutely nothing to do." One of the main attractions of moving to the suburbs is acquiring ground of your own, yet you can travel for miles through suburbia and see no one doing anything in a yard other than working on the yard itself (often with the help of a riding lawnmower, one of the few four-wheeled passenger vehicles that get worse gas mileage than a Hummer). The modern suburban yard is perfectly, perversely self-justifying: its purpose is to be taken care of.

In 1801, in his first Inaugural address, Thomas Jefferson said that the American wilderness would provide growing room for democracy-sustaining agrarian patriots "to the thousandth and thousandth generation." Jefferson didn't foresee the interstate highway system, and his arithmetic was off, in any case, but he nevertheless anticipated (and, in many ways, embodied) the ethos of suburbia, of anti-urbanism, of sprawl. The standard object of the modern American dream, the single-family home surrounded by grass, is a mini-Monticello. It was the car that put it within our reach. But what a terrible price we have paid—and have yet to pay—for our liberation from the city.

DISCUSSION QUESTIONS

1. According to Owen, how is "compactness" of people and buildings an important component in living green?

2. How is Manhattan unlike many American cities in automobile use? And how does that difference affect the environment?

3. Why do people in cities use less electricity than people who live outside of cities?

4. What problems would many American cities have if they moved toward public transit?

COLLECTIVE BEHAVIOR AND SOCIAL MOVEMENTS: SOURCES OF SOCIAL CHANGE

COLLECTIVE BEHAVIOR
Fads and Fashions
Publics and Public Opinion
Responses to Disaster
Panic and Mass Hysteria
Crowds: Mobs, Riots, Audiences, Gatherings, and Other Collections
The Role of Rumor
SOCIAL MOVEMENTS
Types of Social Movements
The Structure of Social Movements
The Natural History of Social Movements
Social Movements as Agents of Social Change
READING: "THE LURE OF URBAN MYTHS," BY NEAL GABLER

W hat do "mooners" (who bare their backsides in public) have in common with flood victims attempting to recover from their disaster? What do both mooners and flood victims have in common with urban rioters and early Christians? These examples may appear a strange collection, but they all have one important similarity within the sociological outlook: all of them are norm breakers. It's true they break (or have broken) different norms, and flood victims do not choose to become refugees, but all of them replace standard patterns of behavior with something new. They also engage in these creative activities with collections of other people; neither mooners nor rioters can exist in the singular, and flood victims generally band together as the early Christians did. In the sociological outlook, such group norm-breaking activities come together to form the field of *collective behavior*. As we will see in this chapter, the existence of collective behavior raises some important questions about the degree to which social coordination controls our lives.

Collective behavior is unpatterned (or non-norm-governed) behavior that is typically transitory and spontaneous. The "collective" part of collective behavior is significant because this behavior emerges from the interactions among people. These interactions may occur in the same physical setting, as with a crowd, or they may cross both time and space, as with people who follow a fad because they know that others have done so. Breaking into a store is an individual crime, but looting is collective behavior. Believing that you are the son of God may win you a quick trip to a mental hospital, but belonging to a religious movement that believes in the second coming is collective behavior. Turning your hair orange and fashioning it into spikes could be the work of a berserk hairdresser or it could be a statement by a "with-it" member of the punk community. In each case the size of the group changes the way we think about the behavior. Moreover, the group itself can cause behavior to happen. An individual who might never think to break into a store might join in with looters during a protest rally. An individual who was never particularly religious might become so from associating with the members of a religious movement.

We have seen throughout this book that socialization results in people's becoming attached to their norms and values, and it usually takes something fairly forceful to push them out of their groove. It is easy to see how floods, tornadoes, and other disasters provide this push, but an economic depression or a political decision can also force people out of the norms of everyday life. In a strange twist of logic, social groups can keep people in line through social control measures while simultaneously creating conditions that drive people into spontaneous and often creative forms of collective behavior.

Even though collective behavior involves new or nonpatterned behavior, you should keep in mind that "new" is being used here in a relative sense. Is there in fact anything really new under the sun? Is there a form of behavior that has no relation to norms or roles that have gone before? Collective behavior might better be thought of as behavior governed by very loose norms in which participants engage in a great deal of behavioral improvisation. But the longer the behavior continues, the more likely norms are to develop. Who was the first mooner? Was that truly "new" behavior? Whether it was or not, many people copied the behavior in following months and years. A somewhat related form of collective behavior—streaking—began in the early 1970s yet was still with us in 1996 during the Wimbledon Tennis Tournament. By that time, the behavior had become somewhat ritualized (norm governed) and the nude woman streaker evoked smiles rather than shock from the crowd. And what of streaking today? The "new behavior" that sociologists label "collective behavior" often becomes fully ritualized. Consider the case of "professional" streaker Mark Roberts who streaked the 2004 Super Bowl and often carries advertising painted on his body.

While streaking began as spontaneous collective behavior in the 1970s, it has now moved into the mainstream. Professional streaker Mark Roberts carries advertising on his body while streaking large public occasions such as this sporting event.

Beyond being important in its own right, collective behavior is an important source of social change as that collective behavior that continues becomes more ritualized. The norms we follow today were created by someone who broke the norms that prevailed yesterday. In its early days Christianity was collective behavior, although today it is commonly found in rigidly structured formal organizations; the government of the United States was generated through collective behavior over two centuries ago. This chapter explores the wide range of collective behaviors, focusing in particular on their causes and the way they develop once they get started. Of the many forms collective behavior may take, the particular form known as the social movement is treated in a separate section because of its importance for social change.

COLLECTIVE BEHAVIOR

All collective behavior is spontaneous and collective; beyond these common characteristics it can comprise a wide range of human behaviors. It can be fairly trivial (such as doing "the wave" at football or baseball games) or highly significant (such as urban rioting). It can be looked on as fine and exemplary behavior by societal authorities (such as altruism in the face of a natural disaster), or it can receive the full force of repression from those same authorities (as is often the experience of revolutionary social movements). It can occur in small groups (as in a work group's effort to get their superior fired), or it can affect the whole society (such as a response to famine). The sociological outlook reveals a great variety of manifestations of collective behavior in everyday life.

FADS AND FASHIONS

Fads and fashions make up a separate category of collective behavior primarily because of their triviality. **Fads** are new forms of behavior that catch on among certain groups of people for a limited time. Fads break norms but not important norms, which means they usually do not upset societal authorities to any great extent; they also tend to disappear almost as quickly as they arise. Within this category we would include such examples as streaking, "Valley girl" talk, body piercing, and the like. Fads generally develop within specific social groups, with one of their functions being boundary maintenance; the group that follows the fad reminds itself and others that it is different from groups that don't. Interestingly, behavior that catches on primarily in poor or powerless social groups—such as young people or the urban poor—tends to be labeled as a fad; punk standards of dress and hair are a good example. If the behavior catches on in more influential social groups, it becomes fashion.

Fashion is basically the same as fads except that it characterizes the behavior of more powerful social groups and it tends to last longer than fads (probably because those social groups have more influence in "selling" their behavior as a model to the rest of society). Fashions include clothing styles (the most common use of the term),

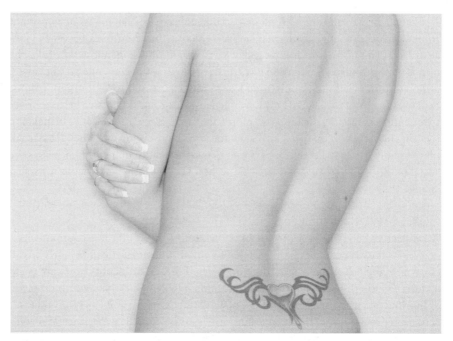

Following fashion can be painful, but perhaps not as painful as when the fashion fades but the tattoo doesn't.

but they also include hair length, leisure activities (such as jogging or tennis), reading preferences, styles of verbal expression, taste in art, and a whole variety of behaviors that certain social groups look upon as correct for certain times and places. As noted, fads can become fashions if they spread to the right groups. Longer hair for men, for example, first appeared as a fad with young people and then spread as a fashion to older people. Similarly, slang expressions can move from "the hood" to high society. Like fads, fashions also serve to maintain boundaries between groups. Wearing last year's clothes means either that you can't afford to change to this year's clothes or, even worse, that you're too "out of it" to know there has been a change. Part of the reason fashions change is to serve this boundary maintenance function (see Veblen, 1899).

Fads and fashions are collective behavior in that they introduce new forms of behavior and spread through the interactions of people. They are also somewhat trivial in terms of the norms they break—being "out of fashion" may result in your not being invited to the cool parties, but it will seldom result in a call to the police. Nevertheless, these forms are interesting to the sociologist in that they illustrate the persistence of social change within social groups. Collective behavior is not limited to deviants; it is an ongoing part of everyday life.

PUBLICS AND PUBLIC OPINION

One important kind of behavior generated within social groups and spread through interactions is people's attitudes and opinions about current issues. A **public** is a collection of people that forms because of their common concern about a current issue. Laws concerning abortion, for example, have led to the creation of publics as individuals have formed opinions through their interactions with others, ultimately finding themselves on one side or the other of the issue. These formed attitudes are referred to as **public opinion.**

As with ideas about clothing or hairstyles, opinions move through already existing social groups. Opposition to legal abortion, for example, formed a public from among American Catholics, who already had religious objections to it. On the other side of the coin, people already dedicated to women's rights favored legalized abortion as consistent with other attitudes they had already formed. There are comparable occurrences in regard to almost every major issue.

Just as members of social groups attempt to influence others to adhere to their fads and fashions, similar techniques are used in the formation of publics. The most notable technique is **propaganda**—the conscious attempt to manipulate public opinion through control over the nature and flow of information. Societal authorities are in an excellent position to use propaganda to sway public opinion toward support of their interests. A famous example is the systematic efforts by Hitler's propaganda minister, Joseph Goebbels, to maintain loyalty to the Third Reich. Such extreme examples, however, should not prevent us from being aware of the use of propaganda in everyday life in all societies. The United States today, for example, is a vast sea of propaganda representing almost every conceivable viewpoint on every imaginable issue. Unlike in Nazi Germany, however, more than one side is presented in most cases, which gives publics the right to choose which propaganda they wish to believe.

The measurement of public opinion is of interest to all members of society, not just sociologists (see Hart and Downing, 1992). In the United States the Gallup Poll and the Roper Poll are just two examples of the many full-time organizations devoted to collecting public opinion on a variety of issues. These organizations use standard sampling techniques: a small portion of a population is questioned with fairly reliable assumptions that the range of opinions within the sample will be the same as the range within the wider population. The programs we watch on television are determined in this manner, as the selections made on a relatively few television sets are assumed to represent the viewing preferences of the whole society. Within certain bounds of sampling error such sampling techniques are amazingly efficient.

The best-known use of public opinion polls in the United States is probably in the realm of politics. Every election produces endless polls on public preferences regarding candidates and ballot issues. Political polling raises an interesting question with regard to public opinion: when we find out that a majority of the people feel a certain way about something, are we more likely to join in, thus adding to the majority?

Polls give us remarkably accurate information, but they may also have an effect on the very information they hope to collect. This question becomes increasingly important when we notice newscasters confidently predicting results from voter polls before all the votes are cast.

RESPONSES TO DISASTER

Within the study of collective responses, *disaster* normally includes the human experience of such occurrences as earthquakes, hurricanes, floods, tornadoes, fires, and volcanic eruptions. With the exception of some fires and a very few floods, all these examples are natural and tend to strike quite rapidly. Some sociologists might also include some of the slower moving (and usually human-made) threats under this heading, such as overpopulation or famine. One reason they are not usually included is that their long-term impact gives people time to organize their behavior in response. Natural disasters, on the other hand, often strike an unprepared group of people who must be collectively creative at short notice. In such responses to disaster we find some of the classic examples of collective behavior.

Nevertheless, most disasters allow for some warning. Fires, earthquakes, and volcanic eruptions are currently exceptions, but scientific research improves constantly, bringing even those disasters somewhat under human control. At the other extreme, hurricanes can be tracked over great distances, giving people considerable time to prepare. Somewhere between these extremes are tornadoes—we can be warned of tornado-producing conditions though not of tornadoes themselves. The ambiguity in disaster warning produces collective behavior among the individuals involved as they attempt to verify the warnings. Rumors (which will be examined later) often accompany disaster warnings as individuals search for information and enthusiastically pass it on when they find it, accurate or not. Disaster warnings are most effective when they come from societal authorities who have had a good record in the past without too many false alarms.

People's experience with a particular kind of disaster plays a major role in their response to it. Hurricanes in the United States, for example, typically hit the southern Gulf states, and people who live in those areas gain experience from past hurricanes that they can use in coping with future ones (although massive hurricanes such as Katrina can go beyond normal preparations and produce collective behavior). The more experience a group of people has with a particular disaster in their immediate environment, the less their response will be an example of collective behavior. In fact, their disaster response may become routine, with particular members of the community taking on specific roles and following certain norms whenever the disaster hits. Consider, however, how people in Minnesota might respond to a hurricane, or how people in Florida might cope with a severe blizzard.

Responses to disaster most clearly take on the character of collective behavior when the people involved are unprepared for and inexperienced with the situation they face. Under these circumstances it is common for people who normally play

The flooding of New Orleans following hurricane Katrina in the summer of 2005 produced one of the least effective disaster responses imaginable and led to significant conflict regarding the assignment of blame.

insignificant roles to take on positions of authority. In a 1977 fire at the Beverly Hills Supper Club in northern Kentucky a busboy was instrumental in evacuating many people who otherwise would have died. This kind of role reversal is common in disaster response as those who had been in authority find their normal activities interrupted and useless in the new situation. It is also common to find ongoing social groups turning as groups to disaster recovery activities. A group of construction workers, for example, might work as a rescue unit during tornado recovery, leaving their old roles behind.

Disasters also have an effect on social groups after the initial impact. Generally, a disaster will create unity among those affected as it gives them a dramatic feeling of having shared an important common experience. The more they encounter outsiders who didn't share their experience, the more they may tend to have these feelings, which can last for years. The winter of 1977, a difficult one for many people, was particularly so in Buffalo, New York. After the snow cleared, T-shirts appeared that identified the wearer as having been through the winter of 1977 in Buffalo, and "survivors" celebrated their common experience at annual parties. Such occurrences are not unlike the veterans' organizations that form around common survival of the war experience.

The unity caused by disaster may turn to disunity if survivors attempt to assign blame for failures in the disaster recovery. Police departments and fire departments

SOCIAL CHANGE

PART 5 SOCIAL CHANGE

may be held accountable if residents feel they didn't respond properly in their assigned duties. As blame is assessed, its target may change. The 2003 fire at The Station nightclub in Rhode Island was initially blamed on the pyrotechnics employed by the band on the stage; later investigations found building code violations in the nightclub itself that may have contributed to the loss of life (CBS News, 2003). The destruction of coal mining communities in West Virginia by the flood of the Buffalo Creek is another good example of this phenomenon. The Buffalo Creek had been held back by an earth dam that had previously been called unsafe; when the dam gave way, it seemed fairly clear that efforts by the coal company to save a few dollars on dam construction cost many their lives and property. Not surprisingly, the coal company found itself facing lawsuits (Erikson, 1976).

As this book went to press, it had been one year since Hurricane Katrina hit the Gulf Coast of the United States and left massive damage in its wake. Government authorities at all levels were not prepared for an effective response, either before or after the impact, producing immediate disunity throughout the United States as blame for the response failure found its way to practically every conceivable door. Undoubtedly, the response failure will be investigated and responsibility will settle at some levels more than others. Perhaps another outcome will be improved hurricane response for future storms, moving that type of disaster response away from collective behavior and closer to routine behavior.

PANIC AND MASS HYSTERIA

Panic is a nonrational response to a threatening situation; specifically, it occurs when individuals perceive a danger, feel that escape is possible, and believe that the passing of time will make that escape less possible. The classic example of panic is probably the fire in the crowded theater, where the audience flees in a group toward the exits and clogs them, with the result that no one gets out. This hypothetical example is not so hypothetical; it comes from the Iroquois Theater fire of December 1903. A curtain caught fire, someone shouted "Fire!" and everyone ran toward the exits. There were too many people, and many of the doors would not open. Approximately six hundred people died in the crush; the fire itself was quickly put out and harmed no one.

Panic is believed to be a common response to disaster. We envision people wildly fleeing the oncoming flood, hurricane, or tornado. Actually, a much more common response to disaster (although far less colorful) is that people diligently go to work to limit the damage to people and property. The violence of many disasters often makes this response active and emotionally charged, but it should not be confused with panic. Agitated behavior can be rational, as there are times when it is rational to move quickly.

Mass hysteria refers to the spread of some nonrational belief or behavior throughout a group of people. It is similar to panic in many ways. Seeing the person in the seat next to you rush to an exit in a crowded theater can convince you to join in for fear

Panic, which is an emotional response to a threatening situation, may not always be irrational. The crowd shown here is reacting with panic—trying to get out of town—after poisonous fumes from a chemical plant began filling the air. The town is Bhopal, in India, 1984. The poison killed 2,000 people.

of being left behind in a fire; in that case, the form of escape spreads throughout the crowd as more and more people follow the modeled behavior. Mass hysteria also takes in other kinds of phenomena, however. In one incident investigated by Kerckhoff et al. (1965), sixty-two factory workers came to believe they were being bitten by bugs. The bugs didn't exist, but the workers' physical symptoms of rashes and nausea were very real. A similar study of mass hysteria in the workplace is described in Box 15.1.

Mass hysteria can take over in communities as well as in the smaller confines of the workplace. Medalia and Larsen (1958) studied a situation in Seattle in which people became convinced that some foreign substance was pitting the windshields of their cars. Conjecture was that meteors or perhaps radioactive fallout were responsible. The story appeared in newspapers and on the radio. People began covering their cars, and the mayor of Seattle ultimately appealed to President Eisenhower for help. As it turned out, Seattle had an average number of cars with pitted windshields. People tend to look through their windshields rather than at them; a concern such as windshield pitting can cause people to notice an ever-present aspect of their environment for the first time.

BOX 15.1

Take This Job and Shove It: Job Dissatisfaction and Mass Hysteria

Mass hysteria can occur wherever people congregate and face some kind of stress. The world of work commonly supplies both. On-the-job hysteria provides a natural setting for the sociologist of collective behavior, as some jobs are more stressful than others and people respond differently to the work they are given to do. Sidney Stahl and Marty Lebedun (1974) set out to study the relationship between on-the-job stress and mass hysteria.

On one day in March 1972, thirty-five women who worked at a university data-processing center became ill, suffering from fainting, nausea, and dizziness; ten of them required medical treatment. The cause of this mass illness was believed to be a gas (of unknown origin) in the atmosphere of the work setting. The building was evacuated and the air inside tested. No unusual gas could be detected. In addition, the blood and urine of the affected workers were tested. Nothing was found in any of the tests, and the building was opened again. The next day more women became ill, and the building was once again closed. Again, no physical reason for the illness was found. Enter the sociologists.

Comparing the symptoms of illness the workers exhibited with how much they liked their work, Stahl and Lebedun found an interesting correlation: the more dissatisfied a woman was with her job, the more severe her symptoms. Apparently a job can make you sick in more ways than is commonly thought. For these women the spreading illness was apparently an appealing alternative to work they would rather not do. Stahl and Lebedun do not suggest that the illness was a charade by the women but rather that mass hysteria spreads more quickly in ground made fertile by social stress.

A similar study by Kerckhoff and his colleagues (1965) found that hysteria on the job spread primarily among friends; if your friend got sick, you would be much more likely to follow suit. Stahl and Lebedun checked these findings with the women in the data-processing center and found similar results. The women with the most severe symptoms tended to be friendly with other women with severe symptoms; women less affected by the gas were friendly with other women less affected. These women did not sit together on the jobs, so location in the building was not a factor.

What can we learn from such studies of mass hysteria? First, collective behavior may be new and different, but it often follows old paths. In both of these studies the hysteria spread through the chains of friendship that existed prior to the outbreak. Second, the study by Stahl and Lebedun suggests that certain social circumstances "encourage" collective behavior to occur. In particular, the change brought about by collective behavior becomes more appealing when we wish to avoid stress in our everyday lives.

A similar case of community-wide hysteria occurred in Mattoon, Illinois, in September 1944 (Johnson, 1945). A woman reported that someone had opened her bedroom window and sprayed her with a gas that made her feel ill and partially paralyzed her legs. The story of the "phantom anesthetist" appeared in the newspapers. On the next day the police were notified of another attack, and two days later of two more. Over a space of about a week, the police received twenty-three reports of attacks by the phantom anesthetist. Scientists reported that no known gas could have produced the symptoms that people reported. The only other conclusion is that the residents of Mattoon were the victims of a mass hysteria in which their collective beliefs made them sick.

Probably the most famous case in this group of phenomena has been called both panic and mass hysteria, highlighting the similarity between these two kinds of behavior. On October 30, 1938, Orson Welles produced a radio program dramatizing H. G. Wells's novel *The War of the Worlds*. The novel described an invasion of earth by alien creatures. Welles gave the program a sense of reality (as a Halloween joke) by presenting the story in the form of news bulletins and changing the locale from England to New Jersey. Many people became highly agitated upon hearing the program, believing that a real invasion was occurring, and some of them even attempted to flee the areas described in the program as the site of the invasion (Cantril, 1966).

A more recent version of mass hysteria concerns the spread of belief in Satanism by Americans. With the help of talk shows and tabloids, many Americans have become convinced that an elaborate body of Satan worshippers exists in the United States. Children have come forth with tales (sometimes remembered through hypnosis) of strange Satanic happenings in their childhood. Others have produced stories of witnessing strange rites carried out by their friends and neighbors. Efforts to track down these cases, however, have proved largely fruitless; the attractiveness of the hysteria as well as its spread are generally attributed to fundamentalist Protestant groups for whom the belief provides consistency with religious beliefs (Jenkins and Maier-Katkin, 1992).

The causes of panic and mass hysteria in various cases have been linked to overwork, economic insecurity, boredom, and lack of intelligence. Their spread is also associated with group phenomena, however. Hysteria in the workplace follows pre-existing friendship groups; people get sick by following models provided by their friends. In the case of panic the actions of the person next to you can influence your behavior. As with most forms of collective behavior, the collective part is a major factor. This brings us to probably the ultimate object of study within the field of collective behavior: the crowd.

CROWDS: MOBS, RIOTS, AUDIENCES, GATHERINGS, AND OTHER COLLECTIONS

The **crowd situation** is one in which a large number of people are in face-to-face contact with each other in a particular physical setting. As we've seen, collective behavior can occur even when people are not together—as in the case of publics, fads, or fashions. The crowd situation, however, is considered the ultimate form of collective behavior because of the immediacy with which communication occurs and because of the social pressure generated by the physical presence of others.

Types of Crowds Not all crowds are examples of collective behavior. Collective behavior is determined by the degree to which behavior follows norms. Some crowds, such as audiences, behave pretty much the same way from one situation to the next. Performers, who are most acutely aware of this, use their knowledge of audience norms to manipulate the experience of people in the audience. A political speaker wishing to generate enthusiasm will alter the content of a speech as well as the style of delivery to suit the audience at hand; out-of-work factory workers will be addressed differently than business leaders. Rock musicians want to produce certain audience experiences so that individuals will have a good time and subsequently buy their records. Musical material will be presented in such an order that excitement builds; if the performer has a popular number everyone is waiting for, it may be saved for the supposedly spontaneous encore, giving the audience the illusion that they provoked their favorite number themselves through the enthusiasm of their ovation. Everyone leaves happy. Members of the audience have an enthusiastic, spontaneous experience that is carefully planned for them. Yelling and shouting does not necessarily make for collective behavior.

A similar example of planned spontaneity occurs in religious gatherings. Some fundamentalist religious services rely on growing excitement and enthusiasm within the crowd. The leader may typically be a trained evangelist who travels from town to town for such services. Wimberly and his colleagues (1975) studied one gathering from the Billy Graham Crusade and discovered that much of the spontaneity is carefully planned. In particular, the experience of "coming forward" to be saved is encouraged by behavioral models provided by "counselors." The authors observed, however, that these models may not even have been necessary, as many people in the audience seemed to have made advance plans for being saved at a particular point in the ritual set aside for that event. In short, it is necessary to look closely at crowds to determine the degree to which people are breaking new ground or following old norms.

Crowds can be active or expressive. **Acting crowds** are those with an apparent goal outside the crowd itself. Riots or lynch mobs would fall under this heading. **Expressive crowds** are those formed solely for the self-expression of the members. Some religious gatherings are expressive in that their members come together solely for the communal expression of religious faith.

When crowds are examples of collective behavior, the norms that are broken may be important or trivial from the point of view of societal authorities. Sports fans throwing trash onto the playing field during a game would be violating a relatively trivial norm, whereas rioters engaged in arson, violence, and looting would receive a much more violent response. But both are examples of collective behavior.

While soccer can produce angry and violent crowds, the destruction in France
during the fall of 2005 had its roots in the lack of social and economic acceptance
faced by French citizens of African and Middle Eastern ancestry.

Finally, we should note a learning factor in crowd behavior. A certain crowd behavior may be novel and inventive today but governed by norms tomorrow. Sociologists who study collective behavior are particularly interested in the formation of novel behavior in the group setting and the way that behavior spreads. After it happens once, it can be planned the next time or at least more easily picked up on by crowd participants. At some time in the distant past, for example, a college football crowd decided to tear down the goal posts after a game; that was collective behavior. But how about the many instances of the same crowd behavior that have occurred since the first? Are they collective behavior, or do they fall closer to the heading of norm-governed behavior? At what point is repeated behavior norm-governed and no longer inventive? The type of crowd under study must be examined carefully in this light.

Theories of Crowd Behavior The first serious theorist of crowd behavior has influenced sociological theory ever since. Gustave LeBon presented his theory in his 1897 work *The Mind of Crowds*. To LeBon crowds were far more than the sum of their members; they had an existence in their own right. He pictured crowd members as having lost all sense of rational thought and being highly suggestible to whatever ideas dominated the crowd. LeBon spoke of the law of mental unity in crowds, in which individuals were "leveled" into the common denominator of a "group mind." This state was brought about by an effective leader who, according to LeBon, "hypnotized" the crowd members through rhetoric, flattery, and the repetition of important symbols. In this situation crowd members came to see themselves as anonymous parts of the whole, ignored the norms and values that had previously governed their lives, and developed an irrational sense of their own invincibility ("No one can stop us now," etc.). In short, LeBon pictured crowd members as a herd of sheep likely to do anything their leader directed.

LeBon's theory is the basis for most popular conceptions of crowd behavior, particularly those fostered by Hollywood. In movies, people in crowds are swayed by persuasive speakers, begin making noises like a bunch of animals, and march off to lynch some poor devil in the local jail. If the victim turns out to be innocent (which is usually the case), the mob participants individually search their consciences at the end of the movie, wondering how they could have done such a thing. The famous western novel (and subsequent film) *The Ox-Bow Incident* by Walter Van Tilburg Clark is a classic example of this perspective. The crowd is pictured as a totally uncontrolled and irrational creature capable of dangerous acts, and individuals within it are given no credit for thinking for themselves.

Modern theories of crowd behavior have been heavily influenced by LeBon, but many of them have moved away from this extreme position to some degree. American sociologist Herbert Blumer (1969) followed fairly close to LeBon with his idea of circular reaction. Ignoring LeBon's emphasis on the hypnotic leader, Blumer maintained that irrational crowd behavior is generated among the crowd members themselves as they react to each other in a circular manner. In panic, for example, my running for an exit would encourage you to do the same. When I see you begin to run, I become all the more convinced that my behavior was correct in the first place and begin to run faster and so on. In this way, says Blumer, crowd behavior operates by **contagion:** as with a virus, its spread is apparently beyond the control of the individual members.

Neil Smelser is another American sociologist of crowd behavior and one of the most famous; his book *Theory of Collective Behavior* (1962) generated considerable research in crowd behavior (see Box 15.2). Smelser maintains that a series of events must occur for crowd collective behavior to occur:

1. There must first be *structural conduciveness.* An urban race riot, for example, could not occur without the urban concentrations of two or more races; student draft protests could not occur without colleges that concentrate people of draft age.
2. There must be *structural strain,* described by Smelser as tensions or contradictions that are built into society. For example, Americans value equality, yet inequalities exist between the sexes and among different ethnic and racial groups.
3. A *generalized belief* must develop. In many ways the central element of Smelser's theory, the generalized belief is a definition of the situation that develops among crowd members as to what they dislike and what should be done about it. According to Smelser, the generalized belief short-circuits reality, often producing an irrational picture and an unjustified victim for crowd violence.
4. A *precipitating event* must occur. In an urban race riot, for example, the arrest of an African American might set things off.
5. *Mobilization* comes next. The crowd must be able to assemble, spread the generalized belief, and act.
6. The *response by societal authorities* (such as police) may serve to end the crowd violence or to promote it, depending on how the authorities act. For example, police efforts to disperse crowds are an attempt to interrupt the assembly process; bluffing force and not carrying through encourages rioters.

According to Smelser, a break in the action at any point in this chain will end the episode of collective behavior. This can even be accomplished at the first stage of structural conduciveness. College campuses, for example, commonly have centralized meeting places (usually around the library or a student union building) where students gather and pass through between classes. Such a meeting place, says Smelser, invites collective behavior. If universities were built without such areas (and some are), university authorities could save themselves a lot of trouble. At the other extreme, we've already noted that police interference in the assembly process can terminate the collective behavior episode. As simple a matter as cutting off the

BOX 15.2

A Study of a Riot: The Kent State Incident

The Vietnam War was the cause of considerable political activity on college campuses during the 1960s. President Nixon's announcement in the spring of 1970 that the United States had invaded Cambodia caused violent activity on campuses throughout the country, but the deaths that occurred on the campus of Kent State University are the most remembered today.

What happened at Kent State? That particular question raises many of the general problems faced by sociologists who study collective behavior. For many reasons riots are very difficult to study; some of the reasons for these difficulties will be apparent as we try to piece together what happened at Kent State, following the research of sociologist Jerry M. Lewis (1972).

After Nixon's announcement, political activities began to build at Kent State. On Friday, May 1, two peaceful rallies were held. That night, in downtown Kent, Ohio, people began gathering in the streets, shouting antiwar chants, and throwing bottles. They were joined by people from the downtown bars. This larger crowd was in turn joined by the local police in riot gear, who attempted to disperse the crowd. The crowd grew and became more violent. During this time the police closed the bars, which resulted in putting still more people into the street and forming a larger crowd.

On Saturday morning rumors began to fly. One persistent rumor was that members of a radical and sometimes violent left-wing organization, the Weathermen, were in town; the rumor was never substantiated. Saturday evening a crowd gathered on the University Commons, a central meeting point on the Kent State campus. The crowd grew to over a thousand and began to take notice of the nearby ROTC building, an old barracks structure. Some rocks were thrown at the building, and it was finally set on fire. Firemen arrived and had their hoses cut. The riot police arrived with tear gas and dispersed the crowd. And while all of this was going on, the National Guard was quietly moving onto the campus.

On Sunday morning Governor James Rhodes of Ohio arrived in Kent and announced, "I think we are up against the strongest, well-trained militant group that has ever assembled in America," repeating the rumor that moved throughout Kent the day before (Lewis, 1972, 90). Sunday evening there was a brief sit-in, which was dispersed by the National Guard.

Classes resumed on Monday morning, but people began to gather on the Commons around noon. The Guard believed that rallies had been prohibited on campus, though there is some evidence that not all the students knew this (Taylor et al., 1971), and many students who did know of the prohibition felt the Guard had no right to make or enforce rules on campus. The rally grew. In response to this apparent threat to their authority, the National Guardsmen moved to disperse the crowd.

The crowd broke up into several groups and took to throwing rocks and tear-gas canisters, the latter in an attempt to return the canisters to their source (the Guardsmen). At one point the Guard marched to the top of a hill and began firing on the crowd, leaving four dead and nine wounded. Five hours later, the campus was closed and most students had gone home. Shortly thereafter, most campuses around the country closed as well to prevent similar occurrences.

Once again, what happened at Kent State? All those involved have vested interests in presenting an account that reflects well on them. The Guardsmen were young and untrained. Were they ordered to fire, or was firing on the crowd a mini-act of collective behavior within the overall scene? The Guardsmen aren't saying, since no one wants to take responsibility. Did the students really know about the rule prohibiting rallies on campus, or is ignorance of the rule a convenient excuse after the fact? The students believed (or later said they believed) the Guardsmen would never shoot, but they did. The Guardsmen believed the student rally was carefully orchestrated by a militant group, but it wasn't. The flow of information was not smooth.

Were the students a herd of sheep led by a hypnotic leader, or were they a mixed bag with a variety of motives for being there? According to Lewis, there were different kinds of crowd members—the active core, the cheerleaders, and the spectators; members of all three groups became victims of rifle fire. Furthermore, there was no single effective leader of the crowd; the events that occurred emerged from the collective situation and not through careful planning.

Lewis was particularly interested in Neil Smelser's (1962) theory of collective behavior and wanted to see whether it applied to Kent State. Much of it did, he discovered, with the major exception of Smelser's emphasis on a generalized belief. According to Smelser, the crowd situation thrives on ambiguity and anxiety; the generalized belief is a belief generated within the crowd that eliminates this ambiguity and anxiety by assigning blame to whichever societal authority happens to be handy. At Kent State the National Guard was forced into the role of facing student hostility toward the government. Anger toward the Nixon administration had turned to anger toward the presence of the Guard on campus. On the other hand, says Lewis, the predicted anxiety was missing. Students at Kent were not the subjects of some nameless confusion and worry; they were very angry and knew exactly what angered them. They were, in short, not a herd of sheep.

speaker's microphone or turning off lights at night during a political rally, for example, would prevent communication within the crowd and could break up the crowd behavior.

Smelser makes two important departures from LeBon and Blumer. First, his emphasis on structural strain suggests that crowd members may actually have some reason for their behavior, particularly in the case of violent outbursts such as riots.

Interestingly, neither LeBon nor Blumer assumes that rioters have any justification whatsoever for their behavior. Second, through his idea of the generalized belief, Smelser focuses on the ideas that motivate crowd members. This concept takes away somewhat from his emphasis on strain since he assumes that the belief will probably have little to do with the actual source of the strain. He also assumes that all crowd members will adhere to this belief equally rather than thinking for themselves. Nevertheless, he does raise the issue of how crowd members think, which is at least a step away from LeBon's herd of sheep.

A differing view of the crowd is provided by Turner and Killian's *emergent norm perspective* (Turner and Killian, 1972). According to this theory, norm-governed behavior develops (or emerges) within the crowd situation as the crowd members interact; individuals look to each other for models of action and ultimately come to agreement and act in concert. They do not, however, necessarily do so with the same motives or for the same reasons. Crowd members may vary considerably in their commitment to the crowd and its emerging actions. Some may be little more than spectators, while others may have hopes of manipulating the crowd and exploiting it for their own purposes. A crowd viewed through the emergent norm perspective may appear unified in action, but not because it is a herd of sheep.

At the far extreme from LeBon we find the theories of Richard Berk (1974a, 1974b). Berk believes that crowd members are as rational as anyone else and enter the crowd situation with the same question we would have in entering a game: how can I win? Say you are in a crowd and interested in acquiring a little free merchandise from the nearby electronics store through looting. You know that if thousands of people begin looting, the chances of your getting caught will go down. If no one else joins in, however, you may very likely get caught. Therefore, you will be interested in estimating the number of other crowd members who might go along with such behavior, and they will be watching you with the same interests. According to Berk, all the crowd members are asking themselves these same questions, deciding what they want to achieve and trying to estimate the chances for their personal success or failure in reaching this end. The contagion described by LeBon and Blumer is not the result of irrational thinking, says Berk, but rather the product of a great many individual thinking processes coming to the same conclusion at the same time.

Berk differs from all other theorists in two major ways. First, he assumes that crowd members have concerns vital to them and that they use the crowd situation to satisfy those concerns. Reasons for crowd behavior will be found not in hypnotic leaders or animal instincts but in perceived injustices and inequalities in society. Second, Berk says that crowd members are rational in their thinking processes and they may not all think the same way (as opposed to Smelser's generalized belief). For instance, some may loot for the goods, while others may join in for the excitement. All this individual behavior becomes sociologically important in the ways individuals estimate support for various courses of action. My engaging in a given behavior may encourage you to join in, and, together, we may encourage a third party. Each new person joins in more readily, since a large number of people engaging in the same behavior lowers the potential costs to each new person. Crowds are contagious, says Berk, but not for the reasons normally assumed.

Berk's observation that crowd members may not think the same way is illustrated by the 1999 protests in Seattle, Washington, against a World Trade Organization meeting. The AFL-CIO organized thousands of marchers into peaceful protests. Meanwhile, other groups instigated property damage—a result definitely opposed by organized labor. The protests in the streets brought together anarchists, labor organizers, environmentalists, and other diverse groups that normally have different interests and different organizational strategies. The overall result in Seattle was major disruption, but the pieces of that puzzle were complex indeed (Levi and Olson, 2000).

Another perspective on crowds is offered by the social behavioral/interactionist perspective of Clark McPhail and his students (see McPhail, 1991). The social behavioral/interactionist perspective also brings us some distance from LeBon in that it suggests that there is no real difference between crowd behavior and any other kind of human behavior. People enter into crowds (according to this perspective) as they enter into any social situation, depending upon their interests, their free time, their personal connections with other people involved, and their knowledge that the situation exists for them to join. Once in the crowd, people respond to forms of communication (either from other crowd members or from outsiders, such as police) about upcoming behaviors and subsequent movements (termed *collective locomotion*). McPhail's perspective is extremely sensitive to physical factors that affect these processes. For example, the presence of a wide open area (such as a square or campus central area) facilitates a crowd's assembling by providing open space and not interfering with communication processes necessary for crowd instructions. Narrow, closed-in areas make these processes difficult. If smoke is added to such closed-in areas, as in a burning building, communication is further hindered, collective locomotion (here, evacuation of the building) is difficult, and deaths occur. From McPhail's point of view, crowds are full of normal people engaging in normal interaction in sometimes unusual and unclear settings.

Theories of Crowd Formation Questions about why crowds form are related to questions about how they act. If you assume crowds behave as they do because of some herd instinct, your theory of crowd formation will look into why people become susceptible to joining the herd. If you assume that crowd members have valid complaints about their social situation, your theory of crowd formation will focus on how people in social groups come to develop those complaints. Though it may seem that theories of crowd formation should logically come before theories of crowd behavior, in practice most sociologists have studied the matter the other way around.

At the most basic level crowds draw crowds. You can test this proposition easily with a few friends. First, go to a busy pedestrian thoroughfare, stop, and fix your eyes on anything up high (a building if there is one). Have a confederate note how many people look where you are looking and how many people stop to look where you are looking. You probably won't attract too many. Then try the same experiment with six or eight friends all looking at the same thing. According to most sociological research, a much higher percentage of passersby should become interested in your behavior, perhaps stopping to ask a few questions. In other words, once a crowd gets started, there appears to be a momentum factor that helps keep it going. But what gets people there in the first place or keeps them there after they've stopped out of curiosity?

The *outside agitator explanation* ties in with the herd instinct theories. According to this perspective, outsiders trained in crowd-formation techniques may systematically get a local population worked up with untrue rumors and effective speaking techniques. This theory of crowd formation is adequate only if you believe that a few trained organizers can effectively control (or hypnotize) a group of basically unwilling crowd participants. Today this theory most commonly comes from societal authorities who have just had a riot on their hands and wish to make it clear that local problems were not the cause (for example, see Box 15.2 on explanations surrounding the Kent State killings).

The *riff-raff theory* of crowd formation blames the crowd members rather than the leaders. This theory assumes that crowd members are typically the malcontents and ne'er-do-wells of the community who have never accomplished anything and who generally look for trouble. This particular theory has been studied a little more than some of the others and has been found wanting in most cases. In the United States urban riots of the late 1960s, for example, it was found that rioters were more likely than nonrioters to be educated, long-term residents of the city and have high occupational aspirations; they tended to be roughly the same as nonrioters in income and community activities (Perry and Pugh, 1978). In the student rebellions of the 1960s the students who took part tended to have higher grade point averages and parents of higher occupational prestige than those who did not take part (Middleton and Putney, 1963). According to most research, those who are really down and out don't actively complain about it too much.

The *mass society theory* was first applied to crowd formation by LeBon. According to this theory, modern society tends to cut people adrift from their traditional moorings in small, stable social groups characteristic of smaller, less urban environments. As society has changed from a collection of many small groups to a collection of individuals, there have been two important results. First, individuals are no longer insulated from persuasive leaders by the confines of their small groups. Second, the social control function of the small group is gone, which makes individuals more likely to get carried away in the crowd situation, thinking little of the consequences of their actions. In short, modern society leaves individuals open to manipulation from outsiders. Mass society theory assumes that manipulation is the key to crowd behavior; not surprisingly, it fits in well with the theories of LeBon and Blumer.

Absolute deprivation theory is the first of the crowd-formation theories to focus on reasons for participants to join the crowd. This very simple theory states that people deprived of social rewards (jobs, money, respect, etc.) will be the most likely to join acting crowds. It also predicts that the greater the deprivation, the more likely the participation. The theory makes sense—but it doesn't work well. As we've seen, people who are really down and out rarely take any action at all. In many societies researchers have noted a strange conservatism among those at the bottom when they are faced with the possibility of change. It would seem that, from their perspective, any change would have to be for the better, but they don't appear to see it that way.

Relative deprivation theory turns away from actual deprivation and focuses on perceived deprivation (Morrison, 1971). In other words, it's not so much a matter of how deprived you are but how deprived you think you are—which will probably be determined by which people you compare yourself to. Most Americans, for example, compare themselves not to Bill Gates (against whom we would all feel terribly deprived) but to the people down the block. If the neighbors get a new car and you can't afford one, you will feel deprived. The real question for relative deprivation theory is the reasons people select particular others for purposes of comparison. In the United States today the mass media have widened the scope for most of us in the kinds of comparisons we make. For example, we become aware of the hourly wages a certain union has achieved for its members. We also become aware of how much others in our own occupation make in other locations. If we're in a minority group, we become aware of the political gains made by other minorities elsewhere. The relative of relative deprivation is a rapidly changing social phenomenon.

The *J-curve theory of rising expectations* is one of the more sophisticated of the modern deprivation theories (Davies, 1969). According to the J-curve theory, what we want (or expect) is generally one step ahead of what we get. If our situation has been improving over time, our expectations will begin to rise at the same speed. Normally, this creates a gap we can tolerate. Collective behavior occurs when something happens to the satisfaction of our needs. For example, if our society experiences a severe depression, our economic situation will go down (thus creating the J of the J-curve), yet our expectations will continue to rise at the same rate they had been; most of us have expectations rising well into the future, based on the current rate of improvement in our experience. If we have been enjoying increasing degrees of political freedom and are then faced with less, once again the gap will occur. Whatever the case, the source of our perceived deprivation has little to do with our objective situation; it is the product of our rising expectations. This theory has been used to explain the urban riots of the late 1960s, in which black inner-city residents took to the streets in many American cities just a few years after the passage of the 1964 Civil Rights Act. The new law caused expectations to rise but did little to elevate the satisfaction of needs in the black community.

These theories reflect some of the variety and some of the contradictions in the sociological explanations of crowd formation. (Many of them can also be applied to the formation of social movements, which sometimes emerge from crowd situations.) Nevertheless, there are still more unanswered than answered questions about crowd formation. For example, the economic situation of most black Americans was little better in the 1970s and 1980s than in the 1960s, yet there was little crowd violence in those two decades. The J-curve would have predicted it with the rising unemployment and high inflation that characterized that period. Relative deprivation theory would also have predicted crowd violence due to the increased knowledge we all have of each other and the tendency we have to take a more global perspective on our problems. No doubt sociologists will add new theories to our list, and those additions will be very welcome.

THE ROLE OF RUMOR

We come finally to an aspect of collective behavior that colors all others: rumor. A **rumor** is a piece of information that spreads among members of a group. It is neither accurate nor inaccurate by necessity; it can be either, and is often partly both. Sociologists of collective behavior are interested in how rumors spread, why they spread, and how they affect other instances of collective behavior.

Rumors typically are unconfirmed pieces of information. Unconfirmed means that societal authorities have either not taken a stand on the information or are unable to convince people when they do. Rumors travel most readily in social situations that are ambiguous to the participants (Buckner, 1965). People who are unsure as to "what's going on" will be the most likely to turn to rumor for answers. Generally, people believe what they see on television or read in the papers, and through these media societal authorities can pass on information that may end a rumor by making the situation less ambiguous. It should be kept in mind, however, that people do not always believe such information. Societal authorities may also present inaccurate information intentionally if it serves their purposes; thus, an accurate rumor may be replaced by inaccurate "official information."

Just as important as situation ambiguity is the importance of the information (Buckner, 1965). People are unlikely to spend their time receiving or passing on information they don't care about. Generally speaking, the greater the importance of a particular piece of information, the more quickly the rumor will spread.

The third factor influencing the spread of rumor is the critical ability of the individuals among whom the rumor is spreading—the ability of an individual (or a group of individuals) to determine the truth or falsity of a rumor from past experience (Buckner, 1965). Important information in a highly ambiguous social situation may be ignored if the participants have good reasons for not believing the rumor they receive. Different groups of people will have different critical abilities about different kinds of information. Nuclear scientists, for example, would probably respond to rumors of a meltdown at the local nuclear power plant differently than you or I would. Those same scientists, however, might have an uncritical ability in relation to rumors about local politics.

Rumors can be accurate, but they are more prone to inaccuracies. According to Gordon Allport and Leo Postman (1947), three processes help good information "go bad": leveling, sharpening, and assimilation. Leveling eliminates detail from the rumor as it passes from person to person. Sharpening, working in concert with leveling, is the process by which elements of the rumor become emphasized in the telling. Finally, assimilation refers to the changes rumors go through to fit the prejudices of the teller. People commonly want to alter rumors somewhat to make them more interesting or to illustrate an important concern they have.

The accuracy of rumor is greatly affected by the social network within which it moves. A rumor can move from person to person with each person hearing it only once. In this instance the rumor can change meaning greatly as each person has a chance to alter it. On the other hand, a rumor can move within a social group in which all members interact with each other. The rumor bounces off all group members as A tells it to B, B tells it to C, and C tells it back to A. In such a situation group members will notice changes in the rumor's content.

Rumors can be a form of harmless recreation or can have devastating results for the individuals or groups involved. An example of the former would be the growing number of urban legends that have grown and spread throughout the United States. Urban legends are stories that are generally presented as having happened to a friend or a friend of a friend (see the reading by Gabler at the end of this chapter). The stories are typically harmless but have a punch line that helps them spread. One such famous rumor concerns a pet lover who comes across (or sometimes runs over) a cat, which soon dies. The pet lover places the dead cat in a brown paper sack (not wanting to leave it on the road) and the sack is subsequently stolen. The thief is located when she (or he) faints after looking in the sack some blocks away (Brunvand, 1981).

An example of rumors in less playful senses would be rumors about products or corporations. The McDonald's wormburger episode is one of the more famous. The rumor spread that McDonald's hamburgers contained worm meat—the Big Mac had become the Crawling Mac. Business at McDonald's fell rapidly until the rumor faded away. And lest you think the rumor might have been started by a competitor of McDonald's, the rumor actually began about Wendy's hamburgers and, for some reason, switched victims. Of the corporation rumors, the most famous is the rumor connecting Procter & Gamble to Satan worship. This old rumor has been spread through church newsletters as well as word of mouth. There is always someone who claims to have seen some top executive from the company on a television talk show (the show varies) claiming that a portion of Procter & Gamble's profits is donated to Satan worship every year. Even the corporate logo is interpreted as symbolizing this devotion. While these rumors may seem crazy or silly, they cost American business dearly in lost sales and extra advertising designed to combat the rumors.

The process of rumor transmission is a form of collective behavior itself. In addition, rumors also play roles in disaster recovery, mobs, riots, mass hysteria, panic, and other forms of collective behavior. Disaster warnings typically are accompanied by rumors; the less accurate or dependable the official warnings, the more common the rumors. Mass hysteria and some kinds of panic depend on the spread of rumor for the spread of the collective behavior. It is probably in mobs and riots, however, that rumors have one of the clearest and most important roles.

Almost all sociologists of collective behavior agree that riots form around some kind of precipitating event, or spark, that sets things off. As with checking a gas tank with a lighted match, the cause of the conflagration is more the gas than the match, but both are necessary. In the case of race riots, precipitating events typically have a heavy symbolic meaning, such as the arrest of an African American by a white police officer. Such precipitating events gain importance through their spread by rumor. For example, a riot that occurred in Harlem, New York, in 1935 began with the arrest of an African American youth for stealing a knife from a department store. The boy's hand was cut during the arrest, and he was taken to the basement of the store to wait for an ambulance. A rumor spread that the boy had been taken to the basement for the police to beat him up. This rumor was supported by the arrival of the ambulance (Perry and Pugh, 1978).

A similar event and rumor occurred at the beginning of the Newark, New Jersey, riot of 1967. An African American cab driver was arrested for driving with a revoked license. Upon arriving at the police station, he either refused or was unable to walk and was dragged into the station in full view of a housing project across the street. Residents in the project started the rumor that the cab driver had been beaten by the police. In addition, the cab company was notified of the arrest, and the news spread to cab drivers all over town on their car radios. Complaints were received by local African American leaders, but by the time they arrived at the police station to check on the cab driver, a crowd was already beginning to form on the grounds of the housing project. The riot began that night and escalated on following nights. The rumor escalated along with the riot, proclaiming by then that the cab driver had died of his beating (National Advisory Commission on Civil Disorders, 1968). There were longstanding divisions between the police department and the black community of Newark, and police brutality was not unknown. Thus the rumor fit in well with already existing prejudices held by the black community toward the police, was spread for that reason, and helped set off the riot that followed.

While rumors often accompany urban disturbances, a definite word or two of caution is in order here. First, not all riots contain rumors that have any impact on the riot's outcome. Second, and more important, riots often have very real causes in community tensions that can be overlooked or trivialized by a focus on rumors. By way of example, the Miami riot of 1980 began over the trial of several white policemen. Race relations had never been good between the black community of Miami and the largely white police force. Events came to a head when an African American, Arthur McDuffie, attempted to elude police on a motorcycle and was beaten to death by a group of policemen when they caught him. Enough were involved that some testified (under immunity) against the others. Medical evidence supported the testimony; the injuries could not have been caused by a motorcycle accident. Nevertheless, the officers were acquitted. On that day, a riot began in the Liberty City black area of Miami and lasted for several days, leaving a number of both whites and blacks dead (Porter and Dunn, 1984). If this sounds familiar, it should. The riots following the trial of the police accused of beating Rodney King in Los Angeles seem to be a close repeat of history.

The study of rumor focuses on one aspect of collective behavior—communication—and shows how communication processes affect other aspects of collective behavior. Information spreads in much the same way (and at the same time) as riot behavior, disaster responses, or mass hysteria.

SOCIAL MOVEMENTS

Social movements are organized efforts by groups of people to bring about social change, either in the members themselves or in members and society alike. Social movements are considered to be a type of collective behavior because they deviate from societal norms and values, yet their often high degree of social organization makes them look very much like the organized social life they seek to change. Unlike mobs, riots, or disaster responses, in which group behavior emerges on the spur of the moment, social movements develop leaders and followers, goals and tactics, and their own set of norms and values to govern all these roles and activities. Because they are highly coordinated forms of group life, social movements are easier for sociologists to study than other forms of collective behavior; some would even argue that they are not collective behavior at all since they lack spontaneity compared with crowds. Nevertheless, social movements often emerge from other forms of collective behavior and, perhaps more important, are responsible for a major portion of the social change that arises from collective behavior in general. Riots rarely bring about lasting change, but social movements can change the whole fabric of society when they are successful in attaining their goals.

TYPES OF SOCIAL MOVEMENTS

Though all social movements seek to bring about social change, they vary considerably in the kind and degree of change they seek. Those movements that seek change in the outside society (that is, outside the movement) can vary from revolutionary movements to reform movements. **Revolutionary movements** seek massive change in the society. The Communist Party in Czarist Russia, for example, brought about the end of the ruling family and of the whole system of politics and economics governed by that family; rule by the aristocratic elite was replaced by rule of the Communist Party, and private ownership of property was largely replaced by state ownership. **Reform movements,** by contrast, seek far less radical change, preferring to work within the existing system. In the United States, for example, the civil rights movement sought equal rights and opportunities for African Americans within the democratic capitalistic system already in force. The goal was not to change the operation of the society but to include blacks within that operation. Reform movements typically want to change the way the pie is sliced rather than create a different pie.

Reform and revolutionary movements are ideal types in that few actual social movements fit perfectly into either category. Rather, they represent a range in terms of the amount of social change they seek. Any but the smallest reforms will have some lasting effect on the structure of society, while even the most vocal revolutionary movements retain some traces of the old order if they are successful. This range is an important one to keep in mind, however, for the way societal authorities perceive the social movement will determine the way they respond to it. Not surprisingly, revolutionary movements often receive violent repression from established authorities since their goal is the overthrow of those authorities; reform movements, on the other hand, can even lean toward respectability if their means and goals agree with established values and don't threaten authorities.

Social movements also vary in the kind of social change they seek. Specifically, some social movements seek to transform only their own members and have no desire for any social change outside the boundaries of their movement. This is particularly common with some religious movements that seek to change the spiritual life of individuals but care little about political power or the distribution of economic rewards in society. The Shakers, for example, were a religious movement that reached a peak in the nineteenth century in the United States. Their most notable attribute from the outsider's perspective was their ban on sexual intercourse; they formed Shaker communities in which men and women lived together yet sexually separate. Not surprisingly, they had a problem keeping up their membership after a time. But more interesting are the many peaceful economic relations they had with members of the outside society. The Shakers didn't approve of sex for themselves but were willing to tolerate it in others.

As we have noted, the 1970s saw the proliferation of religious cults in the United States. Krishna Consciousness, Scientology, the Unification Church, and Synanon all found their way into the news at one time or another, primarily as a result of parental complaints over the resocialization of their children (see Chapter 4). With the exception of the Unification Church (which has been accused of lobbying illegally for the Republic of South Korea), such cults appear to be interested primarily in increasing their membership and keeping their movements economically viable (which is a concern of all social movements). Social movements that seek to change only individuals who join the movement are generally tolerated more than those that seek to change the larger society, all else being equal. In terms of deviating from traditional American values, all of the religious cults are more extreme than Martin Luther King Jr.'s civil rights activities of the 1950s and 1960s, yet none received the political oppression that King faced. Nevertheless, many new religious cults have provoked widespread opposition in the United States, particularly from parents who feel that their children have been "brainwashed" by charismatic movement leaders.

Through a variety of controversial court decisions, parents have been allowed by law to kidnap their own adult children for the purposes of "deprogramming"—a technique designed to alter their values away from the cult and back to mainstream values of American culture (Shupe, 1980).

It should be kept in mind that all social movements must transform their individual members from "outsiders" to "movement followers" if they are to get anything accomplished. Movements that seek only to change their members can stop at that, but movements that seek to change elements of society must first acquire the loyalty and dedication of their members before they can turn their attention outward. Extreme revolutionary movements will even use resocialization techniques since the dedication they require will be so much greater; a movement that seeks to change basic values in society will first have to change the basic values of its members. At the other extreme, a reform movement that seeks additional resources for the eradication of a specific disease conforms to basic American values and will have less difficulty converting members to the "rightness" of its cause. It will, however, have the same problems that all movements have in keeping members interested and working for the movement. Whatever type the social movement, loss of interest among the members is a far greater enemy than the armed might of any nation.

THE STRUCTURE OF SOCIAL MOVEMENTS

Social movements are coordinated social groups, however strange or revolutionary their ideas may be. And like any such group, social movements have a social structure with different roles, activities, norms, and values. Unlike other groups, however, social movements emerge from a collective desire for change among the organizers and develop over time in relation to that desire. Studying the structure of social movements turns our attention to the way in which social coordination develops among groups that seek change.

Some mobs and riots produce leaders on the spot, but all social movements have specially created leadership roles and follower roles. One of the leader's jobs is to maintain group cohesion and efficiency of operation. The way in which this job is approached can vary considerably; there are, in short, different types of leadership roles.

The most colorful type of social movement leader is the **charismatic leader.** The charismatic leader rules by virtue of great personal charm, persuasiveness, and magnetism (which is about as near as sociologists can come to defining charisma). Charismatic leaders are typically moving speakers, have exciting personalities, and are talented at attracting new membership along with maintaining the loyalty of the old. Social movements are rarely lucky enough to find more than one charismatic leader over time, and if they do have one, it will almost always be the first (or founding) leader.

An extremely different kind of social movement leader is the **administrative leader** who, in social movements or elsewhere, sits at the head of a bureaucracy, overseeing the activities below. The administrative leader governs by virtue of bureaucratic position and legal authority within the movement's social organization. As we will see shortly, social movements that survive long enough often become bureaucracies, making an administrative leader necessary; it is in fact a classic case for a charismatic leader to run a loose-knit, dedicated group for a generation and then be replaced by an administrative leader who heads a by-then more formal organization. If a social movement has a formal organization, it must have an administrative leader. Remember, however, we are talking about roles and not people. An initial leader with charismatic qualities could learn administrative duties as the movement changed and become both kinds of leader simultaneously. A social movement could also have two different individuals in leadership roles simultaneously, one charismatic and the other administrative, each having very specific duties.

A third type of social movement leadership role is the **intellectual leader,** who takes charge of the movement's ideas. Why does the movement exist? Why is it necessary? How will the movement bring about change? What should those changes be? All these questions must have answers if the social movement is to survive, and it is the job of the intellectual leader to see that the answers are forthcoming. Again, remember that the intellectual leader is a role and that either a charismatic or an administrative leader could fulfill this function. One individual could, in fact, perform all three roles.

Thinking accomplished by the intellectual leader produces other important elements in the social movement's structure. At the most general level this thinking becomes the ideology and propaganda of the social movement. The movement's **ideology** is basically its worldview; it includes a picture of what's wrong with the world (and why), who's responsible, and what the movement could (and should) do to make things right. Like all ideologies, the ideology of a social movement supports the interests of the movement. *Propaganda* is often a close relative of ideology; in many cases the movement's propaganda is a simplified version of the ideology (often including catchphrases) used in, among other ventures, the recruitment of new members. There can be substantial differences between the two, however, if the movement's leaders feel the true ideology is too radical and might scare off potential recruits. Followers might not be let in on "what's really going on" until they prove themselves loyal; in extreme cases they might be viewed as only expendable tools for the movement's leadership and might never be told.

The ideology/propaganda will make up the public presentation of the social movement. It will generally include an interpretation of the past and a vision of the future with and without the benefits of the social movement. For example, the Ku Klux Klan believes that problems in the United States can be traced to a conspiracy of Jewish people who wish to take over the country and destroy Christianity. Because they think that Jews are manipulating African Americans to achieve this end, the Klan doesn't think too highly of them either. These ideas are part of the Klan's interpretation of the past. Their vision of the future without the changes they propose is a black-white race war in which blacks will rape and murder a disarmed white population, leaving the way clear for Jews to take over. If the Klan becomes strong, say their leaflets, all this can be prevented. This ideology tells you how the movement sees the world and why the movement is necessary for the future.

Within its vision of the future a movement's ideology/propaganda must specify tactics and goals. The goals are included within the vision of the future if the movement is successful; the tactics describe how the movement intends to bring that happy vision about. Both tactics and goals must be marketable if the movement is to be successful. The goals (at least the stated goals contained in movement propaganda) must generally tie in with accepted values of the society. All religious movements, for example, claim to make people happy and content. Political movements generally claim they will produce equality, prosperity, freedom, and, again, happiness. Stated goals should be general enough to leave room for everyone but specific enough for prospective members to get their teeth into. They should also be somewhat flexible so that they can change with the times. Perhaps most important, they should also appear at least possible to achieve (see King, 1956).

If anything, tactics are even more important to the movement's success than goals. You can claim to support total revolution but never be bothered by authorities if you don't do anything. Like goals, tactics must appear acceptable in terms of dominant values, but they must also appear to be workable. This is a particularly difficult problem for most social movements, since almost by definition, they are relatively powerless; otherwise, they would be benefiting from the status quo and less interested in bringing about change. What kinds of tactics can a relatively powerless group employ to force changes on societal authorities? Box 15.3 presents the ideas of one noted social activist.

Ralph Turner (1970) points out that social movement tactics fall under three general headings. *Coercion* is possible only when the social movement controls something of value to the authorities. Labor unions coerce with the strike, removing their valuable labor from management. A boycott removes consumers from a particular product. The civil rights movement began in the 1950s when blacks in Montgomery, Alabama, refused to ride the city buses until the buses were desegregated. Because blacks in that city tended to be poorer and more likely than whites to be bus riders, the city transit system was hurt by the boycott.

Bargaining is the positive side of coercion; it also requires movement control over something of value but emphasizes rewards rather than penalties for societal authorities. An ethnic minority social movement, for example, can use votes to bargain with politicians for favors. And finally, perhaps the least effective tactic, *persuasion* occurs when the movement attempts to enlist support for its goals by presenting the goals as advantageous to all. A telethon to raise money to fight disease would fall under this heading; persuasion generally works only when movement goals are highly respectable in the minds of most people.

BOX 15.3

Rules for Radicals: The Social Movement Tactics of Saul Alinsky

Effective tactics are prime commodities in the world of social movements. Social movements are typically poor and powerless groups that, by definition, are limited in the kinds of pressure they can exert. Moreover, the wrong kinds of tactics might alienate prospective movement members or result in harsh repression from societal authorities. A good tactic is practical, effective, and tailored to the social environment within which it will be applied.

Saul Alinsky (1971) was one of the most creative tacticians ever to give advice to social movements. He describes his approach as "mass jujitsu"—you use the strength of your aggressive opponent to your advantage. The following describes Alinsky's approach to dealing with a Chicago department store that discriminated against African Americans in hiring:

> There is a particular department store that happens to cater to the carriage trade. It attracts many customers on the basis of its labels as well as the quality of its merchandise. Because of this, economic boycotts had failed to deter even the black middle class from shopping there. At the time its employment policies were more restrictive than those of the other stores. Blacks were hired for only the most menial jobs.
>
> We made up a tactic. A busy Saturday shopping date was selected. Approximately 3,000 blacks all dressed up in their good churchgoing suits or dresses would be bused downtown. When you put 3,000 blacks on the main floor of a store, even one that covers a square block, suddenly the entire color of the store changes. Any white coming through the revolving doors would take one pop-eyed look and assume that somehow he had stepped into Africa. He would keep right on going out of the store. This would end the white trade for the day.
>
> For a low-income group, shopping is a time-consuming experience, for economy means everything. This would mean that every counter would be occupied by potential customers, carefully examining the quality of merchandise and asking, say, at the shirt counter, about the material, color, style, cuffs, collars, and price. As the group occupying the clerks' attention around the shirt counters moved to the underwear section, those at the underwear section would replace them at the shirt counter, and the personnel of the store would be constantly occupied.
>
> Now pause to examine the tactic. It is legal. There is no sit-in or unlawful occupation of premises. Some thousands of people are in the store "shopping." The police are powerless and you are operating within the law.
>
> This operation would go on until an hour before closing time, when the group would begin purchasing everything in sight to be delivered C.O.D.! This would tie

up truck-delivery service for at least two days—with obvious further heavy financial costs, since all the merchandise would be refused at the time of delivery.

The threat was delivered to the authorities through a legitimate and "trustworthy" channel. Every organization must have two or three stool pigeons who are trusted by the establishment. The stool pigeons are invaluable as "trustworthy" lines of communication to the establishment. With all plans ready to go, we began formation of a series of committees: a transportation committee to get the buses, a mobilization committee to work with the ministers to get their people to their buses, and other committees with other specific functions. Two of the key committees deliberately included one of these stoolies each, so that there would be one to back up the other. We knew the plan would be quickly reported back to the department store. The next day we received a call from the department store for a meeting to discuss new personnel policies and an urgent request that the meeting take place within the next two or three days, certainly before Saturday!

The personnel policies of the store were drastically changed. Overnight, 186 new jobs were opened. For the first time, blacks were on the sales floor and in executive training.

This is the kind of tactic that can be used by the middle class too. Organized shopping, wholesale buying plus charging and returning everything on delivery, would add accounting costs to their attack on the retailer with the ominous threat of continued repetition. This is far more effective than canceling a charge account. Let's look at the score: (1) sales for one day are completely shot; (2) delivery service is tied up for two days or more; and (3) the accounting department is screwed up. The total cost is a nightmare for any retailer, and the sword remains hanging over his head. The middle class, too, must learn the nature of the enemy and be able to practice what I have described as mass jujitsu, utilizing the power of one part of the power structure against another part.

(From *Rules for Radicals* by Saul Alinsky. Copyright © 1971 by Saul Alinsky. Reprinted by permission of Pantheon Books, a division of Random House, Inc.)

THE NATURAL HISTORY OF SOCIAL MOVEMENTS

In looking at various leadership roles, we noted that different kinds of leaders are appropriate for different types of social movement organization; the more formal the organization, the more necessary it is for the movement to have an administrative leader. Movements tend to have different kinds of organizations as a result of their goals or their size. The hippie movement of the 1960s, for example, contained groups with goals of "doing your own thing" and "hanging loose"; these goals made formal organization impossible—which ultimately made the hippie movement impossible. Many of these same individuals, however, altered their lifestyles and goals when the war in Vietnam became a salient political issue, joining forces in both organized and effective protest groups (Kohn, 1986; Levitt, 1984). Size is another variable. Terrorist revolutionary movements generally have to remain small and emotionally tight-knit because of the danger in which their activities place them. At the other extreme, nationwide reform movements, such as a political party, require elaborate formal organizations to coordinate all the varied activities required to elect candidates. Beyond these requirements the internal structure of all social movements tends to change over time.

Social movements have a natural history of their own. Movements that survive tend to become increasingly formally organized over time. Many sociologists have attempted to depict this change in terms of stages, but the change is actually continuous. Before we look at this process more closely, one good example to keep in mind is the world history of the Christian religion. Based on a charismatic leader and a loose-knit group of twelve followers over two thousand years ago, Christianity developed from small persecuted groups into formalized international churches with tremendous power and influence. Those groups that were once on the outside looking in have now become societal authorities in their own right; like the Romans over two thousand years ago, Christian churches now have the right to pass judgment.

The earliest stage of most social movements is a premovement stage, sometimes termed the *incipient* or the *preliminary* stage of social excitement (Hopper, 1950; King, 1956). This period is usually a classic case of collective behavior in which groups of people face a dilemma but don't quite know what to do about it. Americans have been shown in laboratory research to react in significant fashion when confronted by situations structured to include elements of injustice or illegality (Gainson, Fireman, and Rytina, 1982). Martin Luther King Jr. described his initial entry into the civil rights movement as typical of this first stage. A black woman, Rosa Parks, had refused to give up her bus seat to a white man as the law required in Montgomery, Alabama. Her subsequent arrest antagonized the black community and led them to search for ideas and a leader in order to make some kind of response. King, a new Baptist minister in town, was asked to help. When he began, he had no idea that their efforts would have any impact beyond the city limits of Montgomery.

When leaders, goals, and tactics begin to emerge, the budding social movement starts to take shape. People begin to congregate around the leader and the movement's new ideas, but behavior is far from set at this point. Jobs that need doing get done by whoever is around to do them; there are as yet no formal roles with assigned responsibilities. As in the case of the Montgomery bus boycott, goals may still be in their infancy and limited to immediate matters. As goals are still growing, so too is the movement's ideology, which is highly fluid. The boundaries of the movement are loose, with people coming and going from movement activities, with no one having a sense of formal movement membership. The vast majority of social movements never make it past this point largely because of the organizational problems of keeping people working and getting the jobs done.

As the movement seeks to make its activities more efficient and effective, it moves into a stage of formal organization of some sort. This is the stage where an intellectual leader will emerge with an ideology, and some sort of administrative leader will emerge to handle the growing complexity of movement operations. It will become quite clear who is a member of the movement and who is not. Movement symbols begin to be used that identify members, and rituals develop among members as an aid in reminding them of their membership. One of the main problems the movement will face at this point is a question of priorities: is it more important to spend time keeping the movement together or to continue forging ahead with original movement goals? Margaret Sanger, an early advocate of women's rights, organized the Birth Control League in the late 1800s to give women more control over pregnancy. This accepted position today was considered quite sinful in her time, and she had quite a sales job on her hands. In her autobiography she describes returning from a trip to Europe to discover that other members had their eyes fixed on the movement's bank balance and were spending little effort on anything else (Sanger, 1938).

As in the example of Christianity, a social movement can survive indefinitely into the institutionalized stage when it becomes established as a societal authority. This fourth and last stage sees the movement turn from attacker of the status quo to its defender. Before the Russian Revolution, the Communist Party was in favor of all types of revolutionary activity; once the Communists came into power themselves, the last thing they wanted was revolutionaries running around. One of their foremost agitators during the revolution, Leon Trotsky, ended his life in exile in Mexico because he had become unwelcome at home. Even in exile Trotsky was apparently still viewed as a threat, and he was assassinated. Similarly, the established Catholic Church rejected Martin Luther, which led to the Protestant Reformation.

Individual social movements may seem to come to an end at this point, but the cycle of social movement formation goes on as new ones continue to develop. The importance of social movements can also be seen clearly from this perspective: many of the dominant ideas of almost any age were once the wild and crazy ideas proposed by a social movement some time in the past. The right to birth control that Margaret Sanger fought for is now taken for granted—as are Christianity, the U.S. Constitution, scientific research, the illegality of slavery, and the legality of organized labor (see Box 15.4).

One modern theory of social movements that attempts to integrate many of these observations is *resource mobilization theory* (McCarthy and Zald, 1973, 1977; Zald, 1979). In the terms of this perspective, a *social movement* is redefined as a collection of opinions and beliefs regarding social change; a *social movement organization,* on the other hand, refers to the actual organization of individuals (what has been referred to as a "social movement" in this chapter) that forms to fight for the goals of those opinions and beliefs. Often many organizations form with similar beliefs and goals and must then compete with one another for members who already occupy the same social movement. Such a collection of movement organizations is termed a

BOX 15.4

Social Movements by Occupation: The Natural History of the Labor Movement

Sociologists have noted the tendency of social movements to become increasingly formally organized over time. There is also a tendency, if the movement survives, for its goals to appear less and less radical to the rest of society. One of the best examples of this overall tendency can be found in the history of labor unionism.

The organization of industrial workers is about as old as the industrial revolution itself. In 1769 the British Parliament passed a law making the intentional destruction of an industrial machine a capital offense. The organization of workers for the purpose of raising wages also was against the law; such organization was viewed as a "conspiracy."

The United States had labor laws similar to Britain's. In 1806, for example, boot- and shoemakers in Philadelphia were indicted for their attempts to secure higher wages. The first large-scale labor organizations were the Knights of Labor, formed in 1869, followed by the American Federation of Labor (AFL), formed in the 1880s. The latter, which has survived to this day, was formed around particular craft occupations. The unions were far from accepted, however, and often met with considerable violence. The Chicago Haymarket Square bombing and shooting of May 3, 1886, played a major role in the demise of the Knights of Labor. In 1894 Eugene Debs and his American Railway Union had a confrontation with federal troops; the meeting left thirty strikers dead.

In the 1930s the Congress of Industrial Organizations (CIO) gained strength. Unlike the AFL, the CIO focused on the organization of workers within particular industries rather than particular occupations, including many blue-collar workers who previously had no union open to them. The 1930s also brought the labor movement some of the strongest support it had ever received from the federal government. Under new legislation from the Roosevelt administration, workers were guaranteed the right to organize, strike, and bargain collectively. Not long after World War II, the AFL and the CIO merged and settled into a highly respectable and accepted corner of the American society. As this respectability grew, the more radical elements of the labor movement either drifted away or were expelled. The earlier, charismatic leaders, such as Eugene Debs and John L. Lewis of the United Mine Workers, gave way to the newer administrative leaders of today. Union leaders who used to go to jail for organizing workers now face prison terms for the mismanagement of union funds. Respectability and success have their price.

Some of the newer unions in the United States found themselves in almost the same boat older unions occupied earlier this century. The most noted example has been the United Farm Workers, led by the late Cesar Chavez (see Jenkins, 1986).

Organizing a group of workers to whom unions had previously been closed, Chavez gained recognition for his union through a successful nationwide boycott of table grapes. It is curious, however, that not all established unions welcomed this addition to their ranks. The Teamsters Union was brought in by farm owners in an attempt to break the United Farm Workers by having workers switch to the Teamsters; the hope among farm owners was that the Teamsters would settle more easily than the United Farm Workers (*U.S. News and World Report,* 1975). As with all social movements, older versions at the stage of formal organization may resist newer models still in the early stages of organization.

The future of labor unions should prove interesting. Currently, more and more professional and white-collar occupations are turning from loose-knit and largely powerless "associations" to unions. One of the best-known cases is the American Federation of Teachers, which adopted a strike policy in the early 1960s and has since closed schools many times by calling strikes. Public employees such as police and firefighters have become better organized and increasingly militant. At the same time, however, membership in American unions is today at an all-time modern low, having fallen off considerably since its high point during the 1940s. Activism and enthusiasm in a few select unions can hardly suggest a growing social movement interest in the face of such widespread lack of interest among most American workers.

Perhaps the most interesting trend comes from the Polish workers' strike that began in the summer of 1980. Beyond higher wages, their primary goal was to achieve the right to organize and strike outside the control of the government. After initial success, martial law was imposed and the union leaders were imprisoned, silenced, or forced to go underground. A new generation of workers brought the union back to life in 1988, however, leading ultimately to the overthrow of the Communist Party in Poland and the rise of union leaders—most notably Lech Walesa—to governmental positions.

---

social movement industry. They may operate within a subset of a society, as, for example, a labor union will be limited to organizing certain kinds of workers. They may also potentially have an entire society from which to draw members, as was the case with movement organizations fighting for nuclear arms limitations (Katz, 1986; Price, 1982). McCarthy and Zald emphasize that social movement organizations should be viewed in terms of their abilities to control societal resources and mobilize those resources to bring about social change.

SOCIAL MOVEMENTS AS AGENTS OF SOCIAL CHANGE

All forms of collective behavior can leave their marks on society, but social movements tend to have the most far-reaching effects. A group of unorganized rioters may not last long against trained military personnel, but an organized social movement stands a chance. It is sometimes difficult, however, to know just how much social change can be attributed to social movements and how much would have occurred anyway. Social movements, after all, are the products of social change as well as creators of it. On the other hand, there are times when they appear to be clearly successful in reaching their goals with only minimal help from outside trends.

However much hard work may pay off, the most successful social movements are those that hop aboard ongoing social change. Consider the women's movement. Social movements supporting women's rights have been in existence for over a century, concentrating first on political freedom and more recently on ending economic discrimination. The twentieth century was also a period of great advances for women. At first glance, it would appear that these social movements have been phenomenally successful. At second glance, however, a question arises as to the role of industrialization in this change in women's status. Industrialization altered living areas, lifestyles, occupations, fertility rates, mortality rates, and political processes, to name just a few of the changes. Women were less needed in the family and as mothers while being both more useful and more needed as workers. They certainly didn't have to become equal workers with men; the growing equality of women workers with men obviously has been affected by the existence of women's movements. But the basic changes in women's roles were probably already in the cards before the first women's social movements were formed. Movements that capitalize on such trends will have advantages that others won't.

If a trend doesn't appear in the offing for your particular issue, another strategy for success is to align your social movement with a built-in societal contradiction. Martin Luther King Jr. was a master of this technique. "All men are created equal" is a dominant American theme, and King found dramatic ways for illustrating how this value was limited in its application to African Americans. Americans want strong law enforcement but they also value equal rights. King's tactic of nonviolence made very public how law enforcement agencies used violence against unarmed demonstrators. Contradictions are inherent in all human societies, but people generally develop the ability to ignore them. A well-organized social movement removes these blinders and exploits the situation.

Finally, one of the most important roles played by social movements is changing habits of thought. Social movements create and publicize issues. Even the most radical issue tends to sound less radical after it has been expressed a few hundred times. Social movements keep questions alive and allow people to get used to them. So many of the issues important only ten or twenty years ago are taken for granted today. The apparently ironclad structure of coordination in human society appears a little less solid viewed in light of history.

Social change brought about by social movements provides an appropriate moment to recall the introductory discussion in Chapter 1 on coordination in society. The sociological outlook on society presents a picture of norms, roles, social control, and authority, explaining much of the coordination we see in everyday life. As we've seen throughout this book, however, the sociological outlook also presents a picture of social strains, individual creativity, deviance, and collective efforts to produce social change. As noted at the outset of this book, the individual cannot be understood outside of society, but neither can a society be understood without coming to terms with individual creativity and the dynamic nature of social change.

SUMMARY

Collective behavior is unpatterned behavior that occurs within, or emerges from, collections of people. It is distinctive through its collective nature (as being the product of group interactions) and its norm-creating characteristics.

Collective behavior can take many forms. Fads and fashions are forms of behavior that develop within social groups for limited periods of time and serve to distinguish group members and separate them from others. Publics form around the existence of an issue. Public opinion refers to the opinions that develop through the interactions of publics. Natural and human-made disasters produce collective behavior by forcing people out of their normal routines and requiring that they attend to problems they have not encountered before. Collective behavior can also occur in any situation with a perceived threat as people panic to remove themselves from that threat. Rumor—the spread of information within ambiguous social situations—takes on the characteristics of collective behavior as uncertainties create new information and new social interactions as the rumors spread.

Face-to-face interaction of a crowd is probably the ultimate form of collective behavior. In this situation behavior develops through the simultaneous interactions of crowd members. Theories of crowd behavior range from those that picture crowd members as suggestible sheep subject to the contagion of social behavior to those that portray crowd members as rationally calculating personal benefits from the crowd situation. Theories of crowd formation range from those that depict crowd members as confused or marginal members of society to those based on social deprivation. Of the latter much attention lately has been paid to the perceived deprivation of the crowd member and the relation of deprivation to other social factors.

Social movements are particular forms of collective behavior, occurring when that behavior becomes organized for the purpose of bringing about social change. Social movements can vary in the kinds and amounts of change they seek. Some movements seek change only in their memberships, whereas others seek change in the outside society. Of the latter, reform movements seek relatively minor change, whereas revolutionary movements hope to change the basic structure of society. Social movements are characterized by the emergence of specific norms and roles that define leaders and followers as well as organizing labor within the movement. Types of leadership roles include the charismatic leader, the administrative leader, and the intellectual leader. Movement ideologies describe the worldview typical of the movement and, along with propaganda, provide tools for the recruitment of new members.

Over time social movements change internally. The typical progression is from some form of collective behavior to a loosely knit group that, if it survives, develops some kind of formal organization. Over time social movements become institutionalized and commonly become part of society. Related to their varying degrees of success, social movements are important in bringing about social change.

GLOSSARY

Acting crowds Crowds with apparent goals outside the crowd gathering itself.

Administrative leader Social movement leadership role that governs by virtue of bureaucratic position and legal authority within the movement's social organization.

Charismatic leader Social movement leadership role that governs through great personal charm, persuasiveness, and personal magnetism.

Collective behavior Unpatterned (or non-norm-governed) behavior, typically transitory and spontaneous.

Contagion The spread of an idea or behavior among the members of a crowd.

Crowd situation A social situation in which a large number of people are in face-to-face contact with each other in a particular physical setting.

Expressive crowds Crowds that are formed solely for the self-expression of the members.

Fads New forms of behavior that catch on among certain groups of people for a limited time.

Fashion Forms of behavior that are popular with certain groups of people (typically upper class) for a limited period of time, typically longer than a fad.

Ideology An idea or set of ideas that represents a particular interest of a particular social group. (As defined by Karl Marx, it refers specifically to the set of beliefs that supports the interests of a ruling class in society.) Within a social movement, an ideology represents the movement's worldview, including their perception of the world, along with a proposed role for the movement.

Intellectual leader Social movement leadership role that takes charge of the movement's ideas, specializing in the construction of movement ideology and propaganda.

Mass hysteria The spread of a nonrational belief or behavior throughout a group of people.

Panic A nonrational response to a threatening situation that can occur when inaction is perceived to be dangerous, escape is perceived to be possible, and escape seems less possible with the passage of time.

Propaganda (1) The conscious attempt to manipulate public opinion through control over the nature and flow of information. (2) In a social movement, typically a simplified version of the movement's ideology designed to attract new members or to further the movement's goals.

Public A collection of people that forms because of their common concern about a current issue.

Public opinion The attitudes common to the members of a public.

Reform movements Social movements that seek moderate amounts of social change and work within the existing system.

Revolutionary movements Social movements that seek massive change in society.

Rumor Information, typically unconfirmed, that spreads among members of a group.

Social movements Organized efforts by groups of people to bring about social change, either in the members themselves or in members and society alike.

STUDY QUESTIONS

1. What separates collective behavior from typical social behavior? Why is collective behavior so hard to study?
2. What are the similarities and differences between fads and fashions? How do they both relate to social group boundaries?
3. How is propaganda a significant part of understanding the formation of publics and public opinion?
4. Why do disasters force people into acts of collective behavior?
5. Many people confuse panic with disaster response. While panic can be a part of a disaster response, why are they generally very different?
6. What produces mass hysteria?
7. What are the basic types of crowds? What are the theories regarding crowd behavior? How do those theories provide very different perspectives on how crowds operate?
8. What are the theories of crowd formation?
9. Discuss the nature of rumor transmission and show how rumor can be a part of other types of collective behavior.
10. What are the two basic types of social movements?
11. How do social movements vary in terms of structure and leadership?
12. How do social movements typically change over time? What stages do they go through?
13. How can social movements be agents of social change?

Neal Gabler

THE LURE OF URBAN MYTHS

Urban myths are those curious stories that are always told as having happened to a friend of a friend. They are always told as true stories when passed along. But they are seldom true. They represent a kind of modern folklore that expresses the hopes and (especially) the fears that thrive in any culture. Some of them are object lessons—a kind of adult boogieman story. Others reflect our fears of embarrassment. And yet still more, at least in the sexually absorbed United States, reflect our fascination with and fears of sex. Like rumors, urban myths pass along from person to person. If the "catch" of the story is good enough, people cannot wait to tell their neighbors. Some stories span years. The story described below involving baseball player Reggie Jackson on an elevator can now be heard with Eddie Murphy in the starring role.

Why do sociologists study such things? In part because we want to learn more about how and why rumors spread. But we also want to learn more about human culture in general. Urban myths allow people to say things they would otherwise never express; they allow us to pass the myth along only because it is "true." And in so doing, the myths tell us something about ourselves.

By now you may have heard the story of Gunther Burpus, a hapless 41-year-old man in Bremen, Germany, who couldn't find his house keys and decided to crawl through the cat flap in his front door. Unfortunately, Burpus got stuck. When he called for help, he managed to attract the attention only of some passing students who decided to play a prank. Instead of freeing Burpus, they pulled off his trousers, painted his bottom bright blue, stuck a daffodil between his cheeks, and then placed a sign nearby: GERMANY RESURGENT, AN ESSAY IN STREET ART. PLEASE GIVE GENER-OUSLY. There poor Burpus remained for two days, his pleas for help disregarded by passersby who thought them part of the "exhibition." "People just said, 'Very good! Very clever!' and then threw coins at me," Burpus remarked afterward. It was only when a dog started licking his genitals that an old woman complained to the police and Burpus was finally freed.

Or maybe a friend of yours who happens to be a friend of a friend of one of the guests told you the one about the shocking wedding party. It seems that during a big reception at the Pierre

Hotel in New York, the groom stood and called for silence. The guests naturally assumed he was about to propose a toast. Instead, he announced that the marriage was going to be annulled. If the guests wished to know the reason, they had only to turn over their dinner plates. When the stunned guests flipped their plates, they discovered photographs taped there of the bride flagrante delicto with the best man.

At least that's the way it was told to me. But a similar story circulating at the same time set the reception at a banquet hall in New Hampshire. Another version set it in Medford, Massachusetts. Another placed the incident near Schenectady, New York. A version set outside St. Paul, Minnesota had two significant differences: At the altar, before the vows were taken, the bride announced the ceremony would not continue because the prospective groom had slept with the maid of honor.

Each version of this story comes branded as truth right down to places, dates and sources. Each was told by someone who knew someone who knew someone at the ceremony or reception. The trouble is, the wedding, which was supposed to have occurred sometime last year, has been the subject of newspaper columns and radio call-in shows since at least 1985. Despite the story's decade-long existence, no one has provided one scintilla of evidence that it ever really happened. Indeed, an intrepid Washington *Post* reporter who investigated the tale last fall found that none of the facts jibed—not New Hampshire nor Schenectady, not a reception nor a ceremony.

As for the story of Gunther Burpus, which has been printed as fact in *The Vancouver Sun, The Palm Beach Post, The Providence Journal-Bulletin* and the January 1998 issue of *Playboy,* a debunker named Barbara Hamel has found it to be a complete fabrication. Hamel says that the German magazine *Der Spiegel,* which has been cited as a source for the story, had never heard of Gunther Burpus. Neither had the police in Bremen. As for Burpus' quotes, someone obviously invented them to give the story more texture.

In short, the story of Gunther Burpus, like that of the wedding revenge, is what is known as an urban legend—a tall tale that is purportedly absolutely true but isn't. By one estimate there are now more than 400 of these legends. University of Utah folklorist Jan Harold Brunvand, perhaps the preeminent urban folklorist, has published five volumes' worth of them with titles such as *The Choking Doberman* and *The Baby Train.* No one seems to know exactly where these yarns originated. They just seem to erupt spontaneously in Europe and across America. They then get retold in newspapers and magazines (*Reader's Digest* is a frequent source), on the radio (Paul Harvey trades in these tales), on the Internet (there is a rabid urban folklore newsgroup) and, most of all, by word of mouth—from what urban legend professionals call an FOAF ("friend of a friend" to whom the incident is alleged to have happened).

Although they have grabbed the attention of academics only recently—some trace their scholarly intent to Richard Dorson's *American Folklore* in 1959—contemporary legends are an old phenomenon. A few, such as the story of the butcher who stuck a sausage in his pants fly and shocked his customers by hacking off the end of the sausage with a cleaver, can be traced to before the turn of the century.

Many of the hoarier ones sound as if they had been perfected around the campfire. There's the favorite about the man driving alone one night when he stops to pick up a beautiful young hitchhiker. She gives him her destination, then falls silent during the rest of the trip. When the driver arrives at the girl's house, he turns to find that his passenger has vanished. Baffled, he gets out, knocks on the door and tells his strange tale to the woman who answers. She isn't shocked. Her daughter had died some years before in a car accident, but every so often the girl's spirit tries to make her way back home by hitching a ride with an unsuspecting driver.

And there's the one Brunvand calls the Hook that dates from the late Fifties. Two high school kids drive to lovers' lane one dark evening and are just about to begin their amour when they hear on the radio that a madman has escaped from the local asylum. The catch is that the madman has a hook for a hand. The boy peels out and speeds his date home. When he gets out to open his girlfriend's door, he sees a bloody hook dangling from the handle.

Then there's the classic about the babysitter who has tucked the children into bed upstairs and settled down in front of the television when she gets a prank call from a man laughing hysterically. She hangs up, but the phone rings again. Again she hears the hysterical laugh. She slams down the receiver, but the phone rings a third time and again there is the laugh. Unnerved, she calls the phone company. The operator tells her that the next time the crank phones, the girl should keep him on the line so they can trace him. Of course, the fiend calls and laughs, then hangs up. The next time the phone rings, however, it is the operator. "Get out of the house!" she screams. "The call is coming from upstairs!"

These classics may sound preposterous today, but there are other contemporary legends that are plausible enough to pass muster as fact. Nearly everyone has heard about the alligators that prowl the New York sewers. Supposedly they are descendants of baby gators that children brought back from Florida vacations. When the children returned to New York, their parents realized they couldn't exactly have a pet alligator, so they flushed the critters down the toilet and into the sewer system, where, feasting on rats, they soon formed a colony of predators. In some versions, the gators in the subterranean darkness have turned into blind albinos.

There is another "true" story about the high school coed with the beehive hairdo that she proudly sprays until it is as lacquered as a Chinese cabinet. Unfortunately, the girl begins to have fainting spells during class. One day she can't be revived. At the hospital a nurse notices a small spider crawling from the hairdo of the comatose young woman. Cracking open the beehive, the nurse finds a black widow and hundreds of her young nesting there. The girl, who hadn't washed her hair in months, later dies of the spider bites.

Still another legend that has the elements of truth is the one about the California couple eating at an outdoor café in Tijuana. They see a flea-bitten Chihuahua begging under the table. Taking pity on the animal, the woman feeds it a few scraps. When she and her husband leave the restaurant, the Chihuahua tags along. By the end of the day, the woman is so smitten with the dog that she decides to take it home as her pet and smuggles it across the border, either under her blouse or in a bundle in the backseat. Back home in suburban California, the woman washes and grooms her new pet and retires for the night. In the morning, however, she finds it listless—in some versions oozing mucus—and rushes it off to her veterinarian. Later that day, she gets the vet's call: "Where did you get that dog?" he wants to know. The woman, realizing it is illegal to transport an animal across the border, at first lies and says she found it wandering the streets nearby, but the vet calls her bluff. "You didn't find this animal here," he says. "This is a long-haired Mexican sewer rat."

Those of us who have heard and then retold these legends know that they provide entertainment at the water cooler, at the tavern after work or during dormitory bull sessions. But where they once were dismissed as nothing more than amusing balderdash, they are now perceived by folklorists as expressions of the national psyche. "We project our fears into the stories," says University of Georgia sociology professor Gary Alan Fine, a leading interpreter of folklore. He specifically cites as a propelling theme "the mistrust we have of contemporary society, the fact that so much of our culture is beyond our control."

One story that sprouted around the country in the summer of 1994 tells of a lonely, friendless woman working in an office. Taking pity, her co-workers plan a surprise birthday party for her. They manage to get her apartment key and hide before she arrives home. When she does, they hear her go into the kitchen and call her dog. It sounds as if she is feeding him so they prepare to emerge, but when they burst into the kitchen to yell "Surprise," they find her sitting naked on the floor, with peanut butter spread on her vagina and her dog lapping away. As the story goes, the young woman, mortally embarrassed, never returns to work.

Or there is the story making the rounds just this year about the Samaritan in the supermarket parking lot who sees a woman in a car slumped over the steering wheel one sweltering afternoon. (In fact, Brett Butler has been telling it as having happened to her sister.) Asked if she needs help, the poor woman moans that she has been shot in the head and reaches up to show gray matter oozing from the wound. The Samaritan immediately summons police and paramedics, but when they arrive they find that the woman has not been shot after all. She has actually been hit in the head by the end of a tube of oven-ready Pillsbury biscuits that had exploded in the heat, and she mistook the dough that had splattered on her hair for her brains.

There are scores of legends dealing with miscalculation and embarrassment. Consider the story about the man who goes home with his secretary and, expecting romance, disrobes when she leaves the room, only to discover that the secretary and his wife have arranged a surprise birthday party for him. Or the one about the couple trysting in a small car when the man gets stuck inside the woman (*penis captivus,* Brunvand calls it) and rescuers have to remove the car's top to free them. Or the one about the young man meeting his girlfriend's parents for the first time. He accidentally sits on their pet Chihuahua, crushing it. He then hides the deed by stuffing the carcass under the cushions.

The preponderance of contemporary legends, however, seem to tap a much darker reservoir of terror. According to Patricia Turner, a folklore scholar at the University of California at Davis: "They are definitely about the ambivalence and anxiety and uncertainty that people have about

one another." These sorts of legends portray a dangerous world in which anything can happen, a world of unrelenting horror.

Seen this way, contemporary legends can practically be cataloged by the terrors they exploit. To those who regard the city as ominous there is the story, usually told of New York City (though it has lately been making the rounds in California with either Reno or Las Vegas as the setting), of the group of fraternity boys who spend a wild weekend in the Big Apple. One of them meets a woman at a club and leaves with her for the night. The next morning his buddies get a distress call from their cohort: He is in a hotel room and he begs them to come and get him. They arrive at a seedy hotel to find their friend in bed, the sheets soaked with blood, and a fresh surgical scar on his back. They rush him to the hospital, where they are informed that the man had apparently been drugged and had one of his kidneys removed. A ring of thieves has been harvesting organs to sell on the black market for transplants. Anyone is fair game.

To those who live in dread of crime, there is the story Brunvand calls the Choking Doberman. In this one a woman finds her pet Doberman breathing heavily and takes the dog to the vet for observation. The woman soon gets an urgent call from the vet: She must leave the house immediately and call the police. Why? Because he found three fingers lodged in her Doberman's throat. Rushing to the scene, the police discover a burglar hiding in the woman's closet—sans three of his fingers.

Another story suggests that crime follows you, even into paradise. In this one, a couple honeymooning in Jamaica find that their room has been burgled and that all their possessions—except for their camera and their toothbrushes—have been stolen. Vowing to make the best of their vacation, the couple decide to stick it out. But when they arrive home and develop their pictures, they find a photo of the thieves mooning the camera. Stuck up their rectums are the toothbrushes.

One tale—again, usually told by a friend of a friend of one of the participants—has three women getting on an elevator in a New York hotel when they see a black hand prying open the elevator doors. The doors part and a towering black man enters the elevator with a large dog. "Sit," the man commands, and the three woman immediately hit the ground. The man apologizes. He had been talking to his dog. It turns out that the man is Reggie Jackson. (In one version, he's O. J. Simpson.) And in most tellings Jackson winds up paying for the women's dinner.

The elevator legend—of course, it never happened—may actually serve to defuse racial tension. But these days more contemporary legends exploit issues of race, largely because they enable us to express racial fear safely. "It is illegitimate to make a blanket statement like 'Blacks are criminals,'" explains Fine. "One would be tarred in such a case for being a racist. What one can do, however, is talk specifically about, say, gang initiations: 'Did you hear that in order to get into this gang, they rape white women?' There is no evidence for it, but it seems plausible because gang members may do something like that."

One legend making the rounds, in fact, has a black gang in Chicago cruising the streets at night with their headlights out, waiting for a driver to flash his lights at them. Any driver who does, however, is executed. Another legend that has been taken quite seriously in some suburban communities tells of a black clown dressed like Homey of the old *In Living Color* TV series who attacks or abducts children. (In several versions there is a whole vanload of sinister black clowns.) Some more traditional urban legends have even been revised to reflect racist fears. The Choking Doberman, for example, is often said to have three black fingers in its gullet.

Drugs have also fueled contemporary legends, specifically legends about drug-crazed loons who do harm to themselves or others. Almost everyone has heard about the people who went blind by staring at the sun during LSD trips or those who wind up gouging out their own eyes. (There is no proof that either happened.) More heinous

are the stories of the drugged-out babysitter—sometimes the boyfriend of a sister tending her siblings—who assures the parents checking in that everything is under control. The babysitter tells them she has even put a turkey in the oven. When the parents return home, however, they discover that the turkey is actually their baby.

While these legends address our personal sense of vulnerability at the hands of psychos and criminals, other legends express a dread of the vast impersonal forces of Corporate America. "The rumors," Fine observes, "spring from uneasiness about what is perceived to be the complete amorality of American corporate life." Sometime in the early Eighties, a rumor began circulating that Procter & Gamble, one of the world's largest manufacturers of household products, was in league with the devil. One variation of this rumor has the company contributing to a satanic cult allegedly because its founder back in the 19th-century made a pact with the devil to ensure the company's success. The proof was supposedly right there in Procter & Gamble's trademark, which features stars around a crescent moon bearing a face. (The association between the moon and Moonies is thought to have been a trigger for the story.)

Back in the Seventies Church's Fried Chicken, a popular fast-food franchise—particularly in the South—was identified as being owned by Ku Klux Klan supporters who added a secret ingredient to sterilize black males! The Adolph Coors Co. has also been identified in legends as connected to the Klan. A more recent legend has Snapple donating a share of its profits to white supremacist groups—a story Patricia Turner, author of *I Heard It Through the Grapevine: Rumor in African American Culture,* believes may have sprung from Snapple's association with radio commentators Rush Limbaugh and Howard Stern.

A more elaborate but equally fictitious story told in the black community is one about how Oprah Winfrey ordered designer Liz Claiborne off her show when Claiborne admitted to the studio audience that she purposely cut her clothes narrowly so that black women couldn't wear them. And a bigger legend still is the widespread belief among African Americans and some whites that AIDS is either the result of a government biological experiment gone awry in Africa and Haiti or that the virus was released intentionally by our government to destroy the gay and black communities.

Understandably, technology is another growth area for contemporary legends, clearly reflecting anxieties about the brave new world we face. One urban legends staple is the story of the woman who washes her pet poodle and decides to hasten the drying by putting the dog in her new microwave. The poodle explodes. There is a similar story about a woman who wants a fast tan and begins visiting a tanning salon—more frequently than the salon advises—to get one. In one version the woman begins feeling woozy and goes to her doctor to find out why. In another her husband tells her that she has a peculiar odor. In both the doctor gives her the bad news: She has broiled her insides and now will certainly die.

Based on sheer numbers, however, the most terrifying of all our fears are sexual. From the story of the man who slips his date some Spanish fly and later finds her impaled on the gearshift to the one about the honeymoon hotel that secretly videotapes couples for pornography, there are more legends involving sexual embarrassment, sexual compromise and sexual danger than any other subject. Now homophobia seems to have inspired a whole new cluster of tales.

The most nakedly homophobic is the one, first appearing in the late Eighties, about the college student who goes to the doctor after feeling some rectal pain. At the end of the examination, the doctor tells the young man that he has obviously engaged in anal sex, but the man protests that he has not and is absolutely straight, though his roommate is gay. Concerned by the diagnosis, the student roots around his dorm room. He finds a bottle of ether among his roommate's effects and comes to the conclusion that his roommate has been drugging him while he sleeps and then having intercourse with him.

Another homophobic legend, this one dating from 1990, is the story of the gay man rushed to the emergency room. It seems that, using a plastic tube, he had inserted a live gerbil up his rectum to stimulate his prostate but couldn't extricate the animal once it was inside. The doctor must then perform a gerbilectomy. One variation of this tale that adds to its veracity actually puts a name on the hospital, Cedars-Sinai in Los Angeles, and on the victim, Richard Gere. Although she refers to Gere as "Jerry" to conceal his identity, California State University professor Norine Dresser discovered that Gere's name began to be linked to the legend about the time he resurfaced with an unexpected hit (*Pretty Woman*) and at a time when the actor had joked to a magazine about having performed some youthful indiscretion with a chicken.

Of all the contemporary sex legends, however, the ones that draw most powerfully on modern hysteria are those incorporating AIDS. In the most widely told AIDS legend, a recently divorced man meets a woman at a bar and winds up spending the night with her, making love repeatedly. In another version, the man and the woman continue seeing each other over the course of a month or so, though the woman insists that the man not drive her home. Either the next morning or one morning after a night of lovemaking, depending on the story, the man wakes up alone. He stumbles into the bathroom. There scrawled on the mirror in red lipstick he finds a message: WELCOME TO THE WORLD OF AIDS! It seems that the woman had contracted AIDS from a boyfriend and had vowed to avenge herself on every man she could.

One could, of course, go on to tell the legends about medical catastrophes, terrible accidents, police escapades, college anxieties—each adding to the miasma of dysfunction and paranoia. But while the themes of these stories are generally transparent and familiar, it is far less clear why people feel the need to relate them in the first place. Fairy tales at least help us conquer our amorphous childhood fears by projecting them onto tangible villains vanquished by heroes and heroines. Traditional folktales usually offer some moral instruction. But contemporary legends do neither. At best they are cautionary—wash your hair, watch what you bring back from Mexico, don't sleep around—but seem a rather weak foundation to sustain what is obviously so strong an institution.

It is more probable that contemporary legends aren't intended to provide us with a way to surmount the anxieties of modern life. They are intended to demonstrate to us that these terrors are so ubiquitous and inexplicable that we do not have any way to deal with them. Thus, we shouldn't bear any responsibility for them.

What intensifies the power of this awful, amoral vision of modern life is that, as the critic Digby Diehl once wrote, "At the time of the telling we believe the story to be true." Hypothetically, we can trace it to an eyewitness who told it to a friend who told it to a friend. Newspapers report these legends as if they were true. Radio talk shows discuss them as if they were true. Soon these stories enter the realm where their truth needn't be proved even in the face of logic.

Perhaps, though, our insistence on the truth of these legends is itself a form of revenge against the helplessness and lack of control the stories purvey. Whatever else contemporary legends are, they may be the last vestige of an oral folk culture that operates from the grass roots up. They are expressions of a culture generated by us rather than for us. As Roger Angell recently lamented in a *New Yorker* piece attacking debunkers:

> In a time when almost every fresh plot, exaggerated demise or weirdly victimized citizen seem to come to us from Buttafuoco-land or from another TV cops serial or the latest, sound-blasting, overweaponed movie release, let me hold onto whatever scraps come my way by word of mouth, from across the dinner table, or while I'm waiting by the Xerox machine.

Angell expresses here not only the joy of authentic folktales but also the pride of authorship. These stories are ours. And if in telling them, embellishing them and reconfiguring them we insist on their truth, that is only an author's prerogative in casting his spell. We want them to be believed as we half-believe in them ourselves. We do so not because we are manipulators or fools, but because in allowing us to transform our collective anxieties these contemporary legends grant us one of the few powers left to us in the anemic society they describe: the power to tell stories about our world.

In narrating our terrors, we console ourselves.

DISCUSSION QUESTIONS

1. Many of the stories you just read involve people doing stupid things and paying the price. Are they just "object lessons" (as in, "Be careful, don't make this mistake"), or are they also ways for the storyteller to feel superior to his or her subject matter?

2. In many of the stories, the main characters act on basic assumptions that the world is as it should be and learn differently. Sometimes they are only embarrassed; other times, the results are more serious. Are we being told that nothing is as it seems to be? And why would we want to hear that?

3. The Procter & Gamble story falls generally under the heading of product rumors. Product rumors are those that specifically attack a company or a company's product (e.g., "Big Macs contain worms"). Are product rumors just extensions of the kinds of myths described in discussion question 2?

4. Consider the butcher and the sausage story (or really most of the sex-related urban myths). Imagine telling such stories a hundred years ago in the United States when sexual expression was much less open. Are urban myths a way to talk about things you are not supposed to discuss?

BIBLIOGRAPHY

Abrahamson, Mark, Ephraim Mizruchi, and C. Harnung. *Stratification and Mobility*. New York: Macmillan, 1976.

Ackerman, Diane. *A Natural History of Love*. New York: Random House, 1994.

———. "Fifty Years of Family Research: What Does It Mean?" *Journal of Marriage and the Family* 50 (1988): 5–17.

Adams-Curtis, Leah E., and Gordon B. Forbes. "College Women's Experiences of Sexual Coercion." *Trauma, Violence & Abuse* 5 (2004): 91–123.

Adorno, T. W., E. Frenkel-Brunswik, Daniel Levinson, and R. Nevitt Sanford. *The Authoritarian Personality*. New York: Harper & Row, 1950.

Agnew, Robert. "A Longitudinal Test of Social Control Theory and Delinquency." *Journal of Research in Crime and Delinquency* 28 (1991): 126–156.

Alexander, Karl, Doris R. Entwisle, and Maxine S. Thompson. "School Performance, Status Relations, and the Structure of Sentiment: Bringing the Teachers Back In." *American Sociological Review* 52 (1987): 665–682.

Alinsky, Saul D. *Rules for Radicals*. New York: Random House, 1971.

Allen, James Paul, and Eugene James Turner. *We the People: An Atlas of America's Ethnic Diversity*. New York: Macmillan, 1988.

Allen, Tim. "War, Famine and Flight in Sudan." *Disasters* 15 (1991): 133–136.

Allison, Paul D. "The Cultural Evolution of Beneficent Norms." *Social Forces* 71 (1992): 279–301.

Allport, Gordon W. *The Nature of Prejudice*. Reading, Mass.: Addison-Wesley, 1954.

Allport, Gordon W., and Leo J. Postman. *The Psychology of Rumor*. New York: Holt, 1947.

Ancoma, Deborah G., and David F. Caldwell. "Bridging the Boundary: External Activity and Performance in Organizational Teams." *Administrative Science Quarterly* 37 (1992): 634–665.

Andrews, L. "Family Violence in Florida's Panhandle." *Ms* 12 (1984): 23.

Arendell, Terry. "After Divorce: Investigations into Father Absence." *Gender and Society* 6 (1992): 562–586.

Asch, Solomon E. "Effects of Group Pressures upon the Modification and Distortion of Judgments." In Eleanor Maccoby, Theodore Newcomb, and Eugene Hartley (eds.). *Readings in Social Psychology* (3rd ed.). New York: Holt, Rinehart and Winston, 1958.

Ashley, David. "Class Struggle in the P.R.C. Before and After Tiananmen Square." *Humanity and Society* 15 (1991): 156–182.

Astley, W. Graham, and Edward J. Zajac. "Intraorganizational Power and Organizational Design: Reconciling Rational and Coalitional Models of Organization." *Organizational Science* 2 (1991): 399–411.

Austin, Roy L., and Hiroko Dodge. "Despair, Distrust and Dissatisfaction Among Blacks and Women, 1973–1987." *The Sociological Quarterly* 33 (1992): 579–598.

Backlund, Eric, and Paul D. Sorlie. "A Comparison of the Relationships of Education and Income with Mortality." *Social Science & Medicine* 49 (1999): 1373–1385.

Baker, James H. "Raises, Reform and Respect." *Newsweek* 110 (1987): 92.

Bakken, Linda, and Charles Romig. "Interpersonal Needs in Middle Adolescents: Companionship, Leadership and Intimacy." *Journal of Adolescence* 15 (1992): 301–316.

Banks, Adelle. "Official Presbyterian Church U.S.A. News: Presbyterian Gains Two Seats, Now Total 49." *Religion News Service, 2001*. www.pcusa.org/pcnews/01004.htm.

Banton, Michael. "The Culture of Poverty." *Social Studies Review* 5 (1990): 112–114.

Barnard, Wendy Miedel. "Parent Involvement in Elementary School and Educational Attainment." *Children & Youth Services Review* 26 (2004): 39–63.

Barnett, Steven W., and Jason T. Hustedt. "Head Start's Lasting Benefits." *Infants & Young Children: An Interdisciplinary Journal of Special Care Practices* 18 (2005): 16–25.

Barrera, Mario. *Race and Class in the Southwest: A Theory of Racial Inequality.* Notre Dame, Ind.: University of Notre Dame Press, 1979.

Barrow, Georgia M., and Patricia A. Smith. *Aging, Ageism and Society.* St. Paul, Minn.: West, 1979.

Bartlett, Bruce. "Americans Scorn Class Envy." *Human Events,* June 2, 2000, 21.

Basso, K. H. "To Give Up on Words: Silence in Western Apache Culture." *Southwestern Journal of Anthropology* (Autumn 1970).

Baum, Alice S., and Donald W. Burnes. *A Nation in Denial: The Truth About Homelessness.* Boulder, Colo.: Westview Press, 1993.

Baxter, Leslie A. "Forms and Functions of Intimate Play in Personal Relationships." *Human Communication Research* 18 (1992): 336–363.

Becker, Howard S. *Outsiders: Studies in the Sociology of Deviance.* New York: The Free Press, 1963.

Bell-Villada, Gene H. "Is the American Mind Getting Dumber?" *Monthly Review* 43 (1991): 41–55.

Bellah, Robert N. *Beyond Belief.* New York: Harper & Row, 1970.

Bellair, Paul E., and Vincent J. Roscigno. "Local Labor-Market Opportunity and Adolescent Delinquency." *Social Forces* 78 (2000): 1509–1539.

Benson, Michael L., and Elizabeth Moore. "Are White-Collar and Common Offenders the Same? An Empirical and Theoretical Critique of a Recently Proposed General Theory of Crime." *Journal of Research in Crime and Delinquency* 29 (1992): 251–272.

Berger, Peter L. *The Noise of Solemn Assemblies.* Garden City, N.Y.: Doubleday, 1961.

———. *The Capitalist Revolution: Five Propositions about Prosperity, Equality, and Liberty.* New York: Basic Books, 1986.

Berk, Richard A. *Collective Behavior.* Dubuque, Iowa: Wm. C. Brown, 1974a.

———. "A Gaming Approach to Crowd Behavior." *American Sociological Review* 39 (1974b): 355–373.

Bernard, Jesse. *The Future of Marriage.* New Haven, Conn.: Yale University Press, 1982.

Berry, J. W., and J. A. Bennett. "Cree Conceptions of Cognitive Competence." *International Journal of Psychology* 27 (1992): 73–88.

Best, Raphaela. *We've All Got Scars: What Boys and Girls Learn in Elementary School.* Bloomington: Indiana University Press, 1985.

Biggar, Jeanne C. "The Sunning of America: Migration to the Sunbelt." *Population Bulletin* 34. Washington, D.C.: Population Reference Bureau, 1979.

Bingham, Shereen G. "Communication Strategies for Managing Sexual Harassment in Organizations: Understanding Message Options and Their Effects." *Journal of Applied Communication Research* 19 (1991): 88–115.

Bishop, Meredith. "Why Johnny's Father Can't Read: The Elusive Goal of Universal Adult Literacy." *Policy Review* 55 (1991): 19–25.

Blanchflower, David G., and Richard B. Freeman. "Unionism in the United States and Other Advanced OECD Countries." *Industrial Relations* 31 (1992): 56–79

Blau, Peter M., and W. Richard Scott. *Formal Organizations: A Comparative Approach.* San Francisco: Chandler, 1962.

Blau, Peter, and Otis Dudley Duncan. *American Occupational Structure.* New York: Wiley, 1967.

Blauner, Bob. *Still the Big News: Racial Oppression in America.* Philadelphia: Temple University Press, 2001.

Bloom, Allan. *The Closing of the American Mind.* New York: Simon & Schuster, 1987.

Bluestone, Barry, and Bennett Harrison. *The Deindustrialization of America.* New York: Basic Books, 1982.

Blumer, Herbert. "Collective Behavior." In Alfred McClung Lee (ed.). *Principles of Sociology* (3rd ed.). New York: Barnes & Noble, 1969.

Boeker, Warren. "Power and Managerial Dismissal: Scapegoating at the Top." *Administrative Science Quarterly* 37 (1992): 400–421.

Bogal-Allbritten, Rosemarie, and William L. Allbritten. "An Examination of Institutional Responses to Rape and Acquaintance Rape on College Campuses." *Family Violence and Sexual Assault Bulletin* 8 (1992): 20–23.

Bohanon, Cecil. "The Economic Correlates of Homelessness in Sixty Cities." *Social Science Quarterly* 72 (1991): 817–825.

Bonacich, Edna. "A Theory of Ethnic Antagonism: The Split Labor Market." *American Sociological Review* 37 (1972): 547–559.

——. "Advanced Capitalism and Black/White Relations." *American Sociological Review* 41 (1976): 34–51.

Boocock, Sarene Spence. "The Social Organization of the Classroom." In Ralph Turner, James Coleman, and Renee C. Fox (eds.). *Annual Review of Sociology,* 1–28. Palo Alto, Calif.: Annual Reviews, 1978.

Boone, Sherle L. "Aggression in African-American Boys: A Discriminant Analysis." *Genetic, Social, and General Psychology Monographs* 117 (1991): 203–228.

Bouvier, Leon F., and Robert W. Gardner. "Immigration to the U.S.: The Unfinished Story." *Population Bulletin,* Vol. 411, No. 4 (November 1986).

Bowers, William L., Glenn Pierce, and John McDevitt. *Legal Homicide: Death as Punishment in America, 1964–1982.* Boston: Northeastern University Press, 1984.

Boyd, Robert L. "Effects of Relative Group Size, Increase, and Segregation on the Earnings of Blacks and Asians." *Sociological Focus* 24 (1991): 175–195.

Brand, David. "This Is the Selma of the Deaf." *Time,* March 21, 1988.

Braun, Denny. "Income Inequality and Economic Development: Geographic Divergence." *Social Science Quarterly* 72 (1991): 520–536.

Bridges, Judith S., and Ann Marie Orza. "The Effects of Employment Role and Motive for Employment on the Perceptions of Mothers." *Sex Roles* 27 (1992): 331–343.

"British Parliamentary Papers, Shipping Casualties (Loss of the Steamship 'Titanic'), 1912, cmd. 6352." In *Report of a Formal Investigation into the Circumstances Attending the Foundering on the 15th April, 1912, of the British Steamship "Titanic," of Liverpool, After Striking Ice in or Near Latitude 41 Degrees 46' N., Longitude 50 Degrees 14' W., North Atlantic Ocean, Whereby Loss of Life Ensued.* London: His Majesty's Stationery Office, 1912.

Brodeur, Paul. "Asbestos." *The New Yorker,* June 10, 1985/July1, 1985.

Bromley, David G., and Anson D. Shupe, Jr. *New Christian Politics.* Macon, Ga.: Mercer University Press, 1984.

Bronfenbrenner, Urie. "Socialization and Social Class Through Space and Time." In Eleanor Maccoby, T. Newcomb, and E. L. Hartley (eds.). *Readings in Social Psychology.* New York: Holt, 1958.

Brown, Bernard. "Head Start: How Research Changed Public Policy." *Young Children* 40 (1985): 9–13.

Brown, Jane D., and Susan F. Newcomer. "Television Viewing and Adolescents' Sexual Behavior." *Journal of Homosexuality* 21 (1991): 77–91.

Brown, Lester R. "Population and Affluence: Growing Pressures on World Food Resources." *Population Bulletin* 29. Washington, D.C.: Population Reference Bureau, 1973.

Brown, Peter J. "Culture and the Evolution of Obesity." *Human Nature* 2 (1991): 31–57.

Brown, Phillip, and Hugh Lauder. "Education, Economy and Social Change." *International Studies in Sociology of Education* 1 (1991): 3–23.

Brown, R., and A. Gilman. "The Pronouns of Power and Solidarity." In T. A. Sebeok (ed.). *Style in Language.* New York: Wiley, 1960.

Brown, W. K., Timothy P. Miller, Richard L. Jenkins, and Warren A. Rhodes. "The Human Costs of 'Giving the Kid Another Chance.'" *International Journal of Offender Therapy and Comparative Criminology* 35 (1991): 296–302.

Brunvand, Jan H. *The Vanishing Hitchhiker: American Urban Legends and Their Meanings.* New York: W. W. Norton, 1981.

Bucher, Rue, and Joan Stelling. "Characteristics of Professional Organizations." *Journal of Health and Social Behavior* 10 (1969): 3–15.

Buckner, H. Taylor. "A Theory of Rumor Transmission." *Public Opinion Quarterly* 29 (1965): 54–70.

Bukowczyk, John J., and Nora Faires. "Immigration History in the United States, 1965–1990: A Selective Critical Appraisal." *Canadian Ethnic Studies* 23 (1991): 1–23.

Burgoon, Judee K., and Stephen B. Jones. "Toward a Theory of Personal Space Expectations and Their Violations." *Human Communication Research* 2 (1976): 131–146.

Burkitt, Ian. "Social Selves: Theories of the Social Formation of Personality." *Current Sociology* 39 (1991): 1–225.

Cantril, Hadley. *The Invasion from Mars: A Study in the Psychology of Panic.* New York: Harper & Row, 1966.

Cappell, Charles L., and Gresham Sykes. "Prison Commitments, Crime and Unemployment: A Theoretical and Empirical Specification for the United States, 1933–1985." *Journal of Quantitative Criminology* 7 (1991): 155–199.

Caputo, Richard K. "Income Inequality and Family Poverty." *Families in Society* 76 (1995): 604–615.

——. "Assets and Economic Mobility in a Youth Cohort." *Families in Society* 84 (2003): 51–61.

Carley, Kathleen. "Organizational Learning and Personnel Turnover." *Organization Science* 3 (1992): 20–46.

Carli, Linda L. "Gender, Language and Influence." *Journal of Personality and Social Psychology* 59 (1990): 941–951.

Carlson, Bonnie E. "Dating Violence: A Research Review and Comparison with Spouse Abuse." *Social Casework* 68 (1987): 16–23.

Carrier, James G. *Social Class and the Construction of Inequality in American Education.* New York: Greenwood, 1986.

Carrington, Christopher. *No Place Like Home: Relationships and Family Life among Lesbians and Gay Men.* Chicago: University of Chicago Press, 1999.

Casanova, José. "Roman and Catholic and American: The Transformation of Catholicism in the United States." *International Journal of Politics* 6 (1992): 75–111.

Cassell, Joan. "Doing Gender, Doing Surgery: Women Surgeons in a Man's Profession." *Financial Management* 25 (1996): 47–53.

Caton, Carol L. M. *Homeless in America.* New York: Oxford University Press, 1990.

CBS News. "R.I. Nightclub Fire Probe Continues." March 4, 2003. www.cbsnews.com/stories/2003/03/04/national/main542796.shtml.

Centers, Richard. *The Psychology of Social Classes.* New York: Russell & Russell, 1949.

Chambliss, William J. "The Saints and Roughnecks." *Society* 11 (1973): 24–31.

Checchi, Daniele. "Education and Intergenerational Mobility in Occupations: A Comparative Study." *American Journal of Economics & Sociology* 56 (1997): 331–352.

Chinoy, Ely. "The Tradition of Opportunity and the Aspirations of Automobile Workers." *American Journal of Sociology* 57 (1952): 453–459.

Chiricos, Theodore G., and Miriam A. Delone. "Labor Surplus and Punishment: A Review and Assessment of Theory and Evidence." *Social Problems* 39 (1992): 421–446.

Clinton-Davis, Lord, and Yohannes Fassil. "Health and Social Problems of Refugees." *Social Science and Medicine* 35 (1992): 507–513.

Cloward, R. A., and L. E. Ohlin. *Delinquency and Opportunity: A Theory of Delinquent Gangs.* New York: The Free Press, 1960.

CNN. "Judge: Evolution stickers unconstitutional." www.cnn.com/2005/LAW/01/13/evolution.textbooks.ruling/, 2005.

Cohen, Albert K. *Delinquent Boys: The Culture of the Gang.* Glencoe, Ill.: The Free Press, 1955.

Cohen, Cathy J., and Claire E. Nee. "Educational Attainment and Sex Differentials in African American Communities." *American Behavioral Scientist* 43 (2000): 1159–1201.

Colclough, Glenna, and E. M. Beck. "The American Educational Structure and the Reproduction of Social Class." *Sociological Inquiry* 56 (1986): 456–476.

Coleman, James S. "The Rational Reconstruction of Society." *American Sociological Review* 58 (1993): 1–15.

Coleman, James S., and Thomas Hoffer. *Public and Private High Schools: The Impact of Communities.* New York: Basic Books, 1987.

Coleman, James S., Thomas Hoffer, and Sally Kilgor. *High School Achievement: Public, Catholic, and Other Private Schools Compared.* New York: Basic Books, 1982.

Coleman, James S., et al. *Equality of Educational Opportunity.* Washington, D.C.: U.S. Office of Education, 1966.

Collins, Patricia Hill. "Learning from the Outsider Within: The Sociological Significance of Black Feminist Thought." *Social Problems* 33 (1986): S14 S32.

_____. *Black Feminist Thought.* Cambridge, Mass.: Unwin Hyman, 1990.

_____. "It's All in the Family: Intersections of Gender, Race and Nation." *Hypatia* 13 (1998): 62–82.

Collins, Randall. *The Credential Society: An Historical Sociology of Education and Stratification.* New York: Academic Press, 1979.

———. "The Geopolitical and Economic World-Systems of Kinship-Based and Agrarian-Coercive Societies." *Review* 15 (1992): 373–388.

Coltrane, Scott. "Research on Household Labor: Modeling and Measuring the Social Embeddedness of Routine Family Work." *Journal of Marriage and the Family* 62 (2000a): 1208–1233.

———. "Fatherhood and Marriage in the 21st Century." *National Forum* 80 (2000b): 25–29.

Coltrane, Scott, and Michele Adams. "Men's Family Work: Child-Centered Fathering and the Sharing of Domestic Labor." In Rosanna Hertz and Nancy L. Marshall (eds.). *Working Families: The Transformation of the American Home.* Berkeley: University of California Press, 2001.

Coltrane, Scott, Ross D. Parke, and Michele Adams. "Complexity of Father Involvement in Low-Income Mexican American Families." *Family Relations* 53 (2004): 179–190.

Condry, John, and Sandra Condry. "Sex Differences: A Study of the Eye of the Beholder." *Child Development* 47 (1976): 812–819.

Conrad, Omar Greg. "The Social Psychology of Anti-Semitism." *Mid-American Review of Sociology* 16 (1992): 37–56.

Cooley, Charles Horton. *Human Nature and the Social Order*. New York: Scribner's, 1902.

——. *Social Organization*. New York: Scribner's, 1909.

Copeland, Emily. "Global Refugee Policy: An Agenda for the 1990s." *International Migration Review* 26 (1992): 992–999.

"Corporate Crime and Punishment." *Multinational Monitor,* July/August 1999, 5.

"Corporate Perjury and Obstruction of Justice." *Multinational Monitor,* December 1998, 5.

Courtwright, David T. "Drug Legalization, the Drug War, and Drug Treatment in Historical Perspective." *Journal of Public Policy* 3 (1991): 393–414.

Cox, Harvey. *The Secular City*. New York: Macmillan, 1971.

——. *Religion in the Secular City*. New York: Simon & Schuster, 1984.

Cuber, John F., and William Kenkel. *Social Stratification in the United States*. New York: Appleton, 1954.

Cunningham, James S., and Nadja Zalokar. "The Economic Progress of Black Women, 1940–1980: Occupational Distribution and Relative Wages." *Industrial and Labor Relations Review* 45 (1992): 540–555.

Dabelko, David D., and Robert J. Sheak. "Employment, Subemployment and the Feminization of Poverty." *Sociological Viewpoints* 8 (1992): 31–66.

Dadant and Sons (eds.). *The Hive and the Honey Bee*. Hamilton, Ill.: Dadant and Sons, 1975.

Dahl, Robert A. *Democracy and its Critics*. New Haven, Conn.: Yale University Press, 1989.

——. *Who Governs?* New Haven, Conn.: Yale University Press, 1961.

——. *Dilemmas of Pluralist Democracy*. New Haven, Conn.: Yale University Press, 1982.

Dahrendorf, Ralf. *Class and Class Conflict in Industrial Society*. Stanford, Calif.: Stanford University Press, 1959.

Daniel, Pete. *The Shadow of Slavery: Peonage in the South 1901–1969*. New York: Oxford University Press, 1972.

Daniels, Lee A. "Diversity, Correctness, and Campus Life: A Closer Look." *Change* 23 (1991): 16–20.

Danzger, M. Herbert. *Returning to Tradition: The Contemporary Revival of Orthodox Judaism*. New Haven, Conn.: Yale University Press, 1989.

Davenport, Douglas R. "Environmental Constraints and Organizational Outcomes: Modeling Communities of Municipal Police Departments." *Police Quarterly,* September 1, 2000, 174–200.

Davies, James D. "The J-Curve of Rising and Declining Satisfactions as a Cause of Some Great Revolutions and Contained Rebellion." In Hugh Davis Graham and Ted Robert Gurr (eds.). *Violence in America* (Vol. 2). Washington, D.C.: National Commission on the Causes and Prevention of Violence, 1969.

Davis, Cary, Carl Haub, and JoAnne Willette. "U.S. Hispanics: Changing the Face of America?" *Population Bulletin,* Vol. 38, No. 3 (June 1983).

Davis, James, and Tom Smith. *General Social Survey Cumulative File, 1972–1982*. Ann Arbor, Mich.: Inter-University Consortium for Political and Social Research, 1984.

Davis, Kingsley. "The Amazing Decline of Mortality in Underdeveloped Areas." *American Economic Review* 46 (1956): 305–318.

Davis, Kingsley, and Wilbert E. Moore. "Some Principles of Stratification." *American Sociological Review* 10 (1945): 242–249.

Day, Jennifer, and Andrea Curry. *Educational Attainment in the United States: March 1995*. Washington, D.C.: U.S. Government Printing Office: U.S. Bureau of the Census, Current Population Reports P20–489, 1996.

De Francisco, Victoria Leto. "The Sounds of Silence: How Men Silence Women in Marital Relations." *Discourse and Society* 2 (1991): 413–423.

Delaney, John Thomas. "The Future of Unions as Political Organizations." *Journal of Labor Research* 12 (1991): 373–387.

Dentler, Robert A., and Susan N. Hunt. "The Los Angeles Riots of Spring 1992: Events, Causes, and Future Policy." *Sociological Practice Review* 3 (1992): 229–244.

Desimone, Laura. "Linking Parent Involvement with Student Achievement: Do Race and Income Matter?" *Journal of Educational Research* 93 (1999): 11–31.

Ditton, Jason. "Learning to 'Fiddle' Customers: An Essay on the Organized Production of Part-time Theft." *Sociology of Work and Occupations* 4 (1977): 427–451.

Domhoff, William G. *Who Rules America?* New York: McGraw-Hill, 2002.

Douglas, Jack D., and Frances C. Waksler. *The Sociology of Deviance: An Introduction*. Boston: Little, Brown, 1982.

Downey, Douglas B., and James W. Ainsworth-Darnell. "The Search for Oppositional Culture Among Black Students." *American Sociological Review* 67 (2002): 156–165.

Drutman, Lee, and Charlie Cray. "The Top 10 Financial Scams of the 2002 Corporate Crime Waves." *Multinational Monitor* 23 (2002): 20–24.

Duff, John B. *The Irish in the United States*. Belmont, Calif.: Wadsworth, 1971.

Duke, James T., and Barry L. Johnson. "Religious Affiliation and Congressional Representation." *Journal for the Scientific Study of Religion* 31 (1992): 324–329.

Durham, William H. "Applications of Evolutionary Culture Theory." *Annual Review of Anthropology* 21 (1992): 331–335.

Durkheim, Emile. *Suicide*. Trans. John A. Spaulding and George Simpson. New York: The Free Press, 1951. (Originally published 1897.)

———. *The Elementary Forms of the Religious Life*. Trans. Joseph W. Swain. Glencoe, Ill.: The Free Press, 1954. (Originally published 1915.)

Dusek, Jerome B. (ed.). *Teacher Expectancies*. Hillsdale, N.J.: Erlbaum, 1985.

Edelman, Lauren B., and Mark C. Suchman. "The Legal Environments of Organizations." *Annual Review of Sociology* 23 (1997): 479–516.

Eggebeen, David J., and Daniel T. Lichter. "Race, Family Structure, and Changing Poverty among American Children." *American Sociological Review* 56 (1991): 801–817.

Eggers, Mitchell L., and Douglas S. Massey. "The Structural Determinants of Urban Poverty: A Comparison of Whites, Blacks, and Hispanics." *Social Science Research* 20 (1991): 217–255.

Ehrlich, Paul R., Gretchen C. Daily, and Lawrence H. Goulder. "Population Growth, Economic Growth, and Market Economics." *Contention: Debates in Society, Culture, and Science* 2 (1992): 17–35.

Elam, George A., and David M. Kleist. "Research on the Long-Term Effects of Child Abuse." *Family Journal* 7 (1999): 154–161.

Ellis, Dean S. "Speech and Social Status in America." *Social Forces* 45 (1967): 431–437.

Emery, Robert E., et al. "Divorce, Children and Social Policy." In Harold W. Stevenson and Alberta E. Siegel (eds.). *Child Development Research and Social Policy*. Chicago: University of Chicago Press, 1984.

Engel, Robin Shepard, and Jennifer M. Calnon. "Examining the Influence of Drivers' Characteristics During Traffic Stops with Police: Results from a National Survey." *Justice Quarterly* 21 (2004): 49–91.

Enloe, Cynthia. "The Growth of the State and Ethnic Mobilization: The American Experience." *Ethnic and Racial Studies* 4 (1981): 123–136.

Erickson, Carlton K. "A Pharmacologist's Opinion— Alcoholism: The Disease Debate Needs to Stop." *Alcohol and Alcoholism* 27 (1992): 325–328.

Erikson, Kai. *Wayward Puritans: A Study in the Sociology of Deviance*. New York: Wiley, 1966.

———. *Everything in Its Path: Destruction of Community in the Buffalo Creek Flood*. New York: Simon & Schuster, 1976.

Etzioni, Amitai. *A Comparative Analysis of Complex Organizations: On Power, Involvement and Their Correlates*. New York: The Free Press, 1961.

Evans, Arthur S., Jr. "Black Middle Classes: The Outlook of a New Generation." *International Journal of Politics, Culture and Society* 6 (1992): 211–228.

Evans, William M. "The Organizational Set: Toward a Theory of Interorganizational Relations." In James D. Thompson (ed.). *Approaches to Organizational Design*. Pittsburgh: University of Pittsburgh Press, 1966.

"Falling Behind: An Interview with Jonathan Kozol." *Christian Century*, May 19, 2000, 541–543.

Fallows, James. "American Industry: What Ails It, How to Save It." *Atlantic Monthly*, September, 1980: 111–122.

Falsey, Barbara, and Barbara Heyns. "The College Channel: Private and Public Schools Reconsidered." *Sociology of Education* 57 (1984): 111–122.

Farberman, Harvey A. "Symbolic Interaction and Postmodernism: Close Encounters of a Dubious Kind." *Symbolic Interaction* 14 (1991): 471–488.

Farkas, George. "Teaching Low-Income Children to Read at Grade Level." *Contemporary Sociology* 29 (2000): 53–63.

Farkas, George, Robert P. Grobe, Daniel Sheehan, and Yuan Shuan. "Cultural Resources and School Success: Gender, Ethnicity, and Poverty Groups Within an Urban School District." *American Sociological Review* 55 (1990): 127–142.

Fauth, Rebecca C., Tama Leventhal, and Jeanne Brooks-Gunn. "Short-Term Effects of Moving from Public Housing in Poor to Middle-Class Neighborhoods on Low-Income, Minority Adults' Outcomes." *Social Science & Medicine* 59 (2004): 2271–2285.

Feldberg, Roslyn. "Comparable Worth: Toward Theory and Practice in the United States." *Signs* 10 (1984): 311–328.

Field, Simon. "The Effect of Temperature on Crime." *British Journal of Criminology* 32 (1992): 340–351.

Fine, Terri Susan. "Public Opinion Toward Equal Opportunity Issues: The Role of Attitudinal and Demographic Forces Among African Americans." *Sociological Perspectives* 35 (1992): 705–720.

Finnigan, David. "Pounding the Kid Trail." *Brandweek*, October 9, 2000, 32–35.

Fisher, Arthur. "Sociobiology: Science or Ideology?" *Society* 29 (1992): 67–79.

Fishman, Joshua A. *Advances in the Sociology of Language* (2 vols.). The Hague: Mouton, 1971.

Flake, Carol. *Redemptorama: Culture, Politics and the New Evangelicalism.* Garden City, N.Y.: Anchor, 1984.

Ford, Donna Yvette, J. John Harris III, and William I. Turner. "The Extended African American Family: A Pragmatic Strategy that Blunts the Blade of Injustice." *The Urban League Review* 14 (1990–1991): 71–83.

Forsyth, Craig J., Shelley B. Roberts, and Craig A. Robin. "Variables Influencing Life Satisfaction among Grandparents." *International Journal of Sociology of the Family* 22 (1992): 51–60.

Fowler, Jerry. "Beyond Humanitarian Bandages— Confronting Genocide in Sudan." *New England Journal of Medicine* 351 (2004): 2574–2577.

Frank, Andre Gunder. "Third World War: A Political Economy of the Gulf War and the New World Order." *Third World Quarterly* 13 (1992): 267–282.

Frankl, Razelle. *Televangelism: The Marketing of Popular Religion.* Carbondale: Southern Illinois University Press, 1987.

Franks, David D., and Viktor Gecas. "Autonomy and Conformity in Cooley's Self-Theory: The Looking Glass Self and Beyond." *Symbolic Interaction* 15 (1992): 49–68.

Freud, Sigmund. *Civilization and Its Discontents.* New York: W. W. Norton, 1930.

Frey, William H. "Immigration and Internal Migration 'Flight' from U.S. Metropolitan Areas: Toward a New Demographic Balkanisation." *Urban Studies* 32 (1995): 733–758.

Frydenberg, Erica, and Ramon Lewis. "Adolescent Coping: The Different Ways in Which Boys and Girls Cope." *Journal of Adolescence* 14 (1991): 119–133.

Gabriel, Brother Angelus. *The Christian Brothers in the United States; 1848–1948: A Century of Catholic Education.* New York: Declan X. McMullen Co., 1948.

Gabrielli, William, and Samoff Mednick. "An Adoption Cohort Study of Genetics and Criminality." *Behavior Genetics* 13 (1983): 435.

Gainson, William, Bruce Fireman, and Steven Rytina. *Encounters with Unjust Authority.* Homewood, Ill.: Dorsey Press, 1982.

Gallup, George, Jr. *The Gallup Report.* Report No. 285. Princeton, N.J.: The Gallup Poll, June 1989a.

———. *The Gallup Report.* Report No. 289. Princeton, N.J.: The Gallup Poll, October 1989b.

Gallup, George, Jr., and D. Michael Lindsey. *Surveying the Religious Landscape: Trends in U.S. Beliefs.* Harrisburg, Pa.: Morehouse Publishing, 1999.

Gallup Poll. Gallup Poll Topics: A Z—Religion. Gallup Web site, 2000.

———. Gallup Poll Topics: Homosexual Relations. Gallup Web site, 2004a.

———. Gallup Poll Topics: A Look at Americans and Religion Today. Gallup Web site, 2004b.

———. Gallup Poll Topics: Religion. Gallup Web site, 2004c.

Gamoran, Adam, and Robert D. Mare. "Secondary School Tracking and Educational Inequality: Compensation, Reinforcement, or Neutrality?" *American Journal of Sociology* 94 (1989): 1146–1183.

Gans, Herbert J. *The Urban Villagers.* New York: The Free Press, 1962.

Gardner, R. Allen, and Beatrice T. Gardner. "Teaching Sign Language to a Chimpanzee." *Science* 165 (1969): 664–672.

Gardner, Robert W., Bryant Robey, and Peter C. Smith. "Asian Americans: Growth, Change and Diversity." *Population Bulletin,* Vol. 40, No. 4 (October 1985).

Garrison-Wade, Dorothy F., and Chance W. Lewis. "Affirmative Action: History and Analysis." *Journal of College Admission* (Summer 2004): 23–27.

Garvey, Marcus. *Philosophy and Opinions of Marcus Garvey.* Amy Jacques-Garvey (ed.). New York: Arno, 1968. (Originally published 1923.)

Gaviria, Alejandro. "Intergenerational Mobility, Sibling Inequality, and Borrowing Constraints." *Economics of Education Review* 21 (2002): 331–341.

Gayle, Jacob A., Richard M. Selik, and Susan Y. Chu. "Surveillance for AIDS and HIV Infection Among Black and Hispanic Children and Women of Childbearing Age, 1981–1989." *Morbidity and Mortality Weekly Report,* Vol. 39 (No. SS-3): 23–30. July 1990.

Gelles, Richard J. "Family Violence." *Annual Review of Sociology* 11 (1985): 347–367.

Gelles, Richard J., and Claire Pedrick Cornell (eds.). *Intimate Violence in Families.* Beverly Hills, Calif.: Sage, 1985.

Gelles, Richard J., and Murray A. Straus. *Intimate Violence.* New York: Simon & Schuster, 1988.

Gerber, Jurg, and Susan L. Weeks. "Women as Victims of Corporate Crime: A Call for Research on a Neglected Topic." *Deviant Behavior* 13 (1992): 325–347.

Gerson, Kathleen. "The Morality of Time." *Dissent* 51 (2004a): 53–56.

———. "Understanding Work and Family Through a Gender Lens." *Community, Work & Family* 7 (2004b): 163–179.

Gerson, Kathleen, and Jerry A. Jacobs. "Changing the Structure and Culture of Work: Work and Family Conflict, Work Flexibility, and Gender Equity in the Modern Workplace." In Rosanna Hertz and Nancy L. Marshall (eds.). *Working Families: The Transformation of the American Home.* Berkeley: University of California Press, 2001.

Gerstel, Naomi. "Divorce and Stigma." *Social Problems* 43 (1987): 172–186.

Giddens, Anthony. *A Contemporary Critique of Historical Materialism,* Vol. 2: *The Nation-State and Violence.* Berkeley: University of California Press, 1985.

Gilbert, Dennis, and Joseph A. Kahl. *The American Class Structure: A New Synthesis.* Belmont, Calif.: Wadsworth Publishers, 1993.

Gilmore, Mary Rogers, J. David Hawkins, L. Edward Day, and Richard F. Catalano. "Friendship and Deviance: New Evidence on an Old Controversy." *Journal of Early Adolescence* 12 (1992): 80–95.

Glass, David, Peverill Squire, and Raymond Wolfinger. "Voter Turnout: An International Comparison." *Public Opinion* 6 (1984): 49–55.

Godwin, Deborah D. "Spouses' Time Allocation to Household Work: A Review and Critique." *Lifestyles* 12 (1991): 253–294.

Goffman, Erving. *Encounters.* New York: Bobbs-Merrill, 1961a.

———. *Asylums.* Chicago: Aldine, 1961b.

Goldfield, Michael. *The Decline of Organized Labor in the United States.* New York: Basic Books, 1987.

Goldman, Ari L. "Mainstream Islam Rapidly Embraced by Black Americans." *The New York Times,* August 21, 1989, A1.

Gomes, Charlene. "Partners as Parents: Challenges Faced by Gays Denied Marriage." *Humanist* 63 (2003): 14–20.

Goode, William J. "A Theory of Role Strain." *American Sociological Review* 25 (1960): 483–496.

Gorden, William I., and Dominic A. Infante. "Test of a Communication Model of Organizational Commitment." *Communication Quarterly* 39 (1991): 144–155.

Gordon, Milton. *Assimilation in American Life.* New York: Oxford University Press, 1964a.

———. "Social Structure and Goals in Group Relations." In Morroe Berger, T. Abel, and C. Page (eds.). *Freedom and Control in Modern Society.* New York: Octagon Books, 1964b.

———. *Human Nature, Class and Ethnicity.* New York: Oxford University Press, 1978.

Gorman, Thomas J. "Cross-Class Perceptions of Social Class." *Sociological Spectrum* 20 (2000): 93–121.

Gottfried, Adele Eskeles, and Allan W. Gottfried (eds.). *Maternal Employment and Children's Development: Longitudinal Research.* New York: Plenum, 1988.

Graves, Paul. "The Persistence of Memory: Dynamics of Sociocultural Evolution." *Cultural Dynamics* 4 (1991): 290–320.

Greeley, Andrew M. *Catholic High Schools and Minority Students.* New Brunswick, N.J.: Transaction Books, 1982.

———. *Religious Change in America.* Cambridge, Mass.: Harvard University Press, 1989.

Greer, Edward. "The 'Liberation' of Gary, Indiana." *Transaction,* January 1971, 30–63.

Griffith, Janet. "Social Pressure on Family Size Intentions." *Family Planning Perspectives* 5 (1973): 237–242.

Grigsby, Jill S. "Adult Children in the Parental Household: Who Benefits?" *Lifestyles* 10 (1989): 293–309.

Grossman, Kate N. "Death of a Renaissance?" *Village Voice,* May 13, 1997, 44–45.

Gruber, Carolyn. "Naturally Occurring Play Patterns in Groups of Latency Aged Children." *Child and Adolescent Social Work Journal* 9 (1992): 35–52.

Gumperz, John J. "The Speech Community." In *International Encyclopedia of the Social Sciences.* London: Macmillan, 1968.

Gwartney-Gibbs, Patricia A., Jean Stockard, and Susanne Bohmer. "Learning Courtship Aggression: The Influence of Parents, Peers, and Personal Experiences." *Family Relations* 36 (1987): 276–282.

Hadden, Jeffrey K. "Religious Broadcasting and the Mobilization of the New Christian Right." *Journal for the Scientific Study of Religion* 26 (1987): 1–24.

Hall, Edward T. *The Silent Language.* Garden City, N.Y.: Doubleday, 1959.

Hall, Edward T., and Mildred Reed Hall. "The Sounds of Silence." *Playboy,* June 1971.

Hallinan, Maureen T., and Richard A. Williams. "Interracial Friendship Choices in Secondary Schools." *American Sociological Review* 54 (1989): 67–78.

Hamilton, Malcolm. "Inequality and Stratification." *Social Studies Review* 5 (1990): 193–196.

Harding, Harry. "China's American Dilemma." *The Annals of the American Academy of Political and Social Science* 519 (1992): 12–25.

Harrigan, Marcia P. "Advantages and Disadvantages of Multigenerational Family Households: Views of Three Generations." *Journal of Applied Gerontology* 11 (1992): 457–474.

Harrington, Michael. *The New American Poverty*. New York: Penguin, 1984.

Harris, Lis. "Lubavitcher Hasidim." *The New Yorker,* September 16, 23, and 30, 1985.

Harrison, Bennett, and Barry Bluestone. *The Great U-Turn: Corporate Restructuring and the Polarizing of America*. New York: Basic Books, 1988.

Harrison, Lana, and Joseph Gfroerer. "The Intersection of Drug Use and Criminal Behavior: Results from the National Household Survey on Drug Abuse." *Crime and Delinquency* 38 (1992): 422–443.

Hart, Roderick P., and John D. H. Downing. "Is There an American Public? An Exchange of Correspondence." *Critical Studies in Mass Communication* 9 (1992): 201–215.

Hartley, E. L. *Problems in Prejudice*. New York: Kings Crown, 1946.

Hartung, Beth, and Kim Sweeney. "Why Adult Children Return Home." *The Social Science Journal* 28 (1991): 467–480.

Hasday, Jill Elaine. "Contest and Consent: A Legal History of Marital Rape." *California Law Review* 88 (2000): 1373–1507.

Haub, Carl, and Mary Mederios Kent. *World Population Data Sheet*. Washington, D.C.: Population Reference Bureau, 1987.

Hauser, Robert M., and David L. Featherman. "Occupations and Social Mobility in the U.S." Data reprinted in *Social Indicators 1976*. Washington, D.C.: U.S. Department of Commerce, 1976.

Hayashi, Reiko. "Floor Structure of English and Japanese Conversation." *Journal of Pragmatics* 16 (1991): 1–30.

Heck, Ramona K. Z. "Employment Location Choices: Factors Associated with the Likelihood of Homebased Employment." *Lifestyles* 12 (1991): 217–233.

Heer, David M. "Economic Development and Fertility." *Demography* 3 (1966): 423–444.

Heintz, Katharine E. "Children's Favorite Television Families: A Descriptive Analysis of Role Interactions." *Journal of Broadcasting and Electronic Media* 36 (1992): 443–451.

Held, David. "The Possibilities of Democracy." *Theory and Society* 20 (1991): 875–889.

Hentoff, Nat. "'Speech Codes' on the Campus." *Dissent* 4 (1991): 546–549.

Henze, Rosemary C. "Segregated Classrooms, Integrated Intent: How One School Responded to the Challenge of Developing Positive Interethnic Relations." *Journal of Education for Students Placed at Risk* 6 (2001): 133–156.

Herman, Nancy J. "The Homeless Mentally Ill: Dilemmas and Possible Solutions." *Humanity and Society* 16 (1992): 480–503.

Hessel, Dieter. *Maggie Kuhn on Aging*. Philadelphia: Westminster Press, 1977.

Higgins, Michael. "Sizing Up Sentences." *ABA Journal* 85 (1999): 42–48.

Higley, John, and Michael G. Burton. "The Elite Variable in Democratic Transitions and Breakdowns." *American Sociological Review* 54 (1989): 17–32.

Hirschi, T., and M. J. Hindelang. "Intelligence and Delinquency: A Revisionist Review." *American Sociological Review* 42 (1977): 571–587.

Hodgkinson, Harold L. "Reform Higher Education? Don't Be Absurd." *Phi Delta Kappan* 68 (1986): 271–274.

Holcomb, Derek R., Linda C. Holcomb, K. Annie Sondag, and Nancy Williams. "Attitudes about Date Rape: Gender Differences among College Students." *College Student Journal* 25 (1991): 434–439.

hooks, bell. *Ain't I a Woman: Black Women and Feminism*. Boston: South End Press, 1981.

_____. *Feminist Theory: From Margin to Center*. Boston: South End Press, 1984.

Hopper, Rex D. "The Revolutionary Process: A Frame of Reference for the Study of Revolutionary Movements." *Social Forces* 28 (1950): 270–279.

Horowitz, Irving Louis. "The Glass Is Half Full and Half Empty: Religious Conviction and Political Participation." *Society* 28 (1991): 17–22.

Horton, Hayward Derrick. "Race and Wealth: A Demographic Analysis of Black Homeownership." *Sociological Inquiry* 62 (1992): 480–489.

Hout, Michael, and Andrew Greeley. "The Center Doesn't Hold: Church Attendance in the United States, 1940–1984." *American Sociological Review* 52 (1987): 325–345.

Huebner, E. Scott. "Correlates of Life Satisfaction in Children." *School Psychology Quarterly* 6 (1991): 103–111.

Hunter, James D. "Conservative Protestantism." In Phillip E. Hammond (ed.). *The Sacred in a Secular Age*, 150–166. Berkeley: University of California Press, 1985.

Hurtado, Aida. "Relating to Privilege: Seduction and Rejection in the Subordination of White Women and Women of Color." *Signs: Journal of Women in Culture and Society* 14 (1989): 833–855.

Hymes, Dell H. *Foundations in Sociolinguistics: An Ethnographic Approach*. Philadelphia: University of Pennsylvania Press, 1974.

Hymowitz, Kay S. "Self-Esteem and Multiculturalism in the Public Schools." *Dissent* 39 (1992): 23–29.

Ikerd, John. "Survival Strategies for Small Farms." Presented at "Survival Strategies for Small and Limited Resource Farmers and Ranchers" conference, sponsored by Risk Management Agency, USDA, Agricenter International, Memphis, Tenn., July 23–25, 2001. Available at www.ucce.ucdavis.edu/files/filelibrary/742/13158.pdf.

Infante, Dominic, and William I. Gorden. "How Employees See the Boss: Test of an Argumentative and Affirming Model of Supervisors' Communicative Behavior." *Western Journal of Speech Communication* 55 (1991): 294–304.

Ireson, Judith, Helen Clark, and Susan Hallam. "Constructing Ability Groups in the Secondary School: Issues in Practice." *School Leadership & Management* 22 (2002): 163–178.

Jackson, Phillip W. *Life in Classrooms*. New York: Holt, Rinehart and Winston, 1968.

Jacobsen, Joyce P., and Laurence M. Levin. "The Effects of Internal Migration on the Relative Economic Status of Women and Men." *Journal of Socio-Economics* 29 (2000): 291–304.

Jacobson, Cardell K., and Tim B. Heaton. "Voluntary Childlessness among American Men and Women in the Late 1980's." *Social Biology* 38 (1991): 79–93.

James, Steven E. "Clinical Themes in Gay- and Lesbian-Parented Adoptive Families." *Clinical Child Psychology & Psychiatry* 7 (2002): 475–487.

Jasinski, Jana L. "Beyond High School: An Examination of Hispanic Educational Attainment." *Social Science Quarterly* 81 (2000): 276–301.

Jencks, Christopher. "Can We Put a Time Limit on Welfare?" *The American Prospect* 11 (1992): 32–40.

Jencks, Christopher et al. *Who Gets Ahead? The Determinants of Economic Success in America*. New York: Basic Books, 1979.

Jenkins, J. Craig. *The Politics of Insurgency: The Farm Workers Movement in the 1960s*. New York: Columbia University Press, 1986.

Jenkins, Philip, and Daniel Maier-Katkin. "Satanism: Myth and Reality in a Contemporary Moral Panic." *Crime, Law and Social Change* 17 (1992): 53–75.

Jennings, M. Kent, and Richard G. Niemi. *Generations and Politics*. Princeton, N.J.: Princeton University Press, 1981.

Jensen, Gary F. "Explaining Differences in Academic Behavior Between Public-School and Catholic-School Students: A Quantitative Case Study." *Sociology of Education* 59 (1986): 32–41.

Jermier, John M., John W. Slocum Jr., Louis W. Fry, and Jeannie Gaines. "Organizational Subcultures in a Soft Bureaucracy: Resistance behind the Myth and Facade of an Official Culture." *Organizational Science* 2 (1991): 170–194.

Jernigan, D. E., and R. F. Kronick. "Intensive Parole: The More You Watch, the More You Catch." *Journal of Offender Rehabilitation* 17 (1992): 65–76.

Johansson, Sten, and Ola Nygren. "The Missing Girls of China: A New Demographic Account." *Population and Development Review* 17 (1991): 33–51.

Johnson, D. M. "The 'Phantom Anesthetist' of Mattoon: A Field Study of Mass Hysteria." *Journal of Abnormal and Social Psychology* 40 (1945): 175–186.

Johnson, Ida M. "Economic, Situational, and Psychological Correlates of the Decision-Making Process of Battered Women." *Families in Society* 73 (1992): 168–176.

Johnson, Ida M., and Robert T. Sigler. "Forced Sexual Intercourse Among Intimates." *Journal of Family Violence* 15 (2000): 95–119.

Johnson, Leanor Boulin. "Job Strain Among Police Officers: Gender Comparisons." *Police Studies* 14 (1991): 12–16.

Jones, Maldwyn Allen. *American Immigration*. Chicago: University of Chicago Press, 1960.

Jones, Stephan R. G. "Was There a Hawthorne Effect?" *American Journal of Sociology* 98 (1992): 451–468.

Joseph, Antoine. "The Resurgence of Racial Conflict in Post Industrial America." *International Journal of Politics, Culture and Society* 5 (1991): 81–93.

Josephy, Alvin M. *Now That the Buffalo's Gone: A Study of Today's American Indians*. New York: Knopf, 1982.

Kaempfer, William H., and Anton D. Lowenberg. "A Threshold Model of Electoral Policy and Voter Turnout." *Rationality and Society* 5 (1993): 107–126.

Kagan, Jerome. *Emotions, Cognition and Behavior*. New York: Cambridge University Press, 1984.

Kakuchi, Suvendrini. "Japan: Amid Shrinking Paychecks, Signs of the 'New Worker.'" *Asia Times*, December 24, 1999.

Kalmijn, Matthijs. "Status Homogamy in the United States." *American Journal of Sociology* 97 (1991): 496–523.

Katz, Milton S. *Ban the Bomb: A History of SANE—The Committee for a Sane Nuclear Policy, 1957–1985.* Westport, Conn.: Greenwood Press, 1986.

Kaufman, Jeanne G., and Cathy Spatz Widom. "Childhood Victimization, Running Away, and Delinquency." *Journal of Research in Crime and Delinquency* 36 (1999): 347–371.

Keefe, Susan E., and Amado M. Padilla. *Chicano Ethnicity.* Albuquerque: University of New Mexico Press, 1987.

Kennichell, Arthur, and R. Louise Woodbum. "Estimation of Household Net Worth Using Model-Based and Design-Based Weights: Evidence from the 1989 Survey of Consumer Finances." Unpublished paper. Washington, D.C.: Board of Governors of the Federal Reserve System, 1992.

Kephart, William. *Extraordinary Groups: The Sociology of Unconventional Life-Styles* (3rd ed.). New York: St. Martin's Press, 1987.

Kerbo, Harold R. *Social Stratification and Inequality: Class Conflict in the United States.* New York: McGraw-Hill, 1983.

Kerckhoff, Alan, Kurt Back, and Norman Miller. "Sociometric Patterns in Hysterical Contagion." *Sociometry* 28 (1965): 2–15.

Kessler, Ronald C., Guilherme Borges, and Ellen E. Walters. "Prevalence of and Risk Factors for Lifetime Suicide Attempts in the National Comorbidity Survey." *Archives of General Psychiatry* 56 (1999): 617–626.

Kessner, Thomas, and Betty Boyd Caroli. *Today's Immigrants: Their Stories.* New York: Oxford University Press, 1982.

Kin, Kwan Weng. "Part-time Worker Trend Worries Japan." *The Strait Times,* June 29, 2003.

King, C. Wendell. *Social Movements in the United States.* New York: Random House, 1956.

Kirat, Thierry. "The Social Mastery of Technology: An Agenda for Research and Action." *Futures* 24 (1992): 615–620.

Kitano, Harry H. L. *Japanese Americans: The Evolution of a Subculture.* Englewood Cliffs, N.J.: Prentice-Hall, 1976.

Kitcher, Philip. *Vaulting Ambitions: Sociobiology and the Quest for Human Nature.* Cambridge, Mass.: MIT Press, 1985.

Klinger, David A. "Demeanor or Crime? Why 'Hostile' Citizens Are More Likely to be Arrested." *Criminology* 32 (1994): 475–493.

Knowlton, Clark. "Land-Grant Problems Among the State's Spanish-Americans." *New Mexico Business* 20 (1967): 1–13.

Kohn, Melvin L., and Carmi Schooler. *Work and Personality: An Inquiry into the Impact of Social Stratification.* New York: Ablex Press, 1983.

Kohn, Melvin L., Atsushi Naoi, Cartie Schoenbach, Carmi Schooler, and Kazimierz M. Slomczynski. "Position in the Class Structure and Psychological Functioning in the United States, Japan and Poland." *American Journal of Sociology* 95 (1990): 964–1008.

Kohn, Stephen M. *Jailed for Peace: The History of American Draft Law Violators 1658–1985.* Westport, Conn.: Greenwood Press, 1986.

Kosmin, Barry, Egon Mayer, and Ariela Keysar. "American Religious Identity Survey (ARIS)." The Graduate Center, City University of New York, 2001. www.gc.cuny.edu/studies/aris.pdf.

Kozol, Jonathan. *Illiterate America.* Garden City, N.Y.: Anchor Press, 1985.

Kriesberg, Louis. *Social Inequality.* Englewood Cliffs, N.J.: Prentice-Hall, 1979.

———. "Transformations in the Soviet Union and in East-West Relations: Epilogue." *Research in Social Movements, Conflicts and Change* 14 (1992): 291–297.

Krohn, Marvin D., Susan B. Stein, Terence P. Thornberry, and Sung Joon Jang. "The Measurement of Family Process Variables: The Effect of Adolescent and Parent Perceptions of Family Life on Delinquent Behavior." *Journal of Quantitative Criminology* 8 (1992): 287–315.

Kruttschnitt, Candace, and Maude Dornfeld. "Will They Tell? Assessing Preadolescents' Reports of Family Violence." *Journal of Research in Crime and Delinquency* 29 (1992): 136–147.

Kubitschek, Warren N., and Maureen T. Hallinan. "Race, Gender and Inequity in Track Assignments." *Research in Sociology of Education and Socialization* 11 (1996): 121–146.

Labov, William. "The Study of Language in Its Social Context." *Studium Generale* 23 (1970): 30–87.

Lance, Larry M. "Changes in Homophobic Views as Related to Interaction with Gay Persons: A Study in the Reduction of Tensions." *International Journal of Group Tensions* 22 (1992): 291–299.

Larson, Robert W. "The White Caps of New Mexico: A Study of Ethnic Militancy in the Southwest." *Pacific Historical Review* 22 (1975): 171–185.

Lazerwitz, Bernard, and Michael Harrison. "American Jewish Denomination: A Social and Religious Profile." *American Sociological Review* 44 (1979): 656–666.

Leavitt, Gregory C. "Sociobiological Explanations of Incest Avoidance: A Critical Review of Evidential Claims." *American Anthropologist* 92 (1990): 971–993.

LeBon, Gustave. *The Mind of Crowds.* London: Unwin, 1897.

Lee, Barrett A., David W. Lewis, and Susan Hinze Jones. "Are the Homeless to Blame? A Test of Two Theories." *The Sociological Quarterly* 33 (1992): 535–552.

Lee, Carol D. "Literacy, Cultural Diversity, and Instruction." *Education and Urban Society* 24 (1992): 279–291.

Lee, Richard B. *The !Kung San: Men, Women, and Work in a Foraging Society.* New York: Cambridge University Press, 1979.

Lemert, Edwin. *Human Deviance, Social Problems and Social Control.* Englewood Cliffs, N.J.: Prentice-Hall, 1967.

Lenski, Gerhard E. "Social Participation and Status Crystallization." *American Sociological Review* 21 (1956): 458–464.

———. *Power and Privilege: A Theory of Social Stratification.* New York: McGraw-Hill, 1966.

Lenski, Gerhard E., and Jean Lenski. *Human Societies: An Introduction to Macro Sociology* (2nd ed.). New York: McGraw-Hill, 1974.

Leonard, Jacqueline. "How Group Composition Influenced the Achievement of Sixth-Grade Mathematics Students." *Mathematical Thinking & Learning.* 3 (2001): 175–201.

Levi, Margaret, and David Olson. "The Battles in Seattle." *Politics & Society* 28 (2000): 309–330.

Levin, Jack. *The Functions of Prejudice.* New York: Harper & Row, 1975.

Levitt, Cyril. *Children of Privilege: Student Revolt in the Sixties.* Toronto: University of Toronto Press, 1984.

Levy, Paul E., and Ann H. Baumgardner. "Effects of Self-Esteem and Gender on Goal Choice." *Journal of Organizational Behavior* 12 (1991): 529–541.

Lewin, Arthur. "A Tale of Two Classes: The Black Poor and the Black Middle Class." *The Black Scholar* 21 (1991): 7–13.

Lewis, Jerry M. "A Study of the Kent State Incident Using Smelser's Theory of Collective Behavior." *Sociological Inquiry* 42 (1972): 87–96.

Liebman, Robert C., John R. Sutton, and Robert Wuthnow. "Exploring the Social Sources of Denominationalism: Schisms in American Protestant Denominations." *American Sociological Review* 53 (1988): 343–352.

Lifton, Robert. "Thought Reform: Psychological Steps in Death and Rebirth." In Alfred Lindesmith and Anselm Strauss (eds.). *Readings in Social Psychology.* New York: Holt, Rinehart and Winston, 1969.

Lipset, Seymour M., and Earl Raab. "The Elections and the Evangelicals." *Commentary* 71 (1981): 26–32.

Lipset, Seymour M., and William Schneider. "Political Sociology." In Neil J. Smelser (ed.). *Sociology: An Introduction* (2nd ed.), 399–491. New York: Wiley, 1973.

Lofland, John. *Doomsday Cult.* New York: Irvington, 1977.

Logan, T. K., Robert Walker, Leah S. Horvath, and Carl Leukefeld. "Divorce, Custody, and Spousal Violence: A Random Sample of Circuit Court Docket Records." *Journal of Family Violence* 18 (2003): 269–280.

Lorber, Judith. *Women Physicians: Careers, Status and Power.* New York: Tavistock, 1984.

Lord, Walter. *A Night to Remember.* New York: Holt, Rinehart and Winston, 1955.

Lowe, John. "International Examinations: The New Credentialism and Reproduction of Advantage in a Globalising World." *Assessment in Education: Principles, Policy & Practice* 7 (2000): 364–378.

Luhman, Reid. "Appalachian English Stereotypes: Language Attitudes in Kentucky." *Language in Society* 19 (1990): 331–348.

———. *Race and Ethnicity in the United States: Our Differences and Our Roots.* Fort Worth, Tex.: Harcourt College Publishers, 2002.

Lundman, Richard J. "Demeanor or Crime? The Midwest City Police-Citizen Encounters Study." *Criminology* 32 (1994): 631–656.

Lyman, Stanford M. "Contrasts in the Community Organization of Chinese and Japanese in North America." In N. Yetman and H. Steele (eds.). *Majority and Minority: The Dynamics of Racial and Ethnic Relations.* Boston: Allyn & Bacon, 1975.

———. "The Assimilation-Pluralism Debate: Toward a Postmodern Resolution of the American Ethnoracial Dilemma." *International Journal of Politics, Culture and Society* 6 (1992): 181–210.

Mahard, Rita E., and Robert L. Crain. "Research on Minority Achievement in Desegregated Schools." In Christine H. Rossell and Willis D. Hawley (eds.). *The Consequences of School Desegregation,* 103–125. Philadelphia: Temple University Press, 1983.

Makepeace, James M. "Gender Differences in Courtship Violence Victimization." *Family Relations* 35 (1986): 383–388.

Marcuse, Peter. "Homelessness and Housing Policy." In Carol L. M. Caton (ed.). *Homeless in America.* New York: Oxford University Press, 1990.

Marmor, Judd. "'Normal' and 'Deviant' Sexual Behavior." *Journal of the American Medical Association* 217 (1971): 165–170.

Marx, Karl. *Selected Writings in Sociology and Social Philosophy.* Trans. T. B. Bottomore. New York: McGraw-Hill, 1956.

———. *Capital.* Trans. Eden Paul and Ceder Paul (Vol. 1). New York: Dutton, 1976. (Originally published 1897.)

Massey, Douglas S. "Segregation, the Concentration of Poverty, and the Life Chances of Individuals." *Social Science Research* 20 (1991): 397–420.

Mayer, Egon, Barry Kosmin, and Ariela Keysar. "American Jewish Identity Survey." The Graduate Center, City University of New York, 2002. www.gc.cuny.edu/studies/ajis.pdf.

McCarthy, Cameron. "Multicultural Approaches to Racial Inequality in the United States." *Curriculum and Teaching* 5 (1990): 25–35.

McCarthy, John D., and Mayer N. Zald. *The Trend of Social Movements in America: Professionalization and Resource Mobilization.* Morristown, N.J.: General Learning Press, 1973.

———. "Resource Mobilization and Social Movements: A Partial Theory." *American Journal of Sociology* 82 (1977): 1212–1241.

McDonald, Theodore W., and Linda M. Kline. "Perceptions of Appropriate Punishment for Committing Daterape: Male College Students Recommend Lenient Punishment." *College Student Journal* 38 (2004): 44–57.

McNeill, William H. *Plagues and Peoples.* Garden City, N.Y.: Anchor Press/Doubleday, 1976.

McPhail, Clark. *The Myth of the Madding Crowd.* New York: Aldine de Gruyter, 1991.

McRae, James A., Jr. "Rasch Measurement and Differences between Women and Men in Self-Esteem." *Social Science Research* 20 (1991): 421–436.

McVittie, Chris, Andy McKinlay, and Sue Widdicombe. "Committed to (Un)equal Opportunities?: 'New Ageism' and the Older Worker." *British Journal of Social Psychology* 42 (2003): 595–613.

Mead, George Herbert. *Mind, Self and Society: From the Standpoint of a Social Behaviorist.* Charles W. Morris (ed.). Chicago: University of Chicago Press, 1934.

Mechanic, David. "Sources of Power of Lower Participants in Complex Organizations." *Administrative Science Quarterly* 7 (1962): 349–364.

Medalia, Nahum Z., and Otto N. Larsen. "Diffusion and Belief in a Collective Delusion: The Seattle Windshield Pitting Epidemic." *American Sociological Review* 23 (1958): 221–232.

Merari, Ariel. "Israel Facing Terrorism." *Israel Affairs* 11 (2005): 223–238.

Mercer, Jane. *Labeling the Mentally Retarded.* Berkeley: University of California Press, 1973.

Merrick, Thomas W. "World Population in Transition." *Population Bulletin,* Vol. 41, No. 2 (1986).

Merton, Robert. *Social Theory and Social Structure.* Glencoe, Ill.: The Free Press, 1956.

———. "Manifest and Latent Functions." In *Social Theory and Social Structure.* New York: The Free Press, 1968.

Meyer, Foy, III. "The Rise and Fall of Affirmative Action." *Texas Review of Law & Politics* 8 (2004): 437–534.

Miceli, Marcia P., and Janet P. Near. "Whistle-Blowing as an Organizational Process." *Research in the Sociology of Organizations* 9 (1991): 139–200.

Middleton, Russell, and Snell Putney. "Student Rebellion Against Parental Political Beliefs." *Social Forces* 41 (1963): 377–383.

Milgram, Stanley. *Obedience to Authority.* New York: Harper & Row, 1974.

Milkie, Melissa A., and Pia Peltola. "Playing All the Roles: Gender and the Work-Family Balancing Act." *Journal of Marriage and the Family* 61 (1999): 476–491.

Miller, David L. *Introduction to Collective Behavior.* Belmont, Calif.: Wadsworth, 1985.

Miller, L. Scott. *An American Imperative: Accelerating Minority Educational Advancement.* New Haven, Conn.: Yale University Press, 1995.

Miller, W. B. "Lower Class Culture as a Generating Milieu of Gang Delinquency." *Journal of Social Issues* 14 (1958): 5–19

Mills, C. Wright. *The Power Elite.* New York: Oxford University Press, 1956.

———. *The Sociological Imagination.* New York: Oxford University Press, 1959.

———. "The Sociology of Stratification." In Irving Horowitz (ed.). *Power, Politics and People: The Collected Essays of C. Wright Mills.* New York: Oxford University Press, 1963.

Mingle, James R. *Focus on Minorities: Trends in Higher Education Participation and Success.* Denver: Education Commission of the States, 1987.

Mokhiber, Russell. "White-Collar Crime Spree." *Multinational Monitor,* July/August 2000, 38.

Monk-Turner, Elizabeth. "The Occupational Achievements of Community and Four-Year College Entrants." *American Sociological Review* 55 (1990): 719–725.

Moore, Joan W. *Mexican Americans*. Englewood Cliffs, N.J.: Prentice-Hall, 1976.

Morgan, Carolyn Stout. "College Students' Perceptions of Barriers to Women in Science and Engineering." *Youth and Society* 24 (1992): 228–236.

Morgan, S. Philip, Diane N. Lye, and Gretchen A. Condran. "Sons, Daughters, and the Risk of Marital Disruption." *American Sociological Review* 52 (1988): 278–285.

Morrison, Denton E. "Some Notes Toward Theory on Relative Deprivation, Social Movements, and Social Change." *American Behavioral Scientist* 14 (1971): 675–690.

Moynihan, Daniel P. *The Negro Family: The Case for National Action*. Washington, D.C.: U.S. Department of Labor, 1965.

Muehlenhard, C. L., and M. A. Linton. "Date Rape and Sexual Aggression in Dating Situations: Incidence and Risk Factors." *Journal of Counseling Psychology* 34 (1987): 186–196.

Muller, Edward N. "Democracy, Economic Development, and Income Inequality." *American Sociological Review* 53 (1988): 50–68.

Murdock, George P. *Ethnographic Atlas*. Pittsburgh: University of Pittsburgh Press, 1967.

Naoi, Atsushi, and Carmi Schooler. "Occupational Conditions and Psychological Functioning in Japan." *American Journal of Sociology* 90 (1985): 729–752.

National Advisory Commission on Civil Disorders. *Report of the National Advisory Commission on Civil Disorders*. New York: Bantam, 1968.

National Center for Health Statistics. *Health, United States, 1996–97 and Injury Chartbook*. Hyattsville, Md.: National Center for Health Statistics, 1997.

National Commission on Excellence in Education. *A Nation at Risk: The Imperative for Educational Reform*. Washington, D.C.: U.S. Government Printing Office, 1983.

National Opinion Research Center. *National Data Program for the Social Sciences, Code Book for the Spring 1976, General Social Survey*. Chicago: University of Chicago Press, 1976.

———. General Social Surveys, 1972–1989. Chicago: National Opinion Research Center, 1989.

Neugebauer, Richard. "Research on Intergenerational Transmission of Violence: The Next Generation." *Lancet* 355 (2000): 1116–1117.

Newman, William M. *American Pluralism: A Study of Minority Groups and Social Theory*. New York: Harper & Row, 1973.

Nichols, Lawrence T. "'Whistleblower' or 'Renegade': Definitional Contests in an Official Inquiry." *Symbolic Interaction* 14 (1991): 395–414.

Nightingale, Narina Nunez, and Elaine F. Walker. "The Impact of Social Class and Parental Maltreatment on the Cognitive Functioning of Children." *Journal of Family Violence* 6 (1991): 115–130.

Noel, Donald L. "A Theory of the Origin of Ethnic Stratification." *Social Problems* 16 (1968): 157–172.

Oakes, Jeannie. "Classroom Social Relationships: Exploring the Bowles and Gintis Hypothesis." *Sociology of Education* 55 (1985): 197–212.

Ogburn, William Fielding. *Social Change*. Gloucester, Mass.: Peter Smith, 1964.

O'Hare, William P. "Poverty in America: Trends and New Patterns." *Population Bulletin,* Vol. 40, No. 3 (June 1985).

O'Hare, William P., Kelvin M. Pollard, Taynia L. Mann, and Mary M. Kent. *African Americans in the 1990s*. Washington, D.C.: Population Reference Bureau, 1991.

Oliver, J. Eric. "The Effects of Metropolitan Economic Segregation on Local Civic Participation." *American Journal of Political Science* 43 (1999): 186–203.

Ollerton, Mike. "Inclusion and Entitlement, Equality of Opportunity and Quantity of Curriculum Provision." *Support for Learning* 16 (2001): 35–41.

Oppenheimer, Valerie Kincaide. "A Theory of Marriage Timing." *American Journal of Sociology* 94 (1988): 563–591.

Orum, Anthony M. *Introduction to Political Sociology: The Social Anatomy of the Body Politic*. Englewood Cliffs, N.J.: Prentice-Hall, 1978.

Osman, Suzanne L. "Predicting Men's Rape Perceptions Based on the Belief That 'No' Really Means 'Yes.'" *Journal of Applied Social Psychology* 33 (2003): 683–693.

Pabon, Edward, Orlando Rodriguez, and Gerald Gurin. "Clarifying Peer Relations and Delinquency." *Youth and Society* 24 (1992): 149–165.

Page, Michael S. "Technology-Enriched Classrooms: Effects on Students of Low Socioeconomic Status." *Journal of Research on Technology in Education* 34 (2002): 389–410.

Pakiz, Bilge, Helen Z. Reinherz, and Abbie K. Frost. "Antisocial Behavior in Adolescence: A Community Study." *Journal of Early Adolescence* 12 (1992): 300–313.

Palley, Howard A., and Dana A. Robinson. "Black-on-Black Crime: Poverty, Marginality, and the Underclass Debate from a Global Perspective." *Social Development Issues* 12 (1990): 52–61.

Parkinson, C. Northcote. *Parkinson's Law and Other Studies in Administration.* Boston: Houghton Mifflin, 1957.

Pederson, D. M. "Developmental Trends in Personal Space." *Journal of Psychology* 83 (1973): 3–9.

Perrow, Charles. *Complex Organization: A Critical Essay* (3rd ed.). New York: Random House, 1986.

Perry, Joseph B., Jr., and M. D. Pugh. *Collective Behavior: Response to Social Stress.* St. Paul, Minn.: West, 1978.

Peter, Laurence, and Raymond Hull. *The Peter Principle.* New York: Bantam, 1969.

Peterson, Ruth D., and William C. Bailey. "Felony Murder and Capital Punishment: An Examination of the Deterrence Question." *Criminology* 29 (1991): 367–395.

Phillips, Bernard. *Sociological Research Methods: An Introduction.* Homewood, Ill.: Dorsey, 1985.

Piaget, Jean. *The Moral Judgment of the Child.* Trans. Marjorie Gabain. New York: The Free Press, 1965.

Pinkney, Alphonso. *Black Americans.* Englewood Cliffs, N.J.: Prentice-Hall, 1975.

Pleck, Joseph H. *Working Wives/Working Husbands.* Beverly Hills, Calif.: Sage, 1985.

Porter, Bruce, and Marvin Dunn. *The Miami Riot of 1980: Crossing the Bounds.* Lexington, Mass.: D. C. Heath, 1984.

Potter, W. James, and Stacy Smith. "The Context of Graphic Portrayals of Television Violence." *Journal of Broadcasting & Electronic Media* 44 (2000): 301–324.

Price, Jerome B. *The Antinuclear Movement.* Boston: Twayne, 1982.

Princeton Religion Research Center. *Religion in America 1990.* Princeton, N.J.: Princeton Religion Research Center, 1990.

Psychological Reports. "Numbers of Homosexual Parents Living with Their Children." *Psychological Reports* 94 (2004): 179–189.

Quinney, Richard. *Class, State and Crime: On the Theory and Practice of Criminal Justice* (2nd ed.). New York: Longman, 1980.

Raschke, Helen J. "Divorce." In Marvin B. Sussman and Suzanne K. Steinmetz (eds.). *Handbook of Marriage and the Family,* 597–624. New York: Plenum, 1987.

Rawlings, Steve W. "Single Parents and Their Children." In *Studies in Marriage and the Family.* Current Population Reports, Series P-23, No. 162, pp. 13–26. Washington, D.C.: U.S. Government Printing Office, U.S. Bureau of the Census, June 1989.

Reckless, W. C. *The Crime Problem* (4th ed.). New York: Appleton-Century-Crofts, 1967.

Reiman, Jeffrey H. *The Rich Get Richer and the Poor Get Prison: Ideology, Class and Criminal Justice.* Boston: Allyn & Bacon, 1998.

Riesman, David, Nathan Glazer, and Reuel Denney. *The Lonely Crowd.* New Haven, Conn.: Yale University Press, 1950.

Roach, Jack L., and Orville R. Gursslin. "The Lower Class, Status Frustration and Social Disorganization." *Social Forces* 43 (1965): 501–507.

Roethlisberger, Fritz, and William Dickson. *Management and the Worker.* New York: Wiley, 1964.

Rodgers, Joseph Lee, Paul A. Nakonezny, and Robert D. Shell. "Did No-Fault Divorce Legislation Matter? Definitely Yes and Sometimes No." *Journal of Marriage and the Family* 61(1999): 803–809.

Rogers, Karen B. "Grouping the Gifted and Talented." *Roeper Review* 24 (2002): 103–108.

Rogers, Patrick, and Maria Eftimiades. "Bearing Witness." *People Weekly* 44 (1995): 42–43.

Rogers, Stacy J., and Paul R. Amato. "Have Changes in Gender Relations Affected Marital Quality?" *Social Forces* 79 (2000): 731–753.

Roiphe, Anne. "Confessions of a Female Chauvinist Sow." *New York Magazine,* October 1972.

Rolle, Andrew F. *The American Italians.* Belmont, Calif.: Wadsworth, 1972.

Roof, Wade Clark, and William McKinney. *American Mainline Religion: Its Changing Shape and Future.* New Brunswick: Rutgers University Press, 1987.

Rose, Nancy E., and Lynn Bravewomon. "Family Webs: A Study of Extended Families in the Lesbian/Gay/Bisexual Community." *Feminist Economics* 4 (1998): 107–110.

Rosen, Lawrence, Leonard Savitz, Michael Lalli, and Stanley Turner. "Early Delinquency, High School Graduation, and Adult Criminality." *Sociological Viewpoints* 7 (1991): 37–60.

Rosenhan, D. L. "On Being Sane in Insane Places." *Science* 179 (1973): 250–258.

Rosenthal, Robert, and Lenore Jacobson. *Pygmalion in the Classroom.* New York: Holt, Rinehart and Winston, 1968.

Ross, Catherine. "The Division of Labor at Home." *Social Forces* 65 (1987): 816–833.

Ross, Catherine E., John Mirowsky, and Joan Huber. "Dividing Work, Sharing Work, and In-Between: Marriage Patterns and Depression." *American Sociological Review* 48 (1983): 809–823.

Rossi, Peter, James Wright, Gene Fisher, and Georgianna Willis. "The Urban Homeless: Estimating Composition and Size." *Science* 235 (1987): 1336–1341.

Rossides, Daniel W. "Knee-Jerk Formalism: Reforming American Education." *Journal of Higher Education* 75 (2004): 667–704.

———. *The American Class System: An Introduction to Social Stratification.* Boston: Houghton Mifflin, 1976.

Roy, Donald. "Quota Restriction and Goldbricking in a Machine Shop." *American Journal of Sociology* 57 (1952): 427–442.

Roy, William G. "The Unfolding of the Interlocking Directorate Structure of the United States." *American Sociological Review* 48 (1983): 248–257.

Ryscavage, Paul. "Recent Data on Job Prospects of College-Educated Youth." *Monthly Labor Review* 116 (1993): 16–26.

Rytina, Steven. "Is Occupational Mobility Declining in the U.S.?" *Social Forces* 78 (2000): 1227–1277.

Sagarin, Edward (ed.). *The Other Minorities.* Waltham, Mass.: Ginn, 1971.

Sanders, Jerry W. "From Solidarity to Cooperation: The German Case." *Research in Social Movements, Conflicts and Change* 14 (1992): 255–289.

Sanger, Margaret. *An Autobiography.* New York: W. W. Norton, 1938.

Schein, Edgar, Inge Schneier, and Curtis Barker. *Coercive Persuasion: A Sociopsychological Analysis of the "Brainwashing" of American Civilian Prisoners by the Chinese Communists.* New York: W. W. Norton, 1961.

Schur, Edwin. *Crimes Without Victims.* Englewood Cliffs, N.J.: Prentice-Hall, 1965.

Schutz, Alfred. *On Phenomenology and Social Relations.* Chicago: University of Chicago Press, 1970.

Schwadel, Philip. "Individual, Congregational, and Denominational Effects on Church Members' Civic Participation." *Journal for the Scientific Study of Religion* 44 (2005): 159–172.

Scott, George M., Jr. "To Catch or Not to Catch a Thief: A Case of Bride Theft among the Lao Hmong Refugees in Southern California." *Ethnic Groups* 7 (1988): 137–151.

Scruton, Roger. *The West and the Rest: Globalization and the Terrorist Threat.* Wilmington, Del.: Intercollegiate Studies Institute, 2002.

Scudder, Richard, and C. Arnold Anderson. "Migration and Vertical Occupational Mobility." *American Sociological Review* 19 (1954): 329–334.

Sedgwick, Mark. "Al-Qaeda and the Nature of Religious Terrorism." *Terrorism & Political Violence* 16 (2004): 795–815.

Seeman, Melvin. "The Signals of '68: Alienation in the Pre-Crisis France." *American Sociological Review* 37 (1972): 385–402.

Seltzer, Judith A., and Deborah Kalmuss. "Socialization and Stress Explanations for Spouse Abuse." *Social Forces* 67 (1988): 473–491.

Selznick, Philip. *TVA and the Grass Roots.* Berkeley: University of California Press, 1949.

Serwatka, Thomas S., Sharian Deering, and Patrick Grant. "Disproportionate Representation of African Americans in Emotionally Handicapped Classes." *Journal of Black Studies* 25 (1995): 492–506.

Sheley, Joseph F. "Structural Influences on the Problem of Race, Crime, and Criminal Justice Discrimination." *Tulane Law Review* 67 (1993): 2273–2292.

Sherrill, Robert. "A Year in Corporate Crime." *Nation,* April 7, 1997, 11–18.

Shrier, Diane K. "Sexual Harassment and Discrimination: Impact on Physical and Mental Health." *New Jersey Medicine* 87 (1990): 105–107.

Shupe, Anson D. *The New Vigilantes: Deprogrammers, Anti-Cultists and the New Religions.* Beverly Hills, Calif.: Sage, 1980.

Shupe, Anson, William A. Stacey, and Lonnie R. Hazelwood. *Violent Men, Violent Couples: The Dynamics of Domestic Violence.* Lexington, Mass.: Lexington Books, 1987.

Simmel, Georg. *Conflict and the Web of Group Affiliations.* Trans. Kurt H. Wolff and Reinhard Bendix. New York: The Free Press, 1955.

———. *The Sociology of Georg Simmel.* Trans. and ed. Kurt H. Wolff. New York: The Free Press, 1950.

Simon, David R., and D. Stanley Eitzen. *Elite Deviance* (2nd ed.). Boston: Allyn & Bacon, 1986.

Simpson, Richard L. "A Modification of the Functional Theory of Stratification." *Social Forces* 35 (1956): 130–139.

Sinclair, Ward. "For Miners the Contract Is the Ace in the Hole." *Los Angeles Times—Washington Post News Service,* 1978.

Singer, Mark I., and David B. Miller. "Contributors to Violent Behavior Among Elementary and Middle School Children." *Pediatrics* 104 (1999): 878–884.

Singh, Vijai P. "The Underclass in the United States: Some Correlates of Economic Change." *Sociological Inquiry* 61 (1991): 505–521.

Smelser, Neil J. *Theory of Collective Behavior.* New York: The Free Press, 1962.

Smith, Anna Marie. "The Politicization of Marriage in Contemporary American Public Policy: The Defense of Marriage Act and the Personal Responsibility Act." *Citizenship Studies* 5 (2001): 303–320.

Smith, Jackie. "The 1989 Chinese Student Movement: Lessons for Nonviolent Activists." *Peace & Change* 17 (1992): 82–101.

Smith, M. Dwayne, Joel A. Devine, and Joseph F. Sheley. "Crime and Unemployment: Effects across Age and Race Categories." *Sociological Perspectives* 35 (1992): 551–572.

Smuts, R. W. "Fat, Sex, Class, Adaptive Flexibility, and Cultural Change." *Ethnology and Sociobiology* 13 (1992): 523–542.

Soltow, Lee, and Edward Stevens. *The Rise of Literacy and the Common School in the United States: A Socioeconomic Analysis to 1870.* Chicago: University of Chicago Press, 1981.

Sowell, Thomas. *The Economics and Politics of Race.* New York: Morrow, 1983.

Spiers, Joseph, and Lenore Schiff. "Where Americans Are Moving." *Fortune,* August 21, 1995, 38–39.

Stacey, Judith, and Timothy J. Biblarz. "(How) Does the Sexual Orientation of Parents Matter?" *American Sociological Review* 66 (2001): 159–184.

Stack, Carol B. *All Our Kin: Strategies for Survival in a Black Community.* New York: Harper & Row, 1975.

Stahl, Sidney, and Marty Lebedun. "Mystery Gas: An Analysis of Mass Hysteria." *Journal of Health and Social Behavior* 15 (1974): 44–50.

Stark, Rodney, and Williams Sims Bainbridge. *The Future of Religion: Secularization, Revival, and Cult Formation.* Berkeley: University of California Press, 1985.

Stark, Rodney, and Charles Y. Glock. *American Piety: The Nature of Religious Commitment.* Berkeley: University of California Press, 1968.

Stebbins, Robert A. "Role Distance, Role Distance Behavior and Jazz Musicians." *British Journal of Sociology* 21 (1969): 406–415.

Stedman, Lawrence C., and Carl F. Kaestle. "Literacy and Reading Performance in the United States from 1880 to the Present." In Carl E. Kaestle, Helen Damon-Moore, Lawrence C. Stedman, Katherine Tinsley, and William Vance Trollinger, Jr. (eds.). *Literacy in the United States.* New Haven, Conn.: Yale University Press, 1991.

Stein, Martin T., Ellen C. Perrin, and Jennifer Potter. "A Difficult Adjustment to School: The Importance of Family Constellation." *Pediatrics* 114 (2004): 1464–1468.

Steinfels, Peter. "American Jews Stand Firmly to the Left." *The New York Times,* January 8, 1989.

Straus, Murray A., and R. J. Gelles. "Societal Change and Change in Family Violence from 1975 to 1985 as Revealed by Two National Surveys." *Journal of Marriage and the Family* 48 (1986): 465–479.

Strauss, Anselm, Leonard Schatzman, Rue Bucher, Danuta Ehrlich, and Melvin Sabshin. *Psychiatric Ideologies and Institutions.* New York: The Free Press, 1964.

Sumner, William Graham. *Folkways.* Boston: Ginn, 1906.

Suro, Roberto. "Movement at Warp Speed." *American Demographics,* August 2000, 60–64.

Sutherland, Edwin. *White Collar Crime.* New York: Dryden, 1949.

———. "Differential Association." In Marvin Wolfgang, Leonard Savity, and Norman Johnston (eds.). *The Sociology of Crime and Delinquency.* New York: Wiley, 1962.

Swadesh, Frances Leon. *Los Primeros Pobladores: Hispanic Americans of the Ute Frontier.* Notre Dame, Ind.: University of Notre Dame Press, 1974.

Tasker, Fiona. "Children in Lesbian-led Families: A Review." *Clinical Child Psychology & Psychiatry* 4 (1999): 153–167.

Taub, Amy, and Robert Weissman. "Oligopoly!" *Multinational Monitor,* November 1998, 9–13.

Taylor, S., R. Shuntich, and R. Genthner. *Violence at Kent State: The Student's Perspective.* New York: College Notes and Texts, 1971.

Teachman, Jay D., and Paul T. Schollaert. "Economic Conditions, Marital Status, and the Timing of First Births: Results for Whites and Blacks." *Sociological Forum* 4 (1989): 27–46.

Tedin, Kent L., and Gregory R. Weiher. "Racial/Ethnic Diversity and Academic Quality as Components of School Choice." *Journal of Politics* 66 (2004): 1109–1134.

Teixeira, Ruy A. *Why Americans Don't Vote: Turnout Decline in the United States, 1960–1984.* Westport, Conn.: Greenwood, 1987.

Thompson, Aaron, and Reid Luhman. "Familial Predictors of Educational Attainment: Regional and Racial Variations." In Peter M. Hall (ed.). *Race, Ethnicity, and Multiculturalism: Policy and Practice*, 63–88. New York: Garland Publishing, 1997.

Thorton, Russell. *American Indian Holocaust and Survival: A Population History Since 1492*. Norman: University of Oklahoma Press, 1987.

Tilly, Chris. "Understanding Income Inequality." *Sociological Forum* 6 (1991): 739–756.

Time. "More Seniority for the Victims." *Time*, April 5, 1976, 65.

Toffler, Alvin. *The New Wave*. New York: Morrow, 1980.

Tolnay, Stewart E., and E. M. Beck. "Racial Violence and Black Migration in the American South, 1910 to 1930." *American Sociological Review* 57 (1992): 103–116.

Tönnies, Ferdinand. *Community and Society*. Trans. Charles P. Loomis. East Lansing: Michigan State University Press, 1957.

Tonry, Michael. *Malign Neglect—Race, Crime, and Punishment in America*. New York: Oxford University Press, 1995.

Traub, Stuart H., and Craig B. Little. *Theories of Deviance* (3rd ed.). Itasca, Ill.: F. E. Peacock, 1985.

Trillin, Calvin. "Louisiana." *The New Yorker*, April 14, 1986.

Tsukamoto, Mary, and Elizabeth Pinkerton. *We the People: A Story of Interment in America*. Elk Grove, Calif.: Laguna Publishing, 1987.

Tumin, Melvin M. "Some Principles of Stratification: A Critical Analysis." *American Sociological Review* 18 (1953): 387–394.

Turner, Ralph. "Determinants of Social Movement Strategies." In Tamatsu Shibutani (ed.). *Human Nature and Collective Behavior*. Englewood Cliffs, N.J.: Prentice-Hall, 1970.

Turner, Ralph H., and Lewis M. Killian. *Collective Behavior* (2nd ed.). Englewood Cliffs, N.J.: Prentice-Hall, 1972.

Tyler, Kimberly A., Dan R. Hoyt, and Les B. Whitbeck. "The Effects of Early Sexual Abuse on Later Sexual Victimization Among Female Homeless and Runaway Adolescents." *Journal of Interpersonal Violence* 15 (2000): 235–251.

Uhlaner, Carole Jean. "Electoral Participation: Summing up a Decade." *Society* 28 (1991): 35–45.

United Nations Department of Economic and Social Development. *The Sex and Age Distribution of the World Popula-tions: The 1992 Revision*. New York: United Nations Publication, 1993.

Updike, John. *Rabbit Run*. New York: Knopf, 1960.

U.S. Bureau of the Census. *Marital Status and Living Arrangements: March 1992*. Washington, D.C.: U.S. Government Printing Office, 1992.

_____. *Statistical Abstract of the United States, 1993*. Washington, D.C.: U.S. Government Printing Office, 1993.

_____. *Marital Status and Living Arrangements, March 1993*. Washington, D.C.: U.S. Government Printing Office, 1994.

_____. *Population Projections of the United States by Age, Sex, Race and Hispanic Origin: 1995 to 2050*. Washington, D.C.: U.S. Government Printing Office, 1996a.

_____. *Marital Status and Living Arrangements, March 1994*. Washington, D.C.: U.S. Government Printing Office, 1996b.

_____. *Marital Status and Living Arrangements, March 1998*. Washington, D.C.: U.S. Government Printing Office, 1998.

_____. *Statistical Abstract of the United States, 1999*. Washington, D.C.: U.S. Government Printing Office, 2000.

_____. *The Hispanic Population in the United States: March 2002*. Washington, D.C.: U.S. Government Printing Office, 2003a.

_____. *The Black Population in the United States: March 2002*. Washington, D.C.: U.S. Government Printing Office, 2003b.

_____. *Children's Living Arrangements and Characteristics: March 2002*. Washington, D.C.: U.S. Government Printing Office, 2003c.

_____. *Poverty in the United States, 2002*. Washington, D.C.: U.S. Government Printing Office, 2003d.

_____. *Statistical Abstract of the United States, 2003*. Washington, D.C.: U.S. Government Printing Office, 2004a.

_____. *Educational Attainment in the United States, 2003*. Washington, D.C.: U.S. Government Printing Office, 2004b.

_____. *Global Population Profile 2002*. Washington, D.C.: U.S. Government Printing Office, 2004c.

U.S. Centers for Disease Control and Prevention. *National Vital Statistics Reports: Births, Marriages, Divorces, and Deaths: Provisional Data for 2003*. Washington, D.C.: U.S. Government Printing Office, 2004a.

———. *Diagnosis of HIV/AIDS—32 States, 2000–2003*. Washington, D.C.: U.S. Government Printing Office, 2004b.

U.S. Department of Agriculture, *Trends in U.S. Agriculture*. Washington, D.C.: U.S. Government Printing Office, 2004

U.S. Department of Education. *21st Annual Report to Congress on the Implementation of the Individuals with Disabilities Education Act*. Office of Special Education Programs. Washington, D.C.: U.S. Government Printing Office, 1999.

———. *The Condition of Education, 2000*. Washington, D.C.: U.S. Government Printing Office, 2000a.

———. *Digest of Educational Statistics, 1999*. Washington, D.C.: U.S. Government Printing Office, 2000b.

———. *Digest of Educational Statistics, 2002*. Washington, D.C.: U.S. Government Printing Office, 2003.

U.S. Department of Justice. *Uniform Crime Reports, 2002*. Washington, D.C.: U.S. Government Printing Office, 2003a.

———. *Criminal Victimization, 2002*. Washington, D.C.: U.S. Government Printing Office, 2003b.

———. *Criminal Victimization in the United States— Statistical Tables*. Washington, D.C.: U.S. Government Printing Office, 2003c.

———. *Sourcebook of Criminal Justice Statistics, 2002*. Washington, D.C.: U.S. Government Printing Office, 2003d.

———. *Prisoners in 2002*. Washington, D.C.: U.S. Government Printing Office, 2003e.

U.S. Equal Employment Opportunity Commission. *Indicators of Equal Employment Opportunity—Status and Trends*. Washington, D.C.: U.S. Government Printing Office, 1995.

U.S. House of Representatives, Committee on Ways and Means. *Tax Progressivity and Income Distribution*. March 26, 1990.

U.S. Immigration and Naturalization Service. *Statistical Yearbook of the Immigration and Naturalization Service*. Washington, D.C.: U.S. Government Printing Office, 1993.

———. *Illegal Alien Resident Population*. Washington, D.C.: U.S. Government Printing Office, 1997a.

———. *Fact Sheet: Operation Gatekeeper: Three Years of Results At-a-Glance*. Washington, D.C.: U.S. Government Printing Office, 1997b.

U.S. News & World Report. "Chavez vs. the Teamsters: Farm Workers' Historic Vote." *U.S. News & World Report* 79 (1975): 82–83.

U.S. Sentencing Commission. *Special Report to the Congress: Cocaine and Federal Sentencing Policy*. Washington, D.C.: U.S. Government Printing Office, 1997.

U.S. Supreme Court Reports. *"McCleskey v. Kemp."* Supreme Court Reports, 95L Ed 2d. Rochester, N.Y.: Lawyers Co-operative Publishing Co., 1987.

Useem, Michael. "Corporations and the Corporate Elite." In Alex Inkeles et al. (eds.). *Annual Review of Sociology*. Vol. 6. Palo Alto, Calif.: Annual Reviews, 1980, 41–77.

Usher, Sean. "Health Care Endangered." In Ed Finn (ed.). *The Facts* 10 (2) Spring 1988. Ottawa: Public Relations Department of The Canadian Union of Public Employees.

van den Berge, Pierre L. "Bringing Beasts Back In: Towards a Biosocial Theory of Aggression." *American Sociological Review* 39 (1974): 777–788.

van Dam, Mary Ann A. "Mothers in Two Types of Lesbian Families: Stigma Experiences, Supports, and Burdens." *Journal of Family Nursing* 10 (2004): 450–485.

Vander Zanden, James W. *American Minority Relations* (3rd ed.). New York: Ronald Press, 1972.

Vanfossen, Beth E. *The Structure of Social Inequality*. Boston: Little, Brown, 1979.

Veblen, Thorstein. *The Theory of the Leisure Class*. New York: Macmillan, 1899.

Venkatakrishnan, Hamsa, and Dylan Wiliam. "Tracking and Mixed-ability Grouping in Secondary School Mathematics Classrooms: A Case Study." *British Educational Research Journal* 29 (2001): 189–215.

Verba, Sidney, Garry Oren, and G. Donald Ferree. *Equality in America: The View from the Top*. Cambridge, Mass.: Harvard University Press, 1985.

Verdugo, Richard R. "Earnings Differentials between Black, Mexican American, and Non-Hispanic White Male Workers: On the Cost of Being a Minority Worker, 1972–1987." *Social Science Quarterly* 73 (1992): 663–673.

Wacquant, Löic J. D., and William Julius Wilson. "The Cost of Racial and Class Exclusion in the Inner City." In William Julius Wilson (ed.). *The Ghetto Underclass: Social Science Perspectives*, 25–42. Newbury Park, Calif.: Sage, 1993.

Wainright, Jennifer L., Stephen T. Russell, and Charlotte J. Patterson. "Psychosocial Adjustment, School Outcomes, and Romantic Relationships of Adolescents With Same-Sex Parents." *Child Development* 75 (2004): 1886–1899.

Wallerstein, Immanuel. *Capitalist World Economy*. Cambridge: Cambridge University Press, 1979.

Wardhaugh, Ronald. *An Introduction to Sociolinguistics*. New York: Basil Blackwell, 1986.

Warner, W. Lloyd, and Paul S. Lunt. *The Social Life of a Modern Community*. New Haven, Conn.: Yale University Press, 1941.

Wax, Rosalie. *Doing Fieldwork*. Chicago: University of Chicago Press, 1978.

Weber, Max. *From Max Weber: Essays in Sociology*. Trans. and ed. H. H. Gerth and C. Wright Mills. New York: Oxford University Press, 1946.

———. *The Protestant Ethnic and the Spirit of Capitalism*. New York: Scribner's, 1958.

Weed, James. "The Life of a Marriage." *American Demographics*, February 1989, 12.

Weicher, John C. "Increasing Inequality of Wealth?" *Public Interest*, Winter 1997, 15–26.

Weinberg, S. Kirson, and Henry Arond. "The Occupational Culture of the Boxer." *American Journal of Sociology* 58 (1952): 460–469.

Weinstein, Deena. *Bureaucratic Opposition: Challenging Abuses at the Workplace*. New York: Pergamon, 1979.

Weitzman, Lenore. *Divorce Revolution: The Unexpected Social and Economic Consequences for Women and Children in America*. New York: The Free Press, 1985.

Wellman, Henry M., and Susan A. Gelman. "Cognitive Development: Foundational Theories of Core Domains." *Annual Review of Psychology* 43 (1992): 337–375.

West, Candace, and Don Zimmerman. "Doing Gender." *Gender & Society* 1 (1987): 125–141.

West, Candace, and Sarah Fenstermaker. "Doing Difference." *Gender & Society* 9 (1995): 8–37.

Westphall, Victor. *The Public Domain in New Mexico, 1854–1891*. Albuquerque: University of New Mexico Press, 1965.

White, Lynn, and Stacy J. Rogers. "Economic Circumstances and Family Outcomes: A Review of the 1990s." *Journal of Marriage & the Family* 62 (2000): 1035–1052.

White, Lynn K., and Alan Booth. "The Quality and Stability of Remarriages: The Role of Stepchildren." *American Sociological Review* 50 (1985): 689–698.

White, Lynn K., and Stacy J. Rogers. "Economic Circumstances and Family Outcomes: A Review of the 1990s." *Journal of Marriage and the Family* 62 (2000): 1035–1051.

Whorf, Benjamin. *Language, Thought and Reality*. Cambridge, Mass.: MIT Press, 1956.

Wilson, Donald O. "Diagonal Communication Links within Organizations." *The Journal of Business Communication* 29 (1992): 129–143.

Wilson, Edward O. *Sociobiology: A New Synthesis*. Cambridge, Mass.: The Belknap Press of Harvard University Press, 1975.

Wilson, William J. *The Truly Disadvantaged: The Inner City, the Underclass, and Public Policy*. Chicago: University of Chicago Press, 1987.

———. "The Plight of the Inner-City Black Male." *Proceedings of the American Philosophical Society* 136 (1992): 320–325.

Wimberley, Ronald C., Thomas C. Hood, C. M. Lipsey, Donald Clelland, and Marguerite Hay. "Conversion in a Billy Graham Crusade: Spontaneous Event or Ritual Performance?" *Sociological Quarterly* 16 (1975): 162–170.

Winter, J. Alan, and Eugene C. Goldfield. "Caregiver-Child Interaction in the Development of Self: The Contributions of Vygotsky, Bruner and Kaye to Mead's Theory." *Symbolic Interaction* 14 (1991): 433–447.

Wirth, Louis. "Urbanism as a Way of Life." *American Journal of Sociology* 44 (1938): 1–24.

Withrow, Brian L. "Driving While Different: A Potential Theoretical Explanation for Race-Based Policing." *Criminal Justice Policy Review* 15 (2004): 344–365.

Wreck Commissioner's Court. *On Formal Investigation Ordered by the Board of Trade into the Loss of the S.S. Titanic*. London: His Majesty's Stationery Office, 1912.

Wright, Erik Olin. *The Politics of Punishment: A Critical Analysis of Prisons in America*. New York: Harper & Row, 1973.

Wuthnow, Robert, and Kevin Christiano. "The Effects of Residential Migration on Church Attendance in the United States." In Robert Wuthnow (ed.). *The Religious Dimension*, 257–276. New York: Academic Press, 1979.

Yankow, Jeffrey J. "The Wage Dynamics of Internal Migration Within the United States." *Eastern Economic Journal* 25 (1999): 265–278.

Yuan, Tien H. "China: Demographic Billionaire." *Population Bulletin* 38 (April 1983).

Zald, Mayer N. (ed.). *The Dynamics of Social Movements: Resource Mobilization, Social Control and Tactics*. Englewood, N.J.: Winthrop, 1979.

Zelizer, Viviana. *Pricing the Priceless Child: The Changing Social Value of Children*. New York: Basic Books, 1985.

Zimbardo, Philip G. "Pathology of Imprisonment." *Society* 9 (1972): 4–8.

Zuo, Jiping, and Shengming Tang. "Breadwinner Status and Gender Ideologies of Men and Women Regarding Family Roles." *Sociological Perspectives* 43 (2000): 29–41.

INDEX